Marxism and Art

Marxism and Art
Writings in Aesthetics and Criticism

Edited by

Berel Lang

and

Forrest Williams

Department of Philosophy
University of Colorado

LONGMAN
New York and London

MARXISM AND ART
Writings in Aesthetics and Criticism

Longman Inc., New York
Associate companies, branches, and
representatives throughout the world.

Copyright © 1972 by Longman Inc.

First published 1972 by David McKay Company, Inc.
Second printing 1978 by Longman Inc.

Library of Congress Catalog Card Number: 77-185134
ISBN: 0-582-28050-8 (previously ISBN: 0-679-30148-8)

Manufactured in the United States of America

MARXISM AND ART: WRITINGS IN AESTHETICS AND CRITICISM
COPYRIGHT © 1972 BY DAVID MCKAY COMPANY, INC.

LIBRARY OF CONGRESS CATALOG CARD NUMBER: 77-185134
MANUFACTURED IN THE UNITED STATES OF AMERICA

Acknowledgments

We should like to thank the following people and publishers for their kind permissions to reprint copyrighted material:

Basic Books, Inc. for Chapter 6 from *Classicism and Romanticism* by Frederick Antal, © 1966 by Evelyn Antal, Basic Books, Inc., Publishers, New York.

Georges Borchardt, Inc. for selection from *Pour une Sociologie du Roman* by Lucien Goldmann (Paris: Gallimard, 1964), translated by Forrest Williams; English language rights in U.S. and Canada: Georges Borchardt, Inc.

George Braziller, Inc. for "The Artist and his Conscience," from *Situations* by Jean-Paul Sartre, translated from the French by Benita Eisler; reprinted with the permission of the publisher. English translation copyright © 1965 by George Braziller, Inc.

Doubleday and Co., Inc. for "My Lady's Visit," copyright © 1968 by Boleslaw Taborski. From the book *Theatre Notebook 1947–1967* by Jan Kott, translated by Boleslaw Taborski.

Editori Riuniti, Rome, for selection from *Il Film e il Risarcimento Marxista dell 'Arte* by Umberto Barbaro, edited by Lorenzo Quaglietti, © 1960, translated by Forrest Williams.

Feltrinelli Editore, Milan, for selection from *Critica del Gusto* by Galvano della Volpe, © 1960, translated by Forrest Williams. (Editors' note: To secure maximum continuity for the selection, a few passages have been relocated, one passage on "semantic loci" has been paraphrased in translation, and an occasional phrase has been added or deleted; the meaning of the original text has in no way been altered.)

Harcourt Brace Jovanovich for *Illuminations: Essays and Reflections* by Walter Benjamin, edited by Hannah Arendt, translated by Harry Zohn, translation copyright © 1968 by Harcourt Brace Jovanovich, Inc., © 1955 by Suhrkamp Verlag, Frankfurt am Main. For selections from *Film Form and Film Sense* by Sergei Eisenstein, translated by Jay Leyda, copyright 1949 by Harcourt Brace Jovanovich, Inc. For selections from *Shooting an Elephant and Other Essays* by George Orwell, copyright 1945, 1946, 1950 by Sonia Brownell Orwell. Reprinted by permission of Harcourt Brace Jovanovich.

Hill and Wang, Inc. for "Theatre for Pleasure and Theatre for Instruction" and "Study of the First Scene of Shakespeare's *Coriolanus*" by Bertolt Brecht, from *Brecht on Theatre*, by John Willett, copyright © 1957, 1963, 1964 by Suhrkamp Verlag, Frankfurt am Main. This translation and notes © 1964 by John Willett. Reprinted by permission of Hill and Wang, Inc.

International Publishers Co. for selection from *Economic and Philosophical Manuscripts of 1844* by Karl Marx, edited by Dirk J. Struik, translated by

Martin Milligan, © 1964. Selection from *German Ideology* by Karl Marx and Friedrich Engels, edited and translated by R. Pascal, © 1939. Selection from *Marxism and Linguistics* by Josef Stalin, © 1951. Selection from *Selected Works of Mao Tse-tung* by Mao Tse-tung. Selection from *On Literature and Art* by Karl Marx and Friedrich Engels, © 1947. "Party Organization and Party Literature" from *Collected Works* of V. I. Lenin, Vol. 10. Reprinted by permission of International Publishers Company, Inc.

Lawrence and Wishart, Ltd. for selection from *Aeschylus and Athens* by George D. Thomson (London: Lawrence and Wishart, Ltd., 1968 and New York: Grossett and Dunlap, 1968). Selection from *Illusion and Reality* by Christopher Caudwell, published in the United States by International Publishers Co. Reprinted by permission of Lawrence and Wishart.

Hermann Luchterhand Verlag, Neuwied and Berlin, for selection from *Über die Besonderheit als Kategorie der Ästhetik* by Georg Lukács, © 1967, translated by Berel Lang.

The Merlin Press Ltd. for selection from *The Historical Novel* by Georg Lukács, translated by Hannah and Stanley Mitchell, © 1962.

Monthly Review Press for selection from *Further Studies in a Dying Culture* by Christopher Caudwell, © 1949.

Penguin Books Ltd. for selections from *The Necessity of Art: The Marxist Approach* by Ernst Fischer; reprinted by permission of Penguin Books, Ltd., © 1964.

Random House, Inc. for selection from *The Philosophy of Art History* by Arnold Hauser, copyright © 1958 by Arnold Hauser; reprinted by permission of Alfred A. Knopf, Inc. For selection from *Mannerism* by Arnold Hauser, copyright © 1965 by Arnold Hauser; reprinted by permission of Alfred A. Knopf, Inc.

Russell and Russell for selection from *Historical Materialism: A System of Sociology* [1925] by Nicholas Bukharin, authorized translation from the 3rd edition. (New York: Russell and Russell, 1965.)

Suhrkamp Verlag for "On Non-Objective Painting" and "On Socialist Realism" from *Schriften Zur Literatur und Kunst* by Bertolt Brecht, copyright © 1967 by Suhrkamp Verlag, Frankfurt am Main, translated by Berel Lang, copyright 1970 by Stefan Brecht; reprinted by permission of Suhrkamp Verlag and Stefan Brecht.

University of Michigan Press for selection from *Literature and Revolution* by Leon Trotsky, translated by Rose Strunsky, © 1960.

Contents

C. *Genres*

D. *Critical Practice*

Appendix

Marxism and Art

Introduction

CLOSELY intertwined in its career with political and international developments, Marxist philosophy has had the reputation of bearing almost exclusively on the issues of political and economic theory. The truth of the matter is, of course, quite different; and a major purpose of our anthology is to amend that misconception—from one direction, at least—by exhibiting the critical subtlety and philosophical importance of Marxist writing on various aspects of art.

Among the writings which would ordinarily be placed under the rubric of Marxist aesthetics, one finds, to be sure, tendentious and pious expositions of *"truly"* Marxist art, deliberately extravagant encomiums of *"truly"* Marxist theoreticians and artists, and the use of aesthetic theory as a political testing-ground. But for the student of Marxism *or* of aesthetics, much more significant than these abuses is the existence of general Marxist theories and their concrete application: attempts to account philosophically, critically, and historically for the phenomenon of art in Marxist terms. Such theories have undertaken to define art, to distinguish and study various genres, to formulate general principles of art criticism, and to apply them in critical practice. Through its overt adherents, and by its influence beyond its own circles, Marxism has in fact proved to be an extraordinarily rich source for aesthetic theory, criticism, and art history. One need only glance at the names represented in this volume alone to realize that Marxist aesthetics and criticism promise much more than newspaper promotion-pieces for Socialist Realism and political denunciations of "bourgeois art." Art historians, philosophers, and critics are citing more and more often such thinkers as Gyorgy Lukács, the Hungarian theorist of the arts described by Thomas Mann as perhaps the greatest literary critic of our time; or the late Lucien Goldmann, one of Europe's foremost authorities on seventeenth-century French theater; or Christopher St. John Sprigg, who, killed in the Spanish Civil War at the age of thirty, had yet written under his pen-name of Christopher Caudwell a series of masterful essays on aesthetics combining Marxist principles with a deep understanding of psychoanalysis and an exceptional poetic sensibility.

The individual writings included in the anthology must, of course, speak for themselves; we make no claim either for doctrinal consistency

1

among the various selections, or for the equal value of everything said by each writer in its bearing on either Marxism or art. We believe, rather, that each of the selections contributes to an appreciation and understanding of Marxism and art in some important way. At the same time, a general, philosophical principle underlies the selections compiled in the anthology, which should be considered together with the readings that follow.

The principle is concise and straightforward in its assertion: that neither the interest nor the productivity of the Marxist tradition of thought as it bears on aesthetics and art is a matter of chance. We contend, rather, that the extent and quality of Marxist writing in these areas reflect an overall concern of Marxist thought for art objects and artistic processes. That concern appears both in the most general philosophical categories of Marxism and in its specific references to art.

This thesis stands in apparent contradiction, admittedly, to the lack of explicit theorizing on art by Marx and Engels themselves. Although sensitive and responsive to the arts, neither found much to say along these lines in an otherwise voluminous body of writings and correspondence.[1] There are in fact only a few full-length treatises on art by other "founding" figures of Marxism, let alone attempts to demonstrate formally the intrinsic concern of Marxism for art. This sparseness, it might seem, is highly significant; surely, Marx was sufficiently self-conscious a writer that when he was talking about artistic activity or art objects, he could be expected to say so.

The few explicit acknowledgments in the historically central texts, however, are only the visible tip of a much larger substructure. Aesthetic categories and schematisms seem in fact crucial to Marx's reckoning in at least two ways: first, by way of the roles assigned creativity and sensibility in the eventual classless society toward which Marxist theory as a whole points, and second, in the aesthetic tenor of the general philosophical categories at work in his thought.

1

The concept of alienation, and an idea of what the alternative to alienation promises, are central to Marx's thought.[2] A recurrent theme in his writing asserts the inevitability and desirability of change in the social order, and thus in the condition of individual men. It is true, and has frequently been noted, that Marx himself, and later elaborators of the Marxist eschatology as well (for example, Lenin in State and Revolution), do not say a great deal about the precise condition of man in the classless society to come; but the question nevertheless pervades Marxist thought as a crucial issue. The terms in which the issue is formulated, furthermore—explicitly or tacitly—suggest that the concepts of art and aesthetic experience are relevant to understanding it.

Two principal and related features dominate the account of man as he would be, once the oppressiveness of class society—that takes its toll of the master no less than the slave—had been eliminated. For one, the integrity of the self would be reasserted. That is to say, the self, divided within itself and from others by the original terms of the division of labor and the consequent antagonism of classes, could become whole again. The human being would reassert an integrity defying compartmentalization, reclaiming himself as a unity able "to become accomplished in any branch of labor he wishes . . . , to do one thing today and another tomorrow, to hunt in the morning, fish in the afternoon, rear cattle in the evening, criticize after dinner . . . without ever becoming hunter, fisherman, shepherd, critic." [3] This capacity alone, however, would be sterile were it not accompanied by the possibility (rooted both in the character of the individual and in external conditions) of reaping the fruits of its efforts. In a classless society (by implication, materially affluent), the human self realized will still be active, not passive. Though not forced to commit itself permanently to any single activity, it is essentially committed to activity. The grounds of such activity, however, the outcome, and the very manner of it are different from those of human activity in any other era. For the self that is cut off from the products of its labor, the object of labor "exists independently, outside himself, and alien to him, and stands opposed to him as an alien power." [4] The non-alienated, integral self, on the other hand, truly "possesses" its products: precisely *not* in the sense of legal rights of ownership, but in the much deeper sense that the self *enjoys* them. Man, alienated, discerns objects only in terms of their utility, as "possessed, eaten, drunk, worn, inhabited." [5] The ending of class antagonism—the most radical change possible for man, in Marx's view, tantamount to a true beginning of human *history*—must profoundly alter men's experiences of objects. Neither compulsion nor need will darken the transactions between man and object. The human being acts freely; and, once created, the object of his efforts remains available to him as an elaborated aspect of himself, as continued assurance of the integrity, indeed the inviolability of the self. The true realm of freedom, Marx asserted in *Das Kapital,* is a development of human power "which is its own end." [6]

The way in which this new integrity asserts itself is the second of the characteristic features of human experience in the classless society. It emerges in a variety of experience which is predominantly (and distinctively) sensuous in character. The human situation then is one in which "the wealth of subjective human sensibility (a musical ear, an eye which is sensitive to the beauty of form, in short, senses which are capable of human satisfaction and which confirm themselves as human faculties) is cultivated or created." [7] Marx does not refer here to a *merely* sensuous pleasure (what he terms "abstract" pleasure), such as the pleasure of a cold drink when one is thirsty; the examples cited are far more complex, the sensuous pleasure they bespeak less evanescent and superficial than slaking one's thirst. It is a pleasure which, like the self experiencing it, reflects an origin not in external compulsion or mere need, but somehow in its own structure. It has the quality of a free gift. It exhibits, in a word, aesthetic quality.

The suggestion was made earlier that in Marx art is not only taken seriously as object and activity, but also underlies the general philosophical categories which operate in his system as a whole. This is a much more delicate determination to make, not only with respect to Marxist thought, but for any system. It is illuminating, in considering the question, to look to the enduring influence of Hegel on Marx, and in particular to the dialectical movement ascribed by Hegel to the evolution of spirit. Admittedly, in the Hegelian development of "Absolute Spirit," art plays but a brief and early role: religion, and finally philosophy, supersede it as moments on the way to the full realization of the human spirit. Looked at for its *form*, however, for the categories which govern the whole, the dialectical process—in Hegel, the pattern as well as the source of all historical judgments—is aesthetic in character. To be sure, the Hegelian tradition is not alone in conceiving the work of art as organic, a whole of integrally related parts which alters with the alteration of any one of them. Nor is it the Hegelian tradition alone that views the experience of art as "funding" diffuse elements of experience into a final, consummatory experience. But in the last 200 years, at least, only within the Hegelian tradition are those characteristics ascribed to history or experience as such. In the dialectical process of history (both in the articulation of its individual moments and in the overall process), spirit evolves by first objectifying itself, and then synthesizing the objectification —that is, by integrating the object into a fuller, more complex and novel whole. If the end of the dark "pre-history" of class exploitation means, for Marx, that all men are artists, for Hegel, spirit itself is an artist, unifying and relating whatever offers itself as an independent and innovative element. It is true enough that Hegel's emphasis on abstract consciousness in the late stages of the development of spirit is different from— and, finally, at odds with—Marx's emphasis on experience as sensuous. One understands both the difference and the similarity between the two in this regard, however, by recalling Marx's own words to the effect that Hegel had to be turned upside down. For, if a form is organically unified, turning it upside down (whatever other differences result) will make no difference to its unity.

The discussion so far has centered on the intrinsic importance of art and aesthetic categories for Marxism. This is not to deny an extrinsic or instrumental role to art or the connection between the two types of function. Its instrumental character is emphasized more in later writers than in Marx himself, undoubtedly because they, more than he, were obliged to think of means for actually effecting political change; but there is no inconsistency between, for example, Trotsky's conception of the uses of art in a class society and Marx's view of experience once that society disappears. When Trotsky writes of the dangers of "intellectual Marxism" —that is, a Marxism which ends only in thinking and not in acting—he is elaborating a theme of Marx's; and when Trotsky then suggests the importance of art as a means for effecting a unity in the individual of different, sometimes conflicting elements, he is arguing for a version of the aesthetic relation quite consonant with that ascribed above to Marx himself. There has been much (and much nonsense) written about the Marxist conception of art as instrument of propaganda (some of it by Marxists); underneath the cant, it is important to see that the function assigned art on the way to the integration of man's divided self is quite consistent with the conception of that final goal.

It may be objected at this point that the position ascribed to Marx need not and perhaps does not hold for Marxism as such. One would of course agree that for Marxism, more readily even than for most "isms," the phrase *as such*, if it is at all pertinent, is difficult to apply. There exists, it seems, only individual accounts by individual writers, each making his own assortment of the elements of Marx's work. But the point is not that all Marxist writers on art *have* agreed on certain principles, or even that they *ought* to do so, but that where they have, this is explicable in terms of Marx's own work.

2

Our contention is, of course, not only that a concern with art and aesthetic theory is important to Marxism, but that the Marxist handling of that concern is important, historically and systematically, for aesthetic theory and art criticism in general. Marxist thinking on specific issues concerning the arts is in many ways opposed to the methods and principles of the tradition of aesthetics and criticism descended from the Enlightenment and still pervasive in Western thought. To understand this complex state of affairs, we must now turn from the overall, categorial aspects of Marxist thinking to its more specific contribution, which has been nothing less, it seems, than a major redefinition of the substance of art theory, art history, and art criticism. In so doing, moreover, we turn to what seems *most original* about Marxist theory of art.

The theoretical discipline that has earned the name of "aesthetics" in Western philosophy was a child of Enlightenment preoccupations in name and in content. Enlightenment philosophy approached issue after issue, in the area of political theory, ethics, the analysis of beauty, and so on, from a perspective already fixed by a prior commitment to a specific issue in the theory of knowledge. For the British empiricists, the neo-Cartesians, and Kant, the most fundamental philosophical problem was to analyze how an individual consciousness succeeds in knowing the properties or laws of a given object of experience. The motivation for this consuming interest in individual acts of cognition arose, of course, from the extraordinary achievements and solid promise of the savants of the seventeenth and eighteenth centuries. Turning to the analysis of beauty, these philosophers went directly to an analogous moment: the individual consciousness at the peak of its contemplative enjoyment of a sensuously and formally entrancing object. Thus, most of the various theories of "aesthetics" of the last 250 years bear a certain family resemblance, revealing their common conceptual origin in a specific epistemological preoccupation of the Enlightenment. The individual subject's moment of appreciation before a completed or at least pre-formed object of beauty—a flower, perhaps, or a painting, a poem, a song—has been their central theme. Consequently, theirs has been largely the perspective of the ideal critic, reflecting on and discoursing about a private, yet—given a keen sensibility—widely relevant experience of a thing of beauty. Other plausible themes, such as the creative process, the attitudinal or ideological formation of the artist, relations between artistic content or significance and historical conditions, although often treated extensively, have usually taken shapes previously dictated by the principal perspective. To be sure, consensus is rare in any philosophical tradition, and the tradition of "aesthetics" is no exception. Divergent approaches have arisen from and sometimes against this dominant perspective, for example, physiological theories, environmental theories (e.g., Taine), depth-psychological theories (Nietzsche, Freud, Rank, Jung). But such has, nevertheless, been the main approach of modern writers on art.

The true *originality* of Marxist philosophy of art derives from a radical change of perspective, the shift it proposes from an emphasis on art and aesthetic judgment as isolated and autonomous "moments" in the world and in feeling, to one in which those moments are seen as rooted fundamentally in the social and political existence of men. This reorientation in aesthetic theory springs then from the most general and most important substantive principle of Marxism that *all parts of the ideo-*

logical superstructure—art being one of these—are crucially determined in content and style by the behavior of a more basic structure which is economic in nature.

Familiar to the general public in a variety of simplified formulas, this Marxist principle of the "economic determination" of the ideological superstructure is far from self-explanatory. It admits, moreover, of no facile application in aesthetics and criticism.

The simplest possible interpretation would begin by referring the term "economy" to the visible facts of the ownership, manufacture, and consumption of goods. A Marxist theory of art might then be taken to assert that works of art are merely other such commodities, bearing all the obvious marks of the business enterprise; the relation between the "economy" and the arts would then be causal in the most mechanical sense. Art criticism would concern itself almost entirely with the particular subjects, images, and ideas—or their absence—of the work of art. The criteria of evaluation on this account become directly and openly didactic in texture: "good" art represents "good" men, ideas, or emotions. The party official who criticized Sergei Eisenstein's masterpiece, *The Old and the New,* because the peasant in the famous cream-separator sequence did not smile *enough,* would be in the right.

Such simplistic appraisals of art works often do appear in avowedly Marxist publications, and it is this species of criticism which comes most immediately to public view. But there exists, of course, another and more sophisticated variety of Marxist aesthetics which holds that the relationship between economic base and artistic superstructure is *neither direct nor mechanically determined.* One of the main *advances* over classical political economics claimed by Marx was precisely his treatment of the economic sphere *as a dialectical process* rather than as a mere aggregate of mechanical forces. This master-process is not a sum total of readily visible facts of manufacture and consumption of material goods, as in the classical theories, but a cycle of collective human relations which keep a particular society producing and reproducing daily its material substance.

This important difference between the pre-Marxist and the Marxist views can be seen clearly with reference to a sample concept, that of "capital." On the classical analyses, capital is essentially an accumulated amount of wealth, thus quite literally a physical quantity existing in some place, e.g., in banknotes, or in the market value of machinery or land. But for Marx and Engels, "capital" is, strictly speaking, the name of *a collective social process;* it is not a thing, but (through things) a socially mediated relationship between persons.[8] It consists, not simply of material products in motion, but (in Marx's words) of "social magnitudes." The effective determining process is thus held to be the collective activity of a social class in its exploitative conflict with another social class. Such activity involves, even in the technically most primitive societies, an extraordinarily complex network of mutually reinforcing behavior. For so great an historical venture, the owning class must marshal and shape to its needs every available resource: political power, weaponry, education, moral and artistic influence. The laws of such vast historical complexes are not mechanical causes, but dialectical interactions, tensions, resolutions, and renewed conflicts, as the internal contradictions between a privileged class structure and the objective possibilities of a society dissolve old orders and inaugurate new orders, almost always by violent as well as by evolutionary means.[9]

From this rich, dialectical sense of "economic determination," the Marxist thesis extends naturally into aesthetic theory and art criticism. So, for example, it seems evident that this dialectical and social conception of the economic base led a theorist and critic of literature like Lucien Goldmann to study the plays of Racine, not simply in terms of the content of the particular images, but in terms of their implicit "world vision," that is, "their manner of seeing and feeling a concrete universe of persons and things." [10] This Marxist principle of criticism gained special persuasiveness in Goldmann's analyses of Racine, for it enabled him to demonstrate, contrary to previous critical opinion, that the tragedian's most Christian dramas are just those in which the component images are overtly pagan. Thus, what finally counts in Goldmann's theory and criticism is not a particular setting, or what or who is represented, or the component images as such, but the implicit ideology. On this view, to understand a work of art is precisely not to display it as a direct effect or reflection of some economic cause. It is, rather, to relate the structure of its dominant "universe" to an extra-artistic ideological structure. Racine, for example, expressed in dramatic terms a Jansenist "vision" of things. Jansenist ideology (i.e., theology) is in its turn comprehended by relating its structure to the history of the French nobility of the robe, a specific social-class formation that in turn can only be understood by reference to the specific dialectical structure of emergent capitalism in seventeenth-century France. A simple, linear argument from the economic to the artistic is thus out of order, and even a contradiction in terms. To explain, for Goldmann, consisted in discovering how one dynamic structure fits into a more comprehensive one, with economic class interests serving as the guiding concept.

To a non-Marxist, such reference to the economic structure of a class, a collectivity, often seems on the face of it an utter irrelevance in art criticism, a patent violation of the uniquely individual character of artistic creation, aesthetic object, and immediate enjoyment. Goldmann, like his acknowledged master, Lukács, and Plekhanov (among others), replied that the concept of social class, far from being extraneous to pertinent art criticism, is in fact the only theoretical principle powerful enough and detailed enough in its content to guide the critic to a satisfactory grasp of the full aesthetic structure imaged by a Racine, a Pascal, a Balzac, a Tolstoi, a Mann, a Boucher, a Leonardo. These are universes of a magnitude and an intricacy quite inexplicable by the individualistic categories of either traditional aesthetics or psychoanalytic biography.[11] Inclusive visions of such complexity and generous proportions, the Marxist argument goes, surely can only be the work of many. One might, of course, recoil in justified horror from an apparent proposal for "creation by committees." But the concept of "the many" necessary to illuminate the character of a masterpiece is nothing so arbitrary. It is a concept of many men, whether privileged or deprived, who are collectively organized into a formation pervading every breath they take. Even the concepts of nation, generation, and indeed region remain too loose and abstract to enable the critic to penetrate the organic structure of a work of art. These can account for some common elements of form—there is typically Spanish music, typically Irish music, typically Ozark music, and so on. But the extraordinary unity of an artistic "universe," the concrete coherence of a masterpiece, demands a base in real life far more vastly and powerfully organized: nothing less than the base or medium in which man actually makes his own historical existence, day after day, generation after generation. That base or medium is work: productive relationships in the dynamic class-structured sense outlined above. Far from being an intrusion into aesthetic argument, therefore, detailed reference to the class design of a society provides an important conceptual framework for doing justice to the full complexity of what such geniuses as Racine and Balzac have imagined and written, and is thus the best way for the critic to facilitate for the rest of us—as his calling demands—an adequate grasp of that artistic complexity. Such is the claim made by Marxist aesthetics and criticism on behalf of its substantive principle.

3

Within this general conceptual framework of economic determination of art, particular inquiries can be identified which suggest the characteristic approach and peculiar value of a Marxist perspective on aesthetic theory and criticism. One such item is Marxism's contribution to the theory of genres. It is not much of an exaggeration to claim that Marxist writers have been responsible for both the renewed attention given to

such analysis in the twentieth century and its modern accomplishments.
A striking example is the important work on the genre and sub-genres of
film by such writers as Walter Benjamin, Luigi Chiarini, Raymond Borde,
André Boissy, and Sergei Eisenstein; the theory of genres *qua* theory
(as distinguishable from its specific applications) has been greatly
enlarged by the work of such thinkers as Theodor Adorno and Gyorgy
Lukács. The logical reasons for such achievements seem evident. With
its philosophical emphasis on material conditions, Marxist analysis quite
naturally attends carefully to the artistic medium (to what in Aristotelian
terms would be called the "material cause"), and to the conditions set
by the medium for work done on it as with the medium itself. This issue
of itself yields the basic set of problems confronting the theory of genres.

Correlated to the emphasis on medium is a characteristic Marxist insistence on concreteness in historical analysis. This can be seen, for example,
in Leon Trotsky's rejection of sweeping theses about "Futurism in general," in favor of particular analyses of Russian, German and Italian
forms, each involving a different socio-economic base. For Marxism
displays an inherited (and heightened) Hegelian distaste for the abstract
generality, as compared to the universal which is discoverable in the
concrete situation.[12] When the Marxist aesthetic does exhibit the dogmatism with which the whole enterprise of aesthetic theory has sometimes been charged by artists and critics, the fault can only be committed
by the artist or critic who flies in the face of Marxist principles, which
clearly prohibit merely *a priori* reckonings of concrete empirical phenomena.

Another theme for which Marxist aesthetics is widely known is its
specific opposition to doctrines of "art for art's sake." If that dictum
means that society exists for the artist, that its survival should be sacrificed to the filling of museums with more and more paintings, that, in the
words of Mallarmé, "the world exists to be written in a book," clearly
Marxists are not alone in holding that, on the contrary, art is for mankind's sake. Art as a human enterprise involves an expenditure of human
energy and material goods, and therefore is not exempt from the general
necessity of moral justification. On the other hand, if the dictum means
that "artistic form" alone counts, Marxism generally objects that form
and content cannot be thus separated. Again, many non-Marxists would
agree. However, there exists still another more serious thesis often intended by the phrase, "art for art's sake," which cannot be so easily
answered. One of the classic principles of the discipline of aesthetics
since the Enlightenment is that the audience should accord a work of
art full and exclusive attention, without heed to momentary, practical
needs. One attends to the poem in all its concrete imagery, sound and

cadence, "for its own sake," not as a means to some imported purpose of ours. This is the disinterestedness stressed by Kant, for example, in his celebrated analysis of aesthetic judgment. At this juncture, Marxist opposition seems almost to vanish. Thus Plekhanov, one of the most influential of Marxist theorists on art, stressed in an essay devoted to eighteenth-century French painting and drama that Kant was quite right in banishing the individual spectator's utilitarian responses from a valid aesthetic judgment.[13] That a portrait resembles one's grandmother, or is worth a great deal of money, is perfectly irrelevant to an aesthetic evaluation. According to Plekhanov, then, a man can fairly be asked to set aside such references as extrinsic, and in that sense, to take a "disinterested" stance, to view the work of art "for its own sake."

At the same time, Plekhanov and other Marxists deny that the social character of the work and the experience may be similarly ignored. For man's *essence*, as Marx wrote, resides in the ensemble of social relations. Whatever the precise construction placed upon that phrase, which is currently a topic of philosophical controversy among Marxists,[14] clearly social tendencies and structure are thereby stated to be integral to the very make-up of human experience and, *a fortiori*, of works of art. What anyone "perceives" as "objective" reality, quite apart from any didactic aim on his part, *already* embodies social theses. There can be no such thing as "pure art," in the sense of art without any aesthetically relevant social ingredients (so-called "abstract art" notwithstanding), if man's nature is irrevocably social. In a class-ridden society, moreover, a man's nature is not social *tout court*, but class-social. Even the sciences display such class-social determination. There it appears due to the critical importance of basic concepts and methods; not in experimental verifications and conclusions, which are a matter of simple logic and conscientiousness, but in the very posing of the questions, and once in a while in the interpreting of the results. The phenomenon is central, however, to the creation and appreciation of works of art, where it is a matter, as Leon Trotsky noted, of "feeling the world in images." That is why, Trotsky went on to observe, a man's thoughts may diverge, in their social determination, from his feelings, so that one may well "think as a revolutionary and feel as a philistine."[15] In one sense, then, a Marxist can (and Plekhanov did) endorse the trans-individual, disinterested, non-utilitarian character of the aesthetic that most theorists have deemed essential. But not in any sense that would deny the fundamentally social texture of man and man's works.

Limitations of space preclude more than brief mention of a number of other themes of Marxist theories of art to which it may be important to call attention. For example, whereas aesthetics from the Enlightenment to the present has generally assumed certain "faculties" (Kant) or "moments" (Croce)—the sensibility, the understanding, the intuition-expression, the imagination, the will—to be simply "given" and full capacities, Marx and others have insisted on their historical character. Thus, in *Theses on Feuerbach*, Marx stresses that the senses are specific powers accrued in the course of man's practical struggles with nature and with his social milieu.[16] Another theme brought to the forefront of modern consciousness by Marxist thought is the profound antagonism which exists between bourgeois ideology and artistic creativity. This constitutes a far deeper matter for reflection than merely recognizing, as Plekhanov himself pointed out, that every society with a government standing over against some of the governed—in short, every society in which the Marxist ideal remains unrealized—is bound to adopt a narrowly utilitarian attitude toward the arts. For nothing less than the entire society of the capitalist era has been largely an object of dislike by its artists. Our great art has almost never been socially celebrative, this or that particular government aside. Indeed, it has almost always been overtly hostile, bitterly satirical, coldly indifferent, or patently fearful. We may recall here Marx's laconic observation that a capitalist economy will never have a Hesiod.

Yet another important theme of Marxism, following from its insistence on the social character of artistic creation, is the vexed question of the moral dimension of art. Bertolt Brecht's imaginary discussion concerning a projected presentation of Act I of *Coriolanus* reveals an educative preoccupation at work in the mind of one of the greatest playwrights of our time, and demonstrates the opportunities for developing certain moral-political implications in Shakespeare's play that a non-Marxist would be likely to overlook.[17] Along similar lines, Ernst Fischer reminds us that in societies on the upswing, artists generally aim not only to represent reality but to shape it actively. The "Moses" of Michelangelo, Fischer notes, was not only the artistic image of Renaissance man, the embodiment in stone of a new, self-aware personality; it was also "a commandment in stone to Michelangelo's contemporaries and patrons: 'That is what you ought to be like. The age in which we live demands it. The world at whose birth we are all present needs it.'" [18]

Turning to yet another theme, we may safely say that opposition to Idealism and Romanticism has stimulated Marxist critics to forge important distinctions between "naturalism" and "social realism." From the standpoint of historical materialism, there cannot be "given facts" to reproduce.[19] That would be, as Z. G. Apresian has noted, positivism, not Marxism. Marxism thus aligns itself with the numerous opponents of copy theories of art. Marx himself admired Balzac's "realistic" delineations of "prototypes," of "men of the future," precisely because the French novelist penetrated to concealed social tendencies, and never failed to make value judgments.[20] Some Marxists have attempted to treat this difficult subject of realism in art by introducing such notions as "typicality"[21] and, with regard to arts employing language, "polysignificant symbols."[22]

Finally, we call attention to the fact that Marxist writings have made critics in many quarters more keenly aware than ever of the theoretical problems surrounding programmatic or thesis art; an issue that goes back in philosophy to Plato's *Republic* and *Phaedrus,* and to Aristotle's *Poetics* and *Rhetoric,* but which had been almost removed from traditional aesthetics by wholesale condemnation of any kind of moral or rhetorical effect. In our selections, this particular debate ranges from Engels' strictures against forcing theses (which, he wrote to Kautsky, "must spring from the situation and action itself, without being explicitly displayed"); to Trotsky's attempt to acknowledge simultaneously the "absolute right to exist" of the most personal lyrics and his revolutionary hopes for the arts; to Lenin's demand in 1905 that "literature become party literature"; to Brecht's deliberate provocation of intellectual response in his "epic theater."[23]

4

It should be clear from what has been said that a precise definition of Marxist aesthetics or Marxist criticism is impossible. Interpreters argue over the works of Marx and Engels as energetically as (and more sharply than) any interpreters of Plato or Kant. For Marxism is no abstract formula but a live tradition. As Antonio Gramsci, the Italian man of letters and Communist parliamentary delegate who died a political prisoner during the Mussolini regime, observed on the occasion of the centenary of Marx's birthday:

Marx did not write a vestpocket doctrine, is not a messiah who left a string of parables loaded with categorical imperatives, of indisputable norms, absolutes outside the categories of time and space.[24]

Thus, there can be no such thing as *the* aesthetics of Marxism—just as there is no such thing as *the* aesthetics of phenomenology, of pragmatism, or of neo-Thomism (witness the major disagreements between Jacques Maritain and Étienne Gilson): a lively state of affairs that secures anthologies of this nature against monotony. Moreover, our title refers, not to "Marxists," but to "writings," that is, to Marxist essays as such rather than to Marxist authors as such. The question of who was or is a Marxist is much less pertinent for the purposes of our anthology than whether a given piece of writing in aesthetics, art history, or criticism, itself of value, is significantly indebted to the dialectical-materialist approach to history and society of Marx and Engels. Even here we do not think it useful to limit ourselves exclusively to writings with an overriding commitment to Marxism, although such commitment is evident in the work of figures like Gyorgy Lukács, Galvano della Volpe, or Ernst Fischer. A significant effect of Marxist thought has been to generate ideas which, without belonging in any Marxist fold, could hardly have existed apart from the continual presence of Marxism on the intellectual scene. George Orwell's "Politics and the English Language" is an example of a non-Marxist position for which Marxist theory seems to have served such a background function.

Because it is applied to content rather than to author, our broad criterion also permits us to omit in good conscience otherwise valuable writings of famous artists (for example, the late architect Le Corbusier) whose Marxist political sympathies were not in fact paralleled by any particularly Marxist ideas or influence in their books. And we are able, for the same reason, to include thinkers, such as Jean-Paul Sartre, who are strongly Marxist in certain writings, but much less so in others. In "The Artist and His Conscience," for example, Sartre turned specifically to a dilemma that can be genuinely agonizing only from a Marxist standpoint: the possible conflict between the cultural needs of a revolutionary social class and the expressive style of a contemporary artist who may find himself addressing the proletariat in an idiom alien to their ears.

These are the standards, then, for Part Two, "The Elements," that is, for the selections dealing with theoretical concepts, with art history and criticism, with genres, and with critical practice. The selections in Part One, "The Sources," necessarily require a slightly different rationale. There the aim is rather to provide some fundamental texts that have in fact been historically decisive in the development of Marxist thought on the arts. Not all Marxist essays on art have by any means been in agreement with all these basic texts; indeed, it would seem difficult, for example, for anyone to agree with both Lenin and Engels on the subject of programmatic art. But all are nevertheless basic writings, present to the mind of any Marxist-influenced thinker concerned with the arts. The inclusion of Marx, Engels, Lenin and Trotsky among "The Sources" requires no comment. G. Plekhanov and N. Bukharin were, in turn, two of the principal theoreticians to attempt an explicit formulation of the scattered observations on the arts which had been accumulating, for three-quarters of a century, since Marx's own writings. Joseph Stalin's remarks on the peculiar status of language and literature in the "ideological superstructure" were probably motivated in 1950 by nationalistic aims, but they remain extremely interesting in their own right, and have been widely studied. A similarly twofold justification applies to the inclusion of texts by the Chinese political leader and poet, Mao Tse-tung. In a word, then, relaxing slightly in places the criterion of intrinsic intellectual worth, we introduce in "The Sources" an overriding standard of exceptional historical relevance.

If what we say in this Introduction falls even close to the mark, the essays which follow should, taken together, contain some of the most germinal and sophisticated writings in contemporary aesthetics, criticism, and art history. We are trying to show that their appearance in the Marxist fold, or their bearing the imprint of Marxist thought, is no mere accident. These essays, moreover, should also exhibit the distinctive instruments which Marxist analysis offers to scholars and readers in the field who may not otherwise be aware of them. These aims do not imply, of course, a plea for general acceptance of the tenets of Marxism. The anthology claims, rather, that for anyone interested in the philosophical, critical and historical features of art, Marxism provides a valuable entrée.

We can do no better in concluding than to quote once more from Antonio Gramsci:

> Marx was great, his activity was fruitful, not because he invented out of nothing, not because he extracted an original vision of history from his fancy, but because in him the fragmentary, the incomplete, the immature became maturity, system, comprehension.[25]

The truth of any such claim for Marxist aesthetic theory as a whole remains of course for continuing reflection on art to determine, as its students look to Marxism for an account of art which they might not otherwise have contemplated.

Notes

[1] We know that Marx wrote poetry and could recite long passages of Shakespeare from memory. Even late in life, he planned, once *Das Kapital* was completed, to write a study of Balzac's *Comédie Humaine*. He had worked carefully through the writings on aesthetics of G. W. F. Hegel and of the latter's most prominent follower, F. T. Vischer, and studied Lessing's *Laocoön* and Winckelmann's *History of Ancient Art*. It would be surprising if such interests were not reflected in the structure and direction of his thought; but our question is a systematic, not a biographical one.

[2] The last decade has seen a persistent, often acrimonious controversy among interpreters of Marx concerning the relation between the early and the late writings, especially regarding the place in his systematic thinking of the *Economic and Philosophic Manuscripts of 1844*. One need not take sides in that controversy to admit that the *Manuscripts* were, after all, written by Marx, and that there is a substantial affinity between them and other of his early writings, for example, *Critique of Political Economy* and (with Engels) *German Ideology*. This affinity is especially

marked as concerns the concept of alienation and what the alternatives to it are. Even where the specific aspects of alienation worked out in these early writings are not enumerated, moreover, the necessity (and possibility) of a means for overcoming that condition is, of course, a constant theme in Marx's writing—both early and late.

[3] *The German Ideology*, reprinted in L. Feuer (ed.), *Marx and Engels* (New York: Doubleday and Co., 1959), p. 254.

[4] "First Economic and Philosophic Manuscript." (Cf. E. Fromm, *Marx's Concept of Man* [New York: Frederick Ungar, 1961]).

[5] "Third Economic and Philosophic Manuscript." (Cf. E. Fromm, *Marx's Concept of Man*).

[6] Cf. Mikhail Lifshitz, *The Philosophy of Art of Karl Marx* (New York: Critics Group, 1938), tr. Winn, p. 94.

[7] "Third Economic and Philosophic Manuscript." (Cf. E. Fromm, *Marx's Concept of Man*).

[8] K. Marx, *Capital* (Vol. 1), ed. by F. Engels, tr. by S. Moore and E. Aveling (New York: International Publishers, 1967), p. 73.

[9] Cf. K. Marx, *Communist Manifesto* (Chicago: Charles H. Kerr, 1947), pp. 19–20.

[10] Lucien Goldmann, *Recherches Dialectiques* (Paris: Gallimard, 1959), p. 30.

[11] See chapter 20, Lucien Goldmann, "Genetic-Structuralist Method in History of Literature."

[12] Cf. Gyorgy Lukács, "Einführung in die ästhetischen Schriften von Marx und Engels," (1945) in *Probleme der Ästhetik* (Neuwied: Luchterhand, 1969), pp. 205–31.

[13] Cf. G. Plekhanov, *Art and Society* (New York: Critics Group, 1936), pp. 49–52.

[14] Cf. Stanley Pullberg, "Note pour une lecture anthropologique de Marx," in *Dialectique Marxiste et Pensée Structurale* (Paris: Cahiers du Centre d'Etudes Socialistes, 1968), pp. 113–63 (esp. pp. 115–33, and p. 117, n. 16).

[15] Cf. Leon Trotsky, *Art and Revolution* (Ann Arbor: University of Michigan Press, 1960), tr. Rose Strunsky, p. 147.

[16] Cf. T. B. Bottomore (ed.), *Karl Marx* (New York: McGraw-Hill, 1964), p. 67.

[17] See chapter 35, B. Brecht, "Study of the First Scene of Shakespeare's *Coriolanus*."

[18] See chapter 13, Ernst Fischer, "The Necessity of Art."

[19] Cf. Gyorgy Lukács, "Einführung," p. 225.

[20] Cf. Z. P. Apresian, "An Appraisal of the Work Done in the 1930's on the Foundations of Marxist Aesthetics," in *Soviet Studies in Philosophy* (V, No. 4, 1967), 46.

[21] Cf. Gyorgy Lukács, "Einführung," p. 221; and chapter 4, F. Engels, "Letter to Margaret Harkness, April 1888." See also, G. Malenkov, XIX Congress of the Communist Party of the Soviet Union (October, 1952): "The typical is not only what one encounters most frequently, but what expresses with the most plenitude and in maximum relief the very essence of a given social force. . . . [It] corresponds to the essence of a social and historical phenomenon, it is simply the most widespread phenomenon, the most often repeated, the most day-to-day. A deliberate exaggeration, a more acute presentation of the image does not exclude its typical character, but on the contrary, reveals it more fully and brings it out." (*Cahiers du Communisme*, Paris, Special No., n.d., pp. 137–38.)

[22] Cf. Galvano della Volpe, *Critica del Gusto* (Milan: Feltrinelli, 1960), esp. Ch. II, "La chiave semantica della poesia," pp. 89–158; and chapter 15, "Theoretical Issues of a Marxist Poetics, in this anthology."

[23] See elsewhere in this anthology: chapter 4, F. Engels, "Letter to Minna Kautsky, 26 November 1885"; chapter 6, L. Trotsky, "Proletarian Culture and Proletarian

Art"; chapter 5, V. I. Lenin, "Party Organization and Party Literature"; chapter 25, B. Brecht, "Theatre for Pleasure and Theatre for Instruction"; also, "The Modern Theatre Is the Epic Theatre," in J. Willett, ed., *Brecht on Theatre* (New York: Hill & Wang, 1964), esp. pp. 37, 41–42.

[24] Antonio Gramsci in *II Grido del Popolo,* May 4, 1918.

[25] *Ibid.*

The Sources

1. Karl Marx

Property and Alienation

KARL MARX (1818–83) unquestionably stands as the most important figure in the history of socialist thought. Born in Trier, Germany, he studied at the universities of Bonn and Berlin, receiving his doctorate in philosophy from Jena in 1841 with a dissertation on classical materialism. When the newspaper he edited (1842–43) was suppressed, he emigrated to Paris, and it was there he met Friedrich Engels, who was to be a lifelong friend and co-worker. In 1848, he and Engels wrote the *Communist Manifesto*. From 1849 to the end of his life, Marx lived in London, mostly in relative poverty, studying and writing, when he could, at the British Museum. The first volume of his principal work, *Das Kapital*, appeared in 1867; the last two volumes were published posthumously. Other important works include *The Holy Family* (1845), *The German Ideology* (1845–46), and *Economic and Philosophic Manuscripts of 1844*, from which the selection is taken. The *Manuscripts* shows both Marx's indebtedness to, and his critical attitude toward, the philosophies of Hegel and Feuerbach. Of particular importance to Marx's views on art was his rejection of Feuerbach's "passive" or "contemplative" notion of sensuous experience in favor of a notion of the sensuous as a practical and active mode of experience.

Communism [is] the *positive* transcendence of *private property, as human self-estrangement,* and therefore [is] the real *appropriation of the human* essence by and for man; communism therefore [is] the complete return of man to himself as a *social* (i.e., human) being—a return become conscious, and accomplished within the entire wealth of previous development. This communism, as fully developed naturalism, equals humanism, and as fully developed humanism equals naturalism; it is the *genuine* resolution of the conflict between man and nature and between man and man—the true resolution of the strife between existence and essence, between objectification and self-confirmation, between freedom and necessity, between the individual and the species. Communism is the riddle of history solved, and it knows itself to be this solution.

The entire movement of history is, therefore, both its *actual* act of genesis (the birth act of its empirical existence) and also for its thinking consciousness the *comprehended* and *known* process of its *becoming*. That other, still immature communism, meanwhile, seeks an *historical* proof for itself—a proof in the realm of what already exists—among disconnected historical phenomena opposed to private property, tearing single phases from the historical process and focusing attention on them as proofs of its historical pedigree. . . By so doing it simply makes clear that by far the greater part of this process contradicts its own claim, and that, if it has ever existed, precisely its being in the *past* refutes its pretension to being *essential being*.

It is easy to see that the entire revolutionary movement necessarily finds both its empirical and its theoretical basis in the movement of *private property*—more precisely, in that of the economy.

This *material*, immediately perceptible private property is the material perceptible expression of *estranged human* life. Its movement—production and consumption—is the *perceptible* revelation of the movement of all production until now, i.e., the realization of the reality of man. Religion, family, state, law, morality, science, art, etc., are only *particular* modes of production, and fall under its general law. The positive transcendence of *private property*, as the appropriation of *human* life, is therefore the positive transcendence of all estrangement—that is to say, the return of man from religion, family, state, etc., to his *human*, i.e., *social* existence. Religious estrangement as such occurs only in the realm of *consciousness*, of man's inner life, but economic estrangement is that of *real life;* its transcendence therefore embraces both aspects. It is evident that the *initial* stage of the movement amongst the various peoples depends on whether the true and *authentic* life of the people manifests itself more in consciousness or in the external world—is more ideal or real. Communism begins from the outset (Robert Owen) with atheism; but atheism is at first far from being *communism;* indeed, it is still mostly an abstraction.

The philanthropy of atheism is therefore at first only *philosophical*, abstract, philanthropy, and that of communism is at once *real* and directly bent on *action*.

We have seen how on the assumption of positively annulled private property man produces man—himself and the other man; how the object, being the direct embodiment of his individuality, is simultaneously his own existence for the other man, an existence of the other man, and that existence for him. Likewise, however, both the material of labor and man as the subject, are the point of departure as well as the result of the movement (and precisely in this fact, that they must constitute the *point of departure*, lies the historical *necessity* of private property). Thus the *social* character is the general character of the whole movement: *just as* society itself produces *man as man*, so is society *produced* by him. Activity and mind, both in their content and in their *mode of existence*, are *social: social* activity and *social* mind. The *human* essence of nature first exists only for *social* man; for only here does nature exist for him as a *bond* with *man*—as his existence for the other and the other's existence for him—as the life-element of human reality. Only here does nature exist as the *foundation* of his own *human* existence. Only here has what is to him his *natural* existence become his *human* existence, and nature become man for him. Thus *society* is the unity of being of man with nature—the true resurrection of nature—the naturalism of man and the humanism of nature both brought to fulfillment.

Social activity and social mind exist by no means *only* in the form of some *directly* communal activity and directly *communal* mind, although *communal* activity and *communal* mind—i.e., activity and mind which are manifested and directly revealed in *real association* with other men— will occur wherever such a *direct* expression of sociability stems from the true character of the activity's content and is adequate to its nature.

But also when I am active *scientifically*, etc.—when I am engaged in activity which I can seldom perform in direct community with others— then I am *social*, because I am active as a *man*. Not only is the material of my activity given to me as a social product (as is even the language in which the thinker is active): my *own* existence *is* social activity, and therefore that which I make of myself, I make of myself for society and with the consciousness of myself as a social being.

My *general* consciousness is only the *theoretical* shape of that of which the *living* shape is the *real* community, the social fabric, although at the present day *general* consciousness is an abstraction from real life and as such confronts it with hostility. The *activity* of my general conscious- ness, as an activity, is therefore also my *theoretical* existence as a social being.

Above all we must avoid postulating "Society" again as an abstraction *vis-à-vis* the individual. The individual *is the social being.* His life, even if it may not appear in the direct form of a *communal* life in association with others—is therefore an expression and confirmation of *social life.* Man's individual and species life are not *different*, however much—and this is inevitable—the mode of existence of the individual is a more *particular*, or more *general* mode of the life of the species, or the life of the species is a more *particular* or more *general* individual life.

In his *consciousness of species* man confirms his real *social life* and simply repeats his real existence in thought, just as conversely the being of the species confirms itself in species-consciousness and exists for *itself* in its generality as a thinking being.

Man, much as he may therefore be a *particular* individual (and it is precisely his particularity which makes him an individual, and a real *individual* social being), is just as much the *totality*—the ideal totality—the subjective existence of thought and experienced society for itself; just as he exists also in the real world as the awareness and the real mind of social existence, and as a totality of human manifestation of life.

Thinking and being are thus no doubt *distinct*, but at the same time they are in *unity* with each other.

Death seems to be a harsh victory of the species over the *definite* individual and to contradict their unity. But the particular individual is only a *particular species being*, and as such mortal.

Just as *private property* is only the perceptible expression of the fact that man becomes *objective* for himself and at the same time becomes to himself a strange and inhuman object; just as it expresses the fact that the assertion of his life is the alienation of his life, that his realization is his loss of reality, is an *alien* reality: so, the positive transcendence of private property—i.e., the *perceptible* appropriation for and by man of the human essence and of human life, of objective man, of human *achievements*—should not to be conceived merely in the sense of *immediate*, one-sided *gratification*—merely in the sense of *possessing*, of *having*. Man appropriates his total essence in a total manner, that is to say, as a whole man. Each of his *human* relations to the world—seeing, hearing, smelling, tasting, feeling, thinking, observing, experiencing, wanting, acting, loving—in short, all the organs of his individual being, like those organs which are directly social in their form, are in their *objective* orientation or in their *orientation to the object*, the appropriation of that object. The appropriation of *human* reality; [1] its orientation to the object is the *manifestation of the human reality*, it is human *activity* and human *suffering*, for suffering, humanly considered, is a self-indulgence of man.

Private property has made us so stupid and one-sided that an object is only *ours* when we have it—when it exists for us as capital, or when it is directly possessed, eaten, drunk, worn, inhabited, etc.—in short, when it is *used* by us. Although private property itself again conceives all these direct realizations of possession only as *means of life*, and the life which they serve as means is the *life of private property*—labor and conversion into capital.

All these physical and mental senses have therefore—the sheer estrangement of *all* these senses—the sense of *having*. The human being had to be reduced to this absolute poverty in order that he might yield his inner wealth to the outer world. . . .

The transcendence of private property is therefore the complete *emancipation* of all human senses and qualities, but it is this emancipation precisely because these senses and attributes have become, subjectively and objectively, *human*. The eye has become a *human* eye, just as its *object* has become a social, *human* object—an object made by man for man. The *senses* have therefore become directly in their practice *theoreticians*. They relate themselves to the *thing* for the sake of the thing, but the thing itself is an *objective human* relation to itself and to man,[2] and vice versa. Need or enjoyment have consequently lost their *egotistical* nature, and nature has lost its mere *utility* by use becoming *human* use.

In the same way, the senses and minds of other men have become my *own* appropriation. Besides these direct organs, therefore, *social* organs develop in the *form* of society; thus, for instance, activity in direct association with others, etc., has become an organ for *expressing* my own *life*, and a mode of appropriating *human* life.

It is obvious that the *human* eye enjoys things in a way different from the crude, non-human eye; the human *ear* different from the crude ear, etc.

To recapitulate: man is not lost in his object only when the object becomes for him a *human* object or objective man. This is possible only when the object becomes for him a *social* object, he himself for himself a social being, just as society becomes a being for him in this object.

On the one hand, therefore, it is only when the objective world becomes everywhere for man in society the world of man's essential powers —human reality, and for that reason the reality of his *own* essential powers—that all *objects* become for him the *objectification of himself*, become objects which confirm and realize his individuality, become *his* objects: that is, *man himself* becomes the object. The manner in which they become *his* depends on the *nature of the objects* and on the nature of the *essential power* corresponding *to it;* for it is precisely the *determinate nature* of this relationship which shapes the particular, *real* mode of affirmation. To the *eye* an object comes to be other than it is to the *ear*, and the object of the eye is another object than the object of the *ear*. The specific character of each essential power is precisely its *specific essence*, and therefore also the specific mode of its objectification, of its *objectively actual* living *being*. Thus man is affirmed in the objective world not only in the act of thinking, but with *all* his senses.

On the other hand, let us look at this in its subjective aspect. Just as music alone awakens in man the sense of music, and just as the most beautiful music has *no* sense for the unmusical ear—is no object for it, because my object can only be the confirmation of one of my essential powers. It can therefore only be so for me as my essential power exists for itself as a subjective capacity, because the meaning of an object for me goes only so far as *my* senses go (has only a meaning for a sense corresponding to that object)—for this reason the *senses* of the social man are *other* senses than those of the non-social man. Only through the objectively unfolded richness of man's essential being is the richness of subjective *human* sensibility (a musical ear, an eye for beauty of form —in short, *senses* capable of human gratification, senses affirming themselves as essential powers of *man*) either cultivated or brought into being. For not only the five senses but also the so-called mental senses—the practical sense (will, love, etc.)—in a word, *human* sense—the human nature of the senses—comes to be by virtue of its object, by virtue of *humanized* nature. The *forming* of the five senses is a labor of the entire history of the world down to the present.

The *sense* caught up in crude practical need has only a restricted sense. For the starving man, it is not the human form of food that exists, but only its abstract being as food. It could just as well be there in its crudest form, and it would be impossible to say wherein this feeding activity differs from that of *animals.* The care-burdened man in need has no sense for the finest play; the dealer in minerals sees only the commercial value but not the beauty and the unique nature of the mineral: he has no mineralogical sense. Thus, the objectification of the human essence, both in its theoretical and practical aspects, is required to make man's *sense human,* as well as to create the *human sense* corresponding to the entire wealth of human and natural substance.

Just as through the movement of *private property,* of its wealth as well as its poverty—or of its material and spiritual wealth and poverty —the budding society finds at hand all the material for this *development,* so *established* society produces man in this entire richness of his being —produces the *rich* man *profoundly endowed with all the senses*—as its enduring reality.

We see how subjectivism and objectivism, spiritualism and materialism, activity and suffering, only lose their antithetical character, and thus their existence as such antitheses in social centers; we see how the resolution of the *theoretical* antitheses is *only* possible *in a practical* way, by virtue of the practical energy of man. Their resolution is therefore by no means merely a problem of understanding, but a *real* problem of life, which *philosophy* could not solve precisely because it conceived this problem as *merely* a theoretical one.

We see how the history of *industry* and the established *objective* existence of industry are the *open book* of *man's essential powers,* the exposure to the senses of human *psychology.* Hitherto this was not conceived in its inseparable connection with man's *essential being,* but only in an external relation of utility, because, moving in the realm of estrangement, people could only think of man's general mode of being—religion or history in its abstract-general character as politics, art, literature, etc. —as the reality of man's essential powers and *man's species activity*. We have before us the *objectified essential powers* of man in the form of *sensuous, alien, useful objects,* in the form of estrangement, displayed in *ordinary material industry* (which can be conceived as well as a part of that general movement, just as that movement can be conceived as a *particular* part of industry, since all human activity hitherto has been labor—that is, industry—activity estranged from itself).

A *psychology* for which this, the part of history most contemporary and accessible to sense, remains a closed book, cannot become a genuine, comprehensive and *real* science. What indeed are we to think of a science which *airily* abstracts from this large part of human labor and which fails to feel its own incompleteness, while such a wealth of human endeavor, unfolded before it, means nothing more to it than, perhaps, what can be expressed in one word—*"need," "vulgar need"?*

The *natural sciences* have developed an enormous activity and have accumulated an ever-growing mass of material. Philosophy, however, has remained just as alien to them as they remain to philosophy. Their momentary unity was only a *chimerical illusion.* The will was there, but the means were lacking. Even historiography pays regard to natural science only occasionally, as a factor of enlightenment, utility, and of some special great discoveries. But natural science has invaded and transformed human life all the more *practically* through the medium of industry; and has prepared human emancipation, although its immediate effect had to be the furthering of the dehumanization of man. *Industry* is the *actual,* historical relationship of nature, and therefore of natural science, to man. If, therefore, industry is conceived as the *exoteric* revelation of man's *essential powers,* we also gain an understanding of the *human* essence of nature or the *natural* essence of man. In consequence, natural science will lose its abstractly material—or rather, its idealistic—tendency, and will become the basis of *human* science, as it has already become the basis of actual human life, albeit in an estranged form. *One* basis for life and another basis for *science* is *a priori* a lie. The nature which develops in human history—the genesis of human society—is man's *real* nature; hence nature as it develops through industry, even though in an *estranged* form, is true *anthropological* nature.

Sense-perception (see Feuerbach) must be the basis of all science. Only when it proceeds from sense-perception in the twofold form both of *sensuous* consciousness and of *sensuous* need—that is, only when science proceeds from nature—is it *true* science. All history is the preparation for "man" to become the object of *sensuous* consciousness, and for the needs of "man as man" to become [natural, sensuous] needs. History itself is a *real* part of *natural history—*of nature developing into man. Natural science will in time incorporate into itself the science of man, just as the science of man will incorporate into itself natural science: there will be *one* science.

Man is the immediate object of natural science; for immediate, *sensuous nature* for man is, immediately, human sensuousness (the expressions are identical)—presented immediately in the form of the *other* man sensuously present for him. Indeed, his own sensuousness first exists as human sensuousness for himself through the *other* man. But *nature* is the immediate object of the *science of man:* the first object of man—man—is nature, sensuousness; and the particular sensuous human essential powers can only find their self-understanding in the science of the natural world in general, since they can find their objective realization in *natural* objects only. The element of thought itself—the element of thought's living expression—*language*—is of a sensuous nature. The *social* reality of nature, and *human* natural science, or the *natural science about man,* are identical terms.

It will be seen how in place of the *wealth* and *poverty* of political economy comes the *rich human being* and the rich *human* need. The *rich* human being is simultaneously the human being *in need* of a totality of human manifestations of life—the man in whom his own realization exists as an inner necessity, as *need.* Not only *wealth,* but likewise the *poverty* of man—under the assumption of socialism—receives in equal measure a *human* and therefore social significance. Poverty is the passive blood which causes the human being to experience the need of the greatest wealth—the *other* human being. The dominion of the objective being in me, the sensuous outburst of my life activity, is *passion,* which thus becomes here the *activity* of my being.

A *being* only considers himself independent when he stands on his own feet; and he only stands on his own feet when he owes his *existence* to himself. A man who lives by the grace of another regards himself as a dependent being. But I live completely by the grace of another if I owe him not only the maintenance of my life, but if he has, moreover, *created* my *life—*if he is the *source* of my life. When it is not of my own creation, my life has necessarily a source of this kind outside of it. The *Creation* is therefore an idea very difficult to dislodge from popular consciousness. The fact that nature and man exist in their own account is *incomprehensible* to it, because it contradicts everything *tangible* in practical life.

The creation of the *earth* has received a mighty blow from geogeny—i.e., from the science which presents the formation of the earth, the further development of the earth, as a process, as a self-generation.

Generatio aequivoca [many-sided generation] is the only practical refutation of the theory of creation.

Now it is certainly easy to say to the single individual what Aristotle has already said: You have been begotten by your father and your mother; therefore in you the mating of two human beings—a species-act of human beings—has produced the human being. You see, therefore, that even physically, man owes his existence to man. Therefore you must not only keep sight of the *one* aspect—the *infinite* progression which leads you further to enquire: "Who begot my father? Who is grandfather?" etc. You must also hold on to the *circular movement* sensuously perceptible in that progression, by which man repeats himself in procreation, *man* thus always remaining the subject. You will reply, however: I grant you this circular movement; now grant me the progression which drives me ever further until I ask: Who begot the first man, and nature as a whole? I can only answer you: Your question is itself a product of abstraction. Ask yourself how you arrived at that question. Ask yourself whether your question is not posed from a standpoint to which I cannot reply, because it is wrongly put. Ask yourself whether that progression as such exists for a reasonable mind. When you ask about the creation of nature and man, you are abstracting, in so doing, from man and nature. You postulate them as *non-existent,* and yet you want me to prove them to you as *existing.* Now I say to you: Give up your abstraction and you will also give up your question. Or if you want to hold on to your abstraction, then be consistent, and if you think of man and nature as *non-existent,* then think of yourself as non-existent, for you too are surely nature and man. Don't think, don't ask me, for as soon as you think and ask, your *abstraction* from the existence of nature and man has no meaning. Or are you such an egotist that you conceive everything as nothing, and yet want yourself to exist?

You can reply: I do not want to conceive the nothingness of nature, etc. I ask you about *its genesis,* just as I ask the anatomist about the formation of bones, etc.

But since for the socialist man the *entire so-called history of the world* is nothing but the creation of man through human labor, nothing but the emergence of nature for man, so he has the visible, irrefutable proof of his *birth* through himself, of the *process of his creation.* Since the *real existence* of man and nature—since man has become for man as the being of nature, and nature for man as the being of man has become practical, sensuous, perceptible—the question about an *alien* being, about a being above nature and man—a question which implies the admission of the unreality of nature and of man—has become impossible in practice. *Atheism,* as the denial of this unreality, has no longer any meaning, for atheism is a *negation of God,* and postulates the *existence of man* through this negation; but socialism as socialism no longer stands in any need of such mediation. It proceeds from the *practically and theoretically sensuous consciousness* of man and of nature as the *essence.* Socialism is man's *positive self-consciousness,* no longer mediated through the annulment of religion, just as *real life* is man's positive reality, no longer mediated through the annulment of private property, through *communism.* Communism is the position as the negation of the negation, and is hence the *actual* phase necessary for the next stage of historical development in the process of human emancipation and rehabilitation. *Communism* is the necessary pattern and the dynamic principle of the immediate future, but communism as such is not the goal of human development—which goal is the structure of human society.

Notes

[1] For this reason it is just as highly varied as the *determinations* of human *essence* and *activities.*

[2] In practice I can relate myself to a thing humanly only if the thing relates itself humanly to the human being.

2. Karl Marx

Production and Consumption

KARL MARX composed several slightly varying versions of his *Introduction to the Critique of Political Economy* during the years 1857–59. The title "Production and Consumption" has been supplied by the editors for the passages selected from the *Introduction*. Biographical information may be found on page 21.

THE subject of our discussion as first of all *material* production by individuals as determined by society, naturally constitutes the starting point. The individual and isolated hunter or fisher who forms the starting point with Smith and Ricardo, belongs to the insipid illusions of the eighteenth century. They are Robinsonades which do not by any means represent, as students of the history of civilization imagine, a reaction against over-refinement and a return to a misunderstood natural life. They are no more based on such a naturalism than is Rousseau's *contrat social*, which makes naturally independent individuals come in contact and have mutual intercourse by contract. They are the fiction and only the aesthetic fiction of the small and great Robinsonades. They are, moreover, the anticipation of "bourgeois society," which had been in course of development since the sixteenth century and made gigantic strides towards maturity in the eighteenth. In this society of free competition the individual appears free from the bonds of nature, etc., which in former epochs of history made him a part of a definite, limited human conglomeration. To the prophets of the eighteenth century, on whose shoulders Smith and Ricardo are still standing, this eighteenth century individual, constituting the joint product of the dissolution of the feudal form of society and of the new forces of production which had developed since the sixteenth century, appears as an ideal whose existence belongs to the past; not as a result of history, but as its starting point.

Since that individual appeared to be in conformity with nature and [corresponded] to their conception of human nature, [he was regarded] not as a product of history, but of nature. This illusion has been characteristic of every new epoch in the past. Steuart, who, as an aristocrat, stood more firmly on historical ground, contrary to the spirit of the eighteenth century, escaped this simplicity of view. The further back we go into history, the more the individual and, therefore, the producing individual seems to depend on and constitute a part of a larger whole: at first it is, quite naturally, the family and the clan, which is but an enlarged family; later on, it is the community growing up in its different forms out of the clash and the amalgamation of clans. It is but in the eighteenth century, in "bourgeois society," that the different forms of social union confront the individual as a mere means to his private ends, as an outward necessity. But the period in which this view of the isolated individual becomes prevalent, is the very one in which the interrelations of society (general from this point of view) have reached the highest state of development. Man is in the most literal sense of the word a *zoon politikon,* not only a social animal, but an animal which can develop into an individual only in society. Production by isolated individuals outside of society—something which might happen as an exception to a civilized man who by accident got into the wilderness and already dynamically possessed within himself the forces of society—is as great an absurdity as the idea of the development of language without individuals living together and talking to one another. We need not dwell on this any longer. It would not be necessary to touch upon this point at all, were not the vagary which had its justification and sense with the people of the eighteenth century transplanted in all earnest into the field of political economy by Bastiat, Carey, Proudhon and others. Proudhon and others naturally find it very pleasant, when they do not know the historical origin of a certain economic phenomenon, to give it a quasi historico-philosophical explanation by going into mythology. Adam or Prometheus hit upon the scheme cut and dried, whereupon it was adopted, etc. Nothing is more tediously dry than the dreaming *locus communis.*

Whenever we speak, therefore, of production, we always have in mind production at a certain stage of social development, or production by social individuals. Hence, it might seem that in order to speak of production at all, we must either trace the historical process of development through its various phases, or declare at the outset that we are dealing with a certain historical period, as, e.g., with modern capitalistic production which, as a matter of fact, constitutes the subject proper of this work. But all stages of production have certain landmarks in common, common purposes. *Production in general* is an abstraction, but it is a rational abstraction, insofar as it singles out and fixes the common features, thereby saving us repetition. Yet these general or common features discovered by comparison constitute something very complex, whose constituent elements have different destinations. Some of these elements belong to all epochs, others are common to a few. Some of them are common to the most modern as well as to the most ancient epochs. No production is conceivable without them; but while even the most completely developed languages have laws and conditions in common with the least developed ones, what is characteristic of their development are the points of departure from the general and common. The conditions which generally govern production must be differentiated in order that the essential points of difference be not lost sight of in view of the general uniformity which is due to the fact that the subject, mankind, and the object, nature, remain the same. The failure to remember this one fact is the source of all the wisdom of modern economists who are trying to prove the eternal nature and harmony of existing social conditions. Thus they say, e.g., that no production is possible without some instrument of production, let that instrument be only the hand; that none is possible without past accumulated labor, even if that labor consist of mere skill which has been accumulated and concentrated in the hand of the savage by repeated exercise. Capital is, among other things, also an instrument of production, also past impersonal labor. Hence capital is a universal, eternal natural phenomenon; which is true if we disregard the specific properties which turn an "instrument of production" and "stored up labor" into capital. The entire history of production appears to a man like Carey, e.g., as a malicious perversion on the part of governments.

If there is no production in general, there is also no general production. Production is always some special branch of production or an aggregate, as, e.g., agriculture, stock raising, manufactures, etc. But political economy is not technology. The connection between the general destinations of production at a given stage of social development and the particular forms of production, is to be developed elsewhere (later on).

Finally, production is not only of a special kind. It is always a certain body politic, a social personality that is engaged on a larger or smaller aggregate of branches of production. The connection between the real process and its scientific presentation also falls outside of the scope of this treatise. [We must thus distinguish between] production in general, special branches of production and production as a whole.

Production is at the same time also consumption. Twofold consumption, subjective and objective. The individual who develops his faculties in production, is also expending them, consuming them in the act of production, just as procreation is in its way a consumption of vital powers. In the second place, production is consumption of means of production which are used and used up and partly (as, e.g., in burning) reduced to their natural elements. The same is true of the consumption of raw materials which do not remain in their natural form and state, being greatly absorbed in the process. The act of production is, therefore, in all its aspects an act of consumption as well. But this is admitted by economists. Production as directly identical with consumption, consumption as directly coincident with production, they call productive consumption. This identity of production and consumption finds its expression in Spinoza's proposition, *Determinatio est negatio*. But this definition of productive consumption is resorted to just for the purpose of distinguishing between consumption as identical with production and consumption proper, which is defined as its destructive counterpart. Let us then consider consumption proper.

Consumption is directly also production, just as in nature the consumption of the elements and of chemical matter constitutes production of plants. It is clear that in nutrition, e.g., which is but one form of consumption, man produces his own body; but it is equally true of every kind of consumption, which goes to produce the human being in one way or another. [It is] consumptive production. But, say the economists, this production which is identical with consumption, is a second production resulting from the destruction of the product of the first. In the first, the producer transforms himself into things; in the second, things are transformed into human beings. Consequently, this consumptive production—although constituting a direct unity of production and consumption —differs essentially from production proper. The direct unity in which production coincides with consumption and consumption with production, does not interfere with their direct duality.

Production is thus at the same time consumption, and consumption is at the same time production. Each is directly its own counterpart. But at the same time an intermediary movement goes on between the two. Production furthers consumption by creating material for the latter which otherwise would lack its object. But consumption in its turn furthers production, by providing for the products the individual for whom they are products. The product receives its last finishing touches in consumption. A railroad on which no one rides, which is consequently not used up, not consumed, is but a potential railroad, and not a real one. Without production, no consumption; but, on the other hand, without consumption, no production; since production would then be without a purpose. Consumption produces production in two ways.

In the first place, in that the product first becomes a real product in consumption; e.g., a garment becomes a real garment only through the act of being worn; a dwelling which is not inhabited, is really no dwelling; consequently, a product as distinguished from a mere natural object, proves to be such, first *becomes* a product in consumption. Consumption gives the product the finishing touch by annihilating it, since a product is the [result] of production not only as the material embodiment of activity, but also as a mere object for the active subject.

In the second place, consumption produces production by creating the necessity for new production, i.e., by providing the ideal, inward, impelling cause which constitutes the prerequisite of production. Consumption furnishes the impulse for production as well as its object, which plays in production the part of its guiding aim. It is clear that while production furnishes the material object of consumption, consumption provides the ideal object of production, as its image, its want, its impulse and its purpose. It furnishes the object of production in its subjective form. No wants, no production. But consumption reproduces the want.

In its turn, production

First, furnishes consumption * with its material, its object. Consumption without an object is no consumption, hence production works in this direction by producing consumption.

Second. But it is not only the object that production provides for consumption. It gives consumption its definite outline, its character, its finish. Just as consumption gives the product its finishing touch as a product, production puts the finishing touch on consumption. For the object is not simply an object in general, but a definite object, which is consumed in a certain definite manner prescribed in its turn by production. Hunger is hunger; but the hunger that is satisfied with cooked meat eaten with fork and knife is a different kind of hunger from the one that devours raw meat with the aid of hands, nails, and teeth. Not only the object of consumption, but also the manner of consumption is produced by production; that is to say, consumption is created by production not only objectively, but also subjectively. Production thus creates the consumers.

Third. Production not only supplies the want with material, but supplies the material with a want. When consumption emerges from its first stage of natural crudeness and directness—and its continuation in that state would in itself be the result of a production still remaining in a state of natural crudeness—it is itself furthered by its object as a moving spring. The want of it which consumption experiences is created by its appreciation of the product. The object of art, as well as any other product, creates an artistic and beauty-enjoying public. Production thus produces not only an object for the individual, but also an individual for the object.

Production thus produces consumption: first, by furnishing the latter with material; second, by determining the manner of consumption; third, by creating in consumers a want for its products as objects of consump-

* The manuscript reads "production."

tion. It thus produces the object, the manner, and the moving spring of consumption. In the same manner, consumption [creates] the *disposition* of the producer by setting him up as an aim and by stimulating wants. The identity of consumption and production thus appears to be a threefold one.

First, direct identity: production is consumption; consumption is production. Consumptive production. Productive consumption. Economists call both productive consumption, but make one distinction by calling the former reproduction, and the latter productive consumption. All inquiries into the former deal with productive and unproductive labor; those into the latter treat of productive and unproductive consumption.

Second. Each appears as the means of the other and as being brought about by the other, which is expressed as their mutual interdependence; a relation, by virtue of which they appear as mutually connected and indispensable, yet remaining outside of each other.

Production creates the material as the outward object of consumption; consumption creates the want as the inward object, the purpose of production. Without production, no consumption; without consumption, no production; this maxim figures in political economy in many forms.

Third. Production is not only directly consumption and consumption directly production; nor is production merely a means of consumption and consumption the purpose of production. In other words, not only does each furnish the other with its object; production, the material object of consumption; consumption, the ideal object of production. On the contrary, either one is not only directly the other, not only a means of furthering the other, but while it is taking place, creates the other as such for itself. Consumption completes the act of production by giving the finishing touch to the product as such, by destroying the latter, by breaking up its independent material form; by bringing to a state of readiness, through the necessity of repetition, the disposition to produce developed in the first act of production; that is to say, it is not only the concluding act through which the product becomes a product, but also [the one] through which the producer becomes a producer. On the other hand, production produces consumption, by determining the manner of consumption, and further, by creating the incentive for consumption, the very ability to consume, in the form of want. This latter identity mentioned under point 3, is much discussed in political economy in connection with the treatment of the relations of demand and supply, of objects and wants, of natural wants and those created by society.

The unequal relation between the development of material production and art, for instance. In general, the conception of progress is not to be taken in the sense of the usual abstraction. In the case of art, etc., it is not so important and difficult to understand this disproportion as in that of practical social relations, e.g., the relation between education in the United States and Europe. The really difficult point, however, that is to be discussed here is that of the unequal development of relations of production as legal relations. As, e.g., the connection between Roman civil law (this is less true of criminal and public law) and modern production.

This conception of development appears to imply necessity. On the other hand, justification of accident. Varia. (Freedom and other points.) (The effect of means of communication.) World history does not always appear in history as the result of world history.

The starting point [is to be found] in certain facts of nature embodied subjectively and objectively in clans, races, etc.

It is well known that certain periods of highest development of art stand in no direct connection with the general development of society, nor with the material basis and the skeleton structure of its organization. Witness the example of the Greeks as compared with the modern nations or even Shakespeare. As regards certain forms of art, as e.g., the *epos*, it is admitted that they can never be produced in the world-epoch-making form as soon as art as such comes into existence; in other words, that in the domain of art certain important forms of it are possible only at a low stage of its development. If that be true of the mutual relations of different forms of art within the domain of art itself, it is far less surprising that the same is true of the relation of art as a whole to the general development of society. The difficulty lies only in the general formulation of these contradictions. No sooner are they specified than they are explained. Let us take for instance the relation of Greek art and of that of Shakespeare's time to our own. It is a well known fact that Greek mythology was not only the arsenal of Greek art, but also the very ground from which it had sprung. Is the view of nature and of social relations which shaped Greek imagination and Greek [art] possible in the age of automatic machinery, and railways, and locomotives, and electric telegraphs? Where does Vulcan come in as against Roberts & Co.; Jupiter, as against the lightning rod; and Hermes, as against the Crédit Mobilier? All mythology masters and dominates and shapes the forces of nature in and through the imagination; hence it disappears as soon as man gains mastery over the forces of nature. What becomes of the Goddess Fame side by side with Printing House Square? * Greek art presupposes the existence of Greek mythology, i.e., that nature and even the form of society are wrought up in popular fancy in an unconsciously artistic fashion. That is its material. Not, however, any mythology taken at random, nor any accidental unconsciously artistic elaboration of nature

* The site of the "Times" building in London.

(including under the latter all objects, hence [also] society). Egyptian mythology could never be the soil or womb which would give birth to Greek art. But in any event [there had to be] a mythology. In no event [could Greek art originate] in a society which excludes any mythological explanation of nature, any mythological attitude towards it and which requires from the artist an imagination free from mythology.

Looking at it from another side: is Achilles possible side by side with powder and lead? Or is the *Iliad* at all compatible with the printing press and steam press? Does not singing and reciting and the muses necessarily go out of existence with the appearance of the printer's bar, and do not, therefore, disappear the prerequisites of epic poetry?

But the difficulty is not in grasping the idea that Greek art and epos are bound up with certain forms of social development. It rather lies in understanding why they still constitute with us a source of aesthetic enjoyment and in certain respects prevail as the standard and model beyond attainment.

A man cannot become a child again unless he becomes childish. But does he not enjoy the artless ways of the child and must he not strive to reproduce its truth on a higher plane? Is not the character of every epoch revived perfectly true to nature in child nature? Why should the social childhood of mankind, where it had obtained its most beautiful development, not exert an eternal charm as an age that will never return? There are ill-bred children and precocious children. Many of the ancient nations belong to the latter class. The Greeks were normal children. The charm their art has for us does not conflict with the primitive character of the social order from which it had sprung. It is rather the product of the latter, and is rather due to the fact that the unripe social conditions under which the art arose and under which alone it could appear can never return.

3. Karl Marx
and Friedrich Engels

Real Men and Human Ideas

This selection is from *The German Ideology*, by KARL MARX and FRIEDRICH ENGELS. Composed in Brussels in 1845–46, the manuscript was a detailed criticism of post-Hegelian philosophy, and a systematic account of their view of the derivation of ideological notions from economic structures. Unpublished during the authors' lifetimes, it did not appear in print until the mid-thirties. Biographical notes may be found on pages 21 and 48.

THE premises from which we begin are not arbitrary ones, not dogmas, but real premises from which abstraction can only be made in the imagination. They are the real individuals, their activity and the material conditions under which they live, both those which they find already existing and those produced by their activity. These premises can thus be verified in a purely empirical way.

The first premise of all human history is, of course, the existence of living human individuals. Thus the first fact to be established is the physical organization of these individuals and their consequent relation to the rest of nature. Of course, we cannot here go either into the actual physical nature of man, or into the natural conditions in which man finds himself—geological, orohydrographical, climatic and so on. The writing of history must always set out from these natural bases and their modification in the course of history through the action of man.

Men can be distinguished from animals by consciousness, by religion or anything else you like. They themselves begin to distinguish themselves from animals as soon as they begin to *produce* their means of subsistence, a step which is conditioned by their physical organization. By producing their means of subsistence men are indirectly producing their actual material life.

The way in which men produce their means of subsistence depends first of all on the nature of the actual means they find in existence and have to reproduce. This mode of production must not be considered simply as being the reproduction of the physical existence of the individuals. Rather it is a definite form of activity of these individuals, a definite form of expressing their life, a definite *mode of life* on their part. As individuals express their life, so they are. What they are, therefore, coincides with their production, both with *what* they produce and with *how* they produce. The nature of individuals thus depends on the material conditions determining their production.

The fact is, therefore, that definite individuals who are productively active in a definite way enter into these definite social and political relations. Empirical observation must in each separate instance bring out empirically, and without any mystification and speculation, the connection of the social and political structure with production. The social structure and the State are continually evolving out of the life-process of definite individuals, but of individuals, not as they may appear in their own or other people's imagination, but as they really are; i.e., as they are effective, produce materially, and are active under definite material limits, presuppositions and conditions independent of their will.

The production of ideas, of conceptions, of consciousness, is at first directly interwoven with the material activity and the material intercourse of men, the language of real life. Conceiving, thinking, the mental intercourse of men, appear at this stage as the direct efflux of their material behavior. The same applies to mental production as expressed in the language of the politics, laws, morality, religion, metaphysics of a people. Men are the producers of their conceptions, ideas, etc.—real, active men, as they are conditioned by a definite development of their productive forces and of the intercourse corresponding to these, up to its furthest forms. Consciousness can never be anything else than conscious existence, and the existence of men is their actual life-process. If in all ideology men and their circumstances appear upside down as in a *camera obscura,* this phenomenon arises just as much from their historical life-process as the inversion of objects on the retina does from their physical life-process.

In direct contrast to German philosophy which descends from heaven to earth, here we ascend from earth to heaven. That is to say, we do not set out from what men say, imagine, conceive, nor from men as narrated, thought of, imagined, conceived, in order to arrive at men in the flesh. We set out from real, active men, and on the basis of their real life-process we demonstrate the development of the ideological reflexes and echoes of this life-process. The phantoms formed in the human brain are also, necessarily, sublimates of their material life-process, which is empirically verifiable and bound to material premises. Morality, religion, metaphysics, all the rest of ideology and their corresponding forms of consciousness, thus no longer retain the semblance of independence. They have no history, no development; but men, developing their material production and their material intercourse, alter, along with this their real existence, their thinking and the products of their thinking. Life is not determined by consciousness, but consciousness by life. In the first method of approach the starting-point is consciousness taken as the living individual; in the second it is the real living individuals themselves, as they are in actual life, and consciousness is considered solely as *their* consciousness.

This method of approach is not devoid of premises. It starts out from the real premises and does not abandon them for a moment. Its premises are men, not in any fantastic isolation or abstract definition, but in their actual, empirically perceptible process of development under definite conditions. As soon as this active life-process is described, history ceases to be a collection of dead facts as it is with the empiricists (themselves still abstract), or an imagined activity of imagined subjects, as with the idealists.

Where speculation ends—in real life—there real, positive science begins: the representation of the practical activity, of the practical process of development of men. Empty talk about consciousness ceases, and real knowledge has to take its place. When reality is depicted, philosophy as an independent branch of activity loses its medium of existence. At the best its place can only be taken by a summing-up of the most general results, abstractions which arise from the observation of the historical development of men. Viewed apart from real history, these abstractions have in themselves no value whatsoever. They can only serve to facilitate the arrangement of historical material, to indicate the sequence of its separate strata. But they by no means afford a recipe or schema, as does philosophy, for neatly trimming the epochs of history. On the contrary, our difficulties begin only when we set about the observation and the arrangement—the real depiction—of our historical material, whether of a past epoch or of the present. . . .

. . . This beginning is as animal as social life itself at this stage. It is mere herd-consciousness, and at this point man is only distinguished from sheep by the fact that with him consciousness takes the place of instinct or that his instinct is a conscious one.

This sheep-like or tribal consciousness receives its further development and extension through increased productivity, the increase of needs, and, what is fundamental to both of these, the increase of population. With these there develops the division of labor, which was originally nothing but the division of labor in the sexual act, then that division of labor which develops spontaneously or "naturally" by virtue of natural pre-disposition (e.g., physical strength), needs, accidents, etc., etc. Division of labor only becomes truly such from the moment when a division of material and mental labor appears. From this moment onwards consciousness *can* really flatter itself that it is something other than consciousness of existing practice, that it is *really* conceiving something without conceiving something *real;* from now on consciousness is in a position to emancipate itself from the world and to proceed to the formation of "pure" theory, theology, philosophy, ethics, etc. But even if this theory, theology, philosophy, ethics, etc., comes into contradiction with the existing relations, this can only occur as a result of the fact that existing social relations have come into contradiction with existing forces of production; this, moreover, can also occur in a particular national sphere of relations through the appearance of the contradiction, not within the national orbit, but between this national consciousness and the practice of other nations, i.e., between the national and the general consciousness of a nation.

Moreover, it is quite immaterial what consciousness starts to do on its own: out of all such muck we get only the one inference that these three moments, the forces of production, the state of society, and consciousness, can and must come into contradiction with one another, because the division of labor implies the possibility, nay the fact, that intellectual and material activity—enjoyment and labor, production and consumption—devolve on different individuals, and that the only possibility of their not coming into contradiction lies in the negation in its turn of the division of labor. It is self-evident, moreover, that "specters," "bonds," "the higher being," "concept," "scruple," are merely the idealistic, spiritual expression, the conception apparently of the isolated individual, the image of very empirical fetters and limitations, within which the mode of production of life, and the form of intercourse coupled with it, move.

With the division of labor, in which all these contradictions are implicit, and which in its turn is based on the natural division of labor in the family and the separation of society into individual families opposed to one another, is given simultaneously the distribution, and indeed the unequal distribution (both quantitative and qualitative), of labor and its products, hence property: the nucleus, the first form of which lies in the family, where wife and children are the slaves of the husband. This latent slavery in the family, though still very crude, is the first property, but even at this early stage it corresponds perfectly to the definition of modern economists who call it the power of disposing of the labor-power of others. Division of labor and private property are, moreover, identical expressions: in the one the same thing is affirmed with reference to activity as is affirmed in the other with reference to the product of the activity.

Further, the division of labor implies the contradiction between the interest of the separate individual or the individual family and the communal interest of all individuals who have intercourse with one another. And indeed, this communal interest does not exist merely in the imagination, as "the general good," but first of all in reality, as the mutual interdependence of the individuals among whom the labor is divided. And finally, the division of labor offers us the first example of how, as long as man remains in natural society, that is as long as a cleavage exists between the particular and the common interest, as long therefore as activity is not voluntarily, but naturally, divided, man's own deed becomes an alien power opposed to him, which enslaves him instead of being controlled by him. For as soon as labor is distributed, each man has a particular, exclusive sphere of activity, which is forced upon him and from which he cannot escape. He is a hunter, a fisherman, a shepherd, or a critical critic, and must remain so if he does not want to lose his means of livelihood; while in communist society, where nobody has one exclusive sphere of activity but each can become accomplished in any branch he wishes, society regulates the general production and thus makes it possible for me to do one thing today and another tomorrow, to hunt in the morning, fish in the afternoon, rear cattle in the evening, criticize after dinner, just as I have a mind, without ever becoming hunter, fisherman, shepherd or critic.

This crystallization of social activity, this consolidation of what we ourselves produce into an objective power above us, growing out of our control, thwarting our expectations, bringing to naught our calculations, is one of the chief factors in historical development up till now. And out of this very contradiction between the interest of the individual and that of the community the latter takes an independent form as the STATE, divorced from the real interests of individual and community, and at the same time as an illusory communal life, always based, however, on the real ties existing in every family and tribal conglomeration (such as flesh and blood, language, division of labor on a larger scale, and other interests) and especially, as we shall enlarge upon later, on the classes, already determined by the division of labor, which in every such mass of men separate out, and of which one dominates all the others. It follows from this that all struggles within the State, the struggle between democracy, aristocracy and monarchy, the struggle for the franchise, etc., etc., are merely the illusory forms in which the real struggles of the different classes are fought out among one another (of this the German theoreticians have not the faintest inkling, although they have received a sufficient introduction to the subject in *The German-French Annals* and *The Holy Family*).

Like our opponents, Feuerbach still accepts and at the same time misunderstands existing reality. We recall the passage in the *Philosophy of the Future*, where he develops the view that the existence of a thing or a man is at the same time its or his essence, that the conditions of existence, the mode of life and particular activity of an animal or human individual are those in which its "essence" feels itself satisfied. Here every exception is expressly conceived as an unhappy chance, as an abnormality which cannot be altered. Thus if millions of proletarians feel themselves by no means contented in their conditions of life, if their existence [is in contradiction with their "essence," then it is certainly an abnormality, but not an unhappy chance; an historical fact based on quite definite social relationships. Feuerbach is content to affirm this fact; he only interprets the existing sensuous world, has only the relation of a theorist to it], while in reality for the practical materialist, i.e., the communist, it is a question of revolutionizing the existing world, of practically attacking and changing existing things. When occasionally we find such views with Feuerbach, they are never more than isolated surmises and have much too little influence on his general outlook to be considered here as anything else than embryos capable of development.

Feuerbach's "interpretation" of the sensuous world is confined on the one hand to mere contemplation of it, and on the other to mere feeling; he says "man" instead of "real, historical men." "Man" is really "the German." In the first case, the contemplation of the sensuous world, he necessarily lights on things which contradict his consciousness and feeling, which upset the harmony of all parts of the sensuous world and especially of man and nature, a harmony he presupposes.* To push these on one side, he must take refuge in a double perception, a profane one which only perceives the "flatly obvious" and a higher more philosophical one which perceives the "true essence" of things. He does not see how the sensuous world around him is not a thing given direct from all eternity, ever the same, but the product of industry and of the state of society; and, indeed, in the sense that it is an historical product, the result of the activity of a whole succession of generations, each standing on the shoulders of the preceding one, developing its industry and its intercourse, modifying its social organization according to the changed needs. Even the objects of the simplest "sensuous certainty" are only given

* Feuerbach's failing is not that he subordinates the flatly obvious, the sensuous appearance, to the sensuous reality established by more accurate investigation of the sensuous facts, but that he cannot in the last resort cope with the sensuous world except by looking at it with the "eyes," i.e., through the "spectacles" of the *philosopher*.

him through social development, industry and commercial intercourse. The cherry-tree, like almost all fruit-trees, was, as is well known, only a few centuries ago transplanted by commerce into our zone, and therefore only by this action of a definite society in a definite age provided for the evidence of Feuerbach's "senses." Actually, when we conceive things thus, as they really are and happened, every profound philosophical problem is resolved, as will be seen even more clearly later, quite simply into an empirical fact.

For instance, the important question of the relation of man to nature (Bruno goes so far as to speak of "the antitheses in nature and history," as though these were two separate "things" and man did not always have before him an historical nature and a natural history) out of which all the "unfathomably lofty works" on "substance" and "self-consciousness" were born, crumbles of itself when we understand that the celebrated "unity of man with nature" has always existed in industry and has existed in varying forms in every epoch according to the lesser or greater development of industry, just like the "struggle" of man with nature, right up to the development of his productive powers on a corresponding basis. Industry and commerce, production and the exchange of the necessities of life, themselves determine distribution, the structure of the different social classes and are, in turn, determined by these as to the mode in which they are carried on; and so it happens that in Manchester, for instance, Feuerbach sees only factories and machines where a hundred years ago only spinning-wheels and weaving-looms were to be seen, or in the Campagna of Rome he finds only pasture lands and swamps, where in the time of Augustus he would have found nothing but the vineyards and villas of Roman capitalists. Feuerbach speaks in particular of the perception of natural science; he mentions secrets which are disclosed only to the eye of the physicist and chemist: but where would natural science be without industry and commerce? Even this "pure" natural science is provided with an aim, as with its material, only through trade and industry, through the sensuous activity of men. So much is this activity, this unceasing sensuous labor and creation, this production, the basis of the whole sensuous world as it now exists, that, were it interrupted only for a year, Feuerbach would not only find an enormous change in the natural world, but would very soon find that the whole world of men and his own perceptive faculty, nay his own existence, were missing.

Of course, in all this the priority of external nature remains unassailed, and all this has no application to the original men produced by "generatio aequivoca" (spontaneous generation); but this differentiation has meaning only in so far as man is considered to be distinct from nature. For that matter, nature, the nature that preceded human history, is not by any means the nature in which Feuerbach lives, nor the nature which today no longer exists anywhere (except perhaps on a few Australian coral-islands of recent origin) and which, therefore, does not exist for Feuerbach. . . .

Certainly Feuerbach has a great advantage over the "pure" materialists in that he realizes how man too is an "object of the senses." But apart from the fact that he only conceives him as a "sensuous object," not as "sensuous activity," because he still remains in the realm of theory and conceives of men not in their given social connection, not under their existing conditions of life, which have made them what they are, he never arrives at the really existing active men, but stops at the abstraction "man," and gets no further than recognizing "the true, individual, corporeal man" emotionally, i.e., he knows no other "human relationships" "of man to man" than love and friendship, and even then idealized. He gives no criticism of the present conditions of life. Thus he never manages to conceive the sensuous world as the total living sensuous activity of the individuals composing it; and therefore when, for example, he sees instead of healthy men a crowd of scrofulous, over-worked and consumptive starvelings, he is compelled to take refuge in the "higher perception" and in the ideal "compensation in the species," and thus to relapse into idealism at the very point where the communist materialist sees the necessity, and at the same time the condition, of a transformation both of industry and of the social structure.

As far as Feuerbach is a materialist he does not deal with history, and as far as he considers history he is not a materialist. With him materialism and history diverge completely, a fact which explains itself from what has been said.

History is nothing but the succession of the separate generations, each of which exploits the materials, the forms of capital, the productive forces handed down to it by all preceding ones, and thus on the one hand continues the traditional activity in completely changed circumstances and, on the other, modifies the old circumstances with a completely changed activity. This can be speculatively distorted so that later history is made the goal of earlier history, e.g., the goal ascribed to the discovery of America is to further the eruption of the French Revolution. Thereby history receives its own special aims and becomes "a person ranking with other persons" (to wit: "self-consciousness, criticism, the Unique," etc.), while what is designated with the words "destiny," "goal," "germ," or "idea" of earlier history is nothing more than an abstraction formed from later history, from the active influence which earlier history exercises on later history. The further the separate spheres, which interact on one another, extend in the course of this development, the more the original isolation of the separate nationalities is destroyed by the developed mode of production and intercourse and the division of labor naturally brought forth by these, the more history becomes world-history. Thus, for instance, if in England a machine is invented, which in India or China deprives countless workers of bread, and overturns the whole form of existence of these empires, this invention becomes a world-historical fact. Or again, take the case of sugar and coffee which have proved their world-historical importance in the nineteenth century by the fact that the lack of these products, occasioned by the Napoleonic Continental system, caused the Germans to rise against Napoleon, and thus became the real basis of the glorious Wars of Liberation of 1813. From this it follows that this transformation of history into world-history is not indeed a mere abstract act on the part of the "self-consciousness," the world-spirit, or of any other metaphysical specter, but a quite material, empirically verifiable act, an act the proof of which every individual furnishes as he comes and goes, eats, drinks and clothes himself.

4. Friedrich Engels

Realism and Didacticism

FRIEDRICH ENGELS (1820–95) was born at Barmen, Germany, the son of a wealthy textile manufacturer. In 1842 he went to Manchester to take a position in a factory partly owned by his father, and lived mostly in England thereafter. He met Karl Marx on the Continent in 1844, and collaborated with him on the *Communist Manifesto* in 1848. Throughout his life he was a successful businessman, and was able to assist Marx to devote his life to research and study. After Marx's death in 1883, he spent the remainder of his life translating and editing Marx's drafts and notes, including *Das Kapital*. His works include *The Conditions of the Working Class in England* (1845), *Landmarks of Scientific Socialism* (1878), and *The Origins of the Family, Private Property, and the State* (1884).

Letter to Margaret Harkness (April, 1888)

THANK you very much for sending me your *City Girl* through Mr. Vizetelly.

I have read it with the greatest pleasure and avidity. It is indeed, as my friend Eichkof, your translator, calls it, *ein kleines Kunstwerk* [a little work of art]; to which he adds what will be satisfactory to you, that consequently his translation must be almost literal, as any omission or attempted manipulation could only destroy part of the original's value.

What strikes me most in your tale, besides its realistic truth, is that it exhibits the courage of the true artist. Not only in the way you treat the Salvation Army, in your sharp repudiation of the conception of the self-satisfied philistines, who will learn from your story, perhaps for the first time, why the Salvation Army finds such support among the masses of the people, but above all in the unembroidered form in which you have clothed the fundamental basis of the whole book—the old, old story of the proletarian girl seduced by a man from the middle class. A mediocre writer would have attempted to disguise the trite character of the plot under a heap of artificial details and embellishment, and his design would have been seen through, nonetheless. But you felt that you could tell an old story because you were in a position to make it new by the truthfulness of your presentation.

Your Mr. Grant is a masterpiece.

If I have any criticism to make, it is only that your story is not quite realistic enough. Realism, to my mind, implies, besides truth of detail, the truthful reproduction of typical characters under typical circum-stances. Now your characters are typical enough, to the extent that you portray them. But the same cannot be said of the circumstances surround-ing them and out of which their action arises. In *City Girl* the working class appears as a passive mass, incapable of helping itself or even trying to help itself. All attempts to raise it out of its wretched poverty come from the outside, from above. This may have been a valid description around 1800 or 1810 in the days of Saint Simon and Robert Owen, but it cannot be regarded as such in 1887 by a man who for almost fifty years has had the honor to participate in most of the struggles of the fighting proletariat and has been guided all the time by the principle that the emancipation of the working class ought to be the cause of the working class itself. The revolutionary response of the members of the working class to the oppression that surrounds them, their convulsive attempts—semiconscious or conscious—to attain their rights as human beings, belong to history and may therefore lay claim to a place in the domain of realism.

I am far from finding fault with your not having written a purely socialist novel, a *Tendenzroman,* as we Germans call it, to glorify the social and political views of the author. That is not at all what I mean. The more the author's views are concealed the better for the work of art. The realism I allude to may creep out even in spite of the author's views. Let me refer to an example.

Balzac, whom I consider a far greater master of realism than all the Zolas, past, present, or future, gives us in his *Comédie Humaine* a most wonderfully realistic history of French "society," describing, chronicle fashion, almost year by year from 1816 to 1848, the ever-increasing pres-sure of the rising bourgeoisie upon the society of nobles that established itself after 1815 and that set up again, as far as it could (*tant bien que mal*) the standard of the *vieille politesse française* [old French manners]. He describes how the last remnants of this, to him, model society gradu-ally succumbed before the intrusion of the vulgar moneyed upstart or was corrupted by him. How the *grande dame*, whose conjugal infidelities were but a mode of asserting herself, in perfect accord with the way she had been disposed of in marriage, gave way to the bourgeoise, who acquired her husband for cash or cashmere. And around this central picture he groups a complete history of French society from which, even in economic details (for instance, the redistribution of real and private property after the French Revolution) I have learned more than from all the professional historians, economists and statisticians of the period together.

Well, Balzac was politically a legitimist; his great work is a constant elegy on the irreparable decay of good society; his sympathies are with the class that is doomed to extinction. But for all that, his satire is never keener, his irony never more bitter, than when he sets in motion the very men and women with whom he sympathizes most deeply—the nobles. And the only men of whom he speaks with undisguised admiration are his bitterest political antagonists, the republican heroes of the Cloître Saint Méry, the men who at that time (1830–36) were indeed representatives of the popular masses.

That Balzac was thus compelled to go against his own class sympathies and political prejudices, that he *saw* the necessity of the downfall of his favorite nobles and described them as people deserving no better fate; that he *saw* the real men of the future where, for the time being, they alone were to be found—that I consider one of the greatest triumphs of realism, and one of the greatest features in old Balzac.

I must own, in your defense, that nowhere in the civilized world are the working people less actively resistant, more passively submitting to fate, more depressed than in the East End of London. And how do I know whether you have not had your reasons for contenting yourself, for once, with a picture of the passive side of working class life, leaving the active side for another work?

Letter to Minna Kautsky (November 26, 1885)

I have read *Old and New,** for which I am heartily grateful to you. The life of the workers of the salt mines is described in just as masterly a way as the life of the peasants in *Stefan.*† The scenes of Viennese "society" are also mostly very good. Vienna indeed is the only German city where there is any society. In Berlin there are only "certain circles," and still more uncertain ones, and it therefore offers a field only for a novel on the life of the literary circle, bureaucrats, or actors.

Whether the motivation of the action in this part of your work does not develop a little hastily is easier for you to judge than for me. Much of what produces such an impression on one of us may be perfectly natural in Vienna, with its own sort of international character, full of Southern and Eastern European elements. The characters in both milieus

---

* Minna Kautsky's novel *Old and New* was published in 1884.

† Minna Kautsky's novel *Stefan von Grillenhof* was published in 1879.

are drawn with your usual precision of individualization. Each person is a type, but at the same time a completely defined personality—"this one" as old Hegel would say. That is as it should be.

Only for the sake of impartiality I should find something negative, and here I recall Arnold. In truth he is too faultless, and if at last he perishes by falling from a mountain, this can be reconciled with poetic justice only in that he was too good for this world. It is always bad for an author to be infatuated with his hero, and it seems to me that in this case you have given way somewhat to this weakness. Elsa still has traces of personality, although she is also somewhat idealized, but in Arnold personality is entirely dissolved in principle.

The root of this defect is indicated, by the way, in the novel itself. Evidently you felt the need of publicly declaring your convictions, bearing witness to them before the whole world. You have already done this, this is already behind you, and there is no reason to repeat this in such a form.

I am not at all an opponent of tendentious [*Tendenz*] poetry as such. The father of tragedy, Aeschylus, and the father of comedy, Aristophanes, were both decidedly tendentious poets, just as were Dante and Cervantes; and the main merit of Schiller's *Craft and Loves* is that it is the first German political propaganda drama. The modern Russians and Norwegians, who are writing splendid novels, are all tendentious.

But I think that the bias should flow by itself from the situation and action, without particular indications, and that the writer is not obliged to obtrude on the reader the future historical solutions of the social conflicts pictured. And especially in our conditions the novel appeals mostly to readers of bourgeois circles, that is, not directly related to us, and therefore a socialist-biased novel fully achieves its purpose, in my view, if by conscientiously describing the real mutual relations, breaking down conventional illusions about them, it shatters the optimism of the bourgeois world, instills doubt as to the eternal character of the existing order, although the author does not offer any definite solution or does not even line up openly on any particular side.

Your perfect knowledge both of the Austrian peasantry and of Viennese "society" and marvelous freshness is depicting them will find here inexhaustible material. And in *Stefan* you showed that you are able to view your heroes with that fine irony which demonstrates the power of the writer over his creation.

Letter to Ferdinand Lassalle (May 8, 1859)

. . . I come now to *Franz von Sickingen*. I must first compliment you upon the composition and action, which is more than can be said of any modern German play. In the second instance, aside from a critical attitude to the play, it affected me strongly on the first reading, and so on readers more emotional it must have an even stronger effect. And this is the second, very important side. And now the other side of the medal: first of all—a purely formal matter—since you chose to write verse, you could have rounded your measures more artistically. In the main, however, irrespective of how shocking this carelessness will be to the *professional poets,* I consider this really better, as our poetical epigones have nothing left but smooth forms. Secondly the conflict chosen is not only tragic, but is the tragic conflict which basically wrecked the revolutionary party in 1848–49. I can therefore only express my full approval of making this the central theme of a modern tragedy. I ask myself, however: Is the subject chosen by you adequate to present this collision? Balthasar can of course imagine that if Sickingen had not made a secret of his rebellion under the mask of a knightly internecine strife, and had raised the flag of battle against the emperor and open war against the dukes, he would have been victorious. But can we share this illusion? Sickingen (and with him Hutten, more or less) perished not because of this craftiness. He perished because as a *knight and a representative of a perishing class* he rose up against the existing order or rather its new form. If you take away from Sickingen all that is purely personal, his special training, natural gifts, etc., we have left—Goetz von Berlichingen. In this pitiful figure the tragic opposition of the knighthood against the emperor and the dukes is given in its adequate form and Goethe rightly chose him for the hero. In so far as Sickingen—and even to some extent Hutten, although with respect to him, as with respect to all class ideologists, the formulation should be changed considerably—is struggling against the dukes (his démarche against the emperor can be explained only by the fact that from emperor of knights he has become emperor of dukes), he is simply a Don Quixote, although historically justified. The fact that he begins the uprising under the mask of a war of the knights only means that he begins it as a knight. To begin otherwise, he had to appeal directly and at the very outset to the cities and peasants, that is to those very classes the development of which is equivalent to a negation of knighthood.

If then you did not want to reduce the collision to the one portrayed in Goetz von Berlichingen—and this was not your intention—Sickingen and Hutten had to perish because in their own imaginations they were revolutionists (which cannot be said of Goetz) and, like the *educated* Polish nobility of 1830, became on the one hand the instruments of modern ideas, and on the other, actually represented reactionary class interests. But in that case the *nobles* representing the revolution—behind whose slogans of unity and liberty lurks the dream of the old imperial power and fistic right—should not have absorbed all interest, as they do in your play; the representative of the peasantry (they especially) and revolutionary elements in the cities should have formed an appreciable and active background. Then you could have expressed, and in much greater measure, the most modern ideas in their purest form, while actually, as it is, the main idea with you, aside from religious freedom, remains civil *unity*. You would have to Shakespearize more, while at present I consider Schillerism, making individuals the mere mouthpieces of the spirit of the times, your main fault. Did you not to a certain extent, like your Franz von Sickingen, yourself fall into the diplomatic error of putting the Lutheran-knightly opposition higher than the plebeian Muntzer one?

Further, I do not find any characteristic traits in your characters. I leave out Charles V, Balthasar, and Richard of Trier. And yet is there another period with sharper characters than the sixteenth century? Hutten, to my mind, is too much only the representative of "inspiration." This is boring. Was he not at the same time pretty clever, a devilish wit, and did you not therefore treat him most unjustly?

To what extent even your Sickingen, also by the way drawn too abstractly, is a victim of a collision, independent of all his personal calculations, can be seen from the way he must preach friendship with the city, etc., to his knights and on the other hand from the satisfaction with which he takes it out upon the cities himself by right of the fist.

In many places I must reproach you with too much reflection about themselves by the characters, which is also due to your bias for Schiller. Thus, on page 121, where Hutten is telling Maria his life history it would have been highly natural to put into Maria's mouth the words:

"All the gamut of sensation" and so on to "and weightier than load of years it is."

The preceding verses from "They say" to "grown old" could be made to follow, but the reflection "A night is all a maiden needs, to mature and become a woman" (although it shows that Maria knows more than the mere abstraction of love) is entirely unnecessary; but least of all is it permissible for Maria to begin with the reflection about her own "aging." Only after she has said all that she could in "one" hour could she give general expression to her mood in the sentence on her growing old. I am shocked, further, by the following lines and the words "this I considered right" (i.e., happiness). Why rob Maria of her naive views on the world characteristic of her according to earlier speeches and turn her into a doctrine of rights? Some other time I may tell you my opinion more in detail.

I think the scene between Sickingen and Charles V particularly successful although the dialogue on both sides sounds more like lawyers' speeches; the scenes in Trier are also very good. Hutten's verses on the sword are excellent.

But enough for now.

In the person of my wife you have won a warm adherent of your drama. Only she is not satisfied with Maria. . . .

5. V. I. Lenin

Party Organization and Party Literature

V. I. LENIN, original surname Ulyanov (1870–1924), was the dominant figure of the Russian Revolution of 1917, political theoretician and essayist. Exiled to Siberia early for revolutionary activities, he left Russia in 1900. In London, he won the majority (Bolshevik) wing of the Russian Social Democratic Labor Party (1903), arguing that only an elite of professional revolutionaries could bring social revolution to Russia ("What Is To Be Done?" [1902]). With the outbreak of revolution in February, 1917, the Germans financed Lenin's return to Russia, hoping (correctly, as it turned out) to disrupt the Russian war effort. With the overthrow of the Kerensky government, Lenin established a soviet-type government under the guidance of the Council of People's Commissars. He retained the post of Chairman of this Council until his death. His writings include *Materialism and Empirio-Criticism* (1909), *Imperialism, The Highest Stage of Capitalism* (1916), and *The State and Revolution* (1917). The following selection was written in 1905.

THE new conditions for Social-Democratic work in Russia which have arisen since the October Revolution have brought the question of party literature to the fore. The distinction between the illegal and the legal press, that melancholy heritage of the epoch of feudal, autocratic Russia, is beginning to disappear. It is not yet dead, by a long way. The hypocritical government of our Prime Minister is still running amuck, so much so that *Izvestia Soveta Rabochikh Deputatov* is printed "illegally"; but apart from bringing disgrace on the government, apart from striking further moral blows at it, nothing comes of the stupid attempts to "prohibit" that which the government is powerless to thwart.

So long as there was a distinction between the illegal and the legal press, the question of the party and non-party press was decided extremely simply and in an extremely false and abnormal way. The entire

illegal press was a party press, being published by organizations and
run by groups which in one way or another were linked with groups of
practical party workers. The entire legal press was non-party—since
parties were banned—but it "gravitated" towards one party or another.
Unnatural alliances, strange "bed-fellows" and false cover-devices were
inevitable. The forced reserve of those who wished to express party views
merged with the immature thinking or mental cowardice of those who
had not risen to these views and who were not, in effect, party people.

An accursed period of Aesopian language, literary bondage, slavish
speech, and ideological serfdom! The proletariat has put an end to this
foul atmosphere which stifled everything living and fresh in Russia. But
so far the proletariat has won only half freedom for Russia.

The revolution is not yet completed. While tsarism is *no longer* strong
enough to defeat the revolution, the revolution is *not yet* strong enough to
defeat tsarism. And we are living in times when everywhere and in everything there operates this unnatural combination of open, forthright, direct
and consistent party spirit with an underground, covert, "diplomatic" and
dodgy "legality." This unnatural combination makes itself felt even in our
newspaper: for all Mr. Guchkov's witticisms about Social-Democratic
tyranny forbidding the publication of moderate liberal-bourgeois newspapers, the fact remains that *Proletary*, the Central Organ of the Russian
Social-Democratic Labor Party, still remains outside the locked doors
of *autocratic,* police-ridden Russia.

Be that as it may, the half-way revolution compels all of us to set to
work at once organizing the whole thing on new lines. Today literature,
even that published "legally," can be nine-tenths party literature. It must
become party literature. In contradistinction to bourgeois customs, to
the profit-making, commercialized bourgeois press, to bourgeois literary
careerism and individualism, "aristocratic anarchism" and drive for profit,
the socialist proletariat must put forward the principle of *party literature,*
must develop this principle and put it into practice as fully and completely as possible.

What is this principle of party literature? It is not simply that, for
the socialist proletariat, literature cannot be a means of enriching individuals or groups: it cannot, in fact, be an individual undertaking, independent of the common cause of the proletariat. Down with non-partisan
writers! Down with literary supermen! Literature must become *part* of
the common cause of the proletariat, "a cog and a screw" of one single
great Social-Democratic mechanism set in motion by the entire politically-
conscious vanguard of the entire working class. Literature must become
a component of organized, planned and integrated Social-Democratic
Party work.

"All comparisons are lame," says a German proverb. So is my comparison of literature with a cog, of a living movement with a mechanism. And I daresay there will ever be hysterical intellectuals to raise a howl about such a comparison, which degrades, deadens, "bureaucratizes" the free battle of ideas, freedom of criticism, freedom of literary creation, etc., etc. Such outcries, in point of fact, would be nothing more than an expression of bourgeois-intellectual individualism. There is no question that literature is least of all subject to mechanical adjustment or levelling, to the rule of the majority over the minority. There is no question, either, that in this field greater scope must undoubtedly be allowed for personal initiative, individual inclination, thought and fantasy, form and content. All this is undeniable; but all this simply shows that the literary side of the proletarian party cause cannot be mechanically identified with its other sides. This, however, does not in the least refute the proposition, alien and strange to the bourgeoisie and bourgeois democracy, that literature must by all means and necessarily become an element of Social-Democratic Party work, inseparably bound up with the other elements. Newspapers must become the organs of the various party organizations, and their writers must by all means become members of these organizations. Publishing and distributing centers, bookshops and reading-rooms, libraries and similar establishments—must all be under party control. The organized socialist proletariat must keep an eye on all this work, supervise it in its entirety, and, from beginning to end, without any exception, infuse into it the life-stream of the living proletarian cause, thereby cutting the ground from under the old, semi-Oblomov, semi-shopkeeper Russian principle: the writer does the writing, the reader does the reading.

We are not suggesting, of course, that this transformation of literary work, which has been defiled by the Asiatic censorship and the European bourgeoisie, can be accomplished all at once. Far be it from us to advocate any kind of standardized system, or a solution by means of a few decrees. Cut-and-dried schemes are least of all applicable here. What is needed is that the whole of our Party, and the entire politically-conscious Social-Democratic proletariat throughout Russia, should become aware of this new problem, specify it clearly and everywhere set about solving it. Emerging from the captivity of the feudal censorship, we have no desire to become, and shall not become, prisoners of bourgeois-shopkeeper literary relations. We want to establish, and we shall establish, a free press, free not simply from the police, but also from capital, from careerism, and what is more, free from bourgeois-anarchist individualism.

These last words may sound paradoxical, or an affront to the reader. What! some intellectual, an ardent champion of liberty, may shout. What, you want to impose collective control on such a delicate, individual matter as literary work! You want workmen to decide questions of science,

philosophy, or aesthetics by a majority of votes! You deny the absolute
freedom of absolutely individual ideological work!

Calm yourselves, gentlemen! First of all, we are discussing party literature and its subordination to party control. Everyone is free to write and
say whatever he likes, without any restrictions. But every voluntary
association (including a party) is also free to expel members who use
the name of the party to advocate anti-party views. Freedom of speech
and the press must be complete. But then freedom of association must
be complete too. I am bound to accord you, in the name of free speech,
the full right to shout, lie and write to your heart's content. But you
are bound to grant me, in the name of freedom of association, the right
to enter into, or withdraw from, association with people advocating this
or that view. The party is a voluntary association, which would inevitably break up, first ideologically and then physically, if it did not cleanse
itself of people advocating anti-party views. And to define the border-line
between party and anti-party there is the party program, the party's
resolutions on tactics and its rules and, lastly, the entire experience of
international Social-Democracy, the voluntary international associations
of the proletariat, which has constantly brought into its parties individual
elements and trends not fully consistent, not completely Marxist and not
altogether correct and which, on the other hand, has constantly conducted
periodical "cleansings" of its ranks. So it will be with us too, supporters
of bourgeois "freedom of criticism," *within* the Party. We are now becoming a mass party all at once, changing abruptly to an open organization, and it is inevitable that we shall be joined by many who are
inconsistent (from the Marxist standpoint), perhaps we shall be joined
even by some Christian elements, and even by some mystics. We have
sound stomachs and we are rock-like Marxists. We shall digest those
inconsistent elements. Freedom of thought and freedom of criticism within
the Party will never make us forget about the freedom of organizing
people into those voluntary associations known as parties.

Secondly, we must say to you bourgeois individualists that your talk
about absolute freedom is sheer hypocrisy. There can be no real and
effective "freedom" in a society based on the power of money, in a society in which the masses of working people live in poverty and the
handful of rich live like parasites. Are you free in relation to your bourgeois publisher, Mr. Writer, in relation to your bourgeois public, which
demands that you provide it with pornography in frames* and paintings,
and prostitution as a "supplement" to "sacred" scenic art? This absolute
freedom is a bourgeois or an anarchist phrase (since, as a world outlook,

---

* There must be a misprint in the source, which says *ramkalch* (frames), while the
context suggests *romanakh* (novels).

anarchism is bourgeois philosophy turned inside out). One cannot live in society and be free from society. The freedom of the bourgeois writer, artist or actress is simply masked (or hypocritically masked) dependence on the money-bag, on corruption, on prostitution.

And we socialists expose this hypocrisy and rip off the false labels, not in order to arrive at a non-class literature and art (that will be possible only in a socialist extra-class society), but to contrast this hypocritically free literature, which is in reality linked to the bourgeoisie, with a really free one that will be *openly* linked to the proletariat.

It will be a free literature, because the idea of socialism and sympathy with the working people, and not greed or careerism, will bring ever new forces to its ranks. It will be a free literature, because it will serve, not some satiated heroine, not the bored "upper ten thousand" suffering from fatty degeneration, but the millions and tens of millions of working people—the flower of the country, its strength and its future. It will be a free literature, enriching the last word in the revolutionary thought of mankind with the experience and living work of the socialist proletariat, bringing about permanent interaction between the experience of the past (scientific socialism, the completion of the development of socialism from its primitive, utopian forms) and the experience of the present (the present struggle of the worker comrades).

To work, then, comrades! We are faced with a new and difficult task. But it is a noble and grateful one—to organize a broad, multiform and varied literature inseparably linked with the Social-Democratic working-class movement. All Social-Democratic literature must become Party literature. Every newspaper, journal, publishing house, etc., must immediately set about reorganizing its work, leading up to a situation in which it will, in one form or another, be integrated into one Party organization or another. Only then will "Social-Democratic" literature really become worthy of that name, only then will it be able to fulfill its duty and, even within the framework of bourgeois society, break out of bourgeois slavery and merge with the movement of the really advanced and thoroughly revolutionary class.

6. Leon Trotsky

Proletarian Culture and Proletarian Art

LEON TROTSKY—real name Lev Davidovich Bronstein—was born in 1879. Early a revolutionary, he spent most of the years between 1898 and 1917 in exile. A leader in the October Revolution, he emerged immediately after the revolution as a commanding political figure and military leader. He lost out to Josef Stalin in the struggle for succession following the death of Lenin (1924), and was soon exiled by Stalin. He continued to write in defense of his own actions and theories, and against the regime of Stalin, until he fell victim in Mexico in 1940 to the hand of an assassin from the Russian GPU. His works include *Lenin* (1924), *History of the Russian Revolution* (1932), and *The Revolution Betrayed* (1937). The selections brought together under the title "Proletarian Culture and Proletarian Art" are taken from *Literature and Art*, written in 1925, in which Trotsky demonstrated his trenchant critical faculties and his brilliant literary style.

Pre-Revolutionary Art

THE Bolshevist Revolution of October, 1917, did not overthrow the Kerensky government alone, it overthrew the whole social system that was based on private property. This system had its own culture and its own official literature, and its collapse could not but be the collapse of pre-revolutionary literature.

The nightingale of poetry, like that bird of wisdom, the owl, is heard only after the sun is set. The day is a time for action, but at twilight feeling and reason come to take account of what has been accomplished. The idealists and their almost deaf and blind disciples, the Russian subjectivists, thought that mind and critical reason moved the world, or, in other words, that the intelligentsia directed progress. As a matter of fact, all through history, mind limps after reality. Nor does the reactionary stupidity of the professional intelligentsia need to be proven now after our experience of the Russian Revolution. The working of this law can also be seen clearly in the field of art. The traditional identification of poet and prophet is acceptable only in the sense that the poet is about as slow in reflecting his epoch as the prophet. If there are prophets and poets who can be said to have been "ahead of their time," it is because they have expressed certain demands of social evolution not quite as slowly as the rest of their kind.

Before even a tremor of revolutionary presentiment could pass through Russian literature at the end of the last century and the beginning of this, history had to produce the deepest changes in the basis of economics, in land tenure, in social relations, and in the feelings of the masses. There had to be the collapse of the Revolution of 1905 through its own inner contradictions, there had to be the crushing of the workers in December of that year. . . . A whole generation of Russian intelligentsia was formed (or rather deformed) by the efforts to conciliate monarchy, nobility and bourgeoisie, which filled the inter-revolutionary period [between the first Revolution of 1905 and that of 1917]. Social determinism does not necessarily mean conscious self-interest, but the intelligentsia and the ruling class that keeps it are like connecting vessels, and the law of levels is equally applicable here. The old radicalism and iconoclasm of the intelligentsia which during the Russo-Japanese War found expression in a defeatist state of mind, vanished quickly under the star of June 3, 1907 [when Stolypin introduced the so-called "organic reforms"]. With the metaphysical and poetical props of nearly all centuries and all peoples, and with the aid of the Fathers of the Church, the intelligentsia "self-determined" itself and proclaimed that it had its own value, regardless of its relation to the "people." The crudeness with which it turned bourgeois was its revenge on the people for the anguish which they had inflicted on it in 1905 by their stubbornness and their lack of respect towards it. . . . Under the skin of the subtlest individualism, of the unhurried mystic searchings of a well-bred *weltschmerz,* the fat of bourgeois reconciliation to reactionary forces was being deposited. This became manifest in the common patriotic doggerel which our writers began to turn out at once, when the "organic" development of the "reform" régime of June 3rd was upset by the catastrophe of the World War.

The strain of the War, however, proved to be too great, not only for the poetry of the régime of June 3rd, but for its social foundations as well; the military collapse of that régime broke the spine of the inter-revolutionary intelligentsia. . . .

Regardless of the lesson of 1905, the intelligentsia still cherished the hope of re-establishing its spiritual and political hegemony over the masses. The War strengthened it in this illusion. Patriotic ideology was the

psychological cement for this, the cement which the new religious consciousness, scrofulous from the day of its birth, could not produce and
which the vague symbolism did not attempt to produce. The democratic
Revolution of March, 1917, which grew out of the War, and which ended
the War, gave the greatest impetus, though only for a short time, to a
revival on the part of the intelligentsia of the idea of Messianism. But
the March Revolution was its last historic flare. The smoldering wick
began to smell of Kerenskyism. Then came the October Revolution—a
landmark that is more significant than the history of the intelligentsia,
and which at the same time marks its unqualified defeat. . . .

Proletarian Culture and Proletarian Art

Every ruling class creates its own culture, and consequently, its own art.
History has known the slave-owning cultures of the East and of classic
antiquity, the feudal culture of medieval Europe and the bourgeois
culture which now rules the world. It would follow from this, that
the proletariat has also to create its own culture and its own art.

The question, however, is not as simple as it seems at first glance.
Society in which slave-owners were the ruling class, existed for many
and many centuries. The same is true of Feudalism. Bourgeois culture,
if one were to count only from the time of its open and turbulent manifestation, that is, from the period of the Renaissance, has existed five centuries, but it did not reach its greatest flowering until the nineteenth
century, or more correctly, the second half of it. History shows that the
formation of a new culture which centers around a ruling class demands
considerable time and reaches completion only at the period preceding
the political decadence of that class.

Will the proletariat have enough time to create a "proletarian" culture?
In contrast to the régime of the slave-owners and of the feudal lords and
of the bourgeoisie, the proletariat regards its dictatorship as a brief
period of transition. When we wish to denounce the all-too-optimistic
views about the transition to Socialism, we point out that the period of
the social revolution, on a world scale, will last not months and not years,
but decades—decades, but not centuries, and certainly not thousands of
years. Can the proletariat in this time create a new culture? It is legitimate
to doubt this, because the years of social revolution will be years of fierce
class struggles in which destruction will occupy more room than new
construction. At any rate, the energy of the proletariat itself will be spent
mainly in conquering power, in retaining and strengthening it and in
applying it to the most urgent needs of existence and of further struggle.
The proletariat, however, will reach its highest tension and the fullest
manifestation of its class character during this revolutionary period and

it will be within such narrow limits that the possibility of planful, cultural reconstruction will be confined. On the other hand, as the new régime will be more and more protected from political and military surprises and as the conditions for cultural creation will become more favorable, the proletariat will be more and more dissolved into a Socialist community and will free itself from its class characteristics and thus cease to be a proletariat. In other words, there can be no question of the creation of a new culture, that is, of construction on a large historic scale during the period of dictatorship. The cultural reconstruction which will begin when the need of the iron clutch of a dictatorship unparalleled in history will have disappeared, will not have a class character. This seems to lead to the conclusion that there is no proletarian culture and that there never will be any and in fact there is no reason to regret this. The proletariat acquires power for the purpose of doing away forever with class culture and to make way for human culture. We frequently seem to forget this.

The formless talk about proletarian culture, in antithesis to bourgeois culture, feeds on the extremely uncritical identification of the historic destinies of the proletariat with those of the bourgeoisie. A shallow and purely liberal method of making analogies of historic forms has nothing in common with Marxism. There is no real analogy between the historic development of the bourgeoisie and of the working class.

The development of bourgeois culture began several centuries before the bourgeoisie took into its own hands the power of the state by means of a series of revolutions. Even when the bourgeoisie was a third estate, almost deprived of its rights, it played a great and continually growing part in all the fields of culture. This is especially clear in the case of architecture. The Gothic churches were not built suddenly, under the impulse of a religious inspiration. The construction of the Cologne cathedral, its architecture and its sculpture, sums up the architectural experience of mankind from the time of the cave and combines the elements of this experience in a new style which expresses the culture of its own epoch which is, in the final analysis, the social structure and technique of this epoch. The old pre-bourgeoisie of the guilds was the factual builder of the Gothic. When it grew and waxed strong, that is, when it became richer, the bourgeoisie passed through the Gothic stage consciously and actively and created its own architectural style, not for the church, however, but for its own palaces. With its basis on the Gothic, it turned to antiquity, especially to Roman architecture and the Moorish, and applied all these to the conditions and needs of the new city community, thus creating the Renaissance (Italy at the end of the first quarter of the fifteenth century). Specialists may count the elements which the Renaissance owes to antiquity and those it owes to the Gothic and may argue as to which side is the stronger. But the Renaissance only begins when the new social class, already culturally satiated, feels itself strong enough to come out from under the yoke of the Gothic arch, to look at Gothic art and on all that preceded it as material for its own disposal, and to use the technique of the past for its own artistic aims. This refers also to all the other arts, but with this difference, that because of their greater flexibility, that is, of their lesser dependence upon utilitarian aims and materials, the "free" arts do not reveal the dialectics of successive styles with such firm logic as does architecture.

From the time of the Renaissance and of the Reformation which created more favorable intellectual and political conditions for the bourgeoisie in feudal society, to the time of the Revolution which transferred power to the bourgeoisie (in France), there passed three or four centuries of growth in the material and intellectual force of the bourgeoisie. The great French Revolution and the wars which grew out of it temporarily lowered the material level of culture. But later the capitalist régime became established as the "natural" and the "eternal."

Thus the fundamental processes of the growth of bourgeois culture and of its crystallization into style were determined by the characteristics of the bourgeoisie as a possessing and exploiting class. The bourgeoisie not only developed materially within feudal society, entwining itself in various ways with the latter and attracting wealth into its own hands, but it weaned the intelligentsia to its side and created its cultural foundation (schools, universities, academies, newspapers, magazines) long before it openly took possession of the state. It is sufficient to remember that the German bourgeoisie, with its incomparable technology, philosophy, science and art, allowed the power of the state to lie in the hands of a feudal bureaucratic class as late as 1918 and decided, or, more correctly, was forced to take power into its own hands only when the material foundations of German culture began to fall to pieces.

But one may answer: It took thousands of years to create the slave-owning art and only hundreds of years for the bourgeois art. Why, then, could not proletarian art be created in tens of years? The technical bases of life are not at all the same at present and therefore the tempo is also different. This objection, which at first sight seems convincing, in reality misses the crux of the question. Undoubtedly, in the development of the new society, the time will come when economics, cultural life and art will receive the greatest impulse forward. At the present time we can only create fancies about their tempo. In a society which will have thrown off the pinching and stultifying worry about one's daily bread, in which community restaurants will prepare good, wholesome and tasteful food for all to choose, in which communal laundries will wash clean everyone's good linen, in which children, all the children, will be well fed and strong and gay, and in which they will absorb the fundamental elements of science and art as they absorb albumen and air and the warmth of the sun, in a society in which electricity and the radio will not be the crafts they are today, but will come from inexhaustible sources of super-power at the call of a central button, in which there will be no "useless mouths," in which the liberated egotism of man—a mighty force!—will be directed wholly towards the understanding, the transformation and the betterment of the universe—in such a society the dynamic development of culture will be incomparable with anything that went on in the past. But all this will come only after a climb, prolonged and difficult, which is still ahead of us. And we are speaking only about the period of the climb.

But is not the present moment dynamic? It is in the highest degree. But its dynamics is centered in politics. The War and the Revolution were dynamic, but very much at the expense of technology and culture. It is true that the War has produced a long series of technical inventions. But the poverty which it has produced has put off the practical application of these inventions for a long time and with this their possibility of revolutionizing life. This refers to radio, to aviation, and to many mechanical discoveries. On the other hand, the Revolution lays out the ground for a new society. But it does so with the methods of the old society, with the class struggle, with violence, destruction and annihilation. If the proletarian Revolution had not come, mankind would have been strangled by its own contradictions. The Revolution saved society and culture, but by means of the most cruel surgery. All the active forces are concentrated in politics and in the revolutionary struggle, everything else is shoved back into the background and everything which is a hindrance is cruelly trampled under foot. In this process, of course, there is an ebb and flow; military Communism gives place to the NEP, which, in its turn, passes through various stages. But in its essence, the dictator-ship of the proletariat is not an organization for the production of the culture of a new society, but a revolutionary and military system struggling for it. One must not forget this. We think that the historian of the future will place the culminating point of the old society on the 2nd of August, 1914, when the maddened power of bourgeois culture let loose upon the world the blood and fire of an imperialistic war. The beginning of the new history of mankind will be dated from November 7, 1917. The fundamental stages of the development of mankind we think will be established somewhat as follows: pre-historic "history" of primitive man; ancient history, whose rise was based on slavery; the Middle Ages, based on serfdom; Capitalism, with free wage exploitation; and finally, Socialist society, with, let us hope, its painless transition to a stateless Commune. At any rate, the twenty, thirty, or fifty years of proletarian world revolution will go down in history as the most difficult climb from one system to another, but in no case as an independent epoch of proletarian culture. . . .

The bourgeoisie came into power fully armed with the culture of its time. The proletariat, on the other hand, comes into power fully armed only with the acute need of mastering culture. The problem of a proletariat which has conquered power consists, first of all, in taking into its own hands the apparatus of culture—the industries, schools, publications, press, theaters, etc.—which did not serve it before, and thus to open up the path of culture for itself. . . .

But how about the upper strata of the working class? About its intellectual vanguard? Can one not say that in these circles, narrow though they are, a development of proletarian culture is already taking place today? Have we not the Socialist Academy? Red professors? Some are guilty of putting the question in this very abstract way. The idea seems to be that it is possible to create a proletarian culture by laboratory methods. In fact, the texture of culture is woven at the points where the relationships and interactions of the intelligentsia of a class and of the class itself meet. The bourgeois culture—the technical, political, philosophical and artistic—was developed by the interaction of the bourgeoisie and its inventors, leaders, thinkers and poets. The reader created the writer and the writer created the reader. This is true in an immeasurably greater degree of the proletariat, because its economics and politics and culture can be built only on the basis of the creative activity of the masses. The main task of the proletarian intelligentsia in the immediate future is not the abstract formation of a new culture regardless of the absence of a basis for it, but definite culture-bearing, that is, a systematic, planful and, of course, critical imparting to the backward masses of the essential elements of the culture which already exists. It is impossible to create a class culture behind the backs of a class. And to build culture in cooperation with the working class and in close contact with its general historic rise, one has to build Socialism, even though in the rough. In this process, the class characteristics of society will not become stronger, but, on the contrary, will begin to dissolve and to disappear in direct ratio to the success of the Revolution. The liberating significance of the dictatorship of the proletariat consists in the fact that it is temporary— for a brief period only—that it is a means of clearing the road and of laying the foundations of a society without classes and of a culture based upon solidarity.

In order to explain the idea of a period of culture-bearing in the development of the working class more concretely, let us consider the historic succession not of classes, but of generations. Their continuity is expressed in the fact that each one of them, given a developing and not a decadent society, adds its treasure to the past accumulations of culture. But before it can do so, each new generation must pass through a stage of apprenticeship. It appropriates existing culture and transforms it in its own way, making it more or less different from that of the older generation. But this appropriation is not, as yet, a new creation, that is, it is not a creation of new cultural values, but only a premise for them. To a certain degree, that which has been said may also be applied to the destinies of the working masses which are rising towards epoch-making creative work. One has only to add that before the proletariat will have passed out of the stage of cultural apprenticeship, it will have ceased to be a proletariat. Let us also not forget that the upper layer of the bourgeois third estate passed its cultural apprenticeship under the roof of feudal society; that while still within the womb of feudal society it surpassed the old ruling estates culturally and became the instigator of culture before it came into power. It is different with the proletariat in general and with the Russian proletariat in particular. The proletariat is forced to take power before it has appropriated the fundamental elements of bourgeois culture; it is forced to overthrow bourgeois society by revolutionary violence for the very reason that society does not allow it access to culture. The working class strives to transform the state apparatus into a powerful pump for quenching the cultural thirst of the masses. This is a task of immeasurable historic importance. But, if one is not to use words lightly, it is not as yet a creation of a special proletarian culture. "Proletarian culture," "proletarian art," etc., in three cases out of ten is used uncritically to designate the culture and the art of the coming Communist society, in two cases out of ten to designate the fact that special groups of the proletariat are acquiring separate elements of pre-proletarian culture, and finally, in five cases out of ten, it represents a jumble of concepts and words out of which one can make neither head nor tail.

Here is a recent example, one of a hundred, where a slovenly, uncritical and dangerous use of the term "proletarian culture" is made. "The economic basis and its corresponding system of superstructures," writes Sizoff, "form the cultural characteristics of an epoch (feudal, bourgeois or proletarian)." Thus the epoch of proletarian culture is placed here on the same plane as that of the bourgeois. But that which is here called the proletarian epoch is only a brief transition from one social-cultural system to another, from Capitalism to Socialism. The establishment of the bourgeois régime was also preceded by a transitional epoch. But the bourgeois Revolution tried, successfully, to perpetuate the domination of the bourgeoisie, while the proletarian Revolution has for its aim the liquidation of the proletariat as a class in as brief a period as possible. The length of this period depends entirely upon the success of the

Revolution. Is it not amazing that one can forget this and place the proletarian cultural epoch on the same plane with that of feudal and bourgeois culture? . . .

The study of literary technique alone is a necessary stage and it is not a brief one. Technique is noticed most markedly in the case of those who have not mastered it. One can say with full justice about many of the young proletarian writers that it is not they who are the masters of technique, but that the technique is their master. For the more talented, this is merely a disease of growth. But they who refuse to master technique will come to look "unnatural," imitative, and even buffoon-like. It would be monstrous to conclude from this that the technique of bourgeois art is not necessary to the workers. Yet there are many who fall into this error. "Give us," they say, "something even pock-marked, but our own." This is false and untrue. A pock-marked art is no art and is therefore not necessary to the working masses. Those who believe in a "pock-marked" art are imbued to a considerable extent with contempt for the masses and are like the breed of politicians who have no faith in class power but who flatter and praise the class when "all is well." On the heels of the demagogues come the sincere fools who have taken up this simple formula of a pseudo-proletarian art. This is not Marxism, but reactionary populism, falsified a little to suit a "proletarian" ideology. Proletarian art should not be second-rate art. One has to learn regardless of the fact that learning carries within itself certain dangers because out of necessity one has to learn from one's enemies. One has to learn and the importance of such organizations as the Proletcult [the Organization for Proletarian Culture] cannot be measured by the rapidity with which they create a new literature, but by the extent to which they help elevate the literary level of the working class, beginning with its upper strata. . . .

"Style is class." However, style is not born with a class at all. A class finds its style in extremely complex ways. It would be very simple if a writer, just because he was a proletarian, loyal to his class, could stand at the crossing of the roads and announce: "I am the style of the proletariat!"

"Style is class"—not alone in art, but above all in politics. Politics is the only field in which the proletariat has really created its own style. But how? Not at all by means of a simple syllogism: each class has its own style; the proletariat is a class; it assigns to such and such a proletarian group the task of formulating its political style. No! The road is far more complex. The elaboration of proletarian politics went through economic strikes, through a struggle for the right to organize, through the utopian schools of the English and the French, through the workers' participation in revolutionary struggles under the leadership of bourgeois democrats, through the *Communist Manifesto,* through the establishment of the Socialist Party which, however, subordinated itself to the "style" of other classes, through the split among the Socialists and the organization of the Communists, through the struggle of the Communists for a united front, and it will go through a whole series of other stages which are still ahead of us. All the energy of the proletariat which remains at its disposal after meeting the elementary demands of life, has gone and is going towards the elaboration of this political "style" while, on the contrary, the historic rise of the bourgeoisie took place with a comparative evenness in all fields of social life. That is, the bourgeoisie grew rich, organized itself, shaped itself philosophically and aesthetically and accumulated habits of government. On the other hand, the whole process of self-determination of the proletariat, a class unfortunate economically, assumes an intensely one-sided, revolutionary and political character and reaches its highest expression in the Communist Party.

If we were to compare the rise in art with the rise in politics, we would have to say that here at the present time we find ourselves approximately in the same stage as when the first faint movements of the masses coincided with the efforts of the intelligentsia and of a few workers to construct utopian systems. . . .

The Formalist School of Poetry and Marxism

Leaving out of account the weak echoes of pre-revolutionary ideologic systems, the only theory which has opposed Marxism in Soviet Russia these years is the Formalist theory of art. The paradox consists in the fact that Russian Formalism connected itself closely with Russian Futurism, and that while the latter was capitulating politically before Communism, Formalism opposed Marxism with all its might theoretically. . . .

Having declared form to be the essence of poetry, this school reduces its task to an analysis (essentially descriptive and semi-statistical) of the etymology and syntax of poems, to the counting of repetitive vowels and consonants, of syllables and epithets. This analysis which the Formalists regard as the essence of poetry, or poetics, is undoubtedly necessary and useful, but one must understand its partial, scrappy, subsidiary and preparatory character. It can become an essential element of poetic technique and of the rules of the craft. . . . But the Formalists are not content to ascribe to their methods a merely subsidiary, serviceable and technical significance—similar to that which statistics has for social science, or the microscope for the biological sciences. No, they go much further. To them verbal art ends finally and fully with the word, and depictive art with color. A poem is a combination of sounds, a painting is a combination of color spots and the laws of art are the laws of verbal combinations and of combinations of color spots. The social and psychologic approach which, to us, gives a meaning to the microscopic and statistical work done in connection with verbal material is, for the Formalists, only alchemy. . . .

In other words: not city culture, which has struck the eye and the ear of the poet and which has re-educated them, has inspired him with new form, with new images, new epithets, new rhythm, but, on the contrary, the new form, originating arbitrarily, forced the poet to seek appropriate material and so pushed him in the direction of the city! . . . A new artistic form, taken in a large historic way, is born in reply to new needs. To take an example from intimate lyric poetry, one may say that between the physiology of sex and a poem about love there lies a complex system of psychological transmitting mechanisms in which there are individual, racial and social elements. The racial foundation, that is, the sexual basis of man, changes slowly. The social forms of love change more rapidly. They affect the psychologic superstructure of love, they produce new shadings and intonations, new spiritual demands, a need of a new vocabulary, and so they present new demands on poetry. The poet can find material for his art only in his social environment and transmits the new impulses of life through his own artistic consciousness. Language, changed and complicated by urban conditions, gives the poet a new verbal material, and suggests or facilitates new word combinations for the poetic formulation of new thoughts or of new feelings, which strive to break through the dark shell of the subconscious. If there were no changes in psychology produced by changes in the social environment, there would be no movement in art; people would continue from generation to generation to be content with the poetry of the Bible, or of the old Greeks. . . .

The quarrels about "pure art" and about art with a tendency took place between the liberals and the "populists." They do not become us. Materialistic dialectics are above this; from the point of view of an objective historical process, art is always a social servant and historically utilitarian. It finds the necessary rhythm of words for dark and vague moods, it brings thought and feeling closer or contrasts them with one another, it enriches the spiritual experience of the individual and of the community, it refines feeling, makes it more flexible, more responsive, it enlarges the volume of thought in advance and not through the personal method of accumulated experience, it educates the individual, the social group, the class and the nation. And this it does quite independently of whether it appears in a given case under the flag of a "pure" or of a frankly tendencious art. In our Russian social development tendenciousness was the banner of the intelligentsia which sought contact with the people. The helpless intelligentsia, crushed by Tsarism and deprived of a cultural environment, sought support in the lower strata of society and tried to prove to the "people" that it was thinking only of them, living only for them and that it loved them "terribly." And just as the "populists" who went to the people were ready to do without clean linen and without a comb and without a toothbrush, so the intelligentsia was ready to sacrifice the "subtleties" of form in its art, in order to give the most direct and spontaneous expression to the sufferings and hopes of the oppressed. On the other hand, "pure" art was the banner of the rising bourgeoisie, which could not openly declare its bourgeois character, and which at the same time tried to keep the intelligentsia in its service. The Marxist point of view is far removed from these tendencies, which were historically necessary, but which have become historically *passé*. Keeping on the plane of scientific investigation, Marxism seeks with the same assurance the social roots of the "pure" as well as of the tendencious art. It does not at all "incriminate" a poet with the thoughts and feelings which he expresses, but raises questions of a much more profound significance, namely, to which order of feelings does a given artistic work correspond in all its peculiarities? What are the social conditions of these thoughts and feelings? What place do they occupy in the historic development of a society and of a class? And, further, what literary heritage has entered into the elaboration of the new form? Under the influence of what historic impulse have the new complexes of feelings and thoughts broken through the shell which divides them from the sphere of poetic consciousness? The investigation may become complicated, detailed or individualized, but its fundamental idea will be that of the subsidiary role which art plays in the social process.

Each class has its own policy in art, that is, a system of presenting demands on art, which changes with time; for instance, the Macaenas-like protection of court and grand seigneur, the automatic relationship of supply and demand which is supplemented by complex methods of influencing the individual, and so forth, and so on. The social and even the personal dependence of art was not concealed, but was openly announced as long as art retained its court character. The wider, more popular, anonymous character of the rising bourgeoisie led, on the whole, to the theory of "pure art," though there were many deviations from this theory. As indicated above, the tendencious literature of the "populist" intelligentsia was imbued with a class interest; the intelligentsia could not strengthen itself and could not conquer for itself a right to play a part in history without the support of the people. But in the revolutionary struggle, the class egotism of the intelligentsia was turned inside out, and in its left wing, it assumed the form of highest self-sacrifice. That is why the intelligentsia not only did not conceal art with a tendency, but proclaimed it, thus sacrificing art, just as it sacrificed many other things.

Our Marxist conception of the objective social dependence and social utility of art, when translated into the language of politics, does not at all mean a desire to dominate art by means of decrees and orders. It is not true that we regard only that art as new and revolutionary which speaks of the worker, and it is nonsense to say that we demand that the poets should describe inevitably a factory chimney, or the uprising against capital! Of course the new art cannot but place the struggle of the proletariat in the center of its attention. But the plough of the new art is not limited to numbered strips. On the contrary, it must plow the entire field in all directions. Personal lyrics of the very smallest scope have an absolute right to exist within the new art. Moreover, the new man cannot be formed without a new lyric poetry. But to create it, the poet himself must feel the world in a new way. If Christ alone or Sabaoth himself bends over the poet's embraces, then this only goes to prove how much behind the times his lyrics are and how socially and aesthetically inadequate they are for the new man. Even where such terminology is not a survival of experience so much as of words, it shows psychologic inertia and therefore stands in contradiction to the consciousness of the new man. No one is going to prescribe themes to a poet or intends to prescribe them. Please write about anything you can think of! But allow the new class which considers itself, and with reason, called upon to build a new world, to say to you in any given case: It does not make new poets of you to translate the philosophy of life of the seventeenth century into the language of the Acméists. The form of art is, to a certain and very large degree, independent, but the artist who creates this form, and the spectator who is enjoying it, are not empty machines, one for creating form and the other for appreciating it. They are living people, with a crystallized psychology representing a certain unity, even if not entirely harmonious. This psychology is the result of social conditions. The creation and perception of art forms is one of the functions of this psychology. And no matter how wise the Formalists try to be, their whole conception is simply based upon the fact that they ignore the psychological unity of the social man, who creates and who consumes what has been created.

The proletariat has to have in art the expression of the new spiritual point of view which is just beginning to be formulated within him, and to which art must help him give form. This is not a state order, but an historic demand. Its strength lies in the objectivity of historic necessity. You cannot pass this by, nor escape its force. . . .

In fact, the Formalists do not carry their idea of art to its logical conclusion. If one is to regard the process of poetic creation only as a combination of sounds or words, and to seek along these lines the solution of all the problems of poetry, then the only perfect formula of "poetics" will be this: Arm yourself with a dictionary and create by means of algebraic combinations and permutations of words, all the poetic works of the world which have been created and which have not yet been created. Reasoning "formally" one may produce "Eugene Onegin" in two ways: either by subordinating the selection of words to a preconceived artistic idea (as Pushkin himself did), or by solving the problem algebraically. From the "Formal" point of view, the second method is more correct, because it does not depend upon mood, inspiration, or other unsteady things, and has besides the advantage that while leading to "Eugene Onegin" it may bring one to an incalculable number of other great works. All that one needs is infinity in time, called eternity. But as neither mankind nor the individual poet have eternity at their disposal, the fundamental source of poetic words will remain, as before, the preconceived artistic idea understood in the broadest sense, as an accurate thought and as a clearly expressed personal or social feeling and as a vague mood. In its striving towards artistic materialization, this subjective idea will be stimulated and jolted by form and may be sometimes pushed on to a path which was entirely unforeseen. This simply means that verbal form is not a passive reflection of a preconceived artistic idea, but an active element which influences the idea itself. But such an active mutual relationship—in which form influences and at times entirely transforms content—is known to us in all fields of social and even biologic life. This is no reason at all for rejecting Darwinism and Marxism and for the creation of a Formalist school either in biology or sociology. . . .

It is unquestionably true that the need for art is not created by economic conditions. But neither is the need for food created by economics. On the contrary, the need for food and warmth creates economics. It is very true that one cannot always go by the principles of Marxism in deciding whether to reject or to accept a work of art. A work of art should, in the first place, be judged by its own law, that is, by the law of art. But Marxism alone can explain why and how a given tendency in art has originated in a given period of history; in other words, who it was who made a demand for such an artistic form and not for another, and why.

It would be childish to think that every class can entirely and fully create its own art from within itself, and, particularly, that the proletariat is capable of creating a new art by means of closed art guilds or circles, or by the Organization for Proletarian Culture, etc. Generally speaking, the artistic work of man is continuous. Each new rising class places itself on the shoulders of its preceding one. But this continuity is dialectic, that is, it finds itself by means of internal repulsions and breaks. New artistic needs or demands for new literary and artistic points of view are stimulated by economics, through the development of a new class, and minor stimuli are supplied by changes in the position of the class, under the influence of the growth of its wealth and cultural power. Artistic creation is always a complicated turning inside out of old forms, under the influence of new stimuli which originate outside of art. In this large sense of the word, art is a handmaiden. It is not a disembodied element feeding on itself, but a function of social man indissolubly tied to his life and environment. . . .

Materialism does not deny the significance of the element of form, either in logic, jurisprudence, or art. Just as a system of jurisprudence can and must be judged by its internal logic and consistency, so art can and must be judged from the point of view of its achievements in form, because there can be no art without them. However, a juridical theory which attempted to establish the independence of law from social conditions would be defective at its very base. Its moving force lies in economics—in class contradictions. The law gives only a formal and an internally harmonized expression of these phenomena, not of their individual peculiarities, but of their general character, that is, of the elements that are repetitive and permanent in them. We can see now with a clarity which is rare in history how new law is made. It is not done by logical deduction, but by empirical measurement and by adjustment to the economic needs of the new ruling class. Literature, whose methods and processes have their roots far back in the most distant past and represent the accumulated experience of verbal craftsmanship, expresses the thoughts, feelings, moods, points of view and hopes of the new epoch and of its new class. One cannot jump beyond this. And there is no need of making the jump, at least, for those who are not serving an epoch already past nor a class which has already outlived itself. The methods of formal analysis are necessary, but insufficient. You may count up the alliterations in popular proverbs, classify metaphors, count up the number of vowels and consonants in a wedding song. It will undoubtedly enrich our knowledge of folk art, in one way or another; but if you don't know the peasant system of sowing, and the life that is based on it, if you don't know the part the scythe plays, and if you have not mastered the meaning of the church calendar to the peasant, of the time when the peasant marries, or when the peasant women give birth, you will have only understood the outer shell of folk art, but the kernel will not have been reached. The architectural scheme of the Cologne cathedral can be established by measuring the base and the height of its arches, by determining the three dimensions of its naves, the dimensions and the placement of the columns, etc. But without knowing what a mediaeval city was like, what a guild was, or what was the Catholic Church of the Middle Ages, the Cologne cathedral will never be understood. The effort to set art free from life, to declare it a craft self-sufficient unto itself, devitalizes and kills art. The very need of such an operation is an unmistakable system of intellectual decline. . . .

To a materialist, religion, law, morals and art represent separate aspects of one and the same process of social development. Though they differentiate themselves from their industrial basis, become complex, strengthen and develop their special characteristics in detail, politics, religion, law, ethics and aesthetics remain, none the less, functions of social man and obey the laws of his social organization. The idealist, on the other hand, does not see a unified process of historic development which evolves the necessary organs and functions from within itself, but a crossing or combining and interacting of certain independent principles—the religious, political, juridical, aesthetic and ethical substances, which find their origin and explanation in themselves. The (dialectic) idealism of Hegel arranges these substances (which are the eternal categories) in some sequence by reducing them to a genetic unity. Regardless of the fact that this unity with Hegel is the absolute spirit, which divides itself in the process of its dialectic manifestation into various "factors," Hegel's system, because of its dialectic character, not because of its idealism, gives an idea of historic reality which is just as good as the idea of a man's hand that a glove gives when turned inside out. But the Formalists (and their greatest genius was Kant) do not look at the dynamics of development, but at a cross-section of it, on the day and at the hour of their own philosophic revelation. At the crossing of the line they reveal the complexity and multiplicity of the object (not of the process, because they do not think of processes). This complexity they analyze and classify. They give names to the elements, which are at once transformed into essences, into sub-absolutes, without father or mother; to wit, religion, politics, morals, law, art. Here we no longer have a glove of history turned inside out, but the skin torn from the separate fingers, dried out to a degree of complete abstraction, and this hand of history turns out to be the product of the "interaction" of the thumb, the index, the middle finger, and all the other "factors." The aesthetic "factor" is the little finger, the smallest, but not the least beloved. . . .

The Formalist school represents an abortive idealism applied to the questions of art. The Formalists show a fast ripening religiousness. They are followers of St. John. They believe that "In the beginning was the Word." But we believe that in the beginning was the deed. The word followed, as its phonetic shadow. . . .

Revolutionary and Socialist Art

But can a great art be created out of our infidel epoch, ask certain mystics, who are willing to accept the Revolution if it can secure them immortality. Tragedy is a great and monumental form of literature. The tragedy of classic antiquity was deduced from its myths. All ancient tragedy is penetrated by a profound faith in fate which gave a meaning to life. The Christian myth unified the monumental art of the Middle Ages and gave a significance not only to the temples and the mysteries, but to all human relationships. The union of the religious point of view on life with an active participation in it, made possible a great art in those times. If one were to remove religious faith, not the vague, mystic buzzing that goes on in the soul of our modern intelligentsia, but the real religion, with God and a heavenly law and a church hierarchy, then life is left bare, without any place in it for supreme collisions of hero and destiny, of sin and expiation. The well-known mystic Stepun approaches art from this point of view in his article on "Tragedy and the Contemporary Life." He starts from the needs of art itself, tempts us with a new and monumental art, shows us a revival of tragedy in the distance, and, in conclusion, demands, in the name of art, that we submit to and obey the powers of heaven. There is an insinuating logic in Stepun's scheme. In fact, the author does not care for tragedy, because the laws of tragedy are nothing to him as compared to the laws of heaven. He only wishes to catch hold of our epoch by the small finger of tragic aesthetics in order to take hold of its entire hand. This is a purely Jesuitic approach. But from a dialectic point of view, Stepun's reasoning is formalistic and shallow. It ignores the materialistic and historical foundation from which the ancient drama and the Gothic art grew and from which a new art must grow.

The faith in an inevitable fate disclosed the narrow limits within which ancient man, clear in thought but poor in technique, was confined. He could not as yet undertake to conquer nature on the scale we do today, and nature hung over him like a fate. Fate is the limitation and the immobility of technical means, the voice of blood, of sickness, of death, of all that limits man, and that does not allow him to become "arrogant." Tragedy lay inherent in the contradiction between the awakened world of the mind, and the stagnant limitation of means. The myth did not create tragedy, it only expressed it in the language of man's childhood.

The bribe of spiritual expiation of the Middle Ages and, in general, the whole system of heavenly and earthly double bookkeeping, which followed from the dualism of religion, and especially of historic, positive Christianity, did not make the contradictions of life, but only reflected them and solved them fictitiously. Medieval society overcame the growing contradictions by transferring the promissory note to the Son of God; the ruling classes signed this note, the Church hierarchy acted as endorser, and the oppressed masses prepared to discount it in the other world.

Bourgeois society broke up human relationships into atoms, and gave them unprecedented flexibility and mobility. Primitive unity of consciousness which was the foundation of a monumental religious art disappeared, and with it went primitive economic relationships. As a result of the Reformation, religion became individualistic. The religious symbols of art having had their cord cut from the heavens, fell on their heads and sought support in the uncertain mysticism of individual consciousness.

In the tragedies of Shakespeare, which would be entirely unthinkable without the Reformation, the fate of the ancients and the passions of the medieval Christians are crowded out by individual human passions, such as love, jealousy, revengeful greediness, and spiritual dissension. But in every one of Shakespeare's dramas, the individual passion is carried to such a high degree of tension that it outgrows the individual, becomes super-personal, and is transformed into a fate of a certain kind. The jealousy of Othello, the ambition of Macbeth, the greed of Shylock, the love of Romeo and Juliet, the arrogance of Coriolanus, the spiritual wavering of Hamlet, are all of this kind. Tragedy in Shakespeare is individualistic, and in this sense has not the general significance of *Oedipus Rex,* which expresses the consciousness of a whole people. None the less, compared with Aeschylus, Shakespeare represents a great step forward and not backward. Shakespeare's art is more human. At any rate, we shall no longer accept a tragedy in which God gives orders and man submits. Moreover, there will be no one to write such a tragedy.

Having broken up human relations into atoms, bourgeois society, during the period of its rise, had a great aim for itself. Personal emancipation was its name. Out of it grew the dramas of Shakespeare and Goethe's *Faust.* Man placed himself in the center of art also. This theme sufficed for centuries. In reality, all modern literature has been nothing but an enlargement of this theme.

But to the degree to which the internal bankruptcy of bourgeois society was revealed as a result of its unbearable contradictions, the original purpose, the emancipation and qualification of the individual faded away and was relegated more and more into the sphere of a new mythology, without soul or spirit.

However the conflict between what is personal and what is beyond the personal, can take place, not only in the sphere of religion, but in the sphere of a human passion that is larger than the individual. The super-personal element is, above all, the social element. So long as man will not have mastered his social organization, the latter will hang over him as his fate. Whether at the same time society casts a religious shadow or not, is a secondary matter and depends upon the degree of man's helplessness. Baboeuf's struggle for Communism in a society which was not yet ready for it, was a struggle of a classic hero with his fate. Baboeuf's destiny had all the characteristics of true tragedy, just as the fate of the Gracchi had whose name Babouef used.

Tragedy based on detached personal passions is too flat for our days. Why? Because we live in a period of social passions. The tragedy of our period lies in the conflict between the individual and the collectivity, or in the conflict between two hostile collectivities in the same individual. Our age is an age of great aims. This is what stamps it. But the grandeur of these aims lies in man's effort to free himself from mystic and from every other intellectual vagueness and in his effort to reconstruct society and himself in accord with his own plan. This, of course, is much bigger than the child's play of the ancients which was becoming to their childish age, or the mediaeval ravings of monks, or the arrogance of individualism which tears personality away from the collectivity, and then, draining it to the very bottom, pushes it off into the abyss of pessimism, or sets it on all fours before the remounted bull Apis.

Tragedy is a high expression of literature because it implies the heroic tenacity of strivings, of limitless aims, of conflicts and sufferings. In this sense, Stepun was right when he characterized our "on the eve" art, as he called it, that is, the art which preceded the War and the Revolution, as insignificant.

Bourgeois society, individualism, the Reformation, the Shakespearean dramas, the great Revolution, these have made impossible the tragic significance of aims that come from without; great aims must live in the consciousness of a people or of a class which leads a people, if they are to arouse heroism or create a basis for great sentiments which inspire tragedy. The Tsarist War, whose purpose did not penetrate consciousness, gave birth to cheap verse only, with personal poetry trickling by its side, unable to rise to an objectivity and unable to form a great art.

If one were to regard the Decadent and the Symbolist schools, with all their off-shoots, from the point of view of the development of art as a social form, they would appear merely as scratches of the pen, as an exercise in craftsmanship, as a tuning up of instruments. The period in art when it was "on the eve" was without aims. Those who had aims had no time for art. At present, one has to carry out great aims by the means of art. One cannot tell whether revolutionary art will succeed in producing "high" revolutionary tragedy. But Socialist art will revive tragedy. Without God, of course. The new art will be atheist. It will also revive comedy, because the new man of the future will want to laugh. It will give new life to the novel. It will grant all rights to lyrics, because the new man will love in a better and stronger way than did the old people, and he will think about the problems of birth and death.

The new art will revive all the old forms, which arose in the course of the development of the creative spirit. The disintegration and decline of these forms are not absolute, that is, they do not mean that these forms are absolutely incompatible with the spirit of the new age. All that is necessary is for the poet of the new epoch to re-think in a new way the thoughts of mankind, and to re-feel its feelings.

7. Josef Stalin

Marxism in Linguistics

JOSEF STALIN (1879–1953) was successor to Lenin in the Soviet hierarchy until his own death. Son of a shoemaker in Georgia, Stalin became a Marxist while a divinity student. Unlike Lenin and Trotsky, he never left Russia in exile. In 1912, he became an editor of *Pravda*. After the 1917 Revolution, he became Commissar of Nationalities and, in 1929, head of the Communist Party. From that time, he maintained virtually total control of political and military power in the USSR. His written works include *Problems of Leninism* (1926), *Foundations of Leninism* (1924), and *Dialectical and Historical Materialism* (1938).

A GROUP of comrades of the younger generation have asked me to give my opinion in the press on questions relating to the science of language, particularly in reference to Marxism in linguistics. I am not a linguist and cannot of course satisfy these comrades fully. But as to Marxism in linguistics, as well as in other social sciences, this is a subject with which I have a direct connection. I have therefore consented to answer a number of questions put by these comrades.

QUESTION: *Is it true that language is a superstructure on the base?*
ANSWER: No, it is not true.

The base is the economic structure of society at a given stage of its development. The superstructure consists of the political, legal, religious, artistic, and philosophical views of society and the political, legal, and other institutions corresponding to them.

Every base has its own superstructure corresponding to it. The base of the feudal system has its superstructure—its political, legal, and other views and the corresponding institutions; the capitalist base has its own superstructure, and so has the socialist base. If the base changes or is eliminated, then following this its superstructure changes or is eliminated;

if a new base arises, then following this a superstructure arises corresponding to it.

In this respect language radically differs from superstructure. Take, for example, Russian society and the Russian language. During the past thirty years the old, capitalist base was eliminated in Russia and a new, socialist base was built. Correspondingly, the superstructure on the capitalist base was eliminated and a new superstructure created corresponding to the socialist base. The old political, legal, and other institutions were consequently supplanted by new, socialist institutions. But in spite of this the Russian language has remained essentially what it was before the October Revolution.

What has changed in the Russian language in this period? To a certain extent the vocabulary of the Russian language has changed, in the sense that it has been supplemented by a large number of new words and expressions, which have arisen in connection with the rise of a new socialist production, of a new state, a new socialist culture, a new public spirit and ethics, and lastly, in connection with the development of technology and science; a number of words and expressions have changed their meaning; a number of obsolete words have fallen out of the vocabulary. As to the basic vocabulary and grammatical structure of the Russian language, which constitute the foundation of the language, they, after the elimination of the capitalist base, far from having been eliminated and supplanted by a new basic vocabulary and a new grammatical system of the language, have been preserved in their entirety and have not undergone any serious changes—have been preserved precisely as the foundation of modern Russian.

Further, the superstructure is a product of the base; but this does not mean that it merely reflects the base, that it is passive, neutral, indifferent to the fate of its base, to the fate of the classes, to the character of the system. On the contrary, no sooner does it arise than it becomes an exceedingly active force, actively assisting its base to take shape and consolidate itself, and doing everything it can to help the new system finish off and eliminate the old base and the old classes.

It cannot be otherwise. The base creates the superstructure precisely in order that it may serve it, that it may actively help it to take shape and consolidate itself, that it may actively strive for the elimination of the old, moribund base and its old superstructure. The superstructure has only to renounce its role of auxiliary, it has only to pass from a position of active defense of its base to one of indifference toward it, to adopt the same attitude to all classes, and it loses its virtue and ceases to be a superstructure.

In this respect language radically differs from superstructure. Language is not a product of one or another base, old or new, within the given society, but of the whole course of the history of society and the history of bases throughout centuries. It was created not by any class, but by all society, by all the classes of society, by the efforts of hundreds of generations. It was created for the satisfaction of the needs not of only one class, but of all society, of all the classes of society. Precisely for this reason it was created as a single language for society, common to all members of that society, as the common language of its people. Hence the role of language as an auxiliary, as a means of intercourse between people, consists not in serving one class to the detriment of other classes, but in equally serving all society, all classes of society. This, in fact, explains why a language may equally serve both the old, moribund system and the new, nascent system; both the old base and the new base, both the exploiters and the exploited.

It is no secret to anyone that the Russian language served Russian capitalism and Russian bourgeois culture before the October Revolution just as well as it now serves the socialist system and the socialist culture of Russian society.

The same must be said of the Ukrainian, Byelorussian, Uzbek, Kazakh, Georgian, Armenian, Estonian, Latvian, Lithuanian, Moldavian, Tatar, Azerbaijan, Bashkir, Turkmen, and other languages of the Soviet nations; they served the old, bourgeois systems of these nations just as well as they serve the new, socialist system.

It could not be otherwise. Language exists, and it has been created precisely in order to serve society as a whole, as a means of intercourse between people, in order to be common to the members of society and the single language of society, serving members of society equally, irrespective of their class status. A language has only to depart from this position of being the common language of the people and to give preference and support to any one social group to the detriment of other social groups of that society, and it loses its virtue, ceases to be a means of intercourse between the people of that society, and becomes the jargon of some social group, degenerates, and is doomed to disappear.

In this respect, while it differs in principle from the superstructure, language does not differ from the implements of production, from machines, let us say, which may equally serve a capitalist system and a socialist system.

Further, the superstructure is the product of one epoch, an epoch in which the given economic base exists and operates. The superstructure is therefore short-lived; it is eliminated and disappears with the elimination and disappearance of the given base.

Language, on the contrary, is the product of a whole number of epochs, in the course of which it takes shape, is enriched, develops, and is polished. A language therefore exists immeasurably longer than any base or any superstructure. This in fact explains why the rise and disappearance not only of one base and its superstructure, but of several bases and their corresponding superstructures have not led in history to the elimination of a given language, to the elimination of its structure, and to the rise of a new language with a new vocabulary and a new grammatical system.

It is more than one hundred years since Pushkin died. In this period the feudal system and the capitalist system were eliminated in Russia, and the third, a socialist, system has arisen. Hence two bases, with their superstructures, have been eliminated, and a new, socialist base has arisen, with its new superstructure. Yet if we take the Russian language, for example, it has not in this great length of time undergone any fundamental change, and the modern Russian language differs very little in structure from the language of Pushkin.

What has changed in the Russian language in this period? In this period the Russian vocabulary has been much enlarged; a great number of obsolete words have dropped out of the vocabulary; the meaning of a large number of words has changed; the grammatical system of the language has improved. As to the general structure of Pushkin's language, with its grammatical system and its basic vocabulary, it has been preserved in all essentials as the basis of modern Russian.

And this is quite understandable. Indeed, what necessity is there, after every revolution, for the existing structure of the language, its grammatical construction and basic vocabulary, to be destroyed and supplanted by new ones, as is usually the case with the superstructure? Who would benefit if "water," "earth," "mountain," "forest," "fish," "man," "to walk," "to do," "to produce," "to trade," etc., were called not water, earth, mountain, etc., but something else? Who would benefit from the change of words in a language and the combination of words in sentences following not the existing, but some entirely different grammar? What would be the use to the revolution of such an upheaval in language? History, generally, never does anything of moment without some particular necessity. What, one asks, can be the necessity for such a language upheaval, when it is demonstrated that the existing language and its structure are fundamentally quite suitable for the needs of the new system? The old superstructure can and should be destroyed and replaced by a new one in the course of a few years, in order to give free scope for the development of the productive forces of society; but how can an existing language be destroyed and a new one built in its place in the course of a few years without causing anarchy in social life and without creating the threat of the collapse of society? Who but Don Quixotes could set themselves such a task?

Lastly, there is one other radical distinction between superstructure and language. The superstructure is not directly connected with production, with man's productive activity. It is connected with production only indirectly through the economy, through the base. The superstructure therefore does not reflect changes of development of the productive forces immediately and directly, but only after changes in the base, through the prism of changes wrought in the base by the changes in production. This means that the sphere of action of the superstructure is narrow and restricted.

Language, on the contrary, is connected with man's productive activity directly, and not only with man's productive activity, but with all his other activities in all spheres of work, from production to the base and from the base to the superstructure. That is why language reflects changes in production immediately and directly, without waiting for changes in the base. That is why the sphere of action of language, which embraces all spheres of man's activity, is far broader and more varied than the sphere of action of the superstructure. More, it is practically unlimited.

It is this which primarily explains why language, or rather its vocabulary, is in an almost constant state of change. The continuous development of industry and agriculture, of trade and transport, of technology and science, demands that language should supplement its vocabulary with new words and expressions, needed for their operation. And language, directly reflecting these needs, does replenish its vocabulary with new words, and perfects its grammatical system.

Hence:

(a) A Marxist cannot regard language as a superstructure on the base;

(b) To confuse language and superstructure is a serious error.

QUESTION: *Is it true that language always was and is of a class character, that there is no such thing as a non-class language common and uniform to all the people of a society?*
ANSWER: No, it is not true.

It is not difficult to understand that in a society which has no classes there can be so such thing as a class language. There were no classes in the primitive communal clan system, and consequently there could be no class language—the language was then the common and single language of the whole collective body. The objection that the word class should be taken as covering every human collective, including the primitive communal collective, is not an objection but a play on words that is not worth refuting.

As the subsequent development from clan languages to tribal languages, from tribal languages to the languages of nationalities, and from languages of nationalities to national languages—everywhere and at all stages of development, language, as a means of intercourse between the people of a society, was the common and single language of that society, serving its members equally, irrespective of their social standing.

I am not referring here to the empires of the slave and medieval periods, the empires of Cyrus or Alexander the Great, let us say, or of Caesar or of Charles the Great, which had no economic base of their own and were transitory and unstable military and administrative associations. These empires not only did not have, but they could not have a single language common to the whole empire and understood by all the members of the empire. They were conglomerations of tribes and nationalities, each of which lived its own life and had its own language. Consequently, it is not these or similar empires I have in mind, but the tribes and nationalities forming part of an empire which had their own economic base and their own languages, formed in the distant past. History tells us that the languages of these tribes and nationalities were not class languages, but general languages of the people, common languages for tribes and nationalities, used and understood by all people.

Side by side with this, of course, there were dialects, vernaculars, but they were dominated by, and subordinated to, the single and common language of the tribe or nationality.

Later, with the appearance of capitalism, the elimination of feudal division, and the formation of national markets, nationalities developed into nations, and the languages of nationalities into national languages. History tells us that the national languages are not class, but common languages, common to the members of each nation and constituting the single language of the nation.

It was said above that, as a means of intercourse between the people of a society, language serves all classes of that society equally, and in this respect displays what may be called an indifference to classes. But people, the individual social groups, the classes, are far from indifferent to language. They strive to utilize the language in their own interests, to impose their own special vocabulary, special terms, and special expressions upon it. The upper strata of the propertied classes, who are divorced from and detest the people—the aristocratic nobility, the upper strata of the bourgeois—particularly distinguished themselves in this respect. "Class" dialects, jargons, drawing-room "languages" are created. These dialects and jargons are often incorrectly referred to in literature as the "aristocratic language" or "bourgeois language" in contradistinction to "proletarian language" or "peasant language." For this reason, strange as it may seem, some of our comrades have come to the conclusion that national language is a fiction, and that in reality, only class languages exist.

There is nothing, I think, more erroneous than this conclusion. Can these dialects and jargons be regarded as languages? Certainly not. They cannot, firstly, because these dialects and jargons have no grammatical system or basic vocabularies of their own—they borrow them from the national language. They cannot, secondly, because these dialects and jargons are confined to a narrow sphere of members of the upper strata of a given class and are entirely unsuitable as a means of intercourse for society as a whole. What, then, do they have? They have a collection of specific words reflecting the specific tastes of the aristocracy or the upper strata of the bourgeoisie; a certain number of expressions and turns of speech distinguished by refinement and gallantry, and free of the "coarse" expressions and turns of speech of the national language; lastly, a certain number of foreign words. However, the bulk, that is, the overwhelming majority, of the words and the grammatical system are borrowed from the common national language. Dialects and jargons are therefore offshoots of the common national language, possessing no linguistic independence of any kind and doomed to stagnation. Anyone who believes that dialects and jargons can develop into independent languages, that they are capable of ousting and supplanting the national language, has lost all sense of historical perspective and has abandoned the Marxist position.

References are made to Marx, and the passage from his article, *St. Max*,* is quoted where it is said that the bourgeois have "their own language," that this language "is a product of the bourgeoisie," that it is permeated with the spirit of mercantilism and sale and purchase. Certain comrades cite this passage with the idea of proving that Marx believes in the "class character" of language and denied the existence of a single national language. If these comrades were impartial, they should have cited another passage from this same article, *St. Max*, where Marx, touching on the way common national language arose, speaks of "the concentration of dialects into a single national language as the result of economic and political concentration."

Marx, consequently, did recognize the necessity of a *single* national language, as the highest form, to which dialects, as lower forms, are subordinate.

What, then, can this bourgeois language be which, according to Marx, is "a product of the bourgeoisie"? Did Marx consider it as much a language as the national language, with its own specific linguistic structure? Could he have considered it such a language? Of course not. Marx

---

* The second section of the joint philosophical work by Marx and Engels, *The German Ideology*, of which only the first and third sections have been published in English. St. Max is a satirical reference to Max Stirner (1806–56), philosophical anarchist and author of *The Ego and His Own*.

merely wanted to say that the bourgeois had polluted the common national language with their huckster vocabulary, that the bourgeois, in other words, have their huckster jargon.

It thus appears that these comrades have misrepresented Marx. And they misrepresented him because they quoted Marx, not like Marxists, but like dogmatists, without delving into the essence of the matter.

References are made to Engels, and the words from his *Condition of the Working Class in England* are cited where he says that "the English working class has with the course of time become a different people from the English bourgeoisie," that "the working men speak a different dialect, have different ideas and concepts, different morals and moral principles, different religion and politics from the bourgeoisie." Certain comrades conclude from this passage that Engels denied the necessity for a common, national language, that he believed, consequently, in the "class character" of language. True, Engels speaks here of a dialect, not of a language, fully realizing that, being an offshoot of the national language, a dialect cannot supplant the national language. But these comrades, apparently, do not regard with sympathy the existence of a difference between language and dialect. . . .

It is obvious that the quotation is inappropriate, because Engels here speaks, not of "class languages" but chiefly of class ideas, concepts, morals, moral principles, religion, and politics. It is perfectly true that the ideas, concepts, morals, moral principles, religion, and politics of the bourgeois and proletarian are directly antithetic. But where does national language or the "class character" of language come in here? Can the existence of class contradictions in society serve as an argument in favor of the "class character" of language, or against the necessity of a common national language? Marxism says that a common language is one of the most important earmarks of a nation, although knowing very well that there are class contradictions within the nation. Do the comrades referred to recognize this Marxist thesis?

8. Gyorgii Plekhanov

On Art for Art's Sake

GYORGII PLEKHANOV, a founder of Russian Marxism, was born in 1856 in Tambov province. Early one of the Narodniki (Populists), he led the first popular demonstration against the Tsarist government in St. Petersburg in 1876. In 1880 he emigrated from Russia to France, and then to Switzerland. In 1889 he participated in the founding of the Congress of the Second International. In 1900 he edited the revolutionary journal, *Spark*, with Lenin. Although initially allied with Lenin and the Bolsheviks, his support of World War I led to a break with them, and he died in exile soon after the Revolution (1918), leaving behind 26 volumes of commentary on Marxist theory. Among his works were *Anarchism and Socialism* (1894), *Fundamental Problems of Marxism* (1908), and *Art and Society* (1912), from which this selection is taken.

THE tendency toward art for art's sake arises and develops where an insoluble contradiction exists between the artist and his social environment. This contradiction exercises a favorable effect on the work of the artist to the extent that it enables him to rise above his social environment. Such was the case with Pushkin in the time of Nicholas I, as well as with the romanticists, the Parnassians, and the early realists in France. Innumerable examples would prove that this has always been true wherever such a contradiction existed. But while revolting against the morality of the society in which they lived, the romanticists, the Parnassians, and realists were not basically hostile to the social relations which give rise to this morality. On the contrary, while they despised the "bourgeois," they valued the bourgeois order, at first instinctively, later consciously. The stronger the movement for liberation in modern Europe—a struggle directed against the bourgeois order—the stronger the attachment to that social order on the part of French supporters of art for art's sake. And the more conscious the attachment became, the more difficult did they find it to remain indifferent to the ideological content of their works. But their blindness to the new movement directed toward the regeneration of society rendered their concepts erroneous, robbed them of profundity, and impaired the quality of the ideas expressed in their works. As a result, French realism found itself in a hopeless position, which caused decadence and mysticism in many of the writers who had formerly belonged to the realist school.

This conclusion will be verified later in detail. At this point I should like to add a few words about Pushkin.

When Pushkin thunders against "the mob" we find in his words anger, but never triviality. . . . The Poet reproaches the mundane throng, that is, the privileged classes, but not the toiling masses, who at that time were scarcely considered in Russian literature, and who appreciated a good stew steaming on the hearth more than the Apollo Belvedere. This means that for Pushkin's Poet narrow materialism was unbearable, nothing more. His refusal to educate the masses merely indicates his pessimistic lack of faith in them, but in this there is not the slightest suggestion of reaction. And herein lies Pushkin's superiority to such defenders of art for art's sake as Gautier. This superiority is due to conditioning. Pushkin never laughed at the followers of Saint-Simon; it is possible that he never even heard of them. Although honest and magnanimous, he had been steeped since childhood in certain class prejudices. The thought of ending the exploitation of one class by another would have appeared to him ridiculously utopian. Had he been aware of any practical plans to end social exploitation and, moreover, if these plans had created such a furor in Russia as had those of the Saint-Simonists in France, probably he would have opposed them in sharp, polemical articles and biting epigrams. Some of the remarks in his article, "Random Thoughts," on the advantages of the Russian peasant serf over the worker of Western Europe, show that Pushkin could be as mistaken in his reasoning as the less brilliant Gautier. But the economic backwardness of Russia would account for this error.

When one class dominates society completely, and lives by exploiting the class below it in the economic scale, then any progress whatsoever involves retrogression for this dominant class. Herein lies the solution to that phenomenon, at first glance incomprehensible and even incredible, that in economically backward countries the ideology of the ruling class is often more liberal than in more advanced countries.

Today [i.e., at the beginning of the twentieth century], Russia has reached a degree of economic development in which the advocates of the theory of art for art's sake have become conscious defenders of a social order based on the exploitation of one class by another. Thus, in

our country, countless reactionary absurdities are proclaimed in the name
of the "absolute autonomy of art." Fortunately for Pushkin, in his time
such a state of things did not as yet exist.

We have said that there is no such thing as a work of art completely
devoid of ideological content, and also that not every idea can serve as
a theme for a work of art, or truly inspire the artist. Only that which
promotes communion between men can be the basis of a work of art.
The possible limits of such a communion are determined not by the artist
alone but by the cultural level of the social group to which he belongs,
and in a society divided into classes, the extent of this communion is
still further conditioned at any given time by the mutual relations of these
classes and their degree of development.

When the bourgeoisie was still struggling for emancipation from the
yoke of the clergy and the aristocracy, that is, when it was a revolutionary
class, it marched at the head of all the toiling masses, together with
whom it constituted the Third Estate. Consequently the foremost ideologists of the bourgeoisie were also the foremost ideologists of "the
whole nation with the exception of the privileged." In other words, the
limits of communion between men as expressed in the work of artists
who accepted the bourgeois viewpoint, were relatively broad at that time.
The limits of this communion receded considerably, however, when the
interests of the bourgeoisie ceased to be the interests of all the toiling
masses and particularly when they actually came into violent conflict
with the interests of the proletariat. If, then, as Ruskin said, a miser
cannot sing of his lost gold, in much the same way the mental state
of the bourgeoisie has come to approach that of the miser lamenting his
lost treasure. The only difference is that the miser mourns a loss which
has already occurred, while the bourgeoisie is disquieted by the threat
of an imminent loss. Again, in the words of *Ecclesiastes*, "surely oppression maketh a wise man mad." Fear of being deprived of the right to
oppress others has the same harmful effects even on a "wise man." The
ideas of the ruling class lose their intrinsic value at the rate at which
that class approaches extinction, and the art created in the spirit of that
class decays at the same rate. I should like to supplement, at this point,
what I have previously stated, by examining certain important manifestations of the decline of bourgeois art today.

We have seen how French literature became pervaded by mysticism,
because of the realization that it was impossible to be concerned with
form only, and not with content or ideas, and because of the inability
to rise to an understanding of the great emancipatory ideas of our times.
This realization and inability have resulted in other consequences which,
no less than mysticism, have lessened the intrinsic value of the art thus
affected.

Mysticism is the implacable enemy of reason, but reason numbers among its enemies not only mystics but also those who advocate false ideas.

When a work of art is based upon a fallacious idea, inherent contradictions inevitably cause a degeneration of its aesthetic quality.

Knut Hamsun's play, *At the Gate of the Kingdom,* may be mentioned as a work which suffers from the fallaciousness of its basic idea. The hero of this play is the writer Ivar Kareno, an untalented but overbearing young man who fancies his thoughts to be "free as a bird." But "free as a bird" as his thoughts may be, he nevertheless writes of "resistance" and "hatred"—resistance to the proletariat, and hatred of proletarians. Does this make him a new kind of hero? To be sure there have been very few like him, but these few are sufficient to prevent his being regarded as an absolutely new phenomenon in literature. Whoever preaches resistance to the proletariat becomes the exponent of bourgeois ideology in its clearest expression.

Nevertheless, the bourgeois ideologist Ivar Kareno is regarded by himself and his creator, Knut Hamsun, as one of the greatest of revolutionaries. "Revolutionary" sentiments, however, are often a distinctive feature of conservatism, as we have seen from the early French romanticists. Théophile Gautier hated the "bourgeois" but at the same time he denounced the idea that the hour was at hand to eradicate bourgeois social relations. Clearly, Ivar Kareno is a spiritual descendant of the renowned French romanticist; he has even surpassed his ancestor in that he is an avowed enemy of that which Gautier merely hated instinctively.[1]

The romanticists were conservative; but Ivar Kareno is a thorough reactionary, and moreover a utopian, reminiscent of the cruel landowner depicted by Saltykov-Schedrin. The former wishes to exterminate the proletariat just as the latter wishes to exterminate the moujik. Kareno's utopianism reaches the height of absurdity, like most of his "free, soaring thoughts," the most fantastic being that the proletariat is the exploiter of all other classes of society! And Knut Hamsun evidently shares the ideas of his hero who, because of his "resistance" to the proletariat, whom he despises, is made the victim of a series of misfortunes, culminating in his failure to secure a professorship and to publish his book—persecutions visited upon him by the bourgeoisie among whom he lives and teaches. But where on this earth or in what Utopia has there ever been a bourgeoisie that so relentlessly punished "resistance" to the proletariat? No such bourgeoisie has ever existed anywhere, nor could it exist. Kunt Hamsun's play is based on an idea that directly contradicts reality, and this has so affected the drama that it provokes laughter in scenes which the author had intended to be tragic. Knut Hamsun is a writer of great talent, but no amount of talent can ever make truth out of falsity.

The glaring defects of *At the Gate of the Kingdom* are the natural consequences of the utter bankruptcy of its basic idea. And this bankruptcy is due to the author's inability to understand the meaning of that very class struggle of which his play is a literary echo.

Knut Hamsun is not French, but that does not alter the problem. The *Communist Manifesto* states very aptly that in civilized countries, because of the development of capitalism: "National one-sidedness and narrow-mindedness become more and more impossible, and from the numerous national and local literatures there arises a world literature." Hamsun was born and educated in a country which was not among the most economically developed countries of Europe; this explains the truly infantile absurdity of his concept of the position of the proletariat in contemporary society. But the economic backwardness of his native land did not prevent his becoming hostile to the working class and sympathetic with the struggle against it, like the bourgeois intelligentsia in the most developed countries.

Ivar Kareno is merely one of the many varieties of the Nietzsche type, and the Nietzschean cult is but a new edition duly revised and supplemented to meet the exigencies of the latest stage of capitalism, a struggle against the "bourgeois" which harmonizes quite well with unshakable devotion to the bourgeois order. Hamsun's example can be supplemented with examples from contemporary French literature.

One of the most talented of modern French dramatists is François de Curel, whose most significant work is the five-act play, *Le Répas du Lion,* which, as far as I know, has received little attention from Russian criticism. The chief character of this play, Jean de Sancy, was influenced in his childhood by Christian Socialism but later he breaks with its teachings and becomes an eloquent defender of large-scale capitalist production. In a long speech to the workers he tries to prove that "egoism which produces, is the same thing for the toiling masses as charity for the poor." As his listeners express disagreement with this opinion, he becomes more heated and explains to them, in vivid imagery, the role of capitalist and worker in modern production:

It is said that a whole pack of jackals follow the lion in the desert so that they may devour the remains of his prey. Too weak to attack the buffalo, too slow to stalk the gazelle, all the hopes of the jackals lie in the claws of the lord of the desert. In his claws, you understand! At dusk, the lion leaves his lair and runs, roaring in hunger, in search of prey. There! One mighty leap and the furious struggle begins, fight to the death; the earth is red with blood, which is not always the blood of the victim. Then follows the royal feast, the jackals attentive and respectful. When the lion has sated himself, the jackals feed. Do you believe that the latter would be better fed if the lion were to divide his prey equally among them keeping only a small share for himself?

Not at all! Such a tender-hearted lion would no longer be a lion; scarcely a blind man's dog. At the first cry of anguish he would cease to strangle his victim and begin to lick his wounds. As for me, give me a ferocious beast eager for prey, one that dreams only of carnage and butchery. When such a lion roars, the mouths of the jackals water.

The meaning of this allegory is made even clearer by our eloquent orator in this simpler but no less vivid image:

. . . the enterprising man . . . makes the springs of nourishment gush forth and the workers receive the splashings.

I realize that the artist does not necessarily answer for the words of his heroes; nevertheless his attitude toward them is usually revealed in one way or another, so that we can be judge of his own ideas. And the subsequent development of *Le Répas du Lion* shows that de Curel himself considers sound Jean de Sancy's comparison between "enterprising man" and lion, and between workers and jackals. We can well imagine him reiterating with full conviction the words of his hero:

I believe in the lion, I bow before the rights which his claws give him.

De Curel himself is inclined to regard the workers as jackals who fatten on the morsels produced by the efforts of the capitalists and like Jean de Sancy, he conceives the struggle of the workers against the capitalists as a struggle of envious jackals against the mighty lion. It is this very comparison which constitutes the basic idea of the play and which guides the actions of the hero in spite of the fact that in this idea there is not an atom of truth. It distorts the real nature of social relations in modern society far more than the economic sophisms of Bastiat and all his followers right down to Böhm-Bawerk. The jackals are represented as doing absolutely nothing for their share of the lion's spoils with which, in part, they still the pangs of their hunger. But who would dare to suggest that the workers in any given factory do nothing towards the making of its finished products? In spite of all economic sophisms, it is obvious that they are created by the labor of the workers. It is true, of course, that the "enterprising man" also takes part in the productive process as organizer and, in this capacity, contributes to the product of labor. But a factory manager's salary is one thing and a factory owner's profits another. After deducting salary from profits there remains a surplus which falls to the share of capital as such. The whole problem lies in determining why capital obtains this surplus.

In all the grandiloquent speeches of Jean de Sancy, there is not even a hint of a solution to this problem. In fact, Sancy does not seem to realize he could hardly justify his own income from the business in which he owns a good deal of stock, even if it were correct to compare the "enterprising man" with the lion, and workers with jackals. He himself does nothing whatever for the business except to draw large dividends. If anyone is to be compared with the jackals, which feed on what others labor to produce, surely it is the stockholder, whose only "labor" consists in keeping his stock in a safe place, and perhaps also the apologist for the bourgeois social order, who contributes just as little to production but who, nevertheless, gathers up the remains from the festive board of Capital. Unfortunately, the talented de Curel is just such an apologist. In the struggle of the wage-workers against the capitalists he stands firmly with the latter, distorting the actual relationship between capitalists and those whom they exploit.

And what is Paul Bourget's drama, *La Barricade,* if not an appeal addressed to the bourgeoisie by this celebrated and talented writer, calling upon them to rally for the struggle against the proletariat? Bourgeois art becomes belligerent. Its exponents no longer claim that they were not born for "life's base agitation." On the contrary, they now rush into battle with no fear of its violent passions. But for what is this battle being waged? Alas, it is being fought out of cupidity! True, it is not personal greed, for it would be a mistake to suppose that men like Curel or Bourget come forward as apologists of the bourgeoisie in the hope of enriching themselves. It is the cupidity of an entire class, but cupidity, nonetheless. If this be so, let us consider the consequences.

Why did the romanticists despise the "bourgeois" of their time? Because, in the words of Théodore de Banville, the "bourgeois" esteemed the five franc piece above all else. Yet what do such artists as de Curel, Bourget and Hamsun defend in their works? They defend those very social relations which serve the bourgeoisie to garner innumerable five-franc pieces. How far removed these artists are from the days of romanticism! The great distance that separates them is due solely to the inexorable march of social progress. With the sharpening of the contradictions inherent in the capitalist mode of production, it is becoming increasingly difficult for artists who adhere to the bourgeois ideology to defend the theory of art for art's sake and dwell in an ivory tower.

In the civilized world today [i.e., early twentieth century—*Ed.*] there is not a single country where the youth of the bourgeoisie are not in sympathy with the ideas of Friedrich Nietzsche. Nietzsche detested his "sleepy" (*Schläfrigen*) contemporaries perhaps even more than Gautier detested the "bourgeois" of his day. In Nietzsche's eyes his "sleepy" contemporaries were guilty of one crime, one great defect from which all others flowed—their failure to think, to feel, and above all, to act as behooves those who occupy a dominant position in society. Under present day conditions, this reproach can only mean that they are not sufficiently energetic and determined in defending the bourgeois order against the revolutionary attempts of the proletariat. Not without reason was Nietzsche so hostile to the socialists.

Whereas Pushkin and the romanticists of his day reproached the "mob" for valuing their flesh-pots too highly, the neo-romanticists of today reproach them for not defending these flesh-pots more vigorously, that is, for valuing them too little. At the same time the neo-romanticists, like the romanticists of old, also proclaim the absolute autonomy of art. But art consciously devoted to defending a specific social order is obviously not autonomous. Such art unquestionably has a definite purpose. And if its defenders cannot tolerate creations inspired by utilitarian considerations, they are under a delusion. Although they are evidently not motivated by personal considerations, which can hardly determine a true artist, what they really cannot tolerate are considerations involving the interests of the exploited majority, for to them, the supreme law is the interest of the exploiting minority. Thus, although Théophile Gautier and Flaubert, as we know, were by no means free of conservative prejudices, their attitude was the direct opposite of that of Knut Hamsun or François de Curel toward utilitarian art. Due to the intensification of social contradictions since the time of Gautier and Flaubert, these prejudices have grown so strong among artists sharing the bourgeois viewpoint that it is now incomparably more difficult for them to adhere consistently to the theory of art for art's sake. It would be a mistake, however, to imagine that none of them consistently supports this theory today. But, as we shall see presently, this avenue of thought requires further analysis.

The neo-romanticists, under Nietzsche's influence, like to regard themselves as being "beyond good and evil." But to be "beyond good and evil" it is necessary to perform such epoch-making deeds that they cannot be judged according to the concepts of good and evil prevailing in the society in which they are performed. In their struggle against reaction the French revolutionists of 1793 undoubtedly went beyond good and evil. By their actions, they ran counter to the concepts of good and evil which prevailed under the *ancien régime*. Such a course, always fraught with tragic consequences, can be justified only if it leads to less evil and more good in social life. In order to capture the Bastille, it was necessary to engage its defenders in combat; in such a struggle a position above good and evil is inevitable. But the capture of the Bastille, by putting an end to a despotism which could put men in prison on a whim—"because such is our pleasure," as the absolute monarchs of France used to say—led to less evil and more good in French social life, hence this temporary position beyond good and evil was justified. Of course, not everyone who takes such a position can be equally justified. For example, Ivar Kareno would surely not hesitate for a moment to go beyond good and evil to realize his thoughts "as free as a bird." But the sum total of his thoughts, as we know, may be expressed as a relentless opposition to the proletariat's movement for liberation. For him, therefore, to go beyond good and evil would mean to ignore even those few rights which the working class has won in capitalist society. Therefore, since Kareno's position beyond good and evil would lead not to less but to more evil in social life, it would not be justified. Generally speaking, there is never a justification for such an attitude when it is adopted for reactionary ends.

The objection may be raised that while Ivar Kareno would hardly be justified from the viewpoint of the proletariat, he certainly would from the viewpoint of the bourgeoisie. With this I am in complete agreement. Now the viewpoint of the bourgeoisie is that of the privileged minority striving to perpetuate its privileges; the viewpoint of the proletariat is that of the majority demanding the abolition of all privileges. Thus to say that a man is justified from the bourgeois viewpoint is tantamount to saying that he is condemned from the viewpoint of those who refuse to defend the interests of the exploiters. That is sufficient for me; for the inexorable course of economic development guarantees that the number of the exploited will inevitably increase from day to day.

Detesting with all their soul their "sleepy" contemporaries, the neoromanticists have been stirred into activity, but a conservative activity, opposed to the movement for liberation of our time. Herein lies the clue to their psychology as well as the explanation of the fact that even the most talented of them cannot create works of art as great as they might if their social sympathies lay elsewhere and if their thinking were otherwise.

We have seen the fallaciousness of the basic idea in de Curel's play, Le Répas du Lion. An erroneous idea cannot but mar a work of art, because it results in a falsification of the psychology of the characters. It would not be difficult to show how unsound is the psychology of Jean de Sancy, the hero of this play. But to do so would require a digression too long for this paper. I shall therefore take a simpler illustration.

The basic idea of the play La Barricade is that in the class struggle of today each must side with his own class. Yet whom does Bourget regard as "the most appealing figure" in the play? Why, the old worker, Gaucherond, who sides not with the workers but with the employers. The behavior of this worker fundamentally contradicts the basic idea of the play, and he could appeal only to one blinded by infatuation for the bourgeoisie. The feelings which move Gaucherond are those of the slave who regards his chains with respectful awe. Since the appearance of the works of Alexey Tolstoy, we have seen how difficult it is for any one who has not been educated in the spirit of slavery to sympathize with the self-abnegation of the slave. Recall the servant Vassily Shibanov, one of Tolstoy's heroes, who portrays perfectly this "loyalty of the slave." He dies like a hero, notwithstanding the horrible torture he endures at the hands of the Tsar's executioners, who exclaim:

> Tsar, he keeps saying the same thing:
> He has nothing but praise for his master.

This servile heroism fails to move the contemporary reader, who can hardly conceive that a man who is scarcely more than a "tool that talks" can show such self-sacrificing loyalty for his master. Old Gaucherond, in Bourget's drama, is somewhat analogous to a Shibanov turned proletarian. One needs to be blind indeed to call him "the most appealing figure" in the play. In any case, there is no doubt that if Gaucherond is appealing it shows that despite Bourget, each of us must side not with the class to which we belong but with the class whose cause we consider to be most just.

In this play Bourget contradicts his own basic idea. A wise man is foolish when he oppresses others. When a talented artist is inspired by a fallacious idea, his work is marred.

The modern artist will not find inspiration in a sound idea if he seeks to defend the bourgeoisie in its struggle against the proletariat.

I have said that today it is far more difficult than formerly for artists accepting the bourgeois viewpoint to adhere consistently to the theory of art for art's sake. Bourget, among others, recognizes this fact and he expresses it strongly:

> To one who thinks and feels, the role of disinterested chronicler is impossible when it concerns those terrible internal wars, in which it sometimes seems that the whole future of the nation and of civilization are at stake.

This statement, however, requires certain reservations. One who thinks and feels cannot remain a disinterested chronicler of the terrible internal wars raging in society today. If his outlook is limited by bourgeois prejudices, he will be on one side of the "barricade"; if he is free of those prejudices, he will be on the other side. So much is clear. However, not all the children of the bourgeoisie, or of any other class, for that matter, are able to think; and those who can think do not always feel. Today it is easy for such people to be consistent supporters of the theory of art for art's sake. No other theory is so much in keeping with their attitude of indifference to social interests, even their own narrow class interests.

More than any other, the bourgeois social order fosters such a spirit of indifference. Where whole generations are educated on the principle of "every man for himself and the devil take the hindmost," it is very natural that egoists should appear whose thoughts and interests are centered entirely on themselves. In contemporary bourgeois society there are in fact more egoists than in any other society, past or present. On this point we have the exceedingly valuable testimony of Maurice Barrès, a bourgeois thinker of importance:

Our morality, our religion, our national spirit all have collapsed, I find, leaving us nothing from which to borrow rules of life, and until our masters have re-established absolute truths for us, we must cling to the sole reality, the ego.

When a man finds that all has "collapsed"—all, that is, except his ego —there is nothing to prevent him from playing the role of disinterested chronicler of the tremendous social struggle raging today, except, perhaps —and this is clearly reflected in the above words of Barrès—a lack of any interest in social affairs. Why should any man having no interest in society and the struggle raging within it, assume the role of chronicler of that social struggle? Everything about it would bore him to distraction. If he happens to be an artist he will not even mention it in his work: he will give himself over to the "sole reality," his own ego. And since his ego may weary of its own company, he will invent for it a world of fantasy, high above the earth and all mundane matters. This is exactly what many artists do today.

Note

[1] I refer to the period before Gautier wore his famous red waist-coat. Afterwards, however, at the time of the Paris Commune [March 18–May 28, 1871.—Ed.], for example, he became a conscious and open enemy of the revolutionary aspirations of the working class. Flaubert too—perhaps more justifiably—may be considered a precursor of Knut Hamsun and his ideas. In one of Flaubert's notebooks there is this revealing passage: "It is not against God that Prometheus would today revolt, but against the people, the new god. To the old tyrannies, sacerdotal, feudal, and monarchic, there has succeeded another, more subtle, intangible, imperious, which soon will leave not a single corner of the earth free." (See also the chapter "Les Carnets de Gustave Flaubert" in Louis Bertrand: *Gustave Flaubert* [p. 255, Paris: Mercure de France: 1912.—Ed.]). Here is the very thought "free as a bird" expressed by Ivar Kareno. In a letter to George Sand dated September 8, 1871, Flaubert writes: "I believe that the crowd, the herd, will always be despicable. Of importance only is a small group of intellects, always the same, who pass on the torch." [Flaubert: *Correspondance, op. cit.*, p. 73—Ed.] It is in this letter that he brands universal suffrage a disgrace to man's soul, because it would result in numbers prevailing "even over money." [*op. cit.*, p. 74.—Ed.] In these sentences Ivar Kareno would surely

recognize his own thoughts. Flaubert did not express these ideas so directly in his novels. The class struggle in modern society had to grow to greater proportions before the theorists of the ruling class found it necessary to express in literature their detestation of the emancipatory aspirations of "the herd." But those who came to feel this necessity were no longer able to defend "absolute freedom of ideas." On the contrary, they forged all ideas into spiritual weapons for the struggle against the proletariat.

9. N. I. Bukharin

Art and Social Evolution

NICHOLAS I. BUKHARIN (1888–1938) joined the Social-Democratic Party in his youth, and spent many of his years as a young man in prison and in exile from his native Russia. Together with V. I. Lenin he published the newspaper *Pravda* in Austria, and in 1916 went to New York, where he edited the periodical *Novy Mir* ('The New World'). After the 1917 Revolution, he became a central figure in the Communist Party in Russia: a member of its Central Committee, a leader of the Left Wing Bolsheviks, a member of the Politburo from 1918 to 1929, and the head of the Third International from 1926 to 1929. As an advocate of gradualism in collectivization and industrialization, he allied himself initially with Stalin against the opposition of Trotsky, Kamanev, and Zinoviev, but fell from power and was expelled from the Communist Party in 1929 when Stalin altered these policies. Readmitted to favor, he edited the newspaper *Izvestia* briefly in 1934, but was once more expelled from official circles in 1937 on suspicion of supporting the Trotskyite opposition. Arrested and tried in the famous political trials conducted in Moscow in 1938, he was sentenced to death and executed. The following selection is taken from Bukharin's chapter entitled "The Equilibrium between the Elements of Society" in his major work of Marxist theory, *Historical Materialism: A System of Sociology*, originally published in 1925.

WE shall now take up another order of social phenomena—*art*. Art is as much a product of the social life as is science or any other outgrowth of material production; the expression "objects of art" will make this apparent. But art is an outgrowth of the social life in the further sense that it is a form of mental activity. Like science, it can develop only at a certain level of productive labor, in default of which it will wither and perish. But the subject of art is sufficiently complicated to justify an investigation of the manner in which it is determined by the course of social life; the first question requiring an answer is: what is art; what is its fundamental social function?

Science classifies, arranges, clarifies, eliminates the contradictions in, the thoughts of men; it constructs a complete raiment of scientific ideas and theories out of fragmentary knowledge. But social man not only thinks, he also feels; he suffers, enjoys, regrets, rejoices, mourns, despairs, etc.; his thoughts may be of infinite complexity and delicacy; his psychic experiences may be tuned according to this note or that. Art systematizes these feelings and expresses them in artistic form, in words, or in tones, in gestures (for example, the dance), or by other means, which sometimes are quite material, as in architecture. We may formulate this condition in other words: we may say, for example, that art is a means of "socializing the feelings"; or, as Leo Tolstoy correctly says in his book, art is a means of emotionally "infecting" men. The hearers of a musical work expressive of a certain mood will be "infected," permeated, with this mood; the feeling of the individual composer becomes the feeling of many persons, has been transferred to them, has "influenced" them; a psychic state has here been "socialized." The same holds good in any other art; painting, architecture, poetry, sculpture, etc.

The nature of art is now clear: it is a systematization of feelings in forms; the direct function of art in socializing, transferring, disseminating these feelings, in society, is now also clear.

What conditions the development of art? What are the forms of its dependence on the course of social evolution? In order to answer these questions, we must analyze an art—we have selected *Music* for the purpose—into its component parts. Our investigation will show the following elements: 1. the element of *objective material things,* the musical technology: musical instruments and groups of musical instruments (orchestra, quartette, etc.; the combinations of instruments may be likened to combinations of machines and tools in factories); also, physical symbols and tokens: systems of notation, musical scores, etc.; 2. the *human* organization; these include many forms of human association in musical work (distribution of persons in the orchestra, the chorus, in the process of musical creation; also, musical clubs and societies of all kinds); 3. the *formal* elements of music, including rhythm, harmony (corresponding to *symmetry* in the graphic and plastic arts), etc.; 4. the *methods* of uniting the various forms, principles of construction, what corresponds to style in some arts; in a broader sense, the type of artistic *form;* 5. the *content* of the art work, or, if we are dealing with an entire movement or tendency, the content of all the works; we are chiefly concerned here not with the *method* of performance, but with its substance, let us say with the choice of "subject" of presentation; 6. as a "superstructure of the superstructure," we may also include, in music, the *theory of musical technique* (theory of counterpoint, etc.).

Let us now consider the various causal relations between the evolution of music and social evolution in general, which is ultimately based on the economic and technical evolution of society.

First. We shall not again emphasize the fact that art may not flourish before a certain level has been attained in the productive forces of society.

Second. Only in a certain social "atmosphere" may art (and specifically, music) be singled out for development from among the innumerable forms of the superstructure. For example, in discussing the question of technology and art among the Greeks in the fifth and fourth centuries B.C., we found that there was no growth of technical or natural sciences at all, but that philosophical speculation was widespread. There is no doubt that the "superstructure" in general rises at a fast pace if social technology is moving at a fast pace; but there is also no doubt that the superstructure does not move forward (or backward) *uniformly;* nor does *material* production advance uniformly; for instance, the manufacture of sausages may not keep abreast of the evolution of the productive forces to the same extent as the construction of locomotives or the production of castor oil. Certain forms of production usually develop much faster than others; in fact some such forms may be entirely absent, for certain reasons. The "superstructure" shows the same conditions: in Athens, in the fifth century B.C., technology fared badly, while speculative philosophy flourished. In America, in the twentieth century, technology is supreme and philosophy is neglected. Church hymns (a branch of the general field of music) were once universal, but it would be difficult to find many persons today—except a few moldy old men and pious old women—who are fond of the conventional hymns. The mental "shoots" of society are the highest outgrowth of the superstructure, and we naturally expect that shoot to burgeon that happens to receive the most generous supply of sap. In ancient Athens it was an "ignoble" thing, worthy only of stupid artisans, to concern oneself with an investigation of nature by means of experiment; the disfavor in which the natural sciences were held is easy to understand; it was a result of the class alignment, of the social economy, which in its turn was conditioned by the social technology. Similarly, in the case of music, hymns might be quite important at an epoch when music was still the "handmaiden" —as was also philosophy—of religion. But such hymns are as appropriate to a highly developed capitalist society as General Ludendorff's trousers to Father Sergius. The function of music in society is therefore dependent on the state of the latter, on society's mood, means, views, feelings, etc. The explanation of the latter is found in the class alignment and the class psychology, which are ultimately based on the social economy and the conditions of its growth.

Third. The "technique" of music depends in the first place on the technique of production. Savages cannot build pianos; this prevents them from playing the instrument or composing pieces for it. It is sufficient to compare the primitive musical instruments (aside from the natural instrument, the human voice), those developed from horn and pipe, from the needs of the chase, with the complicated construction of the modern piano, to grasp fully the function of these instruments. "Music is not possible as an independent art until appropriate tools have taken shape and developed: the instruments and their development." "Music can express the gamut of emotions only within the scale of the available instruments." The production of such things as the telescope and the piano are a portion of the social material production; it is obvious that musical "technique" (now meaning: the instruments) depends on the technique of this material production.

Fourth. The organization of persons is also directly connected with the bases of the social evolution. For instance, the distribution of the members of an orchestra is determined precisely as in the factory, by the instruments and the groups of instruments; in other words, the arrangement and organization of these members is here conditioned by musical technique (in our restricted sense of the word) and, through it, based on the stage in social evolution, on the technique of material production as such. Similarly, the organization of persons in another musical field, let us say, a musical society, is the result of a number of conditions of social life, principally, a love of music (resulting from the social psychology, as above discussed), the opportunities afforded the various classes to indulge this predilection (for instance, the amount of unoccupied time available to the various classes, i.e., the class alignment and the degree of productivity of social labor), which elements govern the number of members, the extent and nature of their activity, the character of the membership, etc. Or, in the case of the creative process, we also find a number of forms for the human relations involved, the oldest of which is the impersonal stage (individual names are not handed down), the so called "folk-songs." Here the art work is produced in an elemental manner by thousands of nameless artists. Quite different is the case when the individual artist works "on order," by the command of a prince, king or wealthy man. The case is again different when the artist works as an artisan for an unknown market, on whose caprices he depends. An artistic production may also result when the latter assumes the form of a social service, etc. These forms of human relations are obviously based directly on the economic structure. In the slaveholding system, the musicians were slaves; not so long ago, we still had serf musicians in Russia, performing and composing not to satisfy a market requirement, but at the command of a feudal magnate. Of course, these elements are expressed in the art work.

Fifth. The *formal elements* (rhythm, harmony, etc.) are also connected with the social life. Many of these elements are already present in prehistoric times, even in the animal kingdom. Karl Bücher says, concerning rhythm among horses:

Rhythm springs from the organic nature of man. Every normal use of his animal body he seems to control, as a regulating element of economic utilization of energy. The trotting horse and the laden camel move as rhythmically as the rowing fisherman and the hammering blacksmith. Rhythm awakens a feeling of well-being; it therefore not only renders work easier, but is a source of aesthetic pleasure and the element of art to which all persons respond, regardless of their mental nature.

Quite true; but rhythm has also developed—as Bücher points out in his work—under the influence of social relations and particularly under the direct influence of material labor (the workers' songs, like the Russian *Dubinushka*, arose on the same basis; rhythm here is an instrument of labor organization). In other words, while the formal elements (such as rhythm) may have arisen in prehistoric times, i.e., before man became man, they do not evolve from within themselves only, but under the influence of social evolution.

A further circumstance is worth mentioning. At a certain stage of development, only the simplest rhythms are available to man ("as monotonous as the singing of cannibals"), he has *no ear* for the complicated rhythm perceived by a man at a *different* stage of development. A. V. Lunacharsky, in one of his essays on art, says: "From all of the above (i.e., the determining role of economy, N.B.) it by no means follows that . . . the forms of creative work may not have their own immanent psycho-physiological laws; they have such laws and are *entirely* conditioned by them (N.B. editor's italics) in their specific *form*, while the content is given by the social environment." We learn later on what is meant by this: "The immanent psychological law of evolution in art is the law of complication. Impressions of similar energy and intricacy begin, after a number of repetitions, to exert less and less force on the mind, and to be capable of suggesting a lower intricacy. We experience a sense of monotony, of boredom ("it gets on my nerves"); it follows that every school of art will naturally seek to make more complicated and to enhance the effect of its works" (A. V. Lunacharsky: *Further Remarks on the Theatre and Socialism,* in the collection *Vershiny,* p. 196 *et seq.,* in Russian). We thus find the "psycho-physiology" contrasted with the "economy"; the "content" is left to economy, the "form" to psycho-physiology. This point of view seems to us to be at least insufficient, if not wrong. As a matter of fact, if we consider the evolution of those elements that we regard as formal, we shall find that this evolution has by no means proceeded at a uniform rate. The music of the savage, the number of harmonious tones produced by him, was very poor; yet, the social evolution itself was not characterized by great speed; manifestly the musical supply lasted for a long time, did not produce "boredom" for a long time. "Antiquity did not know our modern harmony and made use of unison arrangements; it took a long time for it to become accustomed to the octave. . . . We have reason to believe that it is only recently that the fourth has been recognized as a harmonic interval" (L. Obolensky: *The Scientific Bases of the Beautiful and of Art*, p. 97, in Russian). Therefore, the formal elements become more complicated as a consequence of the *more complicated structure of life,* for *an increasing intricacy of life alters the psycho-physiological "nature" of man.* The "crude" hearing of the savage is as much a function of social evolution as is the "fine" hearing of the inhabitants of the great capitalist cities with their extremely delicate nervous organization. The "immanent laws" therefore, are merely another phase of the social evolution. And since the social evolution is conditioned by the evolution of the productive forces, they constitute "in the last analysis" a function of these productive forces. For, man alters his nature *in accordance with his influence on the external universe.*

Sixth. The type, the *style,* is also conditioned by the course of social life. It embodies the current psychology and ideology; it expresses those feelings and thoughts, those moods and beliefs, those impressions, those current forms of thought, that "are in the air." Style is not only external form, but also "embodied content with its corresponding objective symbols"; the history of the styles is an expression of the "history of the systems of life." "The style of form is a reflex of the social vitality." The religious music of the ancient Hindoo hymns (the *Vedas*) have not the same "style" or construction as—let us say—a French music-hall song or the battle-song of the revolution, the Marseillaise. These productions are the outgrowth of different environments, different social soils, and their form is consequently different; the religious hymn, the battle-song, the vaudeville song, cannot be composed or constructed in the same way; even their form expresses different feelings, thoughts, and views. This difference is a result of the difference in the situation of the societies or classes involved, and this difference is conditioned by the economic development and consequently, by the state of the productive forces. Furthermore, the style depends also in high degree on the material conditions of the specific work of art (for instance, instrumental music is conditioned by the nature of the instrument) as well as by the method of artistic creation (we have already discussed the organization of persons in music), etc. All these phases likewise depend on the fundamental causal relation in social evolution.

Seventh. The content ("subject"), almost impossible to isolate from the form, is obviously determined by the social environment, as may be readily seen from the history of the arts. It is obvious that artistic form will be given to what is engaging the attention of men in one way or another at the given moment. The creative spirit is not stimulated by subjects that do not hold its attention, but those things that constitute the central interest of society or of its various classes are given treatment, thus reflecting this general interest in the form of "mental labor." "There is indeed a certain moral temperature governing the general condition of manners and minds (*des esprits*)." "The artistic family (Taine here means a specific "school" or tendency in art. N.B.) is situated within a larger community; namely, the surrounding world, whose taste conforms with that of the *school*. For the state of morals and of mental life is the same for the public as for the artists; the latter are not isolated men." These statements by Taine are entirely correct, but Taine seems incapable of thinking them out to their ultimate conclusions, which would lead him into the acceptance of impious materialistic inferences. We have again and again discussed, in another shape, this question of the "moral temperature" of the *"milieu,"* of which Taine speaks; both "morals" and "mental life" in general, feelings and moods, do not develop out of themselves; we know that this social consciousness is determined by the social being, i.e., the conditions of existence of society and its various parts (classes, groups). These conditions also give birth to the various "tastes." As a result, the content of art is also determined, in the last analysis, by the fundamental natural law character of social evolution; its content is a function of the social economy, and therefore of the productive forces.

Eighth. Musical theory is obviously directly connected with all the foregoing, and therefore "subject" to the movement of the productive forces of society.

We have outlined the fundamental chains of causality that exist in music; they do not at all exhaust the subject; in the first place, probably not all of these relations have been enumerated above, and, in the second place, there is in addition a mutual interaction of all these elements, resulting in a much more complicated and confused pattern, the general outlines of which, however, follow the scheme above indicated. Nor does it follow that the other arts will show precisely the same pattern as we have traced in the case of music. Each art has certain special earmarks: for instance, the material objects involved in singing are reduced to a minimum (there are notes, but the "musical instrument" remains the human voice alone); in architecture the role of the material, the tools, the purpose of the buildings (temple, residence, palace, museum, etc.), is of immense importance; the student must not neglect such distinctions, but we shall always find that the following holds good: *directly or indirectly, art is ultimately determined in various ways by the economic structure and the stage of the social technology.*

10. Mao Tse-tung

On Literature and Art

MAO TSE-TUNG (1893–   ) was a librarian and school teacher in his early twenties, turned to politics, and by 1921 had contributed to the founding of the Chinese Communist Party. In 1927 the break with the Kuomintang, the nationalist party organized chiefly by Sun Yat-sen, became irretrievable. In subsequent party struggles, and especially through the "Long March" by which he saved the nucleus of the Chinese Red Army, Mao rose to leadership of the Party, and in 1949 led the Party to control of the Chinese mainland. A prolific essayist and poet, his biography appears in *Red Star Over China* (1937) by Edgar Snow. The selection on literature and art was a talk delivered at the Yenan Forum in May, 1942, and appears in *On Literature and Art* (Peking: Foreign Languages Press, 1967).

COMRADES! You have been invited to this forum today to exchange ideas and examine the relationship between work in the literary and artistic fields and revolutionary work in general. Our aim is to ensure that revolutionary literature and art follow the correct path of development and provide better help to other revolutionary work in facilitating the overthrow of our national enemy and the accomplishment of the task of national liberation.

In our struggle for the liberation of the Chinese people there are various fronts, among which there are the fronts of the pen and of the gun, the cultural and the military fronts. To defeat the enemy we must rely primarily on the army with guns. But this army alone is not enough; we must also have a cultural army, which is absolutely indispensable for uniting our own ranks and defeating the enemy. Since the May 4th Movement such a cultural army has taken shape in China, and it has helped the Chinese revolution, gradually reduced the domain of China's feudal culture and of the comprador culture which serves imperialist aggression, and weakened their influence. To oppose the new culture the Chinese reactionaries can now only "pit quantity against quality." In other words, reactionaries have money, and though they can produce nothing good, they can go all out and produce in quantity. Literature and art have been an important and successful part of the cultural front since the May 4th Movement. During the ten years' civil war, the revolutionary literature and art movement grew greatly. That movement and the revolutionary war both headed in the same general direction, but these two fraternal armies were not linked together in their practical work because the reactionaries had cut them off from each other. It is very good that since the outbreak of the War of Resistance Against Japan, more and more revolutionary writers and artists have been coming to Yenan and our other anti-Japanese base areas. But it does not necessarily follow that, having come to the base areas, they have already integrated themselves completely with the masses of the people here. The two must be completely integrated if we are to push ahead with our revolutionary work. The purpose of our meeting today is precisely to ensure that literature and art fit well into the whole revolutionary machine as a component part, that they operate as powerful weapons for uniting and educating the people and for attacking and destroying the enemy, and that they help the people fight the enemy with one heart and one mind. What are the problems that must be solved to achieve this objective? I think they are the problems of the class stand of the writers and artists, their attitude, their audience, their work and their study.

The problem of class stand. Our stand is that of the proletariat and of the masses. For members of the Communist Party, this means keeping to the stand of the Party, keeping to Party spirit and Party policy. Are there any of our literary and art workers who are still mistaken or not clear in their understanding of this problem? I think there are. Many of our comrades have frequently departed from the correct stand.

The problem of attitude. From one's stand there follow specific attitudes towards specific matters. For instance, is one to extol or to expose? This is a question of attitude. Which attitude is wanted? I would say both. The question is, whom are you dealing with? There are three kinds of persons, the enemy, our allies in the united front and our own people; the last are the masses and their vanguard. We need to adopt a different attitude towards each of the three. With regard to the enemy, that is, Japanese imperialism and all the other enemies of the people, the task of revolutionary writers and artists is to expose their duplicity and cruelty and at the same time to point out the inevitability of their defeat, so as to encourage the anti-Japanese army and people to fight staunchly with one heart and one mind for their overthrow. With regard to our different allies in the united front, our attitude should be one of both alliance and criticism, and there should be different kinds of alliance and different kinds of criticism. We support them in their resistance to Japan and praise them for any achievement. But if they are not active in the War of Resistance, we should criticize them. If anyone opposes the Communist Party and the people and keeps moving down the path of reaction, we will firmly oppose him. As for the masses of the people, their toil and their struggle, their army and their Party, we should certainly praise them. The people, too, have their shortcomings. Among the proletariat many retain petty-bourgeois ideas, while both the peasants and the urban petty bourgeoisie have backward ideas; these are burdens hampering them in their struggle. We should be patient and spend a long time in educating them and helping them to get these loads off their backs and combat their own shortcomings and errors, so that they can advance with great strides. They have remolded themselves in struggle or are doing so, and our literature and art should depict this process. As long as they do not persist in their errors, we should not dwell on their negative side and consequently make the mistake of ridiculing them or, worse still, of being hostile to them. Our writings should help them to unite, to make progress, to press ahead with one heart and one mind, to discard what is backward and develop what is revolutionary, and should certainly not do the opposite.

The problem of audience, i.e., the people for whom our works of literature and art are produced. In the Shensi-Kansu-Ningsia Border Region and the anti-Japanese base areas of northern and central China, this problem differs from that in the Kuomintang areas, and differs still more from that in Shanghai before the War of Resistance. In the Shanghai period, the audience for works of revolutionary literature and art consisted mainly of a section of the students, office workers and shop assistants. After the outbreak of the War of Resistance the audience in the Kuomintang areas became somewhat wider, but it still consisted mainly of the same kind of people because the government there pre- vented the workers, peasants and soldiers from having access to revolu- tionary literature and art. In our base areas the situation is entirely different. Here the audience for works of literature and art consists of workers, peasants, soldiers and revolutionary cadres. There are students in the base areas, too, but they are different from students of the old type; they are either former or future cadres. The cadres of all types, fighters in the army, workers in the factories and peasants in the villages all want to read books and newspapers once they become literate, and those who are illiterate want to see plays and operas, look at drawings and paintings, sing songs and hear music; they are the audience for our works of literature and art. Take the cadres alone. Do not think they are few; they far outnumber the readers of any book published in the Kuomintang areas. There, an edition usually runs to only 2,000 copies, and even three editions add up to only 6,000; but as for the cadres in the base areas, in Yenan alone there are more than 10,000 who read books. Many of them, moreover, are tempered revolutionaries of long standing, who have come from all parts of the country and will go out to work in different places, so it is very important to do educational work among them. Our literary and art workers must do a good job in this respect.

Since the audience for our literature and art consists of workers, peasants and soldiers and of their cadres, the problem arises of understanding them and knowing them well. A great deal of work has to be done in order to understand them and know them well, to understand and know well all the different kinds of people and phenomena in the Party and government organizations, in the villages and factories and in the Eighth Route and New Fourth Armies. Our writers and artists have their literary and art work to do, but their primary task is to understand people and know them well. In this regard, how have matters stood with our writers and artists? I would say they have been lacking in knowledge and understanding; they have been like "a hero with no place to display his prowess." What does lacking in knowledge mean? Not knowing people well. The writers and artists do not have a good knowledge either of those whom they describe or of their audience; indeed they may hardly know them at all. They do not know the workers or peasants or soldiers well, and do not know the cadres well either. What does lacking in understanding mean? Not understanding the language, that is, not being familiar with the rich, lively language of the masses. Since many writers and artists stand aloof from the masses and lead empty lives, naturally they are unfamiliar with the language of the people. Accordingly, their works are not only insipid in language but often contain nondescript expressions of their own coining which run counter to popular usage. Many comrades like to talk about "a mass style." But what does it really mean? It means that the thoughts and feelings of our writers and artists should be fused with those of the masses of workers, peasants and soldiers. To achieve this fusion, they should conscientiously learn the language of the masses. How can you talk of literary and artistic creation if you find the very language of the masses largely incomprehensible? By "a hero with no place to display his prowess," we mean that your collection of great truths is not appreciated by the masses. The more you put on the airs of a veteran before the masses and play the "hero," the more you try to peddle such stuff to the masses, the less likely they are to accept it. If you want the masses to understand you, if you want to be one with the masses, you must make up your mind to undergo a long and even painful process of tempering. Here I might mention the experience of how my own feelings changed. I began life as a student and at school acquired the ways of a student; I then used to feel it undignified to do even a little manual labor, such as carrying my own luggage in the presence of my fellow students, who were incapable of carrying anything, either on 'their shoulders or in their hands. At that time I felt that intellectuals were the only clean people in the world, while in comparison workers and peasants were dirty. I did not mind wearing the clothes of other intellectuals, believing them clean, but I would not put on clothes belonging to a worker or peasant, believing them dirty. But after I became a revolutionary and lived with workers and peasants and with soldiers of the revolutionary army, I gradually came to know them well, and they gradually came to know me well too. It was then, and only then, that I fundamentally changed the bourgeois and petty-bourgeois feelings implanted in me in the bourgeois schools. I came to feel that compared with the workers and peasants the unremolded intellectuals were not clean and that, in the last analysis, the workers and peasants were the cleanest people and, even though their hands were soiled and their feet smeared with cow-dung, they were really cleaner than the bourgeois and petty-bourgeois intellectuals. That is what is meant by a change in feelings, a change from one class to another. If our writers and artists who come from the intelligentsia want their works to be well received by the masses, they must change and remold their thinking and their feelings. Without such a change, without such remolding, they can do nothing well and will be misfits.

The last problem is study, by which I mean the study of Marxism-Leninism and of society. Anyone who considers himself a revolutionary Marxist writer, and especially any writer who is a member of the Communist Party, must have a knowledge of Marxism-Leninism. At present, however, some comrades are lacking in the basic concepts of Marxism. For instance, it is a basic Marxist concept that being determines consciousness, that the objective realities of class struggle and national struggle determine our thoughts and feelings. But some of our comrades turn this upside down and maintain that everything ought to start from "love." Now as for love, in a class society there can be only class love; but these comrades are seeking a love transcending classes, love in the abstract and also freedom in the abstract, truth in the abstract, human nature in the abstract, etc. This shows that they have been very deeply influenced by the bourgeoisie. They should thoroughly rid themselves of this influence and modestly study Marxism-Leninism. It is right for writers and artists to study literary and artistic creation, but the science of Marxism-Leninism must be studied by all revolutionaries, writers and artists not excepted. Writers and artists should study society, that is to say, should study the various classes in society, their mutual relations and respective conditions, their physiognomy and their psychology. Only when we grasp all this clearly can we have a literature and art that is rich in content and correct in orientation.

I am merely raising these problems today by way of introduction; I hope all of you will express your views on these and other relevant problems.

In the last analysis, what is the source of all literature and art? Works of literature and art, as ideological forms, are products of the reflection in the human brain of the life of a given society. Revolutionary literature and art are the products of the reflection of the life of the people in the brains of revolutionary writers and artists. The life of the people is always a mine of the raw materials for literature and art, materials in their natural form, materials that are crude, but most vital, rich and fundamental; they make all literature and art seem pallid by comparison; they provide literature and art with an inexhaustible source, their only source. They are the only source, for there can be no other. Some may ask, is there not another source in books, in the literature and art of ancient times and of foreign countries? In fact, the literary and artistic works of the past are not a source but a stream; they were created by our predecessors and the foreigners out of the literary and artistic raw materials they found in the life of the people of their time and place. We must take over all the fine things in our literary and artistic heritage, critically assimilate whatever is beneficial, and use them as examples when we create works out of the literary and artistic raw materials in the life of the people of our own time and place. It makes a difference whether or not we have such examples, the difference between crudeness and refinement, between roughness and polish, between a low and a high level, and between slower and faster work. Therefore, we must on no account reject the legacies of the ancients and the foreigners or refuse to learn from them, even though they are the works of the feudal or bourgeois classes. But taking over legacies and using them as examples must never replace our own creative work; nothing can do that. Uncritical transplantation or copying from the ancients and the foreigners is the most sterile and harmful dogmatism in literature and art. China's revolutionary writers and artists, writers and artists of promise, must go among the masses; they must for a long period of time unreservedly and wholeheartedly go among the masses of workers, peasants and soldiers, go into the heat of the struggle, go to the only source, the broadest and richest source, in order to observe, experience, study and analyze all the different kinds of people, all the classes, all the masses, all the vivid patterns of life and struggle, all the raw materials of literature and art. Only then can they proceed to creative work. Otherwise, you will have nothing to work with and you will be nothing but a phoney writer or artist, the kind that Lu Hsun in his will so earnestly cautioned his son never to become.

Although man's social life is the only source of literature and art and is incomparably livelier and richer in content, the people are not satisfied with life alone and demand literature and art as well. Why? Because, while both are beautiful, life as reflected in works of literature and art can and ought to be on a higher plane, more intense, more concentrated, more typical, nearer the ideal, and therefore more universal than actual everyday life. Revolutionary literature and art should create a variety of characters out of real life and help the masses to propel history forward. For example, there is suffering from hunger, cold and oppression on the one hand, and exploitation and oppression of man by man on the other. These facts exist everywhere and people look upon them as commonplace. Writers and artists concentrate such everyday phenomena, typify the contradictions and struggles within them and produce works which awaken the masses, fire them with enthusiasm and impel them to unite and struggle to transform their environment. Without such literature and art, this task could not be fulfilled, or at least not so effectively and speedily.

What is meant by popularizing and by raising standards in works of literature and art? What is the relationship between these two tasks? Popular works are simpler and plainer, and therefore more readily accepted by the broad masses of the people today. Works of a higher quality, being more polished, are more difficult to produce and in general do not circulate so easily and quickly among the masses at present. The problem facing the workers, peasants and soldiers is this: they are now engaged in a bitter and bloody struggle with the enemy but are illiterate and uneducated as a result of long years of rule by the feudal and bourgeois classes, and therefore they are eagerly demanding enlightenment, education and works of literature and art which meet their urgent needs and which are easy to absorb, in order to heighten their enthusiasm in struggle and confidence in victory, strengthen their unity and fight the enemy with one heart and one mind. For them the prime need is not "more flowers on the brocade" but "fuel in snowy weather." In present conditions, therefore, popularization is the more pressing task. It is wrong to belittle or neglect popularization.

Nevertheless, no hard and fast line can be drawn between popularization and the raising of standards. Not only is it possible to popularize some works of higher quality even now, but the cultural level of the broad masses is steadily rising. If popularization remains at the same level for ever, with the same stuff being supplied month after month and year after year, always the same "Little Cowherd" and the same "man, hand, mouth, knife, cow, goat," will not the educators and those being educated be six of one and half a dozen of the other? What would be the sense of such popularization? The people demand popularization and, following that, higher standards; they demand higher standards month by month and year by year. Here popularization means popularizing for the people and raising of standards means raising the level for the people. And such raising is not from mid-air, or behind closed doors, but is actually based on popularization. It is determined by and at the same time guides popularization. In China as a whole the development of the revolution and of revolutionary culture is uneven and their spread is gradual. While in one place there is popularization and then raising of standards on the basis of popularization, in other places popularization has not even begun. Hence good experience in popularization leading to higher standards in one locality can be applied in other localities and serve to guide popularization and the raising of standards there, saving many twists and turns along the road. Internationally, the good experience of foreign countries, and especially Soviet experience, can also serve to guide us. With us, therefore, the raising of standards is based on popularization, while popularization is guided by the raising of standards. Precisely for this reason, so far from being an obstacle to the raising of standards, the work of popularization we are speaking of supplies the basis for the work of raising standards which we are now doing on a limited scale, and prepares the necessary conditions for us to raise standards in the future on a much broader scale.

Besides such raising of standards as meets the needs of the masses directly, there is the kind which meets their needs indirectly, that is, the kind which is needed by the cadres. The cadres are the advanced elements of the masses and generally have received more education; literature and art of a higher level are entirely necessary for them. To ignore this would be a mistake. Whatever is done for the cadres is also entirely for the masses, because it is only through the cadres that we can educate and guide the masses. If we go against this aim, if what we give the cadres cannot help them educate and guide the masses, our work of raising standards will be like shooting at random and will depart from the fundamental principle of serving the masses of the people.

To sum up: through the creative labor of revolutionary writers and artists, the raw materials found in the life of the people are shaped into the ideological form of literature and art serving the masses of the people. Included here are the more advanced literature and art as developed on the basis of elementary literature and art and as required by those sections of the masses whose level has been raised, or, more immediately, by the cadres among the masses. Also included here are elementary literature and art which, conversely, are guided by more advanced literature and art and are needed primarily by the overwhelming majority of the masses at present. Whether more advanced or elementary, all our literature and art are for the masses of the people, and in the first place for the workers, peasants and soldiers; they are created for the workers, peasants and soldiers and are for their use.

Literary and art criticism is one of the principal methods of struggle in the world of literature and art. It should be developed and, as comrades have rightly pointed out, our past work in this respect has been quite inadequate. Literary and art criticism is a complex question which requires a great deal of special study. Here I shall concentrate only on the basic problem of criteria in criticism. I shall also comment briefly on a few specific problems raised by some comrades and on certain incorrect views.

In literary and art criticism there are two criteria, the political and the artistic. According to the political criterion, everything is good that is helpful to unity and resistance to Japan, that encourages the masses to be of one heart and one mind, that opposes retrogression and promotes progress; on the other hand, everything is bad that is detrimental to unity and resistance to Japan, foments dissension and discord among the masses and opposes progress and drags people back. How can we tell the good from the bad—by the motive (the subjective intention) or by the effect (social practice)? Idealists stress motive and ignore effect, while mechanical materialists stress effect and ignore motive. In contradistinction to both, we dialectical materialists insist on the unity of motive and effect. The motive of serving the masses is inseparably linked with the effect of winning their approval; the two must be united. The motive of serving the individual or a small clique is not good, nor is it good to have the motive of serving masses without the effect of winning their approval and benefiting them. In examining the subjective intention of a writer or artist, that is, whether his motive is correct and good, we do not judge by his declarations but by the effect of his actions (mainly his works) on the masses in society. The criterion for judging subjective intention or motive is social practice and its effect. We want no sectarianism in our literary and art criticism and, subject to the general principle of unity for resistance to Japan, we should tolerate literary and art works with a variety of political attitudes. But at the same time, in our criticism we must adhere firmly to principle and severely criticize and repudiate all works of literature and art expressing views in opposition to the nation, to science, to the masses and to the Communist Party, because these so-called works of literature and art proceed from the motive and produce the effect of undermining unity for resistance to Japan. According to the artistic criterion, all works of a higher artistic quality are good or comparatively good, while those of a lower artistic quality are bad or comparatively bad. Here, too, of course, social effect must be taken into account. There is hardly a writer or artist who does not consider his own work beautiful, and our criticism ought to permit the free competition of all varieties of works of art; but it is also entirely necessary to subject these works to correct criticism according to the criteria of the science of aesthetics, so that art of a lower level can be gradually raised to a higher and art which does not meet the demands of the struggle of the broad masses can be transformed into art that does.

There is the political criterion and there is the artistic criterion; what is the relationship between the two? Politics cannot be equated with art, nor can a general world outlook be equated with a method of artistic creation and criticism. We deny not only that there is an abstract and absolutely unchangeable political criterion, but also that there is an abstract and absolutely unchangeable artistic criterion; each class in every class society has its own political and artistic criteria. But all classes in all class societies invariably put the political criterion first and the artistic criterion second. The bourgeoisie always shuts out proletarian literature and art, however great their artistic merit. The proletariat must similarly distinguish among the literary and art works of past ages and determine its attitude towards them only after examining their attitude to the people and whether or not they had any progressive significance histori- cally. Some works which politically are downright reactionary may have a certain artistic quality. The more reactionary their content and the higher their artistic quality, the more poisonous they are to the people, and the more necessary it is to reject them. A common characteristic of the literature and art of all exploiting classes in their period of decline is the contradiction between their reactionary political content and their artistic form. What we demand is the unity of politics and art, the unity of content and form, the unity of revolutionary political content and the highest possible perfection of artistic form. Works of art which lack artistic quality have no force, however progressive they are politically. Therefore, we oppose both the tendency to produce works of art with a wrong political viewpoint and the tendency towards the "poster and slogan style" which is correct in political viewpoint but lacking in artistic power. On questions of literature and art we must carry on a struggle on two fronts.

Both these tendencies can be found in the thinking of many comrades. A good number of comrades tend to neglect artistic technique; it is therefore necessary to give attention to the raising of artistic standards. But as I see it, the political side is more of a problem at present. Some comrades lack elementary political knowledge and consequently have all sorts of muddled ideas. Let me cite a few examples from Yenan.

"The theory of human nature." Is there such a thing as human nature? Of course there is. But there is only human nature in the concrete, no human nature in the abstract. In class society there is only human nature of a class character; there is no human nature above classes. We uphold the human nature of the proletariat and of the masses of the people, while the landlord and bourgeois classes uphold the human nature of their own classes, only they do not say so but make it out to be the only human nature in existence. The human nature boosted by certain petty-bourgeois intellectuals is also divorced from or opposed to the masses; what they call human nature is in essence nothing but bourgeois individualism, and so, in their eyes, proletarian human nature is contrary to human nature. "The theory of human nature" which some people in Yenan advocate as the basis of their so-called theory of literature and art puts the matter in just this way and is wholly wrong.

"The fundamental point of departure for literature and art is love, love of humanity." Now love may serve as a point of departure, but there is a more basic one. Love as an idea is a product of objective practice. Fundamentally, we do not start from ideas but from objective practice. Our writers and artists who come from the ranks of the intellectuals love the proletariat because society has made them feel that they and the proletariat share a common fate. We hate Japanese imperialism because Japanese imperialism oppresses us. There is absolutely no such thing in the world as love or hatred without reason or cause. As for the so-called love of humanity, there has been no such all-inclusive love since humanity was divided into classes. All the ruling classes of the past were fond of advocating it, and so were many so-called sages and wise men, but nobody has ever really practiced it, because it is impossible in class society. There will be genuine love of humanity—after classes are eliminated all over the world. Classes have split society into many antagonistic groupings; there will be love of all humanity when classes are eliminated, but not now. We cannot love enemies, we cannot love social evils, our aim is to destroy them. This is common sense; can it be that some of our writers and artists still do not understand this?

"Literary and artistic works have always laid equal stress on the bright and the dark, half and half." This statement contains many muddled ideas. It is not true that literature and art have always done this. Many petty-bourgeois writers have never discovered the bright side. Their works only expose the dark and are known as the "literature of exposure." Some of their works simply specialize in preaching pessimism and world-weariness. On the other hand, Soviet literature in the period of socialist construction portrays mainly the bright. It, too, describes shortcomings in work and portrays negative characters, but this only serves as a contrast to bring out the brightness of the whole picture and is not on a so-called half-and-half basis. The writers and artists of the bourgeoisie in its period of reaction depict the revolutionary masses as mobs and themselves as saints, thus reversing the bright and the dark. Only truly revolutionary writers and artists can correctly solve the problem of whether to extol or to expose. All the dark forces harming the masses of the people must be exposed and all the revolutionary struggles of the masses of the people must be extolled; this is the fundamental task of revolutionary writers and artists.

"The task of literature and art has always been to expose." This assertion, like the previous one, arises from ignorance of the science of history. Literature and art, as we have shown, have never been devoted solely to exposure. For revolutionary writers and artists the targets for exposure can never be the masses, but only the aggressors, exploiters and oppressors and the evil influence they have on the people. The masses too have shortcomings, which should be overcome by criticism and self-criticism within the people's own ranks, and such criticism and self-criticism is also one of the most important tasks of literature and art. But this should not be regarded as any sort of "exposure of the people." As for the people, the question is basically one of education and of raising their level. Only counter-revolutionary writers and artists describe the people as "born fools" and the revolutionary masses as "tyrannical mobs."

11. Mao Tse-tung

On the Correct Handling of Contradictions Among the People

"On the Correct Handling of Contradictions Among the People," by MAO TSE-TUNG, dates from 1957. The complete speech appears in *On Literature and Art* (Peking: Foreign Languages Press, 1967). A biographical note may be found on page 108.

"LET a hundred flowers blossom, let a hundred schools of thought contend" and "long-term coexistence and mutual supervision"—how did these slogans come to be put forward? They were put forward in the light of China's specific conditions, on the basis of the recognition that various kinds of contradictions still exist in socialist society, and in response to the country's urgent need to speed up its economic and cultural development. Letting a hundred flowers blossom and a hundred schools of thought contend is the policy for promoting the progress of the arts and the sciences and a flourishing socialist culture in our land. Different forms and styles in art should develop freely and different schools in science should contend freely. We think that it is harmful to the growth of art and science if administrative measures are used to impose one particular style of art or school of thought and to ban another. Questions of right and wrong in the arts and sciences should be settled through free discussion in artistic and scientific circles and through practical work in these fields. They should not be settled in summary fashion. A period of trial is often needed to determine whether something is right or wrong. Throughout history, new and correct things have often failed at the outset to win recognition from the majority of people and have had to develop by twists and turns in struggle. Often correct and good things have first been regarded not as fragrant flowers but as poisonous weeds. Copernicus' theory of the solar system and Darwin's theory of evolution were once dismissed as erroneous and had to win through over bitter opposition. Chinese history offers many similar examples. In a socialist society, conditions for the growth of the new are radically different from and far superior to those in the old society. Nevertheless, it still often happens that new, rising forces are held back and rational proposals constricted. Moreover, the growth of new things may be hindered in the absence of deliberate suppression simply through lack of discernment. It is therefore necessary to be careful about questions of right and wrong in the arts and sciences, to encourage free discussion and avoid hasty conclusions. We believe that such an attitude can help to ensure a relatively smooth development of the arts and sciences.

Marxism, too, has developed through struggle. At the beginning, Marxism was subjected to all kinds of attack and regarded as a poisonous weed. It is still being attacked and is still regarded as a poisonous weed in many parts of the world. In the socialist countries, it enjoys a different position. But non-Marxist and, moreover, anti-Marxist ideologies exist even in these countries. In China, although in the main socialist transformation has been completed with respect to the system of ownership, and although the large-scale and turbulent class struggles of the masses characteristic of the previous revolutionary periods have in the main come to an end, there are still remnants of the overthrown landlord and comprador classes, there is still a bourgeoisie, and the remolding of the petty bourgeoisie has only just started. The class struggle is by no means over. The class struggle between the proletariat and the bourgeoisie, the class struggle between the different political forces, and the class struggle in the ideological field between the proletariat and the bourgeoisie will continue to be long and tortuous and at times will even become very acute. The proletariat seeks to transform the world according to its own world outlook, and so does the bourgeoisie. In this respect, the question of which will win out, socialism or capitalism, is still not really settled. Marxists are still a minority among the entire population as well as among the intellectuals. Therefore, Marxism must still develop through struggle. Marxism can develop only through struggle, and not only is this true of the past and the present, it is necessarily true of the future as well. What is correct invariably develops in the course of struggle with what is wrong. The true, the good and the beautiful always exist by contrast with the false, the evil and the ugly, and grow in struggle with the latter. As soon as a wrong thing is rejected and a particular truth accepted by mankind, new truths begin their struggle with new errors.

Such struggles will never end. This is the law of development of truth and, naturally, of Marxism as well.

It will take a fairly long period of time to decide the issue in the ideological struggle between socialism and capitalism in our country. The reason is that the influence of the bourgeoisie and of the intellectuals who come from the old society will remain in our country for a long time to come, and so will their class ideology. If this is not sufficiently understood, or is not understood at all, the gravest mistakes will be made and the necessity of waging the struggle in the ideological field will be ignored. Ideological struggle is not like other forms of struggle. The only method to be used in this struggle is that of painstaking reasoning and not crude coercion. Today, socialism is in an advantageous position in the ideological struggle. The main power of the state is in the hands of the working people led by the proletariat. The Communist Party is strong and its prestige stands high. Although there are defects and mistakes in our work, every fair-minded person can see that we are loyal to the people, that we are both determined and able to build up our motherland together with them, and that we have already achieved great successes and will achieve still greater ones. The vast majority of the bourgeoisie and intellectuals who come from the old society are patriotic and are willing to serve their flourishing socialist motherland; they know they will be helpless and have no bright future to look forward to if they turn away from the socialist cause and from the working people led by the Communist Party.

People may ask, since Marxism is accepted as the guiding ideology by the majority of the people in our country, can it be criticized? Certainly it can. Marxism is scientific truth and fears no criticism. If it did, and if it could be overthrown by criticism, it would be worthless. In fact, aren't the idealists criticizing Marxism every day and in every way? Aren't those who harbor bourgeois and petty-bourgeois ideas and do not wish to change—aren't they also criticizing Marxism in every way? Marxists should not be afraid of criticism from any quarter. Quite the contrary, they need to temper and develop themselves and win new positions in the teeth of criticism and in the storm and stress of struggle. Fighting against wrong ideas is like being vaccinated—a man develops greater immunity from disease as a result of vaccination. Plants raised in hothouses are unlikely to be sturdy. Carrying out the policy of letting a hundred flowers blossom and a hundred schools of thought contend will not weaken but strengthen the leading position of Marxism in the ideological field.

What should our policy be towards non-Marxist ideas? As far as unmistakable counter-revolutionaries and saboteurs of the socialist cause are concerned, the matter is easy: we simply deprive them of their freedom of speech. But incorrect ideas among the people are quite a different matter. Will it do to ban such ideas and deny them any opportunity for expression? Certainly not. It is not only futile but very harmful to use summary methods in dealing with ideological questions among the people, with questions concerned with man's mental world. You may ban the expression of wrong ideas, but the ideas will still be there. On the other hand, if correct ideas are pampered in hot-houses without being exposed to the elements or immunized from disease, they will not win out against erroneous ones. Therefore, it is only by employing the method of discussion, criticism and reasoning that we can really foster correct ideas and overcome wrong ones, and that we can really settle issues.

Inevitably, the bourgeoisie and petty bourgeoisie will give expression to their own ideologies. Inevitably, they will stubbornly express themselves on political and ideological questions by every possible means. You cannot expect them to do otherwise. We should not use the method of suppression and prevent them from expressing themselves, but should allow them to do so and at the same time argue with them and direct appropriate criticism at them. We must undoubtedly criticize wrong ideas of every description. It certainly would not be right to refrain from criticism, look on while wrong ideas spread unchecked and allow them to monopolize the field. Mistakes must be criticized and poisonous weeds fought wherever they crop up. However, such criticism should not be dogmatic, and the metaphysical method should not be used, but efforts should be made to apply the dialectical method. What is needed is scientific analysis and convincing argument. Dogmatic criticism settles nothing. We are against poisonous weeds of any kind, but we must carefully distinguish between what is really a poisonous weed and what is really a fragrant flower. Together with the masses of the people, we must learn to differentiate carefully between the two and to use correct methods to fight the poisonous weeds.

At the same time as we criticize dogmatism, we must direct our attention to criticizing revisionism. Revisionism, or Right opportunism, is a bourgeois trend of thought that is even more dangerous than dogmatism. The revisionists, the Right opportunists, pay lip-service to Marxism; they too attack "dogmatism." But what they are really attacking is the quintessence of Marxism. They oppose or distort materialism and dialectics, oppose or try to weaken the people's democratic dictatorship and the leading role of the Communist Party, and oppose or try to weaken socialist transformation and socialist construction. After the basic victory of the socialist revolution in our country, there are still a number of people who vainly hope to restore the capitalist system and fight the working class on every front, including the ideological one. And their right-hand men in this struggle are the revisionists.

At first glance, the two slogans—let a hundred flowers blossom and let a hundred schools of thought contend—have no class character; the proletariat can turn them to account, and so can the bourgeoisie or other people. But different classes, strata and social groups each have their own views on what are fragrant flowers and what are poisonous weeds. What then, from the point of view of the broad masses of the people, should be the criteria today for distinguishing fragrant flowers from poisonous weeds? In the political life of our people, how should right be distinguished from wrong in one's words and actions? On the basis of the principles of our Constitution, the will of the overwhelming majority of our people and the common political positions which have been proclaimed on various occasions by our political parties and groups, we consider that, broadly speaking, the criteria should be as follows:

(1) Words and actions should help to unite, and not divide, the people of our various nationalities.

(2) They should be beneficial, and not harmful, to socialist transformation and socialist construction.

(3) They should help to consolidate, and not undermine or weaken, the people's democratic dictatorship.

(4) They should help to consolidate, and not undermine or weaken, democratic centralism.

(5) They should help to strengthen, and not discard or weaken, the leadership of the Communist Party.

(6) They should be beneficial, and not harmful, to international socialist unity and the unity of the peace-loving people of the world.

Of these six criteria, the most important are the socialist path and leadership of the Party. These criteria are put forward not to hinder but to foster the free discussion of questions among the people. Those who disapprove of these criteria can still put forward their own views and argue their case. However, since the majority of the people have clear-cut criteria to go by, criticism and self-criticism can be conducted along proper lines, and the criteria can be applied to people's words and actions to determine whether they are right or wrong, whether they are fragrant flowers or poisonous weeds. These are political criteria. Naturally, in judging the validity of scientific theories or assessing the aesthetic value of works of art, additional pertinent criteria are needed. But these six political criteria are needed. But these six political criteria are applicable to all activities in the arts and the sciences. In a socialist country like ours, can there possibly be any useful scientific or artistic activity which runs counter to these political criteria?

The views set out above are based on China's specific historical conditions. Conditions vary in different socialist countries and with different Communist Parties. Therefore, we do not maintain the other countries and Parties should or must follow the Chinese way.

II

The Elements

A. Theoretical Concepts

12. G. A. Nedozchiwin

What Is Aesthetics?

G. A. NEDOZCHIWIN, the author of "What Is Aesthetics?", is a member of the Academy of Sciences of the USSR.

DURING the historical development of society, a variety of forms of social consciousness shaped themselves various spheres of man's spiritual life and spiritual activity. Included among these, from the earliest stages of human history, are aesthetic feelings, experiences, and perceptions. A specific form of social consciousness developed, as a function of this, in which the aesthetic relations of man to reality established, shaped, and developed themselves. This form is art.

The aesthetic elements mentioned, however, are not only confined to art, although it is there that they find their fullest and most complete expression. Man has aesthetic relations also with reality, with nature and society. Aesthetic experiences appear not only in confrontation with works of art, but also in contacts with a very large class of objects, phenomena, and events of nature and of the social life. It is the task of aesthetics to investigate the regularity of these aesthetic relations between man and the real world. The science of aesthetics must, moreover, investigate the relations which prevail in society between all of the appearances of aesthetic phenomena and such specific domains as that of art. Although art is apparently closely tied to other forms of social activity—to the process of material production, to politics, philosophy, science, ethics, etc.—and sometimes converges on them, it nonetheless retains its own specificity and principles.

All of this belongs to the sphere or, as is said, the "object" of that special discipline named aesthetics.

Aesthetics is a scientific discipline which investigates the general principles of development of man's aesthetic relations to reality, and especially of art as a specific form of social consicousness. In other words: aesthetics examines in general the aesthetic relations of man to reality and in particular their highest form, art.

To which kind of science does aesthetics belong, and what is the connection between it and others of the related and proximate sciences?

Although, as we shall see, aesthetic feelings and experiences often arise by way of quite various objects and of natural phenomena and are qualified by the natural properties of these objects and phenomena, one must not confuse aesthetics with the natural sciences. Aesthetic activity and aesthetic relations are peculiar to man. They emerged in the process of the historical development of society. Thus aesthetics is a social science. It belongs to that group of sciences which Friedrich Engels, in *Anti-Duhring*, describes as historical sciences and which are linked to each other insofar as they "investigate man's living conditions, his social relations, the forms of law and the state, with their superstructure of philosophy, religion, art, etc. in their historical progression and in their present state."

And there surely *is* a link between aesthetics and the other social sciences, above all, philosophy. Aesthetics is a philosophical discipline. It arose as a science within the bounds of philosophy. There is also even a link between the history of aesthetics and the history of philosophy. Scientific aesthetics is tied to Marxist-Leninist philosophy; it rests on its principles and is guided by its methods, especially in two respects.

The first of these is in respect to epistemology: the basis of aesthetics is the theory of knowledge of dialectical materialism. Demonstrably, the principal question of philosophy is the question of the relation between thinking and what is. For the solution of the problem of the aesthetic relation to reality, Marxist aesthetics allows itself to be guided by the central philosophical principles of Marxism-Leninism concerning the primary character of existence and the secondary character of consciousness, and concerning the dialectical interaction between the objective reality and thought in its organic connection with Praxis. In other words: Marxist-Leninist aesthetics, which reveals the essence of aesthetic consciousness, presupposes the Leninist theory of antitheses.

The second respect is that the materialist conception of society and its history is the foundation of aesthetics. One cannot correctly solve the problems of the inception and development of aesthetic consciousness in general or of art in particular, or ascertain the underlying principles of the historical development of art without calling on the materialist theory of historical development, or historical materialism.

Put differently, this means that only as it exists in an organic relation with the Marxist-Leninist philosophy is the fruitful development of aesthetics possible.

On the other hand, one should not conceive of aesthetics as a science which merely illustrates the guidelines set down by philosophy in general. Obviously the laws which in general direct social consciousness are active in full measure in the sphere of aesthetic consciousness. But aesthetic consciousness has its own distinctiveness, its own specific character; and it is precisely this that aesthetics must discover and investigate. The general laws operate on specific ones within that sphere. Accordingly it is false to reduce the interpretation of aesthetics to general philosophical guidelines or laws and to illustrate them only by examples from within the purview of aesthetics; in such a case the richness and the whole complexity of the materials to be analyzed—especially in art—must be lost.

Like every other science, aesthetics also has its history. The history of aesthetic doctrine and thought is also an organic part of the science of aesthetics. Only by studying the development of aesthetic ideas from their points of origin to our own time can one follow exactly the way in which, in the battle among various philosophical impulses and currents, in the battle between materialism and idealism, scientific conceptions of the development of aesthetic ideas and intuitions arose, and how the historical groundwork for the development of Marxist-Leninist aesthetics was laid. Every aesthetic theory is to a certain degree a generalization both on the development of art and on the aesthetic activity of an historical epoch.

In every theory, the interests and needs of one or another class, its taste for art and its artistic conceptions, find expression.

The working class, as the most progressive class in modern society, and for the first time in history, created a proletarian culture in the battle against the bourgeoisie and against the culture of the exploiting class; the highest expression of this is Marxism-Leninism.

The artistic creativity of the working class and of the working masses found expression in the creations of writers, poets, and painters who emerged from the working people and from the ranks of the progressive creators of culture who placed themselves on the side of the working class and of the people.

The emergence of Marxism which is a scientific expression of the interests of the working class and a unified world view unequivocally opposed to all reaction, to every defense of the bourgeois yoke, was a revolutionary turning point for the social sciences as a whole and thus also for aesthetics. The dominance of idealist aesthetics came to an end. Now there opposes it an aesthetic which rests on the sturdy basis of the Marxist-Leninist world view, and which gives expression to the interests, needs, and artistic taste of the working class and of the masses. For the first time, an aesthetics arose that was free of the limitations from which earlier theories—even the progressive ones—suffered.

Marxist-Leninist aesthetics is a new, higher step in the historical development of aesthetic thought. It arose and evolved by critical appropriation and creative reworking of everything accomplished by aesthetics before it; it is a scientific generalization based on the artistic development of mankind and the rich experiences found in the development of socialist art.

Marxist-Leninist aesthetics, which is a scientific expression of the interests, needs, and aesthetic ideals of the masses of people, makes for the development of socialist and all progressive art. It enriches our art, our theory and criticism of art, by progressive social and aesthetic ideas, and gives them perspectives for further progressive development.

Soviet aesthetics is a partisan science. It generalizes on the praxis of progressive artists and formulates the aspirations of the people with respect to artistic creation; it fights to interpose the politics of the Communist Party in the domain of art, against the reactionary bourgeois ideology, against Formalism and Naturalism and in behalf of a continued flowering of Socialist Realism. In this consists the foundation of the organic link between Marxist-Leninist aesthetics and politics.

This conception of the object and aims of the science of aesthetics stands in opposition to modern, reactionary bourgeois conceptions. Such proponents of modern neo-Thomist aesthetics as Jacques Maritain have, for example, reworked—or more correctly, belabored—the Aristotelian theory of the imitation of reality in art in the spirit of medieval scholasticism and with an obvious regard for perverted taste and for the anti-naturalistic efforts of decadent art. For them, the object of aesthetics is the human emotions which lead to a union with the Beyond. They proclaim the absolute freedom of artists from the objective laws of life; they cultivate arbitrariness, subjectivism and extreme formalism, and maintain that this freedom leads to the discovery of invisible spiritual rays of a spirit active but invisible in things.

The Catholic Existentialist Gabriel Marcel understands by aesthetics the attempt to penetrate, with the help of irrational methods, the "secret" of life. A love for art, so Marcel assures us, means that one appropriates it without thought.

For the Pragmatists (John Dewey and others), the task of aesthetics consists of the examination of principles in terms of which the Beautiful is constructed, from the standpoint of a certain "situation." The consequence of such a conception of aesthetics is that the Beautiful loses its objective significance and that subjectivity in art is strengthened. The essence of idealist theories of this type consists of the effort to "dissolve" the objective world in human representations and to justify subjectivism and formalism.

What is the relation between aesthetics and the science of art? Aesthetics investigates the general principles of the aesthetic relations between man and reality and of the development of art; the question accordingly would more correctly read: What are the connections between aesthetics as a science and the various disciplines that are the "sciences" of art?

The science of art divides itself into individual scientific disciplines. The voluminous material accumulated by them demands more or less clear specialization on the part of their investigators. This specialization corresponds principally to the various genres of art (each of which possesses its own peculiarities) which warrant special investigation.

To it belong the theory of literature, the theory of drama, the theory of art in the narrower sense of the word (one frequently understands by this term the plastic arts, that is, painting and sculpture, includi..g architecture and any related art), the theory of the film, the theory of music, etc. Each of these sciences investigates the concrete history of its respective genre of art and at the same time examines the theoretical questions especially pertinent to it.

If art is the highest and specific form of the aesthetic activity of human society, still aesthetics cannot exist or develop fruitfully without falling back on the material gathered and investigated in the study of the development of art's genres as well as of art history and of the artist's practical activity.

Without this connection, aesthetics runs the danger of losing itself in abstract theses and logical constructions.

On the other hand, the historical investigation of art cannot proceed blindly. In his analysis of the concrete material, the investigator of art must rely on certain theoretical principles. In this way, a particular science of art does not only provide material for aesthetics, but itself receives from it the theoretical presuppositions required. In other words, without a theory of art (aesthetics), there is no history of art; without the history of art, there is no theory of art.

Aesthetics is not related only to the history of art. It is also related to the history of culture and history in general, to sciences which study the theoretical problems and the history of other forms of social consciousness—ethics and its history—and to the history of religion and atheism. A relation also exists between aesthetics and psychology, the latter of which studies the principles and forms of man's psyche and its development. Within the context of pedagogy and pedagogical practice, questions of aesthetic education play a decisive role. Aesthetics stands both on concrete material and on the results yielded by other sciences. In turn, it serves other sciences by way of the material provided in its questions and its conclusions as they are necessary or significant for the other sciences.

It is especially important to emphasize the connection between aesthetics and ethics. Among the conditions required for the comprehensive preparation for the transition to communism, the task of cultivating a fully developed human personality and developing a communist consciousness among the masses is a matter of extraordinary importance. Art is one of the most efficacious forms which can help to accomplish this task. With respect to the development and communist education of man, questions of aesthetics and ethics (moral theory) are especially closely intertwined. One must remember that aesthetics not only makes the praxis of communist education practicable, but is itself also a means of that education, since it formulates the aesthetic ideals of the people and helps the masses to understand the fundamental problems of art.

13. Ernst Fischer

The Origins of Art

ERNST FISCHER (1899–   ) was born in Komotau, Austria. After a period as a student of philosophy at Graz and another period doing unskilled labor in a factory, he joined the staff of the *Arbeiter-Zeitung* in Vienna in 1927 and worked there until 1934. At that time, he joined the Communist Party and became active in its affairs. He was a radio commentator in Moscow during the Second World War, returning to Austria in 1945 to serve as Minister of Education until the end of that year. He later served as a member of parliament and founded and served as chief editor of the newspaper *Neues Österreich*. Since 1959 he has concentrated on his own writing, mainly in the area of literature and philosophy. *The Necessity of Art* from which this selection is taken appeared first in 1959.

ART is almost as old as man. It is a form of work, and work is an activity peculiar to mankind. Marx defined work in these terms:

The labor process is . . . purposive activity . . . for the fitting of natural substances to human wants; it is the general condition requisite for effecting an exchange of matter between man and nature; it is the condition perennially imposed by nature upon human life, and is therefore independent of the forms of social life—or, rather, it is common to all social forms.

Man takes possession of the natural by transforming it. Work is transformation of the natural. Man also dreams of working magic upon nature, of being able to change objects and give them new form by magic means. This is the equivalent in the imagination of what work means in reality. Man is, from the outset, a magician.

Tools

Man became man through tools. He made, or produced, himself by making or producing tools. The question of which came first—man or tool—is therefore purely academic. There is no tool without man and no man without tool; they came into being simultaneously and are indissolubly linked to one another. A relatively highly developed living organism became man by working with natural objects. By being put to such use, the objects became tools. Here is another definition of Marx's:

The instrument of labor is a thing, or a complex of things, which the worker interposes between himself and the subject-matter of his labor, and one which serves as the conductor of his activity. He makes use of the mechanical, physical, and chemical properties of things as means of exerting power over other things, and in order to make these other things subservient to his aims. Leaving out of consideration the gathering of ready-made means of subsistence, such as fruits, for which purpose man's own bodily organs suffice him as the instrument of labor, the object of which the worker takes direct control is not the subject-matter of labor but the instrument of labor. Thus nature becomes an instrument of his activities, an instrument with which he supplements his own bodily organs, adding a cubit and more to his stature, scripture notwithstanding. . . . The use and the fabrication of instruments of labor, though we find their first beginnings among certain other animal species, is specifically characteristic of the human labor process, and for that reason Benjamin Franklin defined man as a 'tool-making animal.'

The pre-human being which developed into man was capable of such development because it had a special organ, the hand, with which it could grasp and hold objects. The hand is the essential organ of culture, the initiator of humanization. This does not mean that it was the hand alone that made man: nature, and particularly organic nature, does not allow of such simple and one-sided sequences of cause and effect. A system of complicated relationships—a new *quality*—always comes out of a set of diverse reciprocal effects. The passing of certain biological organisms into the tree stage, favoring as it did the development of vision at the expense of the sense of smell; the shrinking of the muzzle, facilitating a change in the position of the eyes; the urge of the creature now equipped with a more acute and more precise sense of vision to look in all directions, and the erect body posture conditioned by this; the release of the front limbs and the enlargement of the brain due to erect body posture; changes in food and various other circumstances acted together to create the conditions necessary for man to become man. But the directly decisive organ was the hand. Thomas Aquinas was already aware of the unique significance of the hand, that *organum organorum*, and expressed it in his definition of man: '*Habet homo rationem et manum!*' And it is true that the hand released human reason and produced human consciousness.

Gordon Childe points out in *The Story of Tools:*

Men can make tools because their forefeet have turned into hands, because seeing the same object with both eyes they can judge distances very accurately and because a very delicate nervous system and complicated brain enables them to control the movements of hand and arm in precise agreement with and adjustment to what they see with both eyes. But men do not know by any inborn instinct how to make tools nor how to use them; that they must learn by experiment—by trial and error.

A system of completely new relationships between one species and the entire rest of the world came about through the use of tools. In the working process, the natural relationship of cause and effect was, as it were, reversed; the anticipated, foreseen effect became, as 'purpose,' the legislator of the working process. That relationship between events which, as the problem of 'finality' or 'final cause,' has driven many a philosopher to distraction, was developed as a specially human characteristic. But what is this problem? Let me quote once more one of Marx's clear definitions:

We have to consider labor in a form peculiar to the human species. A spider carries on operations resembling those of a weaver; and many a human architect is put to shame by the skill with which a bee constructs her cell. But what from the very first distinguishes the most incompetent architect from the best of bees, is that the architect has built a cell in his head before he constructs it in wax. The labor process ends in the creation of something which, when the process began, already existed in the worker's imagination, already existed in an ideal form. What happens is not merely that the worker brings about a change of form in natural objects; at the same time, in the nature that exists apart from himself, he realizes his own purposes, the purpose which gives the law to his activities, the purpose to which he has to subordinate his own will.

This is a definition of the nature of work by the time it has reached the wholly developed, wholly human stage. But a long distance had to be travelled before this final form of work, and therefore the final humanization of the pre-human being, was attained. Action determined by purpose —and from this the birth of the mind, the birth of consciousness as the prime creation of man—was the outcome of a long and laborious process. Conscious existence means conscious action. The original existence of man was that of a mammal. Man *is* a mammal, but he begins to *do* something different from all other mammals. The animal, too, acts from 'experience,' that is to say from a system of conditioned reflexes; that is what we call the 'instinct' of an animal. The organism which developed into man acquired a new kind of experience leading to a unique turning-point, insignificant though it may have appeared at the outset: the experience that nature can be used as a means to achieve a man's purpose. Every biological organism is in a state of metabolism with the surrounding world—it continually gives and takes something to and from that world. But this taking is always done directly, without an intermediary. Only human work is *meditated metabolism*. The means has preceded the purpose; the purpose is revealed by the use of the means.

Biological organs are not replaceable. True, they were formed as a result of adaptation to the conditions of the outside world; but an animal must manage with the organs it has got and make the best of them. Yet the instrument of labor, which is outside the organism, *is* replaceable, and a primitive one can be discarded in favor of a more efficient one. With a natural organ, the question of efficiency does not arise: it is as it is, the animal must live as its organs will allow and adapt itself to the world in the manner in which its organs are adapted to it. But a being which uses a non-organic object as an instrument need not adapt its requirements to that instrument—on the contrary, it can adapt the instrument to the requirements. The question of efficiency cannot exist until this possibility arises.

Man's discovery that some instruments are more or less useful than others, and that one instrument can be replaced by another, led inevitably to the discovery that an imperfect, available instrument can be made more efficient: i.e., that an instrument need not be taken directly from nature but can be *produced*. The discovery of greater or lesser efficiency in itself requires a special observation of nature. Animals, too, observe nature, and natural causes and effects are reflected or reproduced in animal brains. But, for an animal, nature is a given fact, unchangeable by any effort of will, like its own organism. Only the use of non-organic, replaceable, and changeable means makes it possible to observe nature in a new context, to foresee, anticipate, and bring about events.

There is a fruit to be picked from a tree. The pre-human animal reaches for this fruit, but its arm is too short. It tries everything but cannot reach the fruit; and after repeated, frustrated attempts it is forced to give up and turn its attention elsewhere. But if the animal takes a stick, its arm is extended; and if the stick is too short, it can choose a second and a third one, until at last it has found one that will do the job. What is the novel element here? It is the discovery of varying possibilities and the ability to choose among them, hence the ability to compare one object with another and decide on its greater or lesser efficiency. With the use of tools, nothing is, in principle, any longer impossible. One only needs to find the right tool in order to reach—or accomplish—what was previously out of reach. A new power over nature has been gained, and this power is *potentially unlimited*. In this discovery lies one of the roots of magic and, therefore, of art.

In the brain of the higher mammal, an inherited reciprocal effect has been established between the center which signals hunger—the organism's lack of necessary foodstuffs—and the center which is stimulated by the sight or smell of a piece of food, say a fruit. Stimulation of one of the centers involves the other; the mechanism is delicately attuned: when the animal is hungry, it looks for a piece of food. Through the interposition of the stick—the instrument for fetching the fruit down from the tree —a new contact between the brain centers is established. This new cerebral process is then strengthened by being repeated countless times. At first the process takes place in one direction only: the stimulation of the 'hunger-fruit' complex is extended to include the center which, putting it crudely, reacts to 'stick.' The animal sees the fruit it wants and looks for the stick which is associated with it. This can scarcely yet be called thinking: the element of purpose characteristic of the working process— which is the creator of thought—is still absent. So far it is not yet the purpose of the stick to fetch down the fruit: the stick is only the instrument for doing so. This one-sided process, this inter-dependent working of the brain centers, can, however, be reversed if the mechanism is refined by frequent repetition. In other words, it may then go like this: here is the stick; where is the fruit it can fetch down?

Thus the stick—the instrument—becomes the starting-point. The means now serves the end, which is to fetch down the fruit. The stick is not just a stick; something new has been magically added to it: a *function*, which now becomes its essential content. And so the instrument commands more and more interest; it is examined for its greater or lesser ability to fulfill its purpose; the question arises whether it might not be made more serviceable, more useful, more efficient, whether it cannot be changed so that it may better fulfill its purpose. Spontaneous experimentation—'thinking with the hands,' which precedes all thought as such—now begins gradually to be transmuted into purposeful reflection. This reversal of the cerebral process is the beginning of what we call work, conscious being, conscious doing, anticipation of the result by cerebral activity. All thought is nothing other than a shortened form of experimentation transferred from the hands to the brain, the innumerable preceding experiments having ceased to be 'memory' and having become 'experience.'

A different example may illustrate this idea more conveniently. Gordon Childe writes in *The Story of Tools:*

The oldest surviving or *eolithic* tools are made of stone—those used by Pekin man of quartz deliberately collected and carried to his cave. A tiny fraction only were artificially shaped, better to serve Sinanthropic needs. Even these lack any standardized form and might have served many purposes. One feels indeed that on each occasion when a tool was required, a handy piece of stone was adapted to meet the moment's need. So such might be called *occasional tools.* . . .

Standardized tools emerge. Among the great mass of miscellaneous occasional tools of very varied shapes of lower paleolithic times, two or three forms stand out that occur again and again with very little variation at a vast number of sites in Western Europe, Africa, and Southern Asia; their makers have obviously been trying to copy a recognized standard pattern.

This tells us something of extreme importance. Man, or the pre-human being, had originally discovered—while gathering objects—that, for instance, a sharp-edged stone can take the place of teeth and fingernails for tearing apart, cutting up, or crushing a prey. A stone that happens to be available becomes an *occasional tool* and is thrown away again when it has fulfilled its momentary function. Anthropmorphous apes also sometimes use such occasional tools. Through repeated use, a firm connection is established in the brain between the stone and its usefulness; the creature about to become man begins to collect and preserve such useful stones, although no definite function or concrete purpose is as yet connected with each stone. The stones are all-purpose instruments to be experimented with from case to case and tested for their specific applications. Two things eventually emerge from these repeated and varied experiments, from this 'thinking with the hands': first, the discovery that stones of a particular shape are more useful than others, that it is possible to choose among the accidental offerings of nature, the reference to purpose thus becoming more and more dominant; secondly, the discovery that it is unnecessary to wait for these offerings, because nature can be corrected. Water, climate, the elements can shape a stone so that it becomes 'handy.' When once the almost-man took natural objects 'in hand' and began to use them as instruments, his active hands discovered that he could shape and alter a stone himself, and from this discovery they learned that there is inherent in a piece of flint the *potentiality* of becoming sharp-edged and, hence, a useful tool.

There is nothing in the least mysterious about this potentiality—it is not a 'power' with ˙which the stone is endowed, nor did it, like Pallas Athene, spring from a creative consciousness. On the contrary, creative consciousness developed as a late result of the *manual* discovery that stones could be broken, split, sharpened, given this shape or that. The shape of the hand-axe, for instance, which nature produces from time to time, was useful for a number of activities: and so gradually man began to copy nature. In producing tools like this he was not obeying any 'creative idea' but only imitating; his models were stones he had found and whose usefulness he had experimentally tested. He produced on the basis of his experience of nature. And the thing that was in his mind in this early productive phase was not the end result of an idea; he was not carrying out a plan; what he saw before him was a very real hand-axe, and he tried to make another like it. He was not implementing an idea but imitating an object. Only very gradually did he depart from the natural model. By using the tool and constantly experimenting with it, he slowly began to make it more useful and more efficient. Efficiency is older than purpose; the hand, rather than the brain, has long been a discoverer. (One need only watch a child untying a knot: it does not 'think,' it experiments; only gradually, out of the experience of its hands, comes the comprehension of how the knot is tied and how best to disentangle it.)

The anticipation of a result—the setting of a purpose to a working process—only comes after concentrated manual experience. It is the result of constantly referring back to the natural product and of many more or less successful tests. It is not looking ahead but looking back that produces the idea of purpose. Conscious doing and conscious being developed in work and along with work, and only at a later stage did a clearly recognized purpose emerge to give each tool a specific shape and character. It took man a long time to rise above nature and confront it as a creator.

When he did, the difference was this. His brain no longer reflected things merely literally: because of the experience of work, it could now also reflect natural laws and reckon with *causal* relationships. (It could recognize, for instance, that muscular energy can be transferred to a tool and thence to the working object, or that friction produces heat.) Man took the place of nature. He did not wait to see what nature would offer him: more and more he forced it to give him what he wanted. He made nature more and more his servant. And out of the increasing usefulness of his tools, out of their increasingly specific character, out of their increasingly successful adaptation to the human hand and the laws of nature, out of their increased *humanization,* objects were created which could not be found in nature. More and more the tool lost its resemblance to any natural object. The function of the tool displaced its original nature-likeness, and as a result of growing efficiency its purpose—the intellectual anticipation of what it could do—became more and more important. This transformation of the nature of work could only occur when work had reached a comparatively highly developed stage.

Without work—without his experience of using tools—man could never have developed language as an imitation of nature and as a system of signs to represent activities and objects, i.e., as an *abstraction*. Man created articulate, differentiated words not only because he was a being capable of pain, joy and surprise, but also because he was a *working* being.

Language and gesture are very closely interconnected. Bücher deduced from this that speech evolved from reflex actions of the vocal organs incidental to the muscular efforts involved in the use of tools. As the hands became more finely articulated, so did the vocal organs, until the awakening consciousness seized on these reflex actions and elaborated them into a system of communication. This theory emphasizes the significance of the collective working process, without which systematic language could never have been formed out of the primitive signals, mating cries, and cries of fear that were the raw material of language. The animal's signal notifying some change in the surrounding world developed into a linguistic 'work reflex.' This was the turning-point from passive adaptation to nature to active changing of nature.

Among hundreds of 'occasional tools' of various kinds it is impossible to distinguish each by a specific sign; but if a few standard tools are evolved, then a specific sign—or name, or *noun*—becomes both possible and necessary. When a standard tool is imitated time and time again, something completely new happens. All the imitations, made to resemble each other, contain within them the same prototype; the prototype, in its function, its form, and its usefulness to man, recurs again and again. There are many hand-axes yet there is only one. Man can take any of the imitations instead of the original hand-axe because all of them serve the same purpose, produce the same effect, and are similar or identical in their function. It is always this tool that is meant, and none other; it does not matter which particular sample of the standard hand-axe happens to come to hand. Thus the first abstraction, the first conceptual form, was supplied by the tools themselves: prehistoric man 'abstracted' from many individual hand-axes the quality common to them all—that of being a hand-axe; in so doing, he formed the 'concept' of a hand-axe. He did not know he was doing it. But he was nevertheless creating a concept.

Making Alike

Man made a second tool resemble the first and by so doing produced a new, equally useful and equally valuable tool. Thus 'making alike' grants man a *power over objects*. A stone which was previously useless acquires value because it can be made like a tool and so recruited into man's service. There is something magical in this process of 'making alike.' It brings mastery over nature. Other experiences confirm this strange discovery. If you imitate an animal, make yourself look and sound like that animal, you can attract it and stalk it more closely, and the prey falls more easily into your hands. Here again, resemblance is a weapon of power, of magic. The primeval instinct of the species adds still greater force to the discovery. This instinct makes all animals suspicious of those of their own species that deviate from the normal, the albinos, the freaks of every kind. They are instinctively seen as rebels against the tribe. They have to be killed or driven out of the natural collective. Thus similarity is universally significant, and prehistoric man—who had by now acquired practice in comparing, choosing, and copying tools—began to attach enormous significance to *all* similarity.

Advancing from one similarity to another, he arrived at an ever-increasing wealth of abstractions. He began to give a single name to whole groups of related objects. It is the nature of such abstractions that they often (though not always) express a real connection or relationship. All tools of a particular kind, it will be remembered, came out of the first tool of which they were an imitation or copy. The same is true of many other abstractions: the wolf, the apple, etc. Nature is reflected in newly discovered connections. The brain no longer reflects each tool as something unique; nor does it reflect every seashell in that way. A *sign* has been evolved to cover all tools, all seashells, all objects and living beings of the same kind. This process of concentration and classification in language makes it possible to communicate more and more freely concerning the outside world, which man shares with all other men.

The same is true of processes and, above all, of the social process of work. The emerging human collective repeated the same process many hundreds of times. Gradually it found a sign—a means of expression—for this collective activity. It may be assumed that this sign came out of the working process itself, reflecting some sort of rhythmic regularity. It indicated a specific activity and was so directly connected with it that its sound or sight immediately excited all the brain centers in which the activity was registered. Such signs were of immense importance to early man; they had an organizing function within the working group or collective, because they meant the same thing to all its members.

A collective working process requires a coordinating working rhythm. This working rhythm is supported by a more or less articulate unison chant. Such chants, be they the English 'Heave-o-ho!,' the German '*Horuck*,' or the Russian '*E-uch-nyem*,' are essential to the rhythmic accomplishment of the work. In such refrains, which have a certain magic attaching to them, the individual preserves the collective even if he is working outside it. George Thomson (with whose splendid work *Studies in Ancient Greek Society: The Prehistoric Aegean* I was unfortunately not acquainted until this book was practically finished, so that I can only refer to it in passing) analyzes the ancient work songs as a combination of refrain (collective unison chant) and individual improvisation. He quotes *inter alia* a chant recorded by the Swiss missionary Junod. A Thonga boy breaking stones at an African roadside for his European employers sang:

> *Ba bi shani-sa, ebé!*
> *Ba ku bi blupba, ebé!*
> *Ba nwa makbofi, ebé!*
> *Ba nga bi njiki, ebé!*
> They treat us badly, *ebé!*
> They are hard on us, *ebé!*
> They drink their coffee, *ebé!*
> And give us none, *ebé!*

The first word-signs for working processes—chanted sounds providing a uniform rhythm for the collective—were probably, at the same time, command signals intended to arouse the collective to action (in the same way as a warning cry produces an immediate passive reaction, e.g., the flight of the herd). Thus there was *power* stored up in every linguistic means of expression—power over both man and nature.

It was not only a question of prehistoric man believing that words were a powerful tool—they actually did increase his control over reality. Language not only made it possible to coordinate human activity in an intelligent way and to describe and transmit experience and, therefore, to improve working efficiency: it also made it possible to single out objects by attaching particular words to them, thus snatching them out of the protective anonymity of nature and bringing them under man's control. If I make a notch in a tree growing in a forest, that tree is doomed. I can instruct someone else to go and cut down the tree. I have marked; he will recognize it by the notch. A name given to an object has a similar effect: the object is *marked,* distinguished from other objects, and delivered into the hands of man. There is an unbroken line of development from the making of tools to the marking and taking possession of those tools (by a notch, say, or a series of notches or a primitive ornament) and thence to their naming, whereby they become recognizable and graspable to every member of the collective.

The standard tool was reproduced by imitation, which singled it out by a kind of magic from among other stones, hitherto subject to the power of nature alone. It may be assumed that the first linguistic means of expression, too, were nothing other than imitation. The word was regarded as largely identical with the object. It was the means of grasping, comprehending, mastering the object. We find that nearly all primitive races believed that by naming an object, a person, a demon, they would exercise some power over them (or else incur their magic hostility). This idea is preserved in innumerable folk tales: we need only remember the sly Rumpelstiltskin with his triumphant

> Glad I am that no one knows
> That Rumpelstiltskin I am styled.

A means of expression—a gesture, an image, a sound, or a word—was as much a tool as a hand-axe or a knife. It was only another way of establishing man's power over nature.

Thus a being evolved out of nature through the use of tools and through the collective working process. This being—man—was the first to confront the whole of nature as an active *subject*. But before man became his own subject, nature had become an *object* for him. A *thing* in nature becomes an object only through becoming the object, or the instrument, of work. A subject-object relationship occurs only through work.

The gradual separation of man from nature, whose creature he remains although he faces it more and more as a creator, gave rise to one of the most profound problems of human existence. It is perfectly reasonable to speak of man's 'double nature.' While still belonging to nature, he has created a 'counter-nature' or 'super-nature.' Through his work, he has made a new kind of reality: a reality which is sensory and suprasensory at one and the same time.

Reality is never an accumulation of separate units existing side by side without connection. Every material 'something' is interconnected with every other material 'something'; between objects there exists a vast variety of relationships. These relationships are as real as the material objects, and only in their relationships to each other do objects constitute reality. The richer and more complex these relationships become, the richer and more complex is the nature of reality. Let us take an object produced by work. What is it? In terms of mechanical reality it is nothing other than a 'mass' gravitating towards other 'masses' ('mass' itself also being the term for a relationship). In terms of physico-chemical reality it is a fragment of concrete matter composed in a certain way of certain atoms and molecules and subject to certain rules peculiar to those particles. In terms of human and social reality it is a tool, an object of utilitarian value, and, if it is exchanged, it gains an exchange value. Man's new relationships with nature and with his fellow-men have penetrated this fragment of matter and endowed it with a new content and quality which it previously did not possess. And so man, the working being, is the creator of a new reality, a super-nature, whose most extraordinary product is the mind. The working being elevates itself, by work, into a thinking being; thought—i.e., mind—is the necessary result of man's mediated metabolism with nature.

By his work, man transforms the world like a magician: a piece of wood, a bone, a flint is fashioned to resemble a model and thereby transformed into that very model; material objects are transformed into signs, names, and concepts; man himself is transformed from an animal into a man.

This magic at the very root of human existence, creating a sense of powerlessness and at the same time a consciousness of power, a fear of nature together with the ability to control nature, is the very essence of all art. The first toolmaker, when he gave new form to a stone so that it might serve man, was the first artist. The first name-giver was also a great artist when he singled out an object from the vastness of nature, tamed it by means of a sign, and handed over this creature of language as an instrument of power to other men. The first organizer who synchronized the working process by means of a rhythmic chant and so increased the collective strength of man was a prophet in art. The first hunter who disguised himself as an animal and by means of this identification with his prey increased the yield of the hunt, the first stone-age man who marked a tool or a weapon by a special notch or ornament, the first chieftain who stretched an animal's skin over a lump of rock or the stump of a tree in order to attract animals of the same kind—all these were the forefathers of art.

The Power of Magic

The exciting discovery that natural objects could be turned into tools capable of influencing and altering the outside world was bound to lead to another idea in the mind of early man, always experimenting and slowly awakening to thought: the idea that the impossible, too, could be achieved with magic tools—that nature could be 'bewitched' without the effort of work. Overwhelmed by the immense importance of similarity and imitation, he deduced that, since all similar things were identical, his power over nature—by virtue of 'making alike'—could be limitless. The newly acquired power to grasp and control objects, to prompt social activity and bring about events by means of signs, images, and words, led him to expect the magical power of language to be infinite. Fascinated by the power of the will—which anticipates and brings about things that are not yet there but exist only as an idea in the brain—he was bound to ascribe an immensely far-reaching, boundless power to acts of will. The magic of tool-making led inevitably to the attempt to extend magic to infinity.

In Ruth Benedict's book *Patterns of Culture* there is a good example of the belief that imitation must bring power. A sorcerer on the island of Dobu wants a fatal illness to strike an enemy.

In communicating the spell the sorcerer imitates in anticipation the agony of the final stages of the disease he is inflicting. He writhes upon the ground, he shrieks in convulsion. Only so, after faithful reproduction of its effects, will the charm do its destined work.

And we read further:

The charms themselves are almost as explicit as the action that accompanies them. . . . The following is the incantation for causing gangosa, the horrible disease which eats away the flesh as the hornbill, its animal patron from which the disease is named, eats the tree trunks with its great rending beak:

> Hornbill dweller of Sigasiga
> in the Iowana tree top,
> he cuts, he cuts,
> he rends open,
> from the nose,
> from the temples,
> from the throat,
> from the hip,
> from the root of the tongue,
> from the back of the neck,
> from the navel,
> from the small of the back,
> from the kidneys,
> from the entrails,
> he rends open,
> he rends standing.
> Hornbill dweller of Kokuku,
> in the Iowana tree top,
> he crouches bent up,
> he crouches holding his back,
> he crouches arms twined in front of him,
> he crouches hands over his kidneys,
> he crouches head bent in arms twined about it,
> he crouches double twined.
> Wailing, shrieking,
> it flies hither,
> quickly it flies hither.

Art was a magic tool, and it served man in mastering nature and developing social relationships. It would be wrong, however, to explain the origins of art by this element alone. Every newly formed quality is the result of a set of new relationships, which may sometimes be highly complex. The attraction of shining, gleaming, glittering things (not only for human beings but also for animals) and the irresistible attraction of light may have played their part in the birth of art. Sexual allurement—bright colors, pungent smells, splendid coats and feathers in the animal world, jewels and fine clothes, seductive words and gestures among humans—may have provided a stimulus. The rhythms of organic and inorganic nature—of heartbeat, breathing, sexual intercourse—the rhythmic recurrence of processes or elements of form and the pleasure derived from these, and, last but not least, working rhythms—may have played an important part. Rhythmical movement assists work, coordinates effort, and connects the individual with a social group. Every disturbance of the rhythm is disagreeable because it interferes with the processes of life and work; and so we find rhythm assimilated in the arts as the repetition of a constant, as proportion and symmetry. And, lastly, an essential element of the arts is the fearsome, the awe-inspiring, and that which is supposed to confer power over an enemy. Clearly the decisive function of art was to exert power—power over nature, an enemy, a sexual partner, power over reality, power to strengthen the human collective. Art in the dawn of humanity had little to do with 'beauty' and nothing at all to do with any aesthetic desire: it was a magic tool or weapon of the human collective in its struggle for survival.

It would be very wrong to smile at the superstitions of early man or at his attempts to tame nature by imitation, identification, the power of images and language, witchcraft, collective rhythmic movement, and so on. Of course, because he had only just begun to observe the laws of nature, to discover causality, to construct a conscious world of social signs, words, concepts, and conventions, he arrived at innumerable false conclusions and, led astray by analogy, formed many fundamentally mistaken ideas (most of which are still preserved in one form or another in our language and philosophy). And yet, in creating art, he found for himself a real way of increasing his power and enriching his life. The frenzied tribal dances before a hunt really did increase the tribe's sense of power; war paint and war cries really did make the warrior more resolute and were apt to terrify the enemy. Cave paintings of animals really helped to build up the hunter's sense of security and superiority over his prey. Religious ceremonies with their strict conventions really helped to instill social experience in every member of a tribe and to make every individual part of the collective body. Man, the weak creature confronting dangerous,

incomprehensible, terrifying Nature, was greatly helped in his development by magic.

The original magic gradually became differentiated into religion,
science, and art. The function of mime altered imperceptibly: from imitation intended to bestow magic power it came to replace blood sacrifice
by enacted ceremonies. The song to the hornbill on the island of Dobu,
which I have quoted, is still pure magic; but when certain Australian
aboriginal tribes appear to prepare for an act of blood vengeance while,
in fact, appeasing the dead by means of mime, this is already a transition
to drama and to the work of art. Another example: Djagga Negroes
felling a tree. They call it the sister of the man on whose plot of land it
is growing. They represent the preparation for felling as preparations
for the sister's wedding. On the day before the tree is actually felled they
bring it milk, beer, and honey, saying 'mana mfu' [departing child], my
sister, I give you a husband, he shall marry you, my daughter.' And when
the tree has been felled the owner breaks out in lamentations: 'You
have robbed me of my sister.' Here the transition from magic to art is
clear. The tree is a living organism. By felling it, the members of
the tribe prepare for its rebirth, just as initiation and death are regarded as the individual's rebirth out of the maternal body of the collective. It is a performance delicately balanced between serious ceremonial
and artistic play; the owner's simulated distress carries echoes of an
ancient dread and magical imprecations. Ceremonial rite has been preserved in drama.

The magic identity of man and earth was also at the root of the
widespread custom of sacrificing the king. The status of a king originated,
as Frazer proved, first and foremost in fertility magic. In Nigeria, kings
were at first only the queens' consorts. The queens had to conceive so
that the earth might bear fruit. After the men—who were seen as earthly
representatives of the moon god—had done their duty, they were
strangled by the women. The Hittites sprinkled the blood of the murdered
king over the fields and his flesh was eaten by nymphs—the queen's
followers, wearing masks of bitches, mares, and sows. As matriarchy
developed into patriarchy, the king took over more and more of the
queen's power. Wearing female dress and equipped with artificial breasts,
he represented the queen. An *interrex* was killed instead of him and
finally this *interrex* was replaced by animals. Reality became myth, the
magic ceremony became religious enactment, and finally magic itself
became art.

Art was not an individual but a collective production, although the first
characteristics of individuality began to declare themselves tentatively
in the sorcerer. Primitive society meant a dense, close-knit form of

collectivism. Nothing was more terrible than to be cast out of the collective and to remain alone. Separation of the individual from the group or tribe meant death; the collective meant life and the content of life. Art in all its forms—language, dance, rhythmic chants, magic ceremonies—was the social activity *par excellence,* common to all and raising all men above nature and the animal world. Art has never wholly lost this collective character, even long after the primitive collective had broken down and been replaced by a society of classes and individuals.

Art and the Class Society

Stimulated by the discoveries of Bachofen and Morgan, Marx and Engels described the process of disintegration of collective tribal society, the gradual growth of productive forces, the progressive division of labor, the birth of barter trade, the transition to patriarchal rule, and the beginnings of private property, social classes, and the State. Countless scholars have since analyzed every detail of this process on the basis of abundant evidence. George Thomson's *Aeschylus and Athens* and *Studies in Ancient Greek Culture* are of immense importance in this field. In ancient Greece, increased labor productivity led to a situation in which laborers, the *demiurgoi,* 'those working for the community,' were accepted as part of the community consisting of the chief, the elders, and the land cultivators. The chief was empowered to dispose of any surplus agricultural products. The chiefs received regular tribute. Barter of goods developed imperceptibly out of friendly relations between tribes. Gifts and counter-gifts assumed the character of barter. Chiefs and laborers were the first to discard the bonds of the clan: the former became landowners, the latter organized themselves in guilds. The tribal village was transformed into a city state ruled by the landowners. That was the beginning of class society.

Just as magic corresponded to man's sense of unity with nature, of the identity of all existing things—an identity implicit in the clan—so art became an expression of the beginnings of alienation. The totemistic clan represented a *totality.* The clan totem was the symbol of the immortal clan itself, the ever-living collective from which the individual emerged and to which he returned. The uniform social structure was a 'model' of the surrounding world. The world order corresponded to the social order. Some races call the lowest social unit the *womb.* The social collective is a union of the living and the dead. Father van Wing writes in *Études Bakongo:*

The land belongs, undivided, to the entire tribe, that is to say not only to the living but also—or rather, primarily—to the dead, i.e., the Bakulu. The tribe and the land on which it lives from an indivisible whole, and this whole is ruled by the Bakulu.

G. Strehlow wrote of the Aranda and Loritja tribes in Central Australia:

As soon as a woman knows that she is pregnant, i.e., that a *ratapa* (totem) has entered her, the grandfather of the expected child . . . goes to a *mulga* tree and cuts off a small *tjurunga* (the secret, hidden totem body that unites the individual with his ancestors and with the universe), on which he carves, with an opossum tooth, signs connected with the totem ancestor or his totem. . . . The totem, the totem ancestor and the totem descendant, that is to say the performer (who, in the ceremonies, embodies the totem by his ornaments and his mask) appear in the *tjurunga* songs as a single unit. . . .

The perfect unity of man, animal, plant, stone, and source, of life and death, collective and individual, is a premise of every magic ceremony.

As human beings separated themselves more and more from nature, as the original tribal unity was gradually destroyed by division of labor and property ownership, so the equilibrium between the individual and the outside world became more and more disturbed. Lack of harmony with the outside world leads to hysteria, trances, fits of insanity. The characteristic posture of the maenad or bacchante—the body arched, the head thrown back—is the classic posture of hysteria. In a letter written from prison on 15 February 1932, the great Italian Marxist Antonio Gramsci spoke of the psycho-analytical method, which, he thought, could only be usefully applied to the social elements described in Romantic literature as

the insulted and the injured . . . who are much more numerous than is traditionally believed. That is to say, applied to persons caught up in the iron contradictions of modern life (to speak only of the present, but every age has had a present in contrast to a past), who cannot, without help, come to terms with those contradictions, overcome them and find a new moral peace and freedom, i.e., they cannot strike a balance between the impulses of the will and the aims to be attained. . . .

There are times of crisis in which the contrast between the present and the past assumes extreme forms. The transition from the primitive social collective to the 'iron age' of class society with its small stratum of rulers and its masses of 'insulted and injured' was such a time.

The condition of being 'beside oneself,' i.e., of hysteria, is a forcible re-creation of the collective, of world unity. As social differentiation progressed, so, on the one hand, there occurred periods of collective demoniacal possession and, on the other hand, there were individuals (often actually forming associations or guilds) whose social function it was to be possessed or 'inspired.' It is the task of these possessed individuals, both the blessed and the damned, these prophets, sybils, and singers, to restore a disturbed unity and harmony with the outside world. We read in the *Ion* of Plato:

> For the epic poets, all the good ones, have their excellence, not from art, but are inspired, possessed, and thus they utter all these admirable poems. So it is also with the good lyric poets; as the worshipping Corybantes are not in their senses when they dance, so the lyric poets are not in their senses when they make these lovely lyric poems. No, when once they launch into harmony and rhythm, they are seized with the Bacchic transport, and are possessed—as the Bacchantes, when possessed, draw milk and honey from the rivers, but not when in their senses.

God speaks in the possessed, said Plato. God is a name for the collective. The content of demoniacal possession was the collective reproduced in a violent manner within the individual, a sort of mass essence. Thus, in a differentiated society, art developed out of magic precisely as a result of differentiation and of the increasing alienation to which it led.

In a class society the classes try to recruit art—that powerful voice of the collective—into serving their particular purposes. The verbal eruptions of Pythia in her state of ecstasy were very skillfully, very consciously 'edited' by aristocratic priests. Out of the chorus of the collective developed the chorus leader; the sacred hymn became a hymn in praise of the rulers; the clan totem was sub-divided into the aristocracy's gods. Finally the chorus leader with his gift of improvisation and invention developed into a bard, singing without a chorus at the king's court and, later, in the market place. On the one hand we find the Apollonian glorification of power and the *status quo*—of kings, princes, and aristocratic families and the social order established by them and reflected in their ideology as a supposedly universal order. On the other hand there was the Dionysian revolt from below, the voice of the ancient, broken collective which took refuge in secret associations and secret cults, protesting against the violation and fragmentation of society, against the *hubris* of private property and the wickedness of class rule, prophesying the return of the old order and the old gods, a coming golden age of commonwealth and justice. Contradictory elements were often combined within a single artist, particularly in those periods when the old collectivism was not yet too remote and still continued to exist in the consciousness of the people. Even the Apollonian artist, herald of the young ruling class, was not entirely free from this Dionysian element of protest or nostalgia for the old collective society.

The sorcerer in the primitive tribal society was in the most profound sense a representative, a servant of the collective, and his magic power entailed a risk of being put to death if he repeatedly failed to fulfill the collective's expectations. In the young class society the sorcerer's role was shared between the artist and the priest, later to be joined by the doctor, the scientist, and the philosopher. The intimate bond between art and worship was only very gradually loosened, eventually to be discarded altogether. But even after this had happened, the artist remained a representative or spokesman of society. He was not expected to importune his public with his own private affairs; his personality was irrelevant, and was judged only by his ability to echo and reflect common experience, the great events and ideas of his people, his class and his age. This *social function* was imperative and unchallengeable, just as the sorcerer's had been earlier. The artist's task was to expound the profound meaning of events to his fellow-men, to make plain to them the process, the necessity, and the rules of social and historical development, to solve for them the riddle of the essential relationships between man and nature and man and society. His duty was to enhance the self-awareness and life-awareness of the people of his city, his class, and his nation; to liberate men, as they emerged from the security of a primitive collective into a world of division of labor and class conflict, from the anxieties of an ambiguous, fragmented individuality and from the dread of an insecure existence; to guide individual life back into collective life, the personal into the universal; to *restore the lost unity of man.*

For man had indeed paid a colossal price for his rise to more complex and more productive forms of society. As a result of the differentiation of skills, the division of labor, and the separation of classes he was alienated, not only from nature, but from his own self. The complex pattern of society meant also the breaking-up of human relationships; increasing social enrichment meant, in many respects, increasing human impoverishment. Individualization was secretly felt to be a tragic guilt, the longing for a lost unity was inextinguishable, the dream of a 'golden age' and an innocent 'paradise' shone through a dark and distant past. This is not to say that looking back to utopia was the only or the essential content of poetry during the development of class society. The opposite motif—affirmation of new social conditions, praise of 'new gods'—was also powerfully present. In the *Oresteia* of Aeschylus, for example, this is the decisive element. All social problems and conflicts were reflected in literature, usually in the form of some mythological 'alienation' and with shifting emphasis. Those who glorified the past as a 'golden age' were usually the oppressed or disinherited among the poets. Later, with the decay of the ancient world, the theme was also taken over by privileged poets

(Virgil, Horace, Ovid) and, as in the *Germania* of Tacitus, used as an argument against the forces of decay. But the feeling that was present from the outset and came up again and again during the process of differentiation and class division was the fear of *hubris*, the belief that man had lost all balance and measure and that the birth of individuality inevitably led to tragic guilt.

The individualization of human beings was bound in the end to spread to the arts. This happened when a new social class, that of seafaring traders, came into being—the class that had so much to do with evolving the human personality. The aristocratic landed gentry, those grave-diggers of the old tribal collective, had also thrown up a few personalities, but their natural element was war, adventure, heroism. An Achilles or an Odysseus could only be conceived of away from their native soil: at home they were not individual heroes but merely representatives of their noble families, merely the mortal frame of the eternal landowner, impersonal links in a long chain of ancestors and heirs. The seafaring trader was something very different: a reckless self-made man used to staking his life again and again, and owing no allegiance to the conservative land with its unalterable pattern of sowing and harvest but only to the inconstant, moody, perpetually moving sea that could bring him as low as it had swung him high on the crests of its waves. Everything depended on individual skill, determination, mobility, cleverness—and getting back. But the difference went still deeper than that. The landowner and his land did not confront each other as strangers; they were closely bound together, so that a piece of land was almost the extension of its owner's person. Everything came from the earth and was returned to the earth. The trader's relationship with his property was very different. They were *alienated* from each other. It was the very nature of that property not to remain itself but to be constantly exchanged, and therefore transformed. Never in the history of the ancient world—which had regarded the incursions of money into the natural economy as an evil thing—had exchange value triumphed so completely over utility value as it did in the capitalist world. The concrete qualities of the exchanged object—whether it happened to be metal, linen, or spices—became secondary for the merchant; its abstract quality—value—and the most abstract form of property—money—became the essential things. But just because a product was now a commodity, something detached and alien, the merchant's attitude to it was that of a sovereign individual. The depersonalization of property gave him the freedom required to become a personality. In the trading coastal cities of the ancient world we always come across the great merchant prince, the individual 'tyrant,' confronting the aristocratic families, defying the traditional privileges, and claiming his rights as a strong, efficient, and successful personality. Wealth in its monetary form recognized no traditional bonds. It did not care for nobility or loyalty. It fell to the boldest—and the luckiest.

This invasion of money and trade into the conservative feudal world had the effect of dehumanizing relationships between people and loosening the structure of society still further. The self-reliant and self-dependent 'I' came to occupy the foreground of life. In Egypt, a country where work was respected and the worker was not discriminated against as in Greece, profane poetry concerned with individual destinies came into being at an early stage, side by side with sacred poetry and the literature of the collective. Let me quote one of the many love songs of ancient Egypt:

> My heart holds you dear.
> When I lie in your arms
> I do whatever you wish.
> My desire is my mascara:
> When I see you, my eyes shine.
> I cling close to you so as to see your love:
> You, the husband in my heart.
> This hour is beautiful above all others.
> May this hour swell to eternity.
> Since I have slept with you,
> You have raised up my heart.
> Whether my heart be plaintive or jubilant,
> Do not go away from me!

In other countries of antiquity it was trade that brought subjectivism into literature. The individual experience became so important that it could hold its own by the side of the tribal chronicle, the heroic epic, the sacred chant, and the war song. The Song of Songs, ascribed by legend to King Solomon, was an expression of this new age. In the Greek world—a world of sea traders—Sappho wrote poetry full of individual passion, lamenting her own fate and her own sorrows. Later, Euripides revolutionized the magnificent collective drama created by his predecessors by portraying individual human beings instead of collective masks. The myth, once the mirror of a collective of which the individual had been but an anonymous particle, gradually became a formal disguise for individual experience.

This new individualism, however, was still contained within a larger collective framework. The personality was the product of new social conditions; individualization was not something that happened to one man, or a few, but was a development shared by many and therefore communicable, for all communication presupposes a common factor. If there existed in the whole world only one self-aware 'I' pitted against a collective, it would be senseless to try to communicate this unique plight.

Sappho could not have sung of her fate had it been hers alone: intensely subjective though she was, she had something to say which, as yet unsaid, nevertheless applied to others. She expressed an experience common to many—that of the lonely, wounded, rejected personality—in a language common to all Greeks. It was not simply an inarticulate lament: her *subjective* experience was rendered *objective* in the common language, so that it could be accepted as an universally human one. More than that: the famous poem to Aphrodite is, by its nature, a prayer—a magic means of influencing the gods, that is to say, of exercising some power over reality; it is a magic, a sacramental act. The purpose or function of such poems is to affect either gods or men: not merely to describe a condition but effectively to change it. That is why the subjective poet submits to the objective discipline of meter and form, to magic ceremony and religious convention. The fact that a human being does not just cry out in formless protest against the pain and passion of individual fate but deliberately obeys the discipline of language and the rules of custom seems inexplicable—until we realize that art is the individual's way back to the collective.

The new 'I' emerged from the old 'we.' The individual voice broke away from the chorus. But an echo of that chorus still lingers on in every personality. The social or collective element has become subjectivized in the 'I,' but the essential content of personality is and remains social. Love, the most subjective of feelings, is also the most universal instinct of all—that of the propagation of the species. But the specific forms and expressions of love in any particular age reflect the social conditions that allow sexuality to develop into more complex, richer, and more subtle relationships. They reflect either the atmosphere of a society based on slavery, or the atmosphere of a feudal or bourgeois society. They also reflect the degree of feminine equality or inequality, the structure of marriage, the current idea of the family, the contemporary attitude to property, and so on. An artist can only experience something which his time and his social conditions have to offer. Hence an artist's subjectivity does not consist in his experience being fundamentally different from that of others of his time or class, but in its being stronger, more conscious, and more concentrated. It must uncover new social relationships in such a way that others will become conscious of them too. It must say *hic tua res agitur*. Even the most subjective artist works on behalf of society. By the sheer fact of describing feelings, relationships, and conditions that have not been described before, he channels them from his apparently isolated 'I' into a 'we,' and this 'we' can be recognized even in the brimming subjectivity of an artist's personality. Yet this process is never a return to the primitive collective of the past. On the contrary, it is a reaching out into a new collective full of differences and tensions, where the individual voice is not lost in a vast unison. In every true work of art, the division of human reality into the individual and the collective, the specific and the universal, is suspended; but it remains as a suspended factor in a recreated unity.

Only art can do all these things. Art can raise man up from a fragmented state into that of a whole, integrated being. Art enables man to comprehend reality, and not only helps him to bear it but increases his determination to make it more human and more worthy of mankind. *Art is itself a social reality.* Society needs the artist, that supreme sorcerer, and it has a right to demand of him that he should be conscious of his social function. This right was never doubted in any rising, as opposed to decaying, society. It was the ambition of the artist full of the ideas and experiences of his time not only to represent reality but also to shape it. The Moses of Michelangelo was not only the artistic image of Renaissance man, the embodiment in stone of a new, self-aware personality. It was also a commandment in stone to Michelangelo's contemporaries and patrons: 'That is what you ought to be like. The age in which we live demands it. The world at whose birth we are all present needs it.'

Usually the artist recognized a twofold social mission: the direct one imposed by a city, a corporation, or a social group; and the indirect one arising from an experience which mattered to him, i.e., from his own social consciousness. The two missions did not necessarily coincide, and when they conflicted with each other too often, it was a sign of increasing antagonisms within that particular society. But, generally, an artist who belonged to a coherent society and to a class that was not yet an impediment to progress did not feel it as any loss of artistic freedom if a certain range of subjects was prescribed to him. Such subjects were very rarely imposed by an individual patron's whim, but usually by tendencies and traditions deeply rooted in the people. By his original handling of a given subject, an artist could express his individuality and at the same time portray the new processes taking place within society. His ability to bring out essential features of his time and to disclose new realities was the measure of his greatness as an artist.

It has nearly always been characteristic of the great periods of art that the ideas of the ruling class or of a rising revolutionary class have coincided with the development of the productive forces and with the general needs of society. At such periods of equilibrium, a new, harmonious unity has seemed to be just round the corner, and the interests of a single class have seemed to be the common interest. The artist, living and working in a state of magic illusion, anticipated the birth of an all-embracing collective. But as the illusory nature of this expectation became clear, as the apparent unity disintegrated, as the class struggle flared up again, and as the contradictions and injustices of this new situation created acute uneasiness, so the situation of the arts and of the artist became more difficult and more problematic.

In a decaying society, art, if it is truthful, must also reflect decay. And unless it wants to break faith with its social function, art must show the world as changeable. And help to change it.

14. Umberto Barbaro

Materialism and Art

UMBERTO BARBARO (1902–59) was one of Italy's leading film theorists and literary critics. He wrote novels, short stories, film scripts, plays, and several critical works including *L'arte dell'attore* ("The Actor's Art") and *Il cinema e l'uomo moderno* ("Cinema and Modern Man"). He served as Director of the Centro Sperimentale di Cinematografia in Rome (of which he was co-founder) from 1944 to 1947, edited the film journal *Bianco e Nero* during the same period, and in 1948–49 taught at the Lodz Film School near Warsaw. As a translator, he introduced the Italian reading public to works by V. Mayakowsky, Heinrich Wöllflin, Sigmund Freud, V. I. Pudovkin and Sergei Eisenstein. Like so many Italian intellectuals of his generation, he began his career as a Crocean Idealist. After World War II, he moved to a Marxist position. The selection is taken from an unfinished essay, which was cut short by his death, *"Il risarcimento marxista dell'arte"* ("The Marxist Redefinition of Art"). Originally conceived as a full-length book, it was published posthumously in 1960 in a volume of writings collected by Lorenzo Quaglietti under the title, *Il film e il risarcimento marxista dell'arte*.

IN Marxist thought, art is an aspect of the intellectual production of a given period, part of the corresponding ideology at a given time. As such, art is conditioned by the structure, by the base, that is, by the relations of production.

Marxist aesthetics opposes and denies the whole series of previous aesthetic theories which are marred from the start by their more or less direct derivation from Idealist thought, and which consider the forms and products of intellectual activity, above all, art and works of art, as *autonomous* and subjective facts; almost as phenomena in their own right, out of time, out of space, out of absolutely all the conditions of their genesis, of their birth. The work of art, to this way of thinking, is truly a windowless monad, closed off in its "insularity." Neither its place of origin nor the specific techniques of that time and that particular art

161

form, nor imitation of or influence by preceding works, even if carried
to the point of plagiarism, nor the biography and psychology of the artist,
nor that of his times and of the social group to which he belongs, nor his
general ideas, nor his moral and social ones, nor even whether he wished
to propagate them through his work, nor whether he made a thesis of
them which was to be exhibited through images, nor the practical objective which he set for himself in his work, nor the practical effect his
work actually has had: none of this interests Idealist aesthetics, at least
in its most modern and consistent form, which is the aesthetics of Croce
and his principal followers. . . .[1]

The opposing viewpoint, prior to or independently of Marxist thought
on art, was put forth by the determinists, the positivists, the followers of a
mechanistic materialism. The most notable of all these, and also the most
interesting because of his definitive stance, is undoubtedly Hippolyte
Taine [1828–93—Eds.]. In spite of everything, his *Philosophie de l'art*
remains replete with acute observations, and his ability to range through
the regions of art is unquestionably remarkable, even if it sometimes
leads to a penchant for the generic which is precisely opposed to criticism;
for criticism is individuation, and, as the very etymology suggests, distinguishing. . . . But the chief fault lies in his sense of history, which
is antiquated, taking no account of the differentiation of society, regarded
by Taine as an undifferentiated whole, with no sense of even the classic
distinctions, that were sensed, however vaguely, by French historians
of the Restoration such as Mignet, Thierry, and Guizot.

It is a major error to consider the Marxist conception of art as an old
positivist position *à la* Taine, or as some familiar position already worked
out and asserted by other aestheticians. One needs to deepen the concept
of superstructure and art's specific place in it, rather than content
oneself with the superficial observation that art is linked to the time in
which it was thought through and produced. . . . The responsibility for
such a superficial judgment falls on certain theorists who, sincerely
believing themselves Marxists, have picked up from Marxism only its
external features and have thereby acquired a certain generic way of
speaking. They have interpreted Marxism as a species of positivism:
which is certainly true of mechanistic materialism, but not of dialectical
materialism. In their investigations and their theories, they have leaned
on and had recourse to positivizing sociologism which, with a slight re-
vamping of terminology, they have pawned off as Marxism. They have
forgotten the light in which Marx and Engels regarded the positivists and
the mechanistic materialists, among whom was none other than Dührung,
"for whom Hegel never existed," and against whom Engels polemicized in
one of his most profound works. G. Plekhanov, who was the first to
translate and introduce Marx to Russia, and who had an undoubted

complex of indubitable merits, in his aesthetics did not go, on the whole, beyond a crude sociology of art, not too dissimilar in fact from the bourgeois type à la Taine. . . . Plekhanov applied himself to corroborating and supporting the counter-revolutionary system with specific studies of a rather generic and approximate character . . . ; for example, his view of the minuet as "an harmonic expression of the psychology of an unproductive, corrupt class," whereas, as has been noted and often enough repeated, the minuet began much earlier, and was in its origins a peasant dance. . . .

Another misunderstanding . . . is to regard the forms of production (we may recall here the clarifications and analyses of Stalin) as instruments and as, indeed, a single instrument, yielding the foolish notion of deducing the necessity of certain determinate forms of art from particular tools. This way of conceiving the relation between structure and superstructure, and between particular instrument and artistic expression, has given rise to the most egregious blunders. How many times have we heard it repeated, and laid at the door of Marxism, that the transition from Romanesque to Gothic style is explained by the invention of the yoke harness, which increased the traction and work force of draft animals? An amazingly silly statement emanating from a pseudo-Marxism with no understanding of the very meaning of the term, "means of material production." An equally silly and addled statement was made only recently, by a young Italian critic . . . who strutted about for a while making himself out to be a Marxist, and who has since crossed over, with his blunted weapons and his scanty cultural baggage, to anti-Communism. His head filled with confusion and ignorance, both in theories and in the historical data of the problem he formulated, he declared in one of his studies of Cézanne, perhaps still unpublished, that impressionism and the *plein-air* pictorial style derived from the use of tin, which made possible the creation of tubes of prepared paint; for these could be carried conveniently in one's pocket, or in appropriate little boxes, into the countryside. Of the entire historical situation and the various mediations which brought on the great realistic revolution from Caravaggio to Manet and Monet, he neither knows anything nor cares to know anything. To explain one of the finest moments in the history of painting anywhere in the world, he needs only tin and Lefranc tubes! The same critic has also tried to explain a trait, neither exclusive nor even especially typical, incidentally, of impressionist canvases, by the economic law of supply and demand, maintaining that their small dimensions depended on the littleness of bourgeois dwellings for which they were intended, whereas in the feudal period the paintings were large because they were intended for and commissioned by churches, palaces, and castles. Without taking into consideration, among other things, that the impressionists were despised and spat upon by the bourgeoisie, who took great care not to buy their paintings. And how many times has it been repeated simplistically that impressionism was an expression of bourgeois ideology, in complete disregard of the innovative value, in content and in form, of that great movement in painting? And above all in disregard of the history and the taste of the French bourgeoisie who, at that time, found their ideal painters in the Coutures, the Bouguereaus and the Meissoniers, and certainly not in the Monets, the Sisleys, the Pissarros, the Renoirs, and the Cézannes. . . .

The aesthetic currents that connect art to its time of birth are indeed many. This issue is embodied in many works and studies by many historians and theoreticians, especially in the history of the figurative arts. The problem has arisen in various ways, deriving for example from the necessity of a *division* of the history of art into *periods*. Division by centuries, adopted by Adolfo Venturi in his monumental *Storia dell'arte italiana*, is certainly the most obvious; but it does not explain, indeed it totally obscures, the importance of the problem of distinguishing artistic epochs and relative transformations. Gothic, Renaissance, Baroque, Rococco, remain concepts floating in mid-air, purely descriptive terms without any historical motivation.

Another simplistic division sets artistic generations against each other, sons against fathers (Pinder), failing to explain at all the causes and the forms of historical evolution in general and artistic evolution in particular.

A more thorough attempt with a considerable influence in recent times on studies in the history of art was that of the Swiss historian, Heinrich Wöllflin, who deduced a series of *fundamental concepts* (*Grundbegriffe*) of art history from numerous investigations in which he explicated and gathered together causes for the transformation of styles. Spoerri has applied these to literature, and P. Frankl derived from them his theory of *phases of development* (*Entwicklungsphasen*). The measure of art in these inquiries, which are more valuable as concrete artistic and historical analyses than as theories, is *man* in the various historical periods in which he expresses himself, creating art in his own likeness. Alois Riegl, able philologist of the arts, most especially in its industrial forms, and serious connoisseur, was among the first to seek a measure of the baroque linked to the time of production of the work of art, and to try thereby to resolve the problems of style (*Stilfragen*); believing that he had found the answer by introducing into art history the concept of *artistic volitions* of various epochs (*Kunstwollen*). Likewise Ortega y Gasset, starting from his observation of periodicity of historical crises, has offered historians a criterion that some have tried to apply to art. Finally, Max Dvorak, with his followers Brickmann, Pinder, and Dagobert Frey, conceived and gave examples in his numerous writings on the history of art as the *history of the spirit* of various epochs.

We do not need to multiply examples . . . to realize that these aesthetic theories, like Marxist aesthetics, connect things up and make art depend on the historical period in which it was produced. Yet these aesthetic currents, deprived as they are of any rigorous canon of historical interpretation, remain inaccurate and inept in their definitions of the general historical situation and their artistic expressions, for all the multiplicity, sometimes admirable and breathtaking, of the materials mastered. And what is worse from the standpoint of theory—though starting from their premises, it could not be otherwise—they remain gagged and silent when it is a matter of explaining, finally, the formation of this or that particular *psychology*, individual or social, this or that particular *man*, particular *artistic volition*, particular *spirit*. To explain ideologies in general, and art along with them, *man* is not enough: the thin man of the fourteenth century or the fat man of the seventeenth century does not suffice to explain the Gothic or the Baroque. And just as slimness and corpulence are insufficient, so are the convolutions in the man's brain, or the shape of his cranium, insufficient to explain his individual psychology; just as the social psychology is inexplicable when the society is conceived as an undifferentiated whole, so long as society remains divided in antagonistic classes or differentiated in generations; nor does volition suffice, nor the complex of feelings and ideas, the spirit.

Marxism offers the possibility of formulating this problem concretely, which has remained unsettled and mysterious for all preceding aesthetics that have linked art to its times, and of resolving it scientifically. It enables us to consider the world of ideas and of art in particular, not abstractly, like something floating in mid-air, in eternity, in some absolute, but in its roots, deeply immersed in real life, that is, in modes of material production. In the light of Marxism, all intellectual production, all forms of knowledge, no longer appear uprooted from reality, autonomous, ends in themselves. Rather, comprehension of their origin enlightens us on the nature of their final end, explains the needs that they appease and satisfy. These needs may be most simply expressed as: to consolidate, to justify and to celebrate the structure from which productions of the mind are born. The various forms of knowledge generate work (the practical organization of the new means of production) and establish it (technical organization), regulate social relationships by means of juridical norms (law) and moral norms (ethics), coordinate coherent justifications of reality in general systems and theories of being (philosophy) and of knowing (epistemology), and finally celebrate in fantasy and through images, and also criticize and condemn, modes of the structure and social life, and even the other forms of the superstructure (art).

The fact that the various forms of intellectual production depend on the economic factor does not mean that the relation between structure and superstructure is direct and immediate. On the contrary, this relation is realized by way of a fairly complex series of transferences and mediations. Naturally enough, one must keep these in mind and study them carefully one by one; at the very least, they conceal and make it difficult to recognize the more remote origins; to overlook them is unquestionably to condemn oneself to a lack of comprehension of intellectual facts in their fullness and complexity. The few examples of misconceived Marxism cited above are inevitable and typical consequences of such incomprehension. The essential connections and mediations have been synthesized with clarity and concision by Raymond Politzer in his *Cours de Philosophie:* "History is the work of men. The activity that produces history is determined by the will. This will is the expression of their ideas. The ideas are expressions of the social conditions in which they live. The social conditions determine the classes and their conflicts. The classes are determined by economic conditions." To say that art celebrates and exalts or criticizes and rejects the structure is not to say that it does so directly and always consciously. It takes place through the political regime and the ensuing social consciousness. The latter often lags behind the economic development because ideologies have a tendency to accredit themselves and to pose as existing *sub specie aeternitatis;* and also for the practical reason that the bearers of past ideologies, the intellectuals of the past, obviously defend their practical positions, and therefore their ideas. Therefore, as Antonio Gramsci said, "it is an obvious remark that the world of ideology is in its overall character retarded as compared to technological relations of production. . . ." [2] [As Marx asserted,] in *18th Brumaire,* "the traditions of all past generations weigh rather heavily on human brains." The influence of the major works of the past exercise a particularly potent influence on works of art. Their authority is all the greater, the higher the qualitative level they have reached. Two cases cited by Marx may serve as examples. [*The author quotes Marx on the gladiator figures of the Roman Republic, which were invoked as ideals in the eighteenth-century bourgeois revolutions, and on the* "words, passions, and illusions" *of the Old Testament, invoked on behalf of the Cromwellian revolution in seventeenth-century England.—Eds.*]. . . . Thus, the claim that art *also* originates in art is not without some truth. Determined by the base, sometimes it undergoes very powerful influences from past art, which it interprets, utilizes and elaborates in its own fashion.

In general, we see repetitions, variations, and developments of so-called technique. Understood as complexes of norms, techniques are closely tied to artistic cycles, and the noteworthy reason for their transformation (the causes of the transformation of styles so avidly sought by art historians) lies precisely in the collapse of the superstructure when the base crumbles in periods of historical transformation or social revolution. The myth of perspective, of depth, of volume and anatomy, after its decline into mannerism, is followed by the great myth of light. But as we have noted above, the authority of the old works, of the old master-pieces endures. The achievement of the artists of the Renaissance is so great that the whole of nineteenth-century bourgeoisie was still domi-nated by the Academy, that is, by repetitions of their modules. . . .

In the practice of criticism, which is always applied from instance to instance, and not by way of classes and generalities, because it is always concrete, individuating, discriminating, one must take account of all these forces and their combinations. All of which does not in any way affect the truth of the basic assertion, "art as form of superstructure is conditioned by the base," but does create shifts and distortions which are not negligible, and hides the truth from superficial inquiry, both historically and artistically speaking. . . .

Another fundamental aspect of the relations between the structure and the superstructure is their *interaction*. There is no need to suppose that ideas, as determined by the base, have a passive or even merely secondary function in history. . . . To say that art is a part of the superstructure of a given period means . . . that it is determined by the conditions of the economic structure of that period, that it is a particular intellectual expression of the latter; but a more or less mediated expression, which generally is realized by way of a rather rich and complex series of mediations. And thus determined, art is, however, like the rest of the superstructure, determinative for the base, on which it often has a rather potent effect.

Behind the ideological forms and their competition (since there is always a more or less acute conflict within the superstructure of a given historical epoch) are classes and the class struggle; as had already been astutely observed by Chernyshevski, who saw human thought as dependent, not only on history, but on social classes, because "one thinks differently in a palace and in a hut." [3] In a given historical cycle the various artistic ideas and manifestations always have, perhaps unconsciously, a class-character; so much so that one can legitimately group them into two main thrusts: the class in power, which serves, and tends to affirm and consolidate in the superstructure the existing structure, and in art, to exalt it, liquidating the residue of past ideology and past structures; and the opposition, which criticizes it, struggles against it, and tends to overturn it. The battles between various artistic currents, new styles against old, new forms against old, can in sum almost always be traced to this antagonism, which is not always conscious in its authors, but is always profound and substantial. . . .

What we have said so far about art applies to all the forms of the superstructure, and therefore does not yet characterize or distinguish art specifically and exclusively in comparison to other intellectual forms. Like the other forms of intelligent activity, art arises from reality and tries to know it and transform it. But not by way of direct action or direct reflection. It does so . . . by way of images and organizations of images: it does so in fanciful form. This is its specific mode of existence. The specific mode of art, that distinguishes it from the other intelligent activities, is given by its matrix: the imagination. . . .

But what is the imagination?

One reply, which for us is unsatisfactory, has been given by Crocean aesthetics.[4] Imagination or intuition are not human faculties, but a level of the spirit: they are one with expression, that is, with form, that is, with art. We cannot take this view, because the denial of the concept of Spirit, or absolute Idea, is precisely the basis of our concrete philosophy, which considers the real world as real, and does not believe in the sub-jectivity, i.e., the unreality, of the real world. . . . To understand what imagination is, one must above all divest it of that mysterious and hardly convincing character of so-called gratuitous activity, which is supposed to be without any necessity or purposiveness. To clarify the issue, we may well hark back to imagination's remotest origins, looking at, among other things (as Lenin advised in his philosophical notebooks), the life of animals. . . .

Is the song of the birds, the kitten's play, disinterested or not? . . . One often sees the cat that lives in a household among people, do something quite extraordinary: on catching a mouse, instead of killing and eating it, the cat plays with it. If a ball of yarn rolls out across the floor, the cat plays with it, too. A strange thing, that an activity like play is possible for a cat. And, when one thinks about it, a really amazing game: for the house-cat, batting and rolling about the ball of yarn, pursuing and seiz-ing it, reproduces in the most remarkable and faithful way—transfiguring and idealizing, one would almost be tempted to say—the circumstances and aspects of the hunt. So that an old definition of art may begin to steal into one's mind: the transfiguration of reality.

Antonio Gramsci, in one of his extraordinary letters from prison, told of nurturing a small bird.[5] Before eating the nourishment put before it, the little bird "went into a frenetic dance." Is not this disinterested ac-tivity of the bird strange, this activity which can be called a "dance"? What is this game, that transfigures the reality of the hunt? What is this frenetic dance? We need to look closely at these activities, which give every indication of being a remote origin of artistic facts.

These are only apparently gratuitous and disinterested activities. For the cat and bird both have energies determined to come out in the hunt for food. But the domesticated cat and the domesticated bird no longer have any need to get food for themselves; the hunt has been rendered unnecessary by the continual, regular, domestic provision of nourishment. The transfiguration of the hunt and of the dance are only the forms through which is discharged a dynamic tension which, if not manifested in some way, would be harmful or actually destructive and fatal for the organism. The courtship of cats on the rooftops is made up of hisses, meowings, and cries which reproduce, at the same time transforming them, stages in the fights between males, required by the species, in certain past circumstances, for the possession of the females. The game, the dance, the feigned battle are an active energy loosened by new and superior conditions of life from their natural and proper end, and constitute a series of events, neither fortuitous nor gratuitous . . . which may well have never been enacted [in their original function] by the domestic cat born in a household, but belonged to the species when it existed under primitive conditions. It is the sight of food that provokes disturbances and movements in the throat of the bird ("it's mouth-watering"), which become articulated in song, and which become more complicated along with new needs and new gratifications of these, such as the call of sex and so on. Similar situations generate similar stances, the gratuitous reproduction of reality: and a first form of knowledge (even Croce spoke, with a poetic turn, of fantasy as a "dawning form of knowledge," "*una forma aurorale di conoscenza.*") This is the direction in which perhaps we will best discover the birth of that mysterious activity which in higher beings we call "imagination," and which produces arts. . . .

All of human behavior is *conditioned by history;* hence, imagination as well, which is not therefore a category of Spirit which produces forms and thereby art, but is rather a natural form conditioned by history. We may recall at this point what Ludwig Feuerbach wrote (cited by Lenin in *Materialism and Empirio-criticism*): "Surely the projects of fancy are also produced by nature, because the power of the imagination, like all other human forms, is in the last analysis, by nature and by origin, a force of nature." It is a force of nature that in the course of history man has managed to dominate and direct more and more successfully, like the other forces of nature. Thus, from direct energy for the satisfaction of an immediate and practical need, the imagination has become more and more intricately conditioned by the forms of social and individual life, and the forces of production determining these, transforming itself into energy that becomes conscious of the world in its particular way (through images), and at the same time becomes conscious of its own manifestations and work. It becomes conscious of the value of its product, and its effects and weight. It becomes what we commonly call fancy: that is, the matrix of art. Fancy which, realizing and appreciating its own importance, succeeds at its best in allying itself with the will, rendering itself responsible, self-directive, and orientated. From the irrational force of its first appearance, imagination tends to make itself ever more self-aware and rational; it tends to make itself dependent on the will, the prime mover, in Marxist thought, of every human activity. From irrational activity it becomes *a mode of knowledge,* i.e., from a thing *in itself* (not in the Kantian but in the materialist sense), it becomes a *thing for us.* Which is the definition of knowledge given by Engels. . . .

If we look closely at imagination we find that it seems to result from a sum of two moments, which cannot be neatly distinguished, localized, or considered strictly successive in time, . . . and which actually correspond to two different impulses or needs. . . . If we dwell on its *fantastic* aspect, we see the fruit of a free expansiveness, as if the banks of a pre-established symmetry of existence were broken in order to rush over reality, over things, without any guidance, like an impetuous torrent breaking out of its bed, destroying embankments and dykes, moving in free contact with things, pouring indiscriminately over them as if to penetrate and identify itself with them. It multiplies and diversifies, like an unloosing of the elements of a personality; the tendencies of the individual, guided by reason, repressed by civil and social life, its needs channelled and ordered, burst forth. . . . This uncontrolled activity is undoubtedly the first, and necessary portion of imaginative activity. It was well defined by Nietzsche as Dionysian, and thereby aptly placed under the sign of Bacchus and drunkenness. . . . For all its uncontrolled freedom and license, it is a way of entering into contact with reality, but with such reality as it can grasp, and which, rather, it cannot grasp and cannot in truth know, precisely because it flows over reality like water, swirls around it, even penetrates into its details, but does not perceive it as a whole, as an unity. The personages it invents, or even plucks from reality, are not realistic, but phantasms; even those which are real take on the phantomlike quality of shadows because they are not characteristic and typical. . . . The other aspect has been called, in analogous manner, Apollonian, and aptly so, since Apollo is the god of music and harmony in Greco-Roman mythology. We shall call this second moment, imagination: it is a re-entry into oneself, laden with fantastic material, to give form. This is the most specifically creative part of the process of fancy: the act of translating into images. . . .

We must also look at some other factors which likewise are reducible, in the last analysis, to history. Art criticism and art history of materialist tendencies—we are speaking here of mechanistic materialism—have already called attention to the concepts of *materials* and *technique*, seeing in these the specific, determining factors of artistic value and quality. We hold, on the contrary, that the means and the manner in which an artist achieves an expression of reality, achieves knowledge of the reality which he reflects, are a matter of indifference when it comes to the result of his work. That a statue is made of bronze, silver, or gold does not determine its value. . . . Similarly for the objective things which it reproduces. The fact that a painting represents a pear on a plate or a battle scene does not determine its value. It is well enough known that a still life by Cézanne or a row of bottles by Morandi are worth much more than the grand battle scenes of, say, Meissonnier, or, if you will, the slaughters of Sartorio, both painters who certainly did not lack technical capacity in an external sense of the term. It is perfectly clear that the more painters who set out to paint the same landscape with the same technical means, in order to render the same scenery in oils, thus beginning with the same materials and the same means, the more different paintings will be executed. For "oil painting" does not by any means exhaust the notion of "technique": besides this external technique there will be, for each painter, a particular way of coloring and brushing, of sketching and tinting, a particular way of harmonizing the colors, of composing the elements of the painting, and so on. There is no such thing as a technique of painting as such (nor of any other art), but a series of different styles [*manière*], which correspond to certain pictorial (or literary, musical, etc.) *myths* that belong to specific epochs and societies; and within the orbit of a given society of a given period there are also, as we have already noted, two contrasting elements that correspond to the division of classes.

The pretense of laying down norms and technical rules, internal or external, in the belief that art can be produced merely by applying them, is absurd. Technical rules appear, if at all, a posteriori, as a way of understanding the works of art. The fixed and immutable rules that certain artists have accepted and adopted for their work were not rules of art, but originated in needs of another sort; for example, the iconographic characteristics of divine figures of worship generated representational and iconographic canons, fixed and indefeasible. This occurred not only in early times, but also in the application of the principles of the Counter-Reformation in the manuals of Posevino and the like. The length of the angels' wings was a rule, for example, because it covered their posteriors.

It is certainly true that materials in the most external sense often determine technique. A wood-engraving exploits the fiber of the wood as a figurative or abstract element. . . . [But] it is clear that any kind of "technicalism" leads to formalism. On this view, which is one of the least apposite and least fortunate, form . . . would be nothing more than knowing and applying certain artifices, certain rules, discoveries, precepts, or even tricks. . . . The basis of all the "academies," it arises from the mistaken notion that one can extract and codify specific *expressive means* for each art and propose the best ways of employing them. This is to believe that these . . . have an absolute value and validity, whereas they are born of particular artists in specific settings, and therefore can perhaps be taken up again, but can never be reproduced as such. An academy of painting will mainly teach drawing, will look for rules for a well-balanced composition, will teach ways to render the volume of bodies, human and animal anatomy, the rules of perspective, and so on. With the result that Vasari, for example, or Daniele da Volterra have Michelangelo's drawing, Raphael's colors, understand perspective as Giotto did not, and can give weight and volume to bodies as Simone Martini certainly could not; and yet they are strictly zeros by comparison to Giotto, Simone Martini, Raphael or Michelangelo. The fact is that those technical approaches were born of particular poetic worlds which expressed themselves by way of one and not another form, expressing a profound content, while the external content (annunciation, madonna, *dormitio virginis* or what have you) was the same for all of them. . . . In theater, . . . even the seemingly most obvious and acceptable rule of all, that of consistency and congruity of a series of events and a resolution which is an inevitable consequence rather than coming from the outside, from a *deus ex machina,* has no absolute validity. For the *deus ex machina* is precisely the solution to the dramatic crises of some of the loftiest works of art produced by man: Greek plays and Homeric poems. There are no aesthetic norms, then: a normative aesthetics can only regulate non-art. . . .

The materialist historian does not deny the importance of personality, especially of the great personalities of history; and therefore he does not and could not deny its importance in art. But if one conceives art, as we do, not as a subjective, individual game or amusement, but as a force, and certainly not the most negligible in the play of forces in life and in history (which are one and the same thing), one realizes that the emergence in history of a work of art is no mere chance. It has fulfilled a particular function that was not chosen, but was the resultant of a series of factors through which it became necessary. It is born, as we have noted, *in the final analysis* from economic necessity. If we hypothesize as eliminated the particular instance of the great artist who created a given work (who was, of course, born by chance), the work would probably have been accomplished by another artist. . . . The economic situation sets certain tasks, and it is certain that a being particularly endowed with that human quality we call fantasy is thereby stimulated and led to exalt those tasks in fantasy. On the other hand, if he had had a greater measure of practical will instead of a greater measure of fantasy, he would certainly have tried to carry out certain tasks directly in action. . . . These theses concerning temperament, to tell the truth, tend to dissipate into tautologies: if he was a great artist, this is because he had an unusually powerful artistic temperament, and this explains why his works of art are great. Which is a fine tautology worthy of being placed alongside those noted in the old logic manuals, for example, that opium puts us to sleep because of its dormitive value. What kind of investigations can we make regarding this artistic temperament? To demonstrate by way of numerous facts, documented by a biography of the artist, that such a temperament existed, may well be an interesting piece of research: so long as we do not suppose it to be of essential utility, since the existence of the artistic temperament has been definitively, irrefutably, and fully demonstrated by the works of art. One might perhaps try to study how such a temperament was born and how it was reinforced and developed. How it was born: but we have already noted that a greater or lesser measure of imagination is common to all men, that all men, to a greater or lesser degree, are artists, are creators of works of art, and all are in a position to enjoy works of art. If the imagination, as we have said, is an energy cut off from its direct and immediate objective, we can consider how it became cut off from that objective; and in an effort to separate the reality from the storybook, from the erotic satisfaction, we may even consider some investigations into depth-psychology. It may even be (though I leave to others the responsibility for saying so with more scientific certitude than I am in a position to muster) that life is the result of a dialectic of two opposing principles, Eros and Thanatos (to take over and follow up the image-filled terminology of that bizarre artist-scientist Freud), and that imagination as an activity cut off from its goal is a sublimated (destructive?) activity. This may well be. At the same time, this pseudo-scientific terminology may rather easily lead to equivocations and errors. And certainly we do not do much toward a better understanding of the work of Dostoyevski by reading in Freud that he hated his father, that when the old reprobate was killed by his peasants Dostoyevski felt responsible and was stricken with attacks of the *mal sacré*, which disappeared after the condemnation to death, the exile to Siberia, and the tragic farce of the interrupted execution. Who could explain a film like *Open City* by the temperament of Rossellini? Such realism, such pungent realism, such power of inflexible truth, such abnegation and spirit of sacrifice, to have seen this among the noblest men of Italy, in one of the noblest and greatest moments of Italian national history—how explain this by a character like that of Rossellini, hesitant, hypersensible, nervous, contradictory, artful and calculating? How reconcile the reverence for humanity and the love of country expressed in *Paisà* with the episodes of his life which have been the delight and the fortune of the slick magazines? [6]

One part of the superstructure, then, has the task of exalting its own structure in fantasy. . . . But when the ruling class is in a decline, the rising class does not exalt in the superstructure the values of the structure of the constituted order. The structure begins to rot and crumble, . . . the ruling class no longer has a propulsive and progressive function, no longer can employ, channel, and exploit the new productive forces. Contradictions multiply, social injustices become glaringly obvious, discontent, reaction, and open rebellion emerge. The old ideologies make no replies that can be accepted as valid, no longer can they say why events occur as they do, no longer can they suggest means for restoring the ailing body social to health. To the inevitable economic crises correspond moral discords and crises of all kinds. Sensing its precarious position, the ruling class sets out to defend its interests, which no longer coincide with those of the majority and take on the form and substance of hated privileges. The best, the fugitives from their class, take refuge in the ascendant, opposing class, exposing themselves to the vituperation, the calumny, the vendetta without quarter of their class of origin. The superstructure, in turn, feels the ground slipping from beneath its feet, so to speak, as the opposing class gains strength. It is at this point that the ruling class throws overboard its old ideologies and, where art is concerned, hastens to proclaim autonomy. This so-called autonomy of art, which has been asserted in all times by the aesthetes of a declining class, is a mask for performing a function quite different from that which a class demands of art: no longer the exaltation of the class, the impossible exaltation of a discredited world, a discredited reality, but rather the task of drawing the attention of its public from the sight of reality. . . . Naturally the intelligentsia usually does not know or even dream that it is an errand-boy for lowly functions of the ruling class. Why lowly functions? Because at this stage in the existence of the structure, the corresponding superstructure undertakes an anti-historical exercise, trying to impede, as it were, the fatal course of events. . . . This unawareness of what he is doing explains why the intellectual often cuts an other-worldly figure, ineffectual in worldly matters, alien and distracted. . . . There emerge those unrealistic, supercalligraphical, superrefined movements in which art takes itself as its own end, and fights for its independence (which is, in reality, only a harsher, less dignified servitude). Art, shall we say? But art is then no longer art; it is not poetry, but prose, . . . the absence of artistic quality. Formalism holds sway, and aesthetics provides the theory, fitting it into general views of the world. A period of profound decadence begins. Reality everywhere contradicts and reveals the inadequacy of the structure, an inadequacy that becomes, bit by bit, ever more strident, ever more unjust, ever more inhuman. Artists, therefore, no longer explain their activity in terms of the fullness of fantasy-imagination. Fantasy assumes a preponderant role in the turning-out of their productions, to the detriment of imagination. One can no longer speak of artistic productions, but only of pseudo-artistic ones. The function of the imagination having become degraded and exhausted, art becomes mere technicalism, empty virtuosity, cleverness. (*Camées* was the title of a collection of poems by Gauthier who propounded the theory of art for art's sake in its modern form—cameos, that is to say, difficult craftmanship.) The skill becomes hypertrophic, a visible intoxication with technique poisons even the productions of those who do not realize what they are doing and do not understand the essentially retrograde function which they are fulfilling. Academicism and Byzantinism emerge. Without the brake of imagination, poetry sets the "marvelous" as its goal, as in the pseudo-poetry of seventeenth-century Italy. This pseudo-art becomes ever more extravagant, avant-garde movements appear which, symptomatically enough, serve only to keep alive old forms of social order, because it is precisely the avant-gardists who are truly devotees of the past. (Their widely acknowledged value for a "general study of technical means," on which I have written elsewhere in connection with film avant-garde, is only further confirmation of this fact.)

Putting it somewhat oversimply, we may say that the dissociation of the synthesis of fantasy and imagination is characteristic of the condition of the ruling class in its decadent phase. Works are then the fruit of fantasy alone or of imagination alone. One sees on the one hand an empty playing with techniques, on the other hand a pessimistic naturalism, an unremitting insistence on themes of desperation, death, the futility of it all. These two aspects are equivalent, so that one often hears it said by minds given to paradox that Luchino Visconti, for example, is a formalist.[7] These two tendencies are, in substance, the tendency to evasion (escapism), and the distorting of reality, largely in a pessimistic direction.

Notes

[1] Cf. chapter 15, Galvano della Volpe, "Theoretical Issues of a Marxist Poetics," notes 1 and 2. (—*Eds.*)

[2] Antonio Gramsci, Italian Communist Party leader and man of letters, who died a political prisoner under the Mussolini regime. (—*Eds.*)

[3] Nikolai Chernyshevski, nineteenth-century Russian author and revolutionary. (—*Eds.*)

⁴ See note 1, above. (*—Eds.*)

⁵ See note 2, above. (*—Eds.*)

⁶ Cf. Raymond Borde and André Boissy, *Le néo-réalisme italien: une expérience de cinéma social* (Lausanne: Claire fontaine, 1960), esp. pp. 22–23, 26–30, 36–37, 85. (*--Eds.*)

⁷ Luchino Visconti, Italian director associated with neorealist cinema (*Ossessione, La Terra Trema*). See R. Borde, *Le néo-réalisme,* pp. 20–21, 44–45, 121–23. (*—Eds.*)

15. Galvano della Volpe

Theoretical Issues of a Marxist Poetics

GALVANO DELLA VOLPE, born in Imola, Italy, in 1895 is the author of studies of Marx, Rousseau, Hume, and Hegel, and professor in the History of Philosophy. The following selection is taken from a major work, *Critica del gusto* ("A Critique of Taste"), published in 1960, in which Marxist principles and modern concepts of semantic analysis are simultaneously brought to bear on the various arts in order to show their unity and their differences.

But the difficulty is not in grasping the idea that Greek art and epos
are bound up with certain forms of social development. It rather
lies in understanding why they still constitute with us a source
of aesthetic enjoyment and in certain respects prevail as the standard
and model beyond attainment.

> —MARX, Introduction to the *Critique of*
> *Political Economy* (1857)

. . . We placed—and had to place—our main emphasis on the
derivation of the political, legal, and other ideological appearances,
and on the basic economic matters-of-fact underlying them. We
thus neglected the form for the content—the style and manner, how
those appearances, etc. take shape.

> ENGELS, letter to Franz Mehring (July 14, 1893)

I

Art and Concept

A SYSTEMATIC exposition of an historico-materialist aesthetics, and therefore a methodical, sociological reading of poetry and of art in general, . . . presupposes above all a radical critique of the Romantic and Idealist conception of aesthetics; even if not that alone. . . .[1]

The most serious obstacle which today [1960—*Eds.*] still blocks the path of aesthetics and literary criticism (to limit ourselves for the moment to the latter) is the term "image" or (poetic) "imagination," laden with a Romantic heredity and with aesthetic mysticism. Even though the poetic "image" is taken as a symbol or a vehicle for some signification or truth, it is implicitly understood that this has nothing at all to do with any organic compresence, or any effective compresence of any sort, of the intellect, discourse, or ideas, which remain the great enemies of the poetic: and yet one insists upon the "truthfulness" of the "image," hence on its cosmic import, universality, or cognitive value ("intuitive," as the saying goes).[2] An *impasse* connatural to the very substance of the poetic, a fated and insurmountable impasse, one might say (and does say): insurmountable, indeed, were it not for the fact that one is dealing with an historical antinomy, connatural to traditional aesthetic thought, Romantic and spiritualist (bourgeois-Christian) by definition, and therefore surmountable with the surmounting of the latter in its ensemble and in its roots.

The truth is that today we are still substantially at the stage of philosophic criteria of, for example, a George Moore or a Yeats . . . , when the former cried, "Those pests and parasites of artistic work—ideas!", and when the latter rejected Ibsenesque symbolism because he found it too clear and intellectual. If even today—to remain in the camp of Anglo-Saxon criticism—critics such as Cleanth Brooks and Robert Penn Warren, to whom we indeed owe some far from superficial analyses of the intellectual structure of so many modern poems, can preface their analysis of the structure of T. S. Eliot's *Wasteland* with a philosophico-methodological warning that "the discussion that follows, [however], is to be considered as a means to an end: the imaginative apprehension of the poem itself," [3] then we are still with Coleridge and his miraculous "imagination" (of German Romantic origin). Contemporary German aesthetics, for its part, repeats for us through the late Nicolai Hartmann the "autonomy" principle, in all its abstractness and its Kantian aestheticism, with its formula of "specifically artistic pleasure" being "a contemplative attitude." As for Marxist aesthetics, and leaving aside all else, what shall we say of a Lukács for whom "art enables us to intuit with our senses" what science resolves into "abstract elements" and "conceptual definitions," while at the same time he pretends to salvage the claims of "typicality" (i.e., the intellectual character) of the artistic image? . . .

There can be no meaning at all, save a mystical one which leads to the worst sort of dogmatism, in speaking any more (even as Marxists) of artistic knowledge through "images" or "intuitions" alone, rather than in organic connection with concepts. Indeed, what enables us to *know*—and thus to perceive something valid for the whole world—if not the ability to overcome the equivocation or chaos of immediacy or raw stuff which is in itself inexpressible and unformed? if not, in sum, the introduction of an order or unity which is that of the universal or the concept (hence, truth which is universality), the proper attribute of the *rational?* Now, assume images or intuitions in themselves and for themselves, in epistemic abstraction, as data presenting themselves bereft of any conceptual references. You will note, to be sure, that they have their own positive character, their own inexpungeable being. You will see this, for example, in Dante's great song of exile, in the phrase, " *'l gran lume":*

> di fonte nasce il Nilo picciol fiume
> quivi dove 'l gran lume
> toglie a la terra del vinco la fronda, . . .[4]

You may fix upon its merely sensual, *aesthetic,* "visual" aspect. But you will also discover that the inevitable (as we know) adjunct of meaning or concept by way of the common denominators of dictionary (and grammar), not only does not negate their being (sensual or material) as images, but explicates and promotes it. We may well ask, now, how we can grasp and appreciate the beauty of the final image (in which the preceding culminate) if we must take it solely as "image," and therefore (everything else aside) without even the contemporaneous, clarifying *concept* of a shadow almost annulled by the perpendicular path of the sun's rays? The images acquire the vividness and full evidence that belongs to them at the moment, and only at the moment, in which they become *common* in and through the (adequately) corresponding *words:* that is to say, in that *expressivity* which is nothing less than their *communicativeness.*[5] To which both everyday and poetic cognition testify every moment, thus also demonstrating their similarity (in this respect, at any rate). . . .

Let us take, for example, Vico's famous thesis that "poetic characters," Achilles, Ulysses, Orestes, etc., are portraits drawn, not "by abstracting genera," but "by fancy," whereby they become "universals of fantasy."[6] When Vico was led to say that these poetic characters are "certain universals of fantasy naturally dictated by the innate property of the human mind to delight in that which is *uniform,*" and that it belongs to the mind "to enlarge the particular through *imagination,*" and thus "to reduce all the *facts* of powerful warriors to Achilles and *all* the counsels of prudence to Ulysses," etc., he was forced to contradict himself in his most astute observations. For it is contradictory and absurd to recognize the human requirement for *uniformity* or *unity* or rationality, and therefore, for *generalization* or "enlargement" of particulars, and yet assign its fulfillment, not to categories and derived processes of abstraction via genera, not to reason, in short, but to "fantasy" or the sensuous, synonymous with particularity itself or with the *multiple* (as if this might "enlarge itself"!). Correct or nearer the truth here was Vico's direct adversary, Castelvetro,[7] who reminds us, for all his simplistic, scholastic schematism of genera and species, that the universality and hence the poetic character of Orestes, Medea, and Ulysses must follow in some way upon that complex of *abstract qualities* (or Aristotelian *poioi*) which is the human "species," within which they are included. Hence one cannot help but conclude that the poetic character of Orestes, Medea, Ulysses, Achilles and innumerable other tragic, epic (and lyric) personages must consist, then, in their universality. This is nothing but the possibility and necessity inherent in *types* or *genera* resulting from *aesthetic* syntheses, i.e., from *empirical* syntheses performed according to criteria of *categorial abstraction,* that is to say, the primordial abstraction proper to those most general genera which are the categories, the predicates, or the supreme points of view of things (quality, for example, with all that this implies or co-implies). Or, otherwise stated, we are led to conclude that "poetic characters," and along with them every other poetic fancy, far from being those hippogriffs known as "universals of fantasy," as Vico and contemporary Vicoites would have it, are noetic or discursive universals, that is, normal epistemological facts resulting, like every other universal or concept (concretely taken), from a generic abstraction based simultaneously on the *categoriality* of things and on their *materiality,* their empirical or aesthetic standing. But we are then forced, no less, to modify the modern-traditional criterion of this artistic "form," and thus of artistic "content": we must now identify the former with the thought or the concept, instead of with abstract, mystical "images" (not to mention "sound-images"!), i.e., *unmeaning* images which, as we know, are *incommunicable, inexpressive,* and finally *formless;* and we must identify the "content" with the material or the multiple (the images). We thus overturn the entire problematic of the arts inherited from Romanticism. Were this not the case, and if we did not realize this, we would have to admit that there is really no sense at all in speaking of "form" in connection with poetry and art in general. For where there is no *eidos* or *dianoia* or idea or concept (judgment) uttered, there is no *form* worthy of the name, but only chaos. . . . We will have to conclude, therefore, that there is "poetic discourse" just as there is historical discourse, scientific discourse, etc., and that the term "discourse" is to be taken in its rigorous, literal sense—an intellectual-rational procedure—with regard to poetry as well: indeed, in all cases. We will have to admit, more precisely stated, that poetry and art in general, is *reason* (*concrete reason*), like history or science, and that in this respect it does not in fact differ at all from history and science in general. It does not differ from them, in other words, in the cognitive, epistemic, *general* elements which they have in common—sensibility (fancy, or what have you) and reason. We will have to realize that if it makes sense (as it undoubtedly does) to speak of the sensibility or imagination of a historian or a scientist, it makes no less sense, conversely, to speak of the rationality or the discursiveness of poetry. We will have to realize, indeed, that the demand of "coherence," that absolutely fundamental feature of the poetic work as such, which everyone insists on, remains inexplicable if coherence means "imaginative coherence," that is, coherence instituted *by* imagination or fancy rather than *in* imagination. . . . Hence the poet, to be a poet, to give form to his images (even if in his own way, as we shall see later), must think and reason, in the literal sense of these terms, and therefore must reckon with the truth and reality of things (the "plausible" as essential artistic element discovered by Aristotle), no less, certainly, than the historian or the scientist in general. And he must reckon—as poet—with ideologies and events . . . even when he intends to withdraw from them in the manner of an Aristo or a Cervantes. It is the *dialectical* (i.e., real) complex of the poetic work *as such* that we have to confront: such is the inevitable consequence of the poetic work being, no less than a historical or scientific work, a *discourse*. . . .

Metaphor

Let us turn to an examination . . . of a fundamental category of literary poetics: metaphor, in order to develop subsequently the concept of literary truth in terms of literary abstraction, an abstraction involved precisely in poetic or literary *discourse*. . . .

We may say that Aristotle's *Rhetoric* contains at 1405a 5–10 the heart of the philosophical and epistemological issues concerning metaphor . . . in its essential classical features, and therefore in its most embarrassing and burdensome aspects for the heirs of Vico, of German Romanticism, of Idealism, and of the associated aesthetic prejudice of the metaphor as a "nexus of fancy" generated by pure images (the usual contradiction in terms); in sum, a purely imaginal *quid*—"certainly a vividness," says one of our latest decadent aesthetes, Ezra Pound, the founder of Imagism. For in that passage not only is it said that metaphor confers "clarity" (an intellectual virtue!) on a style, even more than "attractiveness and distinction," but that it "has great value in both poetry and prose." The same notion is thoughtfully echoed by Cicero and by Quintilian, the former when he tells us that "adolescence, the flower of our years" is "a sort of *definition*" of adolescence itself; and the latter, stressing the intellectual, cognitive, truthtelling value of figures of speech, when he hastens to assert that hyperboles, "if they lie, *do not lie to deceive us*." Similarly, Quintilian observes, in line with Cicero, that we speak prosaically of "the flower of life" or of "a harsh character," etc., because of simple lack of "apt terms" and not, as Vico (wishing to reserve genera and species for "philosophy") would say, because of a "lack of genera and species." . . .

As it happens, every day we *prefer* to usual terms and their limited generality, those wider and deeper connections among things which are precisely figurative terms. We are not referring here merely to those innumerable dead or dormant metaphors, now wasted away, such as the "leg" of the table, the "saddle" of the mountain, the "neck" of the bottle, the "vale" of life, etc. (which, moreover, appear dead only from a superficial, psychological point of view, but are very much alive . . . from a cognitive and therefore practical point of view). We are thinking, above all, of all the metaphors which so often structure the most subtle reasoning and the most apt definitions (one may think of the famous terms "form" and "content" employed in philosophy), and those to be found in these very lines: "to structure," "subtle," "apt," "are found in." Such arguments and such definitions would lose all truth value (and often enough, they are illustrious arguments and definitions) if one had to admit that a metaphor is but an association *by* images, a play of fancies, rather than an association *of* images. So that one may well say of metaphor that it is like the air which envelops us, without which we would expire as thinkers (and this, too, is a metaphor, spelled out as a simile). And it has been pointed out that it befell Horace to defend, and Hobbes to condemn, metaphor by means of metaphor (*"serendis verbis," "ignis fatui"*).

Rhetoric 1410b 14–15 points out that metaphor provides ready instruction and knowledge "by way of genera." "When the poet calls old age 'stubble,' he informs and instructs us by means of a genus: the 'lost bloom' common to both things." . . . In *Topics*, Aristotle concludes that *similarity*, "by which those who use metaphors make metaphors," is the same categorial norm of similarity or sameness that regulates inductive thinking, hypothetical reasoning, and defining. . . . Here we are dealing, as in the above case of "poetic characters," with abstractive empirical syntheses (aesthetic in nature) by way of genera or types, conditioned by the categories; hence, with a concrete rather than an abstract intellection, in short, with a logico-intuitive complex. This is shown, for example, by the following rather subtle and exceptionally telling cases of Homeric and Empedoclean tropes: from genus to species and from species to species. Aristotle cites as an example of a shift from genus to species: "Here stands my ship," because "being at anchor" (*ormein*), is a specific variety of the generic "standing" or "being in place" (*estanai*) which is used instead. As an example of a shift from species to species, he cites: "Drawing off his life with a bronze knife" and "cutting off (his lifefluid) with a bronze mixing-bowl," noting that the poet said "cut off" (*arusai*) instead of "draw off" (*tamein*) and "draw off" instead of "cut off," both of these being species of the generic "removal" (*aphelein*). In this regard we should note that the metaphor of the ship "standing" is just that, and not an insipid abstraction, . . . only because this referring of the species *ormein* to its genus *estanai* is not a purely formal linking of abstract ideas, but consists in a logico-intuitive nexus of *a variety of species* (and not *ormein* alone) with their various genera. . . . As a result, he who has a mind to, can grasp that the ship stands at anchor as the cart stands on its wheels and the man stands on his legs. In the second example, we should also note that . . . the poetic effect results not only from the concreteness of the specification—which is not, after all, a pure *ratio* or abstract essence (the intuitive or imaginal aspect of "drew off" and "cut off" cannot be eliminated)—but also and equally from the genus, "to remove." The latter, with its categorial values that condition it ("action" implicating "being," etc.), actually constitutes the signification, communicativeness, or universality (i.e., validity) of the metaphor from which the imaginal or intuitive potency of the figure of speech is then inseparable. . . .

We have seen how poetry, even in the metaphor, which is usually said to be its very home, is rationality (in the concrete sense indicated previously) . . . , and hence not at all "on this side of" distinctions between real and unreal and the like, as mysticizing aesthetic theories claim. We must now examine . . . the general notion of literary, poetic abstraction from the problem of the literary *symbol* to that of the *typical*. . . .

Organic-Contextual Meaning

Scientific discourse in general seeks the universal, seeks truth, by way of semantic values which are technical, by way of omnicontextual meanings ("prosaic" ones, if you will). These are most adequate to its undertaking thanks to their interchangeability or heteronomy. In them, scientific reflection—whose *genera* must be *univocal*—may express itself and does in fact express itself. Conversely, poetic discourse seeks the universal, seeks truth, by way of so-called "stylistic" semantic values, that is, organic-contextual ones. Their *genera*, we shall see, must be *polysignificant* [*polisenso*], in order to be "occasional," "connotative," "free," etc., thus providing the autonomy in which literary reflection and abstraction may express itself and does in fact express itself. An inquiry into the semantic aspect of scientific thought and poetic thought thus confirms that the real distinction between science and poetry (and art in general) is *not* the "abstractness" of the thought in the one case and the "concreteness" of the imagination in the other, but rather—as we now begin to see—in the omni-contextual or technical nature of the language used in science, and the organically contextual character of the language used in poetry. . . .

In order to characterize the nature of poetry, we must now concentrate on this particular semantic feature, polysignificant genera or polysignificant discourse, which distinguishes poetry from science and its univocal genera or univocal discourse. We need to clarify in fact, three semantic-epistemological notions, by turning to their respective semantical loci: the equivocal, the univocal, and the polysignificant.

By the semantic locus of the *equivocal*, we mean the semantic linguistic unity, the concrete (not abstract) unity of the sentence (cf. the Aristotelian "proposition")—or the word functioning as a sentence—that appears in everyday discourse. Its meaning is entirely fortuitous, in the sense of varying with the particular linguistic context in which it appears. By the semantic locus of the *univocal*, on the other hand, we mean once more a concrete linguistic unity, a sentence or word-sentence, as above, whose meaning, however, is *not* fortuitously dependent on a particular linguistic context, because it is conditioned, instead, by *innumerable contexts which are mutually interdependent*. This "omni-contextual" linguistic value of the univocal expression accounts for its well-known "uni-versality" and "truth." But this is not universality or truth "*par excellence*," because universality and truth are not limited to univocal genera, that is to say, scientific and philosophical expressions. There also exist *polysignificant genera*, or "polysemes." The semantic locus of the polyseme is, once more, a concrete linguistic unity, a sentence or word-sentence, as in both preceding cases. Its expressive value, however, is conditioned by its capacity to constitute a linguistic context sufficiently individuated and organic to function as a necessary "con-text" for each of its elements. And the polyseme may well be in turn an organic part of a larger structure of this nature, involving still other such linguistic unities. Hence a polyseme has *more* meaning than a sentence in everyday discourse. This added meaning, inseparable from a determinate context, because it is generated by and through the context, constitutes *poetic discourse* or thought, and gives to poetry its autonomy. This autonomy, however, is semantic in character, not metaphysical, and hence is scientifically verifiable.

The poetic symbol, then, cannot be considered any less universal than the scientific symbol simply because it is not omni-contextual, but organically-contextual. Each is a unity-in-multiplicity, or *thought*.

Typicality in Art

. . . By means of the notions of logico-intuitive complex and concrete intellectual activity—that is to say, poetry in the sense of *discourse*—we can also derive the notion of *typicality* (and hence, of *thesis* or *tendency*) from poetic values in general. We must recognize, then, in addition to the typical of science, a typical belonging to art. This would be an ensemble of common and specific features, *a socio-historical essentiality*. Needless to say, it has nothing to do—precisely because of its concretely intellectual nature—with any sort of statistical average. Indeed, if typicality is the essence of a given historical phenomenon, it cannot be simply the most diffuse, the most frequent (or most quantifiable), or most ordinary features. In other terms, this typical, precisely because it is not an average, presents itself as something perceptible or concrete or characteristic, which is therefore expressible or valid by way of an ensemble of traits both common *and* specific, and not simply common, generic. It is, in short, a *characteristic typicality*.

We have already underscored, in connection with the "materialist" aesthetics of Lukács, the basic contradiction of combining art, as "sensible intuition" *without* "conceptual" or intellectual elements, and "typicality". . . . Now we must clear the whole terrain of any possible residual equivocation. Engels, for example, reintroduced as a materialist the question of tendentious or thesis poetry (*die Tendenz*), and cited above all as "tendentious poets" such names as Aeschylus, Aristophanes, Dante and Cervantes. Quite rightly, he did not fail to warn that "it is a poor author who becomes infatuated with his own heros," and that "the poet must not give the reader cut and dried the solution in the future of the social conflicts he describes." But he also over-extended his warning against the merely prosaic, in consequence distorting and unbalancing his correct requirement, that "the tendency or thesis must emerge from the situation and action themselves," by adding an absurd restriction: "without any explicit reference being made to the tendency or thesis." He concluded, oddly enough for a historical materialist, that "the more hidden remain the viewpoints (*Ansichten*), the better for the work of art." One can only explain this as a residue in Engels himself of the Romantic fear of thought within poetry (cf. Goethe, for whom poetry "expresses the particular without thinking of or indicating the universal"). . . . However, one need only think of the *organically artistic* character of the "viewpoints" of poets from Aeschylus to Mayakowsky to Brecht. . . . And one need only think of the threat to the poetics of social realism, so warmly urged by Engels, in such anti-rational restrictions. What, indeed, of the poetic force of the "satire" and "irony," to which Engels himself called attention, in the artist Balzac, to take an extreme and very characteristic case? And the example of Schiller's *Kabale und Liebe*, cited with admiration by Engels as the first political *Tendenzdrama* of Germany, becomes quite embarrassing and counter-productive for Engels if judged today according to Engel's own restrictive criteria. For, paradoxically enough,

it is precisely because the play was *not* sufficiently *thought out,* not sufficiently historically motivated, that this bourgeois drama by Schiller appears to us today in its true light as an unsuccessful artistic work lacking
in social realism. As Auerbach and Korff have noted, it is "not reality,
but melodrama"—a negative ascription from an aesthetic standpoint, needless to say. For "perhaps the most important motif *for understanding the
social structure* . . . , the utter subordination of the subject, who, in
their obtuse and narrow religiosity believe their extreme oppression to be
the expression of an eternal law, *never comes out clearly.*" (Our italics.)
Thus, it was because Schiller did leave so concealed what should have
been a tendentious, critical, bourgeois "viewpoint" on subjection by the
ancien régime, that this (bourgeois!) tragedy is an artistic failure rather
than an artistic success! . . .

Sociological Criticism

Let us draw our conclusion concerning poetry and literature. Given
the preceding analyses, we are in a position to define it as *polysignificant
language* dealing with *characteristic types.* In other words, it is the *sociological* nature of the poetic work which we must consider. And the
reason is clear. Only if the intellectual meanings and articulations *of* the
real, the more or less *historically real* (of what else, otherwise?) are constitutive of the poetic work as such, is there really a possibility of a
sociological (materialist) foundation for poetic values. Only then can the
Platonic or meta-empirical or meta-historical heaven (the Hegelian reign
of the Ideal, the *Geister,* the "shadows" and "spiritual figures"), in which
poetic values have been hypostatized at least from the Romantic era to
the present, be recognized as mythical and illusory. . . . If the sociological character and value of the poetic work were not demanded, or better,
implied by the very substance (structural, intellectual) of the poetic
work, how indeed demonstrate the full humanity of the poetic work itself,
both in the sense of the total human involvement of the artist-individual
as a thinking and moral—as well as sentient and imaginative—being, and
in the sense of his involvement as a real individual, all in all, historically
situated, and thus participant in a society and a civilisation? Were this
not the case, a materialist-realist aesthetics would be nothing more than
an ample dream. . . .

Let us now proceed to a rapid *sociological* reading of the Sophoclean
Antigone, that is, to a demonstration by example of the social, historical
conditioning of the poetic work. . . .

With regard to Greek poetry, and to *Antigone* in particular, Croce insisted that "poetry does not deal with 'problems,' but forms images of
life in action." He reproached Hegel with having been "too caught up in

the urgency and gravity of the problem which he himself was reflecting on and resolving in his own way, that of the State and its antinomies, to observe in his analysis the frontiers between religion, poetry and philosophy." Whatever may be true of Hegel, on which we will have a word to say in a moment, the following points against Croce seem incontestable in this particular case:

1) Without the Greek ethico-religious *concepts* of *hybris,* or human arrogance; of *sophrosyne,* or wisdom in the sense of moderation (its opposite); of *nemesis,* or celestial punishment; of *ananke,* or Necessity (or Destiny) as celestial plan, etc.; and therefore without the *problems* these generate, *Antigone* would actually have no *poetic* substance; nor, by the same token, would any Greek tragedy. Hence, abstracting and separating the "logical unity" from the "lyric unity," as is still done in Crocean fashion by so many aestheticizing critics, is the worst of methods.

2) As further confirmation: whether we take the *hybris* of Antigone, daughter of Oedipus, who disobeyed, in the name of the religious law of reverence for the dead, Creon's edict forbidding the burial of her brother, or whether we take the *hybris* of Creon who, agent and instrument of Gods intent on destroying the entire house of Labdacus, nonetheless committed an injustice exposing him to *nemesis,* by condemning Antigone to death—in either case, we arrive at the fulcrum of the tragic poem, from which radiate lyrical and dramatic aspects that are all the more poetic to the extent that they are the more expressive, precisely, of that specific Greek ethos. Consider, for example:

the sensible "wisdom" of her sister Ismene: So I, asking of those beneath the earth to pardon me, since I am compelled, will bow to those who hold the power. Little wisdom lies in action beyond one's strength. . . . Go, then, if you must. And yet be sure: mad though your going, dearly loved are you by those you love. (11. 65–69, 98–99)

the logic of the divine instrument, Creon: None can fully learn the heart, the mind, the judgment of a man until he proves himself in office. . . . I am no longer man, and she the man, if such power is hers unchallenged. (11. 175–78, 484–85)

Antigone reasoning before Creon: I did not think your orders were so strong, that you, a man, could cross the unwritten and unchanging laws of the gods. . . . Who knows if this be piety below? *C.:* A man hated, even dead, remains unloved. *A.:* Mine is not to hate, but to love. (11. 453–55, 521–23)

the second Chorus, on human hope: Hope ranges far to give help to many a man, but to others brings only the falsity of empty longing, pursuing him in stealth until he burns himself in its flame. He was wise indeed who said "Evil seems good to him a god would ruin." And brief is the time before the doom descends. (11. 615–23) *the logic of Creon confronted by his Haemon: C.:* To him who rules belongs the city. *H.:* A desert only would you rule alone. (11. 738–39)

the Antigone-Niobe lament, and her terrible reply to the Chorus: Pitiful was the end of the Phrygian stranger, Tantalus' daughter, covered over on the mountain by clinging rock that grew like ivy. Rain and snow yet fall upon her neck and from her weeping eyes upon the stones. A god shall bring me too to such an end. *Chor.:* Nay, for she was a goddess and sprang from gods. We are mortals only! To win a godlike lot, even in death, is fame for you. *A.:* You mock me! By our country's gods, can you not wait until I am gone to taunt me? (11. 824–39)

her final cry to the gods: I go, struck down, cut off from friends, to the caverns of the dead. What divine ordinance have I transgressed? Why look in such misery as mine to the gods for help? (11. 919–22)

the moral drawn by the Chorus and a punished Creon: Chor.: The right you see, but see too late! *C.:* I have learned in grief. Some god has struck me, has driven me to disaster, has overthrown my happiness and trampled upon it. Woe, woe for the sorrows of men! (11. 1270–75)

the final admonition of the Chorus to Creon: Pray no more. No man can fly his appointed doom. (11. 1338–39)

3) The most rigorous classical philology demonstrates that nothing was more foreign to the mind of Sophocles than a conflict in *Antigone* between religion and the State, since for him, a Greek, the State, the *polis*, is a part of the divine order itself (and not already, in modern style, a distinct and opposing organism). Antigone, concomitantly, can only incorporate in her feelings and her religious conduct the spirit of the true *polis*. If these are the facts, then we shall have to conclude that Hegel's error in his understanding of *Antigone* was not, as Croce supposed, that of having raised moral and philosophical *problems,* thereby crossing the frontier between poetry and philosophy (i.e., thought!), but rather of mistaking modern problems for those of antiquity. It was, in a word, a philological error. . . . And we are led to a second conclusion as well. What we have noted above concerning the profound relationship of Antigone to the *polis* brings into view the problematic of *Antigone* in its most acute form. Things being as they are, the poet himself (not merely the exemplary believer, Sophocles) recognizes here in the development of the Antigone-Creon *hybris* (far more than in the Oedipal *hybris*) the religious postulate: that misfortune, necessity (*ananke*), can also strike down the pious, the innocent, indeed, an Antigone; or rather, that divinity sees fit (the "game" of the gods with Man) to convert human undertaking and aim (even the noblest) into destiny, fatality, *ate*. This is hardly to say that this poetry does not deal with problems but solely with "images of life in action." Moreover, even if Croce was justified in objecting that in positivist criticism "*Antigone* had succumbed to a sort

of logical 'metabasis into another genus,'" that is, a displacement from the genus of poetry to that of history or philosophy, it remains true that the only alternative to positivist criticism is not, and cannot be, aestheticizing spiritualist criticism, but is, rather, philosophical-semantic criticism of an integrally functional variety, carried out wholly as a function of the *text qua historical product*. Such is . . . the instrument of judgment (critical-historiographic) furnished by a materialist aesthetics, and also the best experimental confirmation of the soundness of this method. . . .

Marx perceived the extreme complexity of the aesthetic problem when he posed it in rigorously materialist terms, and no longer in positivist terms (note that the latter are a critical burden of the Romantic and Idealist formulations). He thereby saw that the historical, social ties of the work of art cannot condition it mechanically or from the outside, but must make up in some way a part of the *sui generis* pleasure which it yields us, and thus must make up a part of the very substance of the work of art as such: its *structural, intellectual* substance, as we have seen. . . . The *cultural superstructure* (to which poetry and art in general belong) is genuinely tied, not mechanically but dialectically, to the socio-economic *base*, and one can *demonstrate*, by bringing to light *structural*-poetic networks, . . . that neither Antigone "nor Achilles nor Vulcan, etc.," would have been "possible" with "Roberts & Co." or "the Crédit Immobilier" or "the hail of shot and shell," as Marx put it.[8] For each of these poetic characters presupposes and contains within its *structure* as a poetically meaningful organism conditions and historical reasons quite other than our modern ones; quite other ideological or cultural conditions (moral, religious, scientific, etc.), as we have seen, and in implicit form, quite other economic and material conditions. This state of affairs, naturally, suggests and even gives support to the law, glimpsed by Engels, which may be called "the law of extended periods." "The further from the economic sphere the particular (cultural) sphere investigated (e.g., a given artistic period), the more it will approximate to a purely abstract ideology, and the more it will show accidents (and also peculiarities) in its development, with a zig-zag curve"; but "if one traces the *mean axis* of the curve, one will find that this axis runs more and more closely parallel to the curve of the economic development the *longer* the (historical) period considered and the *wider* the (ideological) sector examined.". . .

Superstructure and Base

Our theory of the poetic or literary work has led to the problem of the superstructure to which the work belongs, and therefore to the question of its relationships to an infrastructure, the economic and social base.

We have seen the inconceivability and impossibility of the poetry of, for example, Antigone, without the language of the religious-ethical mythology of the caste society of Sophocles' time, and the related institutions implicit in a primitive economy. . . . Similarly, the *Divina Commedia* would have been impossible without the teleological, tropological language of Catholic culture in medieval society, with all its implicit economic institutions ranging from the feudal to the communal; *Faust*, without the language of the ideology of bourgeois humanism, Idealistic and pantheistic, of the age of Goethe (and the related flourishing economy of free enterprise); and Mayakowsky's poem, "V. I. Lenin," without the language of the Marxist ideology of the October Revolution and the related Soviet society, with its socialist economy; and so on. . . .

Our analysis of Antigone enabled us to see, by bringing to light poetic-structural complexes, that neither the literary figure of Antigone nor any other such figures would be possible with Roberts & Co. For each of these poetic organisms refers back—in the name of the very meanings of its structural or poetic values—to historical, social and implicitly economic conditions; the value-contents are coherent with those conditions of Greek antiquity, and not with medieval or modern conditions. Greek art, as Marx said, "does not presuppose just any mythology, just any thoughtless artistic elaboration of nature (objective elements and society included), but Greek mythology." For example, "Egyptian mythology could never have been the terrain or matrix of Greek art." In each case, "*a* mythology was needed." This, in turn, presupposes one economy (primitive, pastoral, etc.) and not another. And yet "the low stage of social (-economic) evolution" in which Greek art matured "does not stand in contradiction to the fascination which, as the art of a people in their 'historical childhood,' it exercises on us." This fascination is, rather, "a result indissolubly connected with the fact that the immature social (-economic) conditions, in which it emerged and could only have emerged, can never return." Such is Marx's reply to the current observation, superficial and abstract, and first reported by Marx himself, that "in art it is notable that particular periods of flourishing do not stand in an absolute relationship to the general development of the society, nor therefore to its material base." Distracted bourgeois critics, for example, René Wellek and Austin Warren, took this observation as Marx's own, and as signifying that "in this passage he seems to renounce unequivocally the Marxist position." Whereas Marx cautions immediately that "the difficulty lies only in the general [i.e., the historical-philosophical] formulation of these contradictions; no sooner are they specified than they are already cleared up." And here Engels' insight (earlier noted) is pertinent: the "mean axis" of the historico-cultural curve of a particular ideology or field of the superstructure (e.g., artistic) becomes more and more "nearly parallel" to the axis of the historical curve of economic and material development "the longer the (historical) period considered and the wider the (ideological) field examined." And Engels had already observed that when one deals, not simply with the State, the Law, or Private Right, but with ideological forms such as "philosophy and religion," and with art, the connection (*Zusammenhang*) of the ideas with their material conditions becomes "ever more complicated and obscure, given all the intermediate links," but it nevertheless *exists*. And in sum it is characteristic of ideologies and cultures worthy of the name to embrace, in their universality, long periods, during which the corresponding types of economic factors have a way, so to speak, of evolving their particular traits in an evident parallelism with the cultural or superstructural factors. (We have referred to this parallelism and the problems it raises by repeatedly using such expressions as "implicit" and "implicitly" to portray the nature of the relationship between the ideology which consists of poetic or literary ideas and the corresponding "existent" economic conditions.) We see once more that only by way of an acknowledgement of the *intellectual* (though always concrete) character of the poetic work can one possibly demonstrate its power to "mirror" the society, and hence, its *ideology*. It is a flagrant contradiction, therefore, to claim such powers and yet to think of art—as some Marxist philosophers of art continue to do—as intuitive knowledge, or knowledge "by images," in abstract antithesis to a science taken to be knowledge "by concepts". . . .

II

Marxist Method: Plekhanov, Lukács, "Critical Realism"

The merits of current Marxist method [are at least three]. First, it has substituted a more concrete method for the Hegelian method of philosophical interpretation of works of art. Plekhanov: "As a follower of the materialist conception of the world, I say that the *first task* of the critic consists in translating the ideas in a work of art from the language of art to the language of sociology, in order to locate what may be called the sociological equivalent of a given literary phenomenon." Lukács: Artistic concentration is "the maximum intensification *qua* content of the social and human essence of any situation whatsoever." Second, Marxist method of interpretation has rediscovered in the modern world the aesthetic problem of *content*, and its bearing on the internal economy of the work of art, in contrast to the formalism of "art for art's sake" and the like. Plekhanov: "The prevalence of form over content: vacuity and harshness; beauty is concordance of form and content." Lukács: "It is superficial to criticize a bad writer solely for his formal deficiencies. If we contrast an empty and epidermal portrayal of life with real human and social life, . . . the formal defects will reveal themselves simply as consequences of a fundamental lack of content: appealing to life shows up of itself the emptiness of insignificant artistic reproductions." Third, Marxist method has made some apt—because well measured—historiographic applications of its criteria. For example, the critical notes of Plekhanov on the novels of Balzac and on their value for an understanding of the society of the French Restoration and Louis-Philippe (though preceded in this direction by Engels, in the famous letter to Margaret Harkness of April 1888) [9]; and also in his notes on *Madame Bovary.* "Here there is no question of indifference to content. Here we have an attentive examination and an accurate representation of the everyday way of life of the bourgeoisie. . . . Here we have an ideal enthusiasm and an impassioned rejection of the milieu. But when the enthusiasm fails, there remains only description for the sake of description, and boredom soon sets in." We must also note the essays by Lukács on European and Russian realism, especially those on Balzac, Stendhal, Zola and Tolstoy. . . .

A defect of current Marxist method lies in those historiographic applications (a majority, indeed) in which the personal taste of the critic fails to remedy in some fashion . . . deficiencies in the criteria. For example, Plekhanov's interpretation of the poetic quality of Ibsen's *Ghosts, Doll House,* and *Pillars of Society* is substantially mistaken. He reproaches Ibsen the artist for his bourgeois moral ideas ("purity of will," ethical "individualism," etc.) and his fundamental "weakness" of not being able to find "any way out of the moral into the political" (read: the socially-militant); *hence* his dramatic moral discourses are marred by nebulous and incoherent oratory, and his poetic symbols are marred by "abstractness," "testifying to a poverty of social thought." Plekhanov fails to recognize in Ibsen a satire of the petty bourgeoisie. Lukács, much more aptly, links Ibsen and the "preacher" Tolstoy, and recognizes in passing that "Ibsen, too, . . . triumphed over his contemporaries, even from a purely artistic point of view, precisely by means of a similar pathos as a preacher." Or consider the lack of understanding by Lukács of *Madame Bovary,* which he accuses of descriptions for their own sake, in a word, of formalism. . . . Or the passage in which Lukács complains that Flaubert tried to "overcome solely with technical (*sic*) and artistic means" the "immobility," the "empty and disconsolate grayness" of his mediocre heros, in an attempt "doomed to failure" because "the mediocrity of the average man stems from the fact that the *social antinomies* which determine his existence objectively do not attain in him their maximum tension, remaining instead obfuscated in a superficial equilibrum." Thus, Flaubert is condemned for having given artistic life to social contents which are not those, presumably, of Zola, and which, in a word, do not correspond to the social ideas of his sociological critic, who meanwhile forgets how much he remains in Flaubert's debt for the sum of (poetic) *truth* possessed by those "two mediocrities" (Flaubert's phrase). . . . For other inadequate interpretations by Lukács, see his studies on Hölderlin, whose Enlightenment-Progressivist aspect is noted, but not the Romanticism into which the former flows to gain strength and character; or his studies on Goethe, in which much of the personage of Mephistopheles escapes, while we dwell in compensation, but excessively, on the "small property" of Philomen and Baucis destined to be swallowed up by the large industrial property of Faust; or his studies on Kleist, etc. . . .

As for the Lukácsian methodological concept of a "critical realism" as precursor to socialist realism, with its major example in Thomas Mann, we must say at once that we are doubtful, if only because of certain of the negative results for literary history to which it leads. The poetic originality of a Proust, a Joyce, a Kafka, the last great narrators of the decadent bourgeoisie, is inadequately appreciated by comparison to the refined but second-hand bourgeois art of a Mann, epigone—however genial—of nineteenth-century realism. To speak in somewhat more detail, consider the quality of the poetic testimony to the bourgeois crises . . . represented by Proust's *Remembrance of Things Past,* with its analysis of the decay of the French *élites* of the time of World War I, an analysis, be it noted, conducted by an intellectual method that could not be more significantly bourgeois-individualistic in its use of inner, contemplative memory (whence a narration that is a sort of *artistic* autobiography of the author-protagonist). Or consider the testimonial quality of Joyce's *Ulysses* which, with its literary technique of an interior monologue in which sounds a negative, ironic, anti-heroic counterpoint of classical myths and everyday facts, is a *Summa* and a judgment of our humanitarian bourgeois civilization, in the sense that its justification is couched in terms of its thoroughly devitalized centers of daily existence. Recall, for example, the declaration that it is love, the opposite of hatred, that is really life; proferred with pathetic absurdity by the lone protagonist Leopold Bloom in that lair of modern Cyclopeans, the Dublin tavern, gathering-place of supremely normal "citizens," superpatriotic and racist. Then compare the positive atmosphere in which Tolstoy's heros move so confidently, so actively, so vibrantly. Consider also the poetic testimony to the bourgeois crisis of *The Trial, The Castle,* and the Kafka tales, with their hallucinatory, satirical allegories of existential anguish, religious and metaphysical. Lukács runs the risk of a profound contradiction regarding this narrative poetry—which he does make some effort to analyze, in contrast to his writing on Proust and Joyce. He invokes the term "allegory" in a pejorative sense, denies that Kafka succeeded in "elevating the singular particular to the particularity of the typical," and at the same time admits that in Kafka "the conceiving of particulars is selective, so as to effectively underscore the essential."

If we reflect on these matters, we may ask ourselves what to make of the drama of *Death in Venice,* or the confession of the dehumanization of the romantic-decadent artist of *Tonio Kröger,* or the tragedy of the end of a great Hanseatic family in *Buddenbrooks*—what to make of the "always immanent" bourgeois writer, Thomas Mann, in Lukács' phrase—in comparison to a section of Proust, or Joyce, or Kafka. We cannot make small of him, to be sure: compared, for example, to the self-satisfied decadent art of a Gide, Mann certainly represents an artistically superior realism. Nevertheless, his are only *episodic* visions of the crisis of our times, because they are visions without a profound, problematic center. Moreover, the legacy of Kafka is plain enough, in Camus, in *The Stranger* and *Cross-Purpose,* for example, as is that of Proust in Virginia Woolf, and that of both Kafka and Joyce in Beckett (*Waiting for Godot,* etc.); and also that of Joyce in the farces of Ionesco. But the art of Mann, though bourgeois and an art of crisis, has no heirs, so far as we know: a fact that is not without significance. . . . Thus, the ultimate alternatives formulated by Lukács, namely: "Franz Kafka or Thomas Mann? Artistically interesting decadence, or veracious critical realism?" is wholly artificial, and leads away from adequate, concrete aesthetic appreciation of the two authors. For neither was a precursor in his art of socialist-realist truth. Moreover, the characteristic of "critical realism" ascribed by Lukács to the art of Mann, for all its bourgeois-decadent character, is superfluous: it can in no way serve to show the *distinctive* character of such art, for the overall reason that authentic poetry is always realistically (sociologically) truthful, and therefore also "critical," which is to say, non-unilateral, being truth. In addition, the art of Mann is not "critical realism" because its "immanent"—hence episodic and chronicling—quality, far from constituting a high merit in the face of the profoundly allegorical (or if you wish, symbolic) art of Kafka, obviously marks its limitations and its relatively inferior value (as truth) compared to Kafka (or to Proust or Joyce, for that matter). Consequently one should, if anything, make the opposite choice than the one suggested by the "alternatives," if there were any aesthetic-methodological sense in speaking about alternatives and choices. . . .

It must be said once more that where there is authentic poetry (but one has to make the effort to find it beyond any preconceived schematism of "contents"), there is always sociological truth and therefore realism, that is to say, a *symbolic* representation rich in multiple, organically-contextually-defined meanings, or "polysignificant" language. The representation is therefore always in one way or another a *judgment:* of a social and historical reality. It may be the optimistic and constructive bourgeois realism of a Fielding or a Balzac, etc., which Lukács recognizes, or the pessimistic-constructive realism of a Swift, as Brecht has remarked (and we are thinking not only, for example, of the Houyhnhnms of *Gulliver's Travels,* but also of the *Modest Proposal*). It can be the variously pessimistic-apocalyptic realism of the Eliots, Prousts, Joyces, and Kafkas, or the modest "immanent" realism, the *"hic et nunc,"* of a Mann. Or finally, the new optimistic and constructive realism which is the socialist realism of Mayakowsky and Brecht (for all their hyperboles and paraboles). . . . Does it perhaps require so great an effort as to seem impossible (though it is not) for the Social Democrats to come to understand, today, the negtaive but very instructive lesson (true by virtue of its artistic, hence sociological, truth) concerning the crisis of our times, furnished by the great literature of decadence of Eliot and Proust and Joyce and Kafka? To stop for a moment on the last of these, how deny the edifying feeling of moral nightmare aroused in us by the representation in *The Castle* of the life of K. and the other personages: sordid to the extreme, almost subhuman, because suffering from an elemental religious alienation, which is consubstantial to every other alienation, accompanying it really, historically, wherever man crouches in fear and trembling of oppressive authorities that are in varying ways as transcendent as the divine authority that sanctifies them? It is difficult to deny the edifying nourishment of truth in this sort of black humor which is the "religious humor" of Kafka (the astute phrase is Thomas Mann's). But to find it one must work from the inside of its artistic expression, from its polysignificant symbols: the inaccessible "castle" and its cruel and hypocritical "administration" of the "village," within which are at work, for example, the Goethean and Ibsenesque (and even Dantesque) motif of the eternal feminine intercessor and savior, etc., which turns into the preordained prostitution of a woman who can procure "bureaucratic" favors, i.e., favors "from on high," and thus becomes a principle of abjectness and frustration without end, etc., etc. One cannot start from external preoccupations, as Lukács does when he invokes *tout court,* "the ancient Hapsburg monarchy," etc., *without the mediation* of the central meaning of the poetic symbols. . . .

Engels, Lenin, and the Poetics of Socialist Realism

If we look at the errors we have noted in the criticism of Plekhanov and Lukács—for example, Plekhanov's mistaken interpretation of the poetry of Ibsen's works, and Lukács' mistaken interpretation of the poetry of Flaubert's works, etc.—we see their lack of comprehension of the fundamental lesson of Engels concerning the realistic art of the reactionary

Balzac, a lesson later applied by Lenin to Tolstoy's work.[10] For Engels
and Lenin had a solution to the issue on which depends the being or
non-being of an Aesthetics of Realism, and consequently, of a Poetics of
Socialist Realism: the matter of the necessary presence in a poetic work
of *ideas* as such, with no qualifiers attached—*not* simply "non-false"
ideas, non-reactionary ideas, or progressive ideas. Their replies are one
and the same: whether we are speaking of a French artist of Legitimist or
Monarchical ideas of 1840 and thereafter, or of a Russian artist of mystical-
populist ideas of 1905, the conclusion is identical, *notwithstanding the
differences* in the lessons of (artistic) truth that emerge from the two
authors: in both cases, one is faced with artistic realism. In Balzac's case,
the truth of his art, which earns him the title of Realist, consists in his
"having seen," *in spite of* his own ideological sympathies, the "true men
of the future," the bourgeois adversaries. In Tolstoy's case, the truth of
his art consists in his having seen men and things *conformably* to his
own ideological sympathies, and yet, in being able to teach the revolutionary proletariat to "know better" their "adversaries," precisely by
having reflected in his poetic work "at least some essential features" of the
"Revolution," that is, the peasant "masses" made "as they were," rebellious in spirit but quite unprepared. In Balzac's case, in other words,
the artistic realism consists in the author's seeing the progressive adversaries not with less but with more truth than his own side. In Tolstoy's
case, it consists in his seeing with the greater truthfulness his own side
and his own ideas, both unprogressive. But the result is the same: the
truth (artistic, be it noted). And the incalculable benefit, particularly for
any revolutionary worthy of the name, lies in *knowing better* (by this
artistic, rather than scientific means) the *reality* of both his progressive
and his reactionary predecessors: knowledge which is quite indispensable
for action. The error of Plekhanov and of Lukács lies in not having understood this fact, the very basis of the teaching of Engels and Lenin. The
error is all the more serious in the case of their substantially unintelligent
interpretation of an Ibsen and a Flaubert. Ibsen was an uneasy liberal
and democrat to whom we owe an unsurpassed representation of cruel
hypocrisy and bourgeois lies, and thus of the *antinomy within* individualistic morality. The antinomy is certainly insoluble *from within,* but without an Ibsen we would understand little enough of a socialist playwright
like Brecht, or better, without Ibsen and the world reflected in Ibsen,
there would be no Brecht, it would be meaningless to speak of a Brecht.
Flaubert was an agnostic in politics to whom we owe the discovery of
one of the most profound features of bourgeois mores: the vice of
romantic evasion of the non-working woman, i.e., *"le Bovarisme."* Neither
of these is surely any less *instructive* for the socialist revolutionary than

a Balzac and a Tolstoy—whereas a Pasternak is not instructive at all, because he is not enough of an artist.

The fundamental issue of a Poetics of Socialist Realism, which was perceived by Engels and Lenin, can be resolved, then, by way of the necessary presence in the poetic work of *ideas* or ideologies—as such, and without qualifying reservations; or, what amounts to the same thing, because *truth* counts *too* in a *poetic* work. Truth, as we have seen, that does not conflict but coincides with *tendentiousness, theses*—and also with relative *typicality*, from Dante to Mayakowsky. This does not exclude, however paradoxical it may seem, a *poetics* (as distinct from an aesthetics) of *socialist* realism, but indeed implies it, on the principle that without *ideas in general*, and therefore our ideas as well, there is no poetry; together with the further principle of the *tendentiousness* or inevitable *historical determination* of every idea. For us, in our time, therefore, the only practical *artistic ideal* is to realize a *socialist* realism. For this, we have the *right* to do battle; and not a mere *claim* because we have *had* to recognize the equal right of artistic and poetic ideals of the past. We have the right in the name of the *sociological and realist truth* of poetry *in general*, which is recognized in the halls of Aesthetics. There would seem to be no other way to ground, that is, to justify rigorously, a Poetics of Socialist Realism. Certainly a host of problems arise, from that of the various modes of poetic or artistic truth (which cannot exclude anachronism, for example), to that of the exact meaning of such expressions as "decadent poetry," etc. But we cannot elude these problems on the ground that they might be pseudo-problems or refinements of contemplative philosophy. The observations by Engels and Lenin on Balzac and Tolstoy should suffice in this regard. Their observations are still waiting for a demonstration that they are not (as the overwhelming majority of Marxists here and abroad believe) happy critical remarks of a merely *particular* value, but are, as we believe, observations from which can be derived a truly objective aesthetic *law*.

Notes

[1] The Romantic and Idealist tradition, with its emphasis since Kant (1724–1804), Vico (1668–1744), Coleridge (1772–1834), and numerous nineteenth-century thinkers on a "poetic imagination" inimical to concepts and reason, dominated Italian aesthetics and criticism during the first half of this century in the powerful philosophical figure of Benedetto Croce (1866–1952). Della Volpe's Marxism proposes to begin, therefore, by meeting this pervasive influence head-on. (—Eds.)

[2] The reference is to Croce (see footnote 1), for whom aesthetic experience was an *intuitional*—vs. conceptual—mode of *knowledge*. (—Eds.)

[3] Brooks, Cleanth, and Warren, Robert Penn, *Understanding Poetry*, rev. ed. (New York: Holt, 1950), p. 645.

[4] From Dante's *canzone*, "Tre donne intorno al cor mi son venute." In prose translation: "From a spring the Nile is born a little river / Where the great light / Denies the earth the osier's leaf. . . ." (*—Eds.*)

[5] Della Volpe's play on the root "common" (found in our "communicativeness") is more evident in Italian than in English (*"communi,"* fem. plur., and *"communicarsi,"* refl. inf.). (*—Eds.*)

[6] See footnote 1. (*—Eds.*)

[7] Lodovico Castelvetro (1505–71), Italian critic. (*—Eds.*)

[8] See chapter 2, K. Marx, "Production and Consumption" from Introduction to the *Critique of Political Economy.* (*—Eds.*)

[9] See chapter 4, F. Engels, "Letter to Margaret Harkness, April 1888," in "Realism and Didacticism." (*—Eds.*)

[10] *Ibid.*

16. Christopher Caudwell

Beauty and Bourgeois Aesthetics

CHRISTOPHER CAUDWELL, pen-name of Christopher St. John
Sprigg (1909–37), an English writer, by training a newspaperman,
who in a career cut short by his death as a member of the International Brigade in the Spanish Civil War, still managed to write a
number of novels and non-fiction works on topics as diverse as art,
the philosophy of science, and aeronautics. His best-known work, on
the social evolution of art, is *Illusion and Reality* (1937). Other books,
also published posthumously, include *Studies in a Dying Culture*
(1938), *The Crisis in Physics* (1939), and *Further Studies in a Dying
Culture* (1949) from which the following essay is taken.

. . . EXCEPT in action, truth is meaningless. To attempt to find it in a mere
scrutiny of the conscious field, by 'pure' thought, results not in truth but in
mere consistency. The contents of the mind are measured against themselves without the incursion of a disturbance from outside, which disturbances in fact, in the past history of the field, are what have created it.
Since innumerable consistent worlds are possible, there would be as
many criteria of reality as there were people with different conscious
experiences.

But action upon nature demands cooperation if it is to be fully effective.
The organism which will be most in possession of truth, which will
most deeply penetrate and widely change the environment, will be an
organism able to cooperate with other organisms in that change. The
very combination, by division of labor, produces a qualitative change.
What millions of organisms do separately is nothing compared to what
they can do in cooperation to a common goal. Truth appears as an
outcome of the labor process, for it is the labor process that demands
and at the same time dictates the cooperation of organisms.

Thus a mediating term now appears in truth, which we first analyzed
as an outcome of the bare organism faced by bare environment. But now
the bare organism faces society and its culture, and the bare environment

199

faces, not the lone organism, but the tremendous apparatus of cooperating men.

In fact this occurred from the very beginning. The labor process itself generates the cooperation which changes and expands the responses of the organism, and gives rise to sufficiently many new situations to make it possible to talk of 'truth'. From the very start the labor process, by the society it generates, acts as a mediating term in the production of truth.

From the very start the labor process gives rise to material capital. Simple enough at first, taking the form of mere tools, customs, magico-scientific objects, seeds, huts, these were yet all-important as the beginnings of culture. To our argument they bear this important relation, that all such enduring products represent social truths. The plough is as much a statement about the nature of reality as the instructions how to use it. Each is useless without the other; each makes possible the development of the other. All these social products are generated by the nature of reality, but their form is given by the organism in its interaction with reality. The nature of fields and plants imposes on the organisms specific types of cooperation in sowing and reaping and determines the shape of the plough. It imposes on them language, whereby they signify to each other their duties and urge each other on in carrying them out. Once established the labor process, extending as remotely as observation of the stars, as widely as organization of all human relations, and as abstractedly as the invention of numbers, gathers and accumulates truth. Faster and faster it proliferates and moves. The bare organism is today from birth faced with an enormous accumulation of social truth in the form of buildings, laws, books, machines, political forms, tools, engineering works, complete sciences. All these arise from cooperation; all are social and common. Generated by this capital, truth is the past relation of society to the environment accumulated in ages of experience. It is actually created by the conflict of social organisms with new situations in the course of the labor process.

But the very richness and complexity of this 'frozen' truth, the very elaborateness of an advanced culture and a functioning society, ensures that the naked organism will be confronted with the greatest possible variety of 'situations'. This will ensure the greatest possible activity of a man's consciousness, and the maximum of mutual transformation of his responses, his instincts, and the material environment. There will be a rapid ingression of newness. This itself will generate new truth. Man, as experiencing individual, will find himself constantly negating the truths given in his social environment.

Thus we see the cause of the apparent antinomies in truth. Truth appears to be in the environment, to be objective and independent of me. Yet the attempt to extract a completely non-subjective truth from experience produces only metrics. Moreover the environment changes only slowly, but the truth of science or reality as known to man has changed rapidly.

Truth, then, is in my environment, that is, in my culture, in the enduring products of the labor process. Thus truths, although similar in their lack of newness and fixation to my inherited responses, are yet different in that responses emerge from the unconscious, *inside* me, whereas the inheritances of culture come to me as 'situations', as things learned, taught, or told me, as experience, as *environment*. But I do not regard myself as bound to the social criteria of truth; on the contrary it is my task to change their formulations, where my experience contradicts them.

But, it will be urged, we were to discuss beauty, and now it is only truth we have obtained. Writing when bourgeois English poetry was at its height at the same time as bourgeois German philosophy was reaching its climax, Keats said:

> 'Beauty is truth, truth is beauty'—that is all
> Ye know on earth, and all ye need to know.

A modern bourgeois poet, T. S. Eliot, has announced himself unable to understand these lines of Keats, just as modern bourgeois philosophers show themselves unable to understand Hegel's dialectics. But we saw that the pursuit of truth was the study of the objective elements in the conscious field. We saw further that completely objective elements could never be obtained. A world built up in such a way dissolved into mere metrics, and truth became consistency. To every percept and thought, an affect or subjective tinge inevitably attached itself. We never had a mere situation but always a response to a situation.

Thus truth never stands by itself as 'pure'. It is always generated in action, in instinctive organismal response going out into the situation and modifying both itself and the situation, begetting emotion as a result. Absolute, static, eternal truth is thus impossible.

But every such action involves a desire, a volition, aim, fear, disgust, or hope. Thus truth is always tinged with the subject and with emotion. This is not a discoloration. As we saw, any thoroughgoing attempt to wash truth clean of such affective discoloration simply washed the world away, for it becomes bare geometry. We do not feel ourselves passively responding to a situation, we feel active and subjective and seats of innovation. Necessarily so, because each transaction with a situation changes us, and therefore makes us a new center of force. This is expressed directly in consciousness.

If we sort out of consciousness all the subjective elements we now orientate the same field *in an entirely different way*. The connection between conscious contexts is no longer outer reality, but the responses. We now group all the conscious contexts into like responses (love, fear, self-preservation). The laws of thought now become the laws of affective association. The affective association of ideas discovered by Freud, which threw a flood of light upon dreams, is not so much the discovery of a secret connection as a law arising from our mode of analysis of conscious contents. If we sort them according to the responses of somatic components, we discover ideas to be affectively associated. If we sort them according to the situation or environmental components, we find them to be associated by contiguity and other laws taken from the environment. Both methods are equally correct. Both affect and thought, both response and situation, are given in the one conscious glow.

When we are concerned with dream and day-dream, attention is introverted; the body ceases to be closely concerned with the situation. The response or instinctive element in consciousness then becomes dominant. Hence the value of the Freudian or affective analysis of consciousness in such states. The 'deeper', and more somatic, the innervations, the more dominating becomes the response. The more external and sensory the innervations, the more dominating becomes the situation. The environment rather than the instinct gives the main clue to the structure of the perceptual field; the response lays bare the secret structure of the fantastic field.

A development may take place. The body may be introverted, and unconcerned with its immediate environment, and yet it will not be dreaming, it will be thinking. It will be striving to mold its dream according to the nature of all past situations, according to its experience of outer reality. It will be attempting to realize the laws of outer reality, and penetrate its nature. This is science. It is a scientist thinking, however crudely, for there has been genuine synthesis between almost unconscious dream full of somatic drives and conscious perception, full of environmental shape. These have been fused in thought. Dream draws vividness and restraint from perception; perception gets a flexibility of recombination, an onward drive to a goal, from dream. The result is thought, as rational scientific thought.

But the same development leads to another. Behavior is not only intra-somatic and conscious; it is also overt and visible in action. The organism is conscious, and is acted on by the environment, but it also behaves and acts on the environment. In its behavior it is guided by perception, but perception cannot present it with a goal. Perception guides it but it is impelled by 'instinct'. The somatic element in consciousness now figures as a program for change—what we 'want to do'. In trying to bring about our wishes, they too are transformed.

But perception is not 'pure' perception—perception *only* of the present situation. By introversion, by stiffening dream with the memories of past perceptions, perception has become 'rational' thought. Perception is widened into a general scheme of reality as experienced over a time. Reason, or congealed cognition, now guides instinct. In helping to change the environment, cognition too is modified and becomes truer and subtler.

But how can I by myself effect more than the slightest change in my environment? I need the cooperation of other men. But this involves perceptions held in common: we must all have similar views of reality. Reason and perception therefore become social, become crystallized in languages, tools, techniques. This has the advantage that I can now draw not only on my brief experience of percepts, but on the combined and sifted experiences of thousands of generations, preserved in language, tool, or technique. This has become dominating. Even from the start it was so; man found himself, by the necessities of the labor process, sharing a common view of reality, and inheriting the seeds, experience, and advice of a preceding generation. Even before language, the labor process, if it involved only common hunting tactics not inherited but taught, would involve a common world-view however crude, and would generate a Truth resident not wholly in oneself but also in one's environment. Thus long before science has a name or a distinct existence, it is generated as a social product. Truth is created and extended before the concept could exist, as part of the labor process.

But the labor process, involving a social view of the necessities of the environment, a general consciousness in man of laws existing outside him in reality, involves also a social unity of response to these necessities and this environment. The interaction produces a change, and as the change becomes more willed, it generates increasing consciousness not only of the structure of reality but also of one's own needs. The goal is a blend of what is possible and what is desirable; just as consciousness is a blend of what is response and what is situation. Or, to be more precise, just as consciousness is the product of a tension between response and situation which do not precisely fit each other, so the goal is a product of a tension between what is possible and what is desirable. They are forced to meet; they are synthesized; and as a result both are changed, are fused into an attainable goal. Of all possibles and all desirables, the laws of reality enforce only one wedding, and the child is a new generation.

But if the desirable is to be held clearly in mind, if all action is somatically motivated, or *willed,* and therefore has an affective as well as a perceptual element—then there must be a community of desire as well as a community of perception. There must be a community of instinct, as well as a community of cognition. The heart, as well as the reason, must be social. The community must share a body in common, as well as an environment in common. Its hopes, as well as its beliefs, must be one. This hope, which is the opposite to science, we may call art. Just as Truth is the aim of science, Beauty is the end of art.

But both deflate abjectly if we attempt to isolate them. If we try to get them 'pure' we get nothing. Both are products of the living organism in the real world, and this means that every element is determined both by organism and environment.

We saw that the pursuit of Truth, and the separation of all environmental elements in the conscious field, produced not Truth but consistency. It produced an unreal dematerialized world, devoid of quality; in fact a mere series of equations. The Pursuit of Beauty, and the separation of all affective elements in the conscious field, produces not Beauty but physiology. We get merely the body with its reactions.

But both Truth and Beauty are in fact generated already blended in action, in the social labor process visualized throughout human history. In this they are indivisible. Both continually play into each other's hands. Science makes the percepts, the possibilities, the world with which the body's desire concerns itself, continually richer and more subtle. Art makes the body's incursions into reality always more audacious, more curious, and more indefatigable.

Of course to the bourgeois with his ideal closed worlds, Truth and Beauty, art and science, appear not as creative opposites but as eternal antagonists. Even Keats, who saw their kinship, could yet complain that science had robbed the rainbow of its beauty. This is because science and art, as long as they seem something distinct, situated in the environment entirely on the one hand (science) and in the heart entirely on the other (art), must seem exclusive and inimical. They seem to raise up two different worlds, of which we can choose one only. One is bare of quality, and the other is destitute of reality, so that we cannot rest easily on either horn of the dilemma. Only when we see that the separation is artificial and that response and situation are involved throughout consciousness and are part and parcel of the social process which generates both truth and beauty—only then can we see that there is no such deadly rivalry as we supposed, but that on the contrary these opposites each create the other. The 'secret' connection between the two is the world of concrete society.

In all social products, therefore, affect and percept, response and situation, inevitably mingle. They do not merely mingle, they activate each other. In language every word has an affective as well as a cognitive value. The weight of each value varies in each case. Some words, such as interjections, are almost entirely affective. Others, such as scientific names, are almost entirely cognitive. But an entirely affective language —that is, sounds having only affective associations—ceases to be language. It becomes music. An entirely cognitive language—that is, sounds having only cognitive associations—also ceases to be a language; it becomes mathematics. In doing so, both seem to exchange roles. Music no longer refers to outer reality; but it does not disappear into the body; it becomes for the body outer reality. For the body, listening to the music, the sounds are now environment; nothing is referred to. Mathematics, though it has no affective reference, does not disappear into the environment. On the contrary it becomes pure thought; it becomes the body operating on the environment. Cognition and affection can never be separated. The attempt to do so simply begets a new thing, in which they are united again.

Not only language but all social products have an affective role. Each society evolves its own gestures, deportment, and manners. These include a reference to reality, a pointing to something, the necessary opening of doors to get through them, or lifting of food to feed oneself, or moving of legs to get from one place to another. But these actions also include an affective element: all can be done 'beautifully' or artistically. One can point with an air, open a door politely, feed oneself quietly and 'off silver', walk slowly and with dignity. All this is beauty; all this is desirable; all this is a social product. Different societies have quite different notions of what is desirable in these things.

All objects, from a house to a hat, share these cognitive and affective elements. A hat has a real cognitive environmental function, so has a house. The hat must keep rain and sun off our heads; the house must keep out wind and weather, resist perhaps the robber and marauder. But both are modified by the affective element. The hat must add honor, dignity and grace to the head. The house must express respectability or power; and must contain rooms of a certain shape and size, because of the manners and social customs of the age.

Action designed only to express an affective purpose becomes, like music, an environment; dancing is a *spectacle*. Action designed only to express a cognitive purpose, and to achieve a goal which is not in itself really desired, becomes action in itself desirable, as in the mock-flights and trivial goals of sport, in which all energies are bent on securing something not really to be desired. Between sport and dancing stretch all the forms of action designed to secure an affective but real goal, that is, all forms of work, from sowing and reaping to factory production.

All forms of representation have the same duality. The faithful congruence of representation to reality, robbed of all affective elements, becomes not really a representation at all, but a symbol—the diagram. The attempt to make representation purely affective, without reference to environment, produces what is in itself an environment—the town and the building. Between lies the richness of pictorial illustration—the painting, the sculpture, the film, and the play.

In primitive civilization this intimate generation of truth and beauty in the course of the labor process and their mutual effect on each other is so clear that it needs no elaboration. The harvest is work, but it is also dance; it deals with reality, but it is also pleasure. All social forms, gestures, and manners have to primitives a purpose, and are both affective and cognitive. Law is not merely the elucidation of a truth in dispute, but the satisfaction of the gods, of the innate sense of rightness in man's desires. Myths express man's primitive instincts and his view of reality. The simplest garment or household utensil has a settled beauty. Work is performed in time to singing, and has its own fixed ceremony. All tasks have their lucky days. Truth and beauty, science and art are primitive, but at least they are vitally intermingled, each giving life to the other.

It is the special achievement of later bourgeois civilization to have robbed science of desirability and art of reality. The true is no longer beautiful, because to be true in bourgeois civilization is to be non-human. The beautiful is no longer real, because to be beautiful in bourgeois civilization is to be imaginary.

This itself is simply a product of the fundamental bourgeois position. Our own proposition about beauty is this: whenever the affective elements in socially known things show social ordering, there we have beauty, there alone we have beauty. The business of such ordering is art, and this applies to all socially known things, to houses, gestures, narratives, descriptions, lessons, songs and labor.

But to the bourgeois this proposition seems monstrous, for he has been reared on the anarchy of the social process. He refuses to recognize it. He recognizes only one social process—commodity-manufacture, and one social tie—the market. The bourgeois produces for and buys from the market, governed as an individual by social relations masquerading as laws of supply and demand.

Thus any attempt at social consciousness which necessarily involves the manipulation of desires, i.e., of 'the laws' of supply and demand, seems to him outrageous. But this is just what art is—the manipulation or social ordering of desires, and therefore of the laws of supply and demand. Art gives values which are not those of the market but are use-values. Art makes 'cheap' things precious and a few splashes of paint a social treasure. Hence the market is the fierce enemy of the artist. The blind working of the market murders beauty. All social products, hats, cars, houses, household utensils and clothes, become in the main unbeautiful and 'commercialized', precisely because the maker in producing them does not consider social process, does not scheme how to order socially their affective values in accordance with their use, but merely how to satisfy a demand for them with the maximum profit to himself. This extends finally to those products which have no other purpose than affective ordering—paintings, films, novels, poetry, music. Because here too their affective ordering is socially unconscious, because it is not realized that beauty is a social product, there is a degradation even of these 'purest' forms of art products. We have commercialized art, which is simply affective massage. It awakens and satisfies the instincts without expressing and synthesizing a tension between instinct and environment. Hence wish-fulfillment novels and films; hence jazz. The bourgeois floods the world with art products of a baseness hitherto unimaginable. Then, reacting against such an evident degradation of the artist's task, art withdraws from the market and becomes non-social, that is *personal*. It becomes 'highbrow' art, culminating in personal fantasy. The art work ends as a fetish because it was a commodity. Both are equally signs of the decay of bourgeois civilization due to the contradictions in its foundation.

The ravages of bourgeois unconsciousness destroy not only the social product but the producer. Labor now becomes, not labor to achieve a goal and to attain the desirable, but labor for the market and for cash. Labor becomes blind and unconscious. What is made, or why it is made, is no longer understood, for the labor is merely for cash, which now alone supports life. Thus all affective elements are withdrawn from labor, and must therefore reappear elsewhere. They now reappear attached to the mythical commodity which represents the unconscious market—cash. Cash is the music of labor in bourgeois society. Cash achieves objective beauty. Labor in itself becomes increasingly distasteful and irksome, and cash increasingly beautiful and desirable. Money becomes the god of society. Thus the complete disintegration of a culture on the affective side is achieved, and has resulted from the same causes as its disintegration on the cognitive side.

Beauty, then, arises from the social ordering of the affective elements in socially known things. It arises from the labor process, because there must not only be agreement about the nature of outer reality, but also agreement about the nature of desire. This agreement is not static. In the social process, outer reality becomes increasingly explored, and this makes the social process more far-reaching and deeply entrenched in the environment, while each fresh sortie into reality alters the nature of desire, so that here, too, fresh integrations are necessary. This pressure, both in science and art, appears as an individual experience. A scientist inherits the hypotheses, and an artist inherits the traditions, of the past. In the scientist's case an experiment, and in the artist's case a vital experience indicates a discrepancy, a tension, whose synthesis results in a new hypothesis or a new art work. Of course the scientist feels the tension as an error, as something in the environment, the artist as an urge, as something in his heart.

Science and art, as we use them in current language, are more partial and restricted than in my use. Science, as generally used, involves not all the cognitive elements in the labor process but only the *new* elements. The scientist is on the border line where new hypotheses are generated to modify technique. In factory, in building, in housework, and all daily occupation, the cognitive elements are familiar and traditional. They are technique rather than science. The world-view is not expanding here; reality is as our fathers knew it; but the scientist is situated on the very expanding edge of the world-view. Here new regions are continually coming into sight; discrepancies in experience continually arise to make him modify yesterday's formulations. The same applies to the artist. In daily life, in manners, desires, morals, hopes and patriotisms we tread the daily round; we feel as our fathers do; but the artist is continually besieged by new feelings as yet unformulated, he continually attempts to grasp beauties and emotions not yet known; a tension between tradition and experience is constantly felt in his heart. Just as the scientist is the explorer of new realms of outer reality, the artist continually discovers new kingdoms of the heart.

Both therefore are explorers, and necessarily therefore share a certain loneliness. But if they are individualists, it is not because they are non-social, but precisely because they are performing a social task. They are non-social only in this sense, that they are engaged in dragging into the social world realms at present non-social and must therefore have a foot in both worlds. They have a specially exciting task, but a task also with disadvantages comparable to its advantages. The scientist pays for his new realms by traveling without affective companionship, with a certain deadness and silence in his heart. The artist explores new seas of feeling; there is no firm ground of cognitive reality beneath his feet; he becomes dizzy and tormented. Those not on the fringes of the social process get their life less new but more solid, less varied but more stable. Their values are more earthy, more sensuous, more mature. They are rooted, certain, and full. It is time for the antagonism between scientist and artist to cease; both should recognize a kinship, as between Arctic and tropical explorers, or between bedouins of the lonely deserts and sailors on the featureless sea.

But they must not suppose that a line can ever be drawn between science and other social cognition, and art and other social affection. The social process is far too closely woven for that. The ingression of new values takes place at all parts; only we call certain operations scientific or artistic because there we see the ingression most clearly. In education cognitive and emotional tradition is chiefly at work, but on the one hand even here there is an ingression of the new, and, on the other hand, the artist and the scientist are being educated as well as learning new things all their lives.

If they remember this, they will not make the mistake of supposing they are opposite poles, between which the whole social process is generated. This is to suppose profit produces capital. In fact profit is produced by capital, and yet continually augments it. Science and art represent the profit on social capital. They are pushed out into the deserts of the unknown by the very workings of society. They lead, but they were instructed; they find new worlds of life, but they were supported by the old. Always we find only terms drawn from the labor process to be adequate to describe their function, and only this can explain the nature of Beauty and Truth, how man can never rest on the truth his eyes tell him or the beauty his heart declares, but must go about finding new truth, and cannot rest until he has created with his hands a new beauty.

The artist takes bits of reality, socially known, to which affective associations adhere, and creates a mock world, which calls into being a new affective attitude, a new emotional experience. New beauty is thus born as the result of his social labor.

But if art works were artificial, and beauty is a social product, how do we find beauty in the natural thing, in seas, skies, a mountain, and daffodils?

To separate in this way natural things from artificial is to make as dangerous a distinction as that between environmental and affective elements in the conscious field, or between mental and material qualities. Society itself is a part of nature, and hence all artificial products are natural. But nature itself, as seen, is a product of society. The primitive does not see seas, but the river Oceanus; he does not see mammals, but edible beasts. He does not see, in the night sky, blazing worlds in the limitless void, but a roof inlaid with patines of bright gold. Hence all natural things are artificial. Does that mean that we can make no distinction between nature and art? On the contrary, we can clearly distinguish two opposites, although we must recognize their interpenetration. In all phenomena, from hats to stars, seasons to economic crises, tides to social revolutions, we can distinguish varying portions of change, varying portions of the ingression of the unlike. The most rapid evolution is that of human society, of its customs, towns and hand-made products. The next that of animals and plants. The next that of the solar system. The next that of our galaxy. The whole universe in fact changes, but it changes at different rates. The region of most change, human society, as it were,

separates itself out from a background of least change, which we call
'nature'—stars, mountains and daffodils. The line can nowhere be precisely
drawn; and in all cases it is man, a social product, confronting nature,
and finding beauty in it. Nature finds no beauty in nature; animals do
not look at flowers or stars. Man dies, and therefore it is the social process
which has generated in him the ability to see beauty in flowers and stars.
This ability changes in character. The sea is beautiful to a European, to
an ancient Athenian, to a Polynesian islander, but it is not the same
beauty; it is always a beauty rooted in their cultures. The frozen sea is
to the Eskimo a different beauty from the warm sea of the Gulf; and the
blazing sun of the Equator a different beauty from the faint six-months-
dead sun of the Arctic.

Those elements in nature which are most universal and have changed
least in the history of man, may be expected to produce, in interaction
with him, the most constant quality. Hence we feel rightly that there is
something simple, primitive, and instinctive in the beauty we see in certain primitive, simple things. This must never be pushed too far. The
richest and most complex appreciation of natural beauty belongs to the
civilized man, not to the primitive. We may oppose the artwork just
made to the enduring mountains as an artificial to a natural beauty, but
the difference is one of degree. In both cases beauty emerges as a quality
due to a man, in the course of social process, gazing at a piece of his
environment. The ancient town, with weathered walls, full of history and
character, is a part of nature, and is yet a completely artificial product;
the sun lights it and the wind weathers it. There is no dichotomy between
nature and art, only the difference between pioneers and settled inhabitants.

Art, then, conditions the instincts to the environment, and in doing so
changes the instincts. Beauty is the knowledge of oneself as a part of
other selves in a real world, and reflects the growth in richness and
complexity of their relations. Science conditions the environment to the
instincts and in doing so changes the environment. Truth is the knowledge of the environment as a container for, and yet known by and partly
composed of, one's own self and other selves.

Both are products of the labor process—that is to say, both are realized
in action. Truth and Beauty are not the goals of society, for directly
they become goals in themselves, they cease to exist. They are generated
as aspects of the rich and complex flow of reality. The scientist or the
artist is only a special kind of man of action: he produces truth or beauty,
not as an end but as the color of an act. Consciousness, society, the
whole world of social experience, the universe of reality, is generated by
action, and by action is meant the tension between organism and environment, as a result of which both are changed and a new movement begins.

This dynamic subject-object relation generates all social products—cities, ships, nations, religions, the cosmos, human values.

Bourgeois culture is incapable of producing an aesthetics for the same reason that most of its social products are unbeautiful. It is disintegrating, because it refuses to recognize the social process which is the generator of consciousness, emotion, thought, and of all products into which emotion and thought enter. Because ideology is rooted in the labor process, the decay of an economy must reappear as a similar disintegration in the art of science which is rooted in it. Bourgeois economic contradictions are bourgeois ideological contradictions. The scientist and artist are forced on by the tension between past and present, tradition and experience. But tradition is the accumulated product of the past labor process as preserved; and experience is an experience in contemporary society.

Such a disintegration can only be revitalized by a transformation of the relations which, at the very roots, are destroying the creative forces of society. Change is dialectic; one quality gives birth to another by the revelation of the contradictions it contains, whose very tension begets the synthesis. The contradiction at the heart of bourgeois culture is becoming naked, and more and more clearly there is revealed the inextinguishable antagonism between the two classes of bourgeois economy, the bourgeoisie and the proletariat. The ruling class, the bourgeoisie, which exploits the labor power of the proletariat for profit, in doing so generates an illusion which sets the pattern for all the structure and ideology of bourgeois civilization. Man is held to be free in proportion to his ignorance of the social process, as a part of which he functions. Instead of bourgeois activity being governed by knowledge of the social process, it is governed by the market, by the 'laws of supply and demand', by the free circulation of cash, in short, by mere 'accident', for accident is man's name for his ignorance of determinism. Man is held to be free by virtue of unrestricted rights over property: but this merely conceals the domination of a few, who own the means of production and can traffick in labor-power, over the many who have nothing but labor-power to sell. The few believe that this dominating power they exercise makes them free, that in the act of domination their actions are not determined; but the event—the internal collapse of their economy in war and crisis and of their ideology in anarchy—reveals that not even they the lords are free, but their desires have disrupted their culture.

And who can transform it? Only those who are conscious of the cause of its collapse, who realize that to be without conscious social organization is not to be free, and that power over men by men is not freedom, even though concealed, but all the more if concealed, is mere ignorance of the necessities of society. It is precisely the proletarians who know all this by the pressure of the economy whose cruel weight they support.

In their struggles against exploitation they learn that only conscious organization, Trade Unions and factory Acts, can give them freedom from oppression. When they see their masters, the bourgeoisie, powerless to prevent war, unemployment, and the decay of the economy they have built up, the proletariat learns that this power of men over men, exercised by a simple act of the will and congealed in a property right, is not freedom for either class. It is only a delusive short cut in which humanity was for a time lost. Freedom appears, socially, when men take no short cuts of 'will' but learn the necessities of their own nature and of external reality and thus share a goal in common. Then the common goal and the nature of reality uniquely determine the only possible action without compulsion, as when two men combine, without 'orders', to lift a stone that lies in their path. In such an understanding, a new science, a new art, and a new society are already explicit, and to build it involves a proletariat which has already overthrown the bourgeoisie, and in revolution and reconstruction has transformed civilization. In a society which is based on cooperation, not on compulsion, and which is conscious, not ignorant, of necessity, desires as well as cognitions can be socially manipulated as part of the social process. Beauty will then return again, to enter consciously into every part of the social process. It is not a dream that labor will no longer be ugly, and the products of labor once again beautiful.

17. Jean-Paul Sartre

The Artist and His Conscience

JEAN-PAUL SARTRE (1905–   ), philosopher, playwright, novelist, political essayist, has been a dominant figure in French intellectual circles since World War II. Active in the Resistance during the war, he also wrote at that time his best-known philosophical work, *Being and Nothingness* (1943). In 1946, together with the novelist Simone de Beauvoir and the phenomenologist Maurice Merleau-Ponty, he founded *Les Temps Modernes,* which rapidly became the most important and controversial journal of ideas in post-war France. At times close in his political position to the Communist Party, recurrent differences have also characterized the relation. Notable among his many literary works are the novel, *Nausea,* and the play, *No Exit.* Important philosophical writings include *Imagination: A Psychological Critique* (1936), *The Transcendence of the Ego* (1936–37), and *Critique of Dialectical Reason* (1960) in which the Marxist influence seems to be far stronger than his earlier existentialism. This selection originally appeared in 1950 as a Preface to a book by his friend René Leibowitz titled *L'Artiste et sa Conscience.*

My dear Leibowitz,

You have asked me to add a few words to your book, since, some time ago I had occasion to write on the subject of literary commitment, and you now hope, through the association of our names, to emphasize the solidarity which unites artists and writers in their common concerns in a given age. Had friendship alone not sufficed, the desire to declare this solidarity would have decided me. But now that I must write, I admit to feeling very awkward.

I have no specialized knowledge of music and no desire to make myself ridiculous by paraphrasing poorly and with the wrong terms what you have so well stated in the appropriate language: nor do I foolishly presume to introduce you to readers who already know you well, following you avidly in your triple activity of composer, conductor and music critic. I would really like to say how good I think your book is: clear and simple, it taught me so much, unraveling the most confusing and involved problems and accustoming us to see them with fresh eyes: And what of it? The reader doesn't need me to tell him the merits of your book, he has only to open it. All things considered, I think the best is to suppose that we are talking just as we have often done and that I unburden myself of the questions and anxieties raised by your book. You have convinced me, yet I still feel certain areas of resistance and uneasiness. I must share them with you. To be sure, I am one of the profane who dares to question an initiate, a pupil who argues with the teacher after class. But the same is true of many of your readers and I can imagine that my feelings reflect theirs. Finally, this preface has no other purpose than to ask, in their name and mine, that you write a new book, or even an article, where you will dispel our last remaining doubts.

I cannot laugh at the nausea of the Communist boa constrictor, unable either to keep down or vomit up the enormous Picasso. In the C.P.'s indigestion, I see the symptoms of an infection which contaminates our entire era.

When the privileged classes are comfortably settled in their principles, when their consciences are clear, and when the oppressed, duly convinced of being inferior creatures, take pride in their servile state, the artist is at his ease. Since the Renaissance, you say, the musician has consistently addressed himself to a public of specialists. But who is this public, if not the ruling aristocracy who, not content with merely exercising military, judicial, political and administrative powers over the whole territory, made itself also a tribunal of taste? Just as that elite determined, by divine right, the human shape, so the cantor or choirmaster produced his symphonies or cantatas for the whole man. Art could call itself humanist because society remained inhuman.

Is the same still true today? This is the question which haunts me, and which, in turn, I put to you. For by now, the ruling classes of our western societies can no longer believe that they themselves provide the measure of man. The oppressed classes are conscious of their power, and possess their own rituals, techniques and ideology. Rosenberg, speaking of the proletariat, has put it admirably:

On one side, the present social order is permanently threatened by the extraordinary virtual power of the workers; on the other, the fact that his power is in the hands of an anonymous category, a historical "zero," is a temptation to all the modern myth-makers to seize upon the working class as the new material of new collectivities, by means of which the society can be subjugated. May not this proletariat without a history be as easily converted into anything other than itself? The pathos of the proletariat, holding in the balance the drama between revolution by the working class on its own behalf, and revolution as an instrument for others, dominates modern history.

Now, it is precisely music—to speak only of this one area—which has been metamorphosed. This art took its laws and limitations from what it conceived to be its essence. You have demonstrated brilliantly how, in the course of a free yet rigorous evolution, music wrenched itself from its alienation and set about creating its essence while freely providing its own laws. In its modest way, couldn't music thus influence the course of history by providing the working class with the image of a "total man," who also has wrenched himself from his alienation, from the myth of a human "nature" and who, through daily struggle, forges his own essence and values according to which he judges himself?   As soon as it recognizes *a priori* limitations, music reinforces alienation in spite of itself, glorifies the *given* and, while proclaiming freedom in its own fashion, declares that this freedom receives its limitations from nature. It is not uncommon that these "myth-makers" use music to fool the listener by inspiring him with holy emotions, as witnessed by the use of martial music or choirs. But, if I understand you correctly, something akin to a show of the naked power of creation must be seen in the most recent forms of this art. I think I have grasped precisely what you would oppose to these Communist musicians who signed the Prague Manifesto. They want the artist to reduce himself to a society-object, they want him to sing the praises of the Soviet world as Haydn sang those of divine Creation. They ask him to copy what *is*, to imitate without transcending, and to set an example to his public of submission to an established order: if music is defined as a permanent revolution, doesn't it threaten, in its turn, to arouse in the listener the desire to carry this revolution into other areas? You, on the contrary, want to show man that he is not manufactured and never will be, that he will everywhere and always retain the freedom to make and to remake himself beyond everything which is ready-made.

But here is what disturbs me: haven't you established the fact that an internal dialectic has carried music from monody to polyphony and from the most simple to the most complex polyphonic forms? This means that it can go forward but not backward: it would be as naïve to hope for its return to previous figurations as to want industrial societies to return to pastoral simplicity. Very good. But by the same token, its increasing complexity reserves it—as you yourself recognized—for a handful of specialists, found, by necessity, among the privileged classes. Schoenberg is farther removed from the workers than Mozart was from the peasants. You will tell me that the majority of bourgeois understand nothing of music, and this is true. But it is equally true that those who can appre-

ciate it belong to the bourgeoisie, profit from bourgeois culture, bourgeois leisure, and in general, practice a bourgeois profession. I know:
amateurs are not rich, they are most often found in the middle classes,
and it is rare to find a big industrialist who is a fanatic music lover.
This does happen, however: but I don't ever recall seeing a worker at
one of your concerts. It is certain that modern music is shattering forms,
breaking away from conventions, carving its own road. But exactly to
whom does it speak of liberation, freedom, will, of the creation of man
by man—to a stale and genteel listener whose ears are blocked by an
idealist aesthetic? Music says "permanent revolution" and the bourgeoisie
hear "Evolution, progress." And even if, among the young intellectuals, a
few understand it, won't their present impotence make them see this liberation as a beautiful myth, instead of their own reality? Let us understand each other. This is neither the fault of the artist nor of art. Art has
not changed internally: its movement, negativity and creative power remain what they have always been. What Malraux wrote remains as true
today as it was then: "All creation is at its origin the struggle between a
form in power and an imitated form." And so it must be. But in the
heavens above our modern societies, the appearance of those enormous
planets, the masses, upsets everything. Transforming artistic activity from
a distance, they rob it of its meaning without even touching it and spoil
the artist's tranquil conscience. Because the masses are *also* fighting for
man, but blindfolded, since they are in constant danger of going astray,
of forgetting who they are, of being seduced by the voice of the myth-
maker, and because the artist has no language which permits them to
hear him. He is speaking of *their* freedom—since there is only one freedom—but speaking of it in a foreign tongue. The difficulties of the cultural
policy of the USSR suffices to prove that this is a question of historical
contradiction inherent to our time and not one of bourgeois disgrace, due
in part to the subjectivism of the artist. Of course, if we believe that the
Soviet Union is the Devil, then it follows that its leaders find perverse
pleasure in carrying out purges which overthrow and decimate the artistic
ranks. Or if we believe that God is a Soviet, then things are just as easy:
God does what is just. That is all. But if, for a moment, we dare to uphold this new and paradoxical thesis, that the Soviet leaders are men,
men in a difficult, indeed, untenable position, who are nevertheless trying
to bring about what they believe is right, who are often outstripped by
events, and who are sometimes carried farther than they might like, in
short, men like all of us, then everything changes. Then we can imagine
that they are not overjoyed by these sudden jerks of the gear which
threaten to derail the locomotive. By destroying classes, the Russian revolution set out to destroy the elite, that is, those refined and parasitic
organisms which are found in all societies of oppression and which pro-

duce values and works of art like papal bulls. Wherever an elite functions, an aristocracy of the aristocracy outlining for aristocrats the shape of the whole man, new values and works of art, far from enriching the oppressed man, increase his absolute impoverishment. The productions of the elite are, for the majority of men, rejection, want and boundaries. The taste of our "art lovers" forcibly defines the bad taste or lack of taste of the working classes, and as soon as refined minds consecrate a work, there is one more "treasure" in the world which the worker will never possess, one more thing of beauty that he is unable to appreciate or understand. Values cannot be a positive determination for each man until they are the common product of all. Any one of society's new acquisitions, whether a new industrial technique or a new form of expression, being created for everyone, must be for each an enriching of the world and a way which opens before him, in short, his innermost potential. But instead, the whole man as defined by the aristocracy is the sum of opportunities taken away from everyone; it is he who knows what others do not know, who appreciates what they cannot appreciate, who does what they cannot do, who is, in short, the most irreplaceable of beings. By contrast, the individual in a socialist society is defined at birth by the totality of possibilities which all give to each one, and at his death, by still new possibilities—small as they may be—which he has given to all. Thus *all* is the road of each man towards himself and *each one* the way of all towards all. But the necessities of administration, industrialization and war forced the Soviet Union into first forming a policy of a trained elite. It needed engineers, bureaucrats and military leaders at the same time that it undertook to realize a socialist aesthetic. And from this follows the danger that this trained elite whose culture, profession and standard of living sharply affects those of the mass, produces in its turn values and myths, that "amateurs" bred in its midst create a special *demand* for artists. The Chinese text which you quote, revised and corrected by Paulhan, sums up quite well the threat hanging over a society in the process of construction: if horse lovers suffice to produce beautiful race horses, an elite which becomes a specialized public would suffice to give rise to an art for the elite. A new segregation threatens to take effect: a culture of *cadres* will rise with its whole procession of abstract values and esoteric works of art, while the mass of workers will again fall into a new barbarism which will be measured exactly by its incomprehension of the products destined for this new elite. This, I think, is the explanation of the infamous purges which revolt us. To the degree that the body of trained specialists is reinforced, in the measure that the bureaucracy threatens to become a class, if not an oppressive elite, to that degree will the artist develop a tendency towards aestheticism. And at the same time that they are obliged to depend upon this elite, the rulers must force themselves to maintain, at least in terms of an ideal, the principle of values produced by the community as a whole. Certainly, this drove them into contradictory actions, since they created a general policy of *cadres* and a cultural policy of the masses; with one hand they create an elite and with the other they are obliged to destroy its ideology which is incessantly reborn and which will always rise again. But there is, conversely, as much confusion in the minds of the enemies of the Soviet Union when they reproach its leaders, at the same time, for creating a class of oppressors and for wanting to destroy the class aesthetic. The truth is that the Soviet leaders and the artist in the bourgeois society are colliding against the same impossibility: music has developed according to its dialectic, becoming an art which depends upon a complex technique. This is a regrettable fact, but *it is a fact*, nevertheless, that it demands a specialized public. To sum up, modern music requires an elite and the working masses require music. How can this conflict be resolved? By "giving a form to the profound sensibility of the people"? But *what* form? Vincent d'Indy wrote serious music "On a French Mountain Air." Do you think the mountain dwellers would recognize their song? Besides, the popular sensibility creates its own forms. Folk songs, jazz and African chants don't need revision and correction by professional musicians. On the contrary, the application of a complex technique to the spontaneous products of this sensibility has the necessary consequence of distorting the products. This is the tragedy of Haitian artists who are unable to weld their formal training to the folk material they want to use. The Prague Manifesto states, more or less, that the level of music must be lowered, while the cultural level of the masses is being raised. Either this is totally meaningless, or it confesses that art and its public will meet in absolute mediocrity. You are right to observe that the conflict of art and society is eternal, stemming from the essence of the one and the other. But it has taken a new and sharper form in our time: art is a permanent revolution, and for forty years now, the fundamental situation of our societies has been revolutionary; but the social revolution calls for a conservative aesthetic whereas the aesthetic revolution demands, in spite of the artist himself, a social conservatism. Picasso, a sincere Communist, condemned by the Soviet leaders, purveyor by appointment to rich American collectors, is the image of this contradiction. As for Fougeron, his paintings have ceased to please the elite, without arousing the slightest interest on the part of the proletariat.

Further, the contradiction widens and deepens as soon as we begin to consider the source of musical inspiration. The problem, states the Prague Manifesto, is "to express the feelings and loftiest progressive ideas of the people." So much for feelings. But as for "lofty progressive ideas," how on earth do you set them to music? For music is a *non-signifying* art. Slovenly minds have taken delight in speaking of a "musical language." But we are perfectly aware that the "musical phrase" has no designated object: it is in itself an object. How then can this mute evoke for man his destiny? The Prague Manifesto suggests a solution which for sheer naïveté is a joy: we shall cultivate "musical forms which allow these goals to be attained, above all, vocal music—operas, oratorios, cantatas, chorales, etc." Good God, these hybrids are nothing but babblers, making small talk to music. What they are really saying is that music should be only a pretext, a means of enhancing the glory of the word. *It is the word* of which Stalin will sing, the Five Year Plan, the electrification of the Soviet Union. Set to other words, the same music could glorify Pétain, Churchill, Truman, the TVA. By changing the words, a hymn to the Russian dead of Stalingrad will become a funeral oration for Germans fallen before the same city. What do the sounds contribute? A great blast of sonorous heroism; it is the word which will speak. There can be no musical engagement unless the work of art is such that it can receive only one verbal commentary. In a word, the sonorous structure must *repel* certain words and *attract* others. Is this even possible? Perhaps, in certain special cases, and you give as an example, *The Survivor of Warsaw*. But even there, Schoenberg could not avoid recourse to words. In that "gallop of wild horses," how would we recognize the enumeration of the dead without the words? We would only hear a gallop. Poetic comparison doesn't reside in the music, but in the rapport of the music with the words. But here, at least, you will say, the words are a part of the work, they are not in themselves a musical element. True, but must we now reject the sonata, quartet and symphony? Must we devote ourselves to "operas, cantatas and oratorios," as urged by the Prague Manifesto? I know that you do not believe this. And I am completely in agreement with you when you write that "the chosen subject should remain a *neutral* element, something akin to raw material which is then subjected to a purely artistic treatment. In the final analysis, it is only the quality of this treatment which will prove or deny the adherence of extra-artistic feelings and concerns to a purely artistic design."

Only now I no longer know wherein lies musical engagement and I fear it has already escaped from the work of art to take refuge in the behavior of the artist, that is, in his attitude towards art. The life of the musician may be exemplary; exemplary of the chosen poverty, the refusal of easy success, the constant state of dissatisfaction and that permanent revolution which he wages against others and against himself. But I'm still afraid that his austere personal morality remains an external commentary to his work. The musical work of art is not, *by itself*, negativity,

rejection of traditions, a liberating movement: it is the positive consequence of this rejection and this negativity. A *sonorous object,* it no more
reveals the composer's doubts and fits of despair than the patent of an
invention reveals the torments and anxieties of the inventor; it does not
show us the dissolution of old rules, but makes us see others which are
the *positive* laws of its development. Moreover, the artist *should not be*
a commentator of his own work for the benefit of the public. If his music
is committed, this commitment will be found in its intuitive reality, in
the sonorous object as it will appear immediately to the ear, without
reference to the artist or to previous traditions. Is this even possible? It
seems to me that we simply stumble again upon the same dilemma which
we found at first: by forcing music, a non-signifying art, to express predetermined meanings, it becomes alienated. But again, by rejecting the
meaning which you call "extra-artistic" musical liberation runs the risk
of leading to abstraction and of offering the composer in question that
purely formal and negative freedom which Hegel characterizes as Terror.
Slavery or Terror. Conceivably our era offers the artist no other alternative.* If a choice must be made, I confess that I prefer Terror: not for
its own sake, but because, in this era of flux, it upholds the exigencies
proper to the aesthetics of art, allowing it to await, without too much
detriment, a more favorable time.

But I must admit that I was less pessimistic before reading your book.
I shall now give you the feelings of a rather uncultured listener; whenever I heard a musical composition performed, I found no significance
of any sort in the sequence of sounds, and it was a matter of complete
indifference to me whether Beethoven composed one of his funeral
marches on "the death of a hero" or that Chopin might have wanted to
suggest Wallenrod's satanic laugh at the end of his first *Ballade.* Conversely, it did seem to me that this sequence had a *meaning* and it was
this meaning which I liked. I have always really distinguished meaning
from significance. It seems to me, an object signifies when an allusion to
another object is made through it. In this case, the mind ignores the
sign itself; it reaches beyond to the thing signified; often it so happens
that this last remains present when we have long since forgotten the
words which caused us to conceive of it. The meaning, on the contrary,
is not distinct from the object itself and is all the more manifest inasmuch
as we are more attentive to the thing which it inhabits. I would say that
an object has a meaning when it incarnates a reality which transcends it
but which cannot be apprehended outside of it and which its infiniteness

---

* To be precise: The artist, for me, differs from the man of letters in that he deals
with non-signifying arts. I have elsewhere shown that the problems of literature are
entirely different.

does not allow to be expressed adequately by any system of signs: it is always a matter of a totality, totality of a person, milieu, time or human condition. I would say that the Mona Lisa's smile does not "mean" anything, but that it has a meaning. Through it, that strange fusion of mysticism and naturalism, evidence and mystery which characterize the Renaissance is materialized. And I have only to look at it to distinguish it from that other smile, equally mysterious but more troubling, more rigid, ironic, naïve and holy, which hovers vaguely about the lips of the Etruscan Apollo, or from the "hideous," secular, nationalist and witty suspicion of a smile on Houdon's Voltaire. Certainly, Voltaire's smile was *significant*. It appeared at specific times, it *meant*, "I'm no fool" or "Just listen to that fanatic!" But at the same time, the smile is Voltaire himself, Voltaire as an ineffable totality. You can talk about Voltaire forever— his existential reality is incommensurate with speech. But let him smile and you *have* him completely and with no effort. Thus does music seem to me, a beautiful mute with eyes full of meaning. When I listen to a Brandenburg Concerto, I never *think* of the seventeenth century, of the austerity of Leipzig, of the puritan stolidity of the German princes, of that moment of the spirit where reason, in full possession of its techniques, nevertheless remained subject to faith and where logic of concept was transformed into logic of judgment. But it is all there, present in the sounds, just as the Renaissance smiles on the lips of the Mona Lisa.

Further, I have always believed that the "average" public who, like me, lacks precise knowledge of the history of musical composition could date to the minute a work of Scarlatti, Schumann or Ravel, even if mistaken in the name of the composer, because of this silent presence, inherent in all sonorous objects, of an entire era and its concept of the world. Isn't it conceivable that musical commitment might reside at this level? I know what you will reply to this: if the artist paints himself entirely into his work—and his century with him—he did so unintentionally: his only concern was to sing. It is today's public who, at a hundred years' remove, finds intentions in the object which were never placed there. The listener of the last century only perceived the melody. He found natural and absolute rules in what we, in retrospect, consider to be postulates reflecting the era. All this is true, but can't one conceive of a more conscious artist today who, by reflecting on his art, would try to endow it with his condition as a man? I only put the question to you: you are the one who is qualified to answer it. But even if, like you, I condemn the absurd Prague Manifesto, I also cannot help being disturbed by certain passages in Jdanov's heralded speech which inspired the Soviet Union's whole cultural policy. You know it as well as I do: the Communists are guilty because they are wrong in their means of being right and they make us guilty because they are right in their means of being wrong. The Prague Manifesto is the stupid and extreme consequence of a perfectly defensible theory of art and one which does not necessarily imply an aesthetic authoritarianism. Jdanov states: "we must know life in order to represent it truthfully through works of art, not just to represent it in a dead scholastic way, not only as objective reality, but to represent reality in its revolutionary development." What does he mean if not that reality is never inert, but always in the process of changing, and that those who understand or portray it are themselves in the process of changing. The profound unity of all these changes which come at will is the future meaning of the entire system. It is the artist who must break the already crystallized habits which make us see in the *present* tense those institutions and customs which are *already out of date*. To provide a true image of our time, he must consider it from the pinnacle of the future which it is creating, since it is tomorrow which will decide today's truth. In one sense, this concept rejoins yours—you have shown that the committed artist is *in advance* of his times and that he looks on the present traditions of his art with the eyes of the future. In you as in Jdanov, there is certainly an allusion to negativity and transcendence. But he is not satisfied with the moment of negation. For him, the work has value, above all, for its positive content: it is a block of the future fallen into the present, anticipating by several years the judgment we shall bring to bear upon ourselves. It releases our future possibilities, and in one move it follows, accompanies and precedes the dialectical progression of history. I have always thought that nothing was sillier than those theories which try to determine the mental level of a person or of a group. There is no such level: to be "his age" for a child, is to be simultaneously below and above that age. The same is true of our habits of intellect and feeling. "Our senses have an age of development which does not come from the immediate environment but from the moment of civilization," Matisse wrote. Yes, and reciprocally, they go beyond this moment and perceive confusedly a crowd of objects which will be seen tomorrow, they discern another world in this one. But this is not the result of some sort of prophetic gift: the contradictions and conflicts of the era stimulate them to the point of bestowing upon them a sort of double vision. Thus is it true that a work of art is at the same time an individual achievement and a social fact. It is not the religious and monarchical orders alone that we find in The Well-Tempered Clavier: to these prelates and barons, both victims and beneficiaries of oppressive traditions, Bach held up the image of a freedom which, at the same time as it appeared to be contained within a traditional framework, transcended tradition towards new creations. Against the closed traditions of little despotic courts, he opposed an open tradition: he taught how to find originality within an established discipline; actually—how to live. He demonstrated the play of moral freedom within the confines of a religious and monarchical absolutism and depicted the proud dignity of the subject who obeys his king and the devout who worships his God. Entirely at one with his era, whose prejudices he accepts and reflects, he is, at the same time, outside it, and judges it wordlessly according to the still-implicit laws of a pietistic morality which will give birth, half a century later, to the ethics of Kant. The infinite variations which he performs, the postulates which he constrains himself to respect, place his successors on the verge of changing the postulates themselves. His own life, certainly, was a model of conformism and I cannot imagine that he ever advocated any very revolutionary views. But from the point of view of a still-unborn individualistic rationalism, isn't his art simultaneously the exaltation of the obedience and the transcendence of this same obedience which he *judges* at the same instant that he claims to demonstrate? Later on, without losing his noble audience, the artist will acquire another. By the reflection which he exercises upon the formulas of his art, by his continuous reworking of worn-out customs, the artist reflects, *in anticipation of* the bourgeoisie, that progression without obstacles or revolution which they hope to bring about. Your conception of musical commitment, my dear Leibowitz, seems appropriate to that fortunate era. The assimilation of the aesthetic needs of the artist to the political ones of his public was so perfect that one critical analysis serves to demonstrate the woeful inadequacy of custom duties, tolls, feudal laws and those of the prescriptions which traditionally regulated the length of the musical theme, the frequency of its recurrence, the mode of its development. At the same time, this critique respects the jurisdictions of art and of society: tonal aesthetics remain the natural law of all music as the law of property remains that of every community. You can be sure that I do not pretend to explain tonal music by the laws of property. I merely indicate that in each age, there are profound correspondences between the objects in every domain upon which negativity is brought to bear and between the limits reached by this negativity, at the same time and in every direction. "There is a human nature, don't touch it." This is the common meaning of the social and artistic injunctions of the eighteenth century. Rhetorical, moving, sometimes verbose, the art of Beethoven gives us, with some delay, the musical image of the Assemblies of the French Revolution. It is Barnave, Mirabeau, sometimes, alas, Lally-Tollendal. And I am not thinking here of the meanings he himself occasionally liked to give his works, but of their meaning which ultimately expressed his way of hurling himself into a chaotic and eloquent world. For in the final analysis these torrential discourses and floods of tears seem suspended in the freedom of an almost mortuary calm. Without shattering the rules of his own art, without crossing its boundaries, we could say that he went beyond the triumphs of the Revolution, beyond even his own failure. If so many people find consolation in music, it seems to me that it is because it speaks to them of their sorrows in the same voice which they will use to speak of them when they are comforted, and because it makes them see these sorrows with the eyes of a future day.

Is it so impossible that an artist will emerge in the world today, and without any *literary* intention, or interest in *signifying*, still have enough passion, to love and hate it, to live its contradictions with enough sincerity, and to plan to change it with enough perseverance, that he will transform even this world, with its savage violence, its barbarism, its refined techniques, its slaves, its tyrants, its mortal threats and our horrible and grandiose freedom into music? And if the musician has shared the rage and hopes of the oppressed, is it impossible that he might be transported beyond himself by so much hope and so much rage that he could sing today of this world with the voice of the future? And if that were so, could one still speak of "extra-aesthetic" concerns? Of "neutral" subject matter? Of "significance"? Would the raw material of music be distinct from its treatment?

I put these questions to you, my dear Leibowitz, to you and not to Jdanov. His answer I know. For at the moment when I believed he would show me the way, I realized that he was lost. Scarcely had he mentioned this transcendence of objective reality, when he added: "Truth must unite with the historical and concrete character of the representation in the task of ideological transformation and education of the workers in the spirit of Socialism." I had thought he was asking the artist to live the problems of his times freely and intensely, *in their totality,* so that the work of art could reflect them to us in his way. But I see now that it was a question only of ordering didactic works of art from bureaucrats which they should execute under the supervision of the party. Since the artist is to have his concept of the future imposed upon him, instead of being allowed to find it himself, it makes little difference, politically, that this future is still to be created: for the musician, it is ready-made. The entire system founders in the past; Soviet artists, to borrow the expression so dear to them, are *passéistes.* They sing the future of Soviet Russia the way our romantics sang the past of the monarchy. Under the Restoration, it was a problem of balancing the immense glory of our revolutionaries by an equal glory which they pretended to discover in the first years of the Old Order. Today, the Golden Age has been displaced by projecting it ahead of us. But, in any case, this shifting Golden Age remains what it is: a reactionary myth.

Reaction or Terror? An art that is free but abstract, or an art that is concrete but indentured? A mass public that is ignorant or a learned listener who is bourgeois? It is for you, my dear Leibowitz, who live in full conscience, without compromise or mediation, to tell us whether this conflict is eternal, or whether it is a moment in history, and in the latter instance, whether the artist has today the means within himself to resolve it, or whether, before we see the outcome, we must wait for a profound change of social life and human relations.

18. Bertolt Brecht

On Socialist Realism

BERTOLT BRECHT (1898–1956) was the greatest of modern German playwrights, and perhaps the most important single influence on modern theater on both sides of the Atlantic. Born in Augsburg, Germany, he studied medicine and philosophy at the Universities of Munich and Berlin. His early plays were realistic in style, but in the twenties he turned toward expressionism; influenced by Japanese Noh theater, he then began to develop a new type of drama requiring detachment and observation from the audience. In this "epic" theater he employed narrative, montage, and self-contained scenes. In 1928 he collaborated with the composer Kurt Weill on the *Dreigroschenoper*, based on John Gay's *Beggar's Opera*, in which he satirized bourgeois materialist society. He left Germany in 1933, upon Hitler's rise to power, lived at first in Denmark, then settled in the United States in 1941. Harassed in 1946 by the House Un-American Activities Committee for his Marxist views, he departed for East Germany in 1948 to assume the directorship of a State theater. There, too, he experienced difficulties with the government, mainly due to the anti-authoritarian implications of his plays. Among his major works were *Mother Courage* (1941), *The Good Woman of Setzuan* (1943), and *The Caucasian Chalk Circle* (1955). The following selection, taken from Brecht's Notebooks (1953–54), appears in Volume III of his *Schriften zur Literatur und Kunst* ("Writings on Literature and Art").

WHAT Socialist Realism is cannot simply be read off from extant works or styles of presentation. The criterion is not whether a work or presentation resembles other works or presentations which are counted as Socialist Realism, but whether it *is* socialist and realistic.

One

Realist art is art of battle: it battles against false views of reality and impulses which subvert man's real interests. It makes correct views possible and reinforces productive impulses.

Two

Realist artists emphasize the measured understanding, the "earthly" in a strong sense, the typical (the historically significant).

Three

Realist artists emphasize the moment of *becoming* and *passing*. In all their work, they think historically.

Four

Realist artists identify the *contradictions* between man and his relationships, and show the conditions under which they arise.

Five

Realist artists are interested in the alterations in man and his relations, in the constant ones and in the desultory ones into which the constant ones turn.

Six

Realist artists present the power of ideas and the material basis of ideas.

Seven

Socialist-realist artists are human—that is, social; they so present the relations among men that their social impulses grow stronger. They gain strength from practicable insights into the drives of society—to the extent that they (the drives) become pleasures.

Eight

Socialist-realist artists have a realistic attitude not only to their themes, but also to their public.

Nine

Socialist-realist artists take into account the level of education and the class identity of their public as well as the state of the class wars.

Ten

Socialist-realist artists treat reality from the standpoint of the laboring people and of the intellectuals committed to them who are for Socialism.

19. Gyorgy Lukács

Art as Self-Consciousness
in Man's Development

GYORGY LUKÁCS (1885–1971) was born in Hungary. Early involved in politics, he served in the government of Bela Kun in 1919;
when Kun fell from power, he fled to Germany and then, with the
rise of Hitler, to the Soviet Union. At the end of World War II, he
became Professor of Aesthetics in the University of Budapest, and
re-entered the government briefly during the Hungarian Revolution.
His major works in English translation include *History and Class Consciousness* (1923), *Studies in European Realism* (1946), and *The
Historical Novel* (1955). He is especially noted for his studies of such
great novelists as Scott, Flaubert, Balzac, Zola, and Mann. The selection, "Art as Self-Consciousness in Man's Development," is taken from
his major recent work in aesthetics, *Über die Besonderheit als Kategorie der Asthetik*.

In this the humanity of the artistic formulation expresses itself. Uniqueness as an aesthetic category includes the whole man as well as outer
world, and quite explicitly the world of men, of mankind: the sensible
forms of appearance in the external world—without detracting from its
own heightened intensity in sensuousness, its unmediated vitality—are always signs of the life of men, of their relations to one another, of the objects which these relations mediate, of Nature in its transactions with
human society. The general is both the embodiment of one of the powers
which determine the life of men and also—if it emerges subjectively as the
content of a consciousness in the world articulated—a vehicle of the life
of men, of the formation of their personality and their destiny.

With this sensory formulation of the unique as well as the general, the
work of art—because of its objective essence independent of the subjective aims which underlie its emergence—presages an inner condition,
in itself sensuous, of human, of earthly existence. It has this essential

character even when on socio-historical grounds the known reasons for its development were of a transcendent character (magical or religious). These reasons—the form is determined by the content—were artistically formulated in such a way that the transcendence conceals itself invisibly in an earthy immanence. We can, accordingly, even today experience the transcendence in works of the past, but as human fate, as human emotion and suffering. The mistrust of art which recurs in extreme Idealists and ideological advocates of religion has its source in this spontaneous tendency of authentic art for earthy immanence.

This problem of the humanity of art is inextricably tied to its objectivity and subjectivity. Here, too, theoretical clarity is hindered by the fact that thinking about art moves back and forth between the poles— in this case, false—of generality and uniqueness, and as a consequence leads from an overemphasis on uniqueness into a false subjectivism (which appears at most as an aesthetic agnosticism), from an overemphasis on generality into dogmatics. Bourgeois decadence has as a theoretical basis this distorting polarization into false subjectivism and false objectivism. The great difference from earlier times is that the intention then of important progressive thinkers, even if they misunderstood the nature of generality or uniqueness, was directed towards an integral aesthetic particularity. The theories of decadence, on the other hand, reify generality and uniqueness as poles isolated and without a center.

Only uniqueness, as the midpoint of the aesthetic reflection of reality, is in a position to illuminate the specific dialectical unity of subjective and objective factors as a principle of opposition animating the whole sphere. We have demonstrated this dialectical transaction between subjectivity and objectivity in the individuality of the work itself as well as in its aesthetic working. The humanity of art posited permits us a further concretization. Insofar as art always and finally forms the world of men; insofar as in each of its acts of representation (as opposed to those of science), man is always determinately present; insofar as the extra-human world emerges in art only as a means for human relations, behavior, feelings, etc.,—there arises from this objective dialectical kind of aesthetic representation, from its crystallization in the individuality of the work, a dialectical two-foldness of the aesthetic subject: a dialectical tension in the subject which presents in its account the representation of the fundamental facts involved in the development of mankind.

What is involved here is the relation between man and humanness. Objectively this relation has always been extant; it must then always have figured somehow in the forms of representation of reality. However, since this objective state in the course of the "pre-history of humanity," in "Ur-communism," in the class societies, turned out to be more in itself than for us (in the awareness of humanity as well as in the consciousness of individual men), its direct expression was of necessity often distorted and unwontedly misleading. So long as for humanity differences in race, nation, etc., were and are the bases of its existence and even of its cultural progress; so long as within each nation the class struggle serves as the impetus for development, each direct, theoretical appeal to humanity that fails to reckon with these objective means had to violate the true contents and forms of reality. (Think here of the current theories of supra-political, supra-national "syntheses" which are nothing but the ideological instruments of American imperialism.) Only with the emergence of Socialism, with the real possibility of the realization of the classless society does this problem raise itself to a higher level: the common socialist content that realizes itself in nationalistic forms already shows humanity in the contours of its concrete becoming and being, the concrete perspective of a single humanity.

In itself this question concerns only the historical exterior of the frame of our thoughts; our interest is still concentrated on the theory of representation. But if matters-of-fact exist in themselves, they must also, in some form, be reflected in the representation of reality. In the representations of science, we find not infrequently an appeal (presented as self-evident, requiring no justification) to that commonality which forms the real substratum of the concept of humanity. One thinks here of the categories of Logic which have never admitted doubt that the underlying forms of thinking comprise a common possession of mankind as a whole. (We do not speak here, of course, of the natural sciences, because the object of their representation is principally a reality independent of man.) Such a common human domain is posited justifiably; because aside from the fact that man has not changed decisively (in the anthropological sense), since he became man, his historical development reveals that despite great variations on even very essential questions, certain stages and steps manifest features which are very closely related and typical, which conform to certain general laws. (The economic structure, their development and dissolution, etc.) By its nature, this commonality lies predominantly in the domain of generality; the closer we come to concrete reality, the more commandingly and strikingly do differences emerge (the development of capitalism in England, France, etc.).

With this observation, we have moved a step closer to the answer to this question for aesthetics. Because for the emergence of every work of art it is precisely the concrete that is crucial in the reality represented. An art, which wishes to transcend objectively its national bases, the class structure of its society, the stuff of the class war in it, and—subjectively—the stance of the author with respect to these issues, can do this only by asserting itself as art. It is meaningful scientifically to investigate the common, general regularities of an economic structure (indeed of all structures). For every work of art, however, only a certain concrete stage of development of a certain concrete structure is involved as an immediate object of creation. This undeniable truth was obscured for a long time in the idealistic account of the subject of art as the "universally human"; a healthy turn away from this was effected only by historical materialism (and its important predecessors) which called art back theoretically to the reality of its actual activity.

At the same time, an opposite distortion also entered the affair. Vulgar Marxism immediately identified the social genesis of art with its essential character, and thereby came at times to conclusions which were quite absurd, for example, that in the classless society, the great art works of the class societies will be unintelligible and unenjoyable. A neglect of the theory of representation and the meager conception of art as the expression of a certain position in the class struggle underlie this narrowing and distortion of the true facts of the matter.[1] Because it is only with representation as an underlying principle of art that the universality of the substance of art, and with it that of art's form, can be theoretically founded. The social determination of the genesis of any creation and its necessary partisanship, can unfold themselves only given such a universality in the world reproduced and by its potential for being reproduced. Addressing this matter, Marx himself put the issue quite differently from the vulgarized versions. For him, too, the point of departure is naturally the genesis of society. After it is accomplished, however, the real work of aesthetics only begins: "The difficulty is not in understanding that Greek art and poetry are tied to certain social forms of development. The difficulty is that they still hold for us the pleasures of art, and stand in a sense as norm and unattainable ideal." [2]

When the issue is put in this way, the conception of the common substratum emerges naturally. (This shows that the theory of a "common humanity" was a false answer to a legitimate question.) In a materialistic-dialectical conception of the process of history, the answer appears without much difficulty: this common substratum is the continuity of development, the real transactional relation of the parts in it, the fact that the development does not originate in its entirety at the beginning, but always proceeds through the results of earlier stages which correspond to present needs, and incorporates them. The implications and incongruities of this development cannot be treated here. The bare delineation of the facts referred to indicates, however, the significant moment which the development of mankind makes available to art for articulation; it is precisely the task of that articulation to discover in the concreteness of the national and class-conscious immediate content anything novel which promises to become a lasting possession of mankind and which in fact becomes such a possession.

This definition is, however, not yet sufficiently concrete for the specific problems of art. The continuity of the development of mankind has its own solid, material basis. For art this serves only as a means for fulfilling its assignment: to give form to men, their fate, their behavior—all this understood in the broadest sense. With this the project, for the first time, assumes its true shape: the development brings out changes in the typical which for the most part, naturally, are transitory. Only a limited number of the newly emerging socio-historical types of people and situations are —in the good as well as in the bad sense—preserved in the memory of mankind, incorporated as a lasting possession. This process would be only a contextual selection with respect to which the qualification must still be made that from the standpoint of its "context-type," the object can only be situated relatively between the ephemeral and the perennial. No type belongs altogether to one or the other category; its membership is decided insofar as the artistic representation succeeds in grasping the typical properties in such a way that a moment of this durability—as good or evil—may be expressed. The mass of typical human characteristics preserved in man's historical development is thus surely greater than the number preserved live in the presentations of art. Accordingly, art has an objective basis for the durability of its typology in reality itself; if types of presentation do develop and persist, this is a result of its own activity.

This question has been considered first from the standpoint of content. The vitality of a work and of the types which take shape in it are in the last analysis naturally a problem for the conception of the artistic perfection of form. How many works are offered us which have been repeatedly considered and displayed by the "professionals" because they are extraordinarily important historical documents of past times and because many specialists are inclined to mistake the interest of historical content for the living artistic reality. Thus we must constantly remind ourselves of the unmediated evocation of artistic form. Of course, Sophocles' *Oedipus* provides for the historian of antiquity a wealth of information. It is just as certain, however, that nine-tenths of the later audiences or readers of this drama know little or nothing of such pertinent historical facts and are yet moved very profoundly by its working. It would be an opposite and also false extreme, however, to hold that it involves in this working exclusively the "magic" of the perfection of form. The latter is present: especially *Oedipus* will always remain a formal model of a certain kind of dramatic composition; by itself, however, it would evoke only an empty and thus ephemeral tension, the effect only of Grand-Guignol. What the audience moved by *Oedipus* experiences is a typical human destiny in which man, even today and even if he can understand the concrete historical conditions only in their crudest outline, perceives immediately, emotionally as *mea causa agitur*.

Of course, this identification with what is presented in art requires further concretization. If some of the Soviet youth crowded into performances of *Nora* or *Romeo and Juliet* would gladly take their figures and fates for their own, it is clear that every viewer must well know that such concrete fates lie completely outside his world of possibilities, that they belong irretrievably to the past. Whence then the evocative power of such dramas? We believe that it lies in this: that just here one's own past comes to life, made present—and not just the personal history of any single individual, but his history as a member of humanity whose fate is also experienced in works constituting the present. The power of art can in this way render what is foreign—spatially or temporally, by nation or by class—to experience. It is incontestable that masses of the proletariat have read Tolstoy entranced—and, on the other hand, as many *bourgeois*, Gorky.

All these examples point unequivocally to the active ground of the process involved. Men experience in great works of art the present and past of humanity, perspectives on its development. They experience them, however, not as external facts which one may acknowledge as more or less important, but as something essential for one's own life, as an important moment also of one's own individual existence. Marx, speaking about Homer's work, generalized this point:

A man cannot become a child again or he becomes childish. But doesn't the naivete of a child please him, and doesn't he have to strive himself to reach a higher level in order to reproduce its truth? Doesn't its own character—in its natural reality—stir in the child's nature for each epoch? Why should man's historical childhood, where he appears at his most beautiful, transpire as a stage which will not recur, as an ephemeral charm? There are backward children and precocious children. Many ancient peoples fitted these categories. The Greeks were normal children. The attraction of their art for us does not consist in its opposition to the stage of society in which it evolved. It is much nearer the result of that stage and is inextricably tied to the fact that the unripe social conditions under which it developed and by which alone it could develop can never recur.[3]

And it is clear from this alone that these hints of Marx do not refer only to the childhood of mankind, that much more, *every* period which is as such a moment in a peculiar and never recurring past, *can* be experienced.

We have already referred to the fact that the creative personality that figures in the emergence of the work of art is not simply or immediately identical with its everyday identity; that the artist's creating demands

from him a generalizing on himself, a movement upward from his particular singularity to aesthetic uniqueness. We see now that the effectiveness of important works, at their most striking—when the formed content
is alien in spatio-temporal terms, or in terms of nationality or class—
conveys a broadening and deepening, a transcending of the unmediated
everyday individuality. And above all, in this enrichment of the "I,"
stands the felicitous experience which genuinely great art provides.

It is generally acknowledged that the efficacy of art is a decisive
moment in the movement upward of the individual enjoying it, a movement from the particularity of the merely subjective to uniqueness. It
awakens realities which would have otherwise been inaccessible to him
in the fullness presented by the work; his conceptions of man, of his real
possibilities for good or evil realize an unparalleled broadening; alien
worlds, in space and in time, historically and economically, reveal themselves to him in the inner dialectic of those for us in whose reflection
something alien is of course experienced, but also, at the same time,
something which can be placed actually in relation to his own life, to
his own inwardness. (Where the latter is lacking, there develops an
interest in the exotic, in a mere curiosity involving the purely external,
often formal or technically artistic—but not, in essence, the aesthetic.)

The real content of this generalization, which (objectively as well
as subjectively) deepens and enriches—but never departs from—the
individuality, is the social character of the human personality. Aristotle
already knew this precisely. It was first in the subjective idealism of the
bourgeois epoch that this social substratum of the aesthetic process and
of its force was mystified in the most diverse ways. The content of the
work and, as a result of this, of its activity, is the experience of the
individual in the manifold riches of life in society and—mediated by the
essentially new features of clearly defined human relations—his existence
as a part and a moment of man's development, as a concise abbreviation
of it.[4] This elevation of the particular subjectivity does not of itself
produce a purely objective generality; to the contrary, it deepens the
individuality, precisely because it brings it into this middle ground of
what is unique. The subject in the audience imitates in his aesthetic
pleasure every movement which receives objective form in the creation
of the individuality of the work: a "reality" which, with respect to differentiation, is more intense than the experienced quality of the objective
reality itself, and which in this intensity immediately reveals the essential
features concealed in reality. Thus, the individuality of the work provides
a basis for such processes. Hegel, in the concept of "pathos," conceives of
the elevation of subjectivity into uniqueness on the part of the recipient
as similar to the process sponsored by the creator. It is clear, then, that
the genuinely aesthetic process depends on the soulful-spiritual-moral

level to which the impulse in the work must rise in order to yield a genuinely aesthetic process: the uniqueness in the individuality of the work reflects the tendency toward uniqueness in the aesthetic act of the enjoyment of art.

Of course, the social, the human process of art does not consist only in a frenzy of direct apprehension. Any such process has a preface and an afterward, and it has been one of the greatest mistakes of most Idealist writers on aesthetics to isolate, on artistic grounds, the immediate artistic process from the whole life of the audience. No person immediately becomes another one in the enjoyment of art or by it. The enrichment by it is, exclusively, of *his* personality. The latter is, however, formed by considerations of class, nation, history, etc., as well as within these considerations by personal experiences; it is, again, the sheer illusion of the aesthetic to assume that only a person with a *tabula rasa* for a soul can appreciate a work of art. No, all his prior experiences, which were alive and at hand in the grounding of his social identity, remain active also in the appreciation of art. In any recognition of the evocative power of the artistic, charity dictates that each recipient should compare the reality reflected by the art with the one held by him until then. Naturally what is involved here is not a mechanical photographic superimposing of individual details experienced earlier in life on those now realized in aesthetic pleasure; the issue is much more the correspondence of two entities—the concrete form and the experience of the past.

Acknowledgement of this state of affairs in no way implies a qualification of what we have asserted about the power of the genuinely artistic production of form. On the contrary. What we have called the joyous enrichment in aesthetic pleasure depends specifically on the fact that no one who enjoys it confronts the work of art as a *tabula rasa*. Understandably, then, a struggle often develops in the process, between older experiences and present artistic impressions. The battlefield is just that correspondence of the two wholes: the details offer an obvious basis for the comparison. The accomplishment of great art is precisely in this —that the new, the original, the significant achieve victory over the old experiences of the recipient. Precisely in this do the broadening and deepening of experiences by the world which is formed in the work proceed.

There are many cases, naturally, where as a result of "non-correspondence," the process referred to doesn't come off, when the work is refused. This can be grounded in the ideal and artistic deficiencies of the work, or, also, in the ideological or artistic immaturity of the audience. Treatment of these questions belongs to the history of the arts and of their general principles—in that part of aesthetics which concerns itself with the analysis of the different aspects of aesthetic receptivity. Here a genuine,

aesthetically-shaped susceptibility to our questions is asserted. That it
deals, in the social reality, with a historical process of the development
of such a capacity; that this development even today has not been long
included; that accordingly not every susceptibility can react to art
adequately, in the manner cited—all this changes nothing in the specifically aesthetic representation of reality. Marx derives the objective
necessity of such a transaction from the whole life of society, interestingly
enough with an appeal directly to art: "The art object—like any other
product—creates a public responsive to art and capable of the enjoyment
of beauty. The production thus produces not only an object for the
subject but also a subject for the object." [5] The expansion of the state of
affairs presented by us here into a universal relation does not in the least
weaken the significance of what is specific in aesthetic receptivity, in
the consumption of art. Marx nonetheless remarks a few lines before those
cited by us: "For the object is not an object in general, but a specific
object which must be consumed in a certain way mediated by the production itself." [6]

For the adequate assessment of the working of art, its consequences are
no less important than its prior conditions. For the *polis* ideology of the
classical writers on aesthetics, this question—self-evidently—was central.
Plato's distrust of art, as well as Aristotle's theory of catharsis, have their
source in it. The idealist theories and the Praxis of the newest art, breaking away more and more sharply from society, first isolated (on the model
of the decadent life as a whole) the aesthetic force of antecedents and
consequences. Put more precisely: they conceived of this force as a single
frenzy which in its aftermath (as also in its preface) is surrounded by
a sea of endless boredom, of depressed hangovers. This situation is best
portrayed in the young Hofmannsthal.

The situation is quite different in the society of normally active men.
The enrichment which aesthetic pleasure secures for them manifests itself
(albeit often diffusely and indirectly) in the whole course of their life,
and also in their relation to art. We can best describe the essence of this
aftermath by repeating Tschernyschewsky's words: art is a "textbook of
life." Obviously there are works—among them many first-rate ones—whose
efficacy is more direct; the enrichment in the aftermath unfolds quite
without mediation: it is quite unmediated, for example, in the "Marseillaise," but also relatively unmediated in other forms like the passionate
veneration of a certain typical behavior, like the attempt to take something as a model in life, as the equally passionate rejection of another
type, etc. It would be laughable to fault such efficacy—as does the
largest part of the decadent theory of art—as "inartistic." One would
then have to expel Aeschylus and Aristophanes, Cervantes and Rabelais,
Goya and Daumier, etc., etc. from the domain of art. It would be, how-

ever, no less one-sided and mistaken to discern in such a direct and straightforward process the single criterion of art. Not only because the list of masterworks "excluded" might be still larger, but also because a number of art works which did exercise in their "present" a similarly direct efficacy, later—on the basis of a more indirect process—also became a live part of the world of art of that later future. It suffices to mention in this regard works like *The Marriage of Figaro* or *Werther*.

What is common to the direct and indirect effect on the audience of aesthetic pleasure is the transformation of the subject already described, his enrichment and deepening, the way in which he is strengthened or moved. And with this we come again to the decisive issue between art and science. As in a representation viewed as object, its grounds, freed from the subjective moments of its genesis, stand opposed (but not unimaginably) to the individuality of the work determined, so also in its efficacy. Science discloses the objective reality in its regularities and independent of consciousness. Art works immediately on the human subject; the representation of the objective reality, that of social man in his transactions with other men and in his exchanges with nature, is one —and in fact indispensable—means (but still only a means) for stimulating this growth in the subject. Thus, it can be said as a decisive characterization of this issue: scientific representation makes form the "In-itself" of its objectivity, its essence, its regularities, an at least determinate "For-us"; its effect on human subjectivity is thus, above all, both an extensive and intensive unfolding, broadening and deepening of consciousness, of the conscious knowledge of nature, society, and man. Artistic representation, on the one hand, creates likenesses of reality in which the "being-in-itself" of objectivity is transformed into a "being-for-itself" of the formed world, into the individuality of the work; on the other hand, there is forthcoming in the appropriate effect of such works an awakening and elevation of human consciousness: while the subject experiences a kind of "reality" existing for itself, there arises in him a "for-itself" of the subject, a self-consciousness which does not stand in hostile separation from the external world. A richly and profoundly conceived external world will open, many times more richly and deeply, on an enriched and deepened self-consciousness of man who as member of society, of a class, of a nation and of a self-conscious microcosm yields to the macrocosm of human development.[7]

If we have in this way fixed the issue between the two kinds of representation, it must be recalled again that both reflect the same objective reality, that both—of course in different ways—are moments of the same socio-historical evolutionary process of man. Thus one should not even here oppose consciousness and self-consciousness as exclusive of each other, as Caudwell does, for example, under the influence of the ideology of decadence; one should rather see in them poles of subjective conceptions of the world, between which innumerable dialectical exchanges and transitions may be effected. Because it is self-evident that also those representational scientific elements which primarily render as a possession of human consciousness a reality independent of consciousness exercise an extraordinary, at times even a revolutionary influence on the development of human self-consciousness. It suffices perhaps if we recall the effect which the scientific discoveries of Copernicus and Darwin exerted on the "what" and "how" of man's self-consciousness—to say nothing of the influence of Marx or Lenin, of the economic and historical information provided by them for social and national self-consciousness. On the other hand, for the unfolding of self-consciousness by the activity of works of art, the path which goes by way of the representation of reality is absolutely indispensable. Even for art forms like music or lyrical poetry, with respect to which the ideologies of decadence tend to deny its existence, a concrete Marxist analysis will determine this state of affairs. That great epic poetry, tragedy, really great painting, etc., do mediate the "worlds" contained in them and act on self-consciousness first by this means, is known. Who can determine whether people make the history of their fatherland their own more by way of art or by way of science?

Confluences and exchanges also play a large role here. Furthermore— or more precisely, because of this—the polarization of consciousness (science) and self-consciousness (art) is a fact, a proper characterization of the differentiation of the two kinds of representation. That this polarization reached its pure form only in the course of a long historical development, that in earlier times science as well as art appeared mingled in many respects with far reaching modes of apprehending reality intermediate between these other areas (magic, religion), rather reinforces our conception than runs counter to it. Because science as well as art could realize its proper form only in this struggle for its integrity, for its specificity in the representation of reality. These adequate forms, historically realized, provide the essential object of analysis for the theory of dialectical materialism; historical materialism has to explain the historical conditions of the development of their polarization.

It follows from this that even the countless junctures, overlaps, etc., which are found in the concrete observations of both types of representation, that even the countless interchanges and interaction in the genesis and in the working of their products, cannot nullify the fundamental object between the poles. This follows first from the commonality of the reality represented; it follows finally from the gradually developed differentiation in the forms of its structure. If one wishes to proceed from the aesthetic representation to the coarsest (and often most one-sided, most confused) generalities, the emphasis still must be placed—naturally in retrospect to the common basis—on the differentiation, on the character of the object as object. In these reflections, this has been attempted by way of the category of uniqueness. The polarization referred to, of the role of science and art in the life and development of humanity, the polarization of consciousness and self-consciousness, is a concluding implication, a grasping together of all the specific determinations which one is able—with the aid of our theory of the category of uniqueness in aesthetic representation—to win from the attentive pursuit of the phenomenon of art.

Notes

¹ When even a theoretician like Plekhanov views the "psychology of men in society" as a mediating element between the economic base and ideology and conceives of ideology (and thereby also art) as a representation of "the characteristics of this psychology," he is co-responsible for such a narrowing of the Marxist conception. Cf. G. Plekhanov, *Die Grundprobleme des Marxismus* (Stuttgart & Berlin, 1922), p. 77.

² Cf. chapter 2, Karl Marx, "Production and Consumption." (—*Eds.*)

³ *Ibid.*

⁴ These connections were first recognized—in large measure—in Hegel's *Phenomenology*, and were embodied in Goethe's *Faust*. Cf. on this the related chapter in my *Jungen Hegel*, and also my study of Faust in *Probleme des Realismus* (*Werke*, Bd. 6, Neuwied, 1965), pp. 575ff.

⁵ See footnote 2, above. (—*Eds.*)

⁶ *Ibid.* (—*Eds.*)

⁷ The expression "being-for-itself" is used here in the sense used by Marx in *The Poverty of Philosophy*.

B. On Art History and Criticism

20. Lucien Goldmann

Genetic-Structuralist Method
in History of Literature

LUCIEN GOLDMANN (1913–70), born in Bucharest, Rumania, was best known for his sociological literary criticism, and for the research center in this field of study which he directed in Brussels, Belgium. A prominent figure in European universities, and a frequent visiting lecturer in the United States, he was the author of numerous books and essays in philosophy, sociology and literary criticism, including *Philosophie et sciences humaines, Le Dieu caché, Recherches dialectiques,* and *Pour une sociologie du roman.* Applying socio-historical methods according to Marxist ideas, his writings on the dramas of Racine are a celebrated example of the testing of a Marxist approach by reference to specific, major works of art. The following essay on methodology in literary history and criticism was originally published in French in 1964, in *Modern Language Notes* (Johns Hopkins University Press), and in *Pour une sociologie du roman* (Gallimard).

GENETIC-structuralist analysis in *history of literature* is only the application to this particular area of a *general* method that we believe to be the only valid one in the sciences of man. This is to say that we consider cultural creation a sector which, though doubtless of a privileged sort, is of the same nature as all the other sectors of human behavior, and as such, subject to the same laws, and presenting to scientific inquiry difficulties that, if not identical, are at least analogous.

In the present essay we will attempt to expound some fundamental principles of genetic structuralism as applied to the sciences of man in general and to literary criticism in particular, as well as some reflections concerning the analogy and opposition between the two large and com-

243

plementary schools of literary criticism that are aligned to this method: Marxism and psychoanalysis.

Genetic structuralism starts from the hypothesis that *all* human behavior is an attempt to give a *significant response* to a particular situation and, by the same token, tends to create an equilibrium between the subject of the action and the object to which it is addressed, the surrounding world. This tendency toward an equilibrium always retains, however, a labile and provisional character to the extent that every more or less satisfactory equilibrium between the mental structures of the subject and the external world culminates in a situation within which the behavior of men transforms the world, this transformation rendering the old equilibrium insufficient and engendering a tendency toward a new equilibrium to be once more superseded.

Thus human realities show themselves as processes with two faces: *destructuring* of ancient structures, and *structuring* of new totalities suitable for creating equilibria which may satisfy the new exigencies of the social groups that elaborate them.

In this perspective, scientific study of the facts of human life, whether economic, social, political, or cultural, implies the attempt to throw light on these processes by disclosing both the equilibria which they disrupt and those they are moving toward. This much said, one need only undertake a concrete investigation in order to come up against a whole series of problems, of which we will sketch some of the most important.

In the first place, the problem of knowing who is actually the *subject* of the thinking and the activity. Three kinds of answers are possible, involving essentially different attitudes. One can see the subject as the *individual,* as in effect in the empiricist and rationalist positions, and recently in phenomenological views. One may also, as is the case in certain kinds of Romantic thought, reduce the individual to a mere epiphenomenon, and see in *the collectivity* the sole real and authentic subject. One can, finally, as in dialectical thought, Hegelian and above all Marxist, admit with romanticism that the collectivity is the real subject, without however forgetting that this collectivity is nothing other than a complex network of interindividual relations, and that one must always specify the structure of this network and the particular place occupied in it by individuals, who manifestly appear as at least the immediate subjects of the behavior studied, if not the ultimate ones.

If we leave aside the Romantic position, oriented toward mysticism, denying all reality and autonomy to the individual to the extent that it believes he can and must identify himself integrally with the whole, the question can be seriously put as to why a work should be ascribed in the first instance to the social group, and not to the individual who wrote it;

the more so because, if the dialectical perspective does not deny the importance of the latter, the rationalist, empiricist and phenomenological positions do not deny the reality of the social milieu, though seeing there only an external conditioning, that is to say, a reality whose action on the individual has a causal character.[1]

The answer is simple: when it tries to grasp the work in what is specifically cultural about it (literary, philosophical, artistic), an inquiry which ascribes it uniquely or in the first instance to its author can, within the existing possibilities of empirical study, account *at best* for its internal unity and the relation between the whole and the parts; but in no event can it establish in a positive fashion a relation *of the same sort* between the work and the man who created it. On this level, taking the individual as the subject, the largest part of the work studied remains accidental, and it is impossible to get beyond the sphere of more or less intelligent and ingenious speculation. For, as we have said elsewhere, psychological structure is too complex a reality to be analyzed in the light of this or that collection of testimony about an individual who is no longer living, or about an author one does not know directly, or even by relying on one's intuitive or empirical knowledge of a person to whom one is linked more or less closely by bonds of friendship.

In a word, no psychological study could account for the fact that Racine wrote precisely the body of his dramas and his tragedies and explain why he could in no case have written the plays of Corneille or Molière.[2]

And, curious though it may seem, when it is a matter of studying the great works of a culture, sociological study manages more easily to draw out the *necessary* links by connecting them to collective unities, whose structuring is much easier to illuminate.

Doubtless these unities are but complex networks of interindividual relations. But the complexity of the psychology of individuals derives from the fact that each one belongs to a larger or smaller number of different groups (familial, professional, national, relations of amity, social classes, etc.). Each of these acts upon the consciousness of the individual, thus helping to engender an unique, complex, and relatively incoherent structure. By contrast, as soon as we study a sufficiently large number of individuals *belonging to one and the same social group*, the action of the various other social groups to which each of them belongs, and the psychological elements following from such membership tend to cancel each other out, and we find ourselves in the presence of a much simpler and more coherent structure.[3] In this perspective, the relations between the really major work and the social group which—through the intermediary of the creator—turns out *to be, in the last analysis, the true subject of the creation,* are of the same order as the relations between the elements of

the work and its ensemble. In the one case as in the other, we find ourselves before relations among the elements of a comprehensive structure
and the whole of that structure, relations which are at once comprehensive and explanatory in type. This is why, if it is not absolutely absurd
to imagine that the individual Racine, given a different education or
brought up in a different milieu, might have written plays like those of
Corneille or Molière, it is by contrast quite inconceivable to imagine the
nobility of the robe elaborating an epicurean or a radically optimistic
ideology.

This is to say that insofar as science is an effort to discern *necessary*
relations between phenomena, attempts to relate cultural works to social
groups as the creating subjects prove—at the present level of knowledge
—far more workable than all the attempts to consider the individual as
the true subject of the creation.

However, once this position is accepted, two problems arise. The first
is to determine the order of relations obtaining between the social group
and the work, the second, to determine between what works and what
groups such relations can be established.

Regarding the first point, genetic structuralism (and more precisely
the work of Gyorgy Lukács) represents a real turning-point in the sociology of literature. All the other schools of literary sociology, ancient or
recent, try in effect to establish relations between the *contents* of literary
works and those of collective consciousness. This procedure, which can
sometimes arrive at some results, to the extent that some such transfers
do actually occur, has two major drawbacks:

(a) The writer's reinstatement of elements of the content of collective
consciousness, or quite simply, of the immediate empirical aspect of the
social reality surrounding him, is almost never either systematic or general, and appears only at certain points in his work. This is to say that
to the extent sociological study addresses itself exclusively or mainly to
seeking correspondence *in content,* it allows the unity of the work to
escape, indeed, its *specifically literary* character.

(b) Reproduction of social reality and the collective consciousness in
their immediate aspects is generally the more frequent, the less the creative power of the writer, who is satisfied to describe or recount his
personal experience without transposing it.

This is why literary sociology oriented toward *content* often has an
anecdotal character, and appears workable and effective when it studies
more commonplace works or *literary currents,* but becomes less and less
interesting to the degree that it approaches the great creations.

On this issue, genetic structuralism has signified a total reorientation,
its fundamental hypothesis being precisely that the collective character

of literary creation stems from the fact that the *structures* of the universe of a work are homologous to the mental structures of certain social groups or stand in an intelligible relation to them, whereas on the level of content, that is to say, of the creation of imaginary universes ruled by these structures, the writer has total freedom. The use of the immediate aspect of his individual experience to create these imaginary universes is no doubt possible and frequent, but in no wise essential, and its clarification constitutes only a helpful but secondary task of literary analysis.

In reality, the relation between the creative group and the work most often takes shape according to the following model: the group sets up a structuring process which elaborates in the consciousness of its members effective, intellectual, and practical tendencies toward a coherent response to the problems posed by their relations with nature and their inter-human relations. Save in exceptional cases, however, these tendencies are far from achieving real coherence, to the degree that they are counteracted, as we have already said above, in the consciousness of individuals by membership in numerous other social groups.

Moreover the mental categories exist in the group only in the form of more or less developed tendencies toward a coherence which we have called a world vision. The group thus does not create the vision, but the group deploys (and is alone capable of deploying) its constitutive elements and the energy for uniting these. The great writer is precisely the exceptional individual who succeeds in creating in a certain realm, that of the literary (or pictorial, conceptual, musical, etc.) work, an imaginary universe, rigorously coherent, or nearly so, whose structure corresponds to that toward which the group as a whole tends. As for the work itself, it is, among other things, all the more mediocre or the more worthwhile as its structure lacks or acquires rigorous coherence.

One can see the considerable difference that separates content-sociology from structuralist sociology. The former sees in the work a *reflection* of a collective consciousness, the second on the contrary sees therein *one of its constitutive elements*, one of the most important, enabling the members of the group to become aware of what they had been thinking, feeling, and doing without having objectively realized its significance. One can understand why content-sociology turns out to be more effective when it is a matter of the more ordinary works and contrastingly why genetic-structuralist literary sociology proves to be more efficacious when it is a question of studying the masterpieces of world literature.

Still, an epistemological problem must be faced: if *all* human groups affect the awareness, the feelings, and the behavior of their members, only the agency of certain particular, specific groups is of a nature to favor cultural creation. It is therefore especially important for concrete research to circumscribe these groups in order to know in what direction to turn one's investigation. The nature itself of great cultural works indicates what their characteristics must be. These works represent in effect, we have already noted, the expression of visions of the world, that is to say, imaginary or conceptual slices of reality, structured in such fashion that without essentially having to complete their structures one can develop them into global universes. This is to say that such structuring can only be attributed to groups *whose consciousness tends toward a global vision of man.*

From the standpoint of empirical research it is certainly true that throughout a very long period social classes have been the only groups of this type; even if the question can be raised whether this statement also applies to non-European societies, to Greco-Roman antiquity and preceding periods, and even perhaps to certain sectors of contemporary society. But once more we want to underline that this is a problem for positive empirical research, not for ideological sympathies or antipathies such as underlie too many sociological theories.

Be that as it may, the assertion of a bond between great cultural works and the activity of social groups oriented toward a global restructuring of the society, or toward its conservation, eliminates from the outset every attempt to connect them with a number of other social groups, notably the nation, generations, regions, and the family, to cite only the most important. Not that these groups do not act on the consciousness of their members and, under the circumstances, on that of the writer. But they could explain only certain peripheral elements of a work and not its essential structure.[4] The empirical data support this contention, moreover. Belonging to seventeenth-century French society can neither explain nor render comprehensible the works of Pascal, of Descartes and Gassendi, or that of Racine, of Corneille, and of Molière, to the very degree that these works express different and even opposed visions, even though their authors all belonged to seventeenth-century French society. By way of compensation, their common membership can account for certain formal elements shared by the three thinkers and the three writers.

After these preliminary considerations, we arrive at the most important problem of all sociological research of the genetic-structuralist type: demarcating its object. Where the sociology of economic, social or political life is concerned, this problem is especially difficult and absolutely primordial. For one can examine structures only if one has delimited more or less rigorously the set of immediate empirical data which are included; and, conversely, one could delimit these empirical data only to the extent that one is already in possession of a more or less developed hypothesis about the structure which unifies them.

From the standpoint of formal logic, the circle may seem insoluble; in practice it is well enough resolved, like all circles of this sort, by a series of successive approximations. One starts from the hypothesis that one can assemble a certain number of facts in a structural unity; tries to establish among these facts a maximum of comprehensive and explanatory relations, attempting also to encompass other facts that seem alien to the structure which is being adduced; thus comes to the elimination of some of the facts with which one began, adding others and modifying the initial hypothesis; and repeats this procedure in successive approximations until one arrives (an ideal more or less realized in different cases) at a structural hypothesis capable of accounting for a perfectly coherent ensemble of facts.[5]

When one studies cultural creations one is in a privileged position, it is true, regarding the initial hypothesis. It is likely that great literary, artistic or philosophical works constitute coherent meaningful structures, so that the first demarcation of the object is, as it were, already provided. However, one must warn against the temptation to trust too absolutely in this supposition. A work may contain hetereogeneous elements which in fact must be distinguished from the essential unity. Furthermore, if the hypothesis of the unity of the work is highly plausible for really major works taken in isolation, this likelihood diminishes considerably when it is a matter of the ensemble of *writings of one and the same writer*. That is why one must begin in concrete research with the analysis of each of a writer's works, studying them in the chronological order of their composition insofar as this can be established. Such a study makes it possible to group writings together provisionally, and then seek in the intellectual, political, social and economic life of the epoch those structured social groupings within which the works studied could be integrated, as partial elements, by establishing intelligible relations between them and the whole, and under the most favorable conditions, by establishing homologies.

Progress in a genetic-structuralist inquiry consists in the delineation of sets of empirical data which constitute structures, relative wholes,[6] and in subsequently inserting these as elements into other, vaster structures, of a like nature, and so on.

This method offers, among other things, the dual advantage of conceiving, to begin with, the ensemble of human facts in a unitary manner, and then, of being at once *comprehensive* and *explanatory*. The illumination of a meaningful structure constitutes a process of *comprehending*, while insertion of it into a vaster structure is to *explain* it. As an example:

to throw light on the tragic structure of Pascal's *Pensées* and Racinian
theater is a process of *comprehending;* inserting them in extremist Jansenism, while setting forth the structure of the latter, is a process of comprehending the latter, but is a process of explaining the writings of Pascal
and Racine; inserting extremist Jansenism into the global history of
Jansenism is to explain the first and comprehend the second. To insert
Jansenism, as an ideologically expressive movement, into the history of
the nobility of the robe of the seventeenth century is to explain Jansenism
and to comprehend the nobility of the robe. To insert the history of the
nobility of the robe into the global history of French society is to explain
it, while comprehending the latter, and so on.

Explanation and comprehension are thus not *two* different intellectual
processes, but a single process related to two frames of reference.

Let us underscore, finally, that in this perspective—where the passage
from appearance to essence, from the abstract and partial empirical given
to its concrete and objective significance, is accomplished by insertion
into relative wholes, structured and meaningful—each human fact can,
and even must, have a certain number of concrete meanings, different
according to the number of structures within which it can be inserted
in a way that is both positive and workable. Thus, for example, if Jansenism is to be inserted, through the mediations already indicated, into
seventeenth-century French society, where it represents a retrograde and
reactionary ideological current opposing the progressive historical forces
incarnated above all in the bourgeoisie and the monarchy, and on the
ideological level in Cartesian rationalism; then it is equally legitimate
and necessary to insert it into the global structure of Western society
as it has developed until today, a perspective in which Jansenism becomes progressive to the extent that it constitutes one of the first steps
toward superseding Cartesian rationalism in the direction of dialectical
thinking. And these two meanings are, of course, neither exclusive nor
mutually contradictory.

In the same order of ideas, we would like to pause, in concluding, over
two problems which are particularly important in the current state of
literary criticism:

(a) the insertion of literary works into two real and complementary
wholes both of which can furnish elements of comprehension and explanation, namely, the individual and the group, and,

(b) in consequence, the problem of the function of cultural creation
in the lives of men.

Regarding the first point, we have today two scientific schools of a
genetic-structuralist type, corresponding to attempts to insert works into

collective structures and into individual biography: Marxism and psychoanalysis.

Passing over the difficulties of disengaging individual structures already remarked on, let us begin by considering these two schools at the methodological level. Each proposes to comprehend and to explain human facts by insertion into the structured wholes of, respectively, collective life and individual biography. Thus they constitute allied and complementary methods, and the results of each should, to all appearances at least, reinforce and complete those of the other. Unfortunately, as a genetic structuralism psychoanalysis, at least as Freud evolved it,[7] is not consistent enough, and is far too marred by the scientism that dominated academic life at the end of the nineteenth and the beginning of the twentieth century. This is especially apparent in two central points.

First of all, in Freudian explanations the temporal dimension of the future is completely and radically absent. Subjected in this respect to the influence of the deterministic scientism of his time, Freud wholly neglected the positive, equilibrating forces that function in every human structure, individual or collective. To explain, for him, was to turn back to childhood experiences, to repressed or suppressed instinctive forces, whole wholly neglecting the positive function that consciousness and our relation to reality might have.[8]

Secondly, the individual is, for Freud, an absolute subject, for whom other men can only be *objects* of satisfaction or frustration. This fact may be the basis for the absence of the future just noted.

No doubt it would be erroneous to reduce the Freudian libido too narrowly to the sexual domain; yet it remains true that the libido is always *individual* and that in the Freudian vision of humanity the collective subject and the satisfaction collective action may bring to the individual are completely lacking.

One could develop at length, with the help of many concrete examples, the distortions engendered by these perspectives in Freudian analyses of cultural and historical facts. From this standpoint, Marxism seems to us incomparably more advanced in the degree to which it integrates not only the future as an explanatory factor, but also the individual meaning of human facts alongside their collective meaning.

Finally, on the level which interests us here, that of the works of culture, and particularly literary works, it seems to us undeniable that the latter can be validly integrated into meaningful structures of an individual sort and of a collective sort. Only, it goes without saying, the actual and valid meanings which can be discerned through these two integrations are at once different and complementary in nature. The integration of works into an individual biography could in effect reveal only their individual signification and their relationship with biographical and psychic problems regarding the author. This amounts to saying that, whatever the validity and the scientific rigor of studies of this type, they must necessarily situate the work outside its cultural context and its apposite aesthetic, in order to put it on the same level as any of the individual symptoms of this or that ill person treated by a psychoanalyst.

Supposing—without granting—that on the individual level one might validly refer the writings of Pascal to his relations with his sister, or those of Kleist to his relations with his sister and his father, *one would have brought out an emotional and biographical meaning of those writings, but one would have neither touched upon nor even come close to their philosophical or literary meaning.* Thousands and tens of thousands of individuals have certainly had analogous relationships with family members, and we do not see to what degree at all a psychoanalytic study of these symptoms could account for the difference *in kind* between the writings of this or that madman and the *Pensées* or *The Prince of Homburg.*

The only use, and a rather limited one at that, of psychological and psychoanalytic analyses for literary criticism seems to us to be their capacity to explain why, in such and such a concrete situation, where such and such a social group has elaborated a certain vision of the world, such and such an individual was particularly prone, thanks to his individual biography, to create some conceptual or imaginary universe to whatever degree he could find therein, among other things, a derivative or sublimated satisfaction for his own unconscious aspirations.[9] This means that it is only out of a historico-sociological analysis that the philosophical significance of the *Pensées*, the literary and aesthetic significance of the dramas of Kleist, and the genesis of each can be *comprehended as cultural facts.*

As for psychological studies, these can at most help us to comprehend how, among the hundreds of Jansenists, it was precisely Racine and Pascal who were able to express the tragic vision on the literary and philosophical plane; without, however, yielding the slightest information (unless on this or that secondary and minor detail) regarding the nature, the content, and the meaning of the expression.

It remains, in conclusion, to broach schematically a particularly important problem: that of the individual function (play, dreams, morbid symptoms, sublimations) and the collective function (literary, cultural and artistic values) of the imaginary, in relation to meaningful human structures that commonly present all the marks of being dynamic and structured relations between a subject (individual or collective) and a surrounding milieu.

The problem is complex, and little studied. In closing this essay, we can only formulate a vague and provisional hypothesis. It seems to us in effect that on the psychic level the activity of the subject always takes shape as an ensemble of aspirations, of tendencies, or desires prevented by reality from achieving integral satisfaction.

Marx and Lukács, at the collective level, and Piaget, at the individual level, have studied closely the modifications introduced into the very nature of these desires and aspirations by the difficulties and obstacles raised by the object. Freud showed that on the individual level, desires, even modified, cannot rest content with partial satisfaction and accept repression with no problems. His great merit lay in having discovered that a rational relationship to reality requires the complement of an imaginary satisfaction, which may take the most diverse forms, from the adaptive structures of slips and dreams to the maladaptive structures of derangement and madness. It may be that, despite all the differences (for we do not believe that there can be a collective unconscious), the function of culture is analogous. Human groups might not be able to act rationally on reality and adapt themselves to the frustrations or partial satisfactions imposed by this activity and the obstacles they collide with, save to the degree to which rational and transforming action is accompanied by integral satisfactions at the level of conceptual or imaginary creation.

It must be added here that if, on the individual level, the repressed instincts subsist *in the unconscious* and tend toward a symbolic satisfaction which is always *possession of the object*, collective tendencies, which are often implicit but not unconscious, do not aim at *possession*, but at *realization of coherence*.

Cultural creation thus compensates the compromises and the mix imposed by reality on subjects, and facilitates their insertion into the real world, which is perhaps the psychological foundation of catharsis.

A hypothesis of this sort, which would integrate without difficulty what is valuable in Freudian analyses and in Marxist studies of art and cultural creation, might account for both the parentage—so often sensed by numerous theorists—and the disparity in kind which likewise exists, between play, dream, or even certain forms of morbid imagination, and the great literary, artistic, and even philosophical creations.

Notes

[1] From this perspective sociological inquiry can, at the outside, help to explain the *genesis* of the work, but could in no way help in a *comprehension* of it.

[2] However, if it is impossible to insert into the biographical structure the content

and the form, in sum, the specifically literary, philosophical or artistic structure of great works of a culture, a psychological school of the genetic-structuralist type, psychoanalysis, does succeed to a certain extent in disclosing *alongside this specific cultural essence* an *individual* structure and meaning for these works, which it believes itself capable of inserting into the biographical career. We will return briefly at the end of this essay to the possibilities and limitations of such an insertion.

³ Sheer statistical empiricism is acquainted with analogous consequences of the very same factor: it is practically speaking impossible to predict without a large margin of error whether Peter, James or John will get married, will have an automobile accident, or will die next year, but it is not difficult, in contrast, to predict within a very small margin of error the number of marriages, accidents, and deaths which will occur in France in such and such a week of the year.

This said, and even though they are comparable phenomena, there are considerable differences between such statistical predictions regarding a reality whose structures have not been brought out, and a genetic-structuralist analysis.

⁴ Sociological inquiries of this sort are on the same plane as content-sociology, which likewise can account only for certain secondary and peripheral elements of a work.

⁵ As an example, one might start with the hypothesis of the existence of a significant structure known as dictatorship; one would thus come to a grouping of phenomena such as, for example, political regimes in which the government has absolute powers. But if one tries to account for the genesis of all these regimes with a single structural hypothesis, one soon sees that dictatorship is not a significant structure, and that one must distinguish groups of dictatorships which are different in kind and meaning; so that, for example, the concepts of revolutionary dictatorship, or to the contrary post-revolutionary Bonapartist dictatorship, seem to constitute workable concepts.

Similarly any attempt at a unitary interpretation of the writings of Pascal (and they have been numerous) fails before the fact that his two most important works, *les Provinciales* and the *Pensées,* express essentially different perspectives. If one wishes to understand them, one must consider them as expressions of two structures which are distinct, even if, from certain angles, comparable.

⁶ On this level, especially in the sociology of culture, it is wise to use an external and quantitative safeguard. In interpreting a piece of writing, it goes without saying that there can be a certain number of different interpretations which take account of sixty to seventy percent of the text. This is why a result of that sort must not be deemed scientific confirmation. On the other hand, only rarely can one find two different interpretations that integrate eighty to ninety percent of a text, and the hypothesis which does so has every likelihood of being valid. This probability greatly increases if one succeeds in inserting the structure disclosed through the genetic analysis into a larger whole; if one succeeds in using it effectively to explain other texts one did not have in mind; and above all if, as occurred in our study of seventeenth-century tragedy, one succeeds in illuminating and even predicting a certain number of facts unknown to specialists and historians.

⁷ We know too little of its later developments to venture to discuss them.

⁸ It is no doubt tempting to explain this characteristic of the work of Freud by the fact that he was a doctor, who studied mainly sick persons, that is to say, persons in whom past forces and resistances predominate over positive forces oriented toward equilibration and the future. Unfortunately, the criticism we have formulated applies also to Freud's philosophical and sociological studies.

The word "future" appears in the title of only one of his writings, and—a telling fact regarding the body of his works—that book is called *The Future of an Illusion*. Its content shows, moreover, that that future does not exist.

[9] Conversely, sociological inquiry can furnish no information on the individual and biographical meaning of a work, and could supply psychoanalysts only with relatively secondary information on the forms of real or imaginary satisfaction favored or imposed by the collective structures in a given period or in a given society.

21. Frederick Antal

Remarks on the Method
of Art-History

The Hungarian art historian FREDERICK ANTAL (1887–1954) has perhaps been more influential in his field in the years since his death than he was during his lifetime. The posthumous publication of many of his writings revealed a mind whose close and detailed studies of certain artists and their social backgrounds showed an exemplary sense of historical method. He pioneered in the study of the evolution of Mannerism, and in the period of painting from the French Revolution through Géricault. He wrote illuminating essays on Bronzino, Watteau, Fuseli, the place of Hogarth in European art, and Florentine painting in relation to its social setting. The essay on method in art history first appeared in *The Burlington Magazine* in 1949, and has been republished in a collection of the late author's writings entitled *Classicism and Romanticism*.

THE following are a few casual thoughts, in no sense systematic, on the method of art-history, which have occurred to me while looking through some art-historical literature of the past years.

It is, of course, platitudinous to say that art-history deals with the history of art, that it combines and connects art and history. It is equally obvious that the method used in art-history, as in other disciplines, undergoes certain changes from generation to generation. That of each generation depends on how it views art and how it views history and on the differing combination and proportion of the two components which, as a result, arise afresh in every generation.[1] So the method of art-history naturally constitutes a part of the prevailing intellectual outlook, the problems and interests, of successive periods. Alterations in art-historical methods do not in the least cancel out achievements of previous generations, but only effect a shift of accent which brings into relief ideas in art, as in history, which the particular generation considers most important. For not only do the various methods differ in the importance they accord to history, but they are also largely determined by the preoccupations of historical research itself in the period in question.

Compared with earlier methods (say, with Karl Justi, who described the cultural background and the personal character of great artists), Wölfflin's formalistic method conceded, relatively, the smallest place to history. His approach, to a greater degree than that of his predecessors, tended ultimately to reflect the then prevailing doctrine of art for art's sake. This thesis, as is well known, had been conceived by a group of French Romantics and propagated mainly in the fifties and sixties of the nineteenth century by writers and poets, who believed in erecting an ivory tower for themselves, who considered art to be detached from the ideas of their time, and who stressed in art the 'eternal,' the 'absolute,' that is, the purely formal values.[2] Wölfflin's very lucid, formal analyses, behind which is an undisguised bias in favor of the classicist Cinquecento composition, reduced the wealth of historical evolution to a few fundamental categories, a few typified schemes. The Viennese school of art-history, to which Riegl, Wickhoff, and Dvořák belonged, gave a far more prominent place than did Wölfflin to history and the historical development of style.[3] Here, works of art were treated as threads in the stylistic development, and so great was the value placed upon the continuity of this evolution that so-called 'dark periods,' 'periods of decay,' like those of the late antique, of mannerism, of baroque, that is, periods of which previous art-historians had disapproved, were no longer recognized as such, but were studied constructively and with particular thoroughness. Although scholars of the Viennese school made most exact, formal analyses, even as inexorably logical as Riegl's, they—the late Riegl himself and particularly Dvořák—combined them with analyses of themes and of thematic features. Continuing Riegl, who, in his late phase, regarded his notion of the 'art-will' as dependent on the outlook of the period in question, Dvořák, in his later years, dealt with art-history as part of the history of ideas, of the development of the human spirit. As I was myself a pupil first of Wölfflin and then of Dvořák, I can still feel the great difference in the spiritual atmosphere of these two scholars. I should like to mention a characteristic example of the wide-embracing scope of Dvořák's approach. When writing of the art of the Van Eycks as early as 1904 he remarked that art-history had so far offered no explanation of its sudden emergence, but that the exploration of the sources of the new bourgeois culture in Flanders, of which this art was a product, could only be found in books of economic history. Wölfflin would never have said anything approaching this.

However, it has been chiefly in recent decades since Dvořák's death, as a more general interest has been taken in economic and social ques-

tions, that economic and social history within history has made such
rapid strides—parallel to the sudden rise of sociology and the social sciences. It was almost twenty years after writing his *History of England*
that G. M. Trevelyan gave us, in 1942—a sign of the new trend—his
English Social History. How the history of ideas, which previously led
a comparatively isolated existence, has come to be closely connected with
social history, so that certain types of outlook, in a given period, take on
a clear outline, is well seen in R. H. Tawney's *Religion and the Rise of
Capitalism* (London, 1926), a justly renowned example of this new
tendency. The importance of social and religious history for an understanding of the history of literature and the entirely new interpretations
resulting from it are shown—to name one book among many—by G.
Thomson's *Aeschylus and Athens* (London, 1941).[4] The favorite field of
art-history, the Italian Renaissance, has lately been worked through, from
the new angle, in A. v. Martin's *Sociology of the Italian Renaissance*
(English translation, London, 1944). Like the other historical sciences,
the history of religion or the history of literature, art-history too is now
taking notice of, and using for its own purposes, the ever closer cooperation between the various historical disciplines and the broadening that
has taken place in historical research through a mounting interest
in social history. All the more, since our views not only on history but
also on art have been modified. We have come to look at art, just as
history, in a less esoteric light, associated more closely, in devious ways,
with problems of real, everyday life; hence, for instance, the increasing
attention given to the subject-matter of works of art—a clear indication
that the art for art's sake point of view has much weakened.[5] It is this
new combination of the two components which characterizes the method
of art-history in our generation.

Here it was Warburg, with his wide range of interest in many cultural
and historical disciplines, who did most of the pioneering work and whose
life-long activity so clearly contained the germs of a new method of art-
history. I will confine myself here to recalling his numerous well-known
essays, between 1902 and 1907, devoted to the examination of the mental-
ity and artistic taste of the Florentine middle-class patrons at the time of
Lorenzo de' Medici. Since his death his research work has been continued
in the same spirit by the Institute which bears his name and which is
now incorporated into London University. Warburg's point of view is
best summarized in the words of his own disciples. In her introduction
to Warburg's writings, Dr. Gertrude Bing describes how, aided by
material in the Florentine archives, he succeeded in rescuing the work of
art from the isolation with which it was threatened by a purely aesthetic
and formal approach. In examining in each case the inter-dependence
between the pictorial and literary evidence, the relation of the artist to

the patron, the close connection between the work of art, its social milieu and its practical purpose, Warburg took into consideration not only the products of great art but also minor and aesthetically insignificant works of pictorial art. Or, to use the terminology of another scholar associated with the school of Warburg, Edgar Wind: [6] Warburg was just as averse to the autonomy of a Wölfflinian, isolationist art-history as to the artificial boundaries between the 'purely artistic' and the 'non-artistic' factors, constructed by art-historians. In fact, works of popular and half-popular art were, and are, constantly adduced by Warburg himself and by scholars of the Warburg Institute, in particular by the late F. Saxl, for an understanding of the whole art and the whole world of thought of a period. [7]

The severely historical spirit of the school of Vienna and the resolutely anti-art-for-art's-sake attitude of Warburg together paved the way for a deeper, richer and less nebulous study of art-history, which can draw upon the very tangible results of the historical disciplines, in particular of social and economic, of political and religious history (not exclusively of the history of literature and philosophy) as well as of an historically-intentioned social psychology. Art-historians are now in a position to take seriously into account the many-sidedness of any one period, the complexity of types of outlook, and the mode of thought among various sections of the public,[8] in order to discover which style belongs to which outlook on life—the notion of style, of course, not being restricted to formal features, but including subject-matter. If we look at the whole of society, not only its topmost layers, we come to understand the *raison d'être* of all pictures, not only the best, the most famous, the full meaning of which cannot, indeed, be really grasped in isolation. The more carefully it is scrutinized, the more easily and naturally does the social, intellectual, and artistic picture throughout a period slowly unfold itself and the way in which its parts are connected become increasingly clarified. This, then, is the kind of process now taking place in art-historical literature, particularly, but by no means exclusively, in America.

The various authors represent very different individual shades and manners of approach, yet, historically speaking, they all form part of one trend. I cannot, of course, list the multiplicity of themes which have been examined of recent years in closest connection with the actual life and thought of different periods. But readers would, I think, like to cast a rapid glance at a few suggestive examples.

Herbert Read, treating the function of art in society, has explored the general nature of the links between the forms of society at any given period and the forms of contemporary art.[9] R. Krautheimer has shown that the purely formal approach of recent times to medieval architecture had entirely obscured the elements which, in the view of medieval men, were outstanding in an edifice: namely, its religious implications, that is, its 'content.'[10] Meyer Schapiro's numerous writings have also thrown completely new light on certain aspects of the art of the Middle Ages: he has associated, for instance, the style of the Ruthwell Cross of seventh-century Northumbria, or the differences between the Mozarabic and the Romanesque styles practised concurrently at the end of the eleventh century in the monastery of Silos in Castille, with the religious struggles and the social and political transformations of those times.[11] For the past decade or so, an ever-increasing literature has been appearing on the working conditions of artists of the Italian Renaissance, particularly in Florence, on their position within the guilds, on the various kinds of commissions, on patronage, on the prices received, etc.[12] Above all, we begin to see more clearly than before how the various styles within Italian art of this period were deeply rooted in the types of outlook and in the social and political condition of the period.[13] M. Meiss, for instance, when enumerating the characteristics of Tuscan painting in the second half of the Trecento—abandonment of three-dimensionality and of perspective, limitation of the movements of figures, contrasting colors, ascetic or emotional expressions—has defined them as expressing a state of mind influenced by the economic crisis beginning in the forties and by the shift of power from the merchants and bankers to the lesser guilds and the lower middle class, bearers of a more conservative culture.[14] It is worth mentioning that, working independently through the same historical sources and the same literature of social history, I came to identical results myself, contrasting the Florentine painting of this period with the realist classicism of the early fourteenth (Giotto) and early fifteenth centuries (Masaccio) when the more rationalist upper middle class was in power.[15] E. Gombrich, having demonstrated how Botticelli's mythological pictures are firmly rooted in the literary and philosophical outlook of Lorenzo di Pierfrancesco de' Medici's circle, suggests an important parallel between the different political views of Lorenzo il Magnifico and Lorenzo di Pierfrancesco and their differing artistic tastes: Ghirlandaio and Bertoldo in contrast to Botticelli. Anthony Blunt has sketched the connection between the social and political events, the mode of thought and the artistic theories in fifteenth- and sixteenth-century Italy.[16] In an article on Greco's so-called *Dream of Philip II*, the same author derives the formal features from the complex thematic elements, theological (Adoration of the Holy Name of Jesus) as well as political (Holy League of the Papacy, Spain, and Venice).[17] Again, in his book on Mansart, Blunt points out how the somewhat romantic classicism of this architect was suited to the court aristocracy and the rich financiers imitating them, for whom he worked;[18] and further, how the style of Mansart's churches differs according to the particular type of religious belief of the Order in question.[19] Saxl has equally sought the explanation of Aniello

Falcone's realistic battle pictures which contain no specific hero, in the social type and taste of the particular Neapolitan patrons of this artist in the second third of the seventeenth century.[20] Wind has demonstrated that Reynolds' grand solemn style and Gainsborough's simple, natural style corresponded to the two types of outlook then prevailing: the first to the heroic nature of Dr. Johnson's and Beattie's attitude, the second to the human and sceptical conception of Hume.[21] In another of his writings the same author has shown how a new trend in history painting, based on an accurate rendering of contemporary events, drew its impulse from the democratic ideas proclaimed by the American artists, West and Copley, at the time of the War of Independence; further, he makes revealing comparisons between the styles of history painting as they arose from the American and French Revolutions.[22] Schapiro has indicated how the discovery and appreciation of the folk art of the lower classes took place in a circle of radical artists and writers, among them Courbet, who sympathized with the Revolution of 1848, and how a knowledge of this art had a definite bearing upon Courbet's realism.[23] 'Backward' pictures, even of recent epochs, are now considered to be interesting and worth explaining on account of the particular outlook they represent. For instance, in 1938, two exhibitions were organized at the Baltimore Museum of Art and the Walters Art Gallery: one centering around Courbet, the other displaying his contemporary adversaries, the academic counter-movement; the explanatory lectures by members of different faculties of Baltimore University, later published, discussed at length the point of view not only of the naturalists, but also of the conservative official artists of the Second Empire.[24] And finally, to include a work which deals with modern art, S. Giedion has examined the relation between architecture and social development in Europe, particularly in London, and in America in the nineteenth and twentieth centuries.[25]

To acknowledge the significance of social development and of different types of outlook for understanding the diversity of styles and stylistic evolution does not, of course, carry with it an underestimation of the formal features nor detract from the enjoyment of their quality nor imply that real results already achieved in art-historical literature through formal analyses have lost their validity. Rather the contrary.[26] We can foresee that within two or three generations a new overall pattern of stylistic developments will have been evolved. Such a pattern will buttress and clarify the purely formal evolutions already established by pegging them to a basis wider than previously thought possible.

Why is it, we may ask, that a tendency still remains among some art-historians to put a brake upon efforts to broaden art-history by a study of social history? As regards England, since the seventeenth and eighteenth

centuries an admirable tradition of art theory, art criticism, and connoisseurship has flourished here. Art-history, on the other hand, as a
university discipline, obliged to stand on its own feet, work out its own
field of research and its own method, is of very recent growth. The new
science necessarily originated in previous art criticism; at first, towards
the end of the nineteenth century, in its more impressionistic form, art
criticism was largely concerned to describe the fleeting reactions of a
sensitive beholder before a work of art, while later, in the early twentieth
century, an attempt was made to modify this extreme subjectivism by a
more controlled, more constructed, but still unhistorical approach. The
historical point of view naturally came into the new discipline where it
was the most urgently needed, the most obviously lacking, and where a
transition from the previous stage of art criticism could be most easily
effected: in the construction of the historical development on a formal
basis. So the space allotted to history within art-history was relatively
small, as it had been in the Wölfflin school. But, while in the Wölfflin
school the theory of art for art's sake could only be sensed as a distant
though necessary phenomenon, here art-history, because of its later origin
in an esoteric art criticism, was still closely and directly bound up with
it. It is almost a hundred years since Ruskin, than whom none could
have been more averse to the art for art's sake attitude, considered art as
expressive of the society which produced it, if mainly of the ethical life
of society, and was stimulated in consequence of his study of art to a
thorough study of the social structure and social economy.[27] In contrast
to Ruskin not only many writers during his later life-time and after him,
but even some art-historians of our own day have still been apt to believe,
fundamentally, that art is a world by itself which has, and should have,
as little contact as possible with the tangible world. Since they cannot
be consistently historical, these latter still adhere to the supposition that
the art for art's sake point of view is unchangeable. They cannot imagine
that art-history is a piece of history [28] and that the art-historian's task
is primarily not to approve or to disapprove of a given work of art from
his own point of view, but to try to understand and explain it in the
light of its own historical premises; and that there is no contradiction
between a picture as a work of art and as a document of its time, since
the two are complementary. Nor can they appreciate that familiarity
with outlook and taste aids us in comprehending, not only the complete
style of a picture, but ultimately, even its quality: partly because the
quality of a given picture, in its special nuance, can only be seriously
judged if compared with other pictures of the same style and even more
so because knowledge historically-grounded is the only sure means of
neutralizing our subjective judgment on the quality of works of art of the
past, even on the significance of individual styles, which otherwise is too

exclusively conditioned by our penchant for one tendency or another in contemporary art akin to them.[29]

In recent years, as is well known, historical scholarship in England has tended to emphasize the economic and social aspects. Yet, for instance, though Tawney's book, which we have mentioned, is one of the most widely-read, art-historians of the older persuasion appear to be unacquainted with the fruitful achievements of modern historical research which is to be found, so to speak, on their doorsteps.[30] It is distasteful to them to find, embedded in art-historical literature, facts and terms, commonplaces in every historical book, with which they are unfamiliar and the art-historical implications and consequences of which they fail to grasp.[31] Living in their ivory tower, they think that to adduce the results of social or ecclesiastical history must degrade an art-history which should, at least theoretically, be reserved to masterpieces and in which the diversity of styles is explained by the diversity of styles. The sensitiveness and esoteric nature of their spiritual ancestors has by now become a search for precious, if possible, unusual words. We can feel no surprise, therefore, under such conditions, if the non-art-historian, in particular the social historian, for example E. Halévy, in the short chapter on art in his *History of the English People*, 1815 (English translation, London, 1924) can make striking, new art-historical observations which, in many ways, are more interesting and revealing than those of some art-historians on the same period.

The whole point of view of art-historians, of whatever country or training, who have not yet even absorbed the achievements of Riegl, Dvořák, and Warburg (let alone tried to go beyond them) is conditioned by their historical place: they cling to older conceptions, thereby lagging behind at least some quarter of a century. And, in the same way are conditioned their step-by-step retreat and the concessions they are willing to make— not too many and not too soon—to the new spirit. Their resistance is all the stronger, their will to give ground, all the less, the greater the consistency and novelty they encounter. They themselves frequently publish weak pictures by fifth-rate masters, provided the period is remote enough: for these are attributions to, say, the Master of the Goodenough Deposition, and thus are justified from the point of view of connoisseurship.[32] Even the abundant literature on popular and semi-popular art is not, I believe, particularly frowned upon so long as this art is kept well apart from the general stylistic development or, at any rate, can be considered diverting and charming, reminiscent of Henri Rousseau. Discussion of the subject-matter seems permissible as long as it is restricted to an iconography in which the explanation of the choice of subject is kept as aloof as possible from living history. Literature on the working conditions of artists is not, I think, objected to, provided it remains detached and conclusions which could be drawn from it are not incorporated into literature dealing with great artists but are limited to isolated and casual reference. The innumerable allusions in art-historical literature to the social and political background usually pass unchallenged as long as the connection between it and art is left, on the whole, comfortably vague.[33] In the case of some artists of more recent centuries, however, practising secular art, the connection is so obvious that constant reference to it in literature has bred familiarity: in the case, for instance, of Hogarth, David or Géricault. Thus, a step further which reaches the precise association of style and outlook, a step so small that it is scarcely noticeable, passes without comment.[34] But when it is no longer a question of secular art of the eighteenth or nineteenth centuries but, let us say, of religious art of remoter times as was, for instance, the case in my book on Florentine painting of the fourteenth and early fifteenth centuries, then there still appears an objection on the part of some art-historians to the discussion of differences in religious sentiment and consequently in religious art, as associated with various social groups; they would prefer to keep Fra Angelico and Botticelli in the dream-world ambient where the pre-Raphaelites put them. Although lately it has become fashionable to introduce a few historical facts, these may only enter the art-historical picture when confined to hackneyed political history, in a diluted form, which gives as little indication as possible of the existing structure of society and does not disturb the romantic twilight of the atmosphere. The last redoubt which will be held as long as possible is, of course, the most deep-rooted nineteenth-century belief, inherited from Romanticism, of the incalculable nature of genius in art. It is, however, characteristic of the strength of the new trend that L. Münz, the best connoisseur of Rembrandt in our day, should have brought out, in 1931, a popular, annotated edition of Riegl's famous essay of 1902, on the Dutch Portrait Group; here, without detracting in any way from his grandeur, Rembrandt is treated as a link in a long chain and subjected to an analysis so exact and so instructive as to horrify every supporter of the genius theory.[35]

Methods of art-history, just as pictures, can be dated. This is by no means a depreciation of pictures or methods—just a banal historical statement. But the time will naturally come when the exclusive formalists will generally be recognized as in the rear of art-history, as today are the antiquarians and anecdotalists.

Notes

[1] This, of course, is over-simplification. It was particularly during the heroic years around 1900, spiritually so rich and complex, that various methods of art-history,

to a certain extent, overlapped. However, seen in perspective, the main trend of development is clearly discernible.

[2] In A. Cassagne's well-documented book, *La Théorie de l'Art pour l'Art en France,* Paris, 1906, we read how this theory, originated by Théophile Gautier, developed and under what social and historical circumstances it finally got the upper hand, in spite of early resistance from Victor Hugo and George Sand.

[3] It is no mere chance that, at the University of Vienna, the Art-Historical Institute took its place within the framework of the Austrian Institute of Historical Research. In his articles on Riegl and Wickhoff, Dvořák describes the struggle of both these scholars against aesthetic dogmatism, and characterizes Riegl's method as the victory of the psychological and historical conception of art-history over an absolute aesthetics.

[4] See chapter 26, G. Thomson, "After Aeschylus." (—*Eds.*)

Some forgotten but valuable books have now become topical for the same reason. In consequence of the interest recently taken in social analyses of the literary public, A. Beljame's book of 1881, *Le Public et les Hommes de Lettres en Angleterre au 18e siècle,* has just been translated and published in English. (—*Eds.*)

[5] That is why—to take an outstanding example—such a widespread interest is now shown among the public in Hogarth, who, not many years ago, was still looked down upon in art-history and dubbed a 'literary' artist.

[6] See his introduction to the *Bibliography on the Survival of the Classics,* edited by the Warburg Institute, London, 1934.

[7] How little Saxl cared for the 'boundaries' of art-history, is shown, to take one instance, in his article 'The Classical Inscription in Renaissance Art and Politics' (*Journal of the Warburg and Courtauld Institutes,* IV, 1940–41), where he has treated together copies made by humanists of ancient inscriptions and of ancient monuments, stressing the political implications of the former for the men of the Renaissance.

As is well known, scholars of the Warburg Institute have often been able, by means of an historical approach, to explain the subject-matter and to re-create the real meaning and spirit of works of art which previously had been entirely misinterpreted by generations of writers. In the case of Botticelli's mythological pictures, this has just been rectified by E. Gombrich ('Botticelli's Mythologies: A Study in the Neoplatonic Symbolism of His Circle,' *Journal of the Warburg and Courtauld Institutes,* VIII, 1945), in that of Mantegna's by Wind (*Bellini's Feast of the Gods,* Cambridge, Mass., 1948). On this occasion, Gombrich writes: 'The beautiful pages which have been written by masters of prose on the emotional import of Botticelli's figures remain purely subjective unless the context in which these figures stand can be established by outside means,' and Wind: 'Mantegna's *Parnassus* has had the singular misfortune of being praised for the very qualities which it attempts to mock.'

[8] What G. M. Trevelyan writes of England is true of all countries: 'In everything the old overlaps the new—in religion, in thought, in family custom. There is never any clear cut; there is no single moment when all Englishmen adopt new ways of life and thought. . . . To obtain a true picture of any period, both the old and the new elements must be borne in mind' (*English Social History*).

[9] *Art and Society,* London, 1947.

[10] 'Introduction to an "Iconography of Medieval Architecture,"' *Journal of the Warburg and Coutauld Institutes,* IV, 1940–41.

[11] In Northumbria, the struggle took place between the Celtic, particularist, monastic Church, shaped by the conditions of tribal society and the Roman Church, which was aiming at the integration of local peoples into the larger ambient of European and Mediterranean life ("The Religious Meaning of the Ruthwell Cross,' *Art Bulletin,*

XXVI, 1944); in his other article ('From Mozarabic to Romanesque in Silos,' *Art Bulletin*, XXI, 1939) Schapiro has explained the coexistence of the fantastic conservative, with the more naturalistic modern, style as due to the steady change then occurring in the outlook of the increasingly centralized Spanish Church and ultimately to the transition of Christian Spain from scattered agricultural communities to powerful centralized states with urban secular middle classes. Dr. Joan Evans' *Art in Medieval France: A Study in Patronage* has just been published by the Oxford University Press (*—Eds.*); she shows French medieval art as the mirror of society for which it was produced, by explaining that this art took the forms it did because of the needs of the different sections of society who commissioned it.

[12] Anthony Blunt has shown that the struggle of the artists to better their social position decisively influenced their art theories (*Artistic Theory in Italy 1450–1600*, Oxford, 1940).

[13] Warburg's friend, the economic historian, Doren, already saw, half a century ago, the emptiness of un-historical discussions on Florentine art. In his book of 1901 on the Florentine woollen industry of the fourteenth and fifteenth centuries, a standard work on this period, he affirms that the knowledge of social and economic history of that time would dispel forever the conception of Florence as a community living in conditions of carefree prosperity, general harmony, and timeless beauty.

[14] 'Italian Primitives in Konopiste,' *Art Bulletin*, XXVIII, 1946.

[15] *Florentine Painting and Its Social Background*, London, 1948.

[16] Alberti's rational art theory, Blunt finds, was dependent upon his political outlook, that of the pre-Medici Florentine city-state, while the mystical Neoplatonic art theory was suited to the state of mind prevailing during the Medici autocracy. He asserts that the irrational, neo-medieval tendencies of mannerism and mannerist art theory, are only comprehensible against the background of political and religious reaction caused by the destruction of the great merchant republics with which the Papacy had been allied and by the Papacy's move from a leading place among the progressive states of Italy to one of reaction, subsequently allied with an almost feudal Spain.

[17] El Greco's "Dream of Philip II": An Allegory of the Holy League,' *Journal of the Warburg and Courtauld Institutes*, III, 1939–40.

[18] He explains its difference from the severe classicism of Poussin and Corneille, who express the progressive and earnest ideals of civil servants and of the merchants of Paris and Lyons (*Mansart*, London, The Warburg Institute, 1941).

[19] In his book on the artistic theories in Italy, Blunt has shown that the worldly, emotional religion of the Jesuits preferred the emotional, pre-baroque tendencies in mannerist painting (*Barocci*).

[20] Wealthy gentry and cool-headed businessmen, not warrior types nor politicians but closely associated with and affected by warfare and civil strife (Masaniello) and having a preference for violent and descriptive realistic art, such as was produced in various parts of Europe ('The Battle Scene without a Hero: Aniello Falcone and His Patrons,' *Journal of the Warburg and Courtauld Institutes*, III, 1939–40).

[21] 'Humanitätsidee und heroisiertes Porträt in der englischen Kultur des 18. Jahrhunderts,' *Vorträge der Bibliothek Warburg*, IX, 1930–31.

[22] 'The Revolution of History Painting,' *Journal of the Warburg and Courtauld Institutes*, II, 1938–39. In his *English Expressionist Artists in the 19th Century* (Thesis at the Courtauld Institute, 1938), E. M. Zwanenberg-Phillips bases his explanation of Blake and his followers upon an analysis of the social background.

[23] Schapiro has further noted how the difference in the social and political constellations existing before and under Napoleon III caused Courbet's friend, Champ-

fleury, who had also belonged to this circle, to give different interpretations of popular art during the two periods ('Courbet and Popular Imagery,' *Journal of the Warburg and Courtauld Institutes*, IV 1940). The re-discovery of the le Nains by Champfleury ('The Revival of the le Nains,' *Art Bulletin*, XXIV, 1942) and that of Vermeer by Bürger-Thoré, when a political exile under Napoleon III, have equally been shown by S. Meltzoff to be a result of the predilection for realism of the same circle, whose aesthetics were influenced by their democratic ideas ('The Rediscovery of Vermeer,' *Marsyas*, II, 1942, New York University).

²⁴ *Courbet and the Naturalistic Movement.* Essays read at the Baltimore Museum of Art, edited by G. Boas, Baltimore, 1938.

²⁵ *Space, Time, and Architecture*, Cambridge, Mass., 1941.

²⁶ The results on re-gothicization during the Quattrocento at which I arrived some twenty-five years ago through formal analyses have now been confirmed through my study of the whole historical material. In a recent article ('Observations on Girolamo da Carpi.') I have also tried to show how the continuation of Quattrocento Gothic in Mannerism, which I saw in my earlier writings mainly as a formal process, was ultimately based on the social changes.

²⁷ In his Ruskin lecture, "Ruskin's Politics," London, 1921, Bernard Shaw drew attention to this evolution remarking, incidentally, that this marked his own development too.

²⁸ I purposely employ the expression 'piece of history' because Saxl (himself a product of the school of Vienna) used it in conversation with me.

²⁹ Interest in baroque and mannerist art, which originated, as we have mentioned, within the Viennese school of art-history, was a consequence of the growing historical thoroughness of this school's own researches, while at the same time reflecting contemporary art tendencies. The analysis of baroque art began with Riegl in the last years of the nineteenth century, that of mannerism with Dvořák in the years preceding World War I. Though recognition of the qualities of the latter style, of course, coincided with the taste for contemporary expressionist art, as time goes on and with the growth of our knowledge of the spiritual and social background of mannerism, we shall obtain an increasingly objective idea of this style.

³⁰ Nor, to take an example nearer to art-history, do they appear to be conversant with the writings of the outstanding prehistoric archaeologist, V. Gordon Childe, which extend not only to oriental but even to classical antiquity and which establish the closest possible relations between social structure, religion, mental outlook, and art.

³¹ The connection between religious and economic thought, as Tawney has demonstrated, can no longer be disputed today. Yet, it is apparently only the historian who is allowed to be aware of this, not the art-historian, and, if the pure formalists had it their own way, art-history would be destined to carry on in a water-tight compartment cut off from the other historical disciplines. This is even true of terminology. In the 1937 preface to his book, *Religion and the Rise of Capitalism*, originally published in 1926, Tawney wrote: 'When this book first appeared, it was possible for a friendly reviewer, writing in a serious journal, to deprecate in all gravity the employment of the term "Capitalism" in an historical work, as a political catch-word, betraying a sinister intention on the part of the misguided author. An innocent solecism of the kind would not, it is probable, occur so readily today.' It can, however, occur even in 1948 from the same innocence, when it is a question not of historians but of art-historians, who, as regards certain current terms, are fettered by a primitive word fetishism.

³² To avoid any misunderstanding: nothing would be more puerile than to deny

the obvious importance of attributions. What will soon be gone with the wind is that over-accentuation, which tends to confine art-history to attributions almost for attributions' sake.

[33] C. Gutkind's *Cosimo de' Medici*, Oxford, 1938, is a typical case where a well-meaning author has felt the need to adduce far more economic and social history than had previously been done, but has not yet arrived at the stage of drawing any conclusions from them or of connecting them with anything. A large part of the book deals in almost too great detail with the economic conditions in Florence and with Cosimo's business interests, while, in the chapter 'Cosimo in Private Life,' his philosophy of life (and, of course, also his liking for art and learning) remains entirely detached, so that we acquire no all around picture of Cosimo's person and outlook.

[34] Articles I wrote on those three artists and to which no exception was taken were in the same vein as my book on Florentine painting, mentioned below.

[35] I would like to recall here Münz's opinion that a closer understanding of Rembrandt's works is gained by the realization that they are charged with meaning and emotion than by those 'happily now obsolete, aesthetic approaches from which Rembrandt's work was seen either as realism empty of all emotional content or as a magic of light and shade so exalted, so unique and intangible, that all attempts to search for a meaning became irrelevant' ('Rembrandt's "Synagogue" and Some Problems of Nomenclature,' *Journal of the Warburg and Courtauld Institutes*, III, 1939–40).

22. Arnold Hauser

Sociology of Art

ARNOLD HAUSER, born in Hungary in 1892, a British citizen since 1948, and a frequent lecturer at American universities and museums, is a leading figure in the philosophy and history of art. His work reflects the influence of such celebrated thinkers as Henri Bergson, Georg Simmel, Werner Sombart, and Ernst Troeltsch, as well as Karl Marx. He has combined detailed research in art history with an extensive understanding of philosophy, sociology, and economics in his numerous writings on the methods and concepts of art history. The selection is taken from *The Philosophy of Art History*, originally published in Germany in 1958 under the title *Philosophie der Kunstgeschichte*. Theories of both Marx and Freud have been important in the development of his thought, though he has been highly selective in what he has accepted in their theories.

A WORK of art is a challenge, we do not explain it, we adjust ourselves to it. In interpreting it, we draw upon our own aims and endeavors, inform it with a meaning that has its origin in our own ways of life and thought. In a word, any art that really affects us becomes to that extent modern art.

Works of art however are like unattainable heights. We do not go straight toward them, but circle around them. Each generation sees them from a different point of view and with a fresh eye; nor is it to be assumed that a later point of view is more apt than an earlier one. Each aspect comes into sight in its own time, which cannot be anticipated or prolonged; and yet its significance is not lost, for the meaning that a work assumes for a later generation is the result of the whole range of previous interpretations.

We are now living in the day of the sociological interpretation of cultural achievements. This day will not last for ever, and it will not have the last word. It opens up new aspects, achieves new and surprising insights; and yet this point of view evidently has its own limitations and inadequacies. At best perhaps, before its day is over, we may be able to anticipate some of the future criticisms and become aware of its insufficiencies without foregoing the insights that have been and may be gained within these limits.

There are still people who do not feel quite happy when spiritual phenomena, or, as they prefer to call them, the higher spiritual values, are in any way brought into connection with the struggle for existence, class conflict, competition, prestige, and the like. To deal with them fully would take us too far from our subject; here we can only remark that requiring the spiritual to be preserved from all contact with the material frequently turns out to be a way of defending a position of privilege.

Far more worthy of consideration are those who resist a sociological interpretation of spiritual achievements from a conviction that any significant structure, and above all a work of art, is an independent entity, a closed and complete system in itself, the elements of which are to be entirely explained in terms of interdependence, without any recourse to circumstances of its origin or to its influence. For a work of art undoubtedly has an inner logic of its own, and its particular quality is most clearly seen in the internal structural relations of the various levels of organization and the various motifs distinguishable in it. It is further indisputable that consideration of genetic relationships, that is, of the stages by which the artist moved from one idea or motif to another, not merely introduces a different emphasis, but is also likely to blind us to internal connections and alter the values upon which the aesthetic effect of the work depends. The factors that are most important in the actual production of the work are not equally important in giving it artistic value and effectiveness. Again, the practical aims of the artist, that is, the extraneous purposes that the work of art may be intended to serve, are not always in accord with the inner aesthetic structure that the work reveals. But the exponents of the theory of "art for art's sake"—and that is what is at issue here—are not content with asserting that a work of art is a microcosm and exerts a sovereign power over men; they maintain that any reference to actualities beyond the work must irretrievably destroy its aesthetic illusion. That may be correct, and yet this illusion is not all, to produce it is not the exclusive or the most important aim of artistic endeavor. Even if it be true that we have to loosen our hold upon reality to a certain extent in order to fall under the spell of art, it is no less true that all genuine art leads us by a detour, which may be longer or shorter, back to reality in the end. Great art gives us an interpretation of life which enables us to cope more successfully with the chaotic state of things and to wring from life a better, that is, a more convincing and more reliable, meaning.

The purely formal laws of art are not essentially different from the rules of a game. However complicated, subtle, and ingenious such rules may be, they have little significance in themselves, that is to say, apart from the purpose of winning the game. Considered as mere movements, the maneuvers of football players are unintelligible and, in the long run, boring. For a time one can find a certain pleasure in their speed and suppleness—but how meaningless are these qualities compared with those noted by the expert observer who understands the object of all this running, jumping, and pushing. If we do not know or even want to know the aims that the artist was pursuing through his work—his aims to inform, to convince, to influence people—then we do not get much farther in understanding his art than the ignorant spectator who judges the football simply by the beauty of the players' movements. A work of art is a communication; although it is perfectly true that the successful trans- mission of this requires an outward form at once effective, attractive, faultless, it is no less true that this form is insignificant apart from the message it communicates.

The work of art has been compared to the opening of a window upon the world. Now, a window can claim the whole of our attention or none. One may, it is said, contemplate the view without concerning oneself in the very least with the quality, structure, or color of the window-pane. By this analogy, the work of art can be described as a mere vehicle for experiences, a transparent window-pane, or a sort of eyeglasses not noticed by the wearer and employed simply as means to an end. But just as one can concentrate one's attention upon the window-pane and the structure of its glass without taking note of the view beyond, so, it is said, one can treat the work of art as an independent, "opaque" formal structure, complete in itself and in isolation, as it were, from anything external to it. No doubt one can stare at the window-pane as long as one likes; still, a window is made to look out of.

Culture serves to protect society. Spiritual creations, traditions, con- ventions, and institutions are but ways and means of social organization. Religion, philosophy, science, and art all have their place in the struggle to preserve society. To confine oneself to art, it is first of all a tool of magic, a means of ensuring the livelihood of the primitive horde of hunters. Then it becomes an instrument of animistic religion, used to influence good and bad spirits in the interest of the community. Gradually this is transformed into a magnification of the almighty gods and their earthly representatives, by hymn and panegyric, through statues of gods and kings. Finally, in the form of more or less open propaganda, it is employed in the interests of a close group, a clique, a political party, a social class. Only here and there, in times of relative security or of social estrangement of the artists, it withdraws from the world and makes a show of indifference to practical aims, professing to exist for its own sake and for the sake of beauty. But even then it performs an important social function by providing men with a means of expressing their power and their "conspicuous leisure." Indeed, it achieves much more than that, promoting the interests of a certain social stratum by the mere portrayal and implicit acknowledgment of its moral and aesthetic standards of value. The artist, whose whole livelihood, with all his hopes and prospects, depends upon such a social group, becomes quite unintentionally and unconsciously the mouthpiece of his customers and patrons.

The discovery of the propaganda value of cultural creations, and of art in particular, was made early in human history and exploited to the full, whereas thousands of years passed before man was ready to acknowledge the ideological character of art in terms of an explicit theory, to express the idea that art pursues practical aims either consciously or unconsciously, is either open or veiled propaganda. The philosophers of the French, and even of the Greek enlightenment, discovered the relativity of cultural standards, and doubts regarding the objectivity and ideality of human valuations were expressed again and again in the course of the centuries; Marx, however, was the first to formulate explicitly the conception that spiritual values are political weapons. He taught that every spiritual creation, every scientific notion, every portrayal of reality derives from a certain particular aspect of truth, viewed from a perspective of social interest, and is accordingly restricted and distorted. But Marx neglected to note that we wage a continual war against such distorting tendencies in our thought, that in spite of the inevitable partialities of our mental outlook, we do possess the power of examining our own thought critically, and so correcting to a certain extent the one-sidedness and error of our views. Every honest attempt to discover the truth and depict things faithfully is a struggle against one's own subjectivity and partiality, one's individual and class interests; one can seek to become aware of these as a source of error, while realizing that they can never be finally exluded. Engels understood this process of pulling oneself out of the mud by one's own bootstraps when he spoke of the "triumph of realism" in Balzac. But no doubt such correcting of our ideological falsification of the truth operates within the limits of what is thinkable and imaginable from our place in the world, not in a vacuum of abstract freedom. And the fact that there are such limits of objectivity is the ultimate and decisive justification for a sociology of culture; they stop up the last loophole by which we might hope to escape from the influence of social causation.

Apart from its external limitations, the sociology of art also has internal limitations. All art is socially conditioned, but not everything in art is definable in sociological terms. Above all, artistic excellence is not so definable; it has no sociological equivalent. The same social conditions can give rise to valuable or to utterly valueless works, and such works have nothing in common but tendencies more or less irrelevant from the artistic point of view. All that sociology can do is to account in terms of its actual origin for the outlook on life manifested in a work of art, whereas for an appreciation of its quality everything depends upon the creative handling and the mutual relations of the elements expressing that outlook. Such elements may assume the most diverse aesthetic quality, and again the qualitative criteria may be the same in spite of great diversity of outlook. It is no more than an idle dream, a residue of the ideal of *kalokagathia,* to suppose that social justice and artistic worth in any way coincide, that one can draw any conclusions with regard to the aesthetic success or failure of a work from the social conditions under which it has been produced. The great alliance envisaged by nineteenth-century liberalism between political progress and genuine art, between democratic and artistic feeling, between the interests of humanity in general and universally valid rules of art was a fantasy without any basis in fact. Even the alleged connection between truth of art and truth in politics, the identification of naturalism with socialism, which was from the beginning a basic thesis of socialistic art theory and still is part of its creed, is very dubious. It might be very satisfying to know that social injustice and political oppression were punished with spiritual sterility, but this is not always the case. There have indeed been periods such as that of the Second Empire, in which the predominance of a not very sympathetic social type was characterized by bad taste and lack of originality in art; but along with that inferior art much valuable work was being produced as well. Along with Octave Feuillet there was Gustave Flaubert, along with the Bouguereaus and Baudrys, artists of the rank of Delacroix and Courbet. It may, however, be significant that from the social and political point of view Delacroix was no closer to Courbet than to Bouguereau, that the common artistic aims of these two artists did not rest upon any sort of political solidarity.

Still, on the whole one may say that in the Second Empire the *arriviste* bourgeoisie got the artists it deserved. But what is one to say about epochs such as those of the Ancient Orient or the Middle Ages, in which a most severe despotism or a most intolerant spiritual dictatorship, far from preventing the production of the greatest art, created conditions of life under which the artist did not seem to suffer in the least, certainly no more than he now fancies himself to suffer under the compulsions of even a very liberal form of government? Does not this show that the preconditions of quality in art lie beyond the alternatives of political freedom or unfreedom, and that such quality is not to be compassed by sociological methods?

And what of examples that seem to suggest a contrary view: Greek classical art, which had scarcely any connection with the common people and only the very slightest connection with democracy? Or the "democracy" of the Italian Renaissance, which was anything but a democracy in reality? Or cases from our own day which show the attitude of the masses to art?

It is reported that some time ago an English firm published a book of reproductions of paintings of the most various sorts—good and bad, examples of popular and of more refined taste, devotional pictures, illustrations of anecdotes, and genuine pictorial creations all jumbled up together. The purchasers of the book were requested to indicate the pictures they preferred. The result was that, although as book-buyers the persons questioned were more or less cultivated, and although eighty percent of the reproductions fell within the category of "good art," thus loading the scales in its favor, not one of the first six pictures getting the most votes belonged to this category.

If we took this kind of response to signify that the great public is definitely opposed to the better sort of art and prefers the worse, we could at any rate formulate a sociological law establishing a relation—though an inverse relation—between aesthetic quality and popularity; but there is no trace of any consistent attitude to aesthetic quality in this case. Undoubedly there is always a certain tension between quality and popularity, at times—as now with modern art—an open conflict. Art that is worth anything is addressed to those who have attained a certain cultural level, not to the "natural man" of Rousseau; understanding of it depends upon certain educational preconditions, and its popularity is inevitably limited. Uneducated people, on the other hand, do not positively favor bad art over good; they judge success by quite other than aesthetic criteria. They react, not to what is artistically good or bad, but to features that have a reassuring or a disturbing effect upon their course of life; they are ready to accept what is artistically valuable provided that it supplies vital value for them by portraying their wishes, their fantasies, their day-dreams, provided that it calms their anxieties and increases their sense of security. One must not, however, forget that the strange, the unaccustomed, the difficult has, merely as such, a disquieting effect upon an uneducated public.

Thus sociology fails to explain the connections between artistic quality and popularity; and to questions about the material conditions of the creation of works of art it gives answers that are not altogether satisfying.

For sociology is subject to certain limitations common to all those disciplines, notably psychology, which employ the genetic method to deal with cultural forms, limitations arising out of that method. It is in fact likely to lose sight, from time to time, of the work of art as such and to consider it a record of something more important than the work itself. And just as the factors psychologically decisive in the creative process are not always identical with the artistically most important factors in the work, so also the sociologically most significant features of a work or of a school are not always the ones that are aesthetically relevant. From a sociological point of view a second-rate or third-rate artist may occupy a key position in a particular artistic movement. The social history of art does not replace or invalidate art history, or vice versa; each starts from a different set of facts and values. When the social history of art is judged by the standards of art history, the facts begin to seem distorted. To counter this impression, one may point out that even art history adopts standards different from those of simple art criticism, and again from those of immediate aesthetic experience, that there is often a decided tension between historical and aesthetic values. The sociological view of art is to be rejected only if it claims to be the sole legitimate point of view, and if it confuses the sociological importance of a work with aesthetic value.

Apart from this shifting of emphasis, which, though it may confuse is easily compensated for, the sociology of art has in common with other disciplines employing the genetic method a further inadequacy in the eyes of the art-lover: it claims to derive special and unique characteristics of works of art from that which is of quite another order, from something general and artistically indifferent. The worst example of this sort of trespassing is seen in any attempt to show that artistic quality or artistic talent is dependent upon economic conditions. It would be too cheap a retort merely to assert that only a few dogmatic simpletons have proposed to derive spiritual forms directly from economic facts, that the formation of ideologies is a long, complicated, gradual process, far different from that envisaged by vulgar materialism. Complicated, full of interruptions and contradictions the way may be that leads from certain social conditions to the creation of spiritual values, as for instance from Dutch middle-class capitalism to the works of Rembrandt; still, in the end one has to decide whether or not such conditions are relevant. One can put off the decision, conceal one's position, talk of dualism and dialectic, reciprocity and mutual dependence of spirit and matter; but after all one is either an idealist or a realist, and has to face the question of whether genius falls from heaven or fashions itself here on earth.

However one may decide this ultimate question, the translation of economic conditions into ideologies remains a process that can never be completely clarified; at some point or other, it involves a gap or leap. But we should not suppose that only the transition from material conditions to the spiritual involves us in a leap of this sort; all transition from one spiritual form to another, change of style and fashion, collapse of an old tradition and rise of a new, influence of one artist on another, or even a single artist's turns of direction—all these changes are equally discontinuous and inexplicable. Seen from without, every change looks abrupt and remains, strictly speaking, unintelligible. Continuous gradual change is something of which we have only a subjective, inner experience; it cannot be reconstructed from objective data.

The leap from the material to the spiritual is immeasurable, and yet we make this leap within the sphere of social life, even within the sphere of economics. The most primitive economy is a humanly organized economy, not a natural condition; nature once left behind, we do not anywhere encounter the merely material; we may think we are talking about material conditions, but the leap into the realm of spiritual conceptions has already occurred. The distance between natural occurrences and the most primitive economy is thus in a way greater than that from primitive economy to the highest flights of the human spirit, although every stretch of the way is broken by abysses.

One of the most obvious shortcomings of the sociology of art, as of all genetic explanation of spiritual structures, derives from the endeavor to analyze into simple elements an object whose very nature consists in its complexity. No doubt scientific explanation involves simplification, analysis of the complex into such components as occur in other complexes also. Outside the field of art this procedure does not destroy anything really of the essence of the object, but when applied to art, it eliminates the object as presented in its completeness, the only way in which it can be properly presented. If one eliminates or purposely neglects the complexity of the work of art, interweaving motifs, ambiguity of symbols, polyphony of voices, mutual dependence of form and content, unanalyzable fluctuations of cadence and emphasis, then the best of what art offers us is gone. Still, sociology is not alone in incurring this sort of loss, for all scientific treatment of art has to pay for knowledge gained by destroying the immediate, ultimately irretrievable, aesthetic experience. In even the most sensitive and understanding historical analyses of art, that original direct experience has been lost. All this is, of course, no excuse for the special shortcomings to which the sociologist is prone, nor does it liberate him from the duty of correcting the defects of his point of view as best he may, or at least of being aware of them.

The work of art is not only a source of complex personal experience, but also has another kind of complexity, being a nodal point of several different causal lines. It is the outcome of at least three different types of conditions: psychological, sociological and stylistic. As a psychological being, the individual retains not merely the freedom of choosing among the various possibilities permitted by social causation; he is also always creating for himself new possibilities in no way prescribed by his society, even though they may be restricted by the social conditions under which he lives. The creative individual invents new forms of expression, does not find them ready-made. What he takes for granted is of a negative rather than positive character: it is the totality of what cannot be thought, felt, expressed, or understood at that particular historical moment. Undoubtedly, such "blind spots" of an epoch can be established only subsequently; our actual state of affairs always has an anarchical look, as if the individual could do with it just what he fancies. Subsequently one comes to see a social law that has molded the individual choices in accordance with a unitary trend. In a similar way a stylistic line gradually comes to be recognized, along which particular modes of expression which have seemed to be freely selected fall into place. Indeed, stylistic trends, even more than sociological, have definitely the appearance of being objective regularities that impose themselves upon the individual choices; viewed retrospectively, the individuals seem to be little more than carriers of these anonymous stylistic trends.

But the history of style cannot do away with either psychological or sociological causation. It will never be possible to explain by purely formal, stylistic considerations why a line of artistic development breaks off at a certain point and gives place to a completely different one instead of going on to further progress and expansion—in short, why a change occurred just when it did. The "climax" of a line of development cannot be foretold on the basis of formal criteria; revolution occurs when a certain style is no longer adapted to expressing the spirit of the time, something that depends on psychological and sociological conditions. Change of style, no doubt, occurs in a direction determined from within; but there are always a number of possible directions, and in any case the "maturity" of choice is never fixed in advance or secure from the unforeseeable. Among the circumstances governing the occurrence of the change, social conditions are probably pre-eminent; but it would be a mistake to suppose that social conditions produce the forms in terms by which the artistic revolution expresses itself; these forms are just as much the product of psychological and stylistic as of sociological factors. When one considers social causation, psychology appears as a sort of incipient, abortive sociology, when one regards the psychological motivation, sociology looks like a refusal to trace events to their ultimate origins in the

make-up of the human soul. From the stylistic point of view, both psychology and sociology make the same mistake: they derive what is special
to art from motives of a heterogenous character, explain artistic forms in
terms of something that has nothing to do with "form." Only in descriptive
analysis is the uniqueness and complexity of the work of art preserved;
it is inevitably destroyed by attempts at pragmatic explanation, whether
genetic or teleological. In this respect psychology and art history are on
the same footing as sociology.

The inadequacy, however, that we often find in the sociologist's view
of art is not simply the result of the method of research which sociology
shares with psychology and art history. It is also owing to the rather
undeveloped language applied by the sociologist to the subtly differentiated world of art, a language vastly inferior to the far more refined
and appropriate language of the psychologist and the art historian. The
concepts with which the sociologist works are woefully inadequate for
dealing with the wealth and subtlety of artistic production. Categories
such as "courtly," "bourgeois," "capitalistic," "urban," "conservative," and
"liberal" are too narrow and schematic and also too rigid to do justice
to the special character of a work of art. Each category comprehends
such a variety of artistic views and aims that it does not tell us much
that is really relevant. What do we really know about the artistic problems with which Michelangelo had to wrestle, about the individuality
of his means and methods, when we have noted merely that he was
contemporary with the formulae of the Council of Trent, the new political
realism, the birth of modern capitalism and absolutism? When we know
all this, we perhaps understand better his restless spirit, the turn that
his art took in the direction of mannerism, possibly even in some measure
the astounding inarticulateness of his last works. His greatness and the
incomparable quality of his aims are no more explained this way than
Rembrandt's genius is to be explained by the economic and social conditions that were at once the foundation of his artistic career and his
undoing. Here we come up against the definite limits of sociological
inquiry.

But if there are such limits, do they really matter? If sociology is unable
to penetrate to the ultimate secret of the art of a Rembrandt, are we to
dispense entirely with what it can tell us? For example, are we to refuse
to probe into the social preconditions of his art, and so of the stylistic
peculiarities that distinguish it from the art of the contemporary Flemish
painters, notably Rubens? That would be to ignore the only means of
throwing light upon the otherwise unintelligible fact that two such
different types of art as Flemish baroque and Dutch naturalism arose
almost simultaneously, in direct geographical contact with one another,

on the basis of similar cultural traditions and a long political experience in common, but under markedly different economic and social conditions. Certainly, we have here no explanation of Rubens's greatness or the mystery of Rembrandt. But then, what genetic explanation of this stylistic difference is there other than the sociological one that Rubens produced his works in a courtly-aristocratic society, Rembrandt his in a bourgeois world, with its inclination to inwardness? That Rubens, unlike Rembrandt, went to Italy and absorbed the spirit of Italian baroque is rather a symptom than an explanation in itself. Mannerism was in fashion at the turn of the century in the northern provinces as in the southern, and at first Protestant tendencies were to be found in the South just as much as in the North. But in Flanders, in consequence of the Spanish rule, there was an ostentatious court, an aristocracy accustomed to appear in public, a magnificent Church—all things that did not exist in the sober, Protestant Holland that repelled the Spaniards. There, on the contrary, we find a bourgeois capitalism, liberal and without much feeling for prestige, and so ready to let its artists work according to their own fancies, and starve as they pleased. Rembrandt and Rubens are unique and incomparable; not so their styles and their fates. The various turns and changes that we detect in the course of their artistic development and the story of their lives are by no means without parallel, and do not incline us to attribute the difference of type in their art simply to individual disposition and personal genius.

Sociology possesses no philosopher's stone, does not work miracles or solve all problems. Still, it is more than just one departmental discipline among many. As was theology in the Middle Ages, philosophy in the seventeenth century, and economics in the eighteenth, it is a focal discipline in our day, one upon which the entire world-view of the age centers. To recognize the claims of sociology is to decide in favor of a rational ordering of life and for a struggle against prejudices. The idea upon which this cardinal position of sociology is founded is the discovery of the ideological character of thought, a discovery made in several different guises, during the past hundred years, in Nietzsche's and Freud's exposures of self-deception no less than in Marx's historical materialism. To get clear about oneself, to become conscious of the presuppositions of one's own character, thought, and will is the requirement upon which all these different thinkers insist. Sociology endeavors to probe into the preconditions of thought and will which derive from a man's social position. Objections made to such research are mostly due to the fact that correct estimation of these social connections is not a purely theoretical matter; men are inclined to admit them or deny them on ideological grounds. Many of those who will not hear of sociology exaggerate its deficiencies in order that they need not become conscious of their prejudices. Others resist sociological interpretation of everything in the spiritual realm, not wishing to give up the fiction of a timeless validity of thought and a meta-historical destiny for man. Those on the other hand who accept sociology as simply one means toward more perfect knowledge have no reason to minimize either its undeniable limitations or the extent of its unexplored possibilities.

23. Walter Benjamin

The Work of Art in the Age of
Mechanical Reproduction

The fame of the German critic WALTER BENJAMIN (1892–1940) has been largely posthumous, but his insight and brilliance were recognized early by such celebrated writers as Hugo von Hoffmannstahl, Bertolt Brecht, and Theodor Adorno. In 1920 he wrote on the concept of art criticism in German Romanticism, and later, on the origins of German tragedy, and on such varied subjects as Goethe, Brecht, Baudelaire, Kafka, Proust, the German language, nineteenth-century Paris, and the philosophy of history. He took his own life, a victim of the Nazi invasion of France, while attempting to escape with his manuscripts across the Franco-Spanish border. The publication of two volumes of his writings in Germany in 1955 brought his work to international attention among writers, critics, historians and philosophers. His essay on the work of art in our era of mechanical reproductions first appeared in 1936 in the *Zeitschrift für Sozialforschung*, and has recently been published in English translation in a collection of his writings entitled *Illuminations*, edited with a masterful introduction by Hannah Arendt.

Our fine arts were developed, their types and uses were established, in times very different from the present, by men whose power of action upon things was insignificant in comparison with ours. But the amazing growth of our techniques, the adaptability and precision they have attained, the ideas and habits they are creating, make it a certainty that profound changes are impending in the ancient craft of the Beautiful. In all the arts there is a physical component which can no longer be considered or treated as it used to be, which cannot remain unaffected by our modern knowledge and power. For the last twenty years neither matter nor space nor time has been what it was from time immemorial. We must expect great innovations to transform the entire technique of the arts, thereby affecting artistic invention

*itself and perhaps even bringing about an amazing change in our
very notion of art.*

—PAUL VALÉRY, "La Conquète de l'ubiquité,"
Pièces sur l'art, Paris.

WHEN Marx undertook his critique of the capitalistic mode of production, this mode was in its infancy. Marx directed his efforts in such a way as to give them prognostic value. He went back to the basic conditions underlying capitalistic production and through his presentation showed what could be expected of capitalism in the future. The result was that one could expect it not only to exploit the proletariat with increasing intensity, but ultimately to create conditions which would make it possible to abolish capitalism itself.

The transformation of the superstructure, which takes place far more slowly than that of the substructure, has taken more than half a century to manifest itself in all areas of culture the change in the conditions of production. Only today can it be indicated what form this has taken. Certain prognostic requirements should be met by these statements. However, theses about the art of the proletariat after its assumption of power or about the art of a classless society would have less bearing on these demands than theses about the developmental tendencies of art under present conditions of production. Their dialectic is no less noticeable in the superstructure than in the economy. It would therefore be wrong to underestimate the value of such theses as a weapon. They brush aside a number of outmoded concepts, such as creativity and genius, eternal value and mystery—concepts whose uncontrolled (and at present almost uncontrollable) application would lead to a processing of data in the Fascist sense. The concepts which are introduced into the theory of art in what follows differ from the more familiar terms in that they are completely useless for the purposes of Fascism. They are, on the other hand, useful for the formulation of revolutionary demands in the politics of art.

In principle a work of art has always been reproducible. Man-made artifacts could always be imitated by men. Replicas were made by pupils in practice of their craft, by masters for diffusing their works, and, finally, by third parties in the pursuit of gain. Mechanical reproduction of a work of art, however, represents something new. Historically, it advanced intermittently and in leaps at long intervals, but with accelerated intensity. The Greeks knew only two procedures of technically reproducing works of art: founding and stamping. Bronzes, terra cottas, and coins were the only art works which they could produce in quantity. All others were unique and could not be mechanically reproduced. With the woodcut graphic art became mechanically reproducible for the first time, long before script became reproducible by print. The enormous changes which printing, the mechanical reproduction of writing, has brought about in literature are a familar story. However, within the phenomenon which we are here examining from the perspective of world history, print is merely a special, though particularly important, case. During the Middle Ages engraving and etching were added to the woodcut; at the beginning of the nineteenth century lithography made its appearance.

With lithography the technique of reproduction reached an essentially new stage. This much more direct process was distinguished by the tracing of the design on a stone rather than its incision on a block of wood or its etching on a copper plate and permitted graphic art for the first time to put its products on the market, not only in large numbers as hitherto, but also in daily changing forms. Lithography enabled graphic art to illustrate everyday life, and it began to keep pace with printing. But only a few decades after its invention, lithography was surpassed by photography. For the first time in the process of pictorial reproduction, photography freed the hand of the most important artistic functions which henceforth devolved only upon the eye looking into a lens. Since the eye perceives more swiftly than the hand can draw, the process of pictorial reproduction was accelerated so enormously that it could keep pace with speech. A film operator shooting a scene in the studio captures the images at the speed of an actor's speech. Just as lithography virtually implied the illustrated newspaper, so did photography foreshadow the sound film. The technical reproduction of sound was tackled at the end of the last century. These convergent endeavors made predictable a situation which Paul Valéry pointed up in this sentence: "Just as water, gas, and electricity are brought into our houses from far off to satisfy our needs in response to a minimal effort, so we shall be supplied with visual or auditory images, which will appear and disappear at a simple movement of the hand, hardly more than a sign." Around 1900 technical reproduction had reached a standard that not only permitted it to reproduce all transmitted works of art and thus to cause the most profound change in their impact upon the public; it also had captured a place of its own among the artistic processes. For the study of this standard nothing is more revealing than the nature of the repercussions that these two different manifestations—the reproduction of works of art and the art of the film—have had on art in its traditional form.

Even the most perfect reproduction of a work of art is lacking in one element: its presence in time and space, its unique existence at the place where it happens to be. This unique existence of the work of art determined the history to which it was subject throughout the time of its existence. This includes the changes which it may have suffered in physical condition over the years as well as the various changes in its ownership. The traces of the first can be revealed only by chemical or physical analyses which it is impossible to perform on a reproduction; changes of ownership are subject to a tradition which must be traced from the situation of the original.

The presence of the original is the prerequisite to the concept of authenticity. Chemical analyses of the patina of a bronze can help to establish this, as does the proof that a given manuscript of the Middle Ages stems from an archive of the fifteenth century. The whole sphere of authenticity is outside technical—and, of course, not only technical—reproducibility. Confronted with its manual reproduction, which was usually branded as a forgery, the original preserved all its authority; not so *vis à vis* technical reproduction. The reason is twofold. First, process reproduction is more independent of the original than manual reproduction. For example, in photography, process reproduction can bring out those aspects of the original that are unattainable to the naked eye yet accessible to the lens, which is adjustable and chooses its angle at will. And photographic reproduction, with the aid of certain processes, such as enlargement or slow motion, can capture images which escape natural vision. Secondly, technical reproduction can put the copy of the original into situations which would be out of reach for the original itself. Above all, it enables the original to meet the beholder halfway, be it in the form of a photograph or a phonograph record. The cathedral leaves its locale to be received in the studio of a lover of art; the choral production, performed in an auditorium or in the open air, resounds in the drawing room.

The situations into which the product of mechanical reproduction can be brought may not touch the actual work of art, yet the quality of its presence is always depreciated. This holds not only for the art work but also, for instance, for a landscape which passes in review before the spectator in a movie. In the case of the art object, a most sensitive nucleus—namely, its authenticity—is interfered with whereas no natural object is vulnerable on that score. The authenticity of a thing is the essence of all that is transmissible from its beginning, ranging from its substantive duration to its testimony to the history which it has experienced. Since the historical testimony rests on the authenticity, the former, too, is jeopardized by reproduction when substantive duration ceases to matter. And what is really jeopardized when the historical testimony is affected is the authority of the object.

One might subsume the eliminated element in the term "aura" and go on to say: that which withers in the age of mechanical reproduction is the aura of the work of art. This is a symptomatic process whose significance points beyond the realm of art. One might generalize by saying: the technique of reproduction detaches the reproduced object from the domain of tradition. By making many reproductions it substitutes a plurality of copies for a unique existence. And in permitting the reproduction to meet the beholder or listener in his own particular situation, it reactivates the object reproduced. These two processes lead to a tremendous shattering of tradition which is the obverse of the contemporary crisis and renewal of mankind. Both processes are intimately connected with the contemporary mass movements. Their most powerful agent is the film. Its social significance, particularly in its most positive form, is inconceivable without its destructive, cathartic aspect, that is, the liquidation of the traditional value of the cultural heritage. This phenomenon is most palpable in the great historical films. It extends to ever new positions. In 1927 Abel Gance exclaimed enthusiastically: "Shakespeare, Rembrandt, Beethoven will make films . . . all legends, all mythologies and all myths, all founders of religion, and the very religions . . . await their exposed resurrection, and the heroes crowd each other at the gate." Presumably without intending it, he issued an invitation to a far-reaching liquidation.

During long periods of history, the mode of human sense perception changes with humanity's entire mode of existence. The manner in which human sense perception is organized, the medium in which it is accomplished, is determined not only by nature, but by historical circumstances as well. The fifth century, with its great shifts of population, saw the birth of the late Roman art industry and the Vienna Genesis, and there developed not only an art different from that of antiquity but also a new kind of perception. The scholars of the Viennese school, Riegl and Wickhoff, who resisted the weight of classical tradition under which these later art forms had been buried, were the first to draw conclusions from them concerning the organization of perception at the time. However far-reaching their insight, these scholars limited themselves to showing the significant, formal hallmark which characterized perception in late Roman times. They did not attempt—and, perhaps, saw no way—to show the social transformations expressed by these changes of perception. The conditions for an analogous insight are more favorable in the present. And if changes in the medium of contemporary perception can be comprehended as decay of the aura, it is possible to show its social causes.

The concept of aura which was proposed above with reference to historical objects may usefully be illustrated with reference to the aura of natural ones. We define the aura of the latter as the unique phenomenon of a distance, however close it may be. If, while resting on a summer afternoon, you follow with your eyes a mountain range on the horizon or a branch which casts its shadow over you, you experience the aura of those mountains, of that branch. This image makes it easy to comprehend the social bases of the contemporary decay of the aura. It rests on two circumstances, both of which are related to the increasing significance of the masses in contemporary life. Namely, the desire of contemporary masses to bring things "closer" spatially and humanly, which is just as ardent as their bent toward overcoming the uniqueness of every reality by accepting its reproduction. Every day the urge grows stronger to get hold of an object at very close range by way of its likeness, its reproduction. Unmistakably, reproduction as offered by picture magazines and newsreels differs from the image seen by the unarmed eye. Uniqueness and permanence are as closely linked in the latter as are transitoriness and reproducibility in the former. To pry an object from its shell, to destroy its aura, is the mark of a perception whose "sense of the universal equality of things" has increased to such a degree that it extracts it even from a unique object by means of reproduction. Thus is manifested in the field of perception what in the theoretical sphere is noticeable in the increasing importance of statistics. The adjustment of reality to the masses and of the masses to reality is a process of unlimited scope, as much for thinking as for perception.

The uniqueness of a work of art is inseparable from its being imbedded in the fabric of tradition. This tradition itself is thoroughly alive and extremely changeable. An ancient statue of Venus, for example, stood in a different traditional context with the Greeks, who made it an object of veneration, than with the clerics of the Middle Ages, who viewed it as an ominous idol. Both of them, however, were equally confronted with its uniqueness, that is, its aura. Originally the contextual integration of art in tradition found its expression in the cult. We know that the earliest art works originated in the service of a ritual—first the magical, then the religious kind. It is significant that the existence of the work of art with reference to its aura is never entirely separated from its ritual function. In other words, the unique value of the "authentic" work of art has its basis in ritual, the location of its original use value. This ritualistic basis, however remote, is still recognizable as secularized ritual even in the most profane forms of the cult of beauty. The secular cult of beauty, developed during the Renaissance and prevailing for three centuries, clearly showed that ritualistic basis in its decline and the first deep crisis which befell it. With the advent of the first truly revolutionary means of reproduction, photography, simultaneously with the rise of socialism, art sensed the approaching crisis which has become evident a century later. At the time, art reacted with the doctrine of *l'art pour l'art*, that is, with a theology of art. This gave rise to what might be called a negative theology in the form of the idea of "pure" art, which not only denied any social function of art but also any categorizing by subject matter. (In poetry, Mallarmé was the first to take this position.)

An analysis of art in the age of mechanical reproduction must do justice to these relationships, for they lead us to an all-important insight: for the first time in world history, mechanical reproduction emancipates the work of art from its parasitical dependence on ritual. To an ever greater degree the work of art reproduced becomes the work of art designed for reproducibility. From a photographic negative, for example, one can make any number of prints; to ask for the "authentic" print makes no sense. But the instant the criterion of authenticity ceases to be applicable to artistic production, the total function of art is reversed. Instead of being based on ritual, it begins to be based on another practice—politics.

Works of art are received and valued on different planes. Two polar types stand out: with one, the accent is on the cult value; with the other, on the exhibition value of the work. Artistic production begins with ceremonial objects destined to serve in a cult. One may assume that what mattered was their existence, not their being on view. The elk portrayed by the man of the Stone Age on the walls of his cave was an instrument of magic. He did expose it to his fellow men, but in the main it was meant for the spirits. Today the cult value would seem to demand that the work of art remain hidden. Certain statues of gods are accessible only to the priest in the cella; certain Madonnas remain covered nearly all year round; certain sculptures on medieval cathedrals are invisible to the spectator on ground level. With the emancipation of the various art practices from ritual go increasing opportunities for the exhibition of their products. It is easier to exhibit a portrait bust that can be sent here and there than to exhibit the statue of a divinity that has its fixed place in the interior of a temple. The same holds for the painting as against the mosaic or fresco that preceded it. And even though the public presentability of a mass originally may have been just as great as that of a symphony, the latter originated at the moment when its public presentability promised to surpass that of the mass.

With the different methods of technical reproduction of a work of art, its fitness for exhibition increased to such an extent that the quantitative shift between its two poles turned into a qualitative transformation of its nature. This is comparable to the situation of the work of art in prehistoric times when, by the absolute emphasis on its cult value, it was, first and foremost, an instrument of magic. Only later did it come to be recognized as a work of art. In the same way today, by the absolute emphasis on its exhibition value the work of art becomes a creation with entirely new functions, among which the one we are conscious of, the artistic function, later may be recognized as incidental. This much is certain: today photography and the film are the most serviceable exemplifications of this new function.

In photography, exhibition value begins to displace cult value all along the line. But cult value does not give way without resistance. It retires into an ultimate retrenchment: the human countenance. It is no accident that the portrait was the focal point of early photography. The cult of remembrance of loved ones, absent or dead, offers a last refuge for the cult value of the picture. For the last time the aura emanates from the early photographs in the fleeting expression of a human face. This is what constitutes their melancholy, incomparable beauty. But as man withdraws from the photographic image, the exhibition value for the first time shows its superiority to the ritual value. To have pinpointed this new stage constitutes the incomparable significance of Atget, who, around 1900, took photographs of deserted Paris streets. It has quite justly been said of him that he photographed them like scenes of crime. The scene of a crime, too, is deserted; it is photographed for the purpose of establishing evidence. With Atget, photographs become standard evidence for historical occurrences, and acquires a hidden political significance. They demand a specific kind of approach; free-floating contemplation is not appropriate to them. They stir the viewer; he feels challenged by them in a new way. At the same time picture magazines begin to put up signposts for him, right ones or wrong ones, no matter. For the first time, captions have become obligatory. And it is clear that they have an altogether different character than the title of a painting. The directives which the captions give to those looking at pictures in illustrated magazines soon become even more explicit and more imperative in the film, where the meaning of each single picture appears to be prescribed by the sequence of all preceding ones.

The nineteenth-century dispute as to the artistic value of painting versus photography today seems devious and confused. This does not diminish its importance, however; if anything, it underlines it. The dispute was in fact the symptom of a historical transformation the universal impact of which was not realized by either of the rivals. When the age of mechanical reproduction separated art from its basis in cult, the semblance of its autonomy disappeared forever. The resulting change in the function of art transcended the perspective of the century; for a long time it even escaped that of the twentieth century, which experienced the development of the film.

Earlier much futile thought had been devoted to the question of whether photography is an art. The primary question—whether the very invention of photography had not transformed the entire nature of art

—was not raised. Soon the film theoreticians asked the same ill-considered question with regard to the film. But the difficulties which photography caused traditional aesthetics were mere child's play as compared to those raised by the film. Whence the insensitive and forced character of early theories of the film. Abel Gance, for instance, compares the film with hieroglyphs: "Here, by a remarkable regression, we have come back to the level of expression of the Egyptians. . . . Pictorial language has not yet matured because our eyes have not yet adjusted to it. There is as yet insufficient respect for, insufficient cult of, what it expresses." Or, in the words of Séverin-Mars: "What art has been granted a dream more poetical and more real at the same time! Approached in this fashion the film might represent an incomparable means of expression. Only the most high-minded persons, in the most perfect and mysterious moments of their lives, should be allowed to enter its ambience." Alexandre Arnoux concludes his fantasy about the silent film with the question: "Do not all the bold descriptions we have given amount to the definition of prayer?" It is instructive to note how their desire to class the film among the "arts" forces these theoreticians to read ritual elements into it—with a striking lack of discretion. Yet when these speculations were published, films like *L'Opinion Publique* and *The Gold Rush* had already appeared. This, however, did not keep Abel Gance from adducing hieroglyphs for purposes of comparison, nor Séverin-Mars from speaking of the film as one might speak of paintings by Fra Angelico. Characteristically, even today ultrareactionary authors give the film a similar contextual significance—if not an outright sacred one, then at least a supernatural one. Commenting on Max Reinhardt's film version of *A Midsummer Night's Dream*, Werfel states that undoubtedly it was the sterile copying of the exterior world with its streets, interiors, railroad stations, restaurants, motorcars, and beaches which until now had obstructed the elevation of the film to the realm of art. "The film has not yet realized its true meaning, its real possibilities . . . these consist in its unique faculty to express by natural means and with incomparable persuasiveness all that is fairylike, marvelous, supernatural."

The artistic performance of a stage actor is definitely presented to the public by the actor in person; that of the screen actor, however, is presented by a camera, with a twofold consequence. The camera that presents the performance of the film actor to the public need not respect the performance as an integral whole. Guided by the cameraman, the camera continually changes its position with respect to the performance. The sequence of positional views which the editor composes from the material supplied him constitutes the completed film. It comprises certain factors of movement which are in reality those of the camera, not to mention special camera angles, close-ups, etc. Hence, the performance of the actor is subjected to a series of optical tests. This is the first consequence of the fact that the actor's performance is presented by means of a camera. Also, the film actor lacks the opportunity of the stage actor to adjust to the audience during his performance, since he does not present his performance to the audience in person. This permits the audience to take the position of a critic, without experiencing any personal contact with the actor. The audience's identification with the actor is really an identification with the camera. Consequently the audience takes the position of the camera; its approach is that of testing. This is not the approach to which cult values may be exposed.

For the film, what matters primarily is that the actor represents himself to the public before the camera, rather than representing someone else. One of the first to sense the actor's metamorphosis by this form of testing was Pirandello. Though his remarks on the subject in his novel Si Gira were limited to the negative aspects of the question and to the silent film only, this hardly impairs their validity. For in this respect, the sound film did not change anything essential. What matters is that the part is acted not for an audience but for a mechanical contrivance—in the case of the sound film, for two of them. "The film actor," wrote Pirandello, "feels as if in exile—exiled not only from the stage but also from himself. With a vague sense of discomfort he feels inexplicable emptiness: his body loses its corporeality, it evaporates, it is deprived of reality, life, voice, and the noises caused by his moving about, in order to be changed into a mute image, flickering an instant on the screen, then vanishing into silence. . . . The projector will play with his shadow before the public, and he himself must be content to play before the camera." This situation might also be characterized as follows: for the first time—and this is the effect of the film—man has to operate with his whole living person, yet foregoing its aura. For aura is tied to his presence; there can be no replica of it. The aura which, on the stage, emanates from Macbeth, cannot be separated for the spectators from that of the actor. However, the singularity of the shot in the studio is that the camera is substituted for the public. Consequently, the aura that envelops the actor vanishes, and with it the aura of the figure he portrays.

It is not surprising that it should be a dramatist such as Pirandello who, in characterizing the film, inadvertently touches on the very crisis in which we see the theater. Any thorough study proves that there is indeed no greater contrast than that of the stage play to a work of art that is completely subject to or, like the film, founded in, mechanical reproduction. Experts have long recognized that in the film "the greatest effects are almost always obtained by 'acting' as little as possible. . . ." In 1932 Rudolf Arnheim saw "the latest trend . . . in treating the actor as a stage prop chosen for its characteristics and . . . inserted at the proper place." With this idea something else is closely connected. The stage actor identifies himself with the character of his role. The film actor very often is denied this opportunity. His creation is by no means all of a piece; it is composed of many separate performances. Besides certain fortuitous considerations, such as cost of studio, availability of fellow players, décor, etc., there are elementary necessities of equipment that split the actor's work into a series of mountable episodes. In particular, lighting and its installation require the presentation of an event that, on the screen, unfolds as a rapid and unified scene, in a sequence of separate shootings which may take hours at the studio; not to mention more obvious montage. Thus a jump from the window can be shot in the studio as a jump from a scaffold, and the ensuing flight, if need be, can be shot weeks later when outdoor scenes are taken. Far more paradoxical cases can easily be construed. Let us assume that an actor is supposed to be startled by a knock at the door. If his reaction is not satisfactory, the director can resort to an expedient: when the actor happens to be at the studio again he has a shot fired behind him without his being forewarned of it. The frightened reaction can be shot now and be cut into the screen version. Nothing more strikingly shows that art has left the realm of the "beautiful semblance" which, so far, had been taken to be the only sphere where art could thrive.

The feeling of strangeness that overcomes the actor before the camera, as Pirandello describes it, is basically of the same kind as the estrangement felt before one's own image in the mirror. But now the reflected image has become separable, transportable. And where is it transported? Before the public. Never for a moment does the screen actor cease to be conscious of this fact. While facing the camera he knows that ultimately he will face the public, the consumers who constitute the market. This market, where he offers not only his labor but also his whole self, his heart and soul, is beyond his reach. During the shooting he has as little contact with it as any article made in a factory. This may contribute to that oppression, that new anxiety which, according to Pirandello, grips the actor before the camera. The film responds to the shriveling of the aura with an artificial build-up of the "personality" outside the studio. The cult of the movie star, fostered by the money of the film industry, preserves not the unique aura of the person but the "spell of the personality," the phony spell of a commodity. So long as the moviemakers' capital sets the fashion, as a rule no other revolutionary merit can be accredited to today's film than the promotion of a revolutionary criticism of traditional concepts of art. We do not deny that in some cases today's films can also promote revolutionary criticism of social conditions, even of the distribution of property. However, our present study is no more specifically concerned with this than is the film production of Western Europe.

It is inherent in the technique of the film as well as that of sports that everybody who witnesses its accomplishments is somewhat of an expert. This is obvious to anyone listening to a group of newspaper boys leaning on their bicycles and discussing the outcome of a bicycle race. It is not for nothing that newspaper publishers arrange races for their delivery boys. These arouse great interest among the participants, for the victor has an opportunity to rise from delivery boy to professional racer. Similarly, the newsreel offers everyone the opportunity to rise from passer-by to movie extra. In this way any man might even find himself part of a work of art, as witness Vertoff's *Three Songs About Lenin* or Ivens' *Borinage*. Any man today can lay claim to being filmed. This claim can best be elucidated by a comparative look at the historical situation of contemporary literature.

For centuries a small number of writers were confronted by many thousands of readers. This changed toward the end of the last century. With the increasing extension of the press, which kept placing new political, religious, scientific, professional, and local organs before the readers, an increasing number of readers became writers—at first, occasional ones. It began with the daily press opening to its readers space for "letters to the editor." And today there is hardly a gainfully employed European who could not, in principle, find an opportunity to publish somewhere or other comments on his work, grievances, documentary reports, or that sort of thing. Thus, the distinction between author and public is about to lose its basic character. The difference becomes merely functional; it may vary from case to case. At any moment the reader is ready to turn into a writer. As expert, which he had to become willy-nilly in an extremely specialized work process, even if only in some minor respect, the reader gains access to authorship. In the Soviet Union work itself is given a voice. To present it verbally is part of a man's ability to perform the work. Literary license is now founded on polytechnic rather than specialized training and thus becomes common property.

All this can easily be applied to the film, where transitions that in literature took centuries have come about in a decade. In cinematic practice, particularly in Russia, this change-over has partially become established reality. Some of the players whom we meet in Russian films are not actors in our sense but people who portray *themselves*—and primarily in their own work process. In Western Europe the capitalistic exploitation of the film denies consideration to modern man's legitimate claim to being reproduced. Under these circumstances the film industry is trying hard to spur the interest of the masses through illusion-promoting spectacles and dubious speculations.

The shooting of a film, especially of a sound film, affords a spectacle unimaginable anywhere at any time before this. It presents a process in which it is impossible to assign to a spectator a viewpoint which would exclude from the actual scene such extraneous accessories as camera equipment, lighting machinery, staff assistants, etc.—unless his eye were on a line parallel with the lens. This circumstance, more than any other, renders superficial and insignificant any possible similarity between a scene in the studio and one on the stage. In the theater one is well aware of the place from which the play cannot immediately be detected as illusionary. There is no such place for the movie scene that is being shot. Its illusionary nature is that of the second degree, the result of cutting. That is to say, in the studio the mechanical equipment has penetrated so deeply into reality that its pure aspect freed from the foreign substance of equipment is the result of a special procedure, namely, the shooting by the specially adjusted camera and the mounting of the shot together with other similar ones. The equipment-free aspect of reality here has become the height of artifice; the sight of immediate reality has become an orchid in the land of technology.

Even more revealing is the comparison of these circumstances, which differ so much from those of the theater, with the situation in painting. Here the question is: How does the cameraman compare with the painter? To answer this we take recourse to an analogy with a surgical operation. The surgeon represents the polar opposite of the magician. The magician heals a sick person by the laying on of hands; the surgeon cuts into the patient's body. The magician maintains the natural distance between the patient and himself; though he reduces it very slightly by the laying on of hands, he greatly increases it by virtue of his authority. The surgeon does exactly the reverse; he greatly diminishes the distance between himself and the patient by penetrating into the patient's body, and increases it but little by the caution with which his hand moves among the organs. In short, in contrast to the magician—who is still hidden in the medical practitioner—the surgeon at the decisive moment abstains from facing the patient man to man; rather, it is through the operation that he penetrates into him.

Magician and surgeon compare to painter and cameraman. The painter maintains in his work a natural distance from reality, the cameraman penetrates deeply into its web. There is a tremendous difference between the pictures they obtain. That of the painter is a total one, that of the cameraman consists of multiple fragments which are assembled under a new law. Thus, for contemporary man the representation of reality by the film is incomparably more significant than that of the painter, since it offers, precisely because of the thorough-going permeation of reality with mechanical equipment, an aspect of reality which is free of all equipment. And that is what one is entitled to ask from a work of art.

Mechanical reproduction of art changes the reaction of the masses toward art. The reactionary attitude toward a Picasso painting changes into the progressive reaction toward a Chaplin movie. The progressive reaction is characterized by the direct, intimate fusion of visual and emotional enjoyment with the orientation of the expert. Such fusion is of great social significance. The greater the decrease in the social significance of an art form, the sharper the distinction between criticism and enjoyment by the public. The conventional is uncritically enjoyed, and the truly new is criticized with aversion. With regard to the screen, the critical and the receptive attitudes of the public coincide. The decisive reason for this is that individual reactions are predetermined by the mass audience response they are about to produce, and this is nowhere more pronounced than in the film. The moment these responses become manifest they control each other. Again, the comparison with painting is fruitful. A painting has always had an excellent chance to be viewed by one person or by a few. The simultaneous contemplation of paintings by a large public, such as developed in the nineteenth century, is an early symptom of the crisis of painting, a crisis which was by no means occasioned exclusively by photography but rather in a relatively independent manner by the appeal of art works to the masses.

Painting simply is in no position to present an object for simultaneous collective experience, as it was possible for architecture at all times, for the epic poem in the past, and for the movie today. Although this circumstance in itself should not lead one to conclusions about the social role of painting, it does constitute a serious threat as soon as painting, under special conditions and, as it were, against its nature, is confronted directly by the masses. In the churches and monasteries of the Middle Ages and at the princely courts up to the end of the eighteenth century, a collective reception of paintings did not occur simultaneously, but by graduated and hierarchized mediation. The change that has come about is an expression of the particular conflict in which painting was implicated by the mechanical reproducibility of paintings. Although paintings began to be publicly exhibited in galleries and salons, there was no way for the masses to organize and control themselves in their reception. Thus the same public which responds in a progressive manner toward a grotesque film is bound to respond in a reactionary manner to surrealism.

The characteristics of the film lie not only in the manner in which man presents himself to mechanical equipment but also in the manner in which, by means of this apparatus, man can represent his environment. A glance at occupational psychology illustrates the testing capacity of the equipment. Psychoanalysis illustrates it in a different perspective. The film has enriched our field of perception with methods which can be illustrated by those of Freudian theory. Fifty years ago, a slip of the tongue passed more or less unnoticed. Only exceptionally may such a slip have revealed dimensions of depth in a conversation which had seemed to be taking its course on the surface. Since the *Psychopathology of Everyday Life* things have changed. This book isolated and made analyzable things which had heretofore floated along unnoticed in the broad stream of perception. For the entire spectrum of optical, and now also acoustical, perception the film has brought about a similar deepening of apperception. It is only an obverse of this fact that behavior items shown in a movie can be analyzed much more precisely and from more points of view than those presented on paintings or on the stage. As compared with painting, filmed behavior lends itself more readily to analysis because of its incomparably more precise statements of the situation. In comparison with the stage scene, the filmed behavior item lends itself more readily to analysis because it can be isolated more easily. This circumstance derives its chief importance from its tendency to promote the mutual penetration of art and science. Actually, of a screened behavior item which is neatly brought out in a certain situation, like a muscle of a body, it is difficult to say which is more fascinating, its artistic value or its value for science. To demonstrate the identity of the artistic and scientific uses of photography which heretofore usually were separated will be one of the revolutionary functions of the film.

By close-ups of the things around us, by focusing on hidden details of familiar objects, by exploring commonplace milieus under the ingenious guidance of the camera, the film, on the one hand, extends our comprehension of the necessities which rule our lives; on the other hand, it manages to assure us of an immense and unexpected field of action. Our taverns and our metropolitan streets, our offices and furnished rooms, our railroad stations and our factories appeared to have us locked up hopelessly. Then came the film and burst this prison-world asunder by the dynamite of the tenth of a second, so that now, in the midst of its far-flung ruins and debris, we calmly and adventurously go traveling. With the close-up, space expands; with slow motion, movement is extended. The enlargement of a snapshot does not simply render more precise what in any case was visible, though unclear: it reveals entirely new structural formations of the subject. So, too, slow motion not only presents familiar qualities of movement but reveals in them entirely unknown ones "which, far from looking like retarded rapid movements, give the effect of singularly gliding, floating, supernatural motions." Evidently a different nature opens itself to the camera than opens to the naked eye—if only because an unconsciously penetrated space is substituted for a space consciously explored by man. Even if one has a general knowledge of the way people walk, one knows nothing of a person's posture during the fractional second of a stride. The act of reaching for a lighter or a spoon is familiar routine, yet we hardly know what really goes on between hand and metal, not to mention how this fluctuates with our moods. Here the camera intervenes with the resources of its lowerings and liftings, its interruptions and isolations, its extensions and accelerations, its enlargements and reductions. The camera introduces us to unconscious optics as does psychoanalysis to unconscious impulses.

One of the foremost tasks of art has always been the creation of a demand which could be fully satisfied only later. The history of every art form shows critical epochs in which a certain art form aspires to effects which could be fully obtained only with a changed technical standard, that is to say, in a new art form. The extravagances and crudities of art which thus appear, particularly in the so-called decadent epochs, actually arise from the nucleus of its richest historical energies. In recent years, such barbarisms were abundant in Dadaism. It is only now that its impulse becomes discernible: Dadaism attempted to create by pictorial—and literary—means the effects which the public today seeks in the film.

Every fundamentally new, pioneering creation of demands will carry beyond its goal. Dadaism did so to the extent that it sacrificed the market values which are so characteristic of the film in favor of higher ambitions —though of course it was not conscious of such intentions as here described. The Dadaists attached much less importance to the sales value of their work than to its uselessness for contemplative immersion. The studied degradation of their material was not the least of their means to achieve this uselessness. Their poems are "word salad" containing obscenities and every imaginable waste product of language. The same is true of their paintings, on which they mounted buttons and tickets. What they intended and achieved was a relentless destruction of the aura of their creations, which they branded as reproductions with the very means of production. Before a painting of Arp's or a poem by August Stramm it is impossible to take time for contemplation and evaluation as one would before a canvas of Derain's or a poem by Rilke. In the decline of middle-class society, contemplation became a school for asocial behavior; it was countered by distraction as a variant of social conduct.

Dadaistic activities actually assured a rather vehement distraction by making works of art the center of scandal. One requirement was foremost: to outrage the public.

From an alluring appearance or persuasive structure of sound the work of art of the Dadaists became an instrument of ballistics. It hit the spectator like a bullet, it happened to him, thus acquiring a tactile quality. It promoted a demand for the film, the distracting element of which is also primarily tactile, being based on changes of place and focus which periodically assail the spectator. Let us compare the screen on which a film unfolds with the canvas of a painting. The painting invites the spectator to contemplation; before it the spectator can abandon himself to his associations. Before the movie frame he cannot do so. No sooner has his eye grasped a scene than it is already changed. It cannot be arrested. Duhamel, who detests the film and knows nothing of its significance, though something of its structure, notes this circumstance as follows: "I can no longer think what I want to think. My thoughts have been replaced by moving images." The spectator's process of association in view of these images is indeed interrupted by their constant, sudden change. This constitutes the shock effect of the film, which, like all shocks, should be cushioned by heightened presence of mind. By means of its technical structure, the film has taken the physical shock effect out of the wrappers in which Dadaism had, as it were, kept it inside the moral shock effect.

The mass is a matrix from which all traditional behavior toward works of art issues today in a new form. Quantity has been transmuted into quality. The greatly increased mass of participants has produced a change in the mode of participation. The fact that the new mode of participation first appeared in a disreputable form must not confuse the spectator. Yet some people have launched spirited attacks against precisely this superficial aspect. Among these, Duhamel has expressed himself in the most radical manner. What he objects to most is the kind of participation which the movie elicits from the masses. Duhamel calls the movie "a pastime for helots, a diversion for uneducated, wretched, worn-out creatures who are consumed by their worries . . . , a spectacle which requires no concentration and presupposes no intelligence . . . , which kindles no light in the heart and awakens no hope other than the ridiculous one of someday becoming a 'star' in Los Angeles." Clearly, this is at bottom the same ancient lament that the masses seek distraction whereas art demands concentration from the spectator. That is a commonplace. The question remains whether it provides a platform for the analysis of the film. A closer look is needed here. Distraction and concentration form polar opposites which may be stated as follows: A man who concentrates before a work of art is absorbed by it. He enters into this work of art the way legend tells of the Chinese painter when he viewed his finished painting. In contrast, the distracted mass absorbs the work of art. This is most obvious with regard to buildings. Architecture has always represented the prototype of a work of art the reception of which is consummated by a collectivity in a state of distraction. The laws of its reception are most instructive.

Buildings have been man's companions since primeval times. Many art forms have developed and perished. Tragedy begins with the Greeks, is extinguished with them, and after centuries its "rules" only are revived. The epic poem, which had its origin in the youth of nations, expires in Europe at the end of the Renaissance. Panel painting is a creation of the Middle Ages, and nothing guarantees its uninterrupted existence. But the human need for shelter is lasting. Architecture has never been idle. Its history is more ancient than that of any other art, and its claim to being a living force has significance in every attempt to comprehend the relationship of the masses to art. Buildings are appropriated in a twofold manner: by use and by perception—or rather, by touch and sight. Such appropriation cannot be understood in terms of the attentive concentration of a tourist before a famous building. On the tactile side there is no counterpart to contemplation on the optical side. Tactile appropriation is accomplished not so much by attention as by habit. As regards architecture, habit determines to a large extent even optical reception. The latter, too, occurs much less through rapt attention than by noticing the object in incidental fashion. This mode of appropriation, developed with reference to architecture, in certain circumstances acquires canonical value. For the tasks which face the human apparatus of perception at the turning points of history cannot be solved by optical means, that is, by contemplation, alone. They are mastered gradually by habit, under the guidance of tactile appropriation.

The distracted person, too, can form habits. More, the ability to master certain tasks in a state of distraction proves that their solution has become a matter of habit. Distraction as provided by art presents a covert control of the extent to which new tasks have become soluble by apperception. Since, moreover, individuals are tempted to avoid such tasks, art will tackle the most difficult and most important ones where it is able to mobilize the masses. Today it does so in the film. Reception in a state of distraction, which is increasing noticeably in all fields of art and is symptomatic of profound changes in apperception, finds in the film its true means of exercise. The film with its shock effect meets this mode of reception halfway. The film makes the cult value recede into the background not only by putting the public in the position of the critic, but also by the fact that at the movies this position requires no attention. The public is an examiner, but an absent-minded one.

The growing proletarianization of modern man and the increasing formation of masses are two aspects of the same process. Fascism attempts to organize the newly created proletarian masses without affecting the property structure which the masses strive to eliminate. Fascism sees its salvation in giving these masses not their right, but instead a chance to express themselves. The masses have a right to change property relations; Fascism seeks to give them an expression while preserving property. The logical result of Fascism is the introduction of aesthetics into political life. The violation of the masses, whom Fascism, with its *Führer* cult, forces to their knees, has its counterpart in the violation of an apparatus which is pressed into the production of ritual values.

All efforts to render politics aesthetic culminate in one thing: war. War and war only can set a goal for mass movements on the largest scale while respecting the traditional property system. This is the political formula for the situation. The technological formula may be stated as follows: Only war makes it possible to mobilize all of today's technical resources while maintaining the property system. It goes without saying that the Fascist apotheosis of war does not employ such arguments. Still, Marinetti says in his manifesto on the Ethiopian colonial war: "For twenty-seven years we Futurists have rebelled against the branding of war as antiaesthetic. . . . Accordingly we state: . . . War is beautiful because it establishes man's dominion over the subjugated machinery by means of gas masks, terrifying megaphones, flame throwers, and small tanks. War is beautiful because it initiates the dreamt-of metalization of the human body. War is beautiful because it enriches a flowering meadow with the fiery orchids of machine guns. War is beautiful because it combines the gunfire, the cannonades, the cease-fire, the scents, and the stench of putrefaction into a symphony. War is beautiful because it creates new architecture, like that of the big tanks, the geometrical formation flights, the smoke spirals from burning villages, and many others. . . . Poets and artists of Futurism! . . . remember these principles of an aesthetics of war so that your struggle for a new literature and a new graphic art . . . may be illumined by them!"

This manifesto has the virtue of clarity. Its formulations deserve to be accepted by dialecticians. To the latter, the aesthetics of today's war appears as follows: If the natural utilization of productive forces is impeded by the property system, the increase in technical devices, in speed, and in the sources of energy will press for an unnatural utilization, and this is found in war. The destructiveness of war furnishes proof that society has not been mature enough to incorporate technology as its organ, that technology has not been sufficiently developed to cope with the elemental forces of society. The horrible features of imperialistic warfare are attributable to the discrepancy between the tremendous means of production and their inadequate utilization in the process of production—in other words, to unemployment and the lack of markets. Imperialistic war is a rebellion of technology which collects, in the form of "human material," the claims to which society has denied its natural material. Instead of draining rivers, society directs a human stream into a bed of trenches; instead of dropping seeds from airplanes, it drops incendiary bombs over cities; and through gas warfare the aura is abolished in a new way.

Fiat ars—pereat mundus, says Fascism, and, as Marinetti admits, expects war to supply the artistic gratification of a sense perception that has been changed by technology. This is evidently the consummation of *l'art pour l'art*. Mankind, which in Homer's time was an object of contemplation for the Olympian gods, now is one for itself. Its self-alienation has reached such a degree that it can experience its own destruction as an aesthetic pleasure of the first order. This is the situation of politics which Fascism is rendering aesthetic. Communism responds by politicizing art.

C. Genres

24. Christopher Caudwell

The Organization of the Arts

For a biographical note on CHRISTOPHER CAUDWELL, see p. 199. The following selection is taken from *Illusion and Reality*, first published in 1937.

POETRY grasps a piece of external reality, colors it with affective tone, and makes it distill a new emotional attitude which is not permanent but ends when the poem is over. Poetry is in its essence a transitory and experimental illusion, yet its effects on the psyche are enduring. It is able to live in the same language with science—whose essence is the expression of objective reality—because in fact an image of external reality is the distributed middle of both propositions, the other term being *external reality* in the case of science, the *genotype* in the case of poetry. This is not peculiar to poetry; it is general to all the arts. What is peculiar to poetry is its technique, and the particular kind of emotional organization which this technique secures. None the less, an analysis of poetry should also throw light on the technique of the other arts.

The other important artistic organization effected by words is the story. How does the technique of poetry compare with that of the story?

In a poem the affects adhere directly to the associations of the words. The poet has to take care that the reader's mind does not go out behind the words into the external reality they describe before receiving the affects. It is quite otherwise with the story. The story makes the reader project himself into the world described; he sees the scene, meets the characters, and experiences their delays, mistakes and tragedies.

This technical difference accounts also for the more leisurely character of the story. The reader identifies himself with the poet; to both the words arise already soaked with affect, already containing a portion of external reality. But the novel arises as at first only an impersonal *description* of reality. Novelist and the reader stand outside it. They watch what happens. They become sympathetic towards characters. The characters move amid familiar scenes which arouse their emotions. It seems as if they walked into a world and used their own judgment, whereas the world presented by the poet is already soaked in affective color. Novel-readers do not immediately identify themselves with the novelist, as a reader of poetry does with the poet. The reader of poetry seems to be saying what the poet says, feeling *his* emotions. But the reader of the story does not seem to be writing it; he seems to be living through it, in the midst of it. In the story, therefore, the affective tones cling to the associations of external reality. The poem and the story both use sounds which awake images of outer reality and affective reverberations; but in poetry the affective reverberations are organized by the structure of the language, while in the novel they are organized by the structure of the outer reality portrayed.

In music the sounds do not refer to objects. They themselves are the objects of sense. To them, therefore, the affective reverberations cling directly. Although the affective reverberations of poetry are organized by the structure of the language, this structure itself is dependent on the "meaning"—i.e., on the external reality referred to. But the structure of music is self-sufficient; it does not refer to outer reality in a logical way. Hence music's structure itself has a large formal and pseudo-mathematical component. Its pseudo-logical rigor of scale and chord replaces the logical rigor of external meaning. Thus in music, poetry and the novel the sound symbol has three different functions: in the novel it stands for an object in external reality; in poetry for a word-born mental complex of affective reverberation and memory-image; in music for part of a pseudo-external reality.

The social ego or subjective world is realized in artistic fantasy by the distortion of the external world. But for a world to be distorted into an affective organization it must have a structure which is not affective (subjective) but logical (objective). Hence the socially recognized laws of music, which are pseudo-logical laws. They correspond to the laws of language, also socially recognized, which are pseudo-objective and are distorted by poetry, but not by the novel, which distorts the time and space of objective reality.

A logical external world can only exist in space and time. Hence the musical world exists in space and time. The space is the movement of the scale, so that a melody describes a curve in space as well as enduring in time. Although a melody extends in time, it is *organized* spatially. Just as a mathematical argument is static and quantitative, although it "follows on" in time, so a melody is timeless and universally valid. It is a generalization, corresponding to the classificatory content of science. It is colorless and bare of quality in its essence. It draws from the ego a universal emotional attitude within the limits of its argument.

Harmony introduces into music a temporal element. Just as space can only be described in terms of time (a succession of steps), so time can only be described in terms of space (a space of time imagined as existing simultaneously, like a panorama). Time is the emergence of qualities. Hence two qualities sounding simultaneously describe time in terms of space. Just as the evolutionary sciences import from external reality a perspective of a whole field of qualities evolving (yet here visualized by an all-seeing eye as already fully developed), so harmony brings into music a whole rich field of temporal enrichment and complexity. It individualizes music and continually creates new qualities. It was therefore no accident but a result of the way in which the bourgeoisie "continually revolutionizes its own basis," that the richest development of harmony in music should have coincided with the Industrial Revolution, the rise of the evolutionary sciences and a dialectical view of life. There was a parallel temporal movement in story and symphony. It was equally no accident that this musical development should have coincided with a technical development which on the one hand facilitated the instrumental richness of bourgeois orchestras, and on the other hand by its increase of communications made men's lives and experiences interweave and counterpoint each other like a symphony.

In the world of melody undifferentiated man faces a universal nature or static society, precisely as in poetry. In the novel and the world of harmony a man contemplates the rich and complex movement of the passions of men in a changing and developing world.

Rhythm was prior to either melody or harmony if anthropological researches are any guide, and we assumed that a rhythmic dancing and shouting was the parent also of poetry. The external world of music exists, not to portray the world but to portray the genotype. The world has therefore to be dragged into the subject; the subject must not be squeezed out into the object. Rhythm, because it shouts aloud the dumb processes of the body's secret life and negates the indifferent goings-on of the external universe, makes the hearer sink deep down into himself in a physiological introversion. Hence the logical laws of music, in spite of their externality and materiality, must first of all pay homage to rhythm, must be distorted by rhythm, must be arranged round the breath and pulse-beats and dark vegetative life of the body. Rhythm makes the bare world of sound, in all its impersonality, a human and *fleshy* world. Melody and harmony impress on it a more differentiated and refined humanity, but a great conductor is known most surely by his time. The beating baton of the conductor says to the most elaborate orchestra: All this complex and architectural tempest of sound occurs *inside* the human body. The conductor is the common ego visibly present in the orchestra.

When man invented rhythm, it was the expression of his dawning self-consciousness which had separated itself out from nature. Melody expressed this self as more than a body, as the self of a member of a collective tribe standing in opposition to the universal otherness of nature. Rhythm is the feeling of *a* man; melody the feeling of *Man.* Harmony is the feeling of *men,* of a man conscious of himself as an individual, living in a world where the interweaving lives of society reflect the orchestral pageant of growing and developing nature.

Just as the rhythm of music is physiological and distorts the object to its pattern so as to draw it into the body, so the periodicity and order-ing which is the essence of mathematics is "natural" and logical, and squeezes the ego out of the body into the object, so that it follows the grain of external nature.

The collective members of the tribe do not conflict in their broad desires and do not require a mutual self-adjustment to secure freedom for each, because the possibility of large inequalities of freedom does not arise. There is no real surplus of freedom. The life of the primitive corresponds almost exactly to a blind necessity. So small is the margin that to rob him of much is to rob him of life itself. Therefore just because it is, in the sum, so scanty, it is shared equally by all and Nature, not other men, is a man's chief antagonist. But the individuation produced by the division of labor and a corresponding increase in productivity, raises this mutual interplay of different characters in conflict to a vital problem. Appearing first with the static and logical simplicity of tragedy, it is in bourgeois civilization developed as the novel with a more flexible and changing technique. The development of orchestration in music has a similar significance as a road to freedom.

The decay of art due to the decline of bourgeois economy is reflected in music. Just as the novel breeds a characteristic escape from proletarian misery—"escape" literature, the religion of capitalism—so music produces the affective massage of jazz, which gratifies the instincts without propos-ing or solving the tragic conflicts in which freedom is won. Both think to escape necessity by turning their backs on it and so create yet another version of the bourgeois revolt against a consciousness of social relations. In contrast to the escape from proletarian misery in bourgeois literature, there rises an expression of petty bourgeois misery. This characteristic expression is the anarchic bourgeois revolt, the *surréalisme* that attempts to liberate itself by denying all convention, by freeing both the inner and outer worlds from social-commonness and so "releasing" art into the magical world of dream. In the same way, petty bourgeois music advances through atonality to an anarchic expression of the pangs of a dying class. The opium of the unawakened proletariat mixes with the fantastic aspirations of the fruitlessly rebellious lower stratum of the bourgeoisie.

Because the world of music with its logical structure is pseudo-external and drawn out of the genotype, like the logical content of mathematics, the "infant prodigy" is possible in both. The full development of the novel and the evolutionary sciences requires even in genius the maturity of concrete experience. Because the external reality of music is self-generated, it is as if music directly manipulated the emotions of men.

Language expresses both external reality and internal reality—facts and feelings. It does so by symbols, by "provoking" in the psyche a memory-image which is the psychic projection of a piece of external reality, and a feeling which is the psychic projection of an instinct. But language is not a haphazard group of symbols. It must be organized. This organization is given in the arrangement of the symbols but cannot be itself symbolized by these symbols. Wittgenstein, to whom we owe this conception, saw it as a projective correspondence between the symbols and outer reality. But there is also a projective correspondence between the symbols and inner reality, and the final shape or pattern is the result of a tension or contradiction between the two organizing forces. Both orderings are shared in common with the thing projected. If this is a part of external reality, we may say symbols and symbolized share the real world; if it is a projection of internal reality, they share the same affective manifold or social ego. Considered separately, these orderings are only abstractions. They cannot in concrete language be separated. In concrete language only their tense mutual relation is reflected, and this is the subject-object relation—man's active struggle with Nature.

In poetry the manifold distorted or organized by the affective forces of the common ego is the logical or grammatical manifold inhering in the arrangement and syntactical organization of the words themselves. Of course this corresponds to a similar logical arrangement "out there" in the external reality symbolized. It corresponds, but it is not the same, and therefore permits an affective organization more direct, "languagy" and primitive than that of the novel, where the logical manifold organized by common ego is "out there" in the external reality symbolized. Hence poetry is more instinctive, barbaric and primitive than the novel. It belongs to the age when the Word is new and has a mystic world-creating power. It comes from a habit of mind which gives a magical quality to names, spells, formulae and lucky expressions. It belongs to the "taken for granted" knowledge in language which, when we discover it consciously—as in logic's laws—seems to us a new, unhuman and imperious reality. The poetic Word is the Logos, the word-made-flesh, the active will ideally ordering, whereas the novel's word is the symbol, the reference, the conversationally pointing gesture.

In music the logical manifold is the formal or structural element in music, corresponding to the grammatical or syntactical element in language. It comprises the stuff-ness, the conventions, laws, scales, permitted chords, and instrumental limitations of musical theory. It is the impersonal and external element in music. This is distorted affectively in time and space by rhythm, melody and harmony. *Wovon man nicht sprechen kann, darüber muss man schweigen,* ("whereof one cannot speak, thereof one must be silent"), ended Wittgenstein, asserting in a mystical form that since language corresponds to facts, it cannot speak of non-factual entities, but must fall back on mystical intuition. This is untrue. By arbitrarily limiting the function of language Wittgenstein excludes it from the provinces it has long occupied successfully. It is precisely art—music, poetry and the novel—which speaks in the affective manifold what *man nicht sprechen kann* in the logical manifold.

The even pulse of rhythmic time contrasts with the irregularity of time successions observed in the outside world. Man naturally seizes therefore on the few natural periodicities—day and night, months and years. Hence the conception of order and therefore number is given to us physiologically, and mathematical calculation consists in giving different names to different periodicity groups; at first digital symbols, later separate written characters. The ego is projected on to external reality to order it. Subjective affective periodicity is the parent of number, therefore in mathematics affective time must be distorted by orderings found in external reality. The outer manifold is the main organizing force. In music external periodicity is affectively distorted to follow the instinctive ego. The affective manifold is here the organizing force. The musician is an introverted mathematician. The "lightning calculator" is an extraverted conductor.

To summarize:

Mathematics uses spatial orderings of periodicities drawn from subjective sources, these periodicities being distorted to conform with external reality.

Music uses affective orderings of periodicities drawn from objective sources, these periodicities being distorted to conform with internal reality.

In poetry the affective rhythm is logico-spatial, not affective-temporal. Unlike the basic rhythm of mathematics, it is not distorted by cognitive material. It asserts the tempo of the body as against that of environment. Meter denies external time, the indifferent passing on of changing reality —by "marking time" and drawing in the object to it.

Music, language, mathematics, all mere sounds, can yet symbolize the whole Universe and express the active relation of internal to external reality. Why has sound, a simple physical wave system, become so apt a medium for the symbolization of life in all its concreteness?

In the life of animals external reality has been explored by three distance receptors round which, as Sherrington has shown, the brain has evolved; these are physico-chemical smell, sound and sight. On the whole light-wave reception has proved its superiority for this purpose and sound therefore became specialized as a medium of inter-species communication. Among birds and tree-apes this would follow naturally from the engrossment of eye sense by the demands of balance, aerial or arboreal. Long have cries—mere sounds—been the simple voice of the instincts among the warm-blooded animals from which we evolve. Long have our ears been tuned to respond with affective association to simple sounds. Birds, with their quick metabolism the most emotional of animals, express with sound the simple pattern of their instincts in an endlessly repeated melodic line. But man goes a step further, along the line indicated by the warning cry of birds. The demands of economic cooperation —perhaps for hunting—made essential the denomination of objects and processes in external reality not instinctively responded to. Perhaps gesture stepped in, and by a pictographic mimicking of a piece of external reality with lips and tongue, man modified an instinctive sound, a feeling-symbol, to serve also as the symbol of a piece of external reality. Language was born. Man's simple cries, born of feeling, of primitive sympathy, of gesture, of persuasion, became plastic; the same cry now stood for a constant piece of external reality, as also for a constant judgment of it. Something was born which was music, poetry, science and mathematics in one but would with time fly apart and generate all the dynamism of language and fantasy between the poles of music and mathematics, as the economical operation which was its basis also developed.

It is no mere arbitrary ordering of emotion which music performs. It expresses something that is inexpressible in a scientific language framed to follow the external manifold of reality. It projects the manifold of the genotype. It tells us something that we can know in no other way; it tells us about ourselves. The tremendous truths we feel hovering in its cloudy reticulations are not illusions; nor are they truths about external realities. They are truths about ourselves, not as we statically are, but as we are actively striving to become.

In addition to the sound-symbolical arts, there are the visual or plastic arts—painting, sculpture and architecture. It is easier to see how these fit into our analysis. The visual sense—in all animals, eked out by tactile corrections—has been that sense used most consistently to explore external reality, while the hearing sense has been used to explore that particular part of external reality which consists of other genotypes. Sound mediates between genotype and genotype—the animal hears the enemy or the mate. Light mediates also between genotype and non-genotypical portions of external reality.

As a result, when we make a visual symbol of external reality, such as a diagram or a drawing, it is naturally made projective of external reality and not merely symbolic. Except in onomatopoeia, words individually are not mechanically projective of things like a photograph, but are only symbolic and therefore "conventional." A drawing, however, is directly projective of reality without necessarily the mediation of pseudo-grammatical rules or conventions. This is shown by the resemblance between a drawing and a photograph.

In drawing and sculpture bits of external reality are projected into a mock world, as in a drawing of a flower or a sculpture of a horse. This picture must have in common with the external reality from which it is drawn something not describable in terms of itself—the real or logical manifold or, more simply, the "likeness."

But line and color also have affective associations in their own right. These must be organized in an attitude towards the mock world, the "thing" projected. This must be an affective attitude, which is what the painting or sculpture has in common with the genotype, or affective manifold, and cannot be itself symbolized by a drawing, since it is inherent in the drawing. To the naïve observer this appears as a distortion in the drawing, as a non-likeness to external reality. But of course it is really a likeness, a likeness to the affective world of the genotype.

For the purpose of this brief survey, the only distinction that need be made between painting and sculpture is that one is three-dimensional and the other two-dimensional. Thus painting selects two out of the three dimensions of external reality—or rather to be accurate, it selects two out of the four dimensions, for unlike music, poetry and the story, the plastic arts lack the fourth dimension, time. Pictures do not begin at one moment in time and end at another. They are static; they do not change. All arts must select from external reality in some way, otherwise they would not have any looseness at the joints to give play for ego-organization. They must have one degree of freedom.

Line and color, symbolizing real objects, are organized by the ego reality projected. The result is a new emotional attitude to a piece of reality. After viewing a Rembrandt or a Cézanne we *see* the exterior world differently. We still see the same external reality, but it is drenched with new affective tones and shines with a bright emotional coloring. It is a more "appetizing" world, for it is the appetitive instincts which furnish the aesthetic affects.

Plainly the same criteria we have already established for language hold good here. A Michelangelo painting or a Dutch portrait contains more of external reality than a Picasso, just as a story contains more than a poem. But what is the scope and degree of the emotional reorganization in the visual field that it effects? It is chiefly on this that the varying estimates of greatness in painting are based. Just as in music or poetry, so in painting, easy solutions or shallow grasps of reality are poor art.

Painting resembles poetry in this much, that the affects do not inhere in the associations of the things, but in the lines and forms and colors that compose them. Certain scenes—for example a funeral—have affective associations in themselves. But the affective associations used by painting do not pertain to the funeral as an event but to a brownish rectangle in a large transparent box with circles at the end drawn by grayish horse-shapes. The affective associations adhering to ideas of bereavement could quite properly be used in a story, and the novelist could legitimately bring in a funeral in order to utilize its affective associations in his pattern. Again the mere *word* "funeral" as a word has of course inherent affective associations which can be used in poetry—the "funeral of my hopes"— but only if it is thoroughly understood that the whole group of such linguistic associations will be brought into the poem, and must either be utilized or inhibited, e.g., suggestions of *darkness*, of *purple*, of *stuffy respectability*, of a *procession*, or *pomp* and *ceremony*, of *deep wells* (sound association with *funnel* plus the *grave*). The affective associations used by painting are only those of color, line and combinations of color and line, but they are used to organize the meaning—the *real* object represented.

Hence the static plastic arts which are representational are akin to poetry and mathematics—to the classificatory sciences and the universal arts. Just as we slip at once into the "I" of the poem, so we slip at once into the viewpoint of the painter. We see the world both from where the poet and where the painter stands.

We have already explained why this approach leads to a "tribal" primitive attitude to living, why it tends to lead to the realization of a static universal human essence opposed to a static nature, and is therefore the best medium for voicing universal cries of passion or insight. By a paradox which is not really a paradox, but is given in the nature of individuation, poetry and painting are also the best mediums for expressing individuality—the individuality however only of the poet. Painting, poetry and melody all have this in common—this timeless universal quality of the human *genus* rather than the interesting sub-complications of a group of human individuals. Hence too we find painting developed at an early stage in the history of civilization—as early as Paleolithic man.

In its first appearance painting is man's consciousness of affective quality in Nature, hence the "life-like" character of early Paleolithic Art, when it deals with natural subjects. But with the development of man from a group of hunters and food-gatherers to a crop-raising and cattle-rearing tribe, man passes from a cooperating observation of Nature, seeking his own desires in it, to a cooperative power over Nature, by drawing it into the tribe and domesticating it. Hence he is now interested in the power of social forms over reality, which becomes "convention" in perceptual rendering. Therefore naturalistic Paleolithic Art becomes in Neolithic days conventional, arbitrary and symbolic—*decorative*. Not only does this prepare the way for *writing*, but it also expresses a psychic change in culture similar to the passage from rhythm to poetry and to melody.

The passage from the gens or tribe to class society is marked by a further differentiation in pictorial art which takes the form of a return of "naturalism," but man now seeks in Nature, not the affective qualities of the solid tribe, but the heightened and specialized qualities of the ruling class. These are elaborated by the division of labor and the greater technical power and penetration of Nature this makes possible. This naturalism is always ready to fall back into "conventionality" when a class ceases to be vitally in touch with active reality and its former discoveries ossify into dry shells. Naturalism becomes academicism. The most naturalistic pictorial art is bourgeois art, corresponding to its greater productivity and differentiation and more marked division of labor. Hence the rise of naturalism in bourgeois art, and its revolutionary self-movement, is connected with the rise of harmony in music and of the evolutionary sciences generally during the same period. Naturalism must not be confused with realism—for example the realism of bourgeois Flemish painting. This realism too may be conventional. Since painting is like poetry, and not the novel, the vital ego-organization which is the basis of naturalism does not take place in the real world depicted, but flows from the complex of memory-images and affective reverberations awakened by the line or color, and is organized by the "meaning," by the projective characteristics of the painting.

In later bourgeois culture economic differentiation becomes crippling and coercive instead of being the road to individuation or freedom. There is a reaction against content, which, as long as it remains within the bourgeois categories, appears as "commodity-fetishism." The social forms which make the content marketable and give it an exchange value are elevated as ends in themselves. Hence, cubism, futurism, and various forms of so-called "abstract" art.

Finding himself ultimately enslaved by the social form and therefore still "bound to the market," the bourgeois rebel attempts to shake himself free even from the social ego and so to escape into the world of dream where both ego and external world are personal and unconscious. This is *surréalisme*, with the apparent return of a realism which is however fictitious, because it is not the real, i.e., social external world which returns, but the unconscious personal world. We have already explained why *surréalisme* represents the final bourgeois position.[1]

The plastic arts are static. A visual art moving in time is provided in the dance, the drama and (finally) the film. The dance is primitive story —quality separating itself from the womb of rhythm. In the dance rhythm gradually ceases to be physiological and begins to unfold in time and share the qualitative movement of reality, in which things happen.

Painting shares with poetry the quality of having affects organized by the projective structure of the symbols. (A black oblong, *not* a coffin.) But directly the visual arts move in time this spatial or pseudo-grammatical organization is no longer possible and therefore it must take place as in the story—the affective organization is an organization of the real object symbolized by the visual representation. (The *real* coffin.) The courtship of the dance, the murder on the stage, the riot on the films are the material which is affectively organized, and not the linked forms, prostrate figure, or scattered crowd, considered as a projective structure, as would be the case if they were frozen into a static tableau. This confusion between the projective organization of the static arts and the real organization of the temporal arts leads to all kinds of special expressionistic and scenic theories of drama—for example those of Edward Gordon Craig. The development of the ballet, the drama and the film is the equivalent of the development of harmony, of the counterpoint of individuals whose life-experiences criss-cross against a changing background of Nature because the division of labor has wrought a similar differentiation and individuation within the crystal of the collective tribe. Tragedy appears in the rapid evolution of Greek classes out of the Greek gens and blossoms again with the rise of bourgeois productivity in the drama of the Elizabethan stage. In both *poetry* still soaks it because the drama is a transitional stage in class society. It is the product of a society passing from collectivity to individuality.

The dance, the drama and the film are mixed or counterpointed in their techniques as compared to the affective organizations of language and music. Just as music's sounds are the objects of external reality and not symbols of such objects, so the dancing or acting human being or the scenery around him is the real object. Admittedly, the dancing or acting human being also refers to another object (the courting or dying human he mimics). But he is also an object of external reality in himself —a gracefully or attractively moving human being. Hence acting and dancing have a musical "non-symbolical component," but they also have the other component, the characteristic of referring to objects of external reality. There is a double organization—the thing mimicked and the person mimicking. This double organization has a certain danger, and gives rise to a quarrel between actor and author, cast and producer, which can today only be overcome in the film, where the mechanical flexibility of the camera makes the cast wax in a good producer's hands.

However in an era of bourgeois individualism this feature of the film cannot be fully explored, and the film remains a "starring" vehicle, except in Soviet Russia.

The dancer or actor as *himself*, as an object of contemplation, is *static*, like the poetic word. The reality symbolized is like the reality of story's objects—*in movement*. Hence there is a tension in a play or film between the static close-up or actor's instant and the moving action or author's organization—this resembles the tension in an epic between the poetic instant and the narrative movement.

The individual passages in epic or play that we conceive of as particularly poetic or histrionic—Homer's description of the stars of heaven opening out, or the great moment of a Duse—are almost like music: the affects are attached to the words or actions and only released by the meaning, as if a dam had burst. The play or epic halts. There is a poetic instant and as time vanishes, space enters; the horizon expands and becomes boundless. The art reveals itself as double. The things described in turn have their own affects which are organized by the action of the story or the play in time. It is this that makes us think of the *Iliad* and the *Odyssey* as substantial and spacious worlds, stretching back as far as the eye can reach. In the great Shakespearean plays we feel this double organization as a world of vast cloudy significance, not only looming vaguely behind the action but in the poetic passages actually casting lights on it from underneath, so that the action itself is subtly modified and glows with unexpected fluorescence. Hence the difficulty of acting poetic plays. Act*ion* and poetry go together because they live in different structures. But poetry and act*ing*—the "I" of the poet and the "I" of the actor, are in the same structure and blot each other out. Irving's *Hamlet*, or Shakespeare's—we have to choose. In a play which is read, poetry can take the place of acting, hence the satisfaction from reading Shakespeare's plays not to be paralleled by reading Ibsen's. Of course in Shakespeare's time the actor was less dominating, as is shown by the use of boys to take women's parts.

The same characteristic and good mixture of the real and symbolized objects which is to be found in dance and drama is to be distinguished from the same mixture occasionally found in music—the bastard kind of music in which nightingales sing, monastery bells toll, and locomotives whistle. These real objects, mimicked or symbolized by sound, disturb the logical self-consistent structure of music's world, and are therefore here impermissible.

In Paleolithic Art the individual is only self-conscious and is still anchored in the perception of the object, giving rise to an atomic naturalism of exactly portrayed unorganized percept-things. So in the dance of hunting primitives, the natural object—the animal—is mimicked unaltered because it is only sought by man, not changed. The object draws the ego out of man in accurate perception. It is gained in cooperation and so becomes conscious, a fact which differentiates its qualities from those it possesses in brute perception, but it is sought, not created.

In Neolithic Art, when hunting or food-gathering man becomes a crop-raising or cattle-rearing tribe, the object is not merely sought by society but changed by it. The man realizes himself in the percept as social man, as the tribe changing the object according to conventions and forms rooted in the means of communication. The dance becomes the formal hieratic movement of chorus and incipient tragedy. The hunting or food-gathering primitive's dance is violently naturalistic and mimicking; the food-raising or cattle-rearing dance has the formality of a religious rite and reveals the impress of the tribe's soul on Nature. It emphasizes the magical and world-governing power of the gesture. The circling sun obeys the circling dancer; the crop lifts with the leaping of young men; life quickens with the dizzy motion. The tribe draws Nature into its bosom.

The elaboration of class-society causes the dance to develop into a story, into a *play*. The intricacies of the chorus loosen sufficiently to permit the emergence of *individual* players. Individuation, produced by the division of labor in a class society, is reflected in the tragedy. A god, a hero, a priest-king, people, great men, detach themselves from the chorus and appear on the stage, giving birth simultaneously to the static act*ing* and the moving act*ion* which were inseparably one in the danced chorus, just as were the static poem and the moving story one in the ritual chant, where the word is poetically world-creating and yet also relates a mythical story.

Of course the decay and rigidity of a class society is at any moment reflected in a stiffening and typification of the "characters." The individuation is not rooted in the class but in the division of labor. The class cleavage at first makes this division possible but at a certain moment denies its further development and becomes a brake, a source of academic ossification, a corset which society must break or be stifled.

We said that the cathedrals were bourgeois and not feudal, that they were already Protestant heresies in the heart of Catholicism, the bourgeois town developing in the feudal country. Hence the bourgeois play begins in the cathedrals as the mystery play frowned on by the Church authorities. When the monarchy allies itself with the bourgeois class, the mystery moves to court and becomes the Elizabethan tragedy. Here the individual is realized once again naturalistically as the prince, as the social will incarnate in the free desires of the hero.

Because of the special development of bourgeois individuality, after Shakespeare the mimed action falls a victim to the static actor. In Greek tragedy the actor is swaddled in the trappings of cothurni and mask; he is the pure vehicle of poetry and action. In the Elizabethan play the actor's personality is still stifled, and because the actor is subordinate to the mimed action the play is still poetic. In our day the actor's instant conflicts with the poet's; in Shakespeare's the boy-woman, muffled in the collective representations of the feudal court, was still a hollowness which gave room for the poetry of Cleopatra to come forward and expand. The incursion of woman on to the stage marks the rise of acting in the drama, and the death of narrative and poetry. The personal individual actor or actress becomes primary; his social relations with others or with the social ego—which constitute the story or poetry of the play— become secondary. The play, because of the collective basis of its technique, is injured by the individualism of bourgeois culture.

The play, like painting, becomes increasingly realistic and then moves over to commodity-fetishism—the abstract structure of Expressionism in which the conventions or social forms are hypostatized, and the content or "story" is expelled, so that the play aspires towards the impossibility of becoming the pure social ego. And the play finally makes a bid to cut itself off both from social ego and external reality according to the mechanism of *surréaliste* dream-work.

This same basic movement is only what we have already analyzed in poetry. For the cry, reproducing the authentic image (the bird call or animal cry) in the dance of the hunting primitive, becomes the elaborate chant or choral hymn, with strophe, antistrophe and epode, in the crop-raising or pastoral society which has sucked Nature into its undifferentiated bosom. The rise of class society and its individuation, based on division of labor, is reflected in the emergence of the bard, with his epic poetry, glorifying the deeds of heroes, stories in which he does not speak for himself but for a general class and so his own personal instant does not conflict with a poetic instant which is only given in the acts of heroes. But the further individuation of society, due to still greater division of labor, gives rise to the *poet,* with his lyrical verse—amatory, epistolary and personal—in which the poetic instant coincides with the personal instant, in which the collective "I" (formerly general and heroic) has become personal and individual. With this goes a naturalism and "pathos" of the kind for which Euripides was reproached by his contemporaries and which seems to bourgeois culture so appealing and right.

The poet finds his full individuation in bourgeois poetry, where chanted lyrical poetry becomes written study poetry, and the social ego of poetry is identified with the free individual. Here too there is movement through naturalism to escape from the external world (symbolism) and escape also from the social ego (*surréalisme*).

Architecture and the "applied" arts (ceramics, weaving, design of clothes, furniture, machines, cars, printed characters and the like) play a role in the visual field similar to that of music in the aural field in that the "things" are parts of external reality and are "distorted" or organized directly by the affects. But architecture and the other arts are like *inverted* music. The "external" element is not a formal ideal "structure" as in music, with its pseudo-logical laws, but a human and social function. The external reality of a house or vase is its use—its coveringness or its capaciousness. This use-form is organized or distorted affectively either by the symbolization of natural external reality (as when a carpet, vase or house is covered with sculpture or decoration) or when it is given shape, balance, harmony, curves and movement in space. This organization is poetic; the "I" which organizes the use-function is static and collective. Great architecture arises in the womb of a society where social "I" and individual "I" do not conflict but reinforce each other.

Hunting man expresses the use-value realistically. He finds in Nature the correspondence to his use. His house is a cave; his vase a gourd; his weapon a rough flint; his covering a skin. In this sense his applied art is as realistic as his drawings.

Crop-raising or pastoral man imposes on his materialized use-value, a decoration which is conventional and distorting. He takes Nature into the bosom of the tribe, and molds it plastically to his wish. The use-value is given a social form—it is minted. The stone implements are polished. Instead of seeking out a cave, he erects a rough hut in a convenient spot. He no longer clothes himself in skins; his covering is woven. Instead of gourds, he uses pottery, molded to a shape and decorated.

The birth of a class society sees the birth of palaces and temples where "coveringness" is affectively organized to express the majesty and sacredness of a ruling class. This majesty and sacredness has accrued through the division of labor and the alienation of property whereby the increased social power seems to gather at the pole of the ruling class at the same time as the humility and abasement appears at the pole of the slave class. With the merchant classes of Athens and Rome this reflects itself also in municipal buildings. In feudal society castles and basilicas express the affective organization of social power. The cathedral and the *hôtel de ville* of medieval town life already reflect the growing power of the bourgeois class and are rebellious. The bourgeois class is still collective —it is gathered in self-governing and self-arming communes—tribal islands in the pores of feudalism. At first their social expansion appears in the palaces and cathedrals of princes, who wield for a time the power of the bourgeoisie against other feudal powers. Then it passes into aristocratic villas and State structures; finally appears in the form of gentlemen's residences. At first this is a naturalistic movement. Houses become less "formal" and more useful and domestic. This movement too passes into abstraction. Abstraction in painting is functionalism in architecture. Finally even the social ego is negated and architecture shows everywhere freakishness and personal whim, irrespective of the needs of function. The same movement of course takes place in ceramics, textiles and other applied arts. In general the products of a class society in this field show the same rich elaboration and aesthetic idealization of the aims and aspirations of the ruling class as do the other forms of art.

The organization of the arts can be shown schematically:

ART	EXTERNAL REALITY
I. Sound:	
Music	Pseudo-Logical Laws of Musical Structure
Poetry	Syntactical and Grammatical Laws of Language
Story	Real External World Described
II. Visual:	
Painting and Sculpture	Projective Laws of Structural Representation
Dance and the Play and Film	Real Action Imitated by Real People
Architecture, Ceramics, Textiles, Furniture, etc.	Use-Function

Obviously the arts can also be arranged historically—beginning from their confused appearance in food-gathering and hunting man to their complex development in a class society where individuation is possible. We have already dealt with this movement in general. The three main periods are all sublated in modern art's methods of subjective organization which therefore include the consciousness of man seeking himself in Nature, of man drawing Nature into the social but undifferentiated "I" of the tribe, and finally of man splitting the social "I" into living *individuals* and at the same time resolving Nature into a differentiated universe which *evolves*.

If we are asked the purpose of art, we can make an answer, the precise nature of it depending on what we mean by *purpose*. Art has "survived," cultures containing art have outlived and replaced those that have not, because art adapts the psyche to the environment, and is therefore one of the conditions for the development of society. But we get another answer if we ask *how* art performs its task, for it does this by taking a piece of environment and distorting it, giving it a non-likeness to external reality which is also a likeness to the genotype. It remolds external reality nearer to the likeness of the genotype's instincts, but since the instinctive genotype is nothing but an unconscious and dynamic desire it remolds external reality nearer to the heart's desire. Art becomes more socially and biologically valuable and the greater art, the more that remolding is comprehensive and true to the nature of reality, using as its material the sadness, the catastrophes, the blind necessities, as well as the delights and pleasures of life. An organism which thinks life is all "for the best in the best possible of worlds" will have little survival value. Great art can thus be great tragedy, for here reality at its bitterest—death, despair, eternal failure—is yet given an organization, a shape, an affective arrangement which expresses a deeper and more social view of fate. By giving external reality an affective organization drawn from its heart, the genotype makes all reality, even death, more interesting because more true. The world glows with interest, our hearts go out to it with appetite to encounter it, to live in it, to get to grips with it. A great novel is how we should like our own lives to be, not petty or dull, but full of great issues, turning even death to a noble sound:

> Notre vie est noble et tragique
> Comme le masque d'un tyran
> Nul drame hazardeux et magique
> Aucun détail indifférent
> Ne rend notre amour pathétique.

A great picture is how we should like the world to look to us, brighter, full of affective color. Great music is how we should like our emotions to run on, full of strenuous purpose and deep aims. And because, for a moment, we saw how it might be, were given the remade object into our hands, for ever after we tend to make our lives less petty, tend to look around us with a more seeing eye, tend to feel richly and strenuously.

If we ask why art, by making the environment wear the expression of the genotype, comes to us with the nearness and significance it does, we must say still more about art's essence. In making external reality glow with our expression, art tells us about ourselves. No man can look directly at himself, but art makes of the Universe a mirror in which we catch glimpses of ourselves, not as we are, but as we are in active potentiality of becoming in relation to reality through society. The genotype we see is the genotype stamped with all the possibilities and grandeur of mankind—an elaboration which in its turn is extracted by society from the rest of reality. Art gives us so many glimpses of the inner heart of life, and that is its significance, different from and yet arising out of its purpose. It is like a magic lantern which projects our real selves on the Universe and promises us that we, as we desire, can alter the Universe, alter it to the measure of our needs. But to do so, we must know more deeply our real needs, must make ourselves yet more conscious of ourselves. The more we grip external reality, the more our art develops and grows increasingly subtle, the more the magic lantern show takes on new subtleties and fresh richnesses. Art tells us what science cannot tell us, and what religion only feigns to tell us—what we are and why we are, why we hope and suffer and love and die. It does not tell us this in the language of science, as theology and dogma attempt to do, but in the only language that can express these truths, the language of inner reality itself, the language of affect and emotion. And its message is generated by our attempt to realize its essence in an active struggle with Nature, the struggle called life.

All this is only the inverse picture of what science does. Science too has a survival value and a purpose, and it fulfills this by adapting external reality to the genotype just as art adapts the genotype to external reality. Just as art achieves its adaptative purpose by projecting the genotype's inner desires on to external reality, so science achieves its end by receiving the orderings of external reality into the mind, in the fantastic mirror-world of scientific ideology. Necessity, projected into the psyche, becomes conscious and man can mold external reality to his will. Just as art, by adapting the genotype and projecting its features into external reality, tells us what the genotype is, so science, by receiving the reflection of external reality into the psyche, tells us what external reality is. As art tells us the significance and meaning of all we are in the language of feeling, so science tells us the significance of all we see in the language of cognition. One is temporal, full of change; the other spatial and seemingly static. One alone could not generate a fantastic projection of the whole Universe, but together, being contradictory, they are dialectic, and call into being the spatio-temporal historic Universe, not by themselves but by the practice, the concrete living, from which they emerge. The Universe that emerges is explosive, contradictory, dynamically moving apart, because those are the characteristics of the movement of reality which produced it, the movement of human life.

Art and science play contradictory and yet intermingled roles in the sphere of theory. Science in cognition gives art a projected selection from external reality which art organizes and makes affectively appealing, so that the energy of the genotype is directed towards imposing its desires on that external reality. Thus attention, moving inwards from action, through art moves outwards again to action. Attention to change of externals causes the inward movement of cognition; attention to change of internals the outward movement of action. For the outwards-moving energy to effect its aim, science is again needed, and the original memory-images, now modified affectively, must be rescanned to grasp their inner relationships so that the desires of the genotype can be effected. Science in cognition now becomes science in action. In effecting those desires with the aid of existing memory-images, more knowledge is gained of the real orderings of external reality. Its object achieved, attention returns with fresh empirical experience to add to its treasure. This richer content is again organized affectively by the genotype, and again flows outwards as energy directed to an end. Energy is always flowing out to the environment of society, and new perception always flowing in from it; as we change ourselves, we change the world; as we change the world we learn more about it; as we learn more about it, we change ourselves; as we change ourselves, we learn more about ourselves; as we learn more about what we are, we know more clearly what we want. This is the dialectic of concrete life in which associated men struggle with Nature. The genotype and the external reality exist separately in theory, but it is an abstract separation. The greater the separation, the greater the unconsciousness of each. The complete separation gives us on the one hand the material body of a man, and on the other hand the unknown environment. Spreading from the point of interaction, the psyche, two vast spheres of light grow outwards simultaneously; knowledge of external reality, science; knowledge of ourselves, art. As these spheres expand, they change the material they dominate by interaction with each other. The conscious sphere of the genotype takes color from the known sphere of external reality and *vice versa*. This change—change in heart, change in the face of the earth—is not just a consequence of the expansion of the two circles, it *is* the two expansions, just as the flash of light is the electromagnetic wave group. As man becomes increasingly free and therefore increasingly himself by growing increasingly conscious of Necessity, so Necessity becomes increasingly orderly and "law-abiding," increasingly itself, as it falls increasingly within the conscious grasp of the genotype.

Art therefore is all active cognition, and science is all cognitive action. Art in contemplation is all active organization of the subject of cognition, and in action all active organization of the object of cognition. Science in contemplation is all cognitive organization of the subject of action, and in action all cognitive organization of the object of action. The link between science and art, the reason they can live in the same language, is this: the subject of action is the same as the subject of cognition—the genotype. The object of action is the same as the object of cognition—external reality. Since the genotype is a part of reality, although it finds itself set up against another part of it, the two interact; there is development; man's thought and man's society have a history.

Art is the science of feeling, science the art of knowing. We must know to be able to do, but we must feel to know what to do.

Art is born in struggle, because there is in society a conflict between fantasy and reality. It is not a neurotic conflict because it is a social problem and is solved by the artist for society. Psychoanalysts do not see the poet playing a social function, but regard him as a neurotic working off his complexes at the expense of the public. Therefore in analyzing a work of art, psychoanalysts seek just those symbols that are peculiarly private, i.e., neurotic, and hence psychoanalytical criticism of art finds its examples and material always either in third-rate artistic work or in accidental features of good work. In *Hamlet* they see an Oedipus complex; but they do not see that this does not explain the universal power of the great speeches, or the equal greatness of *Antony and Cleopatra,* which cannot be analyzed into an Oedipus complex.

The psychoanalyst can sometimes cure the neurotic who cannot cure himself unaided, because he provides a force or point of leverage outside the psyche of the neurotic. He is a member of society, and can therefore work from the outside inwards, into the socially created conscious psyche, the neurotic's "better self," and so attack the unconscious, his "worse self." The better self, the conscious psyche, the *conscience,* is society's creation, while the "worse self" is genotypical, the animal in us.

The psychoanalyst is only one man, and is also the possessor of a worse self which may get between himself and his patient. He is a luxury who can be afforded only by the well-to-do. In art all society, the sum of all conscious psyches engaged in social creation, speaks to a man's "better self." All the better part of humanity, endlessly attacking and solving life's problems, stands ranged behind the artistic culture of a nation. They are men not gods; like him they suffered and fought, but when they died they left behind the enduring essence of their transitory lives. Hence the consoling, healing and invigorating power of art.

The emotional attitude of the neurotic or the psychotic towards reality is permanent. That of the poet in creation, or the reader in experiencing, is temporary. The essence of genuine illusion is that it is non-symbolic and plastic. The neurotic is deluded because the complex is in his unconscious; he is unfree. The artist is only illuded because the complex is in his conscious; he is free. We take up the attitude when reading a poem, and experience the emotions, and then when the poem has been experienced the attitude is thrown away. The attitude was released by the conscious emotions; as the neurotic attitude may be unfrozen if he becomes conscious of the complex; as the sleeper wakes if the stimulus demands willed action. The artist releases the autonomous complex in a work of art and "forgets" it, goes on to create anew, to experiment again with the eternal adaptation of the genotype to its eternally changing environment. If poetry becomes religion, if the non-symbolic is taken to be symbolic, the emotional attitude becomes frozen like the neurotic attitude. Thus the value of poetry's illusions in securing catharsis, as compared to religion's, is that they are known for illusion, and as compared to dream, that they are social.

If poetry's emotional attitudes pass, what is their value? It is this; experience leaves behind it a trace in memory. It is stored by the organism and modifies its action. The Universe today is not what it was a million years ago, because it is that much more full of experience, and that much more *historic*. Society is not what it was two thousand years ago, because its culture has lived through much and experienced much. So too a wise man, in the course of his life, has endured and experienced. He has not acquired knowledge of external reality only, for such a man we call merely "learned," and think of his learning as something arid, devoid of richness. The wise man has also learned about *himself*. He has had emotional experience. It is because of this double experience that we call him wise, with a ripeness, a poise, a sagacity given to him by all his history. Of course neither science nor art are substitutes for concrete living: they are guide-books to it.

The wisdom of a culture, our social heritage, inheres both in its science and its art. Either alone is one-sided wisdom, but both together give ripe sagacity, the vigor and serenity of an organism sure of itself in the face of external reality.

What, then, is the illusion of art? In what does it consist? Not in the affective element, for artistic emotion is consciously experienced, and is therefore real and true. Real and true as applied to emotion mean simply, Has it existed in reality?—has it been present in a psyche? The emotion of poetry is certainly real in this sense. The illusion of poetry must therefore inhere in the piece of external reality to which the emotion is attached—in poetry to the meaning, in novel to the story. The purpose of this piece of external reality was to provide a subject for the affect, because an affect is a conscious judgment, and must therefore be a judgment of *something*. Art is therefore affective experimenting with selected pieces of external reality. The situation corresponds to a scientific experiment. In this a selected piece of external reality is set up in the laboratory. It is a mock world, an imitation of that part of external reality in which the experimenter is interested. It may be an animal's heart in a physiological salt solution, a shower of electrified droplets between two plates, or an aerofoil in a wind tunnel. In each case there is a "fake" piece of the world, detached so as to be handled conveniently, and illusory in this much, that it is not actually what we meet in real life, but a selection from external reality arranged for our own purposes. It is an "as if." In the same way the external reality symbolized in scientific reasoning is never *all* external reality, or a simple chunk of it, but a selection from it. The difference between art's piece of reality and science's is that science is only interested in the relation of that selected piece to the world from which it is drawn, whereas art is interested in the relation between the genotype and the selected piece of reality, and therefore ignores the whole world standing behind the part. If by the words "mock world," we denote the illusory piece of external reality, the symbolical part alike of poetry and science, we get this relation:

External Reality	Mock World	Social Ego
Science		Art

Hence it is just "illusion" that art and science *have in common.* The *distinctive* concern of science is the world of external reality; art is occupied with the world of internal reality. The ordering or logical manifold characteristic of scientific language is that internal structure in its mock world projected from the relationships of external reality. The ordering or affective manifold characteristic of artistic language is that internal structure in its mock world projected from the relationships of internal reality. Hence another schematic representation:

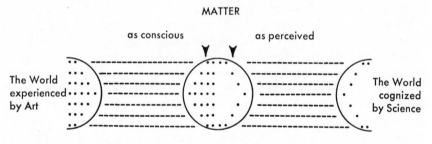

MATTER

as conscious   as perceived

The World experienced by Art   The World cognized by Science

But since the genotype is itself a part of external reality, we can also represent it thus:

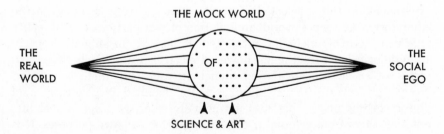

THE MOCK WORLD

THE REAL WORLD   OF   THE SOCIAL EGO

SCIENCE & ART

Hence science and art together are able to symbolize a complete Universe which includes the genotype itself. Each alone is partial, but the two halves together make a whole, not as fitted together, but as they interpenetrate man's struggle with Nature in the process of concrete living.

Note

1 Earlier in this essay, Christopher Caudwell had stated that the poet revolts against capitalist society in a characteristically bourgeois manner by setting his crafts-man skill in opposion to social function, his "art" in opposition to "life." This movement of "art for art's sake" necessarily leads to works of private fantasy, exemplified in France by the progression from the Parnassians (word craft for its own sake), to the Symbolists (generation of a vague aura of distant emotional associations), to the Surrealists (private "unconscious" meanings). (—Eds.)

25. Bertolt Brecht

Theatre for Pleasure and Theatre for Instruction

For a biographical note on BERTOLT BRECHT, see p. 226. The date of the following selection is uncertain, but it was probably written in 1936. It is included in *Brecht on Theatre*, translated and edited by John Willett.

A FEW years back, anybody talking about the modern theatre meant the theatre in Moscow, New York and Berlin. He might have thrown in a mention of one of Jouvet's productions in Paris or Cochran's in London, or *The Dybbuk* as given by the Habima (which is to all intents and purposes part of the Russian theatre, since Vakhtangov was its director). But broadly speaking there were only three capitals so far as modern theatre was concerned.

Russian, American and German theatres differed widely from one another, but were alike in being modern, that is to say in introducing technical and artistic innovations. In a sense they even achieved a certain stylistic resemblance, probably because technology is international (not just that part which is directly applied to the stage but also that which influences it, the film for instance), and because large progressive cities in large industrial countries are involved. Among the older capitalist countries it is the Berlin theatre that seemed of late to be in the lead. For a period all that is common to the modern theatre received its strongest and (so far) maturest expression there.

The Berlin theatre's last phase was the so-called epic theatre, and it showed the modern theatre's trend of development in its purest form. Whatever was labelled 'Zeitstück' or 'Piscatorbühne' or 'Lehrstück' belongs to the epic theatre.

The Epic Theatre

Many people imagine that the term 'epic theatre' is self-contradictory, as the epic and dramatic ways of narrating a story are held, following Aristotle, to be basically distinct. The difference between the two forms was never thought simply to lie in the fact that the one is performed by living beings while the other operates via the written word; epic works such as those of Homer and the medieval singers were at the same time theatrical performances, while dramas like Goethe's *Faust* and Byron's *Manfred* are agreed to have been more effective as books. Thus even by Aristotle's definition the difference between the dramatic and epic forms was attributed to their different methods of construction, whose laws were dealt with by two different branches of aesthetics. The method of construction depended on the different way of presenting the work to the public, sometimes via the stage, sometimes through a book; and independently of that there was the 'dramatic element' in epic works and the 'epic element' in dramatic. The bourgeois novel in the last century developed much that was 'dramatic,' by which was meant the strong centralization of the story, a momentum that drew the separate parts into a common relationship. A particular passion of utterance, a certain emphasis on the clash of forces are hallmarks of the 'dramatic.' The epic writer Döblin provided an excellent criterion when he said that with an epic work, as opposed to a dramatic, one can as it were take a pair of scissors and cut it into individual pieces, which remain fully capable of life.

This is no place to explain how the opposition of epic and dramatic lost its rigidity after having long been held to be irreconcilable. Let us just point out that the technical advances alone were enough to permit the stage to incorporate an element of narrative in its dramatic productions. The possibility of projections, the greater adaptability of the stage due to mechanization, the film, all completed the theatre's equipment, and did so at a point where the most important transactions between people could no longer be shown simply by personifying the motive forces or subjecting the characters to invisible metaphysical powers.

To make these transactions intelligible the environment in which the people lived had to be brought to bear in a big and 'significant' way.

This environment had of course been shown in the existing drama, but only as seen from the central figure's point of view, and not as an independent element. It was defined by the hero's reactions to it. It was seen as a storm can be seen when one sees the ships on a sheet of water unfolding their sails, and the sails filling out. In the epic theatre it was to appear standing on its own.

The stage began to tell a story. The narrator was no longer missing, along with the fourth wall. Not only did the background adopt an attitude to the events on the stage—by big screens recalling other simultaneous events elsewhere, by projecting documents which confirmed or contradicted what the characters said, by concrete and intelligible figures to accompany abstract conversations, by figures and sentences to support mimed transactions whose sense was unclear—but the actors too refrained from going over wholly into their role, remaining detached from the character they were playing and clearly inviting criticism of him.

The spectator was no longer in any way allowed to submit to an experience uncritically (and without practical consequences) by means of simple empathy with the characters in a play. The production took the subject-matter and the incidents shown and put them through a process of alienation: the alienation that is necessary to all understanding. When something seems 'the most obvious thing in the world' it means that any attempt to understand the world has been given up.

What is 'natural' must have the force of what is startling. This is the only way to expose the laws of cause and effect. People's activity must simultaneously be so and be capable of being different.

It was all a great change.

The dramatic theatre's spectator says: Yes, I have felt like that too —Just like me—It's only natural—It'll never change—The sufferings of this man appall me, because they are inescapable—That's great art; it all seems the most obvious thing in the world—I weep when they weep, I laugh when they laugh.

The epic theatre's spectator says: I'd never have thought it—That's not the way—That's extraordinary, hardly believable—It's got to stop—The sufferings of this man appall me, because they are unnecessary—That's great art: nothing obvious in it—I laugh when they weep, I weep when they laugh.

The Instructive Theatre

The stage began to be instructive.

Oil, inflation, war, social struggles, the family, religion, wheat, the meat market, all became subjects for theatrical representation. Choruses enlightened the spectator about facts unknown to him. Films showed a montage of events from all over the world. Projections added statistical material. And as the 'background' came to the front of the stage so people's activity was subjected to criticism. Right and wrong courses of action were shown. People were shown who knew what they were doing, and others who did not. The theatre became an affair for philosophers, but only for such philosophers as wished not just to explain the world but also to change it. So we had philosophy, and we had instruction. And where was the amusement in all that? Were they sending us back to school, teaching us to read and write? Were we supposed to pass exams, work for diplomas?

Generally there is felt to be a very sharp distinction between learning and amusing oneself. The first may be useful, but only the second is pleasant. So we have to defend the epic theatre against the suspicion that it is a highly disagreeable, humorless, indeed strenuous affair.

Well: all that can be said is that the contrast between learning and amusing oneself is not laid down by divine rule; it is not one that has always been and must continue to be.

Undoubtedly there is much that is tedious about the kind of learning familiar to us from school, from our professional training, etc. But it must be remembered under what conditions and to what end that takes place.

It is really a commercial transaction. Knowledge is just a commodity. It is acquired in order to be resold. All those who have grown out of going to school have to do their learning virtually in secret, for anyone who admits that he still has something to learn devalues himself as a man whose knowledge is inadequate. Moreover the usefulness of learning is very much limited by factors outside the learner's control. There is unemployment, for instance, against which no knowledge can protect one. There is the division of labor, which makes generalized knowledge unnecessary and impossible. Learning is often among the concerns of those whom no amount of concern will get any forwarder. There is not much knowledge that leads to power, but plenty of knowledge to which only power can lead.

Learning has a very different function for different social strata. There are strata who cannot imagine any improvement in conditions: they find the conditions good enough for them. Whatever happens to oil they will benefit from it. And: they feel the years beginning to tell. There can't be all that many years more. What is the point of learning a lot now? They have said their final word: a grunt. But there are also strata 'waiting their turn' who are discontented with conditions, have a vast interest in the practical side of learning, want at all costs to find out where they stand, and know that they are lost without learning; these are the best and keenest learners. Similar differences apply to countries and peoples. Thus the pleasure of learning depends on all sorts of things; but none the less there is such a thing as pleasurable learning, cheerful and militant learning.

If there were not such amusement to be had from learning the theatre's whole structure would unfit it for teaching.

Theatre remains theatre even when it is instructive theatre, and in so far as it is good theatre it will amuse.

Theatre and Knowledge

But what has knowledge got to do with art? We know that knowledge can be amusing, but not everything that is amusing belongs in the theatre.

I have often been told, when pointing out the invaluable services that modern knowledge and science, if properly applied, can perform for art and specially for the theatre, that art and knowledge are two estimable but wholly distinct fields of human activity. This is a fearful truism, of course, and it is as well to agree quickly that, like most truisms, it is perfectly true. Art and science work in quite different ways: agreed. But, bad as it may sound, I have to admit that I cannot get along as an artist without the use of one or two sciences. This may well arouse serious doubts as to my artistic capacities. People are used to seeing poets as unique and slightly unnatural beings who reveal with a truly godlike assurance things that other people can only recognize after much sweat and toil. It is naturally distasteful to have to admit that one does not belong to this select band. All the same, it must be admitted. It must at the same time be made clear that the scientific occupations just confessed to are not pardonable side interests, pursued on days off after a good week's work. We all know how Goethe was interested in natural history, Schiller in history: as a kind of hobby, it is charitable to assume. I have no wish promptly to accuse these two of having needed these sciences for their poetic activity; I am not trying to shelter behind them; but I must say that I do need the sciences. I have to admit, however, that I look askance at all sorts of people who I know do not operate on the level of scientific understanding: that is to say, who sing as the birds sing, or as people imagine the birds to sing. I don't mean by that that I would reject a charming poem about the taste of fried fish or the delights of a boating party just because the writer had not studied gastronomy or navigation. But in my view the great and complicated things that go on in the world cannot be adequately recognized by people who do not use every possible aid to understanding.

Let us suppose that great passions or great events have to be shown which influence the fate of nations. The lust for power is nowadays held to be such a passion. Given that a poet 'feels' this lust and wants to have someone strive for power, how is he to show the exceedingly complicated machinery within which the struggle for power nowadays takes place? If his hero is a politician, how do politics work? If he is a business man, how does business work? And yet there are writers who find business and politics nothing like so passionately interesting as the individual's lust for power. How are they to acquire the necessary knowledge? They are scarcely likely to learn enough by going round and keeping their eyes open, though even then it is more than they would get by just rolling their eyes in an exalted frenzy. The foundation of a paper like the *Völkischer Beobachter* or a business like Standard Oil is a pretty complicated affair, and such things cannot be conveyed just like that. One important field for the playwright is psychology. It is taken for granted that a poet, if not an ordinary man, must be able without further instruction to discover the motives that lead a man to commit murder, he must be able to give a picture of a murderer's mental state 'from within himself.' It is taken for granted that one only has to look inside oneself in such a case; and then there's always one's imagination. . . . There are various reasons why I can no longer surrender to this agreeable hope of getting a result quite so simply. I can no longer find in myself all those motives which the press or scientific reports show to have been observed in people. Like the average judge when pronouncing sentence, I cannot without further ado conjure up an adequate picture of a murderer's mental state. Modern psychology, from psychoanalysis to behaviorism, acquaints me with facts that lead me to judge the case quite differently, especially if I bear in mind the findings of sociology and do not overlook economics and history. You will say: but that's getting complicated. I have to answer that it *is* complicated. Even if you let yourself be convinced, and agree with me that a large slice of literature is exceedingly primitive, you may still ask with profound concern: won't an evening in such a theatre be a most alarming affair? The answer to that is: no.

Whatever knowledge is embodied in a piece of poetic writing has to be wholly transmuted into poetry. Its utilization fulfills the very pleasure that the poetic element provokes. If it does not at the same time fulfill that which is fulfilled by the scientific element, none the less in an age of great discoveries and inventions one must have a certain inclination to penetrate deeper into things—a desire to make the world controllable —if one is to be sure of enjoying its poetry.

Is the Epic Theatre Some Kind of 'Moral Institution'?

According to Friedrich Schiller the theatre is supposed to be a moral institution. In making this demand it hardly occurred to Schiller that by moralizing from the stage he might drive the audience out of the theatre. Audiences had no objection to moralizing in his day. It was only later that Friedrich Nietzsche attacked him for blowing a moral trumpet. To Nietzsche any concern with morality was a depressing affair, to Schiller it seemed thoroughly enjoyable. He knew of nothing that could give greater amusement and satisfaction than the propagation of ideas. The bourgeoisie was setting about forming the ideas of the nation.

Putting one's house in order, patting oneself on the back, submitting one's account, is something highly agreeable. But describing the collapse of one's house, having pains in the back, paying one's account, is indeed a depressing affair, and that was how Friedrich Nietzsche saw things a century later. He was poorly disposed towards morality, and thus towards the previous Friedrich too.

The epic theatre was likewise often objected to as moralizing too much. Yet in the epic theatre moral arguments only took second place. Its aim was less to moralize than to observe. That is to say it observed, and then the thick end of the wedge followed: the story's moral. Of course we cannot pretend that we started our observations out of a pure passion for observing and without any more practical motive, only to be completely staggered by their results. Undoubtedly there were some painful discrepancies in our environment, circumstances that were barely tolerable, and this not merely on account of moral considerations. It is not only moral considerations that make hunger, cold and oppression hard to bear. Similarly the object of our inquries was not just to arouse moral objections to such circumstances (even though they could easily be felt—though not by all the audience alike, such objections were seldom for instance felt by those who profited by the circumstances in question) but to discover means for their elimination. We were not in fact speaking in the name of morality but in that of the victims. These truly are two distinct matters, for the victims are often told that they ought to be contented with their lot, for moral reasons. Moralists of this sort see man as existing for morality, not morality for man. At least it should be possible to gather from the above to what degree and in what sense the epic theatre is a moral institution.

Can Epic Theatre Be Played Anywhere?

Stylistically speaking, there is nothing all that new about the epic theatre. Its expository character and its emphasis on virtuosity bring it close to the old Asiatic theatre. Didactic tendencies are to be found in the medieval mystery plays and the classical Spanish theatre, and also in the theatre of the Jesuits.

These theatrical forms corresponded to particular trends of their time, and vanished with them. Similarly the modern epic theatre is linked with certain trends. It cannot by any means be practiced universally. Most of the great nations today are not disposed to use the theatre for ventilating their problems. London, Paris, Tokyo and Rome maintain their theatres for quite different purposes. Up to now favorable circumstances for an epic and didactic theatre have only been found in a few places and for a short period of time. In Berlin Fascism put a very definite stop to the development of such a theatre.

It demands not only a certain technological level but a powerful movement in society which is interested to see vital questions freely aired with a view to their solution, and can defend this interest against every contrary trend.

The epic theatre is the broadest and most far-reaching attempt at large-scale modern theatre, and it has all those immense difficulties to overcome that always confront the vital forces in the sphere of politics, philosophy, science and art.

26. George D. Thomson

After Aeschylus

GEORGE D. THOMSON (1903–   ) has been a Fellow of King's College, Cambridge, and became Professor of Greek at the University of Birmingham (England) in 1937. Since 1947 he has been a member of the Executive Committee of the Communist Party of Great Britain. A noted classicist, historian, and critic, he is the author of *Greek Lyric Meter* (1929), *Marxism and Poetry* (1935), *Studies in Ancient Greek Society* (1949). The selection is taken from his *Aeschylus and Athens*, a study of Greek tragedy in relation to socio-economic conditions originally published in 1941.

GREEK tragedy was one of the distinctive functions of Athenian democracy. In its form and its content, in its growth and its decay, it was conditioned by the evolution of the social organism to which it belonged.

In the Aegean basin, split up into innumerable islands and valleys, the centralization of political power was difficult, and the political units tended to remain autonomous. External expansion being thus restricted, their internal development was proportionately intense. In the democratic city-state, ancient society rose, on a scale necessarily minute, to its highest point. These states had advanced so rapidly that they carried with them copious traditions of the past, and their autonomy favored the persistence of alternative versions of the same events, which provided abundant material for comparison and analysis. Moreover, surrounded as they were by primitive peoples, thoughtful citizens did not fail to perceive that their own ancestors had once lived as these barbarians lived now.* And, finally, the success of the democratic movement predisposed its exponents towards enquiry into its origins, while the strenuous opposition which it had encountered taught them to regard conflict, whether between man and man or man and nature, as the driving-force

---

* Thuc. 1. 6. 6.

of human progress. The result was a view of evolution at once rational and dynamic.

Aeschylus was a democrat who fought as well as wrote. The triumph of democracy over the internal and external enemies allied against it was the inspiration of his art. He was a leading citizen of the most advanced community in Greece; he was also, as a member of the old Attic nobility, the heir to local traditions which had their roots far back in the society of the primitive tribe. The fundamental question which engrossed him all his life was this—how had the tribal society enshrined in those traditions evolved into the democratic city-state which he had helped to establish? It is a question that must concern us, too, if we wish to understand his art, and it is at the same time so vital to the understanding of European civilization as to invest his art with a permanent historical importance.

The Greek view of life was not, as sometimes represented, the expression of qualities inherent in the Greeks as such; it was the rich and varied response of a heterogeneous people to the complex and continuous growth of Greek society itself as determined by the special conditions of its material and historical environment. The use that men make of their leisure, their ideas of the physical world, of right and wrong, their art, philosophy and religion, vary and develop in accordance with variations and developments in their social relations which in turn are ultimately determined by their mode of securing their material subsistence. This is not to deny that there exists an objective reality, or that some men have formed a truer idea of it than others; but every idea of it is relative in so far as it starts from conscious or unconscious assumptions determined by the position of the man himself in the world he contemplates.

To that extent, therefore, not only was the Greek view of life relative, but so is our view of the Greek view. Our view cannot be wholly objective, and the professed impartiality of some modern scholars is an illusion; but it will be more or less objective in proportion as we recognize and analyze our own preconceptions. We must become conscious of our prejudices in order to correct them. The historian of the past is a citizen of the present. Those who as citizens are averse or indifferent to contemporary social changes will seek in the civilization of ancient Greece something stable and absolutely valuable, which will both reflect and fortify their attitude of acquiescence. Others, who cannot acquiesce, will study the history of Greece as a process of continuous change, which, if it can be made to reveal its underlying laws, will help them to understand, and so direct, the forces making for change in the society of today. To such as these, the study of Aeschylus, who was a revolutionary poet, will be especially congenial, and the preconceptions with which they approach him, being akin to his own, will be a positive advantage. . . .

The latest work of Aeschylus marks a turning-point in the evolution of Greek tragedy. In the first place, it concludes that process of expansion and coordination which had begun when the tetralogy first took shape. At this point the tetralogy ceases to develop and splits into its component parts. The satyr play persists, but with diminishing vitality. The new unit is the single tragedy, now self-contained. Thus, in the hands of Sophocles (495–405 B.C.) and Euripides (480–405 B.C.), the art-form reverted to an earlier phase of its development; but at the same time this single tragedy is marked by certain features which can be traced to the distinctive function of the third play of the Aeschylean trilogy. It is therefore not simply a reversion to type, but a reversion to type on a higher plane.

In the second place, it is only at this stage that the art developed what came eventually to be regarded as one of its primary characteristics. According to Aristotle, the tragic plot should consist of a change from good fortune to bad. This principle has only a very limited application to the work of Aeschylus, because the normal conclusion of his trilogy was a change in the reverse direction. From this point of view, therefore, his work is still archaic, preserving the primitive sequence of the passion play, in which the god's death had been followed by his resurrection.

These structural changes in the art can only be explained by reference to external factors; and therefore, before passing on to the work of Sophocles and Euripides, we must pause to consider the developments that were taking place in Athenian society.

The data for the population of Attica in the fifth century B.C. are too fragmentary and uncertain to permit of more than a conjectural estimate. For the time of the Persian Wars all that can be said is that the number of citizens was probably less, the number of resident aliens and slaves certainly much less, than at the outbreak of the Peloponnesian War. In 431 B.C., according to the most recent estimate, there were at least 172,000 citizens, including their women and children, at least 28,500 resident aliens, and not more than 115,000 slaves. This means that the slaves already amounted to over half the free population, and that little more than a quarter of the total number of adults were in possession of the franchise.

Slave labor became one of the most productive fields for the investment of capital. Nikias owned 1,000 slaves, whom he hired out for labor in the mines; Hipponikus owned 600, whom he employed for the same purpose. Of the number employed in the mines, all we know is that in the year 413 B.C. over 20,000 slaves deserted to the Spartans, and it is probable that most of these were miners. Slaves were also employed in large numbers in quarrying and transport.

As the supply of slave labor increased, the demand for free labor declined, with the result that the free laborer was either unable to find employment or else compelled to work in conditions which reduced him to the economic level of a slave. Against this destructive competition, the resident alien had no protection, because he did not possess the franchise, and consequently the poorer aliens sank to a status which Aristotle describes as "limited slavery." But the position of the citizen was different. The lower classes used their newly won political rights to force the state to maintain them without working at all. During the twenty years from 450 to 430 B.C., under the leadership of Pericles, the principle of payment for public services, including attendance at the law courts, was adopted and extended as a permanent policy of state, with the result that, at the end of that period, over 20,000 citizens—that is, between one-third and one-half of the whole citizen body—were supported in one way or another at the public expense. This was the price at which Pericles retained popular support.

Where did the money come from? The fact that the policy was carried through without effective opposition is enough to show that the burden did not fall on the rich. It came partly from imposts on trade and taxes levied from the resident aliens, in whose hands trade was concentrated; and it came partly from the empire into which Athens had now converted the league of free cities which she had organized for the war of liberation against Persia some thirty years before. The internal revenue at this period has been estimated at 400 talents, most of which was raised by taxes of the kind just mentioned, and the average annual assessment of the tribute exacted from the subject states was probably 460 talents. Thus, the wealth of the community was administered by that section of it which had the least part in its production. The citizens of Athens became a class of *rentiers*, living parasitically on the labor of others.

These measures, of course, did nothing to eliminate the tendency, inherent in an economy based on private ownership, for wealth to concentrate at one pole of society; and consequently they only served to intensify the inequalities which they were designed to remove. Fed by cheap corn imported from Athenian dependencies overseas, the city populace was swollen by a constant influx of peasants from the Attic countryside, for whom, owing to the competition of foreign corn, farming had ceased to pay; and so the demand for imported food only grew with the supply. In the same way, many of the impoverished citizens whom the state tried to get off its hands by settling them overseas on lands seized from the subject states, found it profitable to sell their holdings and return to Athens. The state could only maintain itself on this basis by continuous expansion. It had entered on a path which led inevitably to war. And the strongest advocates of this policy were naturally the radicals, representing all those who were struggling to maintain their standard of living against the growing menace of slavery. It was therefore the advanced democrats that now became the most ardent imperialists. So long as their own incomes were not affected, the rich citizens acquiesced, but, when the empire revolted, they were not slow to act. Shortly before the end of the war, when the empire was collapsing, the democracy was overthrown and replaced by a régime whose policy was "to secure for high civil offices men of special competence, to reserve the privileges of the commonwealth to Athenians who could afford them, and deny a voice in political decisions to such as lacked an appreciable property-stake in the community"—in other words, rather than surrender their wealth, the rich aimed at holding the poor in check by depriving them of the franchise, which was their only protection against the competition of slave labor.

Such were the insoluble contradictions on which Athenian democracy wrecked itself. The constitution which had been founded at the beginning of the century in the name of equality was overthrown at the end by the class that had founded it in the name of inequality. The class which had risen to power on the strength of its claim that the state should be ruled by those who produced its wealth now saw its unearned income threatened by rival claimants to the proceeds accruing from the taxation of traders and the exploitation of a multitude of slaves. The cry of liberty, which had been raised with such fervor against the Persian invader, had taken on a hollow ring, because, though Pericles might clothe it in fine words, the policy for which he stood meant that liberty was to be maintained at home by suppressing it abroad. Democracy had been transformed into the negation of democracy.

These contradictions produced in the human consciousness an underlying sense of disillusionment and frustration which it sought to escape by formulating ideas designed to cast a veil over the reality—the idea that Athens was destined to be the "school of Hellas"; the idea that the slave was naturally inferior to the freeman; and, above all, the idea of *sophrosýne*, that virtue of moderation or restraint which was embodied in Athena. The notion of *sophrosýne* is the old aristocratic "nothing too much" in a new guise, but with one difference. In the aristocratic tradition, the man who sought too much had been simply blasted by the thunderbolt of Zeus. What happened to the man whose ambitions or desires led him beyond the limits of *sophrosýne* is that he got the opposite of what he was striving after. This notion, which from the fifth century onwards becomes a dominant element in Greek thought, must be traced back to its origin.

The social contradictions which came to a head after the democratic revolution were insoluble, because they were inherent in an economy based on private property, and it was the growth of private property which through the democratic revolution had brought them to a head. And further, what had facilitated and accelerated the growth of private property was the development of money. In his discussion of this subject, which for depth of insight is one of the most remarkable in the whole range of his work, Aristotle says that the original function of money was to facilitate the process of exchange—selling in order to buy. So long as it was confined to this purpose, the use of money was limited by the fact that it was merely a means to an end—the satisfaction of immediate needs. This use of money (here his own social preconceptions come into play) is regarded as natural and just. But it was not long before money came to be used for a new purpose—buying in order to sell: the merchant buys cheap in order to sell dear. Money-making has become an end in itself, and in this form it has no limit. The same truth has been formulated in modern times by Marx:

> The simple circulation of commodities (selling in order to buy) is a means for carrying out a process which lies outside the domain of circulation—a means for the appropriation of use-values, for the satisfaction of wants. The circulation of money as capital, on the other hand, is an end in itself, for the expansion of value can only occur within this perpetually renewed movement. Consequently, the circulation of capital has no limits.

This, in effect, is what Solon had said at the beginning of the Athenian monetary revolution: "Riches have no limit." And, as Aristotle points out, owing to various causes, such as depreciation in the value of money, the pursuit of wealth for its own sake is liable to result in the opposite of the intention: a man may amass money only to find himself like Midas starving in the midst of his gold.

Under the landed aristocracy, the economic relations between peasant and landowner had been simple and clear. The peasant had paid over so much of his produce to his lord, and this relation was expressed in the simple formula, nothing too much. But with the development of money, economic relations became increasingly complex and obscure. The producer took his goods to market only to find them unsaleable, because others had produced more of the same goods than there were purchasers to buy them. The speculator put his capital into an industrial enterprise only to find that a monetary crisis, which he had unwittingly helped to precipitate, robbed him of the expected return. He found himself the victim of a process which lay outside his understanding and control.

When money was first introduced, it was recognized as a new power destined to increase in an unprecedented degree man's control over Nature. "Man is money": such was the saying of a citizen of one of the first Greek states to strike a coinage. There is nothing money cannot buy; there is nothing the man with money cannot become. But this new power was soon seen to be ambivalent. As Sophocles wrote:

> Money wins friendship, honor, place and power,
> And sets man next to the proud tyrant's throne.
> All trodden paths and paths untrod before
> Are scaled by nimble riches, where the poor
> Can never hope to win the heart's desire.
> A man ill-formed by nature and ill-spoken
> Money shall make him fair to eye and ear.
> Money earns man his health and happiness,
> And only money cloaks iniquity.

And so we find the same poet denouncing money as the root of all evil:

> Of all the foul growths current in the world
> The worst is money. Money drives men from home,
> Plunders great cities, perverts the honest mind
> To shameful practice, godlessness and crime.

The invention has returned to plague the inventor.

As money extended the range of its operations, penetrating every department of human life with its subversive influence, men came to perceive that this yellow slave had become their master; and, since its operation lay outside their control, they could only explain it by idealizing it as a universal law. From this time forward there runs through Greek literature the persistent tradition that the excessive pursuit, not only of riches, but of health, happiness and all things good and desirable in themselves, is liable to produce their opposites. As Isocrates said, men who have acquired great riches cannot rest content, but risk what they have by reaching after more. As Bakchylides said, the spirit of pride or excess bestows on man his neighbor's wealth only to plunge him in the gulf of calamity. As Hippocrates said, extreme conditions of physical well-being are dangerous, because they cannot remain stable. Aeschylus said the same of health and happiness:

> If a man's health be advanced over the due mean,
> It will trespass soon upon sickness, who stands
> Close neighbor, between them a thin wall.
> So doth the passage of life,
> Sped by a prosperous breeze,
> Suddenly founder on reefs of disaster.

The idea received its most precise and comprehensive formulation in the words of Plato: "In the seasons, in plants, in the body, and above all in civil society, excessive action results in a violent transformation into its opposite."

Aeschylus had been able to take the tide of democracy at the flood. His conception of progress as the result of conflict reflected the positive achievement of the democratic revolution; but in his last years, when he urged his fellow citizens to leave their laws unchanged, his outlook was ceasing to be progressive. He failed to see that his reconciliation of opposites was but a transitory equilibrium out of which new opposites must arise. And so the tide began to turn. In his hands, the tragic chorus had still preserved something of its primitive function: it was designed to evoke and organize the attitude of mind appropriate to the ensuing action. In Sophocles, it loses this dynamic quality, and in Euripides it tends to become a musical interlude unrelated to the action. Similarly, the Aeschylean trilogy split up into a group of single tragedies, and the reconciliation survived only in the atrophied form of the *deus ex machina*, a summary conclusion bearing no organic relation to the plot. The center of interest had shifted from the reconciliation to the conflict. And at the same time there emerged the figure of the tragic hero in its mature form —a good man destroyed by his own self-will; and this reversal of his fortune is brought about on the principle of *peripéteia*, which Aristotle defines as "the transformation of the action into its opposite." The hero brings disaster on his own head by doing something which results in the reverse of what he had intended. His tragedy is therefore the tragedy of the community which has created him.

The principle of *peripéteia* can, of course, be traced in Aeschylus. Xerxes lost his empire because he overreached himself, and the circumstances in which Eteocles met his death were of his own making; but the blindness of Xerxes is merely a manifestation of the pride that goes before a fall, and, although the position in which Eteocles finds himself is not what he anticipated, he has the opportunity to withdraw and makes his choice with full knowledge of the consequences. In these plays, therefore, the principle is still rudimentary. To see it in its prime, we must turn to the finest work of Sophocles.

Sophocles raised the single tragedy to a level of technical perfection as high as the Aeschylean trilogy, and what makes this achievement still more remarkable is that, so far from seeking to shun comparison with Aeschylus, again and again he chose as his material the same myths which his predecessor had already dramatized. Just as he adapted the form of the art to his own outlook, so, by reinterpreting its content, he made it thoroughly his own. Further, since his own interpretation was new, he was in a position to exploit the work of Aeschylus, which was, of course,

familiar to his audience, by consciously appealing to it in order to econ-
omize an effect or to point a contrast. A firm grasp of this principle is
indispensable to the understanding of Sophocles. Where the corresponding work of Aeschylus has perished—for example, his *Oedipus* and his
Philoctetes—our appreciation of the Sophoclean plays on those subjects is
necessarily incomplete; but fortunately we possess in the *Electra* a play
which covers exactly the same ground as the *Choephoroi*, and, as Headlam
pointed out many years ago, "in the *Electra* of Sophocles there is hardly
any touch which in one form or another is not already to be found in
Aeschylus."

To Sophocles, meditating on the *Oresteia*, the question presented
itself: What happened to Electra? Aeschylus had shown how, through the
agency of the ancestral curse, an innocent girl had been transformed into
a second Clytemnestra; but there he had left her, because the plan of
his trilogy demanded that the attention of the audience should be concentrated on the consequences to Orestes of obeying the oracle of Apollo.
Sophocles was not interested in working out the implications of the
oracle, which accordingly, in striking contrast to Aeschylus, he states in
such terms as to throw on Orestes the responsibility for interpreting it
as a command to kill his mother. By this means the theological issue,
which for Aeschylus had been fundamental, is carefully excluded. In the
same way, he is not interested in the ancestral curse, or, rather, only in
the reality of which it is a symbol—the effects of upbringing and environment on the characters of a young man and his sister.

In the case of Orestes, the function of the curse is performed by the
Tutor, who accompanies him back to Argos. This energetic and heartless
old man, who has been in charge of Orestes ever since he was sent away
from home and has brought him up of set purpose for the mission on
which he is now engaged, is a fitting embodiment of the political interests
of the royal dynasty. It is he who, after pointing out to the boy the
wealthy palace of his fathers and rehearsing him in the details of the
conspiracy, roughly orders him out of the way when he hears his sister
weeping in the early morning twilight; and it is he who interrupts their
sobs of joy when the forlorn pair are for a moment happily united. He
realizes that, despite all his coaching, he has his work cut out to screw this
tenderhearted boy up to the pitch of murdering his mother; and it is
made quite clear that, without his constant vigilance and timely intervention, the plot would have ended in fiasco. In all this we recognize
a development of one of the functions assigned by Aeschylus to his
chorus; and it is characteristic of Sophocles that this dynamic element is
transferred to one of the actors.

The difference between Orestes and Electra is that, whereas his conduct

has been virtually dictated to him by the manner of his upbringing, hers
is her own choice, obstinately maintained in face of tremendous opposition. By turns sullen and defiant, never ceasing to denounce the
murderers and constantly reminding them of the hope on which she has
staked everything—the coming of Orestes—she is subjected to every insult
and indignity and lives in misery and squalor like a slave, fortified by
the conviction that only by refusing to compromise can she remain true to
her father's memory. The knowledge that in so doing she is forced to
behave in a manner of which she is herself ashamed is a torment to her.
Her sense of decency, which makes it impossible for her to condone her
father's murder, has involved her in a situation in which decency is
impossible. She perceives the contradiction herself, but there is no escape
from it. When her sister Chrysothemis pleads with her to be sensible,
she retorts that to be sensible is to betray her father. Chrysothemis is
what Electra has deliberately chosen not to be—one who has decided
"to obey her masters in all things in order that she may be free." This
allusion to the proverb quoted by Aeschylus in the *Choephoroi*—"Slave,
obey your masters right or wrong"—expresses the heart of the dilemma.
One sister enjoys a life of freedom because she has the spirit of a slave;
the other is treated like a slave because she refuses to submit. And therefore, when the Chorus of her friends warn her that persistence in her
attitude can only result in some fatal calamity, she does not deny it, but
insists that her attitude has been forced upon her by sheer necessity.
Confronted by her mother—a woman hardened by success in crime against
all sense of shame (although even she will feel a momentary pang at
the news of her son's death, showing that her depravity, too, has a history)
—Electra becomes strident and aggressive. "You admit you killed my
father," she declares. "What could be more damning, whether it was
justified or not?" To the audience the answer to this question is so obvious
that it is left to speak for itself in the sequel of the play: The accusations
which Electra levels against her mother sound unpleasantly like the
arguments with which Clytemnestra seeks to justify her murder of her
husband, making us feel that what the mother is the daughter may
become; and, indeed, the same feeling seems to disturb Electra herself,
for she says:

> Though you will not believe me, of all this
> I *am* ashamed—I see that it is wrong,
> Unlike myself. I have been driven to it
> By your misdeeds and by your hatred of me.
> Dishonor is a teacher of dishonor.

The plan of action on which Orestes and his Tutor have agreed has been very thoroughly worked out; yet, when put to the test, it is all but wrecked by an unforeseen contingency. In the *Choephoroi*, when Orestes delivers the report of his own death, Electra knows that it is false, because his identity has already been revealed to her. Sophocles reverses the order of these events. The Tutor dare not let Orestes reveal himself beforehand, because he does not trust him; and therefore he has to leave to chance the effect of the report on the girl who has declared that her hope in her brother is the one thing that enables her to go on living. The Tutor, of course, is quite indifferent to the feelings of Electra, but not so Orestes. Had he possessed more imagination and initiative, he would have foreseen this contingency, which, as it is, takes both him and his adviser by surprise.

The message is that Orestes has been killed by a fall from his chariot when he was leading in the last lap of a race at the Pythian Games at Delphi. This is the mystical charioteer of the *Choephoroi*, who again runs his race under the direction of Apollo; but Sophocles gives a novel turn to the theme by reminding us through his Chorus of the story, ignored by Aeschylus, of the race of Pelops at Olympia; and with this in mind, as we listen to the headlong career of the latest champion of the House of Pelops, we realize that he is doomed.

It is at this point that Sophocles introduces the *motif* of the discovery of the lock of hair which Orestes has laid on his father's tomb, and it is Chrysothemis, not Electra, who discovers it. But when she brings the joyful news to her sister, she is met with the blank assurance that their brother is dead. Meanwhile Electra, exerting all her strength of will to recover herself after the destruction of her sole hope, has conceived the desperate expedient, in which she now appeals to her sister for assistance, of killing Aigisthos herself. Chrysothemis, of course, will not hear of such a thing—as she says quite rightly, it is madness; and so Electra, who had hardly expected any other answer, declares that she will make the attempt single-handed, since the worst that can come of it is her own death. By this time we share the feeling of Chrysothemis and the Chorus that her mind is becoming unhinged.

Orestes appears in disguise, carrying an urn supposed to contain his own ashes. This, too, is part of the prearranged plan, being designed to reinforce the message already delivered in case it should have failed to carry conviction. Electra takes the urn to her breast and breaks into lamentation. This is too much for Orestes. Disregarding his instructions, he tells Electra, who has been pouring out her heart in a flood of passionate despair, that the brother, whose ashes she is still clasping in her arms, stands before her. It was a foolish thing to do, not because it jeopardizes the conspiracy, but because this last stroke drives his sister mad. A few moments ago she heard that he was dead, and on meeting that situation she has spent the last ounce of her strength. The news that he is not dead after all is more than she can bear. She throws herself into his arms, then, tearing herself away, shouts at the top of her voice to all and sundry that Orestes has come home. Her brother strives in vain to calm her, and the situation is only saved by the resourceful Tutor, who, waiting until her fit of hysteria is over, keeps a close watch on the palace door.

The crisis has now come. Aigisthos, who is out in the country, has been sent for. Clytemnestra is at home. Orestes goes in, accompanied by his Tutor. After they have gone, there is a short *stásimon* in which the Chorus, who show as little foresight in this play as in the *Choephoroi,* describe them as "hounds unescapable on the trail of crime," reminding us, both in words and in rhythm, of the opening of the corresponding *stásimon* in the *Choephoroi.* A woman's screams are heard—"Oh, I am struck!"—and Electra shouts back, "Strike, if you have the strength, again!"

Their mother's body is brought out, and a shroud thrown over it. Aigisthos returns. He has heard the report of Orestes' death, and is anxious to have proof. The son and daughter point to the body lying at the door. Aigisthos asks them to call Clytemnestra. Meanwhile he goes up to the body and lifts the veil. "Did you not know," the murderer says, smiling, "you have miscalled the living as though dead?" It is to Aigisthos that Sophocles gives the reading of this riddle: "Surely, it must be Orestes that addresses me?" He asks leave to speak a few words, but Electra intervenes: "For God's sake no more talk. Kill him at once and throw his body into the fields." Ordered into the house, Aigisthos continues to prevaricate, evidently in the hope of catching Orestes off his guard. After some further badinage, he goes in, followed by Orestes, and Electra remains on the stage alone, while the Chorus brings the tragedy to an end with the words: "O seed of Atreus, after much suffering thou hast come forth in freedom, by this enterprise made perfect." These words recall the last *stásimon* of the *Choephoroi,* where the deliverance of the house was acclaimed in an ecstasy of ill-timed jubilation.

In order to bring out the full effect of this last scene, it would be necessary to study it in detail, showing how almost every line vibrates with memories of Aeschylus; but enough has perhaps been said to indicate the method which the dramatist has adopted; and, when that has been understood, we shall hardly be in danger of falling into the egregious blunder of supposing that Sophocles really imagined that these two unhappy creatures were justified in murdering their mother. It is true that he does not expressly tell us that the next thing that happened was that Orestes saw the Erinyes, but that is because he does not wish to distract our attention from the silent figure of Electra. So far as the future of Orestes is concerned, he leaves the audience to draw their own conclusions from the *Oresteia*. But what does the future hold in store for Electra? Her hope has been fulfilled, she has won her deliverance, but the result is her utter desolation:

> O Curse of this sad House, unconquerable,
> How wide thy vision! Even that which seemed
> Well-ordered, safe beyond the reach of harm,
> Thou hast brought down with arrows from afar,
> And left me desolate, stripped of all I loved.

It is not an accident that Sheppard, the first modern scholar to explain this play correctly, was also the first to produce it on the stage; for the stagecraft of Sophocles, who in this respect excelled, is unanswerable. Nor is it an accident that, notwithstanding Sheppard's interpretation, the play continues to be misunderstood, because of all Greek tragedies it presents that sense of contradiction which is the essence of mature tragedy, in its sharpest and most inescapable form. Sophocles and his contemporaries could stand it, but for our dyspeptic culture it is too tough. Of those who seek refuge in the view that Sophocles regarded the murder simply as a justifiable homicide, it must be said that they have been deaf to his appeals to the *Choephoroi*, and that they have no right to father on Sophocles their own predilection for an easy answer to an insoluble problem. Others, less crudely, but with no more success, have tried to find some compromise, some middle point between Electra and Chrysothemis, which will enable them to say that the heroine failed in some way to do what she ought to have done; but these critics (who might well be asked what they would have done in the circumstances themselves) are apparently unaware that they are attempting that very task of reconciling the irreconcilable in which Electra so heroically failed. There is no way out, and that is where the tragedy lies—the tragedy of a passionate nature which by the very exercise of its vitality is caught as in a vise and crushed.

Let us now turn to the *Oedipus Tyrannus*, which Aristotle regarded as the type of all Greek tragedy.

Laios and Jocasta were King and Queen of Thebes. Kreon was Jocasta's brother. To the south of Thebes lies Corinth; to the west, cradled in the cliffs of Parnassus, the Delphic Oracle of Apollo, on whose temple were inscribed the words, "Know thyself." To Laios and Jocasta was born a son, Oedipus, of whom the Oracle predicted that he was destined to murder his father and marry his mother. Rather than rear such a child,

Jocasta handed it over to one of the men-servants with instructions to leave it to perish in the hills. The man-servant, who was a shepherd, took pity on it and gave it to another shepherd, a Corinthian, who took it home with him. The King and Queen of Corinth were childless, and reared it as their own.

Some twenty years later the young Oedipus was taunted by one of his companions with not being the true son of his father. He consulted his supposed parents, who sought to reassure him without revealing the truth. Dissatisfied with their assurances, Oedipus made a pilgrimage to Delphi and consulted the Oracle. The only reply he got was a repetition of the old prophecy, of which he now heard for the first time. Resolving never to set foot in Corinth again, he took the road to Thebes.

At this time the people of Thebes were afflicted by the ravages of the Sphinx, which took a daily toll of human life until some one could be found to read the riddle it had set them. Laios was now on his way to Delphi to consult the Oracle. He was driving a chariot, and one of his attendants was his man-servant, the shepherd. Meeting Oedipus, he tried to force him off the track. A quarrel ensued. Laios struck at Oedipus with his whip. Oedipus struck back and killed him. He killed the attendants, too—all except the shepherd, who took to his heels and brought back to Thebes the panic-stricken story that the King had been murdered by a band of robbers.

Pursuing his journey, Oedipus reached Thebes, where the first thing he did was to deliver the people by reading the riddle of the Sphinx. The answer, as we have seen, was Man. Oedipus knew himself. And yet he did not know himself: that he was yet to learn. The grateful people acclaimed him as their King. At this point the shepherd, who recognized in the deliverer of Thebes his master's murderer, but resolved to keep the truth to himself, obtained Jocasta's leave to spend the rest of his days in retirement in the hills. The new King married the widowed Queen.

Many years passed, and children were born to them. Then once more the Thebans were afflicted, this time with a plague. Determined not to fail them, Oedipus sent Creon to consult the Oracle. The reply was that the plague would cease when the murderer of Laios had been expelled. Oedipus immediately instituted a search for the unknown criminal in their midst, on whom he pronounced a curse. There was one other besides the shepherd who knew the truth and, like him, had decided to keep it dark—the aged prophet, Teiresias. Questioned by Oedipus, he refused to answer. Oedipus lost patience and accused him of disloyalty to Thebes. Then Teiresias lost patience, too, and denounced Oedipus as the murderer. Oedipus flew into a passion, accused Teiresias of having been suborned by Creon, and accused Creon of conspiring against the throne. The quarrel was brought to an end by the intervention of Jocasta, who, in reply to her husband's questions, told him what she had heard of the death of Laios—that he had been killed on the road to Delphi by a band of robbers. The road to Delphi—Oedipus remembered. But a band of robbers—Oedipus had been travelling alone. Jocasta assured him that the second point could be proved by sending for the sole survivor, the old shepherd in the hills. This Oedipus instructed her to do in the hope that his evidence would clear him.

At this point a messenger arrived from Corinth with the news that the King of that city was dead and Oedipus his successor. Oedipus was now at the height of fortune—king of two cities; and Jocasta acclaimed the news as proof that, since his father had died a natural death, the old prophecy was falsified. Reassured on that point, Oedipus nevertheless insisted that he would never return to Corinth for fear of marrying the Queen. Eager to reassure him on this point, too, the messenger explained that he was not her true son, but a foundling.

Meanwhile the old shepherd had arrived and at once recognized the messenger from Corinth as the shepherd he had met long ago in the hills. He tried hard to evade the King's questions, but was forced to answer by the threat of torture. The truth was out at last: Oedipus knew himself. Rushing into the palace, he put out his eyes with brooches torn from the dead body of his mother, who had already hanged herself.

> Ah, generations of men!
> I count your life as nothing.
> None that mortal is hath more
> Of happiness than this—
> To seem and not to be, and then, having seemed, to fail.

Since the beginning of the play, objectively nothing has changed, but subjectively everything has changed. All that has happened is that Oedipus has come to know what he is as apart from what he seemed to be. He ends life as he began it—as an outcast. The interval was only seeming. And yet, if seeming is being, this outcast, who became a king, this king who has become an outcast, has twice become the opposite of what he was. And these strange mutations have been brought about against the intention, yet through the unconscious agency, of the persons concerned. The parents exposed the child to avert the prophecy. The shepherd saved it out of pity, with the result that it grew up ignorant of its parentage. When doubt was cast on his parentage, Oedipus consulted the Oracle, and, when the Oracle revealed his destiny, he sought to escape it by taking the road that led to Thebes. He killed his father in self-defence. When the shepherd recognized him, he said nothing, thus leaving him free to marry his mother. When the Oracle demanded the expulsion of the murderer, Oedipus led the search and followed up each clue until he was brought face to face with himself. Teiresias would not have denounced him if he had not denounced Teiresias. His charges against Teiresias and Creon were unjustified. His vehemence at this point was the error that brought about his fall. And yet this error was but the excess of his greatest quality—his zeal in the service of his people. And, finally, the old shepherd, summoned to disprove the charge that he had killed his father, played into the hands of the Corinthian messenger, who, by seeking to relieve Oedipus of the fear of marrying his mother, proved that what he feared to do he had already done. This constant transmutation of intentions into their opposites, carried on to the catastrophe with the automatic precision of a dream, is the motive that governs the whole conception. The Oedipus of Sophocles is a symbol of the deep-seated perplexity engendered in men's minds by the unforeseen and incomprehensible transformation of a social order designed to establish liberty and equality into an instrument for the destruction of liberty and equality.

This play differs from the *Electra* in that the crisis is followed by an epilogue, which culminates in the prayer dictated by the sufferer to his children:

> Children, out of much
> I might have told you, could you understand,
> Take this one counsel: be your prayer to live,
> Where fortune's modest measure is, a life
> That shall be better than your father's was.

The purpose of this epilogue is, of course, to relieve the tremendous tension created by the crisis, and that purpose it serves perfectly; but the release it provides is, as it was meant to be, purely emotional. The strength of Oedipus is spent. Defeated and crushed by an irresistible and impenetrable power, which out of his own goodness has made the net that has enmeshed him, his wounded spirit instinctively seeks refuge in the simple, idle phrases that he learnt as a child.

Sophocles came of an aristocratic family, and in his conscious life he accepted the conventional outlook of his class. This is shown by his active support of the anti-democratic constitution which placed restrictions on the franchise in the last years of the Peloponnesian War (411 B.C.). It is also shown by his attitude to the Delphic Oracle, to which, owing to its reactionary policy, the democrats were hostile. In the *Oedipus*, as in the

Electra, he evades the religious issue, insisting that the oracle given to Laios is the interpretation put on the will of Apollo by his human agents, who are not infallible. For him, of course, that issue is dramatically irrelevant, but the fact that, unlike Aeschylus and Euripides, he has chosen to make it irrelevant signifies that he accepted the aristocratic view of Apollo, or at least was not prepared to challenge it. It is also true, that he accepted the conventional attitude, which Euripides was already challenging, to slaves and women. These social prejudices were certainly limitations, and more severe in him than in Aeschylus, because their true character was becoming increasingly apparent; but it would be a mistake to suppose that they constituted the essentials of his thought. As one who acquiesced in the privileges of his class, he was bound to accept the moral values designed to protect them, but where he differed from other members of his class, less intellectually gifted, was in his profound sense of the contradictions which those values involved; and this is the conflict that he sublimated in his art. He was far less conscious than Aeschylus had been of his relation to society, but of course this does not mean that the relation was any the less close—merely that it was passive rather than active; and indeed it was partly because of this that he was able to express the conflict in a symbol so true to the reality as the tragedy of Oedipus.

Euripides, like Aeschylus, was actively conscious of his relation to society; but for that very reason his work was fundamentally different, because society had changed. Reared from the cradle in the democratic ideas of liberty and equality, he was dismayed to see them flouted by reality. He saw the decay of the state religion in consequence of the deepening division of interests among the worshippers; he saw the degradation of family life in consequence of the subjection of women; he saw the demoralizing effects of imperialist aggression, waged in the name of democracy; and he even dared to challenge the validity of the distinction between freeman and slave, thus laying bare the irremediable evil which from this time forward was to gnaw at the vitals of ancient society—the condition both of its growth and its decay. Hence his outspoken individualism, the speculative inconsistency of his thought, and the experimental variety of his technique.

As a democrat, he delivered, in the *Ion,* a scathing denunciation of the unscrupulous chicanery by which the Delphic priesthood maintained its hold over the masses. As a rationalist, he boldly declared, in the *Madness of Heracles,* that, in the absence of moral responsibility, the pollution of homicide was merely physical. But, like other rationalists, he failed to see that the evils of society could never be cured by an appeal to reason, because their origin lay, not in ignorance or unenlightenment, but in a conflict of interests. It is therefore not surprising that at the end of his life he turned to mysticism. In his *Hippolytos*, an early play, he had shown little sympathy with the Orphic way of life; but in the *Bacchants*, written shortly before his death in Macedonia, where the worship of Dionysus still survived in its primitive, orgiastic form, his position has changed. The self-abandonment of the mystic is attractive to one who has thought long and earnestly on the riddle of reality, but without achieving any positive result; yet at the same time it is repulsive, because he cannot bring himself to renounce the faculty which has made man what he is. Agaue and her Bacchants escape from the city into the wilds, where, in communion with the divine, they dance their night-long dances, but she returns to the city carrying in her arms the head of her son, whom she has torn to pieces.

We have seen how the position of women at Athens had deteriorated. Lysias gives a picture of Athenian family life in his speech *On the Murder of Eratosthenes*, and it is not a pleasant one. All that was permitted to the wife was housework in the company of slaves and fidelity to a husband who spent most of his time away from home and was free to associate with other women. The result was the rapid growth of concubinage, prostitution and also male homosexuality. This institution, which seems to have been particularly widespread among the aristocratic intellectuals, was an adaptation of the primitive relationship between the newly-initiated boy and the young man who had supervised his initiation —a relationship which, in the conditions of Athenian city life, became predominantly sexual. The extent to which the relations between husband and wife were poisoned by these developments may be judged from the complacent remark of another Athenian orator: "We have courtesans for our pleasure, concubines for the daily needs of our bodies, and wives to keep house for us and bear us legitimate children." And, finally, having been reduced to this condition in the interests of the men, the woman was told to accept it as a dispensation of Nature. Pericles, who had divorced his own wife for an Ionian courtesan, and consequently quarrelled with his son, who then spread scurrilous reports about his father's private life, delivered a public oration in which he exhorted the widows of the men who had died for Athens to make the best of their inferior natures by behaving with such self-effacement as to excite neither applause nor censure. The attitude towards women corresponded to the attitude towards slaves. One wonders how Pericles explained matters to Aspasia, who, being an alien, was free from disabilities declared to be inherent in her sex; and one wonders how Plato felt on the day when by an unlucky stroke of fortune he was sold into slavery himself. The story was that Dionysios of Syracuse, who ordered the sale, told him that no harm would come to him, because, being a just man, he would be happy though a slave. However, the philosopher's capacity to practice what he preached was not put to the test, because, being rich, he was able to buy himself out.

> All trodden paths and paths untrod before
> Are scaled by nimble riches.

There was an Attic proverb that women had no fight in them. Jason returned home with Medea, a woman he had fallen in love with on his travels. After his return he ceased to care for her. She was a foreigner, his children by her were illegitimate, and he wanted a son who would be able to inherit from him. So he made a match with the King's daughter, and, in case Medea should cause trouble, she was told to leave the country and take her children with her. Medea obeyed, but not before she had murdered the bride and her own children by the bridegroom. The arguments advanced by Jason in defence of his conduct are such as would be entirely acceptable to Athenian convention. As Medea says, we have to buy husbands with our money and serve them with our bodies like slaves.

In the year 416 the Athenians delivered an ultimatum to the islanders of Melos, who wished to remain neutral in the war, and, according to Thucydides, this is what the representatives of democratic Athens told the people of Melos:

> As therefore it is not our purpose to amuse you with pompous details—how, after completely vanquishing the Persians, we had a right to assume the sovereignty, we shall waive all parade of words that have no tendency towards conviction, and in return insist from you that you reject all hopes of persuading us by frivolous remonstrances. Let us lay all stress on such points as may on both sides be judged persuasive; since of this you are as strongly convinced as we ourselves are sensible of it, that in all human competitions equal wants alone produce equitable determination, and, in whatever terms the powerful enjoin obedience, to those the weak are obliged to submit.

Since the people of Melos refused to submit, the adult male population was put to the sword and the women and children sold into slavery. In the following year Euripides produced his *Trojan Women,* portraying the helpless misery of the captives and the cynical insolence of the conquerors, who are destined to be destroyed on the voyage home by thunder and lightning. Thus, in the hands of Euripides, the age-old story of the Trojan War became prophetic, for a few years later Athens lost her empire as a result of her disastrous expedition to Sicily.

Euripides was a democrat who saw that democracy was being driven to self-destruction. That is the contradiction that underlies his work. He saw the evils inherent in contemporary society, and courageously exposed them. His influence was therefore disruptive: he helped to undermine the edifice which Aeschylus had labored to construct. But it was also, and for the same reason, progressive: the edifice was crumbling of itself.

After the war, the Greek city-state entered on its last phase, and Athenian thought became sharply divided in accordance with the cleavage between the few who had an interest in maintaining it and the many who had not. On the one hand, the idealists clung to their faith in the city-state at the cost of accepting social inequalities which were becoming less and less compatible with honest thinking. They were driven to deny the validity of the senses as a criterion of truth and to teach that happiness lay, not in pleasure, but in something called "virtue," which involved the acceptance of pain. Plato (428–348 B.C.) made slavery the basis of his ideal state, modelled on the parasitic communism of backward Spartan landowners, and, true to his model, passed imaginary laws narrowly restricting the activities of painters and poets, in whose creative imagination and fertile sense of human possibilities he recognized a danger to the established order; while, for the further security of his ruling class, he drew up a fantastic system of education designed to poison the minds of the people by dissemination of calculated lies. Plato's *Republic* is an implicit confession of the intellectual bankruptcy of the city-state. Similarly, the contradictions in which even Aristotle (384–322 B.C.), less reactionary and more honest than Plato, entangled himself in his justification of slavery is a measure of the extent to which the intellectual integrity of the ruling class was compromised by the maintenance of its privileges. He justified the subordination of slave to freeman by appealing to the subordination of woman to man and of body to soul; but the subordination of woman was a phenomenon of the same nature as slavery, and the subordination of body to soul, or of matter to form, was a projection on to the plane of ideas of the cleavage that confronted him in society. The early Orphics had asserted the independence of the soul as a protest against the enslavement of their bodies; now the same dichotomy was used to reconcile the unfree to permanent subjection. We are reminded of those nineteenth-century thinkers, beginning with Malthus, who, accepting the manufacturers' demand for cheap labor, justified the poverty of the workers by inventing laws of the struggle for existence and the survival of the fittest, and, when on this basis Darwin had founded a new science of biology, they acclaimed his theories as a final proof that the poverty of the workers was a law of nature.

Conversely, the materialists were only able to reaffirm the validity of sense-perception and to maintain their conviction that happiness lies primarily in the satisfaction of material needs, by renouncing their part in a society which no longer conformed to reason and by preaching the self-sufficiency of the individual. Epicurus (342–268 B.C.) taught that justice was relative, rescued the human soul from metaphysical abstractions (even his gods were material), and so completed the work, which Democritos had begun, of formulating the Atomic Theory. The atomism of the Epicureans was the complement of their individualism. They made the elements of the universe impassive and imperturbable, because, in a society torn by discord, that is what they themselves strove to become. Their definition of pleasure as the absence of pain reveals the social desperation of the dying convulsions of the city-state, but it had a positive value in their insistence that the aim of human endeavor *is* pleasure and not self-frustration for an intangible idea or an illusory hereafter. Thus, between the rise and fall of the city-state, idealism and materialism had changed places. At the beginning of the urban revolution, when the Orphics were proclaiming the divinity of the soul, the philosophers of Miletos maintained the primitive notion that the soul is an activity of matter; but now, when the Greek city-states were about to dissolve like crystals into the cosmopolitan empire, the Epicureans suffered persecution in their endeavors to free the masses from the fables of infernal torment with which their rulers cowed them. The heir to Orphic mysticism was Plato; the heir to Ionian materialism was Epicurus. In this, despite their limitations, the Epicureans were in the true line of progress; for at least they recognized that "the supreme being for man is man himself, and consequently all relations, all conditions in which man is humiliated, enslaved, despised, must be destroyed."

There was, however, one tradition which the Epicureans had inherited indirectly from the Orphics. We have seen in a former chapter how, in consequence of the transition from collective to private ownership, Moira had been transformed into Ananke. During the maturity of the city-state, the idea of Ananke was developed and extended. Not only was the slave under the absolute control of his master and denied all share in the surplus product of his labor, but the master himself, in the conditions of a monetary economy, was at the mercy of forces which he was unable to control; and so the freeman, too, was enslaved to the blind force of Necessity, which frustrated his desires and defeated his efforts. But, if Necessity is supreme, and her action incalculable, all change appears subjectively as chance; and so by the side of Ananke there arose the figure of Tyche—opposite poles of the same conception. The belief that the world is ruled by Tyche can be traced through Euripides to Pindar, who declared that she was one of the Moirai and the strongest of them all; and during the next two centuries the cult of Tyche became one of the most widespread and popular in Greece.

It was precisely at this point that Epicurus made his most important advance over the cosmology of Democritos. Parmenides, the forerunner of Plato, had taught that there was no empty space and consequently no motion; that the universe was one and unchanging, its apparent diversity and mutability being an illusion of the senses. Democritos, the forerunner of Epicurus, had reasserted the existence of empty space and attributed the properties of the Parmenidean One to each of an infinite number of atoms, indivisible, indestructible, without weight, falling vertically through the void and by their collisions and combinations creating the world. The result was a mechanistic theory of the universe in which every event is the product of necessity—the slave of Ananke.

In the view of Epicurus, this theory was inadequate, because it failed to take account of one of the faculties which differentiate man from the other animals—what we call freedom of the will. He agreed with Democritos, as against Plato, that matter, not mind, is the *prius*, but he recognized that the human consciousness was capable of reacting on its environment, and hence, by applying what it had learnt from science, of controlling it. Accordingly, endowed in his theory with the property of weight, the atom possesses in itself the cause of its own motion; and, moreover, it possesses, besides the vertical, an oblique motion or swerve from the straight line. Thus, in his system, necessity was superseded by chance, Ananke by Tyche, and in this way the atom became free.

In keeping with this rift in society and thought there was a corresponding rift in art. The old type of comedy, perfected by Aristophanes, which had been intensely political, passed into the comedy of manners, composed almost entirely by resident aliens and devoted to the intrigues of illicit lovers and foundlings, who after many vicissitudes are restored by fortune to their lost heritage. The only other art form that remained popular at Athens after the end of the Peloponnesian War was the dithyramb, which was now developed as an extravagant musical spectacle supplying an opiate to the people's unsatisfied desires. As for tragedy, which by its very nature was at the same time serious and collective, there was no scope for it in a community driven by internal dissensions to seek escape from a conflict that was to remain insoluble until the economic possibilities of slave labor had been exhausted; and, before that point was reached, it was necessary that Imperial Rome should bestride the world like a clay-footed colossus. The tragic festivals were maintained, but with a shift of interest to the stagecraft and the acting, and with an increasing dependence on revivals of the old masters, especially Euripides, whose prophetic individualism appealed far more strongly than the obsolete collectivism of Aeschylus to an audience that had lost faith in social life. As a creative force, the art of tragedy ceased to exist, until the bourgeois revolution of modern Europe brought it once more into being out of conditions similar in certain essential respects to those which had prevailed under the merchant princes of early Athens.

27. Sergei Eisenstein

A Dialectical Approach
to Film Form

SERGEI EISENSTEIN (1898–1948) was recognized by the age of 26 to be one of the greatest artists of the new medium of cinema. He began his career as a set-designer and highly innovative stage director. His film masterpieces are well-known: *Strike* (1924), *Battleship Potemkin* (1925), *October, or Ten Days That Shook the World* (1928), *The Old and the New, or the General Line* (1929), *Alexander Nevsky* (1938), with music by Sergei Prokofiev, and *Ivan the Terrible, Parts I & II* (1944–48). He taught film in state institutes in the USSR from 1928 on, and wrote numerous essays on silent and sound cinema and its relations to theater and literature. His "Dialectical Approach to Film Form" appeared in April, 1929, just before the worldwide advent of the sound film and (as Eisenstein predicted) an era of "highly cultured dramas on the screen." His major written works available in English are *Film Form* (from which the selection is taken) and *Film Sense*.

In nature we never see anything isolated, but everything in connection with something else which is before it, beside it, under it, and over it.

—GOETHE

According to Marx and Engels the dialectic system is only the conscious reproduction of the dialectic course (substance) of the external events of the world.

—RAZUMOVSKY, Theory of Historical Materialism.

Thus:

The projection of the dialectic system of things
into the brain

into creating abstractly
into the process of thinking
yields: dialectic methods of thinking;
dialectic materialism—   PHILOSOPHY.

And also:
The projection of the same system of things
while creating concretely
while giving form
yields: ART.

The foundation for this philosophy is a *dynamic* concept of things:
Being—as a constant evolution from the interaction of two contradictory opposites.
Synthesis—arising from the opposition between thesis and antithesis.
A dynamic comprehension of things is also basic to the same degree, for a correct understanding of art and of all art-forms. In the realm of art this dialectic principle of dynamics is embodied in

CONFLICT

as the fundamental principle for the existence of every art-work and every art-form.

For art is always conflict:
(1) according to its social mission,
(2) according to its nature,
(3) according to its methodology.

According to its social mission *because:* It is art's task to make manifest the contradictions of Being. To form equitable views by stirring up contradictions within the spectator's mind, and to forge accurate intellectual concepts from the dynamic clash of opposing passions.

According to its nature *because:* Its nature is a conflict between natural existence and creative tendency. Between organic inertia and purposeful initiative. Hypertrophy of the purposive initiative—the principles of rational logic—ossifies art into mathematical technicalism. (A painted landscape becomes a topographical map, a painted Saint Sebastian becomes an anatomical chart.) Hypertrophy of organic naturalness—of organic logic—dilutes art into formlessness. (A Malevich becomes a Kaulbach, an Archipenko becomes a waxworks side-show.)

Because the limit of organic form (the passive principle of being) is

Nature. The limit of rational form (the active principle of production) is *Industry*. At the intersection of Nature and Industry stands *Art*.

The logic of organic form *vs.* the logic of rational form yields, in collision,

the dialectic of the art-form.

The interaction of the two produces and determines Dynamism. (Not only in the sense of a space-time continuum, but also in the field of absolute thinking. I also regard the inception of new concepts and viewpoints in the conflict between customary conception and particular representation as dynamic—as a dynamization of the inertia of perception—as a dynamization of the "traditional view" into a new one.)

The quantity of interval determines the pressure of the tension. (See in music, for example, the concept of intervals. There can be cases where the distance of separation is so wide that it leads to a break—to a collapse of the homogeneous concept of art. For instance, the "inaudibility" of certain intervals.)

The spatial form of this dynamism is expression.
The phases of its tension: rhythm.

This is true for every art-form, and, indeed, for every kind of expression.

Similarly, human expression is a conflict between conditioned and unconditioned reflexes. (In this I cannot agree with Klages, who, *a*) does not consider human expression dynamically as a process, but statically as a result, and who, *b*) attributes everything in motion to the field of the "soul," and only the hindering element to "reason." ["Reason" and "Soul" of the idealistic concept here correspond remotely with the ideas of conditioned and unconditioned reflexes.])

This is true in every field that can be understood as an art. For example, logical thought, considered as an art, shows the same dynamic mechanism:

. . . the intellectual lives of Plato or Dante or Spinoza or Newton were largely guided and sustained by their delight in the sheer beauty of the rhythmic relation between law and instance, species and individual, or cause and effect.

This holds in other fields, as well, e.g., in speech, where all its sap, vitality, and dynamism arise from the irregularity of the part in relation to the laws of the system as a whole.

In contrast we can observe the sterility of expression in such artificial, totally regulated languages as Esperanto.

It is from this principle that the whole charm of poetry derives. Its rhythm arises as a conflict between the metric measure employed and the distribution of accents, over-riding this measure.

The concept of a formally static phenomenon as a dynamic function is dialectically imaged in the wise words of Goethe:

Die Baukunst ist eine ertarrte Musik.
(Architecture is frozen music.)

Just as in the case of a homogeneous ideology (a monistic viewpoint), the whole, as well as the least detail, must be penetrated by a sole principle. So, ranged alongside the conflict of *social conditionality*, and the conflict of *existing nature*, the *methodology* of an art reveals this same principle of conflict. As the basic principle of the rhythm to be created and the inception of the art-form.

Art is always conflict, according to its methodology.

Here we shall consider the general problem of art in the specific example of its highest form—film.

Shot and montage are the basic elements of cinema.

Montage

has been established by the Soviet film as the nerve of cinema.

To determine the nature of montage is to solve the specific problem of cinema. The earliest conscious film-makers, and our first film theoreticians, regarded montage as a means of description by placing single shots one after the other like building-blocks. The movement within these building-block shots, and the consequent length of the component pieces, was then considered as rhythm.

A completely false concept!

This would mean the defining of a given object solely in relation to the nature of its external course. The mechanical process of splicing would be made a principle. We cannot describe such a relationship of lengths as rhythm. From this comes metric rather than rhythmic relationships, as opposed to one another as the mechanical-metric system of Mensendieck is to the organic-rhythmic school of Bode in matters of body exercise.

According to this definition, shared even by Pudovkin as a theoretician, montage is the means of *unrolling* an idea with the help of single shots: the "epic" principle.

In my opinion, however, montage is an idea that arises from the collision of independent shots—shots even opposite to one another: the "dramatic" principle.*

* "Epic" and "dramatic" are used here in regard to methodology of form—not to *content* or *plot!*

A sophism? Certainly not. For we are seeking a definition of the whole nature, the principal style and spirit of cinema from its technical (optical) basis.

We know that the phenomenon of movement in film resides in the fact that two motionless images of a moving body, following one another, blend into an appearance of motion by showing them sequentially at a required speed.

This popularized description of what happens as a *blending* has its share of responsibility for the popular miscomprehension of the nature of montage that we have quoted above.

Let us examine more exactly the course of the phenomenon we are discussing—how it really occurs—and draw our conclusion from this. Placed next to each other, two photographed immobile images result in the appearance of movement. Is this accurate? Pictorially—and phraseologically, yes.

But mechanically, it is not. For, in fact, each sequential element is perceived not *next* to the other, but on *top* of the other. For the idea (or sensation) of movement arises from the process of superimposing on the retained impression of the object's first position, a newly visible further position of the object. This is, by the way, the reason for the phenomenon of spatial depth, in the optical superimposition of two planes in stereoscopy. From the superimposition of two elements of the same dimension always arises a new, higher dimension. In the case of stereoscopy the superimposition of two nonidentical two-dimensionalities results in stereoscopic three-dimensionality.

In another field: a concrete word (a denotation) set beside a concrete word yields an abstract concept—as in the Chinese and Japanese languages, where a material ideogram can indicate a transcendental (conceptual) result.

The incongruence in contour of the first picture—already impressed on the mind—with the subsequently perceived second picture engenders, in conflict, the feeling of motion. Degree of incongruence determines intensity of impression, and determines that tension which becomes the real element of authentic rhythm.

Here we have, temporally what we see arising spatially on a graphic or painted plane.

What comprises the dynamic effect of a painting? The eye follows the direction of an element in the painting. It retains a visual impression, which then collides with the impression derived from following the direction of a second element. The conflict of these directions forms the dynamic effect in apprehending the whole.

I. It may be purely linear: Fernand Léger, or Suprematism.

II. It may be "anecdotal." The secret of the marvelous mobility of

Daumier's and Lautrec's figures dwells in the fact that the various anatomical parts of a body are represented in spatial circumstances (positions) that are temporally various, disjunctive. For example, in Toulouse-
Lautrec's lithograph of Miss Cissy Loftus, if one logically develops
position A of the foot, one builds a body in position A corresponding to it.
But the body is represented from knee up already in position A + a. The
cinematic effect of joined motionless pictures is already established here!
From hips to shoulders we can see A + a + a. The figure comes alive and
kicking!

III. Between I and II lies primitive Italian futurism—such as in Balla's
"Man with Six Legs in Six Positions"—for II obtains its effect by retaining
natural unity and anatomical correctness, while I, on the other hand,
does this with purely elementary elements. III, although destroying
naturalness, has not yet pressed forward to abstraction.

IV. The conflict of directions may also be of an ideographic kind. It
was in this way that we have gained the pregnant characterizations of a
Sharaku, for example. The secret of his extremely perfected strength of
expression lies in the anatomical and *spatial disproportion* of the parts—
in comparison with which, our (I) might be termed *temporal disproportion*.

Generally termed "irregularity," this *spatial disproportion* has been a
constant attraction and instrument for artists. In writing of Rodin's drawings, Camille Mauclair indicated one explanation for this search:

The greatest artists, Michelangelo, Rembrandt, Delacroix, all, at a certain
moment of the upthrusting of their genius, threw aside, as it were, the ballast of
exactitude as conceived by our simplifying reason and our ordinary eyes, in
order to attain the fixation of ideas, the synthesis, the *pictorial handwriting* of
their dreams.

Two experimental artists of the nineteenth century—a painter and a poet
—attempted aesthetic formulations of this "irregularity." Renoir advanced
this thesis:

Beauty of every description finds its charm in variety. Nature abhors both
vacuum and regularity. For the same reason, no work of art can really be
called such if it has not been created by an artist who believes in irregularity
and rejects any set form. Regularity, order, desire for perfection (which is
always a false perfection) destroy art. The only possibility of maintaining taste
in art is to impress on artists and the public the importance of irregularity.
Irregularity is the basis of all art.

And Baudelaire wrote in his journal:

That which is not slightly distorted lacks sensible appeal; from which it follows that irregularity—that is to say, the unexpected-surprise and astonishment, are an essential part and characteristic of beauty.

Upon closer examination of the particular beauty of irregularity as employed in painting, whether by Grünewald or by Renoir, it will be seen that it is a disproportion in the relation of a detail in one dimension to another detail in a different dimension.

The spatial development of the relative size of one detail in correspondence with another, and the consequent collision between the proportions designed by the artist for that purpose, result in a characterization —a definition of the represented matter.

Finally, color. Any shade of a color imparts to our vision a given rhythm of vibration. This is not said figuratively, but purely physiologically, for colors are distinguished from one another by their number of light vibrations.

The adjacent shade or tone of color is in another rate of vibration. The counterpoint (conflict) of the two—the retained rate of vibration against the newly perceived one—yields the dynamism of our apprehension of the interplay of color.

Hence, with only one step from visual vibrations to acoustic vibrations, we find ourselves in the field of music. From the domain of the spatial-pictorial—to the domain of the temporal-pictorial—where the same law rules. For counterpoint is to music not only a form of composition, but is altogether the basic factor for the possibility of tone perception and tone differentiation.

It may almost be said that in every case we have cited we have seen in operation the same *Principle of Comparison* that makes possible for us perception and definition in every field.

In the moving image (cinema) we have, so to speak, a synthesis of two counterpoints—the spatial counterpoint of graphic art, and the temporal counterpoint of music.

Within cinema, and characterizing it, occurs what may be described as:

visual counterpoint.

In applying this concept to the film, we gain several leads to the problem of film grammar. As well as a *syntax* of film manifestations, in which visual counterpoint may determine a whole new system of forms of manifestation.

For all this, the *basic premise* is:

The shot is by no means an element of montage.
The shot is a montage cell (or molecule).

In this formulation the dualistic division of

Sub-title and shot
and
Shot and montage

leaps forward in analysis to a dialectic consideration as three different phases of one homogeneous task of expression, its homogeneous characteristics determining the homogeneity of their structural laws.

Interrelation of the three phases:

Conflict within a thesis (an abstract idea)—*formulates* itself in the dialectics of the sub-title—*forms* itself spatially in the conflict within the shot—and *explodes* with increasing intensity in montage-conflict among the separate shots.

This is fully analogous to human, psychological expression. This is a conflict of motives, which can also be comprehended in three phases:

1. Purely verbal utterance. Without intonation—expression in speech.

2. Gesticulatory (mimic-intonational) expression. Projection of the conflict onto the whole expressive bodily system of man. Gesture of bodily movement and gesture of intonation.

3. Projection of the conflict into space. With an intensification of motives, the zigzag of mimic expression is propelled into the surrounding space following the same formula of distortion. A zigzag of expression arising from the spatial division caused by man moving in space. *Mise-en-scène.*

This gives us the basis for an entirely new understanding of the problem of film form.

We can list, as examples of types of conflicts within the form—characteristic for the conflict within the shot, as well as for the conflict between colliding shots, or, montage:

1. Graphic conflict
2. Conflict of planes
3. Conflict of volumes
4. Spatial conflict
5. Light conflict
6. Tempo conflict, and so on.

Nota bene: This list is of principal features, of *dominants.* It is naturally understood that they occur chiefly as complexes.

For a transition to montage, it will be sufficient to divide any example into two independent primary pieces, as in the case of graphic conflict, although all other cases can be similarly divided:

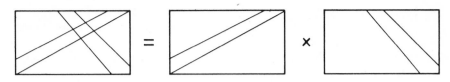

Some further examples:

7. Conflict between matter and viewpoint (achieved by spatial distortion through camera-angle)
8. Conflict between matter and its spatial nature (achieved by *optical distortion* by the lens)
9. Conflict between an event and its temporal nature (achieved by *slow-motion* and *stop-motion*)

and finally

10. Conflict between the whole *optical* complex and a quite different sphere.

Thus does conflict between optical and acoustical experience produce:

sound-film,

which is capable of being realized as

audio-visual counterpoint.

Formulation and investigation of the phenomenon of cinema as forms of conflict yield the first possibility of devising a homogeneous system of *visual dramaturgy* for all general and particular cases of the film problem.

Of devising a *dramaturgy of the visual film-form* as regulated and precise as the existing *dramaturgy of the film-story.*

From this viewpoint on the film medium, the following forms and potentialities of style may be summed up as a film syntax, or it may be more exact to describe the following as:

a tentative film-syntax.

We shall list here a number of potentialities of dialectical development to be derived from this proposition: The concept of the moving (time-consuming) image arises from the superimposition—or counterpoint—of two differing immobile images.

I. Each *moving fragment of montage.* Each photographed piece. Technical definition of the phenomenon of movement. *No composition as yet.* (A running man. A rifle fired. A splash of water.)

II. An *artificially produced image of motion.* The basic optical element is used for deliberate compositions:

A. *Logical*

Example 1 (from *October*): a montage rendition of a machine-gun being fired, by cross-cutting details of the firing.

Combination A: a brightly lit machine-gun. A different shot in a low key.
    Double burst: graphic burst + light burst. Close-up of machine-gunner.
Combination B: Effect almost of double exposure achieved by *clatter* montage
    effect. Length of montage pieces—two frames each.

Example 2 (from *Potemkin*): an illustration of instantaneous action. Woman with pince-nez. Followed immediately—without transition—by the same woman with shattered pince-nez and bleeding eye: impression of a shot hitting the eye.

B. *Illogical*

Example 3 (from *Potemkin*): the same device used for pictorial symbolism. In the thunder of the *Potemkin's* guns, a marble lion leaps up, in protest against the bloodshed on the Odessa steps. Composed of three shots of three stationary marble lions at the Alupka Palace in the Crimea: a sleeping lion, an awakening lion, a rising lion. The effect is achieved by a correct calculation of the length of the second shot. Its superimposition on the first shot produces the first action. This establishes time to impress the second position on the mind. Superimposition of the third position on the second produces the second action: the lion finally rises.

Example 4 (from *October*): Example 1 showed how the firing was manufactured symbolically from elements outside the process of firing itself. In illustrating the monarchist *putsch* attempted by General Kornilov, it occurred to me that his militarist *tendency* could be shown in a montage that would employ religious details for its material. For Kornilov had revealed his intention in the guise of a peculiar "Crusade" of Moslems (!), his Caucasian "Wild Division," together with some Christians, against the Bolsheviki. So we intercut shots of a Baroque Christ (apparently exploding in the radiant beams of his halo) with shots of an egg-shaped mask of Uzume, Goddess of Mirth, completely self-contained. The temporal conflict between the closed egg-form and the graphic star-form produced the effect of an instantaneous *burst*—of a bomb, or shrapnel. Thus far the examples have shown *primitive-physiological* cases—employing superimposition of optical motion *exclusively*.

III. *Emotional* combinations, not only with the visible elements of the shots, but chiefly with chains of psychological associations. *Association montage.* As a means for pointing up a situation emotionally.

In Example 1, we had two successive shots A and B, identical in subject. However, they were not identical in respect to the position of the subject within the frame:

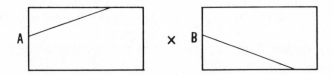

producing *dynamization in space*—an impression of spatial dynamics:

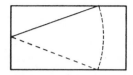

The degree of difference between the positions A and B determines the tension of the movement.

For a new case, let us suppose that the subjects of Shots A and B are not *identical*. Although the associations of the two shots are identical, that is, associatively identical.

This *dynamization of the subject*, not in the field of space but of psychology, i.e., *emotion*, thus produces:

emotional dynamization.

Example 1 (in *Strike*): the montage of the killing of the workers is actually a cross montage of this carnage with the butchering of a bull in an abattoir. Though the subjects are different, "butchering" is the associative link. This made for a powerful emotional intensification of the scene. As a matter of fact, homogeneity of gesture plays an important part in this case in achieving the effect—both the movement of the dynamic gesture within the frame, and the static gesture dividing the frame graphically.

This is a principle subsequently used by Pudovkin in *The End of St. Petersburg*, in his powerful sequence intercutting shots of stock exchange and battlefield. His previous film, *Mother*, had a similar sequence: the ice-break on the river, paralleled with the workers' demonstration.

Such a means may decay pathologically if the essential viewpoint—emotional dynamization of the subject—is lost. As soon as the film-maker loses sight of this essence the means ossifies into lifeless literary symbolism and stylistic mannerism. Two examples of such hollow use of this means occur to me:

Example 2 (in *October*): the sugary chants of compromise by the Mensheviki at the Second Congress of Soviets—during the storming of the Winter Palace—are intercut with hands playing harps. This was a purely literary parallelism that by no means dynamized the subject matter. Similarly in Otzep's *Living Corpse*, church spires (in imitation of those in *October*) and lyrical landscapes are intercut with the courtroom speeches of the prosecutor and defense lawyer. This error was the same as in the "harp" sequence.

On the other hand, a majority of *purely dynamic* effects can produce positive results:

Example 3 (in *October*): the dramatic moment of the union of the Motorcycle Battalion with the Congress of Soviets was dynamized by shots of abstractly spinning bicycle wheels, in association with the entrance of the new delegates. In this way the large-scale emotional content of the event was transformed into actual dynamics.

This same principle—giving birth to concepts, to emotions, by juxtaposing two disparate events—led to:

IV. *Liberation of the whole action from the definition of time and space.* My first attempts at this were in *October*.

Example 1: a trench crowded with soldiers appears to be crushed by an enormous gun-base that comes down inexorably. As an anti-militarist symbol seen from the viewpoint of subject alone, the effect is achieved by an apparent bringing together of an independently existing trench and an overwhelming military product, just as physically independent.

Example 2: in the scene of Kornilov's *putsch,* which puts an end to Kerensky's Bonapartist dreams. Here one of Kornilov's tanks climbs up and crushes a plaster-of-Paris Napoleon standing on Kerensky's desk in the Winter Palace, a juxtaposition of purely symbolic significance.

This method has now been used by Dovzhenko in *Arsenal* to shape whole sequences, as well as by Esther Schub in her use of library footage in *The Russia of Nikolai II and Lev Tolstoy.*

I wish to offer another example of this method, to upset the traditional ways of handling plot—although it has not yet been put into practice.

In 1924–1925 I was mulling over the idea of a filmic portrait of *actual* man. At that time, there prevailed a tendency to show actual man in films only in *long* uncut dramatic scenes. It was believed that cutting (montage) would destroy the idea of actual man. Abram Room established something of a record in this respect when he used in *The Death Ship* uncut dramatic shots as long as 40 meters or 135 feet. I considered (and still do) such a concept to be utterly unfilmic.

Very well—what would be a linguistically accurate characterization of man?

His raven-black hair . . .
The waves of his hair . . .
His eyes radiating azure beams . . .
His steely muscles . . .

Even in a less exaggerated description, any verbal account of a person is bound to find itself employing an assortment of waterfalls, lightning-rods, landscapes, birds, etc.

Now why should the cinema follow the forms of theater and painting rather than methodology of language, which allows wholly new concepts of ideas to arise from the combination of two concrete denotations to two concrete objects? Language is much closer to film than painting is. For example, in painting the form arises from *abstract* elements of line and color, while in cinema the material *concreteness* of the image within the frame presents—as an element—the greatest difficulty in manipulation. So why not rather lean towards the system of language, which is forced to use the same mechanics in inventing words and word-complexes?

On the other hand, why is it that montage cannot be dispensed with in orthodox films?

The differentiation in montage-pieces lies in their lack of existence as single units. Each piece can evoke no more than a certain association. The accumulation of such associations can achieve the same effect as is provided for the spectator by purely physiological means in the plot of a realistically produced play.

For instance, murder on the stage has a purely physiological effect. Photographed in *one* montage-piece, it can function simply as *information,* as a sub-title. *Emotional* effect begins only with the reconstruction of the event in montage fragments, each of which will summon a certain association—the sum of which will be an all-embracing complex of emotional feeling. Traditionally:

1. A hand lifts a knife.
2. The eyes of the victim open suddenly.
3. His hands clutch the table.
4. The knife is jerked up.
5. The eyes blink involuntarily.
6. Blood gushes.
7. A mouth shrieks.
8. Something drips onto a shoe . . .

and similar film clichés. Nevertheless, in regard to the *action as a whole,* each *fragment-piece* is almost *abstract.* The more differentiated they are the more abstract they become, provoking no more than a certain association.

Quite logically the thought occurs: could not the same thing be accomplished more productively by not following the plot so slavishly, but by materializing the idea, the impression, of *Murder* through a free accumulation of associative matter? For the most important task is still to establish the idea of murder—the feeling of murder, as such. The plot is no more than a device without which one isn't yet capable of telling something to the spectator! In any case, effort in this direction would certainly produce the most interesting variety of forms.

Someone should try, at least! Since this thought occurred to me, I have not had time to make this experiment. And today I am more concerned with quite different problems. But, returning to the main line of our syntax, something there may bring us closer to these tasks.

While, with I, II, and III, tension was calculated for purely physiological effect—from the purely optical to the emotional, we must mention here also the case of the same conflict-tension serving the ends of new concepts—of new attitudes, that is, of purely intellectual aims.

Example 1 (in *October*): Kerensky's rise to power and dictatorship after the July uprising of 1917. A comic effect was gained by sub-titles indicating regular ascending ranks (*"Dictator"—"Generalissimo"—"Minister of Navy—and of Army"*—etc.) climbing higher and higher—cut into five or six shots of Kerensky, climbing the stairs of the Winter Palace, all with exactly the *same* pace. Here a conflict between the flummery of the ascending ranks and the "hero's" trotting up the same unchanging flight of stairs yields an intellectual result: Kerensky's essential nonentity is shown satirically. We have the counterpoint of a literally expressed conventional idea with the *pictured* action of a particular person who is unequal to his swiftly increasing duties. The incongruence of these two factors results in the spectator's purely *intellectual* decision at the expense of this particular person. Intellectual dynamization.

Example 2 (in *October*): Kornilov's march on Petrograd was under the banner of "In the Name of God and Country." Here we attempted to reveal the religious significance of this episode in a rationalistic way. A number of religious images, from a magnificent Baroque Christ to an Eskimo idol, were cut together. The conflict in this case was between the concept and the symbolization of God. While idea and image appear to accord completely in the first statue shown, the two elements move further from each other with each successive image. Maintaining the denotation of "God," the images increasingly disagree with our concept of God, inevitably leading to individual conclusions about the true nature of all deities. In this case, too, a chain of images attempted to achieve a purely intellectual resolution, resulting from a conflict between a preconception and a *gradual discrediting of it in purposeful steps*.

Step by step, by a process of comparing each new image with the common denotation, power is accumulated behind a process that can be formally identified with that of logical deduction. The decision to release these ideas, as well as the method used, is already *intellectually* conceived.

The conventional *descriptive* form for film leads to the formal possibility of a kind of filmic reasoning. While the conventional film directs the *emotions*, this suggests an opportunity to encourage and direct the whole *thought process*, as well.

These two particular sequences of experiment were very much opposed by the majority of critics. Because they were understood as purely political. I would not attempt to deny that *this form is most suitable for the expression of ideologically pointed theses,* but it is a pity that the critics completely overlooked the purely filmic potentialities of this approach.

In these two experiments we have taken the first embryonic step towards a totally new form of film expression. Towards a purely intellectual film, freed from traditional limitations, achieving direct forms for ideas, systems, and concepts, without any need for transitions and paraphrases. We may yet have a

synthesis of art and science.

This would be the proper name for our new epoch in the field of art. This would be the final justification for Lenin's words, that "the cinema is the most important of all the arts."

28. Gyorgy Lukács

The Historical Novel
of Democratic Humanism

For a biographical note on GYORGY LUKÁCS, see p. 228. The following selection is from *The Historical Novel*, first published in 1938.

WE see that all problems of form and content alike in the historical novel of our day center upon questions of heritage. All aesthetic problems and valuations in this sphere are determined by the struggle to liquidate the political, ideological and artistic heritage of the period of declining capitalism, by the struggle to renew and fruitfully extend the traditions of the great progressive periods of mankind, the spirit of revolutionary democracy, the artistic grandeur and popular strength of the classical historical novel.

This statement of the problem—both here and, we hope, in our previous analyses—will suffice to show how more than purely artistic these questions are. Artistic form, as the concentrated and heightened reflection of the important features of objective reality, both regulative and individual, can never be treated purely as such, in isolation. Precisely the development of the historical novel shows most clearly how what appear to be purely formal, compositional problems—e.g., whether the great figures of history should be principal heroes or minor figures—so obviously conceal ideological and political problems of the highest importance. Indeed, the whole question of whether the historical novel is a genre in its own right, with its own artistic laws or whether it obeys essentially the same laws as the novel in general can only be solved on the basis of a general approach to the decisive ideological and political problems.

We have seen that the answer to all these questions depends upon the writer's attitude to *popular life*. The resumption of the traditions of the classical historical novel is not an aesthetic quesion in a narrow, professional sense. It does not matter whether Sir Walter Scott or Manzoni was aesthetically superior to, say, Heinrich Mann, or at least this is not the main point. What is important is that Scott and Manzoni, Pushkin and Tolstoy, were able to grasp and portray popular life in a more profound, authentic, human and concretely historical fashion than even the most outstanding writers of our day; that the classical form of the historical novel was a form in which authors could express their feelings adequately; and that the classical manner of story and composition was specially designed to bring out the essentials, the richness and variety of popular life as the basis for changes in history. Whereas in the historical novel even of important writers of the present we are confronted every moment with a conflict between the ideological content, the human attitude that is intended and the literary means that are used.

If then, to judge the outstanding works of contemporary writers, we take our aesthetic measure from a study and analysis of the classics of the historical novel and the laws of epic and drama in general, we are justified in two respects. First of all, the fact that a given literary trend arises as a result of social and economic necessity and the class struggles of its time is still no gauge for aesthetic judgment. To be sure, reactionary-relativist historicism and equally relativist vulgar sociology preach the contrary. Since Ranke all mechanistic vulgarizers say that each product of historical development is "equally near to God" or, in vulgar sociological phraseology, a "class equivalent." This sounds—according to how one likes it—either extraordinarily "deep" in the sense of a mystically irrational conception of history or extraordinarily "scientific" in the sense of a vulgar-bourgeois, liberal-Menshevik theory of progress.

But both conceptions sever the real connection between art and reality. Art appears simultaneously as a fatalistic and purely subjective mode of expression of an individual. Thus it is not a reflection of objective reality. Yet the criteria of a genuine aesthetic derive precisely from this base characteristic of art. Because the historical novel reflects and portrays the development of historical reality the measure for its content and form is to be found in this reality itself. But what is this reality? It is the uneven and crisis-filled development of popular life. Writers like Flaubert and Conrad Ferdinand Meyer create a "new" form of the historical novel for profound and necessary reasons: the development of society produces an ideological decline in their class, they are no longer in a position to see the real problems of popular life in their extended richness, their picture of history is socially and historically impoverished, inadequate, accordingly they fashion it into a "new" form. However, it is the duty of Marxist aesthetics not only to *explain* this impoverishment and inadequacy in a social-genetic way, but also to *measure* them aesthetically against the highest demands of the artistic reflection of historical reality and to find them lacking.

Criticism must be allowed the right to judge and condemn the artistic products of entire periods, while acknowledging their social-historical necessity—indeed, the whole aesthetic judgment rests upon this acknowledgment. But this proclamation of the right of criticism by no means disposes of the problem of the historical novel in our day. For we have repeatedly established the deep ideological *contrast* which separates the literary activity of the important representatives of the historical novel in our own time from that of bourgeois decadence. Thus the problem of assessing the present historical novel is a much more complex one. Our classical yardstick is by no means as opposed and alien to the latter as it is to the products of the beginning decline of bourgeois literature and especially to those of fully-fledged decadence. There are also deep and important similarities between the classical period of the historical novel and the historical novel of our time. Both aim at presenting the movement of popular life in history, in its objective reality and simultaneously in its living relation to the present. This living political and ideological relation to the present is a further important element of outlook which inwardly connects the present-day writing of our humanists with the classical period.

But the unevenness of historical development makes this relation an extremely complicated one. This applies to both important questions, both to the question of popular roots and to that of the connection with the present. It is interesting and characteristic that in a political and ideological respect the views of many humanists of the present are much more radical than those of the classics. One need only think of the contrast between the moderate Tory, Sir Walter Scott, and the revolutionary democrat, Heinrich Mann. But the unevenness of development comes out in the fact that Scott was much more livingly bound up with, much more intimate with, the life of the people than the outstanding writer of the imperialist period, who has had to struggle both against the isolation from popular life imposed upon the writer by the social division of labor of advanced capitalism and the growth of an ever more reactionary liberal ideology under imperialism.

This link with popular life was still a natural, socially given state of affairs for the writers of the classical period of the historical novel. In the period in which they lived the forces of the social division of labor had only just begun to exert a decisive influence upon literature and art in the direction of the writer's isolation from popular life. In many reactionary Romantics of the time this influence is already clearly tangible; however it does not become the dominant basis of literature as a whole until much later.

The humanists of our time start in their writing from a *protest against the dehumanizing influences of capitalism.* An extremely important part is played in this protest by the writer's tragic estrangement from popular life, his isolation, his complete dependence upon himself. However, it is also part of the situation that this protest can advance only gradually, unevenly and contradictorily from *abstractness* to *concreteness*. And this is not only because generally one's links and familiarity with popular life can only be made concrete in a gradual, step-by-step way, but partly because of the inner dialectic of the writer's struggle against the socially isolated position of literature under imperialism.

This dialectic determines the slowness and unevenness of the way in which the writer settles his accounts with the liberal ideology of imperialism. The genuine writers of this period begin with an ardent wish to conquer the isolation of literature and the aestheticism, the artistic self-satisfaction and self-sufficiency which flow from it; and in their desire to make literature an effective force in the society of their time—which they take as given—they naturally look around for allies. The result has been that they have clung passionately to any social current or human manifestation which seemed to offer the slightest hope of being moved to protest against the inhumanity of the social present.

Thus the reawakening of the revolutionary-democratic spirit in German literature has been extremely difficult. The most varied obstacles have been placed in the path of its development by liberal compromise on the one hand and abstract negation of a bohemian-anarchist kind on the other. Hence if, in analyzing the development of the most important anti-Fascist writers, we come across all manner of attempts to ally themselves with currents of this kind—because of insufficient critical judgment or even uncritical over-estimation—we must understand this as part of the general line of development of Germany (and in many respects, though not so markedly, of the rest of Western Europe). The fall of the Hohenzollern régime and the Weimar Republic was able to produce a certain advance in this respect, but no radical change. This took place only with the victory of Fascist barbarism in Germany itself and the experiences and victories of the popular front in France and Spain.

It would be a mistake, however, to see nothing but weaknesses in the earlier literature which everywhere reveals traces of this slow emergence of the revolutionary-democratic spirit. It is not possible here to analyze German literature of the pre-Fascist period in all its detail, particularly since its essential achievements lie outside the scope of this study. But in order to illustrate this general position of protesting humanist literature let us quote one example: that of Thomas Mann. In his youthful work this great writer makes a harsh and deep self-criticism by contrasting the world of the isolated writer with that of the sound, straightforward citizen. Now it would be quite superficial and erroneous to see this as something negative. Thomas Mann discloses deep contradictions in bourgeois life, in its lack of culture, with a dialectic of extreme subtlety and complexity, and there is no doubt that he combats the dominant human type produced by German capitalism. But the more deeply he sees into the problems of isolated literature, the more firmly he repudiates the writer's withdrawal into an "ivory tower" and abstract negation of the present as a whole, the more he is compelled to look around everywhere in reality for positive (at least, relatively) human types. His honesty as a writer also comes out in the fact that while he may present a type positively in one context he will criticize him ironically in another, and in this way add strong reservations to his affirmation; thus his writing never sinks into apologia or glorification of the present.

In all this one has to recognize a double tendency. On the one hand Thomas Mann, like every important writer, endeavors to portray an all-around and comprehensive picture of the society of his time. The universality of this picture depends upon the variety of the characters and whether, even when they are felt to be bearers of hostile principles, they are portrayed as living, many-sided human beings and not as poster-like caricatures. In this respect both Thomas Mann as well as a few of his important contemporaries went far beyond the horizon set by the prejudices of the liberal bourgeoisie. On the other hand, the manner in which these types are humanly and artistically understood reflects the slow and contradictory form in which this separation from the bourgeois-reactionary prejudices of the Wilhelmine period takes place. We stress once again: it is not the fact that hostile types are humanly portrayed that points to this slow and hesitant overcoming of prejudices, but the uncritical attitude to these types in their social and human totality, the failure to recognize their social and human limits. It will suffice if we mention here Thomas Mann's presentation of Frederick the Great's Prussia and its traditions in the First World War.

But we find similar forms of conception and portrayal—admittedly, of a less pronounced kind—even in the earlier period of Heinrich Mann with regard to representatives of the liberal bourgeoisie; and in Arnold Zweig with regard to decent, venerable types of the German military. This sort of artistic conception of reality naturally has its political and ideological roots. Here again a few examples will suffice; it suffices if one mentions the false estimate of Bismarck or Nietzsche. These cases show how certain prejudices of the past period or, at least, their survivals are still alive today.

This slow and contradictory process of overcoming liberal ideology and its estrangement from the people is reflected, too, in the historical novels of the anti-Fascist humanists.

We showed earlier how one of the most important weaknesses of these novels was their portrayal of the problems of popular life from "above"; the people themselves played a part only when they came into direct contact with whatever was going on "above." This gives us a clear picture of the liberal-bourgeois traditions still to be overcome. Thus the return to the traditions of the classical type of historical novel is not primarily an aesthetic-artistic question. It is a consequence rather of the decisive and complete victory of the spirit of revolutionary democracy, of the concrete and close involvement of the important humanists with the destiny of the people. (Our earlier analyses have, we hope, shown the reader sufficiently clearly that the new plebeian tradition in the Latin countries, whose phases are marked by the names of Erckmann-Chatrian, de Coster and Romain Rolland, suffer from a lack of historical concreteness in quite the contrary way. Thus the ideological-artistic problem of reawakening the spirit of the classical historical novel holds good for this tradition, too and is likewise connected with the political and social concretization of revolutionary democracy; except that the literary conclusions to be drawn in this case are of a different, often quite contrary, character.)

The question of the relation of past to present is very closely connected with this problem. Again we must stress sharply the contrast between the present-day historical novel and its immediate predecessors. The historical novel of the humanists of our day is closely linked with the great and urgent problems of the present. It is on the way to portraying the *pre-history of the present*—very much in contrast, say, to Flaubert's type of historical novel. Its topicality—in a large historical sense—is one of the great advances achieved by the anti-Fascist humanists; it marks the beginning of a *change* in the history of the historical novel.

Yet only the *beginning* of a change. For the change itself leads back to the traditions of the classical historical novel. The difference which still exists between the two today has been stressed by us at different points. To recapitulate briefly: the humanist historical novel of today gives only an *abstract prehistory of ideas* and not the concrete prehistory of the destiny of the people themselves, which is what the historical novel in its classical period portrayed.

As a result of this general and conceptual rather than concrete and historical relationship between past and present the distortion of historical figures or movements is at times inevitable; there is thus a falling-away from that superb faithfulness to historical reality which was the strength of the classical historical novel. But beyond that, this all-too-conceptual and therefore all-too-direct relationship with the present has an abstracting effect upon the totality of the world presented. If the historical novel is the concrete prehistory of the present, as it was with the classics, then artistically the popular destiny represented in it should be an end-in-itself. The living relationship to the present should be expressed by the movement of history itself. The relationship is then objective in an artistic sense; it never breaks the limits set by the human-historical frame of the world represented. (That this depends also upon a "necessary anachronism" we have already fully explained.) The direct and conceptual relationship with the present which prevails today reveals an immanent tendency to turn the past into a *parable of the present*, to wrest directly from history a "fabula docet," and this conflicts with the real historical concreteness of the content and the real (not formal) self-containment of the form.

It may sound paradoxical, but is nevertheless true that this direct relationship with the present has an abstracting and hence weakening effect upon the very problems of the present placed in the foreground. This can be seen most clearly of all in Feuchtwanger's novel *The False Nero*. No other artistic work of our time burns with such hatred of Fascism. The satirical pathos of this hatred takes Feuchtwanger a great step forward along the revolutionary-democratic path. But this is not the only merit of the work. Feuchtwanger portrays popular movements here much more concretely than in his Josephus Flavius novels, more so even than in the second part of the cycle. True, these popular movements are also seen and presented from the standpoint of the wirepullers in the background and the leaders in the foreground, yet they have gained a much higher degree of concreteness and differentiation than in his earlier works. Nevertheless, despite its greater liveliness and concreteness this interesting work is but an extensive parable: we see how a pathetic buffoon, incited by the intrigues of big capitalists, assumes the leadership of a popular movement, exercises dictatorial power for a long time and then collapses once the people have come to their senses. No other satire written against Hitler and his gentlemanly and mob accomplices has such deadly accuracy. It is so sharp and convincing, its meaning so immediately clear that *The False Nero* deserves an important place in the anti-Fascist struggle.

But what is missing in this interesting and powerful work? We believe —a sufficiently deep and concrete relationship with the present. It expresses only the immediate emotions aroused by Fascism. For the real and deeper question which stirs all true democrats is this: How could these bands of murderers come to rule in a country like Germany? How was it that thousands and thousands of convinced people could fight fanatically on behalf of these mercenary, murderous hirelings of capitalism? What Feuchtwanger's satirical novel does not do is to unravel the mystery of this mass movement, the mystery of this German disgrace. It simply accepts as a fact that the people may become temporary victims of the crudest demagogy.

But how this crude demagogy was able to exert such an influence upon millions of people is not even asked, let alone answered. And this question is not an academic historical one, but a practical issue of the highest order:

the question of the concrete perspective of the collapse of the Fascist rule of murder. This is indeed shown by Feuchtwanger's novel itself. By not portraying the concrete, social-historical origins of the rule of his false Nero, he is not in a position to portray its concrete, social-historical collapse. A "miracle" occurs: a satirical song travels from mouth to mouth, unmasking the inner hollowness of the usurper and his band, the people come to their senses and the barbaric dictatorship collapses. This perspective of the future no longer expresses the feelings of the progressive anti-Fascist fighters, but—very much contrary to Feuchtwanger's intention —the feelings of those who see in Fascism not so much a concrete political-social movement of the imperialist age as a "social illness," a kind of "mass lunacy" and who hence passively wait for the people to "recover," to "come to their senses"—in a word, for the automatic collapse of the Hitler régime, for a miracle.

We see that there is no substitute for a concrete relationship to the present or, what comes to the same thing, a concrete familiarity with popular life. This is true, however high the intellectual level or brilliant the artistic expression of an abstract relationship to the present. This problem must be emphasized again and again because the way in which it is solved determines the artistic fate of the historical novel in every period. The transformation of the historical novel into an independent genre which plays a considerable part in Feuchtwanger's work—particularly in his theoretical pronouncements—is still a symptom today of the weakness of these relationships. The cause of this weakness is quite different today from when the decline of bourgeois realism began, but the result in both cases is the same: modernization and abstractness in the portrayal of historical characters.

This can be confirmed by positive examples. In the first place, we see that given a deeper and more complex, less direct, abstract and allegorical relationship to at least certain aspects of popular life in the present, a writer may produce more significant and convincing historical portrayals. It is interesting, and characteristic of the new position of the historical novel, that this should come out most clearly in its *positive* characters. The sheer fact that positive characters can be created at all is extraordinarily important. Since Balzac's Michel Chrestien and Stendhal's Palla Ferrante the modern bourgeois novel has been unable to create a positive character who takes an active part in public life. But even Balzac and Stendhal, as clear-sighted and consistent realists, were forced to make their democratic and popular heroes episodic figures.

The anti-Fascist popular front and the spirit of revolutionary democracy which it has revived have once again made it possible to embody a people's yearning for liberation in positive characters. This is the extraordinary historical, political as well as artistic significance of figures like

Heinrich Mann's Henri IV. These positive portrayals are politically deepened polemics against the mendacious demogogic leader-cult of the Fascists; and the breadth and accuracy of their polemical impact depends upon their artistic stature. These characters must visibly embody the deep longing of the broadest popular masses for a solution to the most terrible crisis ever experienced by the German people during the course of their long and arduous history. The less direct the portrayal, the deeper are its roots in these popular sentiments. In this way it brings to light and gives voice to the most varied and obscure popular strivings; in this way it not only expresses what today may be seen upon the surface of life and is consciously known, but can delve into the real origins both of the oppression and degeneration and of the path to liberation. It creates *models* which *accelerate* the consciousness and resoluteness of the longing for liberation.

Bruno Frank's *Cervantes* constitutes a serious coming-to-terms with the divorce of German writing from popular life. Hitherto this kind of self-criticism in literature had been predominantly elegiac and satirical (at its profoundest and most moving in Thomas Mann's *Tonio Kröger*); here a positive example is portrayed. Frank succeeds at many points in portraying the human side of a great writer who was primarily a fighter and for whom literature—literature at its highest cultural and artistic level—was an organic, all-crowning part, yet only a part of his social activity; and by so doing Frank shows a way out of this estrangement not only for writers, but also for the masses who had been painfully deprived of such a literature and such writers, even if for them this has been an unconscious deprivation and they only now realize what they have been missing.

This connection between political-polemical effectiveness and artistic quality is still more striking in Heinrich Mann's Henri IV. Here for the first time after a long period we have before us a figure who is at once popular and significant, wise and resolute, sly yet brave and undaunted. And Heinrich Mann, as we have seen, stresses the fact that Henri IV has drawn his strength and adroitness from his links with popular life, that he has become the leader of the people because of his sensitivity to the real desires of the popular masses and his ability to fulfill them courageously and wisely. The artistic subtlety of this portrayal strikes the Hitler cult far more mortal a blow than the majority of direct attacks. For Mann discloses the connection between people and leader; he answers in an indirect polemic the question which concerns the masses: what is the social content, the human essence of leadership? If one compares Mann's indirect polemic with his direct satire on Hitler in the figure of the Duke de Guise, one sees how much more politically effective is the superior artistic portrayal.

These remarks must not of course be misinterpreted: we are not depreciating negative and satirical portrayals of the enemy. We are simply criticizing the limitations of a too direct, unhistorical approach to these questions. Precisely the lessons of classical literature show how highly artistic, historical and inclusive of all important determinants such portrayals can be. And the positive portrayals, particularly of Heinrich Mann, are so significant because they go a long way towards overcoming a direct, abstract and therefore unhistorical, merely allegorical relationship with the present.

But there is still a long way to go. As we have seen, Bruno Frank and even Heinrich Mann have produced portraits rather than real pictures of the times. The popular character of their heroes, in human terms, in terms of the individual person portrayed, is true and genuine. Yet the real basis, the real interaction with popular forces is not portrayed. Hence the organic link with popular life is lacking, both politically and polemically; there is lacking the concrete interconnection between the concrete popular movement and the hero who leads it. Only when the emergence of the positive, popular hero is shown artistically from a social-historical and not merely individual-biographical standpoint can the full political effect occur: that is, the literary unmasking of the pseudo-hero of Fascism.

This step has already been taken in life, and the literary achievement of a Heinrich Mann is the fact that he has seen this step in German life correctly and embodied it in art. Further advance along this path will again depend solely upon this growing involvement with popular life.

In this way life corrects and guides the work of true writers. And the recognition of this brings us to our second example from contemporary writing of a positive relationship with the present. In the previous chapter we showed how when Maupassant and Jacobsen took their subjects from the present many of their prejudices, which assumed a rigid and abstract form in their "autonomous" historical novels, were corrected by the immediate experience of life; how a "triumph of realism" occurred in their best novels on the present. One can often observe a similar "triumph of realism" in Feuchtwanger. One can criticize in many ways the conception of Fascism both in *Erfolg* (*Success*) and in *Die Geschwister Oppenheim* (*The Oppenheims*). And it would be interesting to show how these false conceptions of Fascism have been enlarged and vulgarized in his historical novels. But this is not so important for us as the fact that Feuchtwanger has created really living and really popular characters in these novels, who express plastically and convincingly all that is best in the popular forces rebelling against Fascist barbarism. Characters such as Johanna Krain in *Erfolg* or the young grammar school boy Bernard Oppenheim are nowhere to be found in Feuchtwanger's historical novels. In these characters especially, but also in many other of his contemporary novels,

Feuchtwanger's outstanding talents emerge unobscured by false theories and contemporary prejudices. He is converted to the historical novel because its self-contained material seems to promise lighter artistic labor and easier success. It seems to us that this "lightness," this insufficient resistance of the historical material to false constructions is one of the sources of the shortcomings of these novels, whereas the contradictory hardness of the living life of the present wrests from the writer his highest artistic talents.

This connection is not an accidental one. If we look at German literature in the imperalist period as a whole, then we have to admit that the historical novel—despite the luminous figure of Henri IV—cannot compare with the monumental portrayals of the present, with Thomas Mann's *Buddenbrooks*, Heinrich Mann's cycle on Wilhelmine Germany, etc. And the same is true for post-war literature. Thomas Mann's *Magic Mountain*, Arnold Zweig's World War cycle, Feuchtwanger's anti-Fascist novels are artistic peaks with which only *Henri IV*, in the field of the historical novel, can compare.

This literary-historical and aesthetic phenomenon tells us something important about the social mission of literature. On what does the significance of these novels rest? On the fact that their authors have tried to show artistically the concrete *historical genesis* of their time. It is this which is so far lacking in the historical novel of German anti-Fascism and in this that its central weakness lies. The great task facing anti-Fascist humanism is to reveal those social-historical and human-moral forces whose interplay made possible the 1933 catastrophe in Germany. For only a real understanding of these forces in all their complexity and intricacy can show their present disposition and the paths which they can take towards the revolutionary overthrow of Fascism. The ever stronger spirit of revolutionary democracy among the best representatives of the literary popular front against Fascism must take this direction ever more insistently if it is to overcome those ideological and literary traditions of liberalism still alive in the imperialist perod today.

The historical novel of the anti-Fascist humanists risks taking the path of least resistance. It enables writers to avoid the question of the historical genesis of the present by resorting to the path of abstraction, the abstract prehistory of problems. To point out this danger, to criticize ideologically and artistically the weaknesses which follow from it, is not to repudiate the historical novel and its great artistic, cultural and political importance for the present. Quite the contrary. Once writers as writers—that is, in terms of the portrayal of characters and destinies—learn to see this concrete, historical genesis of the present in the spirit of revolutionary democracy, the real perspective is opened for the development of the historical novel in the narrower sense. If we have confronted the historical novel of our time with some of the most outstanding works of our time dealing with the present, then it has been chiefly in order to stress how much more *historical* they are compared with the historical novels. Only the consciousness of this historical spirit and its artistic application will conquer the past, in the true sense of the word, on behalf of anti-Fascist humanism.

Here is not the place to subject the above-mentioned contemporary novels to a detailed criticism. These too are products of their time, and though they arose in struggle against imperialism, against the decline of realism in the imperialist period, they could not possibly remain untouched by the weaknesses and limitations of this decline. But whatever criticism is possible and necessary here, it is striking how many of the most important of these works approach the classical type of social novel much more closely than the historical novels of anti-Fascism their corresponding classical type. Our previous arguments have shown why this had to be: the cause was not a purely aesthetic one; it was simply that these works looked at the present much more historically. They did so because of the breadth and wealth of their author's experiences. And this stronger historical spirit became the basis of their greatness.

This historical spirit is the great new principle which Balzac learnt from Walter Scott and passed on to all the really great representatives of the modern social novel. When realism declines this spirit becomes abstract and evaporates, and the problems of the present, its people and its destinies, are conceived metaphysically. The modern social novel is as much a child of the classical historical novel as the latter is of the great social novels of the eighteenth century. The decisive question of the development of the historical novel in our day is how to restore this connection in keeping with our age.

This restoration necessarily leads artistically to a renaissance of the classical type of historical novel. But it will not and cannot be a purely aesthetic renaissance. The classical type of historical novel can only be aesthetically renewed if writers concretely face the question: how was the Hitler régime in Germany possible? Then an historical novel may be achieved which will be fully realized artistically.

The perspective for the development of the historical novel depends then on the resumption of classical traditions, on a fruitful assimilation of the classical inheritance. We have repeatedly shown that this is not an aesthetic question: it does not mean a formal imitation of the manner of Scott, Manzoni, Pushkin or Tolstoy. And since the prospects for the development of the historical novel tie up so closely with the problem of our approach to the classical heritage, we must stress energetically the two closely connected aspects of this heritage: one, its popular, democratic and for this reason truly and concretely historical spirit;

secondly, its high artistic concreteness of form. But popular character, democratic spirit and concrete historicism have a *radically different content* in our time. And, moreover, not only in the Soviet Union where the radically different content follows necessarily from victorious Socialism, but also for the fighting democratic humanists in the capitalist West.

The classical historical novel portrayed the contradictions of human progress, and with the means of history defended progress against the ideological attacks of reaction; in this struggle it depicted the necessary destruction of the old, primitive democracy and the great heroic crises of human history. But its historical perspective could only be that of the *necessary decline of the heroic period,* the necessary march of development into *capitalist prose.* The classical historical novel portrays the *sunset* of the heroic-revolutionary development of bourgeois democracy.

Todays historical novel has arisen and is developing amid the *dawn* of a *new* democracy. This applies not only to the Soviet Union where the tempestuous development and vigorous construction of Socialism have produced the highest form of democracy in human history, Socialist democracy. The struggle of the revolutionary democracy of the popular front, too, is not simply a defence of the existing achievements of democratic development against the attacks of Fascist or near-Fascist reaction. While it is this, it also goes beyond these limits in its defence of democracy; it must give revolutionary democracy new, higher, more advanced, more general, more democratic and more social contents. The revolution unfolding before us in Spain shows this new development at its clearest. It shows that a democracy of a new type is about to be born.

The struggle for this new democracy, which throughout the world is evoking an enthusiastic revival and development of the traditions of revolutionary democracy, everywhere awakens unsuspected and extraordinary heroism in the people. We are in the midst of a heroic period, whose heroism moreover does not rest on historically necessary illusions, as was the case with the Puritans in the English and the Jacobins in the French Revolution, but upon a real knowledge of the needs of the working people and the direction in which society is developing. This heroism does not rest on illusions because its historical conditions are not so constituted that a period of prosaic disenchantment must follow upon its victory. The heroism of the Puritans in England and of the Jacobins in France— much against the will of the revolutionary fighters—helped the prose of capitalist exploitation to victory. The heroism of the fighters of the popular front, however, is a struggle for the true interests of the whole working people; for the creation of material and cultural conditions of life which can guarantee their human growth in every respect.

This perspective; that the heroism of the struggle does not have to be an episode—however historically necessary, yet still an episode—in the triumphal march of capitalist prose, also changes our attitude to the past. If a writer of today, enriched by the experiences of the heroic struggles of the people against imperialist exploitation and oppression throughout the world, depicts the historical forerunners of these struggles, he can do this in a quite different, much truer and deeper historical spirit than Scott or Balzac. For them the heroic periods of mankind could only appear as episodes and interludes, albeit historically justified and historically necessary.

This new perspective which has opened up as a result of the events of recent years not only makes possible a deepened conception of the past, but simultaneously broadens the field of portrayal in our concrete prehistory. Let us refer to just one example. Up to now oriental subjects have necessarily been of an exotic and eccentric character in bourgeois literature. The importation of Indian or Chinese philosophy into the declining ideology of the bourgeoisie could only increase this exoticism. Now, however, when we are contemporaries of the heroic liberation struggles of the Chinese, Indian, etc., people, all these developments flow concretely into the common historical stream of the liberation of mankind and are therefore portrayable in literature. And in the light of this common direction the past of these peoples is illuminated in a new way or at least can be so illuminated through the work of their important writers.

The rule of prose set in after the heroic period because objectively the only result of the people's colossal heroic efforts was the replacement of one form of exploitation by another. From an objective social standpoint the victory of capitalism over feudalism is of course a great historical advance. And the great representatives of the classical historical novel always acknowledged this progressiveness in their work. But precisely because they were great writers, and felt really deeply with the people in their misfortunes, it was impossible for them to be unconditional admirers of capitalist progress. Together with the economic progress they always portrayed the fearful sacrifices which it cost the people.

With this realization of the contradictory character of progress the representatives of the classical historical novel do not glorify the past uncritically. But nevertheless their works do clearly mourn the passing of many moments in the past: in the first place the fruitlessness of the heroic upsurge of past popular movements of liberation; secondly the many primitive democratic institutions, and the human qualities associated with them, which the march of progress has pitilessly destroyed. In really important writers, writers with a really live historical sense, this mourning is very divided and contradictory, dialectical. Humanly, aesthetically and ethically repelled by victorious capitalist prose, they not only feel its necessity, but also, despite all the horrors associated with it, that it marks a step forward in the development of mankind.

This dividedness disappears for the writer of today. His perspective of the future rests neither upon illusions, nor upon a disenchanted awakening from them. It shows not a degradation of heroic and human manifestations of life from the standpoint of a victorious future but on the contrary, the broadening, deepening and raising to a higher level of all the valuable qualities of man which have emerged during his previous development.

It suffices to point to one example in order to show clearly this difference of perspective, which is a difference of development in historical reality. In the first chapter of this work we quoted Maxim Gorky's fine analysis of Cooper's novels. This analysis shows the divided attitude of the classics of the historical novel clearly. They have to affirm the downfall of the humanly noble Indian, the straightforwardly decent, straightforwardly heroic "leather stocking," treating it as a necessary step of progress, and yet cannot help seeing and depicting the human inferiority of the victors. This is the necessary fate of every primitive culture with which capitalism comes into contact.

Now Fadeev, in his new cycle of novels, has raised an enormous problem with a similar theme, although—in those parts of his work so far published—not solved it: namely the fate of the surviving tribe of the Udehe, living still in a state almost of primitive communism, as it comes into contact with the proletarian revolution. Obviously this contact must vigorously transform both the customs and the economic life of the tribe; but it is also obvious that this transformation must take a completely opposite direction from the one which Cooper depicts as movingly tragic.

The revolutionary liberation of the people from the yoke of capitalism produces a heroic upsurge among the masses in exceptionally broad numbers and in a very profound manner. But—and this is the important thing—this upsurge is not an episode to be followed by a fresh suppression of popular energies. On the contrary, it clears away all obstacles which hinder the unfolding of human energies in the popular masses; it creates institutions which help to accelerate and deepen, economically and culturally, this unfolding of the people's energies. This perspective of the real and permanent liberation of the people alters the perspective which historical novels have of the future; it gives quite a different emotional accent to their illumination of the past from that which we find, and inevitably find, in the classical historical novel; it is able to discover entirely new tendencies and features in the past, of which the classical historical novel was not and could not be aware. *In this respect* the new historical novel, born of the popular and democratic spirit of our time, will indeed *contrast* with the classical historical novel.

From what has been said up to now it is clear that this new perspective exists not only for the writers of the Soviet Union, but also for the humanists of the anti-Fascist popular front; although, of course, these tendencies are inevitably more distinct and developed, both objectively and subjectively, in the Soviet Union. But the struggle for a democracy of a new type, the realization that the problems of this democracy are connected with the economic and cultural liberation of the exploited— something we have seen especially vividly in the writings of Heinrich Mann—show that this perspective is also a reality for the fighters of the popular front. Thus, it can also become a reality for their literature.

If these tendencies are to be realized, deep-going changes will have to take place in a formal-artistic respect as well, both in the novel in general and therewith in the historical novel, too. Very generally this tendency may be described as a *tendency towards epic*. This tendency is plainly perceptible in some of the best products of the most recent period. Think of some of the familiar features of Heinrich Mann's *Henri IV*.

This tendency is born of a deep historical necessity. It expresses artistically the same historical phenomenon which led us to contrast the new, emerging historical novel with the classical historical novel. But it must not be overlooked that this is *only* a tendency. Only in fully developed socialism can the cessation of the antagonistic character of contradiction, with its consequences for the whole of human activity, become a determining principle of the structure and movement of social life. As long as there exists a capitalist economy the antagonism of contradictions must prevail. Admittedly, the concrete and actual prospect of liberation does produce a different subjective attitude to the contradictory course of history though of course without being able to change its real character. Thus in such changes of style it can only be a question of tendency.

We are still far from being able to look on capitalist prose as a period we have fully done with, as one which really does belong simply to the past. The fact that a central task of the internal policy of the Soviet Union is the conquest of capitalist survivals in economy and ideology shows that even in socialist reality capitalist prose is still a factor to be reckoned with, although it has suffered defeat and is condemned to ultimate extinction.

What Marx said of legal institutions applies in wide measure to literary forms. They cannot stand higher than the society which brought them forth. Indeed, since they deal with the deepest human laws, problems and contradictions of an epoch they *should* not stand higher—in the sense, say, of anticipating coming perspectives of development by romantic-Utopian projections of the future into the present. For the tendencies leading to the future are in fact more firmly and definitely contained in what really is than in the most beautiful Utopian dreams or projections.

Naturally, this reservation applies still more to the anti-Fascist literature of the West. For there the capitalist system rules in its most repulsive, barbaric, inhuman form. The popular front today can at best only gather together all forces of democracy to resist Fascism, as in Spain. But the victory, the liberation of the people from the Fascist yoke, the new social order of democracy, not to speak of the abolition of exploitation, is today at best an object of struggle, in most cases a real, but nevertheless future, perspective. That a literature of the kind we have seen in the anti-Fascist historical novel could arise in capitalist countries under these social and political conditions is a very important sign of the times—of the maturing revolutionary situation and the enormous international significance of the victorious construction of Socialism in the Soviet Union. But our recognition of this new situation should nevertheless not mislead us into twisting perspectives and tendencies intellectually into present-day realities.

For this reason the contrast between the historical novel today and the classical type is only a very relative one. We had to stress the tendency for this contrast so as to avoid the misunderstanding that we intended a formal revival, an artistic imitation of the classical historical novel. That is impossible. The difference in historical perspectives causes a difference in principles of composition and characterization as well. The more these perspectives and tendencies are transformed into reality, the more therefore the novel develops generally in the direction of epic, the greater will this contrast be. But it would be idle to worry one's head today over how radical a contrast this will be.

The more so, since the principal front of struggle in the artistic sphere, too, is the conquest of harmful legacies. We have shown that in many respects the tendencies present in the new historical novel contrast with those marking the decline of bourgeois realism. So far, however, these tendencies have nowhere been fully realized. The liquidation of harmful legacies is still far from complete. And we have seen how much the problems of the historical novel of our day, both ideological and artistic, depend upon a radical settling-of-accounts with these legacies. At the same time we must stress particularly strongly that any utopian anticipation of the future, any transformation of the future into a supposed reality can very easily cause a slipping-back into the style of the period of decline by blunting the antagonistic contradictions which operate in reality.

In this struggle the study of the classical historical novel will play an outstanding part. Not only because we possess in it a literary standard of a very high level for our portrayal of the real tendencies in popular life, hence a measure for the popular character of the historical novel, but also because the classical historical novel, as a result of this popular character, realized the *general laws of large epic* in a model form, whereas the novel of the period of decline, severed from life, largely destroyed these general laws of narrative art—from composition and characterization down to choice of language. The perspective of the novel's return to true epic greatness, to an epic-like character must re-awaken these general laws of great narrative art, recall them to conscious-ness, translate them again into practice, if they are not to disintegrate into a self-contradictory "problematic." This "problematic" we can observe in the very highest achievement of the modern historical novel, Heinrich Mann's *Henri IV*, where the grand, epic character of the positive hero, the monumentality of the narrative style conflicts strangely and un-resolvably with the necessary, unavoidable and irremovable pettiness of the biographical manner of presentation.

And in a quite different, but—in a large historical sense—similar way, we were able to discern in Romain Rolland's *Colas Breugnon* a contra-dictory combination of this artistic strength, which points to the future, and a specific "problematic" of the present.

This historical novel of our time, therefore, must above all negate, radically and sharply, its immediate predecessor and eradicate the latter's traditions from its own work. The necessary approximation to the classical type of historical novel which occurs in this connection will, as our remarks have shown, by no means take the form of a simple renaissance, a simple affirmation of these classical traditions, but, if one will allow me this phrase from Hegel's terminology, a renewal in the form of a negation of a negation.

D. Critical Practice

29. Arnold Hauser

Alienation as the Key
to Mannerism

The selection is from ARNOLD HAUSER'S noted work, *Mannerism*, published in 1965. A biographical note appears on page 269.

1. The Concept of Alienation

NOTHING better expresses the nature and origin of the cultural crisis of our own time than the concept of alienation. From Rousseau's answer to the celebrated question of the Dijon academy to Freud's *Civilization and Its Discontents* the same notion, if not always the same word, was associated with the threatening or already present danger. The first to use the term alienation, or self-estrangement, in the sense of a criticism of modern culture was Hegel, and in the main it has preserved its original meaning even under the name of reification it received from Marx and that of the sublimation of instincts that it was given by Freud, who took a much more positive view of the outcome of the process of alienation than his predecessors, but nevertheless regarded repression of instinctual urges as an exorbitant price to pay for the protection that civilization provides for us.

The concept of alienation is so much used and misused in modern works on the philosophy of history and culture that its meaning has been somewhat obscured, and special care is needed in disentangling the various levels of meaning that have become confused, and sorting out the essentials in the various aspects of the idea. The individual's sense of uprootedness, aimlessness, and loss of substance is and remains basic to the idea of alienation—the sense of having lost contact with society and having no engagement in one's work, the hopelessness of ever harmonizing one's aspirations, standards, and ambitions.

Its discovery as a cultural phenomenon, as the destiny of civilized man, may date back to Rousseau, and its first authoritative and more or less

still valid definition may be due to Hegel, but alienation certainly did
not begin with its discovery, naming, or definition, even if it is not actually
timeless and does not appear as soon as and whenever contact is made
with the objective world, as Hegel believed. It has existed since man
ceased to live in a natural condition and civilization began, since he
began to subject himself to conventions and traditions, to adapt himself
to institutions and to think in objective terms; in short, ever since he
emerged from the state of nature and became the subject of history.
However, in the narrower sense of the term in which we are interested
in the present context, it originated in the age when the organic unity of
the spiritual world began gradually to disintegrate into a multiplicity of
aspects, interests, and ties. This too is of course a very ancient process,
for it began in about the sixth century B.C., and is only loosely connected
with the alienation of our own cultural period. In the broadly uninterrupted process of development that has since taken place, there have been
some pauses offering rest and relief, as in the Middle Ages, for instance,
as well as a number of sudden, revolutionary leaps, of which the most
striking was that which took place in the sixteenth century. Western man
experienced another such abrupt leap in the nineteenth century, with the
development of modern high capitalism. These two periods are of especial
significance, because of the contemporary awareness of the processes in
train, which not only added a new dimension to the changes objectively
taking place, but also gave them a new meaning.

In conscious form alienation appeared for the first time as the crisis
of the Renaissance, and its effect was so revolutionary and all-embracing
that the concept of alienation is the only possible common denominator
for the various forms of the 'upheaval' that affected every field of culture.
Whichever way one looks, one sees the same phenomenon, of men
suddenly feeling themselves cut off, as it were, from the familiar things
that previously gave meaning and purpose to their lives. They may have
been at the mercy of tyrannical lords before, but now they found themselves at the mercy of forces from which they were estranged. They had
grown estranged from their own work as a consequence of the application
of mechanical methods of production, the replacement of the old patriarchal relationship with their masters by the impersonal forces of the
market and the inscrutable play of economic forces, the turning of state
and administration, economy and society, justice and the military system,
into ruthless automata functioning with inhuman objectivity. The reification of life had gone so far that Georg Simmel's 'tragedy of culture'
became a tangible fact. Man created objects, forms, and values, and
became their slave and servant instead of their master. The works of
his hand and mind assumed an autonomy of their own, and became
independent of him while he became dependent on them, in that he

recognized their meaning, worth, and validity, or strove to possess them without ever being able to acquire them, as Marx complains. In the classical meaning of the term, from which both Hegel and Marx as well as Kierkegaard and the modern existentialists start out, alienation means divesture of the self, the loss of subjectivity; a turning inside out of the personality, exteriorizing and driving out what ought to remain within, with the result that what is ejected in this way assumes a nature completely different from the self, becomes alien and hostile to it, and threatens to diminish and destroy it. Meanwhile the self loses itself in its objectifications, faces an alienated form of itself in them.

But, above all, alienation means the loss of the wholeness or, as Marx called it, the 'universal nature' of man. Men whose world is still homogenous and undivided are not yet alienated and are still whole, but those who have lost that universality and are confronted by independent and autonomous cultural phenomena isolated from the unity of life, like the state, the economy, the sciences, and art, themselves possess no concrete reality, have become 'abstractions' in the sense of the word used by Marx, to whom it is a synonym for alienation and loss of universality. In discussing alienation the cultural philosophers, both the followers of Kierkegaard and those of Marx, that is to say, the irrationalists as well as the rationalists, lay increasing emphasis on the loss of contact with reality. In this sense the whole trend is away from Hegel, who regarded alienation rather as an acceptance of concrete reality than as a departure from it.

Hegel understands by objectification an act of alienation from the self and by alienation a process of turning a subject into an object. He anticipates the basic theme of Simmel's cultural philosophy in that he recognizes that meaningful mental structures or, as he calls them, the forms of the 'objective spirit,' make themselves independent of their creator and thereby become alienated from him. He expresses this by saying that man loses himself in his own creations, works of art, philosophies, religions, sciences, etc., and lives in an alien, spiritually unreal and imaginary world. A work of art, philosophy, or science belongs both to its creator and does not; every such work contains an element of alienation, without which the mind would continue in a state of passivity, a form of being for itself alone. Just as God created the world by an act of self-alienation, so is the human mind confronted by an alien element in his own creations. In this way Hegel derives a positive value from alienation; not only does it lead to everything that is objective to man, but it also represents a necessary and indispensable stage in the mind's journey to itself. Only through alienation does the mind attain awareness of itself; for, in accordance with the laws of dialectics, it is superseded in objectification only to re-establish and realize itself again. The mind constructs a second world for itself by rising above and opposing alienated reality.

But this higher world of self-awareness can come into being only in conflict with the alienated world. Thus alienation is the prerequisite, so to speak, the price, of the mind's ultimate self-realization. For 'the self' is only real after having been superseded.

How close mannerism is to us, not only with its sense of alienation, but also with its theory of it, is shown most clearly by Campanella, who quite literally anticipates Hegel's use of the term as an epistemological principle. When he states that all cognition consists in undergoing external impressions he is still faithful to the imitation theory of the Middle Ages and the Renaissance. But he is original and revolutionary when he states that in the process of cognition the subject becomes alienated from itself, that it conceives things in being seized by them, and that in this process it loses its own true nature and assumes an alien nature in exchange. In his epistemology Campanella goes so far as to deny all difference between knowledge and madness, cognition and distortion. 'Knowing is becoming alienated from one's self,' he writes, 'becoming alienated from one's self is going mad, losing one's own being, and assuming an alien being.'

2. Marx's Concept of Alienation

Both Marx and Hegel mean by alienation the loss of that universality without which, in their view, man is not man. Nevertheless they differ in the important respect that with Hegel alienation is a super-historical process which takes place at every contact between subject and objective reality and is repeated with every such contact, while with Marx it is historically conditioned, that is to say, it first arises with private property, and in the narrower sense of the word originates in modern capitalism or, strictly speaking, the division of labor. The great advance made by Marx in the history of the idea lies chiefly in his stripping the Hegelian concept of its abstract, metaphysical, timeless generality and his defining it historically, that is to say, giving it limits in time. He brings the process of alienation down from the vacuum of logic and epistemology into the reality of history by attempting to derive the whole phenomenon from the worker's separation from the products of his labor, which are no longer his in any real sense of the word and have no real meaning for him. He transforms alienation from a kind of original sin attached to the human spirit from which it has yet to be redeemed, in Hegel's view, into a process with historical limits and dependent on historical conditions. He regards it as having originated with the mechanization of production associated with the division of labor—or, as we should rather say today, tending towards the division of labor—and believed that it would disappear again with it.

Inadequate though Marx's theory of alienation may be in one way or another, it is based on the correct assumption that the fundamental pattern of the alienated world is set by the commodity character of the products of labor. This is nowhere more evident than in the field of art. Works of art were formerly produced for specific purposes arising out of specific personal relationships for specific patrons known personally to the artist. Now they became the object of commercial transactions, a commodity with a market value, expressing thereby the problematic relationship between the artist and his public that so unmistakably differentiates him from the artist of earlier times.

The essence of a 'commodity' in this sense is the circumstance that as a result of neglecting the unequal quality of labor input—its reduction to an abstract common denominator, to mere 'labor,' in fact—it is an article of trade having an exchange value. Marx shows how as a consequence of his alienation from the product of his labor, which becomes a commodity, and his alienation from his work, which is performed solely in the service of others, the worker externalizes and objectifies all that is human in himself, gradually loses all his personal qualities in his relationship with others as well as in relation to himself, acquires an exchange value like everything around him, and becomes a function of money.

The more he gives of himself, the harder he works and produces, the more strength accrues to the alien, objective world that he erects over and against himself, the poorer he becomes, and the less he retains for himself. He puts his life into his work; his life, however, is no longer his own, but belongs to the object that he produces. 'The worker feels himself at home when he is not working, and when he is working he is not at home. . . . His labor is forced labor.' His alienation from the product of his hands thus means, not only that his work has been transformed into an alien object, has a life of its own apart from and independent of him, but also that it has become a hostile force in relation to him.

If Marx's alienation of the worker meant merely that labor was a social activity done for others, and that the product of labor received its deplored commodity character from the social relationships in which the labor was involved, it would be no more than a commonplace. For, ever since man emerged from the state of nature in which he produced solely for his own needs, i.e., left behind him the idyllic conditions of life à la Robinson Crusoe, labor has had a social character, that is to say, has been labor for others. The difference between earlier conditions and those described and criticized by Marx is that in the latter the products of labor are and remain solely the property of others; the worker has no more share in their possession than he has in the raw material and the machinery, which are the property of the employer. At no stage do they belong to the worker, who produces them from beginning to end in the knowledge that there is no bond between him and them. His alienation from the product of his labor is greatly enhanced by a new characteristic of production that makes its first appearance with the beginnings of modern capitalism, namely the division of labor, which Marx regards as a decisive factor in modern economic development. It is impossible to feel any solidarity with work of which one is responsible only for a part, and often only a very unimportant and insignificant part, and in which one is not always able to identify one's share. In these circumstances one is bound to feel like the slave of one's work.

In the sixteenth century there was of course not yet any division of labor in Adam Smith's sense, and his celebrated example, the manufacture of pins, lay in the future. But since the end of the fifteenth century there had been an increasing mechanization of labor resulting from the introduction of machinery. At all events, the Cinquecento can be regarded as the beginning of the technical age, and of the tendency for skilled to be replaced by unskilled labor, though it should not be overlooked that industrial labor was still far from being reduced to simple, mechanical, repetitive tasks. But to bring about the alienation of the worker from his work there was no need for division of labor in the strict sense of the word, in the form in which it first appeared in the eighteenth century; the mechanization of production and the devaluation of skilled craftsmanship were quite sufficient. The importance of the mechanization of labor cannot be over-estimated, even if it is qualified by the consideration that machinery was not invented until it was needed and opportunities for it existed. However that may be, there is no doubt that the rapid growth of capitalism in the sixteenth century was closely connected with technological progress. This advanced at such speed and on so broad a front that the process might well be described as an early industrial revolution. Some time after machinery, and with it a more or less modern and rationalized organization of labor, had been introduced into textile manufacture, it also came to be used in mining, printing, and glass and paper manufacture, leading to the concentration of production in relatively few hands as well as to the more intensive use of labor and the gradual elimination of the small producer.

In his description of the process of alienation Marx, in spite of the basic rationalism of his methods and approach, cannot resist romanticizing the past, obviously in order to bring into sharper relief the intolerable nature of modern conditions. For all the epoch-making impact of the beginnings of mechanization and the division of labor, he should not have overlooked or passed over in silence the fact that for most men labor cannot have been associated with any pleasure even in earlier ages. It is and always has been possible to identify oneself with work only if it is individual and to some extent creative. The failure of the inner impulse to work certainly did not first begin with modern capitalist production; and alienation from work can take place whenever it is done solely to make a living, and production is not for personal consumption but to acquire means of exchange. The slave, the serf, and the servant also worked only because they had to and no more than they had to; not only the serf, but the often so thoughtlessly romanticized medieval craftsman no doubt generally identified himself with his work no more than an industrial worker on a conveyor belt. Nevertheless the development of modern capitalism and the mechanization of production brought about a deep change in this respect. For in different historical periods similar situations do not always have the same results. The patience with which labor is endured depends on the historical situation. In the age of serfdom, when lack of freedom was more or less taken for granted by the whole of feudal society, labor, though it was often far more strenuous and soulless than in later ages, was not by a long way felt to be as oppressive and humiliating as it came to be felt after the liberation of the peasants, the spread of ideas about the rights of the human personality, and the new fluidity of the barriers between the social classes. A beast of burden tolerates more physical labor than man, and primitive man tolerates more than civilized man; there is a relativity about what is felt to be tolerable in any period. What men are willing and able to put up with depends on what they are able to look forward to. Just as the urge to rise in the social scale arises only after the boundaries between the classes have begun to wobble, and social revolutions do not break out when conditions for the oppressed classes are at their worst, but only when their situation becomes comparable to those of the higher classes, so does the sense, if not the fact, of alienation from work hardly become really oppressive until the worker's liberty of movement brings the improvement of his position within the realm of possibility. Thus it was mainly in the subjective respect that conditions deteriorated for the worker with the rise of modern capitalism. In earlier historical periods he was objectively and materially no better off, but he was less aware of the wretchedness of his lot.

Marx was also guilty of romanticizing the past in his assumption that mechanization and mere machine-minding led and was bound to lead to the worker's intellectual frustration. In reality, however, work on a machine was mentally more demanding than ploughing a field, and called for more intelligence than handling a hoe or shovel, or doing the work of many artisans on feudal estates or in small village communities. But the more skilled the worker becomes in the course of time, the more deadening the necessarily monotonous and repetitive processes connected with the use of machinery are felt to be, though these certainly require intelligence and make higher demands on it with the increasing complication of machinery. Leaving modern electric devices entirely aside, a simple mechanical loom such as was used in the early stages of the textile industry was far more complicated and certainly much more absorbing than the tools which he had to handle on a feudal estate in the old days of serfdom. But in the last resort the worker's alienation from his work is not affected by this. The vital factor is that with the change to modern mechanical production, in spite of the more demanding nature of his work, he is robbed of all initiative and all possibility of innovation and change. In considering whether and to what extent an increased degree of alienation is present in any historical period, the decisive factor is the distance that exists between the worker and his work; and this depends, not so much on the nature of his work, as on the totality of his situation, that is to say, the relationship between his economic resources, his chances on the labor market, his social rights, his self-awareness, and his level of intelligence on the one hand, and the actual work he is called on to do on the other. Thus Marx is ultimately correct in his indictment of the mechanization of labor, in spite of his mistake in underestimating the demand made by mechanical production on the worker's capacities.

Though Marx recognizes as the most important symptom of alienation the 'ghost-like objectivity' assumed by products of labor transformed into commodities as a consequence of the mechanization and division of labor of the capitalist age, he is of course very well aware that trade in commodities is much older than modern capitalism. Nevertheless he talks correctly of a hitherto unknown commodity fetishism, that is to say, of a new domination of life by the concept of commodities, a channelling of thought into commodity categories, a revolutionizing of human relationships, now governed by the production and sale of commodities. What was new in the period we are discussing was not so much the fact that both the products of labor and their producers' working-time became saleable commodities, for even in its most exaggerated form this could not have had the revolutionary effect that Marx ascribed to what he understood by 'reification'; the epoch-making upheaval consisted in the fact that the concept of commodities became the fundamental category of social life and reshaped and refashioned every field of human endeavor. Every element in human social relations assumed the quality of a commodity, and not merely in the sense that it became purchasable or saleable like any other commodity, or that the worker's time became a neutral article of commerce measurable by a common standard and comparable with any other worker's time, with the result that the worker himself came to think of his strength and working capacity simply as a saleable object. The essence of the matter, as Marx pointed out, lay in the fact that 'one hour of one man's time equals one hour of any other man's time,' and that 'one man working for one hour was worth as much as any other man working for one hour.' Here we are confronted with something much more fundamental than the sale of working time and the products of labor; we are face to face, not just with loss of work and time, but with loss of personality and individual identity. Not only life and labor were dehumanized and became objectified; the worker himself was dehumanized and became a 'thing' in the same way. It is this that enables one to appreciate the extent to which the commodity concept invades the whole of life and gives a clue to the depth of the spiritual crisis in which it resulted. For conditions that led to such human degradation in an age of social emancipation must have made an impact in fields far wider than the industrial worker's personality, and the pleasure he took in his work; indeed, its revolutionary influence extended to all forms of life and thought, all levels of society, and all areas of culture. The way of thinking of the whole of society was based on the ideology of commodities. There was no form of human relations or human activity that it left untouched or unthreatened.

This, it is true, was also the period when the artist most strikingly differentiated himself from the craftsman, and was increasingly being granted the privileges of individual treatment. Nevertheless his products ceased to be 'bespoke,' and became a commodity, produced for stock or for offer on the open market. Though the greatest works of the age were more strongly marked by individuality than those of any previous age, this was bound to lead to a depersonalization of artistic production in general. Works of art had of course been bought and sold in earlier periods, but the fact that the middle of the sixteenth century saw the real birth of the art trade is highly symptomatic and significant for the future. This was the birth hour, not only of the art dealer and art collector in the modern sense, but also of the modern artist. The latter had to pay for his greater independence with a higher degree of insecurity, and his value was assessed in figures as never before.

3. Alienation from Society

Nothing illustrates the process of alienation in economic and social life more strikingly and significantly than the part played by money in modern capitalism. It is so important and so all-embracing that the whole system could be described as a money economy. Money became the instrument of reification, the means of reducing all values to an impersonal common denominator. It dehumanizes, neutralizes, and quantifies qualitative differences.

Money deprives concrete human relations of their personal character, and turns those engaged in economic activity into strangers to each other. The worker becomes a mere employee, and his master an employer. One sells his work, which the other buys. To the seller the buyer becomes an entity from whom he receives money, to the buyer the seller is a slot-machine from whom he gets labor power in return for the coins inserted.

But money not only depersonalizes economic relationships and the exchange of property; it also depersonalizes possession itself. One bank-note is like another. Money has no face, is not reminiscent of anything, *non olet*. Nothing of its origin clings to the hands of those who inherit it, or even of those who earn it; and the possession of shares is just as impersonal as is the possession of currency. The financier who puts capital into an enterprise has no direct involvement in it, shares pass from hand to hand without affecting the business concerned, and are bought and sold without the buyers or sellers having the slightest real interest in the business.

There is another respect in which money is impersonal, a mere abstraction, quantity without quality. Besides disguising the thing it pays for and the possession that assumes its form, it also disguises the individual who possesses it. In a world ruled by money, in which it has become the universal standard, everyone is valued by the amount of it he possesses. Not only does it make objective values comparable, exchangeable, transferable from one person to another—in other words, make them abstract; it also makes it possible to relate and compare with each other personal values that are qualitatively unique and, as Georg Simmel, Max Weber, and Ernst Troeltsch have shown, accustoms people to an abstract, rational way of thinking in which no account is taken of the individual and the individual case. It encourages, for instance, work in the interests of the 'firm,' which is thought of as existing independently of the employer as an individual; and it plays its part in the building up of an objective, impersonal legal system, an independently functioning bureaucracy, and an army in which irrational feudal principles have been done away with; that is to say, in the multiplication of institutions which alienate themselves from the individual and share the characteristic of freeing themselves from personal influences and considerations.

Money is the very symbol and quintessence of relativism; it expresses the relative value of things by stamping them all as saleable and transforming their utility value into exchange value, thus depriving them of their substance and making them mere bearers of functions, which have their price. Whatever is obtainable for money—and in a society which is organized in capitalist fashion and thinks in capitalist terms most things are obtainable for money—goes to those willing and able to pay the best price for it, without respect to persons or merit or ability. When property, labor, services, become purchasable, they pass out of the sphere of personal relations and enter another sphere in which relations lose their subjective, emotional, and spiritual features. Money serves as a substitute for everything and reduces everything to equality but, however greatly it may succeed in this function, it fails to eliminate the feeling that many things are unique, irreplaceable, and inexchangeable. Nothing could have a more devastating effect on human relations than the fact that nevertheless everything had its price, that one got nothing for nothing, and that one's value in the eyes of others depended on the iron law of inhuman competition. In the old days it had been possible to rely on humane considerations, patriarchal customs, traditional favors. But now all exceptions, concessions, grants of grace and favor, looked like indolence and indulgence. Everything had to be paid for in full, and a full day's work had to be given for a full day's pay, and there was no disposition to be satisfied with less. The laws of the market governed the whole of life.

In recent times the humanitarian element in the treatment of the serfs and the relative security enjoyed even by the lowest sections of society in the Middle Ages, compared with the precarious position of the modern proletariat, has been perhaps somewhat excessively emphasized, obviously to correct the earlier exaggeration of their inhuman treatment. Exploitation is a permanent characteristic of any class society, though often its maintenance imposes certain more or less closely defined limits. On the other hand, when exploitation seems to increase or diminish, it sometimes merely means that methods of exploitation have changed. Since the end of the Middle Ages the lower classes have had to pay for the advantages of freedom of movement with an increased inflexibility and depersonalization of relations with their employers. True, the worker receives more adequate pay, but no bread if there is no work for him. Nobody can force him to work if he does not want to, but there is no law, practice, or custom that obliges or occasions anyone to use services he does not need. Since the end of the feudal system the town laborer has had to accept, in exchange for his sense of a more or less nominal liberty, greater insecurity and a lot that in a number of respects has been much harder than it was in the days of serfdom. He had been freed from the soil, but not from fear, thus resembling the Protestant, who had shaken off the clerical yoke, but was thrown back completely on himself, full of anxiety and suspicion, feeling threatened from everywhere, protected by no one, surrounded by an alienated world, condemned to stand alone.

The medieval forms of loyalty, patriarchal solicitude, corporative solidarity, and Christian and comradely charity gradually disappeared. Not only did the bonds of the manor, the guilds, and other corporations which offered some protection in emergency begin to weaken, but most forms of association lost their human directness. Corporations became rigid institutions, and charitable institutions were motivated less and less by humane and more and more by practical and unemotional considerations. The Protestant ethos of work and the view that poverty was either a sin or the consequence of sloth, negligence, or incompetence, played a part in this, just as did capitalism with its class struggle and ruthless competition. For alienation, a dehumanization of relations, appeared, not only between members of different social classes, but also between members of the same group. Not only did alien, antagonistic, or actually hostile relations—at any rate legal relations from which all trace of patriarchal attachment had vanished—establish themselves between landlord and peasant, master and man, employer and worker, but the employers themselves fought each other and were united only in their struggle against the workers or small craftsmen; and in the more or less homogeneous trade associations and church communities human relations gave way to rigid, impersonal, administrative regulations.

The whole age was dominated by individualism, the discovery, emphasis, and acceptance in principle of the rights of the individual. But, in spite of this principle, the ordinary, anonymous individual counted much less as a person, friend, or brother, than before. No one had legal control over anyone else's life and liberty, but no one was expected to do more for his fellow-men than the law or his contractual obligations required. Human relations were between legal persons and parties to legal contracts, and had all the coldness and distance of contractual relations, and man suffered the more from this the greater his sense of individuality and the greater emphasis he was able to lay on his individual rights. Sensitiveness grew with the sense of vulnerability, and emancipation led to greater susceptibility and a greater readiness to take offense than had ever previously seemed conceivable. There was the more reason and opportunity for grievance as the development of individualism was automatically accompanied by the multiplication of institutions. For the more definitely members of society came forward or claimed to come forward as individuals, the more necessary it became to form new institutions and expand their influence in order to ensure the survival of society.

4. The Process of Institutionalization

Even if nothing were known about the age of mannerism except that it saw the origin of most of the important institutions that prevail in the public life of the present day, it would have to be counted among the most notable and significant periods of history, as one of those which have most profoundly influenced the structure of modern civilization. In the fields of government, military organization, and the administration of justice, private enterprise and social and church organization, as well as that of artistic education, the principle of meeting the problems involved by institutionalization definitely established itself. Modern bureaucracy, the standing army, the new reformed churches as well as the reformed Roman church, exchanges, cartels, academies, and their associated art schools, are all creations of that time. The social institutions that now arose are so numerous and affected so vitally the subsequent development of western culture that it is tempting to describe mannerism, if not as a new beginning, at any rate as the deepest break and the most important turning-point in the history of institutions. The institutionalization of human relations is of course a continuous process, liable to disturbances and sudden accelerations, but it never comes to a complete standstill, and there is never a new beginning for which the ground has not previously been prepared. The history of institutions is indeed as old as that of civilization itself, and it can certainly be claimed that the latter began when institutions developed out of improvisation.

With the birth of institutions man emerged from the state of nature and history began. They ensured the continuity and survival of his cultural attainments. Every habit, every custom, every tradition, is part of the bulwark that he erects against the threat of chaos, the intervention of blind chance; they are defensive arrangements, as Émile Durkheim says, that ensure the objectivity of social action against individual motivation. To complain of dependence on institutions is usually pure romanticism; they often provide a far more reliable guarantee of social security than the most tender conscience. But, in spite of the identity of the history of institutions with that of civilization, and notwithstanding the continuity in the formation of institutions, there are turning-points in their development that give them a new significance, when a quantitative change, that is to say, a multiplication of them, becomes a qualitative change. It was the discovery of such a turning-point that enabled Marx to describe the sixteenth century as the beginning of a new epoch in the history of industrial labor, capitalism, and alienation, and the same insight enables us today to see that a significant transformation in the function of institutions took place in that century.

In spite of the rapid advance of institutionalization in the Cinquecento, not all the institutions of the age were as novel as they seemed to be, though many appeared then for the first time. The Reformation was originally a reaction against the institutional rigidity of the church. But nothing is more indicative of the prevailing trend than the fact that the Reformation itself became rigidly institutionalized, and that the reformed churches developed into the most pedantic and petty-minded institutions of the age. Soulless and inflexible though the older institutions might have been, they were incomparably fewer in number, and exercised far less influence on the individual's life. There were no institutions in the past corresponding to the new bureaucracy and standing armies, the state administration of justice and the princes' fiscal systems, the international banking and credit machinery, the financial operations and exchanges, the academies and schools of art, the art market, and the systematic art collecting; for even the old city administrations, corporations, and guilds, though they ended by functioning almost as mechanically as the new institutions, had originally permitted the individual member to identify himself far more closely with them than was later the case.

The borderline between identification with an institution and alienation from it is as vague and fluctuating as that between 'culture' and 'civilization' or 'community' (*Gemeinschaft*) and 'society' (*Gesellschaft*). Even institutions with which the individual is still able to identify himself contain alienating features, and even the most soulless institutions came into existence to meet a real psychological need. Typologically the same phenomenon continually recurs. The most utilitarian civilization is capable of enriching mental life, and the loftiest culture contains trends leading to formalization, and thus depersonalization and neutralization, of the cultural picture. Similarly, 'social' forms of organization are at work in every form of community, just as something of the original idea of community survives even in the most impersonal forms of social organization. It is nevertheless sensible and useful to distinguish between living and fossilized cultural products, between spontaneous expressions of the human spirit and practically oriented attitudes, between sense of community and social cooperation. For these phenomena mingle with and are relative to each other, and at times one or other of them gains the upper hand, with the result that a period such as that of mannerism can legitimately be described as a period of alienation and the institutionalization of social forms *par excellence*.

It has always been felt that it is in connection with institutions that depersonalization and dehumanization make themselves felt in their most sensitive and wounding way. When one has to adapt oneself to the rules of an institution, one ceases to be oneself, an individual, a person, one is deprived of one's human identity, and often also of one's human dignity. The first thing to be sacrificed to an institution is spontaneity, not merely in those who administer it, but also in most of those who come into contact with it from the outside. It leads a life of its own, as if driven by an internal mechanism. Every mannerist style, and every mannerist vision of life, either bears marks of this deadening of spontaneity and mechanization of reactions, or shows signs of struggle against it by the development of exaggerated forms of individualism, sensibility, and arbitrariness. Simultaneously with their neglect of the individual and the individual case and their loss of direct relationship with concrete actuality, institutions lead to an inherently dangerous but in practice often very useful formalism. Mannerism adopts a similar formalism alienated from reality, but has to pay for the much smaller advantages of ready-made formulas with the much greater disadvantages involved in formalization of artistic expression.

Institutions change very slowly; inertia and inflexibility are among their most characteristic features. They generally outlive their original aim, survive after the conditions which called them into being have completely changed, and their continued existence often harms instead of helping their original cause. There is no cultural formation that more strikingly and tangibly illustrates the process by which a creation of the human spirit assumes independence and becomes a self-governing automaton. In relation to it, whether he is confronted by it in the form of state, church, justice, the economy, society, etc., the individual feels like a puppet moved by invisible and anonymous guiding strings without having the feeling that they are in good hands. Not only does the institution become more and more resourceless and paralyzed in relation to the increasingly complex and heterogeneous reality with which it is faced, but it outgrows its own creators and administrators. Irresistibly and sluggishly it goes on its own uncanny way. But the worst thing about it is its transformation of means into ends, a phenomenon well known to anyone familiar with institutions dating from earlier times in history. Its real and original purpose is neglected and retreats into the background, until administration seems to be carried out for the benefit of the administrators and the office seems to be there for the benefit of the official who sits in it. Exactly the same substitution of means for ends is to be seen in mannerist art. The lack of any directly evident functionalism of detail, the apparently senseless and purposeless play with purely decorative forms, the demonstrative virtuosity in the rendering of the human figure, its postures and movements, the absence of relationship between these forms and the spiritual content of the work, the emphasis laid on individual elements in its structure, e.g., in the treatment of space and the organization of the picture plane or of color and light values, are all examples of the lack of relation between means and ends that is so characteristic of institutions and the way of thinking brought about by them. The question of how far this correspondence depends on direct or indirect influence, and the extent to which mere equivocation may be at the back of it, cannot be answered out of hand; the hazards of making such sweeping transferences from one order of phenomena to another suggest caution, however.

The greatest danger with which institutions are faced is that of bureaucratization, that is to say, lies in the control exercised by officials who do not always use it to the best purpose. Every public institution inclines naturally towards bureaucracy, and all bureaucracies are inclined to misuse their powers. In the age of mannerism, when so many new institutions came into being and bureaucracy in our sense of the word was a new phenomenon, men must have suffered very severely under their pressure. Complaint at the progressive bureaucratization still re-echoes in the Shakespearean phrase 'the insolence of office,' though one has to wait for Franz Kafka for a picture of the full horror of what a bureaucratized world might be. Though Shakespeare and his contemporaries knew nothing of the mythical proportions to be assumed by bureaucracy and officials, courts and authorities in the works of Kafka, that most unmistakable modern counterpart of a mannerist, they were certainly on the way to visualizing the great image in which he sees human life as subject to the preposterous requirements and inscrutable regulations of an unapproachable officialdom, involving the absurdest formalities, following them up through endless and senseless official channels, all the time remaining in complete perplexity about which course of action might harm and which might help. The image culminates in the idea of total alienation in the jungle of institutions, in which private and personal life is overshadowed, obscured, paralyzed, or crushed by unknown, nameless or inadequately named powers that appear in the most absurd disguise.

The age of mannerism was the first to be threatened by a rising tide of institutionalization similar to our own. It struggled against it, but scored only minor successes in stemming it, and that only in the most personal creations of art, literature, philosophy, and science. Even in fields in which the strongest resistance was put up, in Protestantism, it was swept away by the prevailing trend. For, though there was nothing to which Protestantism was more violently opposed than to the depersonalization and institutionalization of religion, the destiny and tragedy of the age lay in the fact that it itself became an instrument of materialization and alienation.

That the Reformation ended by being totally transformed into the reformed churches there can be no doubt. The early history of the movement, and the question of what the church meant in the eyes of the young Luther, are more controversial, however. Luther's well-known shift towards conservatism during and after the Peasants' War, and the inconsistency of his pronouncements about the meaning and function of the church, incline one to the assumption that he moved gradually to the right in this matter too. As has already been mentioned, however, a different view is taken, among others by Ernst Troeltsch, who maintains that Luther, in spite of his religious individualism, his sympathy with lay religion, and his conviction of the subjectivity of the road to salvation, never displayed the slightest inclination towards sectarianism and regarded the community of the church as the only real and true form of religion. Troeltsch argues that, for all the subjectivity and spirituality of his conception of the church, his aspiration was always for an objective, supra-individual institution resting on supernatural foundations. Other scholars still maintain that the institutionalization of Protestantism was a gradual process, and many of them regard its transformation into a system of state churches as a disastrous development which had as little basis in Luther's beginnings as had his final attitude towards the peasants. In his sermon *de virtute excommunicationis* (1518), for instance, he specifically states that the church is no mere institution, but the community of all the faithful; and Karl Holl regards his 'invisible church,' in spite of the various meanings that came to be associated with the term, as having meant the exact opposite of the Catholic church. Troeltsch himself was ultimately forced to admit that 'the objectivity of the institution increasingly prevailed over the original subjectivity' of Luther's conception. But to show that Protestantism shared the historical destiny of institutionalization with the other spiritual movements of the age it is not necessary to appeal to the original meaning of Luther's 'invisible church,' or his much less problematic 'direct filial relationship to God.' The fact that Luther's chief aim, and the mainspring of the Reformation, was the liberation of Christianity from the rigid mechanism of the Roman church is indisputable and not in need of any special proof. In any case, mere quotations do not get one very far in this respect. Luther's statements in relation to the church, as in so many other respects, are contradictory; he speaks now for it and now against it, and often what he says is ambiguous. In this he reflects not only his own doubt-tormented mind, but also his whole generation which, like him, thought in antitheses and was torn by ambivalent impulses.

Moreover, the process of institutionalization and the transition from liberty to coercion that Protestantism underwent corresponded exactly to that by which mannerism, rooted in opposition to the classicism of the High Renaissance, degenerated into dogmatic academicism, or that by which the place of the guilds, from whose ties the artists gradually liberated themselves, was taken by academies which were just as narrow-minded.

A word remains to be said about the closeness of the connection between ideology and alienation. Human thinking has been ideologically determined ever since it represented antagonistic class interests. Apart from serving the purpose of philosophical or scientific orientation, it simultaneously fulfilled the more or less concealed function of serving the economic and social interests of the ruling classes. But, to the extent that men thought and acted in a fashion the motivation of which remained unknown and inscrutable to them, they became alienated from themselves. They did not know what they did, and did not do what they consciously would have liked to have done. But never was ideology more obscured, and alienation consequently deeper, than at the time of the crisis of the

Renaissance, the origins of modern capitalism, the religious struggles of
Protestantism, and the transition from feudalism to centrally administered
national states. Never were men less aware of what lay behind their
efforts and actions than the Protestants, who believed themselves to be
battling solely for freedom of conscience, the artists, who believed themselves to be struggling to liberate themselves from the guilds solely in
the name of free and unfettered creativity, or the thinkers and scientists,
who believed their war on dogma and superstition to be based purely on
rational grounds. They did not know that their aims, though unobjec-
tionable in themselves, were the ideological cloak for economic interests
and social aspirations. However, the true face of the ideals for which they
fought was finally revealed. The liberation of the economy chiefly served
the interests of the employers, and to them it of course represented
progress. The Reformation led to the establishment of churches as intolerant as the old. The successful artists barricaded themselves in their
academies instead of the old guilds, and science produced its own
shackles and blinkers, for it was no more free of prejudices than were the
doctrines of the church or of scholasticism.

5. Art in an Alienated World

Mannerism is not so much a symptom and product of alienation, that
is to say, an art that has become soulless, extroverted, and shallow, as
an expression of the unrest, anxiety, and bewilderment generated by the
process of alienation of the individual from society and the reification of
the whole cultural process. The alienation of the individual does not in
this case exclude the creation of true works of art; on the contrary, it
leads to the most profoundly self-revelatory creations. The sense of alienation is the artists' raw material, not a formal element in his work. He
expresses his concern, dismay, and despair at a world in which the spirit
of alienation, depersonalization, and soullessness prevail, but his work, as
an expression of protest against this world or a way of escape from it,
in the artistic respect need bear no marks of alienation. This of course
does not mean that a large number of works did not simultaneously appear
which were a direct manifestation of alienation, that is to say, themselves
were soulless, impersonal, conventional, mannered, and not merely
mannerist.

One of the contradictory features of mannerism is that it not only
represents a struggle against formalism and what might be called 'fetishism' in art, but is also itself a precious and fetishistic form of art that
alienates itself from the creativity of the individual. Of particular significance in this respect is the circumstance that these conflicting principles,
this polarity and tension, are not only characteristic of the style as a whole,

that is to say, that the signs of stylistic conflict are not only present in different groups of works, different trends, schools, or artists, but also often appear in one and the same work. The greatest, the most vital, the spiritually most significant mannerist works often include devices used with a conventionality and thoughtlessness that are otherwise rarely to be found even in works of the second and third rank. It is precisely this that makes it so difficult to define the stylistic concept and qualitative character of mannerism, which was a desperate attempt to preserve life from alienation and soullessness, mechanization and schematization, but itself partially succumbed to soullessness and materialization.

Its attempt to stem the growing flood of alienation in spite of its own vulnerability, its struggle against the reification and schematization of life, had no real continuation in western culture. With the Counter-Reformation and the baroque it began fading away; the classicism of the seventeenth and eighteenth centuries, the rationalism of the Age of Enlightenment and the scientific outlook of the nineteenth century, led finally to its extinction. The Romantic movement made the embers glow again, but it remained an episode, though the traces it left behind are ineradicable. The consequences of the present revival of mannerism are not foreseeable, but it again seems to be no more than a kind of romanticism.

Whether mannerism presents itself as a positive or negative reaction to alienation, its connection with the social process is unmistakable. In examining its historical and sociological origins it is impossible not to be struck by the parallelism between the loss of personality suffered by the manual worker as a consequence of the mechanization of production and that of the intellectual worker as a consequence of specialization on the one hand, and on the other of the sense of estrangement and loss of self, the doubt about the reality and identity of the self, that are among the principal themes of the literature of the age. Shakespeare's characters, to quote the best known and most striking example, feel lost in this respect; they are continually wondering what they are, whether they really are what they seem to be, and they talk continually of their sense of going about in changed, distorted, unreal form. In most of the plays of which they are the heroes, it is the feeling that they have grown false and untrue to themselves that creates the dramatic crisis, and they set themselves the task of realizing their true nature. 'I am not what I am,' says Iago, and Viola says the same of herself in *Twelfth Night*. 'My Lord is not my Lord,' Desdemona says of Othello, and 'Thou art not thyself,' is the phrase round which the whole drama of *Measure for Measure* seems to revolve. 'This she? . . . No . . . If beauty have soul, this not she. . . . This is, and is not Cressida,' says Troilus; and, after succumbing to Cleopatra's spell, Antony no longer knows himself, and likens himself

to a cloud continually changing in shape. From this idea of man's prob-
lematical identity, his failure to appear what he is, partly because he
must not and partly because he dare not be what he should be, Shakespeare, Cervantes, Calderón, and most of the writers of the age, developed
the theme that it was his nature and destiny to conceal and disguise
himself, to be always playing a part, hiding behind a fictitious identity,
living an illusion, and that it was part of the tragi-comedy of his life that
there might be spectators who were amused at, or even actually
took malicious pleasure in, watching him play his role in dreadful earnest.

Man himself could not tell what part of him was true and real and
what was illusion and self-deception. The core of Shakespearean and the
whole of modern tragedy is the process of man's achieving clarity about
himself, and the moral value of the tragic self-interrogation lies in the
remorselessness with which illusion is shattered and the hero's real nature
is revealed, above all to himself. The reward of the great moment of the
fulfillment of tragic destiny is self-consciousness and self-realization; so
long as these are not attained, or even aspired to, man remains in doubt
about his own nature and the world he lives in. 'Thou art not certain'
says the Duke in *Measure for Measure* and 'nothing that is so, is so' says
the fool in *Twelfth Night,* and these two phrases express the sense of life
of the whole age. Everything is uncertain, questionable, different from
what it seems, and all certitude and bedrock has to be fought for.

Like the novel of the nineteenth century, *Don Quixote,* the novel of
mannerism *par excellence,* the greatest novel of the age and to an extent
the unattained ideal of all subsequent novel writing, is a novel of illusion,
a quality characteristic of the whole literature of the age. *Desengaño*
is not, as is generally assumed, the dominant note only of Spanish
literature, of the works of Cervantes, Góngora, Gracián, and Calderón,
but is also that of Tasso and Marino, John Donne and, broadly speaking,
Shakespeare too. Don Quixote, Segismondo, Faustus, Hamlet, and Troilus
are all ultimately disillusioned, as if on awakening from a dream, facing
an alien and alienated world, a tremendous, disastrous incongruity. The
world, however evil it might otherwise have been, had once seemed
uniform and in harmony with itself and with man, but now it had been
irretrievably split—into a world of illusion and another of dreadful reality.
The generation of mannerism that underwent this bewildering and shattering experience hit on one of the greatest literary themes of all time.

All that Max Weber understands by 'disenchantment,' or everything
that can be connected with it, that is to say, the progressive rationalization
of life, the elimination of magic, mysticism, and metaphysics from the
explanation of natural phenomena, the freeing of the economy and society
from the bonds of tradition, and in particular the relentless domination
of empiricism, can be regarded as a source of alienation. The deep dis-

illusion and dismay at the outcome of the advances in the natural sciences felt at the end of the nineteenth century by many who deplored their exclusively quantitative criteria and their materialism, in spite of the pride felt in their achievements, is a reminder of the shock that must have been caused at the outset of the new age by the beginnings of modern science. Men were alarmed instead of reassured at finding themselves in a disenchanted world, deprived of witches and wizards and spirits, both good and bad. The world had grown empty and barren, and once more the result was a sense of solitude, not a sense of release. There were no more devils to be afraid of, but also there were no more angels and saints to come to man's aid. The desolate, empty space into which Protestantism turned the thickly-populated heavens—the infinite, empty space that still terrified Pascal—yawned everywhere.

One of the most moving things about the adventures and mishaps of Don Quixote, who talks constantly of the enchantments, snares, and deceptions prepared for him by wizards and sorcerers, is that they take place in a completely disenchanted, sober, and sceptical world, in which there are no more sorcerers and no one is left who still believes in them. His monomania and spiritual isolation—the main theme of this novel of alienation—are unaffected by the fact that the arch-realist Sancho Panza ends by becoming infected with his master's madness and begins imagining things himself; Don Quixote remains as mad and solitary as ever. But what gives the novel its universal perspective is the fact that in this disenchanted, sober, and rational world the chivalry and valor which were once men's highest ideal have degenerated into mere folly and madness. So we see the hero of the novel, the personification of that chivalry and valor, now as a sheer madman, now as the symbol of courage and innocence.

᾽ From whatever angle such a figure is looked at, like most of the great figures of mannerist literature it preserves its enigmatic character. Not only is it full of paradoxes, not only does it move on different planes of reality, but also it keeps the reader in suspense and guards its secret even more jealously than other artistic figures. This preservation of mystery, which is one of the fundamental characteristics of mannerist art, appears most strikingly in the genre in which alienation presents itself in its most unmistakable form—in portraiture. The cool, rigid, glassy expressions, the lifeless, 'armor-like' masks of the portraits of Bronzino, Salviati, or Coello, the unconcern with which character is treated in contrast to the care lavished on the incidentals, the architecture, costume, weapons, or jewels, demonstrates a complete withdrawal from the world. The mind, the character is there, but it is concealed behind a mask of indifference. The nerves vibrate, the affects are alive, but they scorn to reveal themselves; nobody must know what goes on behind the mask.

Feeling alienated in this world, men are not resigned to remaining so; they wish to have an alienating and startling effect on others. Therefore the artist not only chooses strange and startling subjects, but also tries to render the most ordinary things in a startling way. The purpose is not merely to surprise and unsettle, but also to state that it is impossible to feel at home among the things of this world or make friends with them.

30. Hsu Min

Feudalism and *The Dream of the Red Chamber*

HSU MIN is a literary critic for the *Peking Review*, published in the People's Republic of China. His essay on a classic Chinese novel appeared in Peking in 1963.

ON New Year's Eve of 1763, the twenty-seventh year of the reign of the Emperor Chien Lung (or, according to a rival view, in 1764), the great Chinese writer Tsao Hsueh-chin died in a mountain village in the western suburbs of Peking. Outside the house the north wind howled as his bereaved and lonely wife wept at his bedside; on his table lay a confused heap of papers—the unfinished manuscript of his now world-famous novel *The Dream of the Red Chamber*. Sick with grief at the early death of his only son, Tsao Hsueh-chin died before reaching his fiftieth year.

This year the bicentenary of his death is being commemorated. The Ministry of Culture, the All-China Federation of Literary and Art Circles, the Union of Chinese Writers and the Palace Museum of Peking have combined to organize a major exhibition in tribute to him and his immortal achievement. The many valuable exhibits and documents now on display in the Palace Museum give one a deeper understanding of the book and its author; they tell of the writer's family and life and describe the era in which the book was written.

The Theme of the Novel

The Dream of the Red Chamber is a great work of critical realism. Through its account of the grandeur and fall of the four big families of the feudal nobility closely linked through marriage—the Chias, the Shihs, the Hsuehs and the Wangs—it incisively reveals the rottenness of a declining feudal society rent by contradictions. The heart of the story is the tragic love in this environment between Chia Pao-yu and the frail Lin

415

Tai-yu, a tragedy of their resistance to the feudal code of behavior, and of their yearning for personal liberation and their search for freedom.

The author portrays the "courtly, rich and noble" Jung and Ning Mansions of the Chia family, showing how, on the surface, high and humble each has his place and there is a strict observance of status; how these aristocrats talk fulsomely about "loyalty to the Emperor" and "honoring Confucius," about official careers and affairs of government; model their speech on ancient classics and use gestures of the utmost politeness. The real doings of these households, however, are screened by a veil of sentimental and kindly feudal morality. In actual fact, these aristocrats are venal and greedy; they twist the laws to their own ends; they have no high ideals and are lacking in ability. Hypocritical tricksters, they struggle for power and profit; both men and women are unbridled in their debauchery. The astonishing grandeur, luxury and extravagance of the feudal nobles of these mighty households depend entirely on ruthless exploitation of the peasantry through land rents, on usury at high interest and on the slavery of their domestics. In these households each day is filled with the bitter tears of the enslaved, the struggles of the oppressed and the reprisals of the oppressors caught up in a web of antagonisms.

Although every year, as the novel describes, "the floods and droughts are bad and the country is infested with bandits," the Jung and Ning households keep up their gross extravagance. In the words of Granny Liu, one of the characters in the novel, the cost of one of their meals would be "enough to feed one of us farmers for a year!" Having squeezed every last drop of sweat and blood out of their peasants, they finally resort to pawning and selling off their property in a desperate attempt to maintain their wealthy display. In the struggle for power within the ruling class, the Chia family suffers a mortal blow—its property is confiscated by an imperial decree. From then it slides down the road to ruin. Such a story of splendor and decline was no isolated phenomenon among the eminent families of the feudal nobility; it is a picture in miniature of the contradictions which rent Chinese feudal society during the "prosperous reign of Yung Cheng and Chien Lung" in the first half of the eighteenth century.

A Work of Great Artistry

An outstanding genius, Tsao Hsueh-chin created several hundred characters, of whom over four hundred have names and about a hundred play active roles. They include old gentlemen, young masters, elderly and young ladies and a multitude of servant girls. . . . Varied according to their social status and different backgrounds, and with their individual personalities freshly drawn, this host of characters come to life on his pages. Writing with deep emotion, the author created in the hero and heroine of the novel, Chia Pao-yu and Lin Tai-yu, two rebellious-minded young people. Through Pao-yu the author gives expression to many of his own ideals. In the eyes of the guardians of feudal morality Pao-yu is "perverse" in his thoughts and improper in his behavior. He bitterly ridicules as "place-seekers" those who pursue official advancement; he attacks the imperial examination system as a complete misuse of talent and makes fun of Confucianist hypocrisy. The inequalities between men and women and between master and servant rouse his bitter indignation and he shows his deep abhorrence of the feudal marriage system. In these respects Lin Tai-yu, the heroine, shares his aspirations and tastes.

The love between these two developed on the basis of a common opposition to feudal ideas, but it was wrecked by the upholders of feudalism and ended in tragedy. With the story of their love as the unifying theme and tracing the growth of their affection for each other, the author unfolds before the reader a richly varied picture of an age. In exposing this hateful environment he turns the spotlight of his criticism onto the statutes and codes of feudal society, its economic life, its culture and education and its morality in general, uttering a great cry for emancipation of the individual and for freedom. But as the urban classes at that time were still weak and the world outlook reflecting their ideology was still in its rudimentary stage, Tsao Hsueh-chin's criticism of feudal society was spontaneous and far from thoroughgoing. Moreover, as the author was born in a family of the feudal nobility, he was intricately linked in many ways in his thoughts and feelings with feudal society, and continued to hanker after his memories of former splendor. These realities and unresolved conflicts resulted in the elements of nihilism and pessimism in his work and a belief in predestination. These negative elements however, are only a minor part of the book; the powerful anti-feudal aspect holds the leading place.

There are many masterpieces in the history of Chinese literature which reveal the darkness of feudalism, but none of them expose that system so penetratingly, or are so well constructed on so great a scale, or have such compelling artistic power as *The Dream of the Red Chamber*.

Tsao Hsueh-chin died after completing the first eighty chapters of his masterpiece. The last forty were added by Kao Ngo on the basis of the fragmentary and incomplete drafts left by Tsao Hsueh-chin. Although these latter chapters have many ideological and artistic shortcomings, they still manage to reach a great tragic ending by following some of the clues in the first eighty chapters. It is not easy for readers to tell that the book was written by two authors.

After the death of Tsao Hsueh-chin *The Dream of the Red Chamber* was circulated in hand-written versions among a small number of readers, and for quite a long time very little was known about the life of its author.

But with the increasing popularity of the book and its publication in print, scholars have increased and deepened their researches so that although it is still very incomplete, the material now available about Tsao Hsueh-chin's life and thought is sufficient to enable some definite conclusions to be drawn about his family and his life.

The Author's Family Background

The Palace Museum exhibition includes a recently discovered copy of the *Tsao Clan Ancestral Register* which proves that Tsao Hsueh-chin's family came originally from Fengjun County in Hopei Province and that the founder of the clan had played a distinguished role in the founding of the Ming Dynasty. His descendants later moved to Northeast China linking their fortunes with those of the Manchu noble house which later became the next, Ching, dynasty of China. In recognition of the military achievements of the Tsao family, the Manchu nobles allowed them to adopt the Manchu nationality and assigned them to the Main White Banner of the army composed of Manchus of Han descent. The exhibition also contains patents of nobility and imperial documents relating to the Tsao clan which show that they had been "a great family of a century's standing."

The office in charge of the Chiang-ning (present-day Nanking) Silk Textile Factories was founded at the beginning of the Ching Dynasty. The nominal responsibility of the commissioner of this office was to superintend the manufacture of silk textiles for use in the imperial palace, but he was in fact an agent of the Ching emperor and his principal task was to woo the support of the people south of the Yangtse River, investigate the local situation and keep the government informed on it, and break up the local people's resistance movement against Ching rule. This post was held in succession by Tsao Hsueh-chin's great-grandfather Tsao Hsi, his grandfather Tsao Yin, his uncle Tsao Yung and his father Tsao Fu, and between them they occupied it for fifty-eight years. The "Imperial Rescript" in which the emperor Kang Hsi ordered mounted messengers to travel day and night with medicine for Tsao Yin and the picture of the Imperial Residency at the Bureau of the Silk Textile Factories shown in the exhibition, illustrate the close relations which existed between the emperor Kang Hsi and the Tsao clan. On four of the six occasions on which Kang Hsi made an imperial tour of the south while the Tsao family held that office, he made the Bureau of the Silk Textile Factories his "temporary palace."

Tsao Hsueh-chin's grandfather Tsao Yin was a high official who was also a connoisseur of the arts. He cultivated the acquaintance of noted scholars of the day and was himself a man of broad and deep learning and an excellent writer of both prose and verse. His father and uncle, too, were learned *literati*-officials at the time. Such was the family into which Tsao Hsueh-chin was born in 1715 (the 54th year of Kang Hsi), and such was the highly cultured atmosphere in which he was brought up.

When Hsueh-chin was eight the emperor Yung Cheng came to the throne. Yung Cheng did not gain the throne through any wish of his father Kang Hsi, who hated him, but seized it with great ruthlessness in a palace coup. After his accession, Kang Hsi's former intimates, who included the Tsao family, became the objects of a special attack. The imperial edict ordering the sequestration of Tsao Fu's property is on display; thus in 1728 (the sixth year of Yung Cheng), when Hsueh-chin was thirteen, his father lost his official post and most of the family's possessions were confiscated. It seems that about this time the Tsaos moved from Nanking up to Peking.

Some years later the family suffered an even more serious blow and from then on was completely ruined. Finding no way to make a living inside Peking, Hsueh-chin moved to a part of the western suburbs near the Western Hills and lived in a village cottage. With his wife and son he lived in dire poverty, "the whole family eating gruel and often buying on credit." Among those who kept up friendship and exchanged verses with him were his close friends the brothers Tun Min and Tun Cheng. Although he was reduced to utter poverty, his contempt for his times and his rugged independence restrained him from ever begging for help from the feudal nobility. With this great change in his life he came to see more clearly the contradictions and crimes of feudal society and his thinking attained a new depth of understanding. It was probably at the age of thirty or so that he began in a spirit of anger to write *The Dream of the Red Chamber*, drawing on his widely varied experience of life. It took him ten years to produce the first eighty chapters. He rewrote them five times. As he said himself, "every word seems to be written in blood: ten years strenuous labor were no light matter."

The Age in Which the Novel Was Written

Many documents in the exhibition show that Tsao Hsueh-chin wrote his masterpiece in a time of the strictest literary controls and in an atmosphere of rampant terror. Taking over the government from the Ming Dynasty, which had been of Han nationality, the Manchu founders of the Ching had encountered vigorous resistance from the Hans. The Ching rulers were determined to stifle all anti-Ching thought and for this purpose used exceptionally harsh methods including large-scale literary persecutions. If the writings of a dead man were found to hold the slightest hint of nostalgia for the Ming or to contain a phrase or even a single word which could be regarded as satirizing the Ching, this was enough for his coffin to be broken open, his corpse mutilated and his remaining household exterminated. If such "errors" were discovered in a live writer he was done to death without mercy and his family butchered to a man. Seeing at the exhibition the extant files of many cases of such huge literary persecutions, one can easily understand the agonized feelings which made Hsueh-chin use so many oblique references and hidden allegories in his novel when writing of forbidden things.

While it carried out these literary inquisitions, the Ching court also used the imperial examination system to keep the intellectuals under tight control. The exhibition includes answer papers as well as "cribs" used for cheating during the examinations—shirts covered with usable "quotes" from the classics and microscopically written books which could be concealed in a shoe. All these show that while the Ching rulers made use of the exams to induce conscientious scholars to bury their heads in idiotic "eight-legged essays" and put aside any anti-Ching thoughts, this system was in fact downright corrupt. In *The Dream of the Red Chamber* Tsao Hsueh-chin attacks it through these thoughts of the hero Pao-yu: "The so-called eight-legged essays have always been heartily detested; they are not the original works of the sages, so how can they expound the sages' profound wisdom? They are nothing but a ladder to fame and fortune." To speak up so militantly in such an environment of terror was an act of courage for which Tsao Hsueh-chin deserves to be honored.

During the lifetime of Tsao Hsueh-chin the Ching empire went through an economic revival. The textile industry, commerce, and foreign trade flourished. But the nobility, the high officials, the big landowners and the leading merchants squeezed vast quantities of wealth from the people to live in the greatest luxury. This led to the polarization of the social economy; the rich got richer and the poor poorer; and, as a result, class antagonism aggravated. When reduced to destitution, the peasants would either be driven as refugees to some other part of the country, or be forced to sell their children, while some desperate men took the course of armed resistance. The many land leases in the exhibition show by what cruel methods the debauched and extravagant life of the nobility was maintained during the Yung Cheng and Chien Lung periods. The account of the life of the four big clans in the novel (the Chia, Wang, Shih and Hsueh families) is a graphic example of what this meant. The sight of the deeds in which the peasants signed away their own children recalls the fate of the many maids of the Chia family, such as Yuan-yang, Ching-wen, Chin-chuan and Ssu-chi as they were brought into the Jungkuo Mansion. The piles of high-interest loan receipts displayed are evidence of the criminal way in which the feudal nobility exploited the people. The four big families in the novel are just such usurious moneylenders. Also on display are bethrothal documents reeking of feudal superstition which denies the young people any freedom of choice. The lucky youngsters of today's China who see them have difficulty in understanding what they are; but in the novel the feudal marriage system destroyed the happy lives of the hero and heroine.

The Dream of the Red Chamber gave such a telling exposure of the corruption of the landowning nobility and was so deeply moving an indictment of their crimes that, as its popularity increased, they slandered it as a "scurrilous book," as an "obscene novel" and as "harmful to public morality"; and even had it officially banned and burnt.

A Focus of Great Interest

The exhibition contains many manuscript and printed editions of the novel. The earliest manuscript editions were circulated among a very small number of readers, but in 1791–92 its popularity led Cheng Wei-yuan and Kao Ngo to supplement the text, bringing it up to 120 chapters, and publish it in woodblock and moveable type printed editions. Between the publication of Cheng and Kao's version to the liberation of China many different editions and sequels came out, as well as vast numbers of commentaries and annotations, romances, dramas, poems, illustrations and pictures and sculptures based on the book. The number of translations in foreign languages is increasing. With the passage of years the influence of the novel is growing ever greater.

A colossal number of works have been written in China on *The Dream of the Red Chamber*. But the investigations of scholars of the feudal classes in the past were little more than elaborate guessing games concerning the elucidation of obscure passages and literary references; they were unable to appreciate fully the true, great value of this work. Beginning with the May 4th Movement of 1919, a number of bourgeois scholars approached the problems of the exegesis of the novel and its origins, and of the life and background of its author. They unearthed many facts about the author's life and proved that the last forty chapters were an addition, with many facts pointing to Kao Ngo as their author. They also found that Tsao Hsueh-chin died leaving one or two of the first eighty chapters unfinished and that there had originally been some incomplete versions of some of the subsequent chapters written by Tsao Hsueh-chin. These scholars, with Hu Shih as their representative, made the mistake, however, of regarding the novel as simply an autobiographical novel, as the author's "confessions of his own sufferings in love," and as a naturalistic record of the author's personal experience in life, since, as they said, Tsao Hsueh-chin wrote the book for the mere purpose of "lamenting his own misfortune." Basing their studies on pragmatism and an idealistic viewpoint, they were blind to the historical background of the novel and completely negated its anti-feudal substance. And this led to many subjective and unfounded judgments and forced and far-fetched conclusions. Whereas the author treated life in all its great complexity as an organic whole they saw the novel as so many isolated, unrelated phenomena and thus veiled the great masterpiece in a cloak of mysticism.

After liberation, China's scholars, following the guidance of Marxism-Leninism, criticized the academic thinking of the bourgeois scholars, as represented by Hu Shih, in the study of *The Dream of the Red Chamber*. In their studies and discussions, they have made a scientific investigation of the age in which the novel was written. While admitting that the novel was essentially based on the author's own experiences they pointed out that it is by no means an autobiographical novel, nor is it a merely naturalistic account of what actually happened in the real life of the author. *The Dream of the Red Chamber* is rather a superb generalization of the typical social phenomena of the time. In it, the author has not only laid bare the ugliness and corruption of the feudal society, but also created a number of ideal, new characters capable of rousing in readers' minds a deep yearning for a more beautiful life. These studies and discussions have succeeded in giving rise to a clear view of the real value of this work and its great anti-feudal significance.

At present, fresh research and critical discussion are still being carried on in the spirit of "letting a hundred schools of thought contend." Several new collated editions have been published and photographic reprints of a number of manuscript editions which had been regarded in the past as "private editions" have reached a wide public.

The proletariat has proved that it is the only class that can critically inherit all that is best in the culture of mankind. Far beyond Tsao Hsueh-chin's fondest dreams, a new society has arisen which can truly appreciate his work.

31. Bertolt Brecht

On Non-Objective Painting

For a biographical note on BERTOLT BRECHT, see p. 226. "On Non-Objective Painting" is taken from Brecht's Notebooks (1935–39), and has been published in Volume II of *Schriften zur Literatur und Kunst*.

I SEE that you have removed the motifs from your paintings. No recognizable objects appear there anymore. You reproduce the sweeping curve of a chair—not the chair; the red of the sky, not the burning house. You reproduce the combination of lines and colors, not the combination of things. I must say that I wonder about it, and especially because you say that you are Communists, going out to reconstruct a world which is not habitable. If you were not Communists but subject spirits of the ruling classes, I would not wonder about your painting. It would seem to me then not inappropriate, even logical. Because things as they now are (people are among them, too) arouse for the most part feelings of repugnance—mixed with thoughts that criticism applies to them which would have them other than they are. Painting, reproducing them as recognizable, would fall into this conflict of feelings and thoughts; and if you were subject spirits of the Establishment, it would be cunning of you to make things unrecognizable, since it is things after all which are vexing, and since your patrons would be blamed for it. If you were subject spirits of the Establishment, you would do well to fulfill the wish of your patrons by representations rather opaque, general, uncommitted. It is the ruling classes who enjoy hearing such expressions as: "One must enjoy one's work, irrespective of what it accomplishes, of how it is to be done, or why": or: "One can enjoy a forest, even if one doesn't own it." It is only those who are ruled who cannot enjoy themselves even in the most beautiful landscapes, if, as road workers, they have to pound stones into it—and among whom such strong emotions as love are lost if their living conditions are too bad. As painters and subject spirits of the

423

Establishment, you could proclaim that the most beautiful and important perceptions are composed of lines and colors (so that anyone can enjoy them, even the most costly things, since lines and colors can be obtained *gratis*). And as court painters, you could drag all objects out of the world of perception, everything that is of value, all needs, anything substantial. You would require as painters for the ruling classes no specific perceptions, like anger in the face of injustice, or desire for certain things which are wanting, no perceptions bound to knowledge which call up other perceptions of a changing world—but just quite general, vague, unidentifiable perceptions, available to everyone, to the thieves and to their victims, to the oppressors and to the oppressed. You paint, for example, an indeterminate red; and some cry at the sight of this indeterminate red because they think of a rose, and others, because they think of a child lacerated by bombs and streaming with blood. Your task is then completed: you have composed a perceptual object of lines and colors. It is clear that motifs, recognizable objects in painting, must, in our world of class conflict, redeem the most diverse perceptions. If the profiteer laughs, the man from whom he made the profit cries. The poor man who lacks a kitchen chair does not lack color and form. The wealthy man who has a beautiful old chair does not regard it as something to sit on, but as form and color. We Communists see things differently than do the profiteers and their lackeys. The difference in our seeing validates things; it is concerned with things not with eyes. If we wish to teach that things should be seen differently, we must teach it to the things. And we want not only that things should simply be seen "differently," but that they should be seen in a certain way; not just differently from every other way, but correctly—that is, as fits the thing. We want to master things in politics and in art; we do not wish simply to "master." Assume that someone comes up and says, "I am mastering." Would not everyone ask, "What?" I hear you say: "With our tubes of oils and our pencils, we can only reproduce the colors and lines of the things, nothing more." This sounds as if you were modest men, honest men, without pretenses. But it sounds better than it is. A thousand examples prove that one can say more about things with tubes of oils and pencils, that one can communicate and expound more than simple solids with lines and colors. Breughel, too, had only tubes of oil and pencils; he, too, reproduced the colors and lines of things—but not only that. The perceptual objects which he composes emerge from his relations to the objects which he reproduces; it is specific objects of perception which may alter the relation of the viewer of his paintings to the objects represented in them. Nor should you say: "There is much good in art which is not understood in its own time." It doesn't follow from this that something must be good *if* it is not understood in its own time. You would do better to show in your paintings how man in our times has been a wolf to other men, and to say then: "This will not be bought in our time." Because only the wolves have money to buy paintings in our times. But it will not always be this way; and our paintings will contribute to seeing that it will not be.

32. George Orwell

Politics and the English Language

GEORGE ORWELL, pen-name of Eric Blair (1903–50), novelist and important essayist of the British Left. Severely wounded in the Spanish Civil War, his *Homage to Catalonia* (1938) remains the most telling account of that war. Other essays and reporting include *The Road to Wigan Pier* (1937) and *Shooting an Elephant* (1950); and in fiction, *Animal Farm* (1946) and *Nineteen Eighty-Four* (1949). "Politics and the English Language" first appeared in 1946, in *Horizon*.

MOST people who bother with the matter at all would admit that the English language is in a bad way, but it is generally assumed that we cannot by conscious action do anything about it. Our civilization is decadent and our language—so the argument runs—must inevitably share in the general collapse. It follows that any struggle against the abuse of language is a sentimental archaism, like preferring candles to electric light or hansom cabs to aeroplanes. Underneath this lies the half-conscious belief that language is a natural growth and not an instrument which we shape for our own purposes.

Now, it is clear that the decline of a language must ultimately have political and economic causes: it is not due simply to the bad influence of this or that individual writer. But an effect can become a cause, reinforcing the original cause and producing the same effect in an intensified form, and so on indefinitely. A man may take to drink because he feels himself to be a failure, and then fail all the more completely because he drinks. It is rather the same thing that is happening to the English language. It becomes ugly and inaccurate because our thoughts are foolish, but the slovenliness of our language makes it easier for us to have foolish thoughts. The point is that the process is reversible. Modern English, especially written English, is full of bad habits which spread by imitation and which can be avoided if one is willing to take the necessary trouble. If one gets rid of these habits one can think more clearly, and to think clearly is a necessary first step towards political regeneration: so that the fight against bad English is not frivolous and is not the exclusive concern of professional writers. I will come back to this presently, and I hope that by that time the meaning of what I have said here will have become clearer. Meanwhile, here are five specimens of the English language as it is now habitually written.

These five passages have not been picked out because they are especially bad—I could have quoted far worse if I had chosen—but because they illustrate various of the mental vices from which we now suffer. They are a little below the average, but are fairly representative samples. I number them so that I can refer back to them when necessary:

(1) "I am not, indeed, sure, whether it is not true to say that the Milton who once seemed not unlike a seventeenth-century Shelley had not become, out of an experience ever more bitter in each year, more alien [sic] to the founder of that Jesuit sect which nothing could induce him to tolerate."

Professor Harold Laski
(Essay in Freedom of Expression).

(2) "Above all, we cannot play ducks and drakes with a native battery of idioms which prescribes such egregious collocations of vocables as the basic *put up with* for *tolerate* or *put at a loss* for *bewilder*."

Professor Lancelot Hogben (Interglossa).

(3) "On the one side we have the free personality: by definition it is not neurotic, for it has neither conflict nor dream. Its desires, such as they are, are transparent, for they are just what institutional approval keeps in the forefront of consciousness; another institutional pattern would alter their number and intensity; there is little in them that is natural, irreducible, or culturally dangerous. But *on the other side*, the social bond itself is nothing but the mutual reflection of these self-secure integrities. Recall the definition of love. Is not this the very picture of a small academic? Where is there a place in this hall of mirrors for either personality or fraternity?"

Essay on psychology in Politics (New York).

(4) "All the 'best people' from the gentlemen's clubs, and all the frantic fascist captains, united in common hatred of Socialism and bestial horror of the rising tide of the mass revolutionary movement, have turned to acts of provocation, to foul incendiarism, to medieval legends of poisoned wells, to legalize their own destruction of proletarian organizations, and

rouse the agitated petty-bourgeoisie to chauvinistic fervor on behalf of
the fight against the revolutionary way out of the crisis."

Communist pamphlet.

(5) "If a new spirit is to be infused into this old country, there is one
thorny and contentious reform which must be tackled, and that is the
humanization and galvanization of the B.B.C. Timidity here will bespeak
cancer and atrophy of the soul. The heart of Britain may be sound and
of strong beat, for instance, but the British lion's roar at present is like
that of Bottom in Shakespeare's *Midsummer Night's Dream*—as gentle
as any sucking dove. A virile new Britain cannot continue indefinitely to
be traduced in the eyes or rather ears, of the world by the effete languors
of Langham Place, brazenly masquerading as 'standard English.' When
the Voice of Britain is heard at nine o'clock, better far and infinitely
less ludicrous to hear aitches honestly dropped than the present priggish,
inflated, inhibited, school-ma'amish arch braying of blameless bashful
mewing maidens!"

Letter in *Tribune*.

Each of these passages has faults of its own, but, quite apart from
avoidable ugliness, two qualities are common to all of them. The first is
staleness of imagery: the other is lack of precision. The writer either has
a meaning and cannot express it, or he inadvertently says something else,
or he is almost indifferent as to whether his words mean anything or not.
This mixture of vagueness and sheer incompetence is the most marked
characteristic of modern English prose, and especially of any kind of
political writing. As soon as certain topics are raised, the concrete melts
into the abstract and no one seems able to think of turns of speech that
are not hackneyed: prose consists less and less of words chosen for the
sake of their meaning, and more and more of *phrases* tacked together
like the sections of a prefabricated hen-house. I list below, with notes
and examples, various of the tricks by means of which the work of
prose-construction is habitually dodged:

Dying Metaphors. A newly invented metaphor assists thought by evoking a visual image, while on the other hand a metaphor which is technically "dead" (e.g., *iron resolution*) has in effect reverted to being an
ordinary word and can generally be used without loss of vividness. But
in between these two classes there is a huge dump of worn-out metaphors
which have lost all evocative power and are merely used because they
save people the trouble of inventing phrases for themselves. Examples
are: *ring the changes on, take up the cudgels for, toe the line, ride
roughshod over, stand shoulder to shoulder with, play into the hands of,*

no axe to grind, grist to the mill, fishing in troubled waters, on the order of the day, Achilles' heel, swan song, hotbed. Many of these are used without knowledge of their meaning (what is a "rift," for instance?), and incompatible metaphors are frequently mixed, a sure sign that the writer is not interested in what he is saying. Some metaphors now current have been twisted out of their original meaning without those who use them even being aware of the fact. For example, *toe the line* is sometimes written *tow the line.* Another example is *the hammer and the anvil,* now always used with the implication that the anvil gets the worst of it. In real life it is always the anvil that breaks the hammer, never the other way about: a writer who stopped to think what he was saying would be aware of this, and would avoid perverting the original phrase.

Operators or *verbal false limbs.* These save the trouble of picking out appropriate verbs and nouns, and at the same time pad each sentence with extra syllables which give it an appearance of symmetry. Characteristic phrases are: *render inoperative, militate against, make contact with, be subjected to, give rise to, give grounds for, have the effect of, play a leading part (role) in, make itself felt, take effect, exhibit a tendency to, serve the purpose of, etc., etc.* The keynote is the elimination of simple verbs. Instead of being a single word, such as *break, stop, spoil, mend, kill,* a verb becomes a *phrase,* made up of a noun or adjective tacked on to some general-purposes verb such as *prove, serve, form, play, render.* In addition, the passive voice is wherever possible used in preference to the active, and noun constructions are used instead of gerunds (*by examination of* instead of *by examining*). The range of verbs is further cut down by means of the *-ize* and *de-* formation, and the banal statements are given an appearance of profundity by means of the *not un-* formation. Simple conjunctions and prepositions are replaced by such phrases as *with respect to, having regard to, the fact that, by dint of, in view of, in the interests of, on the hypothesis that;* and the ends of sentences are saved from anticlimax by such resounding commonplaces as *greatly to be desired, cannot be left out of account, a development to be expected in the near future, deserving of serious consideration, brought to a satisfactory conclusion,* and so on and so forth.

Pretentious diction. Words like *phenomenon, element, individual* (as noun), *objective, categorical, effective, virtual, basic, primary, promote, constitute, exhibit, exploit, utilize, eliminate, liquidate,* are used to dress up simple statement and give an air of scientific impartiality to biased judgments. Adjectives like *epoch-making, epic, historic, unforgettable, triumphant, age-old, inevitable, inexorable, veritable,* are used to dignify the sordid processes of international politics, while writing that aims at glorifying war usually takes on an archaic color, its characteristic words being: *realm, throne, chariot, mailed fist, trident, sword, shield, buckler, banner, jackboot, clarion.* Foreign words and expressions such as *cul de sac, ancien régime, deus ex machina, mutatis mutandis, status quo, gleichschaltung, weltanschauung,* are used to give an air of culture and elegance. Except for the useful abbreviations *i.e., e.g.,* and *etc.,* there is no real need for any of the hundreds of foreign phrases now current in English. Bad writers, and especially scientific, political and sociological writers, are nearly always haunted by the notion that Latin or Greek words are grander than Saxon ones, and unnecessary words like *expedite, ameliorate, predict, extraneous, deracinated, clandestine, subaqueous* and hundreds of others constantly gain ground from their Anglo-Saxon opposite numbers. The jargon peculiar to Marxist writing (*hyena, hangman, cannibal, petty bourgeois, these gentry, lackey, flunkey, mad dog, White Guard,* etc.) consists largely of words and phrases translated from Russian, German or French; but the normal way of coining a new word is to use a Latin or Greek root with the appropriate affix and, where necessary, the -ize formation. It is often easier to make up words of this kind (*deregionalize, impermissible, extramarital, non-fragmentatory* and so forth) than to think up the English words that will cover one's meaning. The result, in general, is an increase in slovenliness and vagueness.

Meaningless words. In certain kinds of writing, particularly in art criticism and literary criticism, it is normal to come across long passages which are almost completely lacking in meaning. Words like *romantic, plastic, values, human, dead, sentimental, natural, vitality,* as used in art criticism, are strictly meaningless in the sense that they not only do not point to any discoverable object, but are hardly ever expected to do so by the reader. When one critic writes, "The outstanding feature of Mr. X's work is its living quality," while another writes, "The immediately striking thing about Mr. X's work is its peculiar deadness," the reader accepts this as a simple difference of opinion. If words like *black* and *white* were involved, instead of the jargon words *dead* and *living,* he would see at once that language was being used in an improper way. Many political words are similarly abused. The word *Fascism* has now no meaning except insofar as it signifies "something not desirable." The words *democracy, socialism, freedom, patriotic, realistic, justice,* have each of them several different meanings which cannot be reconciled with one another. In the case of a word like *democracy,* not only is there no agreed definition, but the attempt to make one is resisted from all sides. It is almost universally felt that when we call a country democratic we are praising it: consequently the defenders of every kind of régime claim that it is a democracy, and fear that they might have to stop using the word if it were tied down to any one meaning. Words of this kind are often used in a consciously dishonest way. That is, the person who uses them has his own private definition, but allows his hearer to think he means something quite different. Statements like *Marshal Pétain was a true patriot, The Soviet Press is the freest in the world, The Catholic Church is opposed to persecution,* are almost always made with intent to deceive. Other words used in variable meanings, in most cases more or less dishonestly, are: *class, totalitarian, science, progressive, reactionary, bourgeois, equality.*

Now that I have made this catalogue of swindles and perversions, let me give another example of the kind of writing that they lead to. This time it must of its nature be an imaginary one. I am going to translate a passage of good English into modern English of the worst sort. Here is a well-known verse from *Ecclesiastes:*

"I returned and saw under the sun, that the race is not to the swift, nor the battle to the strong, neither yet bread to the wise, nor yet riches to men of understanding, nor yet favor to men of skill; but time and chance happeneth to them all."

Here it is in modern English:

"Objective consideration of contemporary phenomena compels the conclusion that success or failure in competitive activities exhibits no tendency to be commensurate with innate capacity, but that a considerable element of the unpredictable must invariably be taken into account."

This is a parody, but not a very gross one. Exhibit (3), above, for instance, contains several patches of the same kind of English. It will be seen that I have not made a full translation. The beginning and ending of the sentence follow the original meaning fairly closely, but in the middle the concrete illustrations—race, battle, bread—dissolve into the vague phrase "success or failure in competitive activities." This had to be so, because no modern writer of the kind I am discussing—no one capable of using phrases like "objective consideration of contemporary phenomena"—would ever tabulate his thoughts in that precise and detailed way. The whole tendency of modern prose is away from concreteness. Now analyze these two sentences a little more closely. The first contains forty-nine words but only sixty syllables, and all its words are those of everyday life. The second contains thirty-eight words of ninety syllables: eighteen of its words are from Latin roots, and one from Greek. The first sentence contains six vivid images, and only one phrase ("time and chance") that could be called vague. The second contains not a single fresh, arresting phrase, and in spite of its ninety syllables it gives only a shortened version of the meaning contained in the first. Yet without a doubt it is the second kind of sentence that is gaining ground in modern English. I do not want to exaggerate. This kind of writing is not yet universal, and outcrops of simplicity will occur here and there in the worst-written page. Still, if you or I were told to write a few lines on the uncertainty of human fortunes, we should probably come much nearer to my imaginary sentence than to the one from *Ecclesiastes*.

As I have tried to show, modern writing at its worst does not consist in picking out words for the sake of their meaning and inventing images in order to make the meaning clearer. It consists in gumming together long strips of words which have already been set in order by someone else, and making the results presentable by sheer humbug. The attraction of this way of writing is that it is easy. It is easier—even quicker, once you have the habit—to say *In my opinion it is a not unjustifiable assumption that* than to say *I think*. If you use ready-made phrases, you not only don't have to hunt about for words; you also don't have to bother with the rhythms of your sentences, since these phrases are generally so arranged as to be more or less euphonious. When you are composing in a hurry—when you are dictating to a stenographer, for instance, or making a public speech—it is natural to fall into a pretentious, Latinized style. Tags like *a consideration which we should do well to bear in mind* or *a conclusion to which all of us would readily assent* will save many a sentence from coming down with a bump. By using stale metaphors, similes and idioms, you save much mental effort, at the cost of leaving your meaning vague, not only for your reader but for yourself. This is the significance of mixed metaphors. The sole aim of a metaphor is to call up a visual image. When these images clash—as in *The Fascist octopus has sung its swan song, the jackboot is thrown into the melting pot*—it can be taken as certain that the writer is not seeing a mental image of the objects he is naming; in other words he is not really thinking. Look again at the examples I gave at the beginning of this essay. Professor Laski (1) uses five negatives in fifty-three words. One of these is super-fluous, making nonsense of the whole passage, and in addition there is the slip *alien* for akin, making further nonsense, and several avoidable pieces of clumsiness which increase the general vagueness. Professor Hogben (2) plays ducks and drakes with a battery which is able to write prescriptions, and, while disapproving of the everyday phrase *put up with*, is unwilling to look *egregious* up in the dictionary and see what it means. (3), if one takes an uncharitable attitude towards it, is simply meaningless: probably one could work out its intended meaning by reading the whole of the article in which it occurs. In (4), the writer knows more or less what he wants to say, but an accumulation of stale phrases chokes him like tea leaves blocking a sink. In (5), words and meaning have almost parted company. People who write in this manner usually have a general emotional meaning—they dislike one thing and want to express solidarity with another—but they are not interested in the detail of what they are saying. A scrupulous writer, in every sentence that he writes, will ask himself at least four questions, thus: What am I trying to say? What words will express it? What image or idiom will make it clearer? Is this image fresh enough to have an effect? And he will probably ask himself two more: Could I put it more shortly? Have I said anything that is avoidably ugly? But you are not obliged to go to all this trouble. You can shirk it by simply throwing your mind open and letting the ready-made phrases come crowding in. They will construct your sentences for you—even think your thoughts for you, to a certain extent—and at need they will perform the important service of partially concealing your meaning even from yourself. It is at this point that the special connection between politics and the debasement of language becomes clear.

In our time it is broadly true that political writing is bad writing. Where it is not true, it will generally be found that the writer is some kind of rebel, expressing his private opinions and not a "party line." Orthodoxy, of whatever color, seems to demand a lifeless, imitative style. The political dialects to be found in pamphlets, leading articles, manifestoes, White Papers and the speeches of under-secretaries do, of course, vary from party to party, but they are all alike in that one almost never finds in them a fresh, vivid, home-made turn of speech. When one watches some tired hack on the platform mechanically repeating the familiar phrases—*bestial atrocities, iron heel, bloodstained tyranny, free peoples of the world, stand shoulder to shoulder*—one often has a curious feeling that one is not watching a live human being but some kind of dummy: a feeling which suddenly becomes stronger at moments when the light catches the speaker's spectacles and turns them into blank discs which seem to have no eyes behind them. And this is not altogether fanciful. A speaker who uses that kind of phraseology has gone some distance towards turning himself into a machine. The appropriate noises are coming out of his larynx, but his brain is not involved as it would be if he were choosing his words for himself. If the speech he is making is one that he is accustomed to make over and over again, he may be almost unconscious of what he is saying, as one is when one utters the responses in church. And this reduced state of consciousness, if not indispensable, is at any rate favorable to political conformity.

In our time, political speech and writing are largely the defense of the indefensible. Things like the continuance of British rule in India, the Russian purges and deportations, the dropping of the atom bombs on Japan, can indeed be defended, but only by arguments which are too brutal for most people to face, and which do not square with the professed aims of political parties. Thus political language has to consist largely of euphemism, question-begging and sheer cloudy vagueness. Defenseless villages are bombarded from the air, the inhabitants driven out into the countryside, the cattle machine-gunned, the huts set on fire with incendiary bullets: this is called *pacification*. Millions of peasants are robbed of their farms and sent trudging along the roads with no more than they can carry: this is called *transfer of population* or *rectification of frontiers*. People are imprisoned for years without trial, or shot in the back of the neck or sent to die of scurvy in Arctic lumber camps: this is called *elimination of unreliable elements*. Such phraseology is needed if one wants to name things without calling up mental pictures of them. Consider for instance some comfortable English professor defending Russian totalitarianism. He cannot say outright, "I believe in killing off your opponents when you can get good results by doing so." Probably, therefore, he will say something like this:

"While freely conceding that the Soviet régime exhibits certain features which the humanitarian may be inclined to deplore, we must, I think, agree that a certain curtailment of the right to political opposition is an unavoidable concomitant of transitional periods, and that the rigors which the Russian people have been called upon to undergo have been amply justified in the sphere of concrete achievement."

The inflated style is itself a kind of euphemism. A mass of Latin words falls upon the facts like soft snow, blurring the outlines and covering up all the details. The great enemy of clear language is insincerity. When there is a gap between one's real and one's declared aims, one turns as it were instinctively to long words and exhausted idioms, like a cuttlefish squirting out ink. In our age there is no such thing as "keeping out of politics." All issues are political issues, and politics itself is a mass of lies, evasions, folly, hatred and schizophrenia. When the general atmosphere is bad, language must suffer. I should expect to find—this is a guess which I have not sufficient knowledge to verify—that the German, Russian and Italian languages have all deteriorated in the last ten or fifteen years, as a result of dictatorship.

But if thought corrupts language, language can also corrupt thought. A bad usage can spread by tradition and imitation, even among people who should and do know better. The debased language that I have been discussing is in some ways very convenient. Phrases like *a not unjustifiable assumption, leaves much to be desired, would serve no good purpose, a consideration which we should do well to bear in mind,* are a continuous temptation, a packet of aspirins always at one's elbow. Look back through this essay, and for certain you will find that I have again and again committed the very faults I am protesting against. By this morning's post I have received a pamphlet dealing with conditions in Germany. The author tells me that he "felt impelled" to write it. I open it at random, and here is almost the first sentence that I see: "The Allies have an opportunity not only of achieving a radical transformation of Germany's social and political structure in such a way as to avoid a nationalistic reaction in Germany itself, but at the same time of laying the foundations of a cooperative and unified Europe." You see, he "feels impelled" to write—feels, presumably, that he has something new to say—and yet his words, like cavalry horses answering the bugle, group themselves automatically into the familiar dreary pattern. This invasion of one's mind by ready-made phrases (*lay the foundations, achieve a radical transformation*) can only be prevented if one is constantly on guard against them, and every such phrase anaesthetizes a portion of one's brain.

I said earlier that the decadence of our language is probably curable. Those who deny this would argue, if they produced an argument at all, that language merely reflects existing social conditions, and that we cannot influence its development by any direct tinkering with words and constructions. So far as the general tone or spirit of a language goes, this may be true, but it is not true in detail. Silly words and expressions have often disappeared, not through any evolutionary process but owing to the conscious action of a minority. Two recent examples were *explore every avenue* and *leave no stone unturned,* which were killed by the jeers of a few journalists. There is a long list of flyblown metaphors which could similarly be got rid of if enough people would interest themselves in the job; and it should also be possible to laugh the *not un-* formation out of existence, to reduce the amount of Latin and Greek in the average sentence, to drive out foreign phrases and strayed scientific words, and, in general, to make pretentiousness unfashionable. But all these are minor points. The defense of the English language implies more than this, and perhaps it is best to start by saying what it does *not* imply.

To begin with it has nothing to do with archaism, with the salvaging of obsolete words and turns of speech, or with the setting up of a "standard English" which must never be departed from. On the contrary, it is especially concerned with the scrapping of every word or idiom which has outgrown its usefulness. It has nothing to do with correct grammar and syntax, which are of no importance so long as one makes one's meaning clear, or with the avoidance of Americanisms, or with having what is called a "good prose style." On the other hand it is not concerned with fake simplicity and the attempt to make written English colloquial. Nor does it even imply in every case preferring the Saxon word to the Latin one, though it does imply using the fewest and shortest words that will cover one's meaning. What is above all needed is to let the meaning choose the word, and not the other way about. In prose, the worst thing one can do with words is to surrender to them. When you think of a concrete object, you think wordlessly, and then, if you want to describe the thing you have been visualizing you probably hunt about till you find the exact words that seem to fit. When you think of something abstract you are more inclined to use words from the start, and unless you make a conscious effort to prevent it, the existing dialect will come rushing in and do the job for you, at the expense of blurring or even changing your meaning. Probably it is better to put off using words as long as possible and get one's meaning as clear as one can through pictures or sensations. Afterwards one can choose—not simply *accept*— the phrases that will best cover the meaning, and then switch around and decide what impression one's words are likely to make on another person. This last effort of the mind cuts out all stale or mixed images, all pre-fabricated phrases, needless repetitions, and humbug and vagueness generally. But one can often be in doubt about the effect of a word or a phrase, and one needs rules that one can rely on when instinct fails. I think the following rules will cover most cases:

(i) Never use a metaphor, simile or other figure of speech which you are used to seeing in print.

(ii) Never use a long word where a short one will do.

(iii) If it is possible to cut a word out, always cut it out.

(iv) Never use the passive where you can use the active.

(v) Never use a foreign phrase, a scientific word or a jargon word if you can think of an everyday English equivalent.

(vi) Break any of these rules sooner than say anything outright barbarous.

These rules sound elementary, and so they are, but they demand a deep change of attitude in anyone who has grown used to writing in the style now fashionable. One could keep all of them and still write bad English, but one could not write the kind of stuff that I quoted in those five specimens at the beginning of this article.

I have not here been considering the literary use of language, but merely language as an instrument for expressing and not for concealing or preventing thought. Stuart Chase and others have come near to claiming that all abstract words are meaningless, and have used this as a pretext for advocating a kind of political quietism. Since you don't know what Fascism is, how can you struggle against Fascism? One need not swallow such absurdities as this, but one ought to recognize that the present political chaos is connected with the decay of language, and that one can probably bring about some improvement by starting at the verbal end. If you simplify your English, you are freed from the worst follies of orthodoxy. You cannot speak any of the necessary dialects, and when you make a stupid remark its stupidity will be obvious, even to yourself.

Political language—and with variations this is true of all political parties, from Conservatives to Anarchists—is designed to make lies sound truthful and murder respectable, and to give an appearance of solidity to pure wind. One cannot change this all in a moment, but one can at least change one's own habits, and from time to time one can even, if one jeers loudly enough, send some worn-out and useless phrase—some *jackboot, Achilles' heel, hotbed, melting pot, acid test, veritable inferno* or other lump of verbal refuse—into the dustbin where it belongs.

33. Franz Mehring

Charles Dickens

FRANZ MEHRING, journalist, historian, critic, was one of Germany's leading Socialists in both word and deed. Born in Pomerania in 1846 of a middle-class family, he completed his university studies with a Doctor of Philosophy degree from the University of Leipzig. His brilliant articles appeared in newspapers which he edited and, beginning in 1890, in Karl Kautsky's *Neue Zeit.* He joined the anti-war "Spartacus" group founded by Karl Liebknecht and Rosa Luxemburg, spent many months in prison, and died in 1919 a few days after hearing of the assassination of his two "Spartacus" friends. His best-known historical works are *History of the German Socialist Democracy* (1897–98), and *Karl Marx, A History of His Life,* published in Germany in 1918 after delays by military censors, and by now a classic biography of Marx. His essay on Charles Dickens was first published in the *Neue Zeit* (Volume 30, no. 1, pp. 621 *et seq.*) in 1912, and was subsequently reprinted in *Für Literaturgeschichte* (Berlin: Universeinbücherei) in 1930.

OF the three great English novelists during the long reign of Queen Victoria—Bulwer, Dickens and Thackeray—Dickens was the most loved and most read, although the literature and philosophy of the Continent were much less familiar to him than to either of his classically educated rivals. Yet he easily outstripped them by his original talent and by that indomitable energy for work and life which was perhaps his most outstanding quality.

He was through and through an Englishman; it has been said, not unjustly, that he never left behind him the Cockney of London. In his letters, published after his death by his friend Forster, he complains repeatedly as he journeys in the Swiss mountains, unmarred then by today's hordes of tourists, of the lack of street noises which were, he felt, indispensable for his creative production. "I cannot say how much

I miss the streets," he wrote in 1846 from Lausanne where he wrote one of his greatest novels, *Dombey and Son*.

It is as though they give something to my brain which it cannot do without if it is to work. For a week or fortnight, I can write wonderfully in a remote place; one day in London suffices then to set me up and off. But the trouble and work of writing day after day without this magic lantern is *enormous*. . . . My characters seem to want to stand still if they do not have a crowd around them. I wrote very little in Genoa and thought I had avoided traces of its influence—but, good God, even there I had at least two miles of streets by the lights of which I could roam around at night, and a great theater each evening.

Dozens of similar complaints appear in the writer's letters. Among his brothers in Apollo he stands, in this respect, quite alone.

The nerve-shattering life of the city was the real spirit of his artistic creation. He knew that life in its heights and depths; with wonderful penetration, he grasped its social types and embodied them in living figures, many of which are still popular in England and beyond England as well. Mr. Pickwick and Sam Weller compare in fame with Don Quixote and Sancho Panza. His heart, even when he was a celebrated dinner guest of Ministers of State and a close friend to all the famous names of England, was with the poor and unfortunate from whose midst he had, by his huge strength of spirit and life, raised himself to brilliant fame. No one could feel more deeply for Nature's stepchildren, the blind, the dumb, and the deaf, nor more deeply—and this says even more—for the stepchildren of society. Even bourgeois aesthetes said of Dickens, partly in accusation, partly in wonder, that he never confused in his sympathy for the working classes crudity, criminality, immorality, or filth.

His creative powers were almost unbelievable. As much as he enjoyed the exciting social life which the fruits of his writing made possible, he still managed to write in scarcely two decades twelve substantial novels as well as a host of stories and sketches, a yearly Christmas tale, travel journals and other things as well; matters which might otherwise occupy the whole of a man's life, such as the founding of a newspaper, the *Daily News*, or of a substantial weekly magazine, *Household Words*, were for him incidental. Attempts were made to explain his productivity as carelessness; he was accused of a lack of economy, of clumsiness in his plots and denouements, of the improbabilities of his stories, of the mannered style, of a broadness in his humor, of exaggerations, and so on. It is difficult in fact to argue with many of these accusations, which are understandable in light of the facility with which Dickens wrote. Still it goes too far to contest on these grounds the honors due him as the author, since in many of his creations (and not in the least of them) he pursued certain moral ends.

One need only mention in this connection *Oliver Twist*, in which he describes the poor-relief with such biting humor, or *Nicholas Nickleby* where he does the same for the school systems, or *Bleak House* in which he does it for the judiciary. As it happens, notwithstanding the shameful conditions which they reveal, these novels remain a claim to fame on behalf of the English people. If a German author, either in Dickens' time or now, had dared to portray the venality and inflexibility of the official institutions of the government as Dickens did with respect to the judiciary in *Bleak House*, he would be defamed in all patriotic circles, including the so-called liberal ones, as a disgrace to the Government; and the insulted judges would prepare their genuine Prussian requital, inviting the malcontent to lengthy afterthoughts in prison. There is something true in the writer's words: "Only a free people is worthy of an Aristophanes." To return to Dickens, however, he did not consider tendentiousness in art to be objectionable, but only that tendentiousness which utilized inartistic means. And in the choice of his own means, Dickens, as his letters edited by Forster show, was extraordinarily deliberate and circumspect. Of course, according to an aesthetic doctrine which he himself had contrived. But Lessing already knew that each genius creates new rules for himself; and as strongly as an aesthetic theory may attempt to draw the boundaries around ethical judgment and artistic taste, in the practice of artistic creation those boundaries are continually overrun, as many of the most famous art works of all people and times attest. "To better and to convert men" is an undeniable drive even in the areas of writing and painting; and to attempt to evade it anxiously can readily lead to opposite extremes represented in those tasteless and bland sauces into which a full blown morality is poured under the guise of art.

How strong the artistic temperament was in Dickens is shown most forcefully by the fact that despite his attentiveness to the most important questions of public life and despite his radically democratic sentiments, he remained himself outside of political life. Other possible grounds for this reticence—lack of insight or even of courage—can be excluded for Dickens, because he so often did touch the most sensitive spots in the sensibilities of the ruling classes. But his democratic convictions were not able to stand where they encountered a total lack of artistic sensibility: how bitterly and unjustly did he condemn the United States. And, on the other hand, the artistic quality of Italian life reconciled him to the harsh conditions of the Italian middle and lower classes. Once when he entered Switzerland from Italy he wrote:

The cleanliness of the small doll houses is really wonderful for someone coming from Italy. But the beautiful Italian manners, the soft language, the swift acknowledgment of a friendly look, of a word in jest, the enchanting expression of a wish to be pleasant to one and all—these I have left behind the Alps. When I think of them, I long too for dirt, brick floors, naked walls, unwhitewashed ceilings and broken windows.

One should not assume, however, that Dickens as artist saw less deeply in his art than the politician might in his—that Dickens fell into the tired game of playing at charities by which the bourgeoisie attempt to quiet their false consciousness. In fact, the recognition of precisely these perverse impulses made him a Democrat: tirelessly he fought "the worst and meanest of all cant, the cant of philanthropy." To the Christian Socialist he called:

Give a man and his family a glimpse of Heaven by a little air and light, give him water; help him to get clean, brighten the dark atmosphere in which he sees himself, and which makes him callous to everything else. . . . Then, but not before, will he be willing to hear of him whose thoughts so readily were with the poor, and who sympathized with all human grief.

When his friend Cruikshank publishes a series of sketches depicting the terrible results of alcoholism, Dickens praises their technical execution, but adds, nonetheless:

The philosophy of the matter, however, as doctrine I take to be quite false— since, to be more accurate, the drinking would have to be seen to originate from worry, poverty or ignorance, the three things from which its awful spectre always sets out. Then the sketches would have been a double edged sword— but too radical, I think, for our good old George.

Dickens regarded alcoholism as the English national vice, but even with respect to it he kept himself free of narrowly partisan fanaticism; he himself enjoyed a drink and was never overcome by the attractions of abstinence. Nonetheless, he basically favored the temperance movements; and it was only as they sought to uproot alcoholism with pietistic and moralistic sermonizing that he poked fun at them, for example in one of the scenes in *Pickwick Papers*. He reiterated constantly the social causes of alcoholism—the confined, unhealthy dwellings with their disgusting odors, the mean working places with their lack of light, air, and water. He felt that if one showed so emphatically the side of the coin on which the common people with their mistakes and crimes were engraved, one was the more obligated to show the other side as well, where the mistakes and crimes of the governments which ruled the people were impressed.

One cannot call him, then, a socialist writer. He lacked any speculative plan or inclination along these lines, quite aside from the fact that it was much more difficult then than now to visualize bourgeois society overthrown and reconstructed on new foundations. Dickens had to work himself up from the most bitter poverty, in the absence of any systematic education; all philosophy would have seemed to him, had he ever troubled himself with the question, a bit foolish. As difficult as the first stages of his life might have been, he was at 27 a famous writer; bourgeois society looked to him uncannily like a stepmother. What it was able to offer, it strenuously heaped on him. He did not, however, become its toady on that account, as did so many like him and for lesser prices; his good heart and his healthy understanding of mankind kept his eyes open to its faults. But with all his passionate words his political credo remained that the institutions of England must be improved, not replaced by new ones.

In the last decade of his life Dickens was overtaken by the *auri sacra fames*, the unholy lust for gold, which was richly enough satisfied. Not only the writer ran afoul of this; the man himself also deteriorated in a version of suicide awful in its details. It was, apparently, certain love affairs which gave him the *idée fixe* that he had to earn more and more in order to assure a lavish living not only in the present but also in the future for whomever he was involved with. The extraordinary talent of representation which Dickens had restricted to playacting, reading aloud, and dinner table talk, he now turned to the public recital of his works. His friend Forster had the courage to tell him honestly that this means of earning money was not worthy of him, but this single friendly voice remained unheard in the storm of approbation which accompanied the writer's new career. He had, however, purchased his own demons, which pursued and scourged him from then on and until, in July, 1870, he broke down.

Thus, a shadow marks the twilight of the writer; but this shadow should not be allowed to obscure the brilliant light of his dawn and midday. The grave of the writer, on February 7th, his hundredth birthday, deserves from the German working class as well, a wreath of homage.

34. Jan Kott

My Lady's Visit

JAN KOTT (1914–   ), Polish critic, poet, and theorist was educated at the Universities of Warsaw, Paris, and Lodz. In World War II he fought in the Polish Peoples' Army and was active in the underground movement. In 1953 he was appointed Professor of History of Polish Literature at the University of Warsaw. He received the State Prize in Literature and Literary Studies in 1955, and the Herder Award (Vienna) in 1964. His works in Polish include *Mythology and Realism* (1946), *School of Classics* (1949), and *As You Like It* (1955). A major work written in 1964 and available in English translation is *Shakespeare, Our Contemporary*. The following selection is from his *Theatre Notebook 1947–1967*.

IN the last general election to the Seym one of the candidates was a young and talented woman writer who had been born in the 'landowner class,' as it is customary to describe it on personnel forms. It is perhaps because of her origins that her novels about squires and peasants are bitterly authentic and seem to reflect vital human experiences. It is not, however, my intention to write about her novels. By some chance—or by some courageous and defiant design—she was a candidate from the same constituency where the now-divided estate of her parents was situated.

I do not know if the manor where she spent her childhood now has a Crops Protection Center, a tractor cooperative, or a village social club. I do not even know if she spent a couple of nights there on her last visit. All I know is that her standing as candidate caused a great commotion in the district. The peasants had not read her books and must have been somewhat stunned when they heard the young lady from the manor encourage them to deliver their compulsory supplies to the State.

It does not matter whether this story is true. It might not have happened exactly the way I have described it. But one thing is certain: it is excellent material for a play, a specifically Polish play.

What kind of play could be written from this material? A comedy, of course. Not only because there was a happy ending and the peasants voted for the woman, but also because an ex-landowner trying to persuade her own peasants to establish a cooperative is a humorous figure.

Or she could be an ex-landowner who is an enemy and creeps into the family manor at night to let the Colorado beetle out of the Crops Protection Center. I can see how that material could be used in a film: the brave boys from the State farm chase the Colorado beetle through the fields and woods on thoroughbreds from the State stud farm.

There could be another variation: the ex-landowner is neither ally nor enemy, but simply the lady from the manor, with a degree in art history and a divorce from her husband. There can be the lady from the manor as a pure Platonic idea—without a life history, without a social background. She is and she is not. What happens then? We have Leon Kruczkowski's *The Visit.*

The first act is mainly about the Colorado beetle. The Wielhorski estate, divided in 1945 among the local peasants, has next to it a State farm and a Crops Protection Center situated in the manor. The old servant, who used to be a butler and is now a laboratory assistant, grinds in a mortar the murderous nitrides to kill the beetles. The young girl assistant who is breeding the beetle in a test-tube is in love with the director of the center, the son of a poor peasant. He is so busy trying to invent a biological means to fight the beetle that he does not even notice her. There are also a peasant, an old man of the village, and an agronomist from the State farm. The old man is a relic of the past. The agronomist, whose name is Pszonka (a word rather similar to the Polish for Colorado beetle) is talking through the window to the noble director of the center. He starts some intrigue. From his first words we can see that he is an enemy.

It is May 1952. The Colorado beetle in the test-tube will hatch any moment now. We have just learned that the offspring of twenty pairs of the beetle can destroy two or three acres of the potato crop. The picture of the village is now complete: everything is as it should be. But we still do not know what Kruczkowski needs it for. Then there is the young lady of the manor. For the last few days a mysterious stranger has been sitting in the evenings at the edge of the woods and looking in the direction of the manor. Just at the point when the Colorado beetles are hatching, a professor of art history visits the manor with his female assistant. On seeing her the old servant who is now a laboratory assistant lets the jar of nitrides he is holding fall to the ground. We know now who the mysterious stranger is: Miss Wielhorski, availing herself of the absence of the director, has decided to spend a night secretly in the manor. The telephone rings: the center announces to the district authorities the news that the beetles have hatched. This is the end of the first act.

The dramatic logic of the exposition is quite clear. The problem of the Colorado beetle and the problem of the young lady of the manor have to meet. Either we will see the continuation of the familiar outline of a 'productivity play,' or Kruczkowski will do a *volte-face* and ridicule the insipid anecdote of the exposition.

Nothing like that happens. Kruczkowski treats the first act only as a framework, and the problem of the Colorado beetle as an allegory. The second act is a new national drama, a great night when consciences are examined and grievances reckoned, when the ghosts of the landowning past appear before the ex-landowner's daughter. There is something here of Wyspianski's *Wedding*, but it does not come off.

The first act is a productivity pseudo-anecdote; the second a national pseudo-drama; the third, a popular pseudo-vaudeville. In the morning, peasants throng in great numbers to the manor drawing-room, now the club, where Miss Wielhorski spent the night. They come arranged in proper Leninist classifications: the poor, the average, the rich, the once-landless and the State farm workers, the party activists and the village authorities. They all say what they ought to say at such a moment.

Are they real people? No. Why not? The answer is simple. Can there be a conflict between a pure Platonic idea and real people? There cannot. What can happen? Well, the pure Platonic idea of an ex-landowner's daughter can see the class divisions of the village. And, indeed, she does see them.

The Visit is a failure, no doubt about it. But could it have been a successful play? Why did Kruczkowski fail in his grand metaphor? The vital question is: Is there a national drama in the visit paid by an ex-landowner to her family home?

Not long ago I was told a story the authenticity of which I can vouch for. In a small district town of southern Poland, a young hooligan got drunk, came out on to the street and began to shout: "When there is a change of régime, I shall hang all communists. They will all hang on the lamp-posts." He was arrested and the case put before the prosecutor. The prosecutor wrote on the act of indictment: "Immediate discharge. His threat was unreal. The régime is strong."

I rather liked what the prosecutor did. The régime is strong indeed. The ex-landowner's visit to her family home can result in nothing. There is simply no drama. The case has been settled by history.

35. Bertolt Brecht

Study of the First Scene of Shakespeare's *Coriolanus*

For a biographical note on BERTOLT BRECHT, see p. 226. This selection was originally published in 1953, and is taken from *Brecht on Theatre*. The scene from *Coriolanus* discussed here may be found in the Appendix, pp. 463–470.

B. How does the play begin?

R. A group of plebeians has armed itself with a view to killing the patrician Caius Marcius, an enemy to the people, who is opposed to lowering the price of corn. They say that the plebeians' sufferance is the patricians' gain.

B. ?

R. Have I left something out?

B. Are Marcius's services mentioned?

R. And disputed.

P. So you think the plebeians aren't all that united? Yet they loudly proclaim their determination.

W. Too loudly. If you proclaim your determination as loudly as that it means that you are or were undetermined, and highly so.

P. In the normal theatre this determination always has something comic about it: it makes the plebeians seem ridiculous, particularly as their weapons are inadequate clubs, staves. Then they collapse right away, just because the patrician Agrippa makes a fine speech.

B. Not in Shakespeare.

P. But in the bourgeois theatre.

B. Indeed yes.

R. This is awkward. You cast doubt on the plebeians' determination, yet you bar the comic element. Does that mean that you think after all that they won't let themselves be taken in by the patricians' demagogy? So as not to seem more comic still?

B. If they let themselves be taken in I wouldn't find them comic but tragic. That would be a possible scene, for such things happen, but a horrifying one. I don't think you realize how hard it is for the oppressed to become united. Their misery unites them—once they recognize who has caused it. 'Our sufferance is a gain to them.' But otherwise their misery is liable to cut them off from one another, for they are forced to snatch the wretched crumbs from each other's mouths. Think how reluctantly men decide to revolt! It's an adventure for them: new paths have to be marked out and followed; moreover the role of the rulers is always accompanied by that of their ideas. To the masses revolt is the unnatural rather than the natural thing, and however bad the situation from which only revolt can free them they find the idea of it as exhausting as the scientist finds a new view of the universe. This being so it is often the more intelligent people who are opposed to unity and only the most intelligent of all who are also for it.

R. So really the plebeians have not become united at all?

B. On the contrary. Even the Second Citizen joins in. Only neither we nor the audience must be allowed to overlook the contradictions that are bridged over, suppressed, ruled out, now that sheer hunger makes a conflict with the patricians unavoidable.

R. I don't think you can find that in the text, just like that.

B. Quite right. You have got to have read the whole play. You can't begin without having looked at the end. Later in the play this unity of the plebeians will be broken up, so it is best not to take it for granted at the start, but to show it as having come about.

W. How?

B. We'll discuss that. I don't know. For the moment we are making an analysis. Go on.

R. The next thing that happens is that the patrician Agrippa enters, and proves by a parable that the plebeians cannot do without the rule of the patricians.

B. You say 'proves' as if it were in quotes.

R. The parable doesn't convince me.

B. It's a world-famous parable. Oughtn't you to be objective?

R. Yes.

B. Right.

W. The man starts off by suggesting that the dearth has been made by the gods, not the patricians.

P. That was a valid argument in those days, in Rome I mean. Don't the interests of a given work demand that we respect the ideology of a given period?

B. You needn't go into that here. Shakespeare gives the plebeians good arguments to answer back with. And they strongly reject the parable, for that matter.

R. The plebeians complain about the price of corn, the rate of usury, and are against the burden of the war, or at any rate its unjust division.

B. You're reading that into it.

R. I can't find anything against war.

B. There isn't.

R. Marcius comes on and slangs the armed plebeians, whom he would like to see handled with the sword, not with speeches. Agrippa plays the diplomat and says that the plebeians want corn at their own rates. Marcius jeers at them. They don't know what they are talking about, having no access to the Capitol and therefore no insight into the state's affairs. He gets angry at the suggestion that there's grain enough.

P. Speaking as a military man, presumably.

W. In any case as soon as war breaks out he points to the Volscian's corn.

R. During his outburst Marcius announces that the Senate has never granted the plebeians People's Tribunes, and Agrippa finds this strange. Enter Senators, with the officiating Consul Cominius at their head. Marcius is delighted at the idea of fighting the Volscians' leader Aufidius. He is put under Cominius's command.

B. Is he agreeable to that?

R. Yes. But it seems to take the Senators slightly by surprise.

B. Differences of opinion between Marcius and the Senate?

R. Not important ones.

B. We've read the play to the end, though. Marcius is an awkward man.

W. It's interesting, this contempt for the plebeians combined with high regard for a national enemy, the patrician Aufidius. He's very class-conscious.

B. Forgotten something?

R. Yes. Sicinius and Brutus, the new People's Tribunes, came on with the Senators.

B. No doubt you forgot them because they got no welcome or greeting.

R. Altogether the plebeians get very little further attention. A Senator tells them sharply to go home. Marcius 'humorously' suggests that they should rather follow him to the Capitol. He treats them as rats, and that is when he refers them to the corn of the Volscians. Then it just says, 'Citizens steal away.'

P. The play makes their revolt come at an unfortunate moment. In the crisis following the enemy's approach the patricians can seize the reins once more.

B. And the granting of People's Tribunes?

P. Was not really necessary.

R. Left alone, the Tribunes hope that the war, instead of leading to Marcius's promotion, will devour him, or make him fall out with the Senate.

P. The end of the scene is a little unsatisfactory.

B. In Shakespeare, you mean?

R. Possibly.

B. We'll note that sense of discomfort. But Shakespeare presumably thinks that war weakens the plebeians' position, and that seems to me splendidly realistic. Lovely stuff.

R. The wealth of events in a single short scene. Compare today's plays, with their poverty of content!

P. The way in which the exposition at the same time gives a rousing send-off to the plot!

R. The language in which the parable is told! The humor!

P. And the fact that it has no effect on the plebeians!

W. The plebeians' native wit! Exchanges like 'Agrippa: Will you undo yourselves? Citizen: We cannot, sir, we are undone already!'

R. The crystal clarity of Marcius's harangue! What an outsize character! And one who emerges as admirable while behaving in a way that I find beneath contempt!

B. And great and small conflicts all thrown on the scene at once: the unrest of the starving plebeians plus the war against their neighbors the Volscians; the plebeians' hatred for Marcius, the people's enemy —plus his patriotism; the creation of the post of People's Tribune— plus Marcius's appointment to a leading role in the war. Well—how much of that do we see in the bourgeois theatre?

W. They usually use the whole scene for an exposition of Marcius's character: the hero. He's shown as a patriot, handicapped by selfish plebeians and a cowardly and weak-kneed Senate. Shakespeare, following Livy rather than Plutarch, has good reason for showing the Senate 'sad and confused by a double fear—fear of the people and fear of the enemy.' The bourgeois stage identifies itself with the patricians' cause, not the plebeians'. The plebeians are shown as comic and pathetic types (rather than humorous and pathetically treated ones), and Agrippa's remark labelling the Senate's granting of People's Tribunes as strange is used for the light it casts on Agrippa's character rather than to establish a preliminary link between the advance of the Volscians and the concessions made to the plebeians. The plebeians' unrest is of course settled at once by the parable of the belly and the members, which is just right for the bourgeoisie's taste, as shown in its relations with the modern proletariat. . . .

R.   Although Shakespeare never allows Agrippa to mention that his parable has managed to convince the plebeians, only to say that though they lack discretion (to understand his speech) they are passing cowardly—an accusation, incidentally, that's impossible to understand.

B.   We'll note that.

R.   Why?

B.   It gives rise to discomfort.

R.   I must say, the way in which Shakespeare treats the plebeians and their tribunes rather encourages our theatre's habit of letting the hero's hardships be aggravated as far as possible by the 'foolish' behavior of the people, and so paving the way in anticipatory forgiveness for the later excesses of his 'pride.'

B.   All the same Shakespeare does make a factor of the patricians' corn profiteering and their inclination at least to conscript the plebeians for war—Livy makes the patricians say something to the effect that the base plebs always go astray in peacetime—also the plebeians' unjust indebtedness to the nobles. In such ways Shakespeare doesn't present the revolt as a piece of pure folly.

W.   But nor does he do much to bring out Plutarch's interesting phrase: 'Once order had been restored in the city by these means, even the lower classes immediately flocked to the colors and showed the greatest willingness to let the ruling authorities employ them for the war.'

B.   All right; if that's so we'll read the phrase with all the more interest: we want to find out as much about the plebeians as we can.

P.   'For here perhaps we have descriptions
Of famous forbears.'

R.   There's another point where Shakespeare refrains from coming down on the aristocratic side. Marcius isn't allowed to make anything of Plutarch's remark that 'The turbulent attitude of the base plebs did not go unobserved by the enemy. He launched an attack and put the country to fire and sword.'

B.   Let's close our first analysis at this point. Here is roughly what takes place and what we must bring out in the theatre. The conflict between patricians and plebeians is (at least provisionally) set aside, and that between the Romans and the Volscians becomes all-predominant. The Romans, seeing their city in danger, legalize their differences by appointing plebeian commissars (People's Tribunes).

The plebeians have got the Tribunate, but the people's enemy Marcius emerges, *qua* specialist, as leader in war.

B.   The brief analysis we made yesterday raises one or two very suggestive problems of production.

W.   How can one show that there has been opposition to the plebeians uniting, for instance? Just by that questionable emphasis on determination?

R.   When I told the story I didn't mention their lack of unity because I took the Second Citizen's remarks as a provocation. He struck me as simply checking on the First Citizen's firmness. But I don't suppose it can be played in this way. It's more that he's still hesitating.

W.   He could be given some reason for his lack of warlike spirit. He could be better dressed, more prosperous. When Agrippa makes his speech he could smile at the jokes, and so on. He could be disabled.

R.   Weakness?

W.   Morally speaking. The burnt child returns to its fire.

B.   What about their weapons?

R.   They've got to be poorly armed, or they could have got the Tribunate without the Volscians' attacking; but they mustn't be weak, or they could never win the war for Marcius and the war against him.

B.   Do they win their war against Marcius?

R.   In our theatre, certainly.

P.   They can go in rags, but does that mean they have to go raggedly?

B.   What's the situation?

R.   A sudden popular rising.

B.   So presumably their weapons are improvised ones, but they can be good improvisers. It's they who make the army's weapons; who else? They can have got themselves bayonets, butchers' knives on broomhandles, converted fire-irons, etc. Their inventiveness can arouse respect, and their arrival can immediately seem threatening.

P.   We're talking about the people all the time. What about the hero? He wasn't even the center of R.'s summary of the content.

R.   The first thing shown is a civil war. That's something too interesting to be mere background preparation for the entrance of the hero. Am I supposed to start off: 'One fine morning Caius Marcius went for a stroll in his garden, went to the market place, met the people and quarrelled,' and so on? What bothers me at the moment is how to show Agrippa's speech as ineffective and having an effect.

W.   I'm still bothered by P.'s question whether we oughtn't to examine the events with the hero in mind. I certainly think that before the hero's appearance one is entitled to show the field of forces within which he operates.

B.   Shakespeare permits that. But haven't we perhaps overloaded it with particular tensions, so that it acquires a weight of its own?

P.   And *Coriolanus* is written for us to enjoy the hero!

R.   The play is written realistically, and includes sufficient material of a contradictory sort. Marcius fighting the people: that isn't just a plinth for his monument.

B.   Judging from the way you've treated the story it seems to me that you've insisted all of you from the first on smacking your lips over the tragedy of a people that has a hero against it. Why not follow this inclination?

P.   There may not be much pretext for that in Shakespeare.

B.   I doubt it. But we don't have to do the play if we don't enjoy it.

P.   Anyway, if we want to keep the hero as the center of interest we can also play Agrippa's speech as ineffective.

W.   As Shakespeare makes it. The plebeians receive it with jeers, pityingly even.

R.   Why does Agrippa mention their cowardice—the point I was supposed to note?

P.   No evidence for it in Shakespeare.

B.   Let me emphasize that no edition of Shakespeare has stage directions, apart from those presumed to have been added later.

P.   What's the producer to do?

B.   We've got to show Agrippa's (vain) attempt to use ideology, in a purely demagogic way, in order to bring about that union between plebeians and patricians which in reality is effected a little—not very much—later by the outbreak of war. Their real union is due to *force majeure*, thanks to the military power of the Volscians. I've been considering one possibility: I'd suggest having Marcius and his armed men enter rather earlier than is indicated by Agrippa's 'Hail, noble Marcius!' and the stage direction which was probably inserted because of this remark. The plebeians would then see the armed men looming up behind the speaker, and it would be perfectly reasonable for them to show signs of indecision. Agrippa's sudden aggressiveness would also be explained by his own sight of Marcius and the armed men.

W.   But you've gone and armed the plebeians better than ever before in theatrical history, and here they are retreating before Marcius's legionaries. . . .

B.   The legionaries are better armed still. Anyway they don't retreat. We can strengthen Shakespeare's text here still further. Their few moments' hesitation during the final arguments of the speech is now due to the changed situation arising from the appearance of armed men behind the speaker. And in these few moments we observe that

Agrippa's ideology is based on force, on armed force, wielded by Romans.

W. But now there's unrest, and for them to unite there must be something more: war must break out.

R. Marcius can't let fly as he'd like to either. He turns up with armed men, but his hands are tied by the Senate's 'ruth.' They have just granted the mob senatorial representation in the form of the Tribunes. It was a marvellous stroke of Shakespeare's to make it Marcius who announces the setting-up of the Tribunate. How do the plebeians react to that? What is their attitude to their success?

W. Can we amend Shakespeare?

B. I think we can amend Shakespeare if we can amend him. But we agreed to begin only by discussing changes of interpretation so as to prove the usefulness of our analytical method even without adding new text.

W. Could the First Citizen be Sicinius, the man the Senate has just appointed Tribune? He would then have been at the head of the revolt, and would hear of his appointment from Marcius's mouth.

B. That's a major intervention.

W. There wouldn't have to be any change in the text.

B. All the same. A character has a kind of specific weight in the story. Altering it might mean stimulating interest that would be impossible to satisfy later, and so on.

R. The advantage would be that it would allow a playable connection to be established between the revolt and the granting of the Tribunate. And the plebeians could congratulate their Tribune and themselves.

B. But there must be no playing down of the contribution which the Volscians' attack makes to the establishment of the Tribunate; it's the main reason. Now you must start building and take everything into account.

W. The plebeians ought to share Agrippa's astonishment at this concession.

B. I don't want to come to any firm decision. And I'm not sure that that can be acted by pure miming, without any text. Again, if our group of plebeians includes a particular person who probably only represents the semi-plebeian section of Rome, then it will be seen as a part representing the whole. And so on. But I note your astonishment and inquisitiveness as you move around within this play and within these complex events on a particular morning in Rome, where there is much that a sharp eye can pick out. And certainly if you can find clues to these events, then all power to the audience!

W. One can try.

B.   Most certainly.

R.   And we ought to go through the whole play before deciding anything. You look a bit doubtful, B.

B.   Look the other way. How do they take the news that war has broken out?

W.   Marcius welcomes it, like Hindenburg did, as a bath of steel.

B.   Careful.

R.   You mean, this is a war of self-defense.

P.   That doesn't necessarily mean the same thing there as usually in our discussions and judgments. These wars led to the unification of Italy.

R.   Under Rome.

B.   Under democratic Rome.

W.   That had got rid of its Coriolanuses.

B.   Rome of the People's Tribunes.

P.   Here is what Plutarch says about what happened after Marcius's death: 'First the Volscians began to quarrel with the Aequi, their friends and allies, over the question of the supreme command, and violence and death resulted. They had marched out to meet the advancing Romans, but almost completely destroyed one another. As a result the Romans defeated them in a battle. . . .'

R.   I.e., Rome without Marcius was weaker, not stronger.

B.   Yes, it's just as well not only to have read the play right through before starting to study the beginning, but also to have read the factual accounts of Plutarch and Livy, who were the dramatist's sources. But what I meant by 'careful' was: one can't just condemn wars without going into them any further, and it won't even do to divide them into wars of aggression and wars of defense. The two kinds merge into one another, for one thing. And only a classless society on a high level of production can get along without wars. Anyhow this much seems clear to me: Marcius has got to be shown as a patriot. It takes the most tremendous events—as in the play— to turn him into a deadly enemy of his country.

R.   How do the plebeians react to the news of the war?

P.   We've got to decide that ourselves; the text gives no clue.

B.   And unhappily our own generation is particularly well qualified to judge. The choice is between letting the news come like a thunderbolt that smashes through everyone's defenses, or else making something of the fact that it leaves them relatively unmoved. We couldn't possibly leave them unmoved without underlining how strange and perhaps terrible that is.

P.   We must make it have tremendous effects, because it so completely alters the situation, if for no other reason.

W.   Let's assume then that at first the news is a blow to them all.

R. Even Marcius? His immediate reaction is to say he's delighted.

B. All the same we needn't make him an exception. He can say his famous sentence 'I'm glad on't; then we shall ha' means to vent / Our musty superfluity,' once he has recovered.

W. And the plebeians? It won't be easy to exploit Shakespeare's lacuna so as to make them seem speechless. Then there are still other questions. Are they to greet their new Tribunes? Do they get any advice from them? Does their attitude towards Marcius change at all?

B. We shall have to base our solution on the fact that there is no answer to these points; in other words, they have got to be raised. The plebeians must gather around the Tribunes to greet them, but stop short of doing so. The Tribunes must want to lay down a line, but stop short of it. The plebeians must stop short of adopting a new attitude to Marcius. It must all be swallowed up by the new situation. The stage direction that so irritates us, 'Citizens steal away,' simply represents the change that has taken place since they came on stage ('Enter a company of mutinous citizens with clubs, staves and other weapons'). The wind has changed, it's no longer a favorable wind for mutinies; a powerful threat affects all alike, and as far as the people goes this threat is simply noted in a purely negative way.

R. You advised us in our analysis to make a note to record our discomfort.

B. And our admiration of Shakespeare's realism. We have no real excuse to lag behind Plutarch, who writes of the base people's 'utmost readiness' for the war. It is a new union of the classes, which has come about in no good way, and we must examine it and reconstitute it on the stage.

W. To start with, the People's Tribunes are included in the new union; they are left hanging useless in mid-air, and they stick out like sore thumbs. How are we to create this visible unity of two classes which have just been fighting one another out of these men and their irreconcilable opponent Marcius, who has suddenly become so vitally needed, needed for Rome as a whole?

B. I don't think we'll get any further by going about it naïvely and waiting for bright ideas. We shall have to go back to the classic method of mastering such complex events. I marked a passage in Mao Tse-tung's essay 'On Contradiction.' What does he say?

R. That in any given process which involves many contradictions there is always a main contradiction that plays the leading, decisive part; the rest are of secondary, subordinate significance. One example he gives is the Chinese Communists' willingness, once the Japanese attacked, to break off their struggle against Chiang Kai-shek's reactionary régime. Another possible example is that when Hitler attacked the USSR even the émigré white Russian generals and bankers were quick to oppose him.

W. Isn't that a bit different?

B. A bit different but also a bit the same thing. But we must push on. We've got a contradictory union of plebeians and patricians, which has got involved in a contradiction with the Volscians next door. The second is the main contradiction. The contradiction between plebeians and patricians, the class struggle, has been put into cold storage by the emergence of the new contradiction, the national war against the Volscians. It hasn't disappeared though. (The People's Tribunes 'stick out like sore thumbs.') The Tribunate came about as a result of the outbreak of war.

W. But in that case how are we to show the plebeian-patrician contradiction being overshadowed by the main Roman-Volscian contradiction, and how can we do it in such a way as to bring out the disappearance of the new plebeian leadership beneath that of the patricians?

B. That's not the sort of problem that can be solved in cold blood. What's the position? Starving men on one side, armed men on the other. Faces flushed with anger now going red once more. New lamentations will drown the old. The two opposed parties take stock of the weapons they are brandishing against one another. Will these be strong enough to ward off the common danger? It's poetic, what's taking place. How are we going to put it across?

W. We'll mix up the two groups: there must be a general loosening-up, with people going from one side to the other. Perhaps we can use the incident when Marcius knocks into the patrician Lartius on his crutches and says: 'What, art thou stiff? stand'st out?' Plutarch says in connection with the plebeians' revolt: 'Those without any means were taken bodily away and locked up, even though covered with scars from the battles and ordeals suffered in campaigns for the fatherland. They had conquered the enemy, but their creditors had not the least pity for them.' We suggested before that there might be a disabled man of this sort among the plebeians. Under the influence of the naïve patriotism that's so common among ordinary people, and so often shockingly abused, he could come up to Lartius, in spite of his being a member of the class that has so maltreated him. The two war victims could recall their common share in the last war; they could embrace, applauded by all, and hobble off together.

B. At the same time that would be a good way of establishing that it is generally a period of wars.

W. Incidentally, do you feel a disabled man like this could perhaps prevent our group from standing as *pars pro toto?*

B. Not really. He would represent the ex-soldiers. For the rest, I think we could follow up our idea about the weapons. Cominius as Consul and Commander-in-Chief could grin as he tested those home-made weapons designed for civil war and then gave them back to their owners for use in the patriotic one.

P. And what about Marcius and the Tribunes?

B. That's an important point to settle. There mustn't be any kind of fraternization between them. The new-found union isn't complete. It's liable to break at the junction points.

W. Marcius can invite the plebeians condescendingly, and with a certain contempt, to follow him to the Capitol, and the Tribunes can encourage the disabled man to accost Titus Lartius, but Marcius and the Tribunes don't look at each other, they turn their backs on one another.

R. In other words both sides are shown as patriots, but the conflict between them remains plain.

B. And it must also be made clear that Marcius is in charge. War is still his business—especially his—much more than the plebeians'.

R. Looking at the play's development and being alert to contradictions and their exact nature has certainly helped us in this section of the story. What about the character of the hero, which is also something that must be sketched out, and in precisely this section of the story?

B. It's one of those parts which should not be built up from his first appearance but from a later one. I would say a battle-scene for Coriolanus, if it hadn't become so hard for us Germans to represent great wartime achievements after two world wars.

P. You want Marcius to be Busch, the great people's actor who is a fighter himself. Is that because you need someone who won't make the hero too likeable?

B. Not too likeable, and likeable enough. If we want to generate appreciation of his tragedy we must put Busch's mind and personality at the hero's disposal. He'll lend his own value to the hero, and he'll be able to understand him, both the greatness and the cost of him.

P. You know what Busch feels. He says he's no bruiser, nor an aristocratic figure.

B. He's wrong about aristocratic figures, I think. And he doesn't need physical force to inspire fear in his enemies. We mustn't forget a 'superficial' point: if we are going to represent half the Roman plebs with five to seven men and the entire Roman army with something like nine we can't very well use a sixteen-stone Coriolanus.

W. Usually you're for developing characters step by step. Why not this one?

B. It may be because he doesn't have a proper development. His switch from being the most Roman of the Romans to becoming their deadliest enemy is due precisely to the fact that he stays the same.

P. *Coriolanus* has been called the tragedy of pride.

R. Our first examination made us feel the tragedy lay, both for Coriolanus and for Rome, in his belief that he was irreplaceable.

P. Isn't that because the play only comes to life for us when interpreted like this, since we find the same kind of thing here and feel the tragedy of the conflicts that result from it?

B. Undoubtedly.

W. A lot will depend on whether we can show Coriolanus, and what happens to and around him, in such a light that he can hold this belief. His usefulness has got to be beyond all doubt.

B. A typical detail: as there's so much question of his pride, let's try to find out where he displays modesty, following Stanslavsky's example, who asked the man playing the miser to show him the point at which he was generous.

W. Are you thinking of when he takes over command?

B. Something like. Let's leave it at that for a start.

P. Well, what does the scene teach us, if we set it out in such a form?

B. That the position of the oppressed classes can be strengthened by the threat of war and weakened by its outbreak.

R. That lack of a solution can unite the oppressed class and arriving at a solution can divide it, and that such a solution may be seen in a war.

P. That differences in income can divide the oppressed class.

R. That soldiers, and war victims even, can romanticize the war they survived and be easy game for new ones.

W. That the finest speeches cannot wipe away realities, but can hide them for a time.

R. That 'proud' gentlemen are not too proud to kowtow to their own sort.

P. That the oppressors' class isn't wholly united either.

B. And so on.

R. Do you think that all this and the rest of it can be read in the play?

B. Read in it and read into it.

P. Is it for the sake of these perceptions that we are going to do the play?

B. Not only. We want to have and to communicate the fun of dealing with a slice of illuminated history. And to have first-hand experience of dialectics.

P.   Isn't the second point a considerable refinement, reserved for a handful of connoisseurs?

B.   No. Even with popular ballads or the peepshows at fairs the simple people (who are so far from simple) love stories of the rise and fall of great men, of eternal change, of the ingenuity of the oppressed, of the potentialities of mankind. And they hunt for the truth that is 'behind it all.'

Appendix

Coriolanus
by William Shakespeare

Act I, Scene 1

Men. = Menenius Agrippa, a friend of Coriolanus
Mar. = Caius Marcius, later to be Caius Marcius Coriolanus
Com. = Cominius,
Lart. = Titus Laritius, } generals against the Volscians
Bru. = Junius Brutus,
Sic. = Sicinius Velutus, } tribunes of the people
Citizens and Senators.

A street in ancient Rome.

Enter a company of mutinous citizens, with staves, clubs, and other weapons.

First Cit.	Before we proceed any further, hear me speak.
All.	Speak, speak.
First Cit.	You are all resolved rather to die than to famish?
All.	Resolved, resolved.
First Cit.	First, you know Caius Marcius is chief enemy to the people.
All.	We know't, we know't.
First Cit.	Let us kill him, and we'll have corn at our own price. Is't a verdict?
All.	No more talking on't; let it be done. Away, away!
Sec. Cit.	One word, good citizens.
First Cit.	We are accounted poor citizens, the patricians good. What authority surfeits on would relieve us. If they would yield us but the superfluity while it were wholesome, we might guess they relieved us humanely; but they think we are too dear: the leanness that afflicts us, the object of our misery, is as an inventory to particularize their abundance; our sufferance is a gain to them. Let us revenge this with our pikes, ere we become rakes; for the gods know I speak this in hunger for bread, not in thirst for revenge.
Sec. Cit.	Would you proceed especially against Caius Marcius?

All.	Against him first; he's a very dog to the commonalty.
Sec. Cit.	Consider you what services he has done for his country?
First Cit.	Very well; and could be content to give him good report for't, but that he pays himself with being proud.
Sec. Cit.	Nay, but speak not maliciously.
First Cit.	I say unto you, what he hath done famously, he did it to that end. Though soft-conscienced men can be content to say it was for his country, he did it to please his mother, and to be partly proud; which he is, even to the altitude of his virtue.
Sec. Cit.	What he cannot help in his nature, you account a vice in him. You must in no way say he is covetous.
First Cit.	If I must not, I need not be barren of accusations; he hath faults, with surplus to tire in repetition. (Shouts within.) What shouts are these? The other side o' th' city is risen; why stay we prating here? To the Capitol!
All.	Come, come.
First Cit.	Soft! who comes here?

Enter Menenius Agrippa.

Sec. Cit.	Worthy Menenius Agrippa, one that hath always loved the people.
First Cit.	He's one honest enough; would all the rest were so!
Men.	What work's, my countrymen, in hand? Where go you With bats and clubs? The matter? Speak, I pray you.
Sec. Cit.	Our business is not unknown to th' Senate: they have had inkling this fortnight what we intend to do, which now we'll show 'em in deeds. They say poor suitors have strong breaths; they shall know we have strong arms too.
Men.	Why, masters, my good friends, mine honest neighbors, Will you undo yourselves?
Sec. Cit.	We cannot, sir, we are undone already.
Men.	I tell you, friends, most charitable care Have the patricians of you. For your wants, Your suffering in this dearth, you may as well Strike at the heaven with your staves as lift them Against the Roman state, whose course will on The way it takes, cracking ten thousand curbs Of more strong link asunder than can ever Appear in your impediment. For the dearth, The gods, not the patricians, make it, and Your knees to them (not arms) must help. Alack, You are transported by calamity Thither where more attends you, and you slander

	The helms o' th' state, who care for you like fathers.
	When you curse them as enemies.
Sec. Cit.	Care for us? True, indeed! They ne'er car'd for us yet:
	suffer us to famish, and their store-houses crammed with
	grain; make edicts for usury, to support usurers; repeal daily
	any wholesome act established against the rich, and provide
	more piercing statutes daily, to chain up and restrain the poor.
	If the wars eat us not up, they will; and there's all the love
	they bear us.
Men.	Either you must
	Confess yourselves wondrous malicious,
	Or be accus'd of folly. I shall tell you
	A pretty tale. It may be you have heard it;
	But, since it serves my purpose, I will venture
	To stale't a little more.
Sec. Cit.	Well, I'll hear it, sir; yet you must not think to fob off our
	disgrace with a tale; but, an't please you, deliver.
Men.	There was a time when all the body's members
	Rebell'd against the belly; thus accus'd it:
	That only like a gulf it did remain
	I' th' midst o' th' body, idle and unactive,
	Still cupboarding the viand, never bearing
	Like labor with the rest, where th' other instruments
	Did see and hear, devise, instruct, walk, feel,
	And, mutually participate, did minister
	Unto the appetite and affection common
	Of the whole body. The belly answer'd—
Sec. Cit.	Well, sir, what answer made the belly?
Men.	Sir, I shall tell you. With a kind of smile,
	Which ne'er came from the lungs, but even thus—
	For, look you, I may make the belly smile
	As well as speak—it tauntingly replied
	To th' discontented members, the mutinous parts
	That envied his receipt; even so most fitly
	As you malign our senators for that
	They are not such as you.
Sec. Cit.	Your belly's answer? What!
	The kingly-crowned head, the vigilant eye,
	The counsellor heart, the arm our soldier,
	Our steed the leg, the tongue our trumpeter,
	With other muniments and petty helps
	In this our fabric, if that they—
Men.	What then?

	'Fore me, this fellow speaks! What then? what then?
Sec. Cit.	Should by the cormorant belly be restrain'd,
	Who is the sink o' th' body,—
Men.	Well, what then?
Sec. Cit.	The former agents, if they did complain,
	What could the belly answer?
Men.	I will tell you.
	If you'll bestow a small—of what you have little—
	Patience a while, you'st hear the belly's answer.
Sec. Cit.	Y'are long about it.
Men.	Note me this, good friend;
	Your most grave belly was deliberate,
	Not rash like his accusers, and thus answered:
	"True is it, my incorporate friends," quoth he,
	"That I receive the general food at first
	Which you do live upon; and fit it is,
	Because I am the store-house and the shop
	Of the whole body. But, if you do remember,
	I send it through the rivers of your blood,
	Even to the court, the heart, to th' seat o' th' brain;
	And, through the cranks and offices of man,
	The strongest nerves and small inferior veins
	From me receive that natural competency
	Whereby they live. And though that all at once,
	You, my good friends,"—this says the belly, mark me,—
Sec. Cit.	Ay, sir; well, well.
Men.	"Though all at once cannot
	See what I do deliver out to each,
	Yet I can make my audit up, that all
	From me do back receive the flour of all,
	And leave me but the bran." What say you to 't?
Sec. Cit.	It was an answer. How apply you this?
Men.	The senators of Rome are this good belly,
	And you the mutinous members; for examine
	Their counsels and thier cares, disgest things right
	Touching the weal o' th' common, you shall find
	No public benefit which you receive
	But it proceeds or comes from them to you
	And no way from yourselves. What do you think,
	You, the great toe of this assembly?
Sec. Cit.	I the great toe! Why the great toe!
Men.	For that, being one o' th' lowest, basest, poorest,
	Of this most wise rebellion, thou goest foremost;

Thou rascal, that art worst in blood to run,
Lead'st first to win some vantage.
But make you ready your stiff bats and clubs;
Rome and her rats are at the point of battle,
The one side must have bale.

                    Enter *Caius Marcius.*

Hail, noble Marcius!

Mar.   Thanks. What's the matter, you dissentious rogues,
That, rubbing the poor itch of your opinion,
Make, yourselves scabs?

Sec. Cit.   We have ever your good word.

Mar.   He that will give good words to thee will flatter
Beneath abhorring. What would you have, you curs,
That like nor peace nor war? The one affrights you,
The other makes you proud. He that trusts to you,
Where he should find you lions, finds you hares;
Where foxes, geese. You are no surer, no,
Than is the coal of fire upon the ice,
Or hailstone in the sun. Your virtue is
To make him worthy whose offense subdues him,
And curse that justice did it. Who deserves greatness
Deserves your hate; and your affections are
A sick man's appetite, who desires most that
Which would increase his evil. He that depends
Upon your favors swims with fins of lead
And hews down oaks with rushes. Hang ye! Trust ye?
With every minute you do change a mind,
And call him noble that was now your hate,
Him vile that was your garland. What's the matter,
That in these several places of the city
You cry against the noble Senate, who,
(Under the gods) keep you in awe, which else
Would feed on one another? What's their seeking?

Men.   For corn at their own rates; whereof, they say,
The city is well stor'd.

Mar.   Hang 'em! They say!
They'll sit by the fire, and presume to know
What's done i' th' Capitol; who's like to rise,
Who thrives, and who declines; side factions, and give out
Conjectural marriages; making parties strong,
And feebling such as stand not in their liking
Below their cobbled shoes. They say there's grain enough!
Would the nobility lay aside their ruth

	And let me use my sword, I'd make a quarry
	With thousands of these quarter'd slaves, as high
	As I could pick my lance.
Men.	Nay, these are almost thoroughly persuaded;
	For though abundantly they lack discretion,
	Yet are they passing cowardly. But, I beseech you,
	What says the other troop?
Mar.	They are dissolv'd, hang 'em!
	They said they were an-hungry; sigh'd forth proverbs,
	That hunger broke stone walls, that dogs must eat,
	That meat was made for mouths, that the gods sent not
	Corn for the rich men only. With these shreds
	They vented their complainings; which being answer'd,
	And a petition granted them,—a strange one
	To break the heart of generosity,
	And make bold power look pale,—they threw their caps
	As they would hang them on the horns o' th' moon,
	Shouting their emulation.
Men.	What is granted them?
Mar.	Five tribunes to defend their vulgar wisdoms,
	Of their own choice. One's Junius Brutus,
	Sicinius Velutus, and I know not—'Sdeath!
	The rabble should have first unroof'd the city,
	Ere so prevail'd with me: it will in time
	Win upon power and throw forth greater themes
	For insurrection's arguing.
Men.	This is strange.
Mar.	Go, get you home, you fragments!

Enter a *Messenger*, hastily.

Mess.	Where's Caius Marcius?
Mar.	Here. What's the matter?
Mess.	The news is, sir, the Volsces are in arms.
Mar.	I am glad on't. Then we shall ha' means to vent
	Our musty superfluity. See, our best elders.

Enter *Cominius, Titus Lartius,* with other
Senators; Junius Brutus and *Sicinius Velutus.*

First Sen.	Marcius, 't is true that you have lately told us;
	The Volsces are in arms.
Mar.	They have a leader, Tullus Aufidius, that will put you 't.
	I sin in envying his nobility,
	And were I anything but what I am,
	I would wish me only he.
Com.	You have fought together ?

Mar.	Were half to half the world by th' ears and he
	Upon my party, I'd revolt, to make
	Only my wars with him. He is a lion
	That I am proud to hunt.
First Sen.	Then, worthy Marcius,
	Attend upon Cominius to these wars.
Com.	It is your former promise.
Mar.	Sir, it is;
	And I am constant. Titus Lartius, thou
	Shalt see me once more strike at Tullus' face.
	What, art thou stiff? Stand'st out?
Lart.	No, Caius Marcius;
	I'll lean upon one crutch and fight with t' other,
	Ere stay behind this business.
Men.	O, true-bred!
First Sen.	Your company to th' Capitol; where, I know,
	Our greatest friends attend us.
Lart.	(To Cominius.) Lead you on.
	(To Marcius.) Follow Cominius; we must follow you;
	Right worthy you priority.
Com.	Noble Marcius!
First Sen.	(To the Citizens) Hence to your homes; begone!
Mar.	Nay, let them follow.
	The Volsces have much corn; take these rats thither
	To gnaw their garners. Worshipful mutiners,
	Your valor puts well forth; pray, follow.
	Citizens steal away. Exeunt all but Sicinius and Brutus.
Sic.	Was ever man so proud as is this Marcius?
Bru.	He has no equal.
Sic.	When we were chosen tribunes for the people,—
Bru.	Mark'd you his lip and eyes?
Sic.	Nay, but his taunts.
Bru.	Being mov'd, he will not spare to gird the gods.
Sic.	Be-mock the modest moon.
Bru.	The present wars devour him! He is grown
	Too proud to be so valiant.
Bru.	Such a nature,
	Tickled with good success, disdains the shadow
	Which he treads on at noon. But I do wonder
	His insolence can brook to be commanded
	Under Cominius.
Bru.	Fame, at the which he aims,
	In whom already he's well grac'd cannot

	Better be held nor more attain'd than by
	A place below the first; for what miscarries
	Shall be the general's fault, though he perform
	To th' utmost of a man, and giddy censure
	Will then cry out of Marcius, "O, if he
	Had borne the business!"
Sic.	Besides, if things go well,
	Opinion that so sticks on Marcius shall
	Of his demerits rob Cominius.
Bru.	Come.
	Half all Cominius' honors are to Marcius,
	Though Marcius earn'd them not, and all his faults
	To Marcius shall be honors, though indeed
	In aught he merit not.
Sic.	Let's hence, and hear
	How the dispatch is made, and in what fashion,
	More than his singularity, he goes
	Upon this present action.
Bru.	Let's along. *Exeunt.*